Financial Accounting

Financial Accounting

Jack L. Smith, Ph.D., C.P.A.
Professor of Accounting, University of South Florida—School of Accountancy

Robert M. Keith, Ph.D., C.P.A.
Professor of Accounting, University of South Florida—School of Accountancy

William L. Stephens, D.B.A., C.P.A.
Professor of Accounting, University of South Florida—School of Accountancy

McGraw-Hill Book Company
New York St. Louis San Francisco Auckland Bogotá Hamburg London
Madrid Mexico Milan Montreal New Delhi Panama Paris São Paulo
Singapore Sydney Tokyo Toronto

FINANCIAL ACCOUNTING

Copyright © 1988 by McGraw-Hill, Inc. All rights reserved. Printed in the United States of America. Except as permitted under the United States Copyright Act of 1976, no part of this publication may be reproduced or distributed in any form or by any means, or stored in a data base or retrieval system, without the prior written permission of the publisher.

1 2 3 4 5 6 7 8 9 0 V N H V N H 8 9 2 1 0 9 8 7

ISBN 0-07-059002-8

This book was set in Times Roman by Progressive Typographers, Inc. The editors were Michael R. Elia, Robert D. Lynch, and Peggy C. Rehberger; the designer was Merrill Haber; the production supervisor was Friederich W. Schulte. Drawings were done by J&R Services, Inc. Von Hoffmann Press, Inc., was printer and binder.

Library of Congress Cataloging-in-Publication Data

Smith, Jack L.
   Financial accounting.

   Includes index.
   1. Accounting.   I. Keith, Robert M.   II. Stephens,
William L.   III. Title.
HF5635.S6445   1988   657   87-17233
ISBN 0-07-059002-8

About the Authors

Jack L. Smith is a professor at the School of Accountancy at the University of South Florida. He received a Ph.D. in accounting at the University of Mississippi and is a CPA. Professor Smith is a member of the American Accounting Association, the AICPA, the Florida Institute of Certified Public Accountants, the National Association of Accountants, and the Florida Association of Accounting Educators, and has been active in a number of state and local professional organizations. Professor Smith was the chamber faculty adviser of the Delta Gamma Chapter of Beta Alpha Psi. He is also active in various local and national professional development programs and has received awards as an outstanding discussion leader. In addition to *Accounting for Financial Statement Presentation,* an MBA-level introductory financial accounting text coauthored with Robert M. Keith, and Accounting Principles, 2nd edition, Professor Smith is the author of a number of articles in the *Journal of Accountancy, The Florida CPA,* and the *Financial Executive,* as well as two award winning articles published in the May and July 1978 issues of *Management Accountant.* In addition to his writing activities, Jack Smith is also an experienced teacher. His 20 years of working closely with students make this textbook one that actively involves students in the learning process.

Robert M. Keith is a professor at the School of Accountancy at the University of South Florida. He received his Ph.D. in accounting from the University of Alabama and holds the CPA certificate. While his research interests center on financial accounting, Professor Keith also has a strong interest in accounting education at both the college and professional levels. He received the first Outstanding Accounting Faculty Award by the Delta Gamma Chapter of Beta Alpha Psi and was voted an outstanding discussion leader four years in a row by CPA participants in continuing professional education seminars sponsored by the Florida Institute of CPAs. In addition to papers presented at regional meetings of the AAA, Professor Keith's research has appeared in the *Journal of Accountancy* and *The Florida CPA.* He was also a coauthor with Jack L. Smith of *Accounting for Financial Statement Presentation,* published in 1979 and *Accounting Principles,* 2nd edition. Professor Keith is a member of the American Accounting Association, the AICPA, and the Florida Institute of Certified Public Accountants, and has served on the editorial board of *The Florida CPA.*

William L. Stephens is a professor at the School of Accountancy at the University of South Florida. He has a DBA from Florida State University and is a CPA. His primary research and teaching interests are in the area of managerial and cost accounting. Active in continuing professional education projects, Professor Stephens is also a member of the American Accounting Association, the National Association of Accountants, and the Florida Institute of Certified Public Accountants. For 13 of the last 14 years, he has been the faculty advisor to the Delta Gamma Chapter of Beta Alpha Psi which has been recognized as a Superior Chapter for 12 straight years. Author of numerous articles in *The Journal of Accountancy,* and *The Accounting Review,* Professor Stephens has also co-authored *Accounting Principles,* 2nd edition, a financial accounting text, and a study guide for a financial accounting text.

To Diane, Kristie, and Scott

To Leanne and Rob

In memory of my parents, Lois and Lewis Stephens, who raised their children
To love and respect their parents
To have empathy for the less fortunate
To develop a "punish" sense of humor, and
To love, honor, and serve the Lord.

CONTENTS

PREFACE

Financial Accounting is designed to be a comprehensive balanced approach to the college or university student's first exposure to accounting. The text and its companion, *Managerial Accounting,* is intended for use in a two-semester or three-quarter sequence by college students who plan a business career, who intend to enter the accounting profession, and who are interested in broadening their business background. Our assumption in writing this text is that the student's exposure to business has been very limited. Therefore, we have carefully explained and illustrated, where appropriate, all business terms and practices as they are first introduced.

We view our texts as being neither conceptual nor procedural but a balanced blend of the two. Students are informed *why* information is accounted for in a certain manner. The why is reinforced by illustrating *how* the accounting is accomplished. Students can better grasp concepts through sufficient attention to the procedures.

IMPORTANT FEATURES OF THIS TEXT

We have incorporated in *Financial Accounting* numerous pedagogical devices and techniques which we describe in this preface as general or specific. In the general category we include items that are presented in all chapters of the text, while the pedagogical items that we describe as specific are features found only in specific chapters.

GENERAL

- We have written this book in a lively style with extensive use of the active voice which we believe makes the material real and interesting and certainly more helpful to the student in learning and understanding it.

- Each of the five parts of the text is introduced by a section explaining the overall purpose of that part and briefly describing its contents.

- Chapter objectives are given at the beginning of each of the 16 chapters.

- Margin notes are used extensively throughout each chapter to describe text material. Margin notes are also used to briefly indicate the objective of each exercise and problem in the back of each chapter.

- The text contains many well illustrated charts, diagrams, and figures designed to help the student easily and quickly visualize concepts, and relationships, and enabling the student to develop the ideas underlying the material as it is explained.

- Real world examples extracted from sources such as *Forbes, Fortune, Harvard Business Review,* Securities and Exchange Releases, and *The Wall Street Journal,* provide the student with an opportunity to see how principles of accounting are foundations of much that happens in the business world.

- After each chapter a decision problem is given to provide the student with a challenging real life problem to solve.

■ Summaries are presented at the end of each chapter.

■ Important terms used in the chapters are presented again at the end of each chapter in the form of a glossary which includes page references to where the term was first introduced.

■ Check figures are located in the margin alongside the exercises and problems where they are most helpful to the student, not on the end covers or in a separate list.

SPECIFIC

■ Accounting principles and concepts are discussed and developed fully as they are introduced.

■ An interlude in the form of a major section entitled *GAAP: Generally Accepted Accounting Principles* is located between Chapters 10 and 11, the point in the text where the student is best prepared for a comprehensive discussion of this important topic.

■ The accounting cycle is reviewed by means of a detailed flowchart at the end of Chapters 3, 4, and 6; the chart is expanded successfully as new procedures are introduced.

■ A full discussion of reversing entries for accruals and transactions initially recorded in nominal accounts is developed in Chapter 4.

■ An extended discussion (with a clear concise example) of the difference between the accrual and cash basis of accounting is located in Chapter 3.

■ Features of the 1986 Tax Reform Act are incorporated wherever appropriate throughout the text and in the appendix.

■ An extensive discussion on the important topic of internal control is an integral part of chapter 6; also included is a reference to the E. F. Hutton case.

■ Chapter 10 on long-lived assets includes a discussion of the impact of income tax depreciation.

■ Chapter 13, "Corporations: Long-Term Liabilities," contains an extended, easy-to-follow treatment of present value analysis. These techniques are then used in finding bond values, amortizing bond premiums and discounts, and accounting for leases.

■ Chapter 15, "Statement of Cash Flows," provides the student with the procedures for developing this new statement by either the T-account method or the worksheet method. In the Solutions Manual the problems are solved using both methods.

■ Chapter 16, "Financial Statement Analysis and Interpretation," includes an ongoing analysis of a corporation.

■ The Appendix focuses on the basics of corporate taxation and includes a reconciliation of book and taxable income.

SUPPLEMENTARY MATERIALS

Accompanying *Financial Accounting* is a full array of supporting materials that includes:

For the Instructor:

■ *Solutions Manual.* Answers to all the questions, exercises, and problems are contained in this comprehensive manual. The type is extra large and extra bold so that any transparencies made from the manual will be clearly seen by the students in the last row of the classroom.

The questions, exercises, and problems follow closely the textual material and learning objectives. Time, estimated difficulty levels, and descriptions of all exercises and problems are provided as an aid to the instructor in selecting material appropriate for the level of course being taught.

■ *Teacher's Manual.* Designed to aid primarily graduate teaching assistants, adjuncts, and other part-time instructors, the *Teacher's Manual* contains comments, notes, illustrations, and examples that the authors have found useful in teaching the financial accounting course. Also included in the *Teacher's Manual* are solutions to *Tests and Exam Set A* and *Tests and Exam Set B* and solutions to *Practice Set, Neptune Swimming Pool Supply Company.*

■ *Tests and Exams.* Two completely different yet parallel sets, *Set A* and *Set B,* are available to provide the instructor with alternative testing options. Both sets include 9 tests that cover two to three chapters each and a final comprehensive examination covering the entire text.

Each shrink-wrapped package contains 20 copies of each test and each exam.

■ *Test Bank.* For those instructors who wish to construct their own examinations, a manual containing over 1,400 true/false, multiple choice, and short problem test questions arranged by chapter is available. These questions are also available in a computerized test-generation system.

■ *Overhead Transparencies.* A complete set of solutions to all problems and exercises in the form of overhead transparencies is available upon request to adopters of the text.

■ *Teacher's Transparencies.* An extensive set of additional teaching transparencies is available for classroom use as an aid in illustrating many of the concepts discussed in the text.

FOR THE STUDENT

■ *Study Guide.* A comprehensive study guide, prepared by Joe Icerman of Florida State University, contains chapter-by-chapter learning overviews, together with an abundance of multiple-choice, fill-in, and true or false questions as well as numerous problems. Solutions to all these self-test items are found in the back of the *Study Guide.*

■ *Practice Set.* A manual practice set, *Neptune Swimming Pool Supply Company,* illustrates the basic accounting system using the periodic inventory method and special journals. The practice set can be used after covering the first six chapters of the text. The set is unique because it contains two beginning trial balances and two sets of amounts for each transaction, thus providing the instructor with the opportunity to assign any one of four practice sets although the student purchases only one set. Solutions to each of the four variations are in the *Teacher's Manual.*

■ *Business Forms Practice Set.* A second practice set, *Decker Avenue Discount Video,* contains various source documents, business forms, and cancelled checks for the student to analyze and process. The set is available for both *Principles of*

Accounting and *Financial Accounting.* (Instructors will find the solution to the Decker Avenue Discount Video practice set in the manual, *Solutions to Practice Sets One and Two, Accounting Principles,* second edition, published 1986.)

■ *Computerized Practice Set.* This practice set utilizes microcomputers to process data inputed by students to generate financial statements.

■ *Microcomputer Spreadsheet.* Templates for solving selected exercises and problems at the end of the chapter are developed using *Accounting/Lotus® Connection* by E. James Meddaugh of The Rochester Institute of Technology.

■ *Worksheets.* Partially filled in accounting worksheets for all problems in the text are preprinted with the problem headings and preliminary data to help students save time and concentrate on working out the essence of each problem.

ACKNOWLEDGMENTS

We wish to express our sincere appreciation to the many individuals who contributed their efforts to this project.

Constructive criticism was gratefully received from Elinor Boer, Vanderbilt University; Sandra Byrd, South Missouri State University; Harold Cannon, SUNY at Albany; Joann Noe Cross, University of Wisconsin; Monica Frizzell, Western Connecticut State University; Dave Greenfield, University of California at Los Angeles; Joseph T. Kastantin, University of Wisconsin; Charles A. Konkol, University of Wisconsin; Marc F. Massoud, Claremont McKenna College; Joseph J. Master, Stetson University; Claudel B. McKenzie, University of North Carolina; Jack Miller, Florissant Valley Community College; Gale Newell, Western Michigan University; Thomas R. Nunamaker, Washington State University; Ginger Parker, University of Nebraska; Ronald Rubin, San Francisco Community College; John R. Simon, Northern Illinois University; Richard H. Simpson, University of Massachusetts; Frederic M. Stiner, Jr., University of Delaware and Robert Zwicker, Pace University.

We are indebted to Mr. Blake Carson, a University of South Florida graduate student, Professor Robert Zwicker of Pace University and Professor David Greenfield of the University of California at Los Angeles who independently checked the accuracy of all the solutions (to text exercises and problems) in the *Solutions Manual.* We are most grateful.

We appreciate the help and encouragement of our colleagues at the University of South Florida. Special thanks to Chairman Robert J. West and Professor James Lasseter.

Once again we are most fortunate to have had the assistance of two outstanding individuals from the McGraw-Hill editorial staff. We enjoyed working with Peggy Rehberger and Mike Elia and, as always, are most impressed by their creative talents.

Jack L. Smith
Robert M. Keith
William L. Stephens

PART ONE

Financial Accounting: Its Environment and Structure

For many years to come you are going to make economic decisions. These decisions may be required of you in your role as a taxpayer, a voter, an employee, a club member, a business manager, and a husband or wife. To make the best economic decisions, you need the appropriate financial facts. Accounting is a service that provides these facts in the form of financial reports. But before you can use financial reports, you need to know how accounting information is generated, processed, and presented. You should also have a basic understanding of accounting principles, be familiar with the terms used by accountants, and understand the limitations of financial reports. Part One of *Financial Accounting* is designed to provide you with this information.

In Part One you will learn that there are many kinds of accounting activities and what each of these activities involves. In this text you will be studying just one of these activities —general financial accounting— which is concerned with recording business transactions and preparing financial reports. You will learn how to record transactions for a business entity. And you will learn how to prepare three financial reports — the income statement, the statement of retained earnings, and the balance sheet.

Financial reports are useful to us only when they are reliable and comparable. Certain ground rules called generally accepted accounting principles have been developed over the years to assure us that business entities prepare financial reports that are reliable and comparable. We will tell you in Part One how these generally accepted accounting principles are developed and discuss with you five important principles that you will need to know even at this early stage in your course of study.

INTRODUCTION
The Accounting Environment

If you are alive, alert, and an active and interested citizen of the free world, you will be expected to make decisions about how you feel your country's economy should operate and how it should affect the economies of other countries. Depending on which hat you wear in your society, and your attitudes, your interests, and your job, you will have to make some decisions like the following:

Economic decisions require accounting information

Taxpayers Should you support your local government's proposed bond issue to finance increased community services?

Club members Should you support the proposed club operating budget for the forthcoming year?

Finance manager of an international company Should you invest funds for a new plant to be located in France?

Investment manager for a large insurance company Should you buy the stocks or bonds of a particular company?

Loan officer of a local bank Should you grant credit to an applicant for an auto loan?

Representative of a labor union Should demands be made on the company for a 6% pay increase? Or a 10% pay increase?

Executive of an appliance manufacturer Should you buy steel from a Japanese firm?

Member of a corporation's board of directors Should you increase the dividends you pay to your stockholders?

Director of a governmental program Should you request additional funding to carry out the program?

These are all economic decisions, and you need to have information in order to make them. Accounting is a service that provides managers, taxpayers, directors, or other users with the financial information they need to make informed decisions.

Financial reports are based on accounting concepts

Like any other discipline, accounting has its own terms and concepts. Financial reports are based on these concepts, and the information in the reports is expressed in accounting terms.

Many beginning students of accounting are surprised to learn that financial reports may not always be a precise measure of actual activity. For example, values presented on financial reports may reflect prices paid several years ago or current prices. Furthermore, accounting involves estimates, and estimates preclude precision.

To make informed decisions among economic alternatives, you must have a basic understanding of accounting concepts and terms; you must know how accounting information is generated, processed, and presented; and you must both realize the limitations of financial reports and know how to deal with them.

USERS OF ACCOUNTING INFORMATION

There are many different users of accounting information. Financial reports are used by investors, creditors, managers, taxpayers, union representatives, regulatory agencies, potential investors and creditors, and many others. Broadly speaking, the principles underlying the gathering and presenting of accounting information are basically similar for all economic entities. *Economic entities* are separate, distinct organizations you encounter in our society. Banks, retail stores, state governments, automobile companies, student organizations, and charitable organizations are economic entities you see or hear of daily.

Accounting principles are basically the same for all economic entities

Business entities and not-for-profit entities are the two types of economic entities

There are two types of economic entities: *profit-motivated* entities such as General Motors, Sears, and McDonald's; and *non-profit-motivated* entities such as the City of New York, the First Methodist Church, the University of Texas, and Mount Sinai Hospital. Entities of the first type are referred to as *business entities,* the second, *not-for-profit entities.* The term *economic entities* refers to both types.

FIGURE I-1
Economic Entities Can Be Either Business or Not-for-Profit Entities

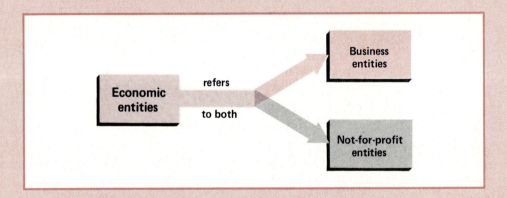

This text will focus on accounting for business entities. After you have achieved an understanding of the principles of accounting as applied to business entities, it will be relatively easy for you to apply the same principles to not-for-profit entities.

Financial reports are used by "inside" and "outside" people

A business entity has "inside" and "outside" people. The inside people are the ones who manage or control the operations and hence the destiny of the business entity. The outside people, who have provided the money to operate the business, are affected in some way by what happens to the business entity or by what it does.

External financial reports provide information needed by users who do not have direct access to the business entity's records. Some users of a business entity's information have the power to generate and enforce laws about what information is made available to them and how such information is to be submitted. As you might well imagine, these users are the Internal Revenue Service, the Securities and Exchange Commission, and the public utility commissions, among others. These agencies

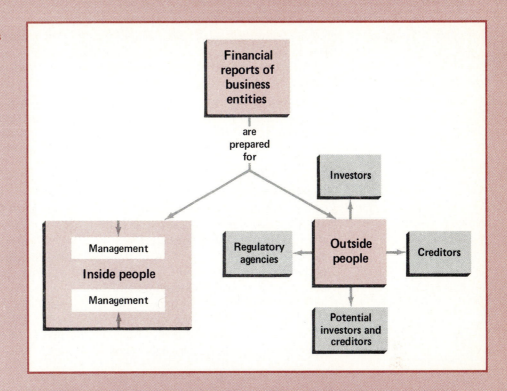

Financial reports of business entities

are prepared for

Inside people

Management

Management

Outside people

Regulatory agencies

Investors

Creditors

Potential investors and creditors

prescribe the exact manner in which the financial information is to be reported, what type of information is to be reported, and when and where it is to be reported.

There are also users who need financial information but have neither direct access to a business entity's records nor legislative power to require a business entity to report to them in a specified manner. These users are investors, potential investors, creditors, and potential creditors. Management of business entities meets the needs of these users by preparing general-purpose financial statements covering for specified periods the results of business activities and listing the economic resources entrusted to the entity and the obligations incurred by the entity.

General-purpose financial statements are prepared for investors and creditors

The area of accounting concerned with the preparation and presentation of general-purpose financial statements is referred to as ***financial accounting*** and is the subject of this text.

Internal financial reports are prepared exclusively for the inside users — the management of the business entity. These reports provide management with information that will help carry out its objectives and its responsibilities.

Internal financial reports are prepared for management

Examples of internal reports include:

■ Reports contrasting the cost of leasing a new computer with the costs of buying a new one

■ Reports showing the results that can be expected from eliminating a department

■ Reports showing the cost to produce a certain product

Management accounting is concerned with internal reporting

The area of accounting concerned with internal reporting is referred to as ***management accounting*** and is the subject of the second volume of this two-volume set.

PREPARERS OF ACCOUNTING INFORMATION

The responsibility for the accounting information contained in the financial reports of business and not-for-profit entities ultimately rests with the entity's chief executive officer. The *chief executive officer* is the president or chairman of the board of directors of a business entity, or the director, head, mayor, president, or some other designee of a not-for-profit entity. Financial reports, however, are generally prepared not by chief executive officers but by accountants engaged or employed by the economic entity. Both business entities and not-for-profit entities employ accountants.

Business Entities

The executive officer of a business entity in charge of the accounting activity is called the *controller.* As you may infer from the title, the controller is responsible for the control of the operations of the business. The controller may have a staff of several hundred accounting and finance employees, as in the case of a large international corporation such as Mobil Oil Company, or a relatively small staff, as with a small enterprise such as a local retail store.

Some small companies operate with only one or two executive officers who, in addition to their other responsibilities, also perform the function of a controller, thus eliminating the need for a separate one. They may employ a full- or part-time accountant to prepare financial reports.

Accounting Activities of Business Entities

In the next few pages, we will describe the following accounting activities of business entities:

- General financial accounting
- Accounting systems design
- Cost accounting
- Budgeting

- Taxation
- Internal auditing
- Data processing

Large international corporations may divide their accounting staffs into departments according to accounting activity. Small departments may perform some of the accounting activities with accountants employed as staff or may hire the services of independent *certified public accountants (CPAs)* for whatever accounting activities management deems necessary.

The descriptions of the accounting activities that follow will provide you with some insight into the important role accountants play in our society.

General financial accounting is concerned with recording business transactions and preparing financial reports

General Financial Accounting Business entities are involved daily with numerous business transactions, such as the purchase and sale of goods and services. General financial accounting is concerned with recording these business transactions and preparing financial reports to be used internally by management and externally by investors and creditors as well as by potential investors and creditors. Accountants working in the general financial accounting area are also responsible for preparing financial reports required by most governmental agencies. These reports must be prepared in compliance with the particular governmental agency's regulations, which are referred to as *compliance requirements.*

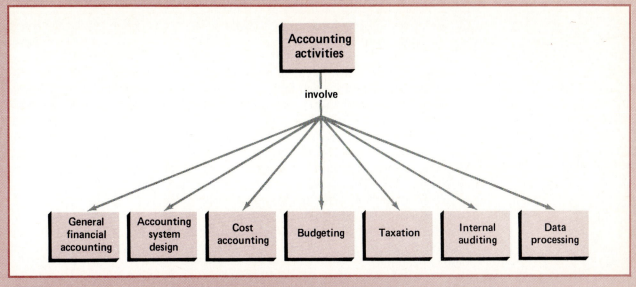

FIGURE I-3 Accounting Involves Numerous Activities

Accounting Systems Design The numerous business transactions that must be processed and recorded by the general financial accounting staff must first be *classified* before financial reports can be issued. By classifying we mean grouping together related financial transactions. For example, all sales transactions must be grouped together and classified as *sales.* Likewise, all transactions involving the purchase of inventory must be grouped together and classified as *purchases.*

Those working in accounting systems help design forms that summarize accounting data; they also develop and implement accounting procedures

In simplest terms, the classifying process is this: Sales are recorded on a sales form, purchases are recorded on a purchase form, and each of the many other business transactions is recorded on forms designed to convey the nature and purpose of the financial transaction. One of the functions of accounting systems design is to design the forms that record business activities, thus enabling the classifying process to work smoothly and efficiently. The result is that the mass of accounting data can be summarized in a meaningful manner in the financial reports. Systems design is also concerned with specifying the procedures for how an accounting system should be operated, for implementing these procedures, and for investigating new means of processing the mass of accounting data.

Cost accountants determine the cost of a product or service and provide information for cost control

Cost Accounting The accounting activity concerned with gathering accounting information for the purpose of planning and controlling and to determine the cost of a product is referred to as *cost accounting.* Not only is it essential to know the cost of a product or a service, it is even more important to control such costs. It is the responsibility of the cost accounting function to provide management with relevant information to help achieve control over cost.

Budgeting is concerned with planning for future activities

Budgeting Business entities can be managed efficiently if they have determined what their objectives are. Expressing these objectives in monetary terms is what the budgeting activity is all about. Budgets covering specific periods of time are prepared. Upon the completion of operating activities for these specific periods of time, what actually happened—the actual results—is compared to what was "budgeted" to happen—the budget. Any differences are analyzed carefully by management with the view toward improving and closing the gap between actual and budget performance in future periods.

Taxation You are well aware that individuals must pay taxes to the federal government. Business entities are also subject to taxes. A business entity must comply with the requirements of not only the Internal Revenue Service (IRS), but also state, local, and foreign tax laws. The various tax laws to which business entities are subject are very complex. Large corporations have separate tax departments staffed by specialists in tax compliance and tax planning. By the term **tax compliance** we mean following the many detailed and specific rules of the taxing authorities in preparing tax returns. The term **tax planning** refers to the study of the possible tax effects of various proposed financial transactions in which management may wish to engage. Small firms may have their general accountants prepare the required tax returns. By now you may get the idea that accountants in small firms do just about everything. They do. Small firms may also use the services of a CPA for tax return preparation and tax planning.

Compliance and planning are the main concerns of taxation

Internal Auditing In order to ensure that transactions are recorded, classified, and summarized properly, the records for each of these accounting activities must be reviewed regularly. Internal auditing is that area of accounting concerned with this review of the records. However, the scope of internal auditing extends beyond a review of the company's records. Internal auditing also encompasses a responsibility to ensure that accounting and operating policies and procedures are being properly and consistently followed. The internal auditing function cannot report to an accounting or financial officer. To do so would destroy the independent nature of the work.

Internal auditors review the accounting records and procedures

Data Processing Although general financial accounting is the activity responsible for recording business transactions, the actual physical activity of recording the mass of accounting data is not done by general financial accounting. It is done as a separate activity by the data processing department. The data processing department simply provides the service necessary to record the thousands upon thousands of business transactions the entity enters into during the year. Small firms may not have a computer installation of their own. These firms often use the services of data processing companies to meet their needs.

Data processing is the physical activity of recording accounting data

Not-for-Profit Entities

Although they don't make a profit, not-for-profit entities buy and sell goods and services and require many of the same kinds of transactions as business entities. Thus, the operating activities, the economic resources (things the entity owns), and the obligations of not-for-profit entities can be described and summarized in financial reports in much the same way that they are described and summarized in the financial reports of business entities.

Operating activities of not-for-profit entities are much the same as those of business entities

Executive officers of hospitals, directors of governmental agencies, taxpayers, elected schoolboard officials, county commissioners, and investors in municipal bonds all need reliable accounting information on which to base decisions. These needs are met by the same accounting activities as are found in accounting for business entities.

CERTIFIED PUBLIC ACCOUNTANTS (CPAs)

Like physicians and lawyers, CPAs are licensed by the state

Certified public accountants (CPAs) are independent professional accountants, licensed by the state, who provide accounting services to clients for a fee in much the same way that other professionals such as physicians and lawyers provide their services to the public. In order to obtain a license, physicians, lawyers, and CPAs must fulfill educational standards and pass certain tests. This assures the public of a high degree of competence in the practice of medicine, law, or accounting. CPAs, like other professionals, are highly regarded by their clients for two basic reasons: the rigorous training that is necessary to become a member of the profession and the self-imposed high degree of ethical standards.

Requirements for the CPA License

In order to become a CPA, an applicant must pass the comprehensive CPA examination. The CPA exam is a uniform examination prepared and graded by the American Institute of Certified Public Accountants (AICPA). The four-part examination is administered over a $2\frac{1}{2}$-day period every May and November on the same dates in all states.

Although all applicants in every state must pass the same test, there are also a number of other requirements, which can vary from state to state. A candidate must fulfill the appropriate requirements of a specific state to be granted a CPA license. The most common requirements are that an individual must be a U.S. citizen, must be of legal age as defined by the state, must be a college graduate with the equivalent of an accounting major, and, of course, must have a passing grade (75%) on all parts of the CPA exam.

The Role of the CPA

Most of the work done by CPAs is auditing, although a majority of CPAs also provide tax and management advisory services.

Auditing

The CPA is a trusted link between inside people and outside people

The major function of the CPA is to serve as a link between the preparers of financial statements and the people who use them. Like most people, most officers of business entities and directors of not-for-profit entities are ethical and honest people. The financial reports they represent to users are prepared with the highest degree of integrity. However, two different officers or directors, given exactly the same information and the same circumstances, may not produce identical reports. You might be inclined to think that one of them must have cheated. Most likely, however, your assumption would prove to be incorrect. Differences of this type result because in accounting there are alternative ways, all of them quite legal, to treat many kinds of business transactions. Of course, and unfortunately, there always have been and always will be cheaters who prepare inexact and dishonest reports. But, although it may take some time, they are usually discovered.

FIGURE I-4
The CPA Reviews a Business Entity's Financial Statements to Provide Assurance to Outside People

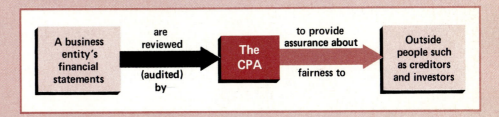

Users of financial statements do not have access to the financial records of the economic entity in which they are interested. They cannot assure for themselves that proper choices of accounting alternatives have been made. Users also need assurance that the statements fairly and honestly represent the results of operating activities as well as resources and obligations. Because users cannot establish these assurances for themselves, they must rely on assurances from someone else.

The CPA provides that assurance by performing an independent audit of the economic entity and issuing an audit report that is an integral part of the financial statements issued by the economic entity. By the term *independent audit* we mean a check of the accounting records of an economic entity by someone who is neither an employee of the entity nor related to an officer of the entity. (The check is not made of 100% of the accounting records: That's not necessary. A statistically selected sample of the records is used.) The audit report is a statement of the CPA saying that the financial reports issued by the economic entity are fairly stated and prepared in accordance with approved accounting rules. An audit report usually must accompany the financial reports issued by a business entity.

The CPA assures the public that financial statements are fair

Tax Services

Tax services provided to a client by the CPA include preparing and filing tax returns and, perhaps of greater importance, tax planning. Tax planning directly affects the prime objective of business entities, which is to make profits. Any business decision about how to make those profits involves another decision about how much taxes will have to be paid. With proper tax planning, decisions can be made to reduce taxes that would affect increased profits. CPAs are uniquely qualified to render service in this area because of their knowledge of the tax laws, tax regulations, and various court decisions regarding taxes.

CPAs play a major role in any business entity's tax planning

Management Advisory Services

Management advisory services are offered by CPAs in addition to auditing and tax services. A CPA, in the course of auditing many different clients, observes many different accounting systems. This experience enables the CPA to analyze any particular client's strengths and weaknesses. Thus, as a CPA audits a business entity, a natural by-product of the audit is suggestions for improving the performance of the business to make profits. Management has come to expect these suggestions as part of

Management advisory services are often a by-product of an audit engagement

**FIGURE I-5
Auditing, Taxes, and
Management Advising Are
Services Offered by CPAs**

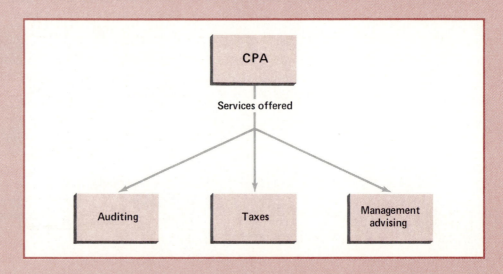

the audit. Moreover, management may often want further help, engaging the CPA for specific management services, such as establishing an accounting system for determining costs, or designing a new payroll system, or designing a system for the firm to help estimate future performance. It is not at all uncommon to find mathematicians, statisticians, and engineers on the management services staff of many large CPA firms.

FINANCIAL STATEMENTS FOR BUSINESS ENTITIES

Financial statements are the end product of the general financial accounting activity

Business entities communicate their financial information to interested users through published financial statements. By *published* we mean reports prepared in a manner similar to a glossy-covered magazine such as *Sports Illustrated.* You would find in these reports not only the financial statements but also color pictures of the companies' products and facilities. The reports are usually 30 to 40 pages long. These statements represent the end product of the general financial accounting activity. The main objective of general financial accounting is to communicate a description of the financial condition and operation of a business entity, and that is done through financial statements. The financial statements, the last step in the accounting process, are the starting point in the study of accounting. As with most other things, by understanding what the ultimate goal is, it is easier to understand the concepts and procedures used to achieve it. You will begin Chapter 1 by studying the basic financial statements.

FIGURE I-6
Information Provided by the Financial Statements

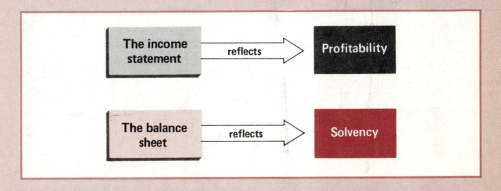

While many of the concepts and procedures of accounting are equally applicable to both business entities and not-for-profit entities, this text will be concerned mainly with business entities, whose objective is to earn a profit. To earn a profit, a business entity must sell its service or product at a price that exceeds its cost. In addition, sufficient funds must be generated to pay debts as they become due and to acquire productive resources when needed. Only then can profits become available to those who have invested in the business entity. There are other objectives of business entities, but earning profits and paying debts when due are the two most important.

Earning profits and paying debts are two important objectives of business entities

If a business entity fails to earn sufficient profits, its owners may dispose of the business and invest their funds in more promising alternatives.

The inability of an entity to pay its current maturing debts is called insolvency

A business entity unable to pay its debts as they become due is said to be ***insolvent.*** When a business entity becomes insolvent, its creditors (the people and firms owed money) can seek payment through legal recourse, which may involve closing the business and selling its equipment and buildings to get some money to pay creditors.

Financial statements are designed to provide users with information concerning the profitability and solvency—the capacity to pay debts—of business enterprises. The *income statement* and the *balance sheet* are the two principal financial statements that contain this information. The income statement tells us about the entity's profitability, while the balance sheet tells us about its solvency. After recording, classifying, and summarizing thousands of business transactions, an accountant represents all that work on an income statement and a balance sheet. These two statements are prepared for managers, owners, creditors, and other users of accounting information for business entities.

The income statement provides information on profitability, while the balance sheet provides information on solvency

THE THREE TYPES OF BUSINESS ENTITIES

There are three main types of business entities: *proprietorships, partnerships,* and *corporations.* Although there are minor differences in the way each type of business entity reports information, all of them use basically the same type of financial statements. These minor differences will be brought to your attention in Part Four, *Accounting for Partnerships and Corporations.*

Proprietorship

A proprietorship is a business entity owned by one person

A business entity that is owned by one person is called a *proprietorship.* Many attorneys, accountants, and physicians do their professional work as individual practitioners, and thus are proprietorships. The proprietorship form of business is also

**FIGURE I-7
Legal and Accounting
Concepts of a
Proprietorship**

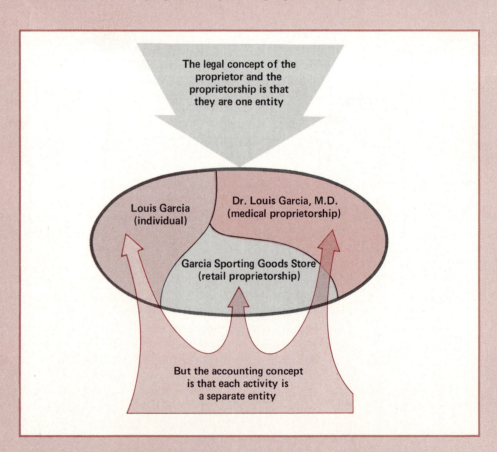

common for small retail enterprises. The main characteristic of a proprietorship is that it can be formed so easily. You simply decide to start a business, obtain an operating license (if necessary), and there it is—the business exists. There are no other requirements.

No legal distinction exists between a proprietorship and its owner, but a distinction is made for accounting purposes

Legally, the owner of a business entity—the proprietor—and the business entity itself—the proprietorship—are considered to be one and the same. If the proprietor were to die, the proprietorship would cease to exist. However, for accounting purposes a distinction must be made between the two. The following example should clarify this for you.

There is this chap, Louis Garcia, who is a physician and who also owns a sporting goods store. That is, he owns the medical proprietorship, Louis Garcia, M.D., and the proprietorship, Garcia Sporting Goods Store. Dr. Garcia needs financial information on three separate entities: his medical practice, the sporting goods store, and his own personal affairs. Since there is no legal distinction among these three entities, income taxes are imposed on him only as an individual. Of course, all the income earned from his medical practice as Dr. Garcia and the income earned from his store must be included together as Louis Garcia's personal income.

Partnership

A partnership is a business entity owned by two or more persons

A business entity that is owned by two or more persons is called a ***partnership.*** Most small businesses and professional service groups are partnerships. For example, there are several CPA firms that have more than 1,000 partners. Like a proprietorship, a partnership is easy to form. The various partners simply agree (preferably in writing) to conduct a business entity as co-owners. The agreement typically specifies how the profits will be shared among partners and provides arrangements for settlements to be made to withdrawing partners or upon the death of a partner. Legally, the

No legal distinction is made between a partnership and its partners, but an accounting distinction exists

owners of a partnership and the partnership itself are not considered to be separate. As you may have guessed, the accounting concept is that they are separate. Financial statements are prepared for the business entity and for the partnership, and may also be prepared for each of the individual partners.

Corporation

A business entity organized as a corporation is considered by law to be an artificial person. By the term ***artificial person*** we mean that the corporation itself has many of the rights and obligations that a person does. It can be sued and can sue, it can borrow money, it can enter into contracts, and it must pay income taxes. Persons wishing to form a corporation must request state officials to grant that privilege. The request is in the form of an application for a corporate charter. The charter is a document issued by the state, if the request is granted, providing legal evidence that the corporation is

A corporation is a legal entity, distinct from its owners

created. Upon creation, the corporation issues shares of stock to its owners, who are referred to as ***shareholders*** or ***stockholders.*** The shareholders receive stock certificates as evidence of their ownership interests. Most large corporations have many thousands of shareholders.

The basic concepts and procedures of accounting apply to all three forms of business entities. So, in the first several chapters we'll simply refer to the business entity in general. There are distinctions in accounting among the three forms, as we mentioned previously, and we will get into them later, in Part Four.

GENERALLY ACCEPTED ACCOUNTING PRINCIPLES

Consider the situation presented by the following facts: Red Company, White Company, and Blue Company are competitors in the data processing industry. Several years ago, each of the three companies acquired identical computers for $100,000. Inflation is such that $100,000 purchasing power several years ago, when the computers were acquired, is equivalent to $120,000 purchasing power today. The computer industry is characterized by rapid technological advances such that new computers equivalent in capacity to the older ones acquired by Red, White, and Blue could be purchased today for $75,000. At the end of the current year, when the balance sheets are presented, the value of the computer is listed among the assets of Red Company at $100,000; Blue Company reports the computer as an asset valued at $120,000; and White Company values it at $75,000. Obviously there exists a need for some type of ground rules that all companies will follow when presenting financial statements. Otherwise the statements will not provide information that is useful to investors and creditors.

Generally accepted accounting principles (GAAP) are the ground rules of accounting

The ground rules used by business entities in presenting financial information are called *generally accepted accounting principles (GAAP).* These principles have been developed by the accounting profession over the years in an attempt to provide a consistent system of financial reporting in a constantly changing business environment. Unlike the physical sciences, where natural laws are universally and eternally true, accounting principles may change to meet the needs of emerging and changing financial situations. What may have provided adequate financial information several years ago may not be adequate today.

The authority of accounting principles rests on their general acceptance by the accounting profession. Generally accepted accounting principles encompass not only accounting principles, but various procedures for applying these principles. For example, one accounting principle tells us that the price we paid for a machine must be spread over the period of time, the *life,* we expect to use the machine. We have several accepted procedures for applying this principle. We could spread the cost over the life in equal amounts per year; we could spread the costs based on the number of hours the machine was used each year; or we could spread the cost based on the number of units the machine produced each year.

Accounting principles develop as members of the accounting profession think about various issues in accounting in an attempt to seek solutions to those issues. What may be a theoretically sound solution to a particular accounting problem may have certain practical limitations. The experience of the members of the accounting profession will determine when a practical rather than a conceptual solution to a problem is required. Thus, generally accepted accounting principles are a blend of theoretical principles and practical considerations.

Development of Accounting Principles: Major Institutions

Several groups have been influential in the development of generally accepted accounting principles for the entire accounting profession: the Financial Accounting Standards Board, the American Institute of Certified Public Accountants, the Securities and Exchange Commission, the American Accounting Association, and the National Association of Accountants.

Financial Accounting Standards Board

The group responsible for developing generally accepted accounting principles today is the *Financial Accounting Standards Board,* commonly referred to as the

A major portion of GAAP is developed by the FASB

FASB. These generally accepted accounting principles are called **Statements** of the Financial Accounting Standards Board and, in effect, must be followed by all business entities issuing financial statements to investors or creditors. The FASB consists of seven full-time members. The FASB members spend a considerable amount of time and effort in developing a standard. **Discussion memorandums,** which are pamphlets explaining the basic issues of the topic under consideration, are prepared; **public hearings,** where accountants and others can express their views orally and in writing, are held; and **exposure drafts,** which are the FASB's planned solutions to the problem, are written. After all this the FASB members vote on the standards, and if four of the seven approve, it is issued to the accounting profession as a new standard.

FIGURE I-8
The FASB, Which Is the Prime Source of GAAP, Receives Input from Several Organizations

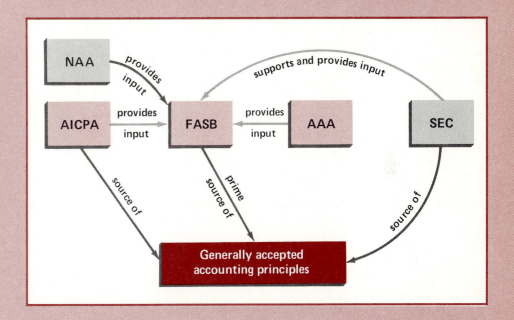

Securities and Exchange Commission

The SEC provides strong support for the FASB

The Securities and Exchange Act of 1934 created an independent quasi-judicial agency of the federal government to administer the various acts concerning the distribution and sale of publicly held securities. This agency is called the **Securities and Exchange Commission (SEC).** Legal authority is vested in the SEC to require whatever specific accounting practices it deems necessary to protect the public. However, the SEC has taken the position that accounting principles are best set in the private sector rather than the public sector. As a consequence the SEC has looked to the FASB to establish generally accepted accounting principles, and thus far most of the FASB statements have been accepted by the SEC as its own requirements for how financial and accounting data must be reported. On occasion the SEC may differ with the FASB over certain accounting principles, and when that happens the SEC may issue its own ruling requiring whatever additional accounting information it believes must be reported to the SEC and perhaps also presented in the annual reports to stockholders. While the SEC could exist without the FASB, most certainly the FASB could not exist without the support of its friendly partner, the SEC, and its power to legislate accounting principles.

American Institute of Certified Public Accountants

As the American Bar Association is to the legal profession and the American Medical Association is to the medical profession, so the ***American Institute of Certified Public Accountants (AICPA)*** is to the accounting profession. The AICPA is the professional organization representing certified public accountants on a national basis.

Here are some of the ways the AICPA contributes to or affects the generally accepted accounting principles:

The AICPA provides input to the FASB and the SEC

■ The AICPA collects reactions of its members to accounting issues and furnishes them to the FASB, which considers them in developing new standards.

■ The AICPA represents the views of the profession in cases of congressional investigations.

■ The AICPA publishes a monthly magazine called the *Journal of Accountancy* and many other materials on accounting.

The APB was the predecessor of the FASB

Prior to the establishment of the FASB in 1973, the AICPA was directly involved with developing generally accepted accounting principles. The predecessor to the FASB, the Accounting Principles Board (APB), was a committee within the AICPA responsible for issuing statements on accounting principles. These statements were called APB *Opinions* and, unless superseded by a later *Opinion* of the APB, or a *Standard* of the FASB, are still in effect today.

American Accounting Association

The AAA provides indirect and long-range influence on GAAP

The ***American Accounting Association (AAA)*** is an organization of accounting professors. As such, its influence on establishing accounting principles is indirect and long-range. The research done by AAA members leans toward the theoretical rather than the practical. The AAA is in continual search for the way accounting issues should be solved. The theoretical solution offered by the AAA today often finds its way into accounting a number of years later. For example, the present concept of the income statement was expressed 20 years ago by the AAA. Articles in the *Accounting Review,* the AAA's quarterly publication, and AAA committee reports may help establish accounting principles in the future.

National Association of Accountants

The ***National Association of Accountants (NAA)*** is an organization of private accountants concerned with managerial accounting issues. Their publication, *Management Accounting,* is issued monthly. The organization conducts research on current topics and develops an extensive educational program. The NAA sponsors the ***Institute of Management Accounting (IMA),*** which prepares and administers an examination similar to the CPA exam. Those passing this examination are issued a ***Certificate in Management Accounting (CMA).***

INTRODUCTION SUMMARY

Accounting is a service that provides financial reports on which informed economic decisions are based.

Financial reports are prepared for two distinct user groups. Internal financial reports are prepared for management of economic entities—this area of accounting is referred to as *management accounting.* External financial reports are prepared for those who do not have direct access to the entity's records — this area of accounting is referred to as *financial accounting.*

There are many different kinds of accounting activities. Principal among them:

■ *General financial accounting* is concerned with recording business transactions and preparing financial reports.

■ *Accounting systems design* is concerned with the development of business forms and records, with writing and implementing operating procedures, and with investigating new means of processing accounting data.

■ *Cost accounting* involves the gathering of accounting information to determine the cost of a product or service.

■ *Budgeting* expresses predetermined business objectives in monetary terms.

■ *Taxation* is concerned with the preparation of various tax returns in compliance with the taxing authority's requirements and with tax planning to minimize the impact of taxes of the business entity.

■ *Internal auditing* provides a continual review of the accounting records, reports, policies, and procedures.

■ *Data processing* is responsible for recording the mass of business transactions generated by a business entity.

Users of external financial statements need assurance that the financial statements have been prepared in a manner that fairly represents the results of activities for the period. Such assurance is provided by the *certified public accountant (CPA),* who issues an audit report based on an independent review of the business transactions underlying the financial report. CPAs are licensed by the various states only after passing the CPA examination. Generally a CPA candidate must have a college degree with a major in accounting to be eligible to take the CPA exam.

There are three main types of entities:

1. *Proprietorship*   A business entity owned by one person
2. *Partnership*   A non-incorporated business entity owned by two or more persons
3. *Corporation*   A business entity incorporated under the laws of one of the states

Generally accepted accounting principles (GAAP) have been developed over the years in an attempt to provide a rational system of financial reporting. These principles can be considered the ground rules of financial accounting. The most influential groups in the development of generally accepted accounting principles are the *Financial Accounting Standards Board (FASB)* and the *Securities and Exchange Commission (SEC).* The *American Institute of Certified Public Accountants (AICPA),* the *American Accounting Association (AAA),* and the *National Association of Accountants (NAA)* also provide input into the development of GAAP.

IMPORTANT TERMS USED IN THIS INTRODUCTION

American Accounting Association   The organization of professional accounting educators. (page 16)

American Institute of Certified Public Accountants   The professional organization of CPAs. (page 16)

Budgeting   The accounting activity concerned with expressing predetermined management objectives in monetary terms. (page 7)

Certified public accountant   An individual who has met the educational and experience requirements as prescribed by state law and has passed the uniform CPA exam. A CPA performs an independent review of business entities' financial transactions (called an audit) and expresses his or her professional opinion on the fairness of the financial statements issued by the business entity. (page 9)

Controller   The executive officer of a business entity in charge of its accounting activity. (page 6)

Corporation   A business entity that is incorporated under the laws of one of the states. (page 13)

Cost accounting   The accounting activity concerned with determining the cost of producing a product or service. (page 7)

Data processing   The accounting activity concerned with the physical act of recording the mass of accounting data. (page 8)

External financial reports   Reports — the income statement, the statement of stockholders' equity, and the balance sheet — prepared to meet the informational needs of those who do not have direct access to the business entity's records. (page 4)

Financial accounting   The area of accounting concerned with the preparation and presentation of general-purpose financial statements. (page 5)

Financial Accounting Standards Board   The independent public board, comprising seven full-time members, which is responsible for the development of generally accepted accounting principles. (page 14)

Generally accepted accounting principles (GAAP)   The ground rules used by economic entities in presenting financial information. (page 14)

Internal auditing   The area of accounting concerned with checking and reviewing the entity's records, reporting policies, and procedures. (page 8)

Internal financial reports   Reports prepared exclusively for management of business entities. (page 5)

Management accounting   The area of accounting concerned with internal reporting. (page 5)

National Association of Accountants   The professional organization of management accountants. (page 16)

Partnership   A non-incorporated business entity that is owned by two or more persons. (page 13)

Proprietorship   A business entity that is owned by one person. (page 12)

Securities and Exchange Commission   An independent quasi-judicial agency of the federal government responsible for administering the various acts concerning the distribution and sale of publicly held securities. (page 15)

Taxation   The area of accounting concerned with preparation of various tax returns and with tax planning to minimize the impact of taxes on the business entity. (page 8)

QUESTIONS

1. The terms *economic entities, business entities,* and *not-for-profit entities* are often used by business persons and accountants. Distinguish among these terms. Are the accounting needs of one different from the others?

2. Corporations and other economic entities prepare two types of financial reports, *internal* and *external*. Explain the difference between the two.

3. Describe the various areas of accounting activity.

4. Corporate financial reports are prepared by accountants, yet the accountants are not responsible for those reports. Comment.

5. The independent certified public accountant plays an important part in issuing external financial statements of corporations. Explain this role.

6. Describe briefly the requirements to become a certified public accountant.

7. What is a corporation? In addition to corporations, two other legal forms of business entities exist. Describe them.

8. Corporate financial statements are prepared using generally accepted accounting principles. What does this term mean? Why are these principles necessary?

9. *Statements* of the Financial Accounting Standards Board and *Opinions* of the Accounting Principles Board are deemed important to corporations. Why?

10. Explain the function of the Securities and Exchange Commission and its relationship to the FASB.

Basic Concepts and the Accounting Model

- The basic purpose of the principal *financial statements* and the type of information contained in each
- What the basic *accounting concepts and principles* are and what they mean
- How business transactions affect the basic accounting model
- How to record business transactions on a financial transaction worksheet
- How to prepare the financial statements

The Introduction to *Financial Accounting* provided you with some insight about the environment of financial accounting. You learned that there are two distinct user groups of financial reports, internal and external, and that there are many kinds of accounting activities.

You also learned about the role the CPA plays in financial reporting and why financial statements must be prepared in accordance with generally accepted accounting principles.

With this background you are now ready to start the study of financial accounting. And we will start at the end — that is, the end result of financial accounting, which is the financial statements. Once we have a basic understanding of these statements, we can introduce a few generally accepted accounting principles on which these statements are based. Finally, we will show you how an entity accumulates the financial data to develop financial statements.

THE PRINCIPAL FINANCIAL STATEMENTS

The principal financial statements are the *income statement,* the *balance sheet,* and the *statement of retained earnings.*

The Income Statement

The financial statement designed to report the profitability of a business entity is the *income statement.* Many consider it more important than the balance sheet because the first question asked by most users is whether or not the business entity achieved its first objective: Did the business earn a profit? The answer to that question is the main purpose of an income statement. The income statement compares the

The income statement compares revenue with expenses

[20]

revenue earned during a specified period of time with the *expenses* incurred during that same period of time, as seen in the following income statement:

The income statement compares revenues and expenses for a period of time

REPAIR & RENTAL CORPORATION Income Statement Year Ended December 31, 1989		
Revenues:		
Service Fees..		$ 72,375
Equipment Rental Fees...		36,100
Total Revenues..		$108,475
Expenses:		
Salaries Expense...	$51,000	
Repairs Expense...	12,450	
Advertising Expense	3,500	
Utilities Expense	1,360	
Total Expenses...		68,310
Net Income		$ 40,165

Revenue

The amount charged for goods sold or services rendered is called **revenue.** Examples of revenue are sales, commissions earned, rental fees, and fees for professional services rendered.

Revenue is the amount charged for goods sold or services rendered

Total revenue earned by Repair & Rental Corporation is $108,475. This revenue resulted from two activities: service fees, $72,375, and equipment rental fees, $36,100.

Expenses

Expenses are the costs of goods sold or the services rendered in the process of generating revenues

Expenses are the cost of goods sold by a business entity or the services rendered to it in the process of generating revenue. Examples of expenses are salaries, delivery expenses, utilities expense, and travel expenses. Repair & Rental Corporation incurred $68,310 of expenses in generating revenue. If revenue earned exceeds expenses incurred, the difference is **net income.** As illustrated in the Repair & Rental Corporation example, revenue exceeds expenses by $40,165, which is the net income. However, if expenses exceed revenue, the result is a **net loss** for the period.

The Heading

Notice that the income statement is identified by a heading and that the heading consists of three lines:

The heading consists of the name of the company, the type of statement, and the time period covered

1. The first line specifies the name of the company.

2. The second line specifies the type of financial statement it is—this financial statement is an income statement.

3. The third line specifies the period of time covered by the financial statement.

The last item is very important. Revenue and expenses are **time concepts.** Revenue is earned and expenses are incurred over a period of time. When we tell you that Repair & Rental Corporation had revenue of $9,500 in January, you will know that we mean Repair & Rental Corporation has accumulated revenue of $9,500 from Jan. 1 to Jan. 31. If we say that the corporation incurred $17,000 of expenses in the second quarter, you will know that this amount was incurred from April 1 to June 30. And if we say that the corporation had revenue of $108,475 for the year, you will know that is the amount of revenue earned from Jan. 1 to Dec. 31. Users of the financial statements need to know if the revenue earned and expenses incurred represent amounts for 1 month, 2 quarters, or a year. Without knowing what period of time the statement covers, users cannot interpret the financial data reported, nor can they compare them with previous financial statements or financial statements of other firms.

The Balance Sheet

The financial statement designed to show a business entity's financial position — what it owns and what it owes — on a particular date is called the **balance sheet.** By reviewing a firm's balance sheet — comparing what it owns with what it owes — users can make judgments about whether or not and how easily the firm pays its bills — and this, we have already learned, is called the **solvency** of the firm.

See the balance sheet for Repair & Rental Corporation at the bottom of this page. For the moment, don't be too concerned about the technical terms listed in it. What we want you to be concerned about is that the balance sheet consists of two sides. The left side represents what the firm owns, its **assets;** the right side represents what the firm owes, its **liabilities,** and the amount the owners have invested in the business, the **stockholders' equity.** In a sense, the business owes the amount shown under stockholders' equity to the stockholders. If the business were sold or dissolved and all the liabilities paid, the remaining money would be paid to the stockholders.

The total of the assets, $108,000, on the left side of the Repair & Rental Corporation balance sheet is indeed equal to the sum of the liabilities, $24,300, and the stockholders' equity, $83,700, on the right side — hence the term **balance sheet.**

Like the income statement, the balance sheet has a heading with three important parts: first, the name of the company; second, what type of financial statement it is; and third, the date of the balance sheet. Unlike the income statement, which covers a specified *period of time,* the balance sheet is a listing of assets, liabilities, and stockholders' equity at a *point in time.* That point in time for Repair & Rental Corporation is the close of business on Dec. 31, 1989.

The balance sheet covers a point in time

REPAIR & RENTAL CORPORATION
Balance Sheet
December 31, 1989

Assets		Liabilities and Stockholders' Equity		
Cash	$ 6,300	Liabilities:		
Accounts Receivable	9,050	Notes Payable		$ 10,000
Supplies on Hand	2,100	Accounts Payable		14,300
Land	18,000	Total Liabilities		$ 24,300
Building	45,300			
Equipment	27,250	Stockholders' Equity:		
		Capital Stock	$30,000	
		Retained Earnings	53,700	
		Total Stockholders' Equity		83,700
		Total Liabilities and Stockholders'		
Total Assets	$108,000	Equity		$108,000

The balance sheet lists what a company owns and what it owes

The Statement of Retained Earnings

This third financial statement is designed to show how the stockholders' equity has changed from the start of a period to the end of a period. It is a connecting link between the income statement and the balance sheet. For Repair & Rental Corporation the statement of retained earnings looks like this:

REPAIR & RENTAL CORPORATION Statement of Retained Earnings Year Ended December 31, 1989	
Retained Earnings, Jan. 31, 1989	$33,535
Add: Net Income...	40,165
Total	$73,700
Less: Dividends	(20,000)
Retained Earnings, Dec. 31, 1989	$53,700

Again, as with the other two statements, the heading is important. It has three parts: the name of the company, the name of the statement, and the period of time covered. This statement is like the income statement in that it too covers a period of time, from Jan. 1, 1989, to Dec. 31, 1989. The statement tells us that the corporation started the year with retained earnings of $33,535. During the year it increased by $40,165; the net income we saw on the income statement. And $20,000 were paid in dividends. The corporation ended up with retained earnings of $53,700 on Dec. 31, 1989, which was also the figure we saw on the balance sheet in the stockholders' equity section.

Assets

The *assets* of an economic entity are the economic resources that are owned by the entity and that are expected to provide future benefits. They may be *physical* in nature, such as cash, merchandise, supplies, equipment, trucks, machines, buildings, and land. Or they may not exist in a tangible or physical form.

Nonphysical assets can be legal claims, such as payments due from customers (called *accounts receivable*), or legal rights, such as patents or copyrights. These nonphysical assets produce future benefits. For example, when we sell a product for $10 to one of our customers, the customer may not pay the amount due today. He or she may charge it, and pay at the end of the month. We have sold our product *on account,* earning revenue of $10, and we have a nonphysical asset—an account receivable of $10—which we anticipate will be collected shortly. The future benefit is the cash we will receive at the end of the month.

To be included on the balance sheet as an asset, an economic resource must be measurable; if it is not measurable, it is not an asset. For example, the managerial ability of the company's president is an economic resource that will provide future benefit, but it is not susceptible to measurement.

Liabilities

The *liabilities* of an economic entity are its debts. The debts may be represented as *formal* claims or *informal* claims. A formal claim is a written contract, such as a written promise to repay a borrowed sum of money plus interest at a specified future date; this is called a *note payable.* Or a debt may be represented as an informal claim such as an amount due to a creditor for goods and services acquired but not yet paid for; this is called an *account payable.*

Stockholders' equity is the difference between an entity's assets and its liabilities

Stockholders' Equity

To convey to you the meaning of stockholders' equity, an example is needed. Assume that several of us decide to go into business and invest $40,000 of our own money to buy an empty factory building. Next, we borrow $60,000 from a bank and buy machines to put in the factory. That's it. We need nothing else; we are ready to operate. At this point we could prepare a balance sheet. If we did, it would look like this:

Assets		Liabilities and Stockholders' Equity	
Assets......................	$100,000	Liabilities	$60,000
		Stockholders' Equity	40,000

The bank has a claim on our assets amounting to $60,000. This is a liability. There are no other creditors' claims on our assets. The difference between the assets and the creditors' claims on those assets, the liabilities, represents the owner's interest in the business. In our business we have a $40,000 interest. This is the ***stockholders' equity.*** Since the creditors' claim on a business entity's assets take precedence over stockholders' claims, stockholders' equity represents a residual amount equal to the difference between assets and liabilities.

Look back at Rental & Repair Corporation for a moment. Notice that the stockholders' equity section has two items: capital stock and retained earnings. Retained earnings are exactly that: earnings (profits) that are retained in the business. If this concept eludes you now, be patient—we will come back to it later in the chapter.

Prior to lending money to a business entity, creditors will study the relationship between the resources provided by other creditors and the resources provided by the owner. Generally, the greater the amount of resources provided by creditors compared to that provided by the owner, the greater the risk to be taken by any new creditors considering lending additional funds.

CERTAIN BASIC ACCOUNTING PRINCIPLES

Now that you have some idea about why generally accepted accounting principles are needed and how and who sets these principles, we'll take a look at some specific and very important accounting principles and the concepts behind them. The principles are the basis for how financial statements are prepared. Of course, there are many principles, and as we take up further topics, we'll also discuss the principles related to those topics. But at this early point, we'll begin with principles that relate to preparing financial statements. As we proceed in this chapter, as well as throughout the entire text, we will regularly refer to the principles relating to the topic under discussion. This will help your awareness and increase your understanding of the reasons why the financial statements are presented as they are.

Five concepts and principles are presented in this section:

1. The cost principle
2. The objectivity principle
3. The business entity concept
4. The going concern concept
5. The stable-dollar concept

The Cost Principle

Assets acquired by a business entity are to be recorded at the exchange price paid for them. The price the buyer pays in exchange for an asset is known as the ***historical***

The cost principle requires that assets be recorded at their exchange price

cost. It is called a historical cost because, once recorded, the cost of the asset remains unchanged.

Applying this cost principle to the situation of the Red Company, White Company, and Blue Company discussed on page 14 would require that the identical computers purchased by each company all be recorded at their historical cost, $100,000. Neither the current market value of $75,000, nor the cost adjusted for inflation of $120,000, would be recorded. Neither value is in accordance with this generally accepted accounting principle.

It is important to realize at this early stage that *the assets listed on the balance sheet are measured in dollar amounts that represent the* historical cost *of those assets,* not *what presently could be obtained from their sale.*

The Objectivity Principle

The cost of an asset is established by an exchange transaction between an informed buyer and an informed seller. Evidence of the exchange price agreed upon and transacted by both parties can be found in documents such as purchase invoices, sales invoices, property deeds, transfers of title, and other similar documents. This exchange price — the historical cost — can be confirmed by any independent party by simply reviewing the information in the documents that describes the transaction. By the term **independent party** we mean a person who is not related to, nor has a financial interest in the business affairs of, either the buyer or seller. The evidence supplies facts on which assets are measured.

The objectivity principle requires that values be determined by verifiable objective evidence

The **objectivity principle** establishes the reason for recording assets at cost. Any value other than cost could not be agreed upon by independent parties who are experts in determining values of assets. Estimated market values are not based on fact and are not objective; they are subjective. **Subjective** means that they rest on the opinion of the one making the estimate.

FIGURE 1-1 Objective vs. Subjective Evidence
To determine the value of the car on July 15, 1988, for financial reporting, the accountant will look to the objective evidence provided by the sales invoice rather than to the subjective evidence provided by appraisals.

The Business Entity Concept

For accounting purposes financial statements are prepared for each individual business entity, as we discussed previously with the Louis Garcia example on page 13. A business entity is considered to be separate and distinct from its owner or owners. Similarly, when a travel agency and a dry cleaning store are operated by the same person but as two separate proprietorships, the business transactions of each must be recorded, summarized, and reported separately, resulting in an income statement and a balance sheet for each enterprise. The purchase of an automobile by the owner of these two establishments for his or her personal use could not be considered as relating to either business entity. Thus, accounting treats each business entity as generating its own revenue, incurring its own expenses, owning its own assets, and owing its own debts. As seen previously, this is not legally true for a proprietorship or a partnership.

The Going Concern Concept

Business entities are established with the basic assumption of continued existence. Even though occasionally the entity may incur a loss, so long as the stockholders can reasonably expect future earnings that will yield profits, a business entity will continue to operate. Thus, it is assumed that a business entity will be in existence for as far into the future as is necessary to complete any projects the business entity plans to undertake. This is the ***going concern*** concept. It is because of this concept that assets are considered to have future economic benefits. Since the business entity will be in existence long enough to complete any project it is now working on, or plans to work on in the future, any assets that will not be used up in 1 year are recorded on the balance sheet. If we did not have this going concern concept, we would be forced to record all assets as expenses on the income statement. We would not know if any future benefit would be received from the asset, since the business entity might not be in operation next year.

For example, a building typically has an estimated useful life of 40 years, but its full cost is not recorded as an expense when acquired. Instead, because the business entity expects to be in existence 40 years hence, the cost of the building will be allocated to each of 40 successive annual income statements as an expense. The market value of the building today, as well as most other assets acquired by the business entity, is not considered relevant to the users of the financial statements since the entity does not plan to sell those assets it needs to operate the business. There is considerable disagreement on this last point.

The Stable-Dollar Concept

The mile and the kilometer are standard units that enable us to measure distances. If we know the distance between two cities, we can use that information to estimate the time to travel between them or how much gasoline is needed to make the trip.

Money is the unit of measure employed in recording financial transactions. Knowing the money values assigned to financial transactions enables the users of financial statements to estimate the profitability or solvency of a business enterprise. The mile and the kilometer are precise units of measure. Every mile or kilometer will measure exactly the same distance. Unfortunately, the same precision is not true for money. A dollar of 1980 is not the same as a dollar of today. As we know, this is due to inflation.

Accountants do not recognize that the value of the dollar changes over time. They prepare financial statements based on the ***stable-dollar concept.***

We use this term *stable dollar* to mean that the dollar of a past year is equal in value to a current dollar. When we compare revenues of 1980 to revenues of 1988, the same dollar is used to measure the revenues from each year. The accounting dollar is thus assumed to be "stable"—it does not change in value over time. This we know is not true! The dollar does change in value over time. We could buy 1 gallon of gasoline for $0.34 in 1972. How much is a gallon of gasoline today? The gallon stayed the same, but the dollar certainly didn't.

It is possible to present financial statements adjusted for current values, but to do so would require subjective judgments on the part of those preparing such statements. We could adjust the $40,000 cost of a building acquired several years ago to a current value by the use of the **consumer price index (CPI)**. If the CPI was 100 when the building was acquired and it is now 250, we would simply multiply the $40,000 by $\frac{250}{100}$ to obtain a current value of $100,000. But is that the true value of the building today? It may cost $125,000 in materials to replace the building today. And why did we use the CPI—why not the wholesale price index or some other index?

While such information concerning current values is useful, accountants generally feel that objectivity in determining historical cost is more important. The FASB has, however, considered the problem of inflation and has in the past required that the basic financial statements of the largest corporations be supplemented with information concerning changing prices. With inflation at relatively low levels this requirement has been rescinded.

THE BASIC ACCOUNTING MODEL

The end result of the accounting activity for a business entity is the financial statements that describe the entity. These statements cannot be prepared until the financial transactions of the business entity have been recorded, classified, and summarized. The framework of the financial statements rests on a basic relationship, referred to as the accounting model, as expressed by the balance sheet equation:

The basic accounting model must always be in balance

$$\text{Assets} = \text{Liabilities} + \text{Stockholders' Equity}$$

This fundamental equality is always true because the left side of the equation is simply another view of the right side. Assets represent resources owned by the business entity; liabilities and stockholders' equity represent the claims of those who supplied the assets.

Financial transactions represent the exchange of goods and services between economic entities. Each financial transaction will affect the balance sheet equation. Consider, for example, the acquisition of an asset. We can list only three ways the asset can be acquired:

1. It could be acquired by paying cash—*giving up an asset already owned.* Buying an office desk for cash would be an example.

2. It could be acquired today with a promise to pay the amount due at some future date—*incurring a liability.* Buying an office desk, but not paying for it until next month, would illustrate incurring a liability.

3. It could be acquired from a stockholder of the business entity—*increasing the stockholders' equity* in the business. If the stockholder of a business used his or her own personal desk in the business, the business would have acquired the desk from the stockholder.

Can you see that each of these financial transactions has two parts?
On the one hand, acquiring the office desk by paying cash would increase the total

assets owned by the business entity by the cost of the desk. But on the other hand, the cash would be reduced by a like amount.

Acquiring the desk by incurring a liability would increase the total assets, but also increase the liabilities.

Acquiring the desk from the stockholder would increase the total assets, but also increase the stockholders' equity.

Since the transaction has two parts, the term *double-entry accounting* is used to refer to the recording of financial transactions.

Remember: The ultimate result of the accounting activity for an entity is its financial statements. The first step required to produce financial statements is to record the financial transactions within the framework of the basic accounting model.

Effects of Financial Transactions on the Accounting Model

Every financial transaction, whether very simple or extremely complex, can be analyzed by or expressed in terms of its effect on the balance sheet equation. Every business entity, whether it's General Meat Market or General Motors, analyzes and reflects financial transactions by the effect of each transaction on the balance sheet equation.

It is essential for you to understand the basic accounting model and the effects on the financial transactions on the model. To help you begin to understand the model, we'll show you an example of how transactions affect the model.

GENERAL CLEANING CORPORATION

Early in 1988, Polly Miller and several of her friends apply for and receive permission to incorporate a business to provide laundry and dry cleaning services. The business is to be called General Cleaning Corporation. During February, the first month of operations, various financial transactions take place, which are analyzed on the following pages.

Transaction 1 Polly and her friends invest $15,000 from their personal savings in the new corporation, depositing the money at the Albany State Bank into an account, "General Cleaning Corporation." As evidence of ownership, Polly and her friends issue to themselves capital stock of the corporation equal to their $15,000 investment.

Let's look at what the friends have done. With this small financial transaction, they have given us a few very important and fundamental things to learn about.

■ A business entity separate and distinct from their personal financial affairs has been created.

■ An economic resource—the $15,000, which is the asset Cash—has been invested in the business entity. The source of this resource is the contribution made by the stockholders, which represents stockholders' equity.

■ The dual nature of the transaction is that cash has been invested and stockholders' equity created. The effect of this transaction on the basic accounting model—the balance sheet equation—is to increase an asset (Cash) from zero to $15,000 and also to increase stockholders' equity, from zero to $15,000.

In this chapter we will analyze financial transactions like these by means of a ***financial transaction worksheet.*** The financial transaction worksheet is a form used to analyze increases and decreases in the assets, liabilities, or stockholders' equity of a business entity. When a specific asset, liability, or stockholders' equity item is created by a financial transaction, it is listed on the financial transaction worksheet under the appropriate heading. These are called ***accounts*** and are used to accumulate money amounts. For example, when the stockholders contribute the $15,000 asset Cash, it is simply listed under the heading Assets.

The following is an illustration of the first transaction for General Cleaning Corporation. The amounts of assets, liabilities, and stockholders' equity are all zero before this first transaction, since the business entity did not exist prior to transaction 1.

The stockholders make an investment in the business

	GENERAL CLEANING CORPORATION Financial Transaction Worksheet Month of February, 1988				
Transaction Number	**Assets**	**=**	**Liabilities**	**+**	**Stockholders' Equity**
	Cash				**Capital Stock**
(1)	+$15,000	=			+$15,000

Transaction 2 Dry cleaning and laundry equipment costing $9,500 is acquired by paying a check in that amount to the vendor.

This exchange transaction results in the decrease in one asset—Cash—but a corresponding increase in another asset—Equipment. Notice that while the value of total assets is unchanged after this transaction, the composition of the assets has changed.

Equipment is acquired by paying cash

	GENERAL CLEANING CORPORATION Financial Transaction Worksheet Month of February, 1988					
Transaction Number	**Assets**		**=**	**Liabilities**	**+**	**Stockholders' Equity**
	Cash	**Equipment**				**Capital Stock**
(1)	+$15,000					+$15,000
(2)	−$ 9,500	+$9,500				
Totals	$ 5,500	+ $9,500	=		+	$15,000

Transaction 3 Used dry cleaning equipment is acquired on account, $1,500.

In this case an asset — Equipment — is increased. However, the equipment was obtained not by reducing another asset — Cash — but by incurring a liability. This is what we mean by the term *on account,* acquiring the equipment with a promise to pay the amount due at a later date. We may also say *on credit* or *for credit* to mean the same thing. When we buy something in this manner, we call the amount we owe the creditor an *account payable.* The dual nature of this transaction is to offset the increase in assets — Equipment — by a corresponding increase in the liability — Accounts Payable. Of course, after this exchange transaction the total of the assets ($5,500 + $11,000 = $16,500) is exactly equal to the total of the liabilities and stockholders' equity ($1,500 + $15,000 = $16,500).

Used equipment is acquired on account

GENERAL CLEANING CORPORATION
Financial Transaction Worksheet
Month of February, 1988

| Transaction Number | Assets | | = | Liabilities | + | Stockholders' Equity |
	Cash	Equipment		Accounts Payable		Capital Stock
(1)	+$15,000					+$15,000
(2)	−$ 9,500	+$ 9,500				
(3)		+$ 1,500		+$1,500		
Totals	$ 5,500 +	$11,000	=	$1,500	+	$15,000

Transaction 4 Cleaning and certain other necessary supplies in the amount of $700 are acquired on account.

As a result of this transaction, a new asset account called Supplies on Hand is created. Whenever the business entity engages in activities that result in the need to establish new accounts, accountants simply do that: They create new accounts. The new account is given a name that describes that account in as few words as possible. The account *Supplies on Hand* is so called to distinguish it as an asset. The term *Supplies* might lead to some confusion, since it is not clear whether the supplies are "on hand" or "used." *Supplies Used* is an expense, not an asset. This transaction results in an increase in assets — Supplies on Hand — and an increase in the liability Accounts Payable.

GENERAL CLEANING CORPORATION
Financial Transaction Worksheet
Month of February, 1988

| Transaction Number | Assets | | | = | Liabilities | + | Stockholders' Equity |
	Cash	Supplies on Hand	Equipment		Accounts Payable		Capital Stock
(1)	+$15,000						+$15,000
(2)	−$ 9,500		+$ 9,500				
(3)			+$ 1,500		+$1,500		
(4)		+$700			+$ 700		
	$ 5,500 +	$700 +	$11,000	=	$2,200	+	$15,000

Supplies are acquired on account

Transaction 5 During the month of June, General Cleaning collects $2,700 in cash for laundry services.

The rendering of services for a fee was a prime motivating factor in establishing the business entity. General Cleaning hopes to receive more money from laundry and dry cleaning services than it has to spend in providing those services. The excess is **profit** or **net income.** The $2,700 collected for laundry services represents revenues and as such reflects an increase in the ownership interest in the business entity. **Revenue** is an inflow of cash or other properties in exchange for goods sold or services rendered. When the inflow of cash or other properties is recorded, another asset is not reduced. Nor is a liability incurred. The stockholders are better off than they were before; this is why stockholders' equity is increased. Specifically, the account Retained Earnings is increased. All revenues and all expenses are reflected in this account. The effect of this transaction—$2,700 cash revenue—on the basic accounting equation is to increase the asset Cash and to increase Retained Earnings, each by $2,700.

Cash is received for laundry services

GENERAL CLEANING CORPORATION
Financial Transaction Worksheet
Month of February, 1988

| Transaction Number | Assets | | | = | Liabilities | + | Stockholders' Equity | | |
	Cash	Supplies on Hand	Equipment		Accounts Payable		Capital Stock	Retained Earnings	Retained Earnings Explanation
(1)	+$15,000						+$15,000		
(2)	−$ 9,500		+$ 9,500						
(3)			+$ 1,500		+$1,500				
(4)		+$700			+$ 700				
(5)	+$ 2,700							+$2,700	Laundry
	$ 8,200 +	$700 +	$11,000	=	$2,200	+	$15,000	+ $2,700	

These two items are expenses. They represent an outflow of resources and a reduction of stockholders' equity. Thus, the asset Cash is decreased by $1,250, and the Retained Earnings account is decreased by $500 for rent and $750 for wages.

GENERAL CLEANING CORPORATION
Financial Transaction Worksheet
Month of February, 1988

Transaction Number	Cash	Assets		=	Liabilities	+	Stockholders' Equity		
		Supplies on Hand	Equipment		Accounts Payable		Capital Stock	Retained Earnings	Retained Earnings Explanation
(1)	+$15,000						+$15,000		
(2)	−$ 9,500		+$ 9,500						
(3)			+$ 1,500		+$1,500				
(4)		+$700			+$ 700				
(5)	+$ 2,700							+$2,700	Laundry
(6)	−$ 1,250							−$ 500	Rent
								−$ 750	Wages
Totals	$ 6,950 +	$700 +	$11,000	=	$2,200	+	$15,000	+ $1,450	

Rent and wages are paid

Even though the company has not received cash, it has earned revenue. General Cleaning has performed its services and is entitled to payment. Once the services are performed, an economic resource is created. This economic resource is the amount owed to General Cleaning and is called *accounts receivable.* As seen in transaction (5), revenue is an increase in stockholders' equity. Thus, this revenue transaction results in an increase in an asset—Accounts Receivable—and a like increase in Stockholders' Equity—Retained Earnings, in the amount of $1,500.

GENERAL CLEANING CORPORATION
Financial Transaction Worksheet
Month of February, 1988

Transaction Number	Cash	Accounts Receivable	Supplies on Hand	Equipment	=	Accounts Payable	Capital Stock	Retained Earnings	Retained Earnings Explanation
		Assets			= Liabilities +		Stockholders' Equity		
(1)	+$15,000						+$15,000		
(2)	−$ 9,500			+$ 9,500					
(3)				+$ 1,500		+$1,500			
(4)			+$700			+$ 700			
(5)	+$ 2,700							+$2,700	Laundry
(6)	−$ 1,250							−$ 500	Rent
								−$ 750	Wages
(7)		+$1,500						+$1,500	Dry cleaning
Totals	$ 6,950 +	$1,500 +	$700 +	$11,000 =		$2,200 +	$15,000 +	$2,950	

Corporate customers are billed for dry cleaning

Transaction 8 At month's end, General Cleaning pays the $1,500 bill for the purchase of the used dry cleaning equipment. The bill for supplies will be paid in early July.

The payment of the $1,500 is an outflow of resources as evidenced by the cash expenditure and the reduction of a liability—Accounts Payable. This payment transaction reduces both cash and accounts payable by $1,500.

GENERAL CLEANING CORPORATION
Financial Transaction Worksheet
Month of February, 1988

Transaction Number	Cash	Accounts Receivable	Supplies on Hand	Equipment	=	Accounts Payable	Capital Stock	Retained Earnings	Retained Earnings Explanation
		Assets			= Liabilities +		Stockholders' Equity		
(1)	+$15,000						+$15,000		
(2)	−$ 9,500			+$ 9,500					
(3)				+$ 1,500		+$1,500			
(4)			+$700			+$ 700			
(5)	+$ 2,700							+$2,700	Laundry
(6)	−$ 1,250							−$ 500	Rent
								−$ 750	Wages
(7)		+$1,500						+$1,500	Dry cleaning
(8)	−$ 1,500					−$1,500			
Totals	$ 5,450 +	$1,500 +	$700 +	$11,000 =		$ 700 +	$15,000 +	$2,950	

An Account Payable is paid

Transaction 9 A check in the amount of $300 is received from a corporate customer for dry cleaning billed in transaction (7).

While the total assets remain unchanged, their composition does change. The asset Cash is increased by $300 and the asset Accounts Receivable is decreased by a like amount. The collection of receivables and the payment of accounts payable are two of the most common business transactions.

GENERAL CLEANING CORPORATION
Financial Transaction Worksheet
Month of February, 1988

Transaction Number	Cash	Assets — Accounts Receivable	Supplies on Hand	Equipment	= Liabilities + Accounts Payable	Stockholders' Equity — Capital Stock	Retained Earnings	Retained Earnings Explanation
(1)	+$15,000					+$15,000		
(2)	−$ 9,500			+$ 9,500				
(3)				+$ 1,500	+$1,500			
(4)			+$700		+$ 700			
(5)	+$ 2,700						+$2,700	Laundry
(6)	−$ 1,250						−$ 500	Rent
							−$ 750	Wages
(7)		+$1,500					+$1,500	Dry cleaning
(8)	−$ 1,500				−$1,500			
(9)	+$ 300	−$ 300						
Totals	$ 5,750 +	$1,200 +	$700 +	$11,000 =	$ 700 +	$15,000 +	$2,950	

An Account Receivable is received

Transaction 10 General Cleaning pays a $1,000 dividend to its stockholders.

This is the means by which stockholders of business entities receive a distribution of the profits. Remember transaction (1), in which the stockholders invested $15,000.

At that time we increased cash by $15,000 and also increased capital stock by a like amount. This was an investment by the stockholders. It was *not* revenue. The stockholders simply transferred funds from their personal accounts to the checking account of the corporation in exchange for capital stock. A dividend, such as we have in transaction 10, is exactly the opposite. Funds are simply transferred from the checking account of the corporation to the checking accounts of the stockholders. This is not an expense. It is a distribution of earnings. It is earnings *not* retained. That's why we must reduce Retained Earnings for dividends.

GENERAL CLEANING CORPORATION
Financial Transaction Worksheet
Month of February, 1988

		Assets			= Liabilities +	Stockholders' Equity		
Transaction Number	Cash	Accounts Receivable	Supplies on Hand	Equipment	Accounts Payable	Capital Stock	Retained Earnings	Retained Earnings Explanation
(1)	+$15,000					+$15,000		
(2)	−$ 9,500			+$ 9,500				
(3)				+$ 1,500	+$1,500			
(4)			+$700		+$ 700			
(5)	+$ 2,700						+$2,700	Laundry
(6)	−$ 1,250						−$ 500	Rent
							−$ 750	Wages
(7)		+$1,500					+$1,500	Dry cleaning
(8)	−$ 1,500				−$1,500			
(9)	+$ 300	−$ 300						
(10)	−$ 1,000						−$1,000	Dividends
Totals	$ 4,750 +	$1,200 +	$700 +	$11,000 =	$ 700 +	$15,000 +	$1,950	

Dividends are paid

Transaction 11 On the last day of June, Polly counts the various supplies and determines that $200 worth of supplies remain on hand. Since she purchased $700 of supplies at the start of the month, $500 of supplies must have been used during the month.

This $500 represents an expense, Supplies Used, and as such reflects a reduction in stockholders' equity. This transaction represents supplies used and is recorded as a reduction in Supplies on Hand and a reduction in Retained Earnings.

	GENERAL CLEANING CORPORATION								
	Financial Transaction Worksheet								
	Month of February, 1988								

Transaction Number	**Assets**				**= Liabilities +**	**Stockholders' Equity**			
	Cash	**Accounts Receivable**	**Supplies on Hand**	**Equipment**	**Accounts Payable**	**Capital Stock**	**Retained Earnings**	**Retained Earnings Explanation**	
(1)	+$15,000					+$15,000			
(2)	−$ 9,500			+$ 9,500					
(3)				+$ 1,500	+$1,500				
(4)			+$700		+$ 700				
(5)	+$ 2,700						+$2,700	Laundry	
(6)	−$ 1,250						−$ 500	Rent	
							−$ 750	Wages	
(7)		+$1,500					+$1,500	Dry cleaning	
(8)	−$ 1,500				−$1,500				
(9)	+$ 300	−$ 300							
(10)	−$ 1,000						−$1,000	Dividends	
(11)			−$500				−$ 500	Supplies used	
Totals	$ 4,750 +	$1,200 +	$200 +	$11,000 =	$ 700 +	$15,000 +	$1,450		

Supplies used during the period are recorded

PREPARING THE FINANCIAL STATEMENTS

At the end of the month, after the last transaction has been recorded on the financial transaction worksheet and the various columns totaled, it is a relatively simple matter to prepare the financial statements—the income statement, the statement of retained earnings, and the balance sheet.

Income Statement

The income statement is prepared first. The data for the income statement are contained under the Retained Earnings account, since revenues are increases in stockholders' equity and expenses represent decreases in stockholders' equity. Only revenue and expenses are shown on the income statement. Dividends are not shown on the income statement, since they are neither revenues nor expenses.

Statement of Retained Earnings

Before the balance sheet is prepared, a statement of retained earnings is developed. This statement reflects the increases in stockholders' equity due to net income—the excess of revenues over expense and the decreases due to dividends. This statement explains how Retained Earnings increased from a zero balance on Feb. 1 to a $1,450 balance on Feb. 29.

EXHIBIT 1-1
The Three Financial Statements

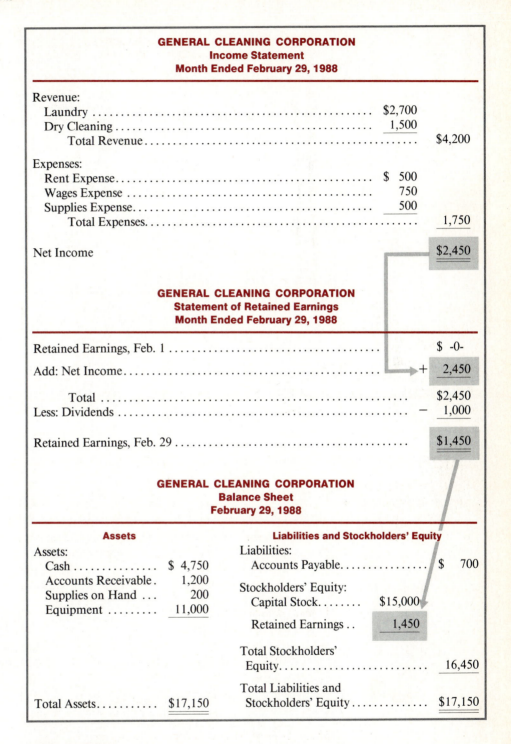

GENERAL CLEANING CORPORATION
Income Statement
Month Ended February 29, 1988

Revenue:		
Laundry	$2,700	
Dry Cleaning	1,500	
Total Revenue		$4,200
Expenses:		
Rent Expense	$ 500	
Wages Expense	750	
Supplies Expense	500	
Total Expenses		1,750
Net Income		$2,450

GENERAL CLEANING CORPORATION
Statement of Retained Earnings
Month Ended February 29, 1988

Retained Earnings, Feb. 1	$ -0-
Add: Net Income	+ 2,450
Total	$2,450
Less: Dividends	− 1,000
Retained Earnings, Feb. 29	$1,450

GENERAL CLEANING CORPORATION
Balance Sheet
February 29, 1988

Assets		Liabilities and Stockholders' Equity	
Assets:		Liabilities:	
Cash	$ 4,750	Accounts Payable	$ 700
Accounts Receivable	1,200		
Supplies on Hand	200	Stockholders' Equity:	
Equipment	11,000	Capital Stock	$15,000
		Retained Earnings	1,450
		Total Stockholders' Equity	16,450
		Total Liabilities and	
Total Assets	$17,150	Stockholders' Equity	$17,150

Balance Sheet

After completion of the statement of retained earnings, the balance sheet is prepared. The balance sheet is simply the totals of the left side of the financial transaction worksheet—the asset accounts—and the right side—the liability and stockholders' equity accounts.

THE BUCS BALANCE SHEET

Tampa Tribune confuses balance sheet with income statement

An article appearing in the Tampa Tribune on October 30, 1983, contained the following information:

The on-field misfortunes of the stumble-footed Tampa Bay Buccaneers have local fans reaching for the collective neck of coach John McKay and owner Hugh Culverhouse.

But any frowns you see on the face of multimillionaire attorney Culverhouse are from the Buccaneer's dismal 0–8 playing ledger, not their flourishing balance sheet.

Even an 0–16 season could not prevent the Buccaneer franchise from showing a profit for the 1983 season, several sources indicate.

Financial figures gathered from five primary National Football sources project a $4.73 million pre-tax profit for the hapless

Bucs Balance Sheet '83	
Projected Home Revenue	$ 3,825,300
Projected Road Revenue	2,378,572
Preseason Gate Revenue	1,139,000
Projected Playoff Revenue	500,000
Projected Lounge Box Revenue	578,000
Network Television Revenue	13,400,000
Home Television/Radio Revenue	250,000
Projected Concession/Parking	162,500
Projected Misc. Revenue	1,300,000
Total Projected Revenue	$23,533,372
Total Projected Expenses	18,800,000
Total Projected Net Income	$ 4,733,372

Buccaneers. A balance sheet compiled by the Tribune showed $23.53 million in revenue and $18.8 million in expenses.

Source: Tampa Tribune-Times, Oct. 30, 1983, by Jeff Smith. Reprinted by permission.

The various types of financial statements are often confused with each other. For example, in the article above, there is a financial statement identified as a *balance sheet.*

Recall that a balance sheet shows an entity's financial position on a particular date. Balance sheets are prepared at the end of the year or, sometimes, at the end of each quarter or month. Balance sheets include assets, liabilities, and stockholders' equity. Individual accounts are classified under these three main categories.

On the other hand, an income statement shows revenue, expenses, and net income or loss for a specific period of time. The difference between the revenue and the expenses will later be shown in the stockholders' equity section of the balance sheet.

The financial statement in the article above is, as you will no doubt recognize, an *income statement.*

CHAPTER SUMMARY

The *income statement* and the *balance sheet* are the principal financial statements generated by the general financial accounting activity.

The *income statement* compares *revenues* (the inflow of cash or other properties) earned during a specified period of time with *expenses,* the cost of goods sold or services rendered during the same period of time.

The *balance sheet* shows the financial position of a business entity at a particular date. The total of the *assets*—the economic resources owned by the entity that are expected to provide future benefits—of a business entity will always equal the sum of its liabilities—its debts—and the *stockholders' equity*—the owners' interest in the business entity.

Generally accepted accounting principles (GAAP) have been developed over the years in an attempt to provide a rational system of financial reporting. These principles can be considered the ground rules of financial accounting.

Five generally accepted accounting principles need to be considered as you begin to develop your understanding of accounting:

1. The *historical cost principle* states that assets acquired by a business entity are to be recorded at the exchange price paid for such assets and this cost, once recorded, will remain unchanged.
2. The *objectivity principle* provides that objective evidence be established for

recording business transactions where the exchange price can be verified by invoice, deeds, transfers of title, or other business documents.

3. The *business entity concept* considers the business to be separate and distinct from its owners.

4. The *going concern concept* assumes that the entity will be in existence for as far into the future as it is reasonable to foresee.

5. Finally, the *stable-dollar concept* assumes that the basic unit of measure employed in recording financial transactions—the dollar—does not change in value over time.

The financial statements of economic entities cannot be prepared until the business transactions have been recorded, classified, and summarized within the framework of the *basic accounting model.*

The basic accounting model is simply expressed by the balance sheet equation:

$$\text{Assets} = \text{Liabilities} + \text{Stockholders' Equity}$$

Each transaction will require two elements to be considered, which will result in increases or decreases in assets, liabilities, or stockholders' equity. This dual nature of business transactions gives rise to the term *double-entry accounting.*

After all business transactions have been recorded and summarized, the financial statements can be prepared. The income statement is prepared first because it yields the net income for the period, and the net income is used to compute the ending balance of retained earnings that will appear on the balance sheet.

IMPORTANT TERMS USED IN THIS CHAPTER

Account A specific asset, liability, stockholders' equity, revenue, or expense item used to accumulate money amounts. (page 29)

Assets The economic resources that are owned by an economic entity and that are expected to provide future benefits. (page 23)

Balance sheet The financial statement that lists the assets owned, liabilities owed, and stockholders' equity at a specific point in time. (page 22)

Basic accounting model The algebraic expression depicting the balance sheet relationship between assets and the sum of liabilities plus stockholders' equity:

$$\text{Assets} = \text{Liabilities} + \text{Stockholders' Equity}$$

(page 27)

Business entity concept The basic generally accepted accounting principle stating that a business entity is considered to be separate and distinct from its owners for accounting purposes. (page 26)

Capital A term often used in accounting to mean stockholders' equity; retained earnings, for example, is a stockholders' equity account. (page 24)

Capital stock The amount that owners—stockholders—invest in a corporation in the form of cash or other assets in exchange for shares of stock. (page 28)

Dividends Distributions of earnings to stockholders. (page 34)

Double-entry accounting The process of recording each business transaction by affecting two elements within the basic accounting model. (page 28)

Expenses The cost of goods sold or services rendered in the process of generating revenues. (page 21)

Generally accepted accounting principles (GAAP) The ground rules used by economic entities in presenting financial information. (page 24)

Going concern concept The assumption that a business entity will be in existence for as far into the future as it is reasonable to foresee. (page 26)

Historical cost principle The principle whereby assets acquired by a business entity are to be recorded at the price paid in exchange for such assets. (page 25)

Income statement The external financial statement designed to report the profitability of a business entity by contrasting revenue earned with expenses incurred in the determination of net income. (page 21)

Liabilities Debts of economic entities. (page 23)

Objectivity principle The principle requiring objective verifiable evidence underlying the recording of business transactions. (page 25)

Retained earnings The excess of revenues over expenses — the earnings of a corporation that have been invested in the business and not distributed to stockholders in the form of dividends. (page 23)

Revenue The inflow of cash or other properties in exchange for goods sold or services rendered. (page 21)

Stable-dollar concept The assumption used in accounting that the unit of measure — the dollar — does not change in value over time. (page 26)

Stockholders' equity The financial interest of the stockholders in a corporation. (page 24)

QUESTIONS

1. What information is contained on an income statement?

2. Explain the meaning of the terms *revenue* and *expense.*

3. What does the term *stockholders' equity* mean? What do the terms *assets* and *liabilities* mean?

4. The corporate balance sheet is a major financial report. What information does it contain?

5. Five basic concepts and principles of accounting were discussed in the chapter. List and explain briefly each.

6. What is the basic accounting model? Why is it important?

7. Each business transaction has two elements. Explain.

8. Describe a business transaction that would:

   a. Increase an asset and increase stockholders' equity
   b. Increase an asset and decrease a second asset
   c. Increase an asset and increase a liability

9. Alpha Corporation reported in November cash sales of $25,000, sales on account of $60,000; and expenses incurred of $52,000, of which $19,000 was paid in cash. Determine the amount of revenue, expenses, and net income for the month.

10. The Jan. 1 balance of the Cola Company Retained Earnings account amounted to $21,000. By the end of the year the balance increased by $40,000. If $10,000 were paid in dividends, what was the amount of net income?

EXERCISES

Exercise 1-1
Transactions that change the basic accounting model

Describe a transaction for each of the five situations that will result in the indicated change in the elements of the basic accounting model.
a. Increase an asset and increase a liability.
b. Decrease an asset and decrease a liability.
c. Increase one asset and decrease another asset.
d. Increase an asset and increase stockholders' equity.
e. Increase an asset, decrease a second asset, and increase a liability.

Exercise 1-2
Computing the missing elements in the basic accounting model

Determine the requested item for each of the following:
a. The assets of a corporation having liabilities of $62,000 and stockholders' equity of $97,350.
b. The liabilities of a corporation having assets of $26,250 and stockholders' equity of $15,975.
c. The stockholders' equity of a corporation having assets of $57,700 and liabilities of $32,400.
d. The revenues of a corporation having expenses of $31,450 and net income of $7,360.
e. The expenses of a corporation having revenues of $47,220 and a net loss of $17,520.

Exercise 1-3
Preparing a balance sheet from a list of accounts

The items listed below were obtained from the records of Pasco Corporation. Using this information, prepare a proper balance sheet to be dated Apr. 30, 1988.

Shop Supplies on Hand	$ 1,040	Accounts Receivable	$ 6,300
Capital Stock	15,000	Retained Earnings	5,460
Notes Payable	5,000	Building	12,070
Rent Expense	4,350	Equipment	?
Cash	2,750	Accounts Payable	11,400
Land	4,200		

(Check figure: Total assets = $36,860)

Exercise 1-4
Determining the effect of transactions on the basic elements of the balance sheet equation

The Mars Company engaged in the 11 transactions listed below during the current month. Indicate for each transaction the effect on the basic elements of the balance sheet equation using (+) for increase, (−) for decrease, and (0) for no change. Use the following headings to record your answer:

Transaction Letter	Assets	Liabilities	Stockholders' Equity

a. Paid a liability.
b. Issued additional capital stock for cash.
c. Collected an account receivable.
d. Acquired office furniture on account.
e. Acquired a service truck paying 25% in cash.
f. Paid dividends.
g. Received cash for services rendered.
h. Acquired supplies for cash.
i. Billed a customer for services rendered.
j. Returned office furniture acquired in transaction (d) above. The furniture had not been paid for as of this date.
k. Received a bill for utilities expense used this month.

Exercise 1-5
Violations of GAAP

Certain generally accepted accounting principles or concepts have been violated in each of the situations described below. Indicate for each situation which principle or concept has been violated.
a. When the Dane Corporation acquired its Albany branch office building for $16,350, the total amount of the cash outlay was recorded as rent expense.
b. The personal automobile of Otto Dane, the corporation's major stockholder, is listed among the corporate assets.
c. Early in the current year the Dane Corporation exchanged its used forklift truck for a second-hand drill press. Since no monetary consideration exchanged hands, Dane Corporation valued the press at $6,325, a price that seemed reasonable to corporate executives.
d. Land, acquired at a cost of $15,250 in 1981, is written up to $43,175. (List three principles.)

Exercise 1-6
Identifying transactions in a completed worksheet

Nine transactions from the October financial transaction worksheet for Wilson Corporation are listed below. Describe each transaction. Transaction (i) is the only transaction affecting the Retained Earnings account that does not affect net income.

	Cash	+	Accounts Receivable	+	Supplies on Hand	+	Office Furniture	=	Accounts Payable	+	Capital Stock	+	Retained Earnings
Bal.													
Oct. 1	+$6,500		+$12,300		+$ 700		+$18,500		+$13,200		+$20,000		+$4,800
(a)	+$1,500		−$ 1,500										
(b)			+$ 4,300										+$4,300
(c)	−$ 650				+$ 650								
(d)							+$ 1,950		+$ 1,950				
(e)	+$5,000										+$ 5,000		
(f)	+$2,500												+$2,500
(g)	−$2,000												−$2,000
(h)	−$ 900								−$ 900				
(i)	−$3,500												−$3,500
Oct. 31													
Bal.	$8,450	+	$15,100	+	$1,350	+	$20,450	=	$14,250	+	$25,000	+	$6,100

Exercise 1-7
Preparing a statement of retained earnings

The Johnson Corporation reported $40,000 net income for the year 1988. On Jan. 1, 1988, the corporation had a balance in the Retained Earnings account of $70,000; at year-end the balance was $95,000. Dividends of $15,000 were paid during the year. Using this information, prepare a statement of retained earnings for the year ended Dec. 31, 1988.

Exercise 1-8
Preparing an income statement

A number of items from the records of the Delaware Corporation are listed below. Using these data, prepare an income statement for the year ended May 31, 1988.

Utilities Expense	$ 9,300		Storage Revenues	$ 65,700
Moving Revenues	43,200		Retained Earnings	6,300
Dividends	5,500		Rent Expense	18,000
Salaries Expense	52,000		Capital Stock	20,000
Totals	$110,000		Totals	$110,000

PROBLEMS: SET A

Problem A1-1
Preparing an income statement and a statement of retained earnings

The revenue and expense accounts of the Stratford Typing and Answering Service, Inc., are listed below.

Advertising Expense	$ 1,800		Telephone Expense	$ 540
Answering Service Fees Earned	27,500		Typing Fees Earned	18,700
Salaries Expense	21,200		Typing Supplies Used	10,300
Rent Expense	1,000			

Required

1. Prepare an income statement for the 3-month period ended Mar. 31, 1988.

(Check figure: Net Income = $11,360)

2. On Jan. 1, 1988, Stratford Typing and Answering Service, Inc., had a balance of $36,700 in its Retained Earnings account. Dividends in the amount of $2,500 were paid on Feb. 15, 1988. Prepare a Statement of Retained Earnings for the 3-month period ended Mar. 31, 1988.

(Check figure: Retained Earnings, Mar. 31, 1988 = $45,560)

Problem A1-2
Preparing a balance sheet

The balance sheet accounts as of June 30, 1988, for the Schuyler Corporation are as follows:

Capital Stock	$30,000	Accounts Receivable	$7,200
Building	29,000	Notes Payable	6,000
Retained Earnings	19,450	Accounts Payable	2,300
Equipment	11,000	Cash	1,500
Land	8,000	Supplies on Hand	1,050

Required

Prepare a balance sheet as of June 30, 1988.

(Check figure: Total Assets = $57,750)

Problem A1-3
Identifying violations of GAAP

During the current year the Baker Company, a newly organized service business, entered into the five transactions described below. Mr. Baker has had no previous business education or experience and is consequently ignorant of current accounting practices.

a. Equipment acquired on Jan. 15 for $10,000 is recorded on the Dec. 31 balance sheet at $11,300. Mr. Baker explains that since at the date of acquisition the consumer price index was 100 and had increased to 113 by year-end, the appropriate value for financial statement presentation would accordingly be $11,300.

b. A calculator purchased in early March for $560 can be purchased at year-end for $395. Mr. Baker has used the latter value on the balance sheet.

c. Land bought on July 1 for $25,000 is valued on the Dec. 31 balance sheet at $42,000, a value obtained by considering recent land sales in the vicinity.

d. A lawnmower used by Mr. Baker for his residence is included among the Dec. 31 assets.

e. Included among the expenses is $750 of office rent paid 3 months in advance on Dec. 31 of the current year.

Required

For each of the transactions above, list the most appropriate generally accepted accounting concept violated, and explain why the treatment of the Baker Company is inappropriate.

Problem A1-4
Recording transactions in a financial transaction worksheet

On Feb. 1, 1988, Nancy Richardson formed the Richardson Pest Control Service by issuing capital stock in the amount of $2,000, receiving cash for a like amount. The cash was obtained from Nancy ($1,000) and two other stockholders, each of whom invested $500.

During the first month of operations the following transactions occurred:

a. Acquired pesticide supplies in the amount of $730 on open account.
b. Received $2,100 cash for pest control service.
c. Paid $350 rent for the month.
d. Ms. Richardson provided a truck for the exclusive use of the corporation. The fair market value of the truck on this date was $7,000. Capital stock in that amount was issued to Ms. Richardson.
e. Paid the telephone bill of $200.
f. Provided pest control services amounting to $2,500 for the Green Company; cash was not received.
g. Paid $425 of the amount due for the pesticide supplies previously acquired.
h. Paid $500 in dividends.
i. Collected $1,200 of amount due from the Green Company.
j. Paid salaries of $2,350.
k. Truck repairs in the amount of $625 were incurred but not yet paid.

Required

1. Establish the following accounts in a financial transaction worksheet: Cash, Accounts Receivable, Pesticide Supplies on Hand, Truck, Accounts Payable, Capital Stock, and Retained Earnings. Record the transactions for the month.

(Check figure: Total Assets = $10,505)

2. Compute the amount of net income for the month.

(Check figure: Net income = $1,075)

Problem A1-5
Recording transactions
and preparing financial
statements

Orville Haberman and two of his friends organized, incorporated, and commenced operating the Haberman Washing and Dry Cleaning Company. The three friends invested a total of $10,000 from their personal savings in the new business, receiving capital stock in a like amount.

During the month of August, 1988, their first month of operations, the following activities took place:

a. Acquired washing and dry cleaning equipment in the amount of $7,500, paying $2,000 in cash. The difference represents a note payable due Feb. 1, 1989.
b. Acquired $750 of cleaning supplies on account from the Keith Company.
c. Billed several corporate clients $3,725 for dry cleaning office building drapes.
d. Acquired $1,290 of cleaning supplies, paying cash.
e. Received $2,500 from clients billed in transaction (c).
f. Received $3,200 cash from customers for washing.
g. Paid telephone bill of $150.
h. Paid salaries of $1,350.
i. Billed Good Food Restaurant $1,170 for washing.
j. Paid rent of $800.
k. Paid Keith Company $300 [see transaction (b)].
l. Paid dividends, $2,250.

Required

1. Using a financial transaction worksheet, record the transactions listed above. Establish the following accounts: Cash, Accounts Receivable, Cleaning Supplies on Hand, Washing and Dry Cleaning Equipment, Notes Payable, Accounts Payable, Capital Stock, and Retained Earnings.
   (Check figure: Total Assets = $19,495)

2. Prepare the following three financial statements:
   a. An income statement for the month ended Aug. 31, 1988
   (Check figure: Net Income = $5,795)
   b. A statement of retained earnings for the month ended Aug. 31, 1988
   (Check figure: Retained Earnings, Aug. 31, 1988 = $3,545)
   c. A balance sheet as of Aug. 31, 1988.

Problem A1-6
Recording transactions
and preparing financial
statements

Christina Gallagher, a master mechanic, obtained the backing of several investors to organize a new business to be called Gallagher Auto Repair and Parts Corporation. Assets of an existing company were acquired with the proceeds of the issuance of $42,000 capital stock to the investors and Ms. Gallagher. Specifically, the following assets were acquired: Accounts Receivable, $13,200; Auto Parts on Hand, $6,500; Land, $9,500; Shop Building, $30,000; and Shop Equipment, $21,600. The land and building were subject to a $25,000 mortgage payable. In addition, two other liabilities existed, Notes Payable, $10,000; and Accounts Payable, $8,000. The difference between the sum of the assets and the sum of the payables and capital stock is cash.

During the last quarter of 1988, the following transactions took place:

a. Acquired $4,250 of auto parts from Johnson Manufacturing Company on account.
b. Collected $8,250 accounts receivable due.
c. Acquired additional shop equipment costing $6,700 by issuing a note payable in the amount of $2,000 and paying cash for the difference.
d. Paid $5,000 due on accounts payable.
e. Billed customers $37,600 for auto repair work performed on account.
f. Received $25,900 from customers for repair work performed for cash.
g. Paid salaries of $14,720.
h. Paid utilities expense of $3,200.
i. Paid dividends of $3,000.
j. Received $6,100 cash for auto parts sales.
k. Reduced auto parts on hand by $5,250, and recorded auto parts expense for parts sold in transaction (j).
l. Collected $1,650 accounts receivable due.

| **Required** | 1. Record the initial account balances in a financial transaction worksheet. Then record the transactions for the last quarter of 1988. *(Check figure: Total Assets = $129,680)* |

2. Prepare: **a.** an income statement; **b.** a statement of retained earnings; **c.** a balance sheet

Problem A1-7
Preparing financial statements from a list of accounts

Listed below are the accounts of Leroy G. Craig Corporation summarizing its business activity for the month of March, 1988:

Land Sales Commissions	$76,300	Professional Devel. Expense	$9,350
Salaries, Staff	61,200	Office Supplies Used	7,150
Office Building	58,270	Entertainment Expense	5,300
Land Development Consulting		Dividends	5,000
Commissions	41,500	Cash	3,650
Capital Stock	40,000	Accounts Payable	3,120
Retained Earnings, Mar. 1, 1988	35,000	Advertising Expense	2,500
Mortgage Payable	32,700	Notes Receivable	2,000
Salaries, Clerical	18,750	Salaries Payable	1,750
Office Furniture	16,230	Utilities Expense	1,470
Travel Expenses	13,150	Office Supplies on Hand	1,230
Land	12,900	Prepaid Insurance	600
Accounts Receivable	11,370	Miscellaneous Expense	250

 Required

1. Prepare an income statement.   *(Check figure: Net loss = $1,320)*
2. Prepare a statement of retained earnings.
                                 (Check figure: Retained Earnings, Mar. 31, 1988 = $28,680)
3. Prepare a balance sheet.   *(Check figure: Total Assets = $106,250)*

PROBLEMS: SET B

Problem B1-1
Preparing an income statement and a statement of retained earnings

Listed below are a number of accounts from the records of Barr Body and Paint Shop, Inc. The accounts represent activities for the 3-month period ending Mar. 31, 1988.

Auto Repair Fees Earned	$47,300	Dividends	$7,500
Salaries Expense	41,150	Equipment Rent Expense	5,700
Painting Fees Earned	33,700	Paint Expense	4,600
Retained Earnings, Jan. 1, 1988	25,000	Utilities Expense	2,550
Repair Parts Used	12,400	Miscellaneous Expense	500

| **Required** | 1. Prepare an income statement for the 3-month period ended Mar. 31, 1988. *(Check figure: Net Income = $14,100)* |

2. Prepare a statement of retained earnings for the 3-month period ended Mar. 31, 1988.
                         (Check figure: Retained Earnings, Mar 31, 1988 = $31,600)

Problem B1-2
Preparing a balance sheet

The balance sheet accounts of Bigger Consulting Service, Inc., are listed below for Oct. 31, 1988:

Accounts Payable	$14,050	Land	$ 7,500
Accounts Receivable	3,900	Notes Payable	7,000
Building	31,500	Office Supplies on Hand	1,600
Capital Stock	20,000	Retained Earnings	16,300
Cash	5,200	Salaries Payable	2,650
Equipment	10,300		

| **Required** | Prepare a balance sheet as of Oct. 31, 1988. |

                                 (Check figure: Total Assets = $60,000)

Problem B1-3
Identifying violations of
GAAP

On Jan. 1 of the current year, three identical companies commenced business. During the year, each company entered into identical transactions. At year-end, the three companies presented the following balance sheets:

Balance Sheets December 31, 1988	Red Company	White Company	Blue Company
Assets			
Assets:			
Cash	$ 5,000	$ 7,000	$ 5,000
Accounts Receivable........................	12,000	12,000	12,000
Prepaid Rent.............................	1,000	-0-	-0-
Office Equipment..........................	15,000	18,000	12,000
Shop Equipment	8,000	8,000	9,000
Goodwill	-0-	10,000	-0-
Total Assets..............................	$41,000	$55,000	$38,000
Liabilities and Stockholders' Equity			
Liabilities:			
Accounts Payable..........................	$ 4,500	$ 4,500	$ 4,500
Notes Payable............................	6,000	6,000	6,000
Total Liabilities	$10,500	$10,500	$10,500
Capital...................................	30,500	44,500	27,500
Total Liabilities and Stockholders' Equity	$41,000	$55,000	$38,000

A review of the underlying data revealed:

a. The White Company included $2,000 in its Cash account from a personal investment made by Mr. White in a savings and loan account with Freedom Exchange Savings & Loan.

b. Rent in the amount of $3,000 was paid in cash by both the White and the Blue Companies on Sept. 1 for the next 6 months.

c. At year-end, equipment costing $15,000 was valued by the White Company at $18,000, an amount reflecting the effects of inflation on the U.S. economy. Blue Company, however, valued the equipment at $12,000, the amount it would cost to replace the equipment at year-end.

d. Shop equipment costing $8,000 was valued by the Blue Company at $9,000, representing the amount offered to the Blue Company if it decided to sell the equipment.

e. The White Company recorded $10,000 of goodwill on Oct. 1. This amount represents Mr. White's best unbiased estimate of his superior managerial talent.

Required

Describe the violations of generally accepted accounting principles made by the three companies.

Problem B1-4
Recording transactions in
a financial transaction
worksheet

Terry Getz formed the Gainesville Sign Company on Oct. 1, 1988, by incorporating the company with the issue of $5,000 capital stock. The stock was issued to several investors in exchange for $2,000 cash and to Mr. Getz for a 1980 panel truck, which had a fair value on Oct. 1, 1988, of $3,000.

During the month of October the following transactions took place:

a. Repaired the truck at the Gator Auto Shop, receiving a bill of $575 for the repair work.

b. Acquired supplies in the amount of $375 on account.

c. Received $950 cash from customers for signs painted.

d. Paid $275 rent.

e. Billed customers $1,725 for signs painted.

f. Paid $210 of amount owed in transaction (b).
g. Paid dividends of $350.
h. Collected $1,150 from customers.
i. Paid $75 of utilities expense.

Required

1. Record the transactions of the Gainesville Sign Company for the month of October, 1988, using a financial transaction worksheet as illustrated in the chapter. Use the following accounts: Cash, Accounts Receivable, Supplies on Hand, Truck, Accounts Payable, Capital Stock, and Retained Earnings. *(Check figure: Total Assets = $7,140)*

2. Determine the amount of net income for the month.
(Check figure: Net Income = $1,750)

Problem B1-5
Recording transactions and preparing financial statements

Helen Haulbrook decided on July 1, 1988, to open a beauty shop. Upon the advice of her lawyer, the business was to be organized as a corporation. Consequently, Helen withdrew $4,000 cash from her personal savings and invested the funds in the business, issuing capital stock to herself for that amount. In addition, she obtained $5,600 from the North Carolina Trust Company as a note payable. The total funds were used to acquire beauty supplies of $2,650 and beauty equipment of $5,300, leaving $1,650 cash for daily business. The corporation is to be operated under the name of the Tar Heel Beauty Shop, Inc.

After incorporation, the following transactions occurred during the month of July:
a. Hairstyling for customers was done on account, $250.
b. Beauty supplies were acquired on account, $410.
c. Beauty equipment costing $975 was acquired; $475 was paid in cash and a $500 note payable was issued for the balance.
d. Cash of $825 was received for hairstyling.
e. Repairs were made to the equipment, $105 on account.
f. Paid $210 cash on amount due for beauty supplies acquired in transaction (b).
g. Paid $150 to the North Carolina Trust Company. Of this amount, $125 is for the note payable, $25 is interest expense.
h. Hairstyling for customers on account, $360.
i. Paid for utilities, $55.
j. Paid $360 in wages.
k. Paid $500 dividends.
l. Collected $175 for hairstyling done in transaction (a).

Required

1. Record the transactions in a financial transaction worksheet. The following accounts will be needed: Cash, Accounts Receivable, Beauty Supplies on Hand, Beauty Equipment, Notes Payable, Accounts Payable, Capital Stock, and Retained Earnings.
(Check figure: Total Assets = $10,670)

2. Prepare the following statements:
   a. An income statement for the month ended July 31, 1988
(Check figure: Net Income = $890)
   b. A statement of retained earnings
(Check figure: Retained Earnings, July 31, 1988 = $390)
   c. A balance sheet as of July 31, 1988.

Problem B1-6
Recording transactions and preparing financial statements

The Dec. 31, 1988, balance sheet for Constanzo Carpet Cleaning Corporation is presented at the top of the next page.

Mr. Constanzo operates his business in Miami, Florida, providing service to office buildings in the downtown area and selling cleaning supplies to condominiums in Miami Beach.

During the month of January, 1989, the following transactions took place:
a. Billed Dade Business Plaza for cleaning services rendered, $1,920.
b. Collected $2,100 from accounts receivable due.
c. Acquired carpet-cleaning supplies on account, $1,150.
d. Acquired carpet-cleaning equipment for $1,675, issuing a note payable for $1,000 and paying the rest in cash.

CONSTANZO CARPET CLEANING CORPORATION
Balance Sheet
December 31, 1988

Assets		Liabilities and Stockholders' Equity		
Assets:		Liabilities		
Cash	$ 1,300	Notes Payable		$ 3,200
Accounts Receivable . . .	2,800	Accounts Payable		1,100
Cleaning Supplies on		Total Liabilities		$ 4,300
Hand	1,750			
Cleaning Equipment . . .	4,100	Stockholders' Equity:		
Truck	3,950	Capital Stock	$5,000	
		Retained Earnings	4,600	
		Total Stockholders'		
		Equity		9,600
		Total Liabilities and		
Total Assets	$13,900	Stockholders' Equity		$13,900

e. Sold cleaning supplies to the Seminole Condominium for $1,300.

f. In connection with transaction (e), recorded a reduction in carpet-cleaning supplies on hand by $650 for the cost of the supplies and correspondingly recorded $650 of cleaning supplies expense.

g. Received $680 from the Orange Exchange Center for cleaning services rendered.

h. Dividends of $2,000 were paid.

i. Paid $1,500 note payable due; in addition, $125 interest on the note was paid.

j. Paid for gasoline used by the truck, $115.

k. Paid salaries, $800.

Required

1. Record the amounts from the Dec. 31, 1988, balance sheet in a financial transaction worksheet, then record the transactions for the month of January, 1989.

(Check figure: Total Assets = $14,760)

2. Prepare the following statements:

   a. An income statement for the month ended Jan. 31, 1989

   (Check figure: Net Income = $2,210)

   b. A statement of retained earnings

   (Check figure: Retained Earnings, Jan. 31, 1989 = $4,810)

   c. A balance sheet as of January 31, 1989

Problem B1-7
Preparing financial
statements from a list of
accounts

Listed in alphabetical order are the accounts of Kathy Krautsack, CPA. Ms. Krautsack's accounting firm is organized as a professional association (PA), which is a corporation.

Accounts Payable	$ 14,350	Office Supplies on Hand	$16,200
Accounts Receivable	38,900	Professional Devel. Expense	36,750
Auditing Fees Earned	216,500	Rent Expense	18,000
Capital Stock	50,000	Retained Earnings, Jan. 1, 1988	64,250
Cash	10,750	Salaries Expense	126,300
Dividends	41,100	Salaries Payable	5,600
Insurance Expense	2,500	Tax Fees Earned	72,175
Notes Receivable	30,000	Taxes Payable	7,200
Office Equipment	51,300	Travel Expenses	35,075
Office Supplies Expense	21,400	Utilities Expense	1,800

Required

Prepare the three statements for the year ended Dec. 31, 1988, from these data.

(Check figure: Total Assets, Dec. 31, 1988 = $147,150)

DECISION PROBLEM

After working a number of years for International Business Corporation as a computer specialist, William McDraw resigned and formed his own computer consulting company, which he named McDraw Consulting Corporation. A small inheritance enabled him to incorporate the business with an investment of $120,000.

Mary McDraw, William's wife, serves as the corporation's financial vice president. At the end of the first year, Mrs. McDraw prepared the following financial statements:

MCDRAW CONSULTING CORPORATION
Balance Sheet
December 31, 1989

Assets		**Liabilities**	
Cash	$127,500	Notes Payable	$ 60,000
Accounts Receivable	21,000	Accounts Payable	10,500
Supplies on Hand	1,500	Salaries Payable	3,000
Equipment	75,000	Total Liabilities	$ 73,500
		Stockholders' Equity	
		Capital Stock	$120,000
		Retained Earnings	31,500
		Total Stockholders' Equity	$151,500
		Total Liabilities and	
Total Assets	$225,000	Stockholders' Equity	$225,000

MCDRAW CONSULTING CORPORATION
For the Year Ended December 31, 1989

	Income Statement	Cash Statement
Revenues:		
Consulting Fees Earned	$90,000	$69,000
Expenses:		
Salaries Expense	$45,000	$37,000
Rent Expense	7,500	5,000
Supplies Used	4,500	3,000
Equipment Purchased	-0-	15,000
Dividends	-0-	1,500
Total Expenses	$57,000	$61,500
Net Income/Cash Increase	$33,000	$ 7,500

Required If William had remained with International Business Corporation for the year 1989, he would have earned a salary of $45,000.

Do you think that Mr. McDraw has made a good decision? Provide reasons to support your answer.

The Accounting System

The basic objective of the financial accounting activity is the preparation of the principal financial statements—the income statement, the statement of retained earnings, and the balance sheet. In Part Two we will show you how accountants gather, classify, summarize, and communicate accounting information.

You will learn that accounting information is gathered in accounts—the basic elements of financial accounting. Business transactions are first recorded as they occur in various journals and then later transferred to the accounts. We will show you how the accounts are conveniently arranged to facilitate the preparation of the financial statements and how worksheets are used to help in this process.

In order for the financial statements to be useful to you in making decisions, you must have the statements in time to make those decisions. You will see how this forces the accountant to divide the life of a business into short time frames called accounting periods—years, quarters, and months. And this causes the accountant to make estimates as to future events and to make other necessary adjustments to the accounts so that the statements can be issued at the end of the accounting periods.

CHAPTER 2

Analyzing and Recording Business Transactions

You will learn the following through studying this chapter:

- The nature and meaning of the *account*
- The distinction between a *ledger* and a *journal* and how each is used in the accounting system
- The rules of *debits* and *credits*
- How business transactions are recorded using the *double-entry accounting system*
- How to determine the *balance* for any account
- How to *prepare financial statements* from the ledger accounts

The primary objective of financial accounting is the preparation of the financial statements

The balance sheet, the income statement, and the statement of retained earnings may all be prepared from the information generated by recording business transactions on financial transaction worksheets. We illustrated how to prepare financial statements from transaction worksheets in the previous chapter. But preparing financial statements in that way for any but the simplest of business entities would be extremely cumbersome and impractical. Consequently a simpler, more efficient system has been developed. This system is the basis for all accounting systems, from the small retail store employing a part-time bookkeeper to the giant multinational corporation using the latest computer technology.

The system, which is referred to by accountants as the ***pen-and-ink – double-entry accounting system,*** is the substance of this and the following four chapters. As its name implies, the pen-and-ink system is entirely manual and has been in use for several hundred years. Of course, anything that can be done manually can also be done by a computer faster and more accurately. Computer systems use machines to record, compile, classify, summarize, and prepare the financial statements. But the programmed instructions for the machines are based on the concepts of the pen-and-ink system. Thus, the study of manual pen-and-ink accounting systems is essential in order to understand a computerized accounting system. And all of you will come into contact with computerized systems. The systems may be on large computers, called **mainframes;** or the systems may be on microcomputers. But the system is in concept what we will study in the next several chapters.

The "pen-and-ink" system is basic to computer systems

THE ACCOUNT

The basic element of the accounting system is the account

The account is used to record increases and decreases in assets, liabilities, retained earnings, and revenue and expense items

The account is the basic building block of any accounting system. A separate record, **an account,** is established for each of the individual items that appear on the three financial statements. An account exists, therefore, for each asset, liability, retained earnings, revenue, and expense item. The account is used to record increases and decreases resulting from business transactions. When cash is received, the transaction is reflected in the Cash account as an increase. When cash is paid, the Cash account is decreased. Thus, a record is available on a day-by-day basis that will provide management with information concerning a particular item. Questions such as, "What is the amount of accounts payable due? Is the inventory level sufficient to meet this week's demand? Is there adequate cash on hand to pay wages due today?" can each be answered by information contained in one of the accounts.

In its most elementary form, *the account has three parts:*

A title, a place for increases, and a place for decreases are the three components of an account

1. ***The account title,*** which is the name of a particular accounting element, such as Cash

2. ***A place to record increases in the monetary amounts*** in the account

3. ***A place to record decreases in the monetary amounts*** in the account

An example of the elementary form of the account is shown below.

The title of the account in this example is Cash. On the left side of the account there are three accounting entries representing increases to this account. On the right side there are two accounting entries representing decreases to this account.

The total of the three left side entries amounts to $8,380, which is indicated by the italicized **footing.** The term *footing* refers to the addition of a column of figures. The total of the entries on the right side of the account is $2,100, also indicated by the italicized footing. You perhaps have noticed in the account that plus (+) and minus (−) signs are not needed. This is because only increases are entered on one side of the account and only decreases are entered on the other side. All increases are added together to obtain the $8,380, and all decreases are added together to obtain the $2,100.

The elementary form of the account, a T-account

These amounts are footings: the total of a column of figures

Cash					
Increases in Cash			**Decreases in Cash**		
Oct. 1	Owner's Investment.....	4,350	Oct. 15	Salaries Paid	1,400
12	Cash Received for Services	2,670	30	Rent Paid.............	700
25	Accounts Receivable	1,360			
		8,380			*2,100*
Bal.		6,280			

The balance of an account is the difference between the increases and decreases

The net difference between increases and decreases in the Cash account is an increase, and that's why the balance of $6,280 is located on the increases in cash side. Of course, total decreases in cash could not have exceeded total increases; as much as we would like this to happen, we cannot spend more cash than we have!

In a textbook we can use italics to show footings. In a pen-and-ink system, footings and balances are shown in pencil, whereas the entries are recorded in ink.

Notice that the elementary form of the account looks like the letter *T*. For this reason it is referred to as a **T-account.** The T-account is used by accountants to analyze accounting problems and by instructors in teaching accounting. It is not used by economic entities to record business transactions. In the classroom we can easily write a dozen T-accounts on the chalkboard to demonstrate an accounting problem. The same can be done on the back of an envelope by a practicing accountant.

T-accounts are used to analyze accounting problems

THE LEDGER

A **ledger** is simply a group of accounts.

The **general ledger** is a book containing all the accounts of an economic entity that appear on the financial statements. In a pen-and-ink system each account would have a separate page in the general ledger. Accounts that have substantial activity, such as the Cash account, may have more than one page. The pages are typically loose-leaf and of heavy construction so that they may be inserted and removed from the ledger as the need arises.

The general ledger contains all the accounts that appear on the financial statements

In some cases, a general ledger is sufficient to report all the transactions of an organization. In other cases, more detail is needed. For example, each account of the general ledger may be *too* general, recording only summary information. Certain transactions can be described with more detail in a separate ledger of their own.

An account such as the Accounts Receivable account contains information that comes from each of the detailed accounts in the subsidiary ledger account. The general ledger Accounts Receivable account provides information on the amount of total accounts receivable but does not show the specific amounts owed by individual customers. The **accounts receivable ledger** would contain this information, since it is a ledger of the individual accounts receivable. The accounts receivable ledger is referred to as a **subsidiary ledger,** and the Accounts Receivable account of the general ledger is referred to as a **control account.** The general ledger account "controls" the subsidiary ledger. By this we mean that the balance in the general ledger account is the amount that the accounts in the subsidiary ledger, when added up, must equal.

Accounts Receivable is the general ledger account for the accounts receivable subsidiary ledger

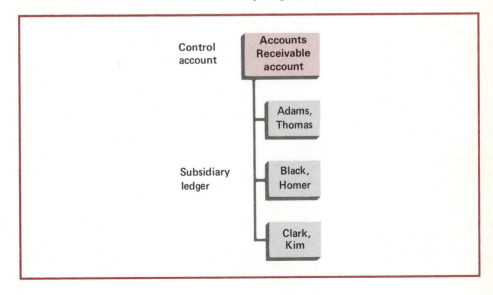

HOW ACCOUNTS ARE CLASSIFIED IN THE GENERAL LEDGER

Accounts in the general ledger are arranged in a certain order

The accounts in the general ledger are arranged in the same order that they would appear in the financial statements. Balance sheet accounts are placed first, followed by the income statement accounts.

Do you remember the financial statements we prepared for General Cleaning Corporation in Chapter 1? Well, in the general ledger we would show the balance sheet accounts first starting with Cash and ending with Retained Earnings and Dividends. The income statement accounts would follow, starting with the revenue account Laundry and ending with the expense account Supplies Expense.

Assets

Assets are divided into current and noncurrent classifications

Assets are commonly subdivided into two major classifications: current assets and noncurrent assets. *Current assets* are generally those that can be expected to provide benefits in the near future (within 1 year). *Noncurrent assets* are those that are used to provide the business entity with benefits over a number of years.

Current Assets

Typical accounts found under the current asset classification are described below in the order in which they would appear in the general ledger.

Cash You all know that cash is the medium of exchange in a civilized society. A company's Cash account includes not only cash on hand (coins, currency, checks, and money orders), but also checking accounts (demand deposits) and savings accounts (time deposits).

Notes Receivable Occasionally an economic entity may loan money or provide goods or services to another entity, receiving in return in each case a *note receivable.* A note receivable is a written agreement between the maker of the note and an economic entity in which the maker promises to pay to the economic entity a specific amount of money on a specified date in the future.

Accounts Receivable Upon accepting goods or services from an economic entity, a customer implies that he or she will pay the agreed price for the goods sold or services rendered. Payment may be made immediately or the customer may be billed, payment to follow within 30 days. The expectation of this future payment is an *account receivable.*

Inventory Retail stores, wholesale companies, and manufacturing concerns all sell a product rather than a service. The price paid by these entities for the product they plan to sell is recorded in the general ledger account Inventory.

Prepaid Expenses Insurance, rent, and supplies are usually paid for in advance. These prepaid items represent future economic benefits—*assets*—until the time they start to contribute to the earning process. They then become expenses. Prepaid rent becomes rent expense day by day as the business entity occupies the space rented. For example, assume that $900 in rent is paid on June 1 for office space. The chart at

	June 1	June 2	June 3	June 29	June 30
Prepaid Rent	$900	$870	$840	$30	$0
Rent Expense	$0	$30	$60	$870	$900

the bottom of the facing page reflects how the $900 asset of June 1 reverts to a $900 expense for the month of June.

Noncurrent Assets

The common noncurrent assets are land, buildings, and equipment.

Land   Land owned and used by the business entity is recorded in the Land account. Since land has an infinite life, no depreciation is recorded.

Buildings   Included in the Buildings account are retail and wholesale stores, factories, warehouses, and office buildings. These structures typically have useful lives up to 40 or more years and, like equipment, must be depreciated over their useful lives.

Equipment   The Equipment account records the acquisition and disposition of office machines, desks, autos, trucks, file cabinets, and similar items. These assets have useful lives exceeding 1 year. Since their useful lives exceed 1 year, the cost of these items should not be assigned to just the year they were acquired. Rather, it makes sense to allocate their cost over their useful lives in some reasonable way. This allocation process is called **depreciation.** Thus, the cost of equipment becomes depreciation expense on a year-by-year basis. Monthly depreciation is typically computed by dividing the yearly depreciation by 12.

Allocating the cost of an asset over its useful life is called depreciation

Liabilities

The second group of general ledger accounts is the liability accounts. They too typically fall into two major groups: **current liabilities** and **long-term liabilities.** The basic distinction between current and long-term liabilities is that current liabilities are due within 1 year. The long-term classification reflects liabilities that will be paid later than 1 year after the balance sheet date.

Liabilities are divided into two classifications: current and long-term

Current Liabilities

The common current liability accounts are Notes Payable, Accounts Payable, Salaries Payable, and Unearned Revenues.

Notes Payable   A note payable is like a note receivable but is a liability, not an asset. In the case of a note payable, the business entity is the maker of the note; that is, the business entity is the party doing the promising, and promises to pay the other party to the agreement a specified amount of money on a specified future date.

Accounts Payable   Accounts Payable represents the reverse relationship of Accounts Receivable. By accepting the goods or services, the buyer agrees to pay for them in the near future.

Salaries Payable   On the date for which a balance sheet is prepared, it is very likely that a number of employees have earned salaries that haven't yet been paid. Unpaid earnings represent a liability to the business entity and are recorded in the Salaries Payable account.

Unearned Revenues   When a business entity receives payment before providing its customers with goods or services, the amounts received are recorded in the *Unearned Revenue* account. When the goods or services are provided to the customer, revenue is recognized. The Unearned Revenue account is reduced and the revenue account is increased. If you understand the concept of prepaid expenses, then you may already have wondered about how the business entities receiving the prepaid expense

Unearned revenues are the opposite of prepaid expenses

amounts characterize and record those receipts. They characterize them as revenues received but not yet earned. Unearned insurance premiums and unearned rent represent the reverse relationship of prepaid insurance and prepaid rent. The Unearned Revenue account represents a liability because the business entity has an obligation to provide goods or services in the future.

Long-Term Liabilities

The common long-term liability accounts are Mortgage Payable and Bonds Payable.

Mortgage Payable The Mortgage Payable account records long-term debt of the business entity for which the business entity has pledged certain assets as security to the creditor. In the event that the debt payments are not paid, the creditor can force the sale of the mortgaged asset to settle the claim.

Bonds Payable Corporations often obtain substantial sums of money from lenders to finance the acquisition of inventories, equipment, and other assets. They obtain these funds by issuing **bonds.** The bond is a contract between the issuer and the lender specifying the terms of repayment and the interest to be charged. Bonds, like mortgage payables, represent a long-term liability, since they will be paid after 1 year from the balance sheet date.

Stockholders' Equity

The third group of general ledger accounts includes the Capital Stock account, the Retained Earnings account, and the Dividends account.

Capital Stock

The Capital Stock account reflects the stockholders' contribution to the business

The Capital Stock account is used to record the amount the stockholders of a corporation have invested in the corporation. The stockholders investment is evidenced by shares of stock issued to the stockholders by the corporation. We will elaborate on this when we discuss corporations in a later chapter, but for now this simple example should help.

Let's assume that four individuals start a business together, obtaining a corporate charter from the state in which they reside. Most likely they engaged a lawyer to do whatever legal work was necessary. Let's say that the first individual, Mr. Blanchard, invests $10,000 cash in the new corporation and is issued 1,000 shares of capital stock. And Mrs. Rameriz and Mr. Levy invest a truck worth $15,000 and a building worth $30,000, respectively. Mrs. Rameriz is issued 1,500 shares of stock, and Mr. Levy is issued 3,000 shares. Finally, Miss Johnson contributes land worth $45,000, receiving 4,500 shares in return.

Now 10,000 shares have been issued (1,000 + 1,500 + 3,000 + 4,500). Mr. Blanchard owns 10% of the corporation (1,000 ÷ 10,000), Mrs. Rameriz 15% (1,500 ÷ 10,000), Mr. Levy 30% (3,000 ÷ 10,000), and Miss Johnson 45% (4,500 ÷ 10,000). The corporation would have a balance sheet that would look like this:

Assets		Stockholders' Equity	
Cash	$ 10,000	Capital Stock	$100,000
Land	45,000		
Building	30,000		
Truck	15,000		
Total Assets	$100,000		$100,000

Notice that the 10,000 shares of capital stock are valued at $100,000, the amount of assets contributed by the four stockholders. That's how it works: The stock is issued at the value of the assets contributed.

Retained Earnings

The Retained Earnings account reflects total earnings of the company since the date of inception less total dividends paid out

The Retained Earnings account is used to record the amount of accumulated earnings the corporation has decided to retain in the business and not pay out to its stockholders in the form of dividends. It is the sum of the earnings of the corporation from its first day of business until today less all the dividends ever paid. It is not cash!! Cash is on the other side of the balance sheets: It's an asset.

Dividends

When cash is distributed to the stockholders we call that a dividend and record it in the Dividend account rather than reducing the Retained Earnings account directly.

Revenue

The fourth group of general ledger accounts is the revenue accounts. These accounts represent earnings during the year. A revenue account is established in the general ledger for each source of revenue. The account titles generally supply an adequate description of the nature of each revenue account. Sales, Commissions Earned, Interest Income, and Fees from Services Rendered are all examples of revenue accounts.

Expenses

Expenses are the fifth and last group of general ledger accounts. Again, the account titles are descriptive of the nature of the account. Typical expenses are: Cost of Goods Sold, Depreciation Expense, Rent Expense, Supplies Expense, Insurance Expense, and Salaries Expense.

THE CHART OF ACCOUNTS

The accounts in the general ledger for one business entity may be different from the accounts found in the general ledger for another entity. The accounts in the general ledger for any business entity depend on several things: the nature of the business and the way it operates; the size of the business entity; the amount of detail needed for management to make its decisions; and, for business entities that must comply with them, rulings of federal or state (or both) regulatory agencies (e.g., the Internal Revenue Service, the Securities and Exchange Commission, and the Federal Power Commission). The amount of detail needed to fulfill compliance with these agencies will also affect the kinds of accounts in the general ledger.

The chart of accounts is a system of organizing and numbering the accounts in the general ledger

To facilitate the recordkeeping process, the accounts in the general ledger are numbered. The use of numbers to identify accounts in business documents is much easier than the use of account titles. Each business entity will normally devise its own numbering system. Numbering the accounts consecutively presents problems in cases where new accounts may have to be added, as often happens with most business entities. So, what is needed is a numbering system that is not necessarily consecutive but is successive and allows for new numbers to be inserted within the succession. For example, a typical numbering system will use a series of multi-digit numbers, the first digit in each number indicating the major classification of the general ledger. Assets may be 1000, liabilities may be 2000, stockholders' equity accounts 3000, revenues 4000, and expenses 5000.

The second digit will be used to represent subclassifications of each major account. For example, within the assets, 1100 may be used to indicate current assets, 1200 to indicate noncurrent assets, and so on.

Specific general ledger accounts can then be identified by the third digit. For example, Cash would be 1110, Notes Receivable 1120, etc.

Finally, the fourth digit can be used to achieve a more detailed classification, such as 1112—Cash in Savings Account; or 1113—Cash on Hand.

With the type of system described above it would be relatively easy to add new accounts as the need arises. For example, if the current asset account Notes Receivable from Officers were to be added, it would be assigned the account number 1121. The use of account numbers is very important in using computerized accounting systems.

Presented below is a typical chart of accounts:

A list of accounts with their account numbers is called a chart of accounts

Assets		**Liabilities**	
Current assets:		Current liabilities:	
1110	Cash	2110	Notes Payable
	1111 Cash in Checking Account	2120	Accounts Payable
	1112 Cash in Savings Account	2130	Salaries Payable
	1113 Cash on Hand	2140	Unearned Rent Revenue
1120	Notes Receivable		
1130	Accounts Receivable	Long-term liabilities:	
1140	Inventory	2210	Mortgage Payable
1150	Prepaid Rent	2220	Bonds Payable
1160	Prepaid Insurance		
1170	Supplies on Hand	**Stockholders' Equity**	
		3100	Capital Stock
Noncurrent assets:		3200	Retained Earnings
1210	Land	3300	Dividends
1220	Building		
1221	Accumulated Depreciation: Building	**Revenue**	
1230	Equipment	4100	Sales
1231	Accumulated Depreciation: Equipment	4200	Commissions Earned
		4300	Rent Income
		4400	Interest Income
		Expenses	
		5100	Cost of Sales
		5200	Salaries Expense
		5300	Depreciation Expense
		5400	Rent Expense
		5500	Interest Expense
		5600	Supplies Expense

DEBIT AND CREDIT

Many students come to this part of their study of accounting with preconceived notions about debits and credits. For the moment, forget what you think you know about these two basic terms. Start from the beginning with us.

And in the beginning, when the accounting profession developed, it was arbitrarily decided that entries recorded on the left side of any account should be called *debits* and entries recorded on the right side of any account should be called *credits*. And that's the way it's been ever since—debits on the left and credits on the right.

Debits are recorded on the left side of any account, credits on the right

Accounts are the basic building blocks of the accounting system. The account must be capable of reflecting increases and decreases in monetary amounts resulting from business transactions. But which side of the account should be used to show increases? Which side should show decreases? Let's think this through together.

We know that the objective of our accounting system is to provide financial statements—an income statement, a statement of stockholders' equity, and a balance sheet. We also know that the accounting system must be based on the basic balance sheet equation, *Assets = Liabilities + Stockholders' Equity.* We used this equation as a basis for the financial transaction worksheet in Chapter 1. We now know that a separate account must be maintained for each item listed in the financial statements. And each account will show increases and decreases.

We have to start somewhere, so why not with the first accounts—assets. It would seem logical to start with increases first, for we cannot decrease something we do not yet have. And it would also seem logical to start with the left side rather than the right because that is the way we read—from left to right.

So we decide that to record an increase in an asset account, we will show this on the debit side of the account. Once this decision is made, then the credit side of an asset account must be used for decreases.

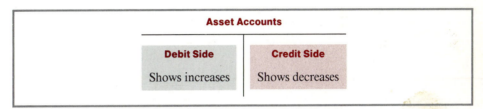

Assets are increased by debits; decreased by credits

Now, we realize that each financial transaction has two parts as we observed in Chapter 1. If an asset is increased, then if the basic model is to remain in balance, something else must happen—namely, one of the following:

1. *Another asset must decrease,* or

2. *A liability must increase,* or

3. *Stockholders' equity must increase.*

Since we selected the debit side of the asset account to show increases resulting in the credit side to show decreases, the first alternative can be solved when one asset is increased—*debited*—and a second asset is decreased—*credited*—by a like amount. The debit equals the credit; the basic equation remains in balance.

If the increase in the asset resulted from an increase in a liability or a stockholders' equity account, we would realize that we must use the credit side of those two accounts to record increases. Why? The basic equation must balance. Liabilities and stockholders' equity accounts are on the opposite side of the basic equation from assets. If debits are used to increase assets, then the opposite, credits, must be used to increase those accounts on the opposite side of the equation to maintain equality, as seen below:

Liabilities and stockholders' equity are increased by credits; decreased by debits

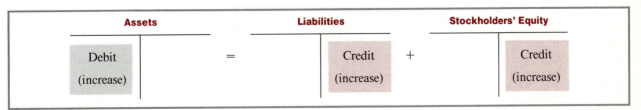

And, if credits increase liabilities and stockholders' equity accounts, then debits must be used to decrease these accounts.

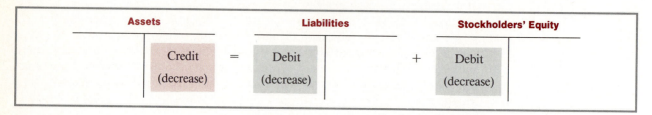

All this, referred to as the ***rules of debit and credit,*** flowed from the initial decision to select debits to record increases in asset accounts.

Now let's summarize and expand on what we have developed.

An account is debited (sometimes the word ***charged*** is used) when an amount is entered on the left side. An account is credited when an amount is entered on the right side. The word *debit* is abbreviated **Dr.,** and similarly, the word *credit* is abbreviated **Cr.** The difference between the sum of the debits in an account and the sum of its credits is the ***account balance.*** A ***debit balance*** results when the sum of the debits exceeds the sum of its credits. If the sum of the credits exceeds the sum of the debits, a ***credit balance*** results.

Debits and credits by themselves do not indicate increases or decreases. Reference must be made to a specific account to determine if the debits or credits represent increases or decreases. This is illustrated in the following chart:

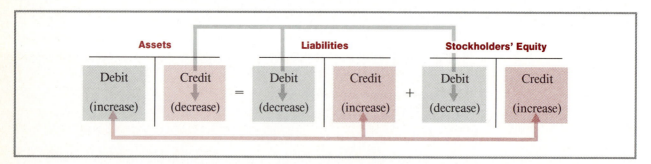

Every single financial transaction affects at least two accounts in the general ledger—an account in which a debit is recorded and an account in which a credit is recorded. The amount recorded in the debit account must equal the amount recorded in the credit account. If one debit account affects more than one credit account, the sum of the credit accounts affected must, of course, equal the amount of the corresponding debit account. Conversely, if one credit account affects more than one debit account, the sum of the debit accounts must equal the amount of the credit account.

This ***law of accounting***—that for every transaction, the sum of the debits must always equal the sum of the credits—is as basic to accounting as Newton's law of motion (for every action there is an equal and opposite reaction) is to physics.

Let's record a transaction in the new accounting system we have just developed to reinforce our understanding. Assume that a new corporation is started with an initial cash investment of $1,000, and capital stock of a like amount is issued. An asset, Cash, is increased, and stockholders' equity, Capital Stock, is also increased as shown at the top of the next page:

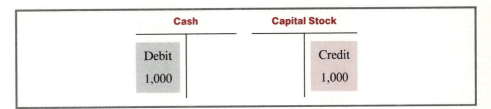

Assets are increased by debits, stockholders' equity is increased by credits. Debits of $1,000 equal credits of a like amount.

Income Statement Accounts

Go back to the financial transaction worksheet prepared in Chapter 1 after transaction (11), page 36. There you can see that revenues increase the Retained Earnings account, and expenses decrease that account. Dividends are also part of the Retained Earnings account.

When we prepared the income statement for General Cleaning Corporation, we used a financial transaction worksheet. All revenue and expense accounts were listed as plus (+) or minus (−) under the Retained Earnings account. In your homework from Chapter 1 you spent considerable time after the transactions had been recorded identifying all revenue and expense accounts listed under the Retained Earnings account.

What do you think? Would it not be much easier if we listed each revenue and expense account separately? Of course it would, and that is what we do.

Revenue, expense, and dividends accounts are part of the stockholders' equity account

But keep in mind that revenue, expense, and dividends accounts are still part of the Retained Earnings account and as such are part of the basic balance sheet equation, Assets = Liabilities + Stockholders' Equity.

Increases and decreases in asset and liability accounts are recorded directly into those accounts; increases and decreases in the retained earnings account are recorded in the revenue, expense, and dividends accounts.

The relationship of revenue, expense, and dividends accounts to the basic accounting model can be illustrated by the following diagram:

This is how the revenue, expense, and dividends accounts relate to the basic accounting equation

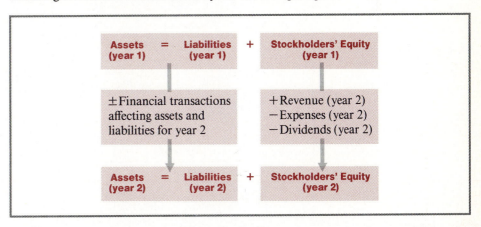

Since revenue, expenses, and the dividends account are part of the retained earnings account, which in turn is part of stockholders' equity, the rules of debit and credit as applied to stockholders' equity also apply to these three component accounts within the retained earnings account.

If we wish to increase a revenue account, which in turn will increase the retained earnings account, the revenue account must be credited. This is so because the

Revenues are increased by debits

retained earnings account is increased by credits. Notice in the diagram below that the revenue account is represented as part of the retained earnings account. Specifically, it is represented as part of the credit side. Can you see why? Revenues will always have credit balances. We either earn some revenue or we earn zero revenue. We do not earn "negative" revenue.

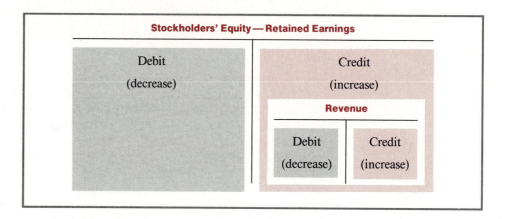

Expenses and dividends are increased by debits

Expenses and dividends decrease retained earnings. If we wish to record a decrease to the retained earnings account we must debit the account. To increase expenses and dividends is to decrease retained earnings; consequently expenses and dividends are increased by debits. Like revenues, expenses and dividends either exist or they do not. And if they exist, they must have debit balances, which explains why they are shown on the debit side of the following diagram:

Expenses and dividends are part of stockholders' equity

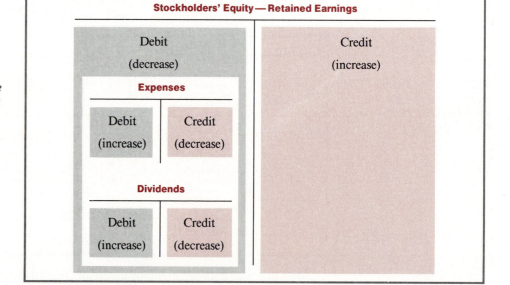

We have now determined how to record increases and decreases for each of the six basic accounts. These rules of increases and decreases are summarized as follows:

		To Increase	To Decrease
	Assets must be	Debited	Credited
	Liabilities must be	Credited	Debited
	Stockholders' equity must be......	Credited	Debited
Part of stockholders' equity	Revenues must be	Credited	Debited
	Expenses must be..........	Debited	Credited
	Dividends must be.........	Debited	Credited

Normal Balances

For any account, the normal situation is for the sum of the increases to the account to exceed the sum of the decreases to the account. The resulting balance is a positive balance rather than a negative balance. The positive balance of an account is referred to as its **normal balance.** Asset accounts typically have total debits in excess of total credits and consequently have a normal debit balance.

The normal balance of any account is the excess of that accounts increases over its decreases

For example, consider the Office Supplies on Hand account. When office supplies are acquired, the Office Supplies on Hand account is debited representing the normal balance. When office supplies are used, the Office Supplies on Hand account must be decreased, and this is done by crediting the account. We cannot use more office supplies than we have. We can credit the Office Supplies on Hand account only to the extent of previous debits, resulting in a zero balance. All supplies have been used. The Office Supplies on Hand account cannot have a credit balance. It must have a debit balance, which is its normal balance.

The normal balance of each type of account is always the "Increase" side of the account, as illustrated below:

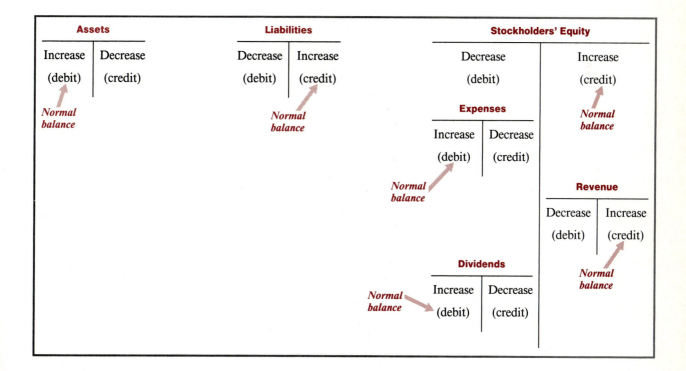

PACIOLI ON ACCOUNTING

In the name of God enter in the Journal the first item of your Inventory, which is the quantity of money that you possess. In order to know how to enter this Inventory in the Journal and Ledger, you must make use of two other terms; one is called Cash, and the other Capital. Cash means the money on hand. Capital means the entire amount of what you now possess.

At the beginning of all business Journals and Ledgers, Capital must always be entered as a credit and Cash always as a debit. In the management of any type of business, Cash may never have a credit balance, but only debit (unless it balances). If, in balancing your book, you find that Cash has a credit balance, an error in the book is indicated. Cash must always be entered in the Journal in the following way:

Source: R. Gene Brown and Kenneth S. Johnston, *Pacioli on Accounting,* McGraw-Hill Book Company, New York, 1963, p. 45. Reprinted by permission.

Examples for Making Journal Entries.

8th day of November, MCCCCLXXXXIII, in Venice.

First
1
2

debit line *

Debit Cash, credit Capital of myself, Mr. Businessman. At present I have cash in a certain place, consisting of gold, coin, silver, and copper of various coinage as shown on the first sheet of the Inventory, in total so many gold ducats and so many ducats in coin. In our Venetian money all is valued in gold, that is, 24 grossi for each ducat and 32 picioli for each grosso, and so many gold lire.

Value:

credit line

L. . (lire) S. . (solidi) G. . (grossi) P. . (picioli)

* Pacioli suggests that when the debit entry is posted to the Ledger, a vertical line be drawn to the left of the journal entry. When the credit is posted, a "credit posting line" be drawn to the right of the journal entry. The two numbers at the left of the debit posting line are the folio references giving, respectively, the ledger page number of the debit and credit entry.

Our present double-entry accounting system can be traced back some 500 years to the writings of Fra Luca Pacioli of Venice, Italy. Here's what he had to say about investing funds in a business entity.

An Illustration

In order to illustrate the application of the rules of debit and credit and how transactions are recorded in the accounts, we will take you through some transactions and analyze them as we apply the rules and record them in the accounts. Prior to being recorded, a transaction must be analyzed to determine which accounts must be increased or decreased. After this has been determined, the rules of debit and credit are applied to effect the appropriate increases and decreases to the accounts.

RESIDENTIAL REMODELING, INC.

Stockholders invest funds

Transaction 1 Several stockholders invest $8,000 of their funds in a new business entity entitled Residential Remodeling, Inc.

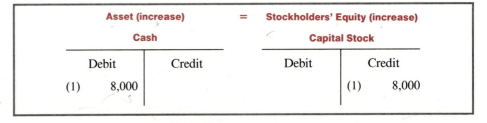

Asset (increase)		=	Stockholders' Equity (increase)	
Cash			Capital Stock	
Debit	Credit		Debit	Credit
(1) 8,000				(1) 8,000

This transaction increases the economic resource, the asset Cash, and also the stockholders' equity account, Capital Stock. According to the rules of debit and credit, debits will increase assets and credits will increase stockholders' equity accounts. Thus the transaction is debit Cash and credit Capital Stock. Notice that the figure (1) is placed by the $8,000 debit and the $8,000 credit. This is a *posting reference* and is used to identify the source (transaction 1 in this case) of the debit or credit in the account.

Assets are acquired for cash

Transaction 2 Residential Remodeling, Inc., purchased the following assets for cash: Supplies, $900; Office Equipment, $700; and Tools, $600.

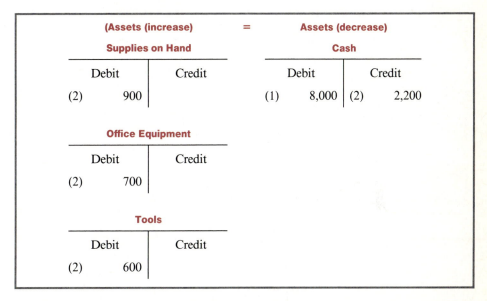

Three assets—Supplies on Hand, Office Equipment, and Tools—are increased by this transaction in the total amount of $2,200. These assets were acquired by payment of $2,200 in cash, reducing the asset Cash by $2,200. Assets are increased by debits and reduced by credits. Therefore Supplies on Hand, Office Equipment, and Tools are debited, each for its appropriate amount, and Cash is credited for the total, $2,200.

A truck is acquired for cash and a note payable

Transaction 3 The corporation acquired a used truck for $7,500, paying $1,500 in cash and issuing a note payable for the difference.

	Asset (increase, decrease)		=		Liability (increase)	
	Cash				**Notes Payable**	
Debit		Credit		Debit		Credit
(1) 8,000		(2) 2,200				(3) 6,000
		(3) 1,500				

	Truck	
Debit		Credit
(3) 7,500		

The asset Truck is created and starts with an increase of $7,500 by this transaction. At the same time the asset Cash is decreased and the liability Notes Payable is created and starts off with an increase. Increases in assets are recorded by debits. Decreases in assets are recorded by credits, and increases in liabilities are recorded by credits. Thus, this transaction is recorded by debiting the account Truck for $7,500, crediting the account Cash for $1,500, and crediting Notes Payable for $6,000.

Rent is paid in advance

Transaction 4   Three months' rent is paid in advance, $1,200.

Asset (increase)		=	Asset (decrease)		
Prepaid Rent			**Cash**		
Debit	Credit		Debit	Credit	
(4) 1,200			(1) 8,000	(2)	2,200
				(3)	1,500
				(4)	1,200

Prepaid Rent, a resource having future economic benefit, has been acquired for the cash payment of $1,200. The future economic benefit is the right to occupy the rented property. (As each month goes by, $400 of Prepaid Rent will be transferred to the Rent Expense account.) Increases in assets are recorded by debits, and decreases in assets are recorded by credits. The transaction is recorded by debiting Prepaid Rent for $1,200 and crediting Cash for $1,200.

Cash is received for services rendered

Transaction 5   Cash is received in the amount of $950 as payment for remodeling services.

Asset (increase)			=	Stockholders' Equity (increase)	
Cash				**Remodeling Services**	
Debit	Credit			Debit	Credit
(1) 8,000	(2)	2,200			(5) 950
(5) 950	(3)	1,500			
	(4)	1,200			

This transaction increases the asset Cash and stockholders' equity by the revenue received as payment for remodeling services. Assets are increased by debits, and revenues are increased by credits. A debit of $950 to Cash and a credit of $950 to Remodeling Services record the transaction.

Services are performed on account

Transaction 6   Remodeling services of $1,350 are performed on account; the customer is billed and will pay later.

Assets (increase)			=	Stockholders' Equity (increase)		
Accounts Receivable				**Remodeling Services**		
Debit		Credit		Debit		Credit
(6)	1,350				(5)	950
					(6)	1,350

Services have been performed entitling Residential Remodeling, Inc., to receive $1,350 payment, which will be paid in the future. Since the service has been completed, revenue is earned. A future economic benefit has been received, the asset Accounts Receivable, in exchange for the service rendered. Assets are increased by debits. Revenues are increased by credits. Debit Accounts Receivable and credit Remodeling Services for $1,350.

Payment is made on a note payable

Transaction 7 The first of five payments in the amount of $1,200 is made for the truck acquired in transaction (3).

Assets (decrease)			=	Liabilities (decrease)		
Cash				**Notes Payable**		
Debit		Credit		Debit		Credit
(1)	8,000	(2)	2,200	(7)	1,200	(3)	6,000
(5)	950	(3)	1,500				
		(4)	1,200				
		(7)	1,200				

The asset Cash and the liability Notes Payable are reduced by $1,200 each by this transaction. Assets are decreased by credits; liabilities are decreased by debits. The transaction is recorded by debiting Notes Payable and crediting Cash.

Tools are acquired on account

Transaction 8 Additional tools are acquired on account, $150.

Assets (increase)			=	Liabilities (increase)		
Tools				**Accounts Payable**		
Debit		Credit		Debit		Credit
(2)	600				(8)	150
(8)	150					

This transaction increases the asset Tools and also the liability Accounts Payable each by $150. Assets are increased by debits. Liabilities are increased by credits. Debit Tools in the amount of $150 and credit Accounts Payable in the amount of $150.

Utilities are paid

Transaction 9   Paid utilities expense of $100.

Assets (decrease)			=	Stockholders' Equity (decrease)	
Cash				Utilities Expense	
Debit	Credit			Debit	Credit
(1) 8,000	(2) 2,200			(9) 100	
(5) 950	(3) 1,500				
	(4) 1,200				
	(7) 1,200				
	(9) 100				

As in the revenue transactions (5 and 6), a separate expense account must be established for each expense item. This transaction increases the expense Utilities and reduces the asset Cash by $100. Expenses are increased by debits, and assets are decreased by credits. Debit Utilities Expense in the amount of $100 and credit Cash in the amount of $100.

Cash is received from a customer

Transaction 10   Received $750 in cash from customers for whom service was rendered in transaction (6).

Asset (increase)			=	Asset (decrease)	
Cash				Accounts Receivable	
Debit	Credit			Debit	Credit
(1) 8,000	(2) 2,200			(6) 1,350	(10) 750
(5) 950	(3) 1,500				
(10) 750	(4) 1,200				
	(7) 1,200				
	(9) 100				

Payments by customers reduce the asset Accounts Receivable and increase the asset Cash. Assets are increased by debits and decreased by credits. Debit Cash for $750, and credit Accounts Receivable for $750.

Dividends are paid

Transaction 11   Dividends of $500 are paid.

Dividends are a reduction of stockholders' equity but are not an expense of the business entity. Nevertheless, they are recorded separately from the Retained Earnings account. This transaction increases the Dividends account and reduces cash. Debits record increases in the Dividends account, and credits record decreases in asset accounts. The transaction is recorded by a debit in the amount of $500 to the Dividend account and a credit of $500 to Cash.

Assets (decrease)			=	Stockholders' Equity (decrease)		
Cash				**Dividends**		
Debit		Credit		Debit		Credit
(1)	8,000	(2)	2,200	(11)	500	
(5)	950	(3)	1,500			
(10)	750	(4)	1,200			
		(7)	1,200			
		(9)	100			
		(11)	500			

Depreciation is recorded

Transaction 12 Depreciation of $750 is recorded on the truck.

Stockholders' Equity (decrease)			=	Assets (decrease)		
Depreciation Expense				**Accumulated Depreciation**		
Debit		Credit		Debit		Credit
(12)	750				(12)	750

The depreciation expense transaction is recorded by increasing an expense and reducing an asset. The reduction of the asset is accomplished by the use of a ***contra-asset*** account, Accumulated Depreciation. Expenses are increased by debits. Assets are reduced by credits. (As a result, contra assets are increased by credits.) To record the transaction, Depreciation Expense is debited in the amount of $750 and Accumulated Depreciation: Truck is credited in the amount of $750.

The 12 transactions of this illustration are shown in the accounts of the general ledger shown on page 72. Notice that the accounts are organized under the basic elements of the financial statements. Also notice that the number identifying each of the transactions provides a cross reference between the accounts debited and the accounts credited. The $100 credit in the Cash account from transaction (9) can be located in the Utilities Expense account by reference to the ***posting reference*** 9.

The Trial Balance

Our objective in using an accounting system was to prepare financial statements more efficiently than we could by use of a financial transaction worksheet. We have reached a stage where all the transactions for a period of time have been recorded. What next?

Before the statements can be prepared, the balance in each account must be determined. Once this is done (and it was done in the general ledger shown on page 72), we may wish to prove that we have recorded all transactions accurately. How? Well, we know that every transaction is recorded by equal debits and credits, and that the total of the debits must equal the total of the credits in the general ledger. Why not make a list of all the account balances, showing which ones have debit balances and which ones have credit balances? Now, let's *try* to see if the total of the debit accounts will equal, *balance,* the total of the credit accounts. We have prepared a *trial balance.*

A trial balance is a listing of all the accounts and their respective balances

RESIDENTIAL REMODELING, INC.
General Ledger

Assets		=	Liabilities		+	Stockholders' Equity	

Cash

(1)	8,000	(2)	2,200
(5)	950	(3)	1,500
(10)	750	(4)	1,200
		(7)	1,200
		(9)	100
		(11)	500
	9,700		6,700
Bal.	3,000		

Accounts Receivable

(6)	1,350	(10)	750
Bal.	600		

Prepaid Rent

(4)	1,200	
Bal.	1,200	

Supplies on Hand

(2)	900	
Bal.	900	

Office Equipment

(2)	700	
Bal.	700	

Tools

(2)	600	
(8)	150	
Bal.	750	

Truck

(3)	7,500	
Bal.	7,500	

Accumulated Depreciation: Truck

		(12)	750
		Bal.	750

Notes Payable

(7)	1,200	(3)	6,000
		Bal.	4,800

Accounts Payable

		(8)	150
		Bal.	150

Capital Stock

		(1)	8,000
		Bal.	8,000

Dividends

(11)	500	
Bal.	500	

Revenues
Remodeling Services

		(5)	950
		(6)	1,350
		Bal.	2,300

Expenses
Utilities Expense

(9)	100	
Bal.	100	

Depreciation Expense

(12)	750	
Bal.	750	

Again, to prepare a trial balance we must first compute the balance of each account in the general ledger. Next, the balance from each account of the general ledger is listed on a two-column work paper in the same order as the accounts appear in the general ledger. The accounts in the general ledger having a debit balance are entered in the first column. The accounts having credit balances are entered in the second column. The debit column is added up and the credit column is added up. The sums of each column should be equal.

The trial balance of Residential Remodeling, Inc., is presented in the trial balance below. The total of the debit column equals $16,000, which is equal to the total of $16,000 for the credit columns. The trial balance does in fact balance.

Now, once the trial balance is prepared and it balances, it should be relatively easy to prepare the financial statements from the trial balance. Just copy the income statement accounts on an income statement and the balance sheet accounts on a balance sheet.

RESIDENTIAL REMODELING, INC.
Trial Balance
October 31, 1989

	Debits	Credits
Cash	$ 3,000	
Accounts Receivable	600	
Prepaid Rent	1,200	
Supplies on Hand	900	
Office Equipment	700	
Tools	750	
Truck	7,500	
Accumulated Depreciation: Truck		$ 750
Notes Payable		4,800
Accounts Payable		150
Capital Stock		8,000
Dividends	500	
Remodeling Services		2,300
Utilities Expense	100	
Depreciation Expense	750	
Totals	$16,000	$16,000

The trial balance provides proof that the general ledger is in balance. This means that the accountant can be sure of three things:

1. For each transaction, the debits and credits were recorded in equal amounts.

2. The balance (debit balances and credit balances) for each account was calculated correctly.

3. The balances of the various debit and credit accounts have been correctly added together to arrive at the total equality of the debits and credits.

If the trial balance does not balance, the accountant knows that an error, or perhaps several errors, exists. When errors do occur, they are usually one of the three following types:

*Recording an incorrect
amount in a general ledger
account is a transaction
error*

1. *Transaction errors* When a transaction is recorded, an error might occur through an incorrect amount's being recorded to the general ledger account. One of the most typical errors is to record a debit entry incorrectly as a credit, or a credit as a debit. Another common transaction error is to record only one portion of the transaction, say, the debit, but forget to record the other portion of the transaction, say, the credit; or to record the credit but not the debit.

2. *Account balance errors* Errors can occur in calculating the balance of a specific account. Another account balance error is simply to misplace a debit balance in the credit column or a credit balance in the debit column.

*Transferring an incorrect
amount from a general
ledger account to the trial
balance is a trial balance
error*

3. *Trial balance errors* Trial balance errors can occur by transferring incorrectly the amount of an account balance to the trial balance. They can also occur by incorrectly recording a debit account balance as a credit on the trial balance, or a credit as a debit. The most simple trial balance error is incorrectly adding the debit or credit column.

Caution: You cannot automatically assume that because the trial balance balances, the accounts are correct. You must realize that it is possible to have errors in the accounts and that errors may be such that all the debits still equal all the credits. Some ways this can happen are as follows:

- If an incorrect amount was recorded as both a debit and a credit to the proper accounts, the trial balance will balance.

*Errors may exist even if
the trial balance balances*

- Either omitting an entire transaction or recording a transaction two times, the second time in error, would be an error but would cause the trial balance to balance.

- The correct amounts may be recorded to the incorrect accounts; for example, a debit to Cash may be recorded as a debit to Accounts Receivable.

THE JOURNAL

The accounting system does not start with the recording of a transaction in the general ledger accounts. A little reflection will reveal the need for a record of each transaction listed in chronological order—day by day, day after day. If an error is made in recording a transaction, it will more than likely come to light when the trial balance does not balance. At this point the accountant knows that there is an error but does not know where to start looking for it. Look back to the general ledger for Residential Remodeling, Inc., on page 72 and assume that the transaction numbers were not recorded in the T-accounts as posting references. Suppose that you wish to know the source of the $1,500 credit to the Cash account. How would you find the corresponding debit? A chronological listing of each transaction together with the use of posting references solves this problem. Such a record is called a *journal.*

In the pen-and-ink system, transactions are first recorded in the journal and later transferred to the general ledger, a process referred to by accountants as *posting.* The journal provides a complete record of each transaction. Most errors in the trial balance can be found by reviewing the postings from the journal to the ledger and the ledger to the trial balance.

Because transactions are initially recorded in the journal, this record—the journal—is referred to as a *book of original entry.* A business enterprise will design a journal to suit its own particular needs. Some entities may use only a few different

A journal is a book of original entry; it records transactions in chronological order

types of journals; others may use more. Common to most entities, however, is the **general journal.** The general journal is the simplest of the journals, and it provides the most flexibility. (Four other specific types of journals are typically used; they will be the subject of Chapter 6.)

Journalizing

Journalizing is the act of recording transactions in the journal

Recording transactions in the journal is called **journalizing.** In the general journal, information such as the date, the account to be debited, the amount to be debited, the account to be credited, the amount to be credited, and an explanation of the business transaction are all recorded in appropriate places. A typical general journal page for the first several transactions of Residential Remodeling, Inc., illustration is shown at the bottom of this page.

1. ***The date*** The year is recorded at the top of the date column of each journal page. The month is written on the first line of the date column. Neither the month nor the year is repeated on the page unless the month or year changes. The date of each transaction is recorded in the journal. Notice that the dates correspond to the transaction numbers of the illustration.

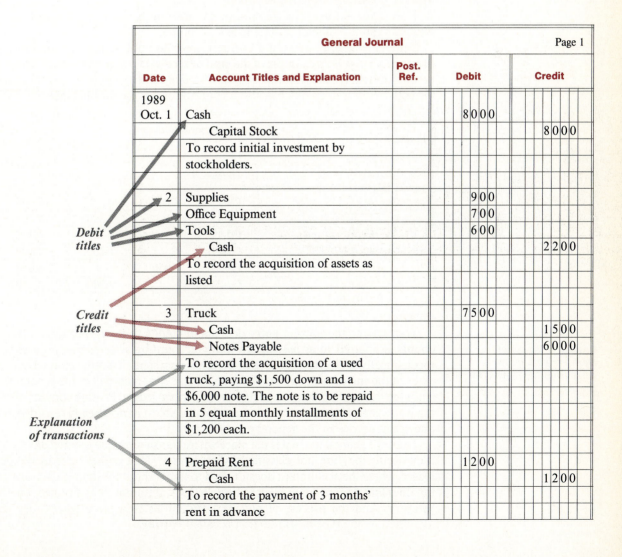

Debit titles

Credit titles

Explanation of transactions

		General Journal			Page 1
Date	Account Titles and Explanation	Post. Ref.	Debit		Credit
1989 Oct. 1	Cash		8000		
	Capital Stock				8000
	To record initial investment by				
	stockholders.				
2	Supplies		900		
	Office Equipment		700		
	Tools		600		
	Cash				2200
	To record the acquisition of assets as				
	listed				
3	Truck		7500		
	Cash				1500
	Notes Payable				6000
	To record the acquisition of a used				
	truck, paying $1,500 down and a				
	$6,000 note. The note is to be repaid				
	in 5 equal monthly installments of				
	$1,200 each.				
4	Prepaid Rent		1200		
	Cash				1200
	To record the payment of 3 months'				
	rent in advance				

2. *Account titles and explanation* The title of the account to be debited is listed at the left of the title and explanation column.

The title of the account to be credited is listed on the line below the account debited, and the title of the credit is indented.

The explanation of the transaction is recorded below the account credited. The explanation should be brief but adequate to explain the transaction.

3. *Amounts debited and credited* The debit amount is recorded in the debit column opposite the title of the account debited. The credit amount is recorded in the credit column opposite the title of the account credited.

The posting reference column (*Post. Ref.*) is not used at the time transactions are recorded in the general journal. When the debits and credits are posted to the general ledger accounts, this column is used to indicate that the posting has been done by placing the account number of the account posted in the posting reference column of the general journal. Only account titles used in general ledgers can be used to record entries in the general journal. If new accounts are needed, they must be added to the general ledger before entries can be recorded under them in the general journal.

Standard Ledger-Account Format

T-accounts are used for classroom demonstration on the chalkboard. They are representations of actual general ledger accounts.

General ledger accounts of a business entity are not maintained in T-accounts. Illustrated below is an example of the kind of account format that is used. This type of account format is called a *balance column account,* since it contains not only columns for both debits and credits but also a column for the account balance.

		Cash in Checking Account			Account No. 1111
Date	Explanation	Post. Ref.	Debit	Credit	Balance
1989 Oct. 1		GJ-1	8,000		8,000
2		GJ-1		2,200	5,800
3		GJ-1		1,500	4,300
4		GJ-1		1,200	3,100
5		GJ-2	950		4,050
7		GJ-2		1,200	2,850

Posting

Posting is the act of transferring a journal entry from the journal to the ledger

Transferring the journal entry debits and credits to their appropriate ledger accounts is referred to as *posting.* In many accounting systems this process is done mechanically or electronically. In a pen-and-ink system, it is done manually. Periodically, at the end of each day or week, the transactions recorded in the general journal since the last posting date are posted to the general ledger. Posting consists of recording in the general ledger accounts the debit and credit items already recorded as debit and credit entries in the general journal.

Thus, the general journal is the place where transactions are entered day by day, as they occur; they are not classified by categories. That comes later in the general ledger, where the accountant doesn't need to know about the date of the transactions but does find it more convenient to begin to look at transactions grouped together by category. And the process of putting transactions in a place where they can be identified by the type of transaction is called *posting.*

The posting process is illustrated below. To get an idea of the posting process, refer to this table as we explain it in the following discussion.

Step in the Posting Process	Explanation
Ⓐ	Locate in the general ledger the account named in the debit portion of the general journal entry.
Ⓑ	Record the date of the transaction in that account in the general ledger.
Ⓒ	Enter the dollar amount of the debit from the journal into the debit column of that particular account in the ledger and determine the new balance.
Ⓓ	Record the general journal page number in the posting reference column of the account debited in the general ledger.
Ⓔ	Enter the account number of the ledger account debited in the posting reference column of the journal on the line of the debit portion of the transaction.
Ⓕ	Repeat the steps above for the credit portion of the journal entry.

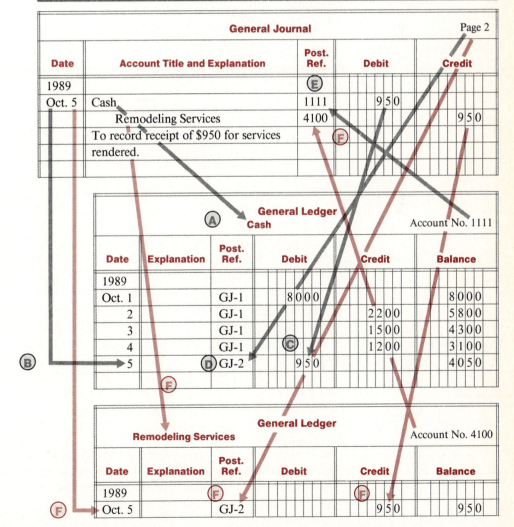

The posting reference columns in both the journal and the ledger serve two purposes. First, a valuable cross reference is achieved. In the event that a question arises concerning an amount in a particular ledger account, the posting reference refers to the journal page where the transaction, the amount, the account titles, and the explanation can be found.

Second, it provides evidence that the accounts have in fact been posted.

Finding Errors

The founding father of accounting once said:

Who does nothing
makes no mistakes;

Who makes no mistakes
Learns nothing

—FRA LUCA PACIOLI (1445–1520)

As you will shortly realize, it is very easy to make errors in working accounting problems. You will also learn, alas, that it is not so easy to find your errors. You can determine an error through chance discovery. More likely, you will learn of errors when the trial balance does not balance.

If your trial balance doesn't balance, subtract the smaller column from the larger column

If an error is discovered because the trial balance did not balance, the difference between the total debit balance and total credit balance should be determined. Often this difference will reveal the nature or location of the error. For example, assume that the debit totals of a trial balance amount to $13,384 and the credit totals $13,700. The difference of $316 might have resulted from the omission of a debit posting of that amount or from a debit of $158 having been posted as a credit. This would cause the credits to be $158 larger than they should be and the debits to be $158 less than they should be, a difference of $316. To check for this type of error, divide the difference by 2 and look for that amount in the trial balance. Check to see if it was recorded correctly.

If the difference is 10, 100, or 1,000, this may be the result of adding the columns incorrectly

Errors of 10, 100, or 1,000 often indicate that the addition of the trial balance columns is in error.

If the difference is divisible evenly by 9, it might be the result of a slide or transposition

If the error is divisible evenly by 9, it is an indication that either a *slide* or a *transposition* has occurred. Moving an entire number either to the right or left is a slide — for example, recording $36 as $360 or $3.60. Reversing the digits in a number is referred to as a transposition. Writing $36 as $63 is an example of a transposition.

Compare the balances in the general ledger to the trial balance. Check the postings from the general journal

The first step to be taken in the process of locating errors is to determine the difference in the trial balance totals. If this does not reveal the error, then each of the various steps in the recording process must be checked, as follows:

- Check the addition of the trial balance.
- Check the transfer of amounts from the general ledger to the trial balance.
- Recompute the account balances.
- Check the posting from the general journal to the general ledger.
- Examine the original transaction to determine if the entry was journalized correctly.

As you proceed through this sequence of steps you will discover the error that causes the trial balance not to balance. Simply retrace your steps starting with the trial balance imbalance.

If an error was made and the trial balance still balances, you will not know that the error exists. Discovery then rests on chance or perhaps on hearing from an irate customer who is billed too much for services rendered or goods sold.

Correcting Errors

Errors must be corrected. If an error is discovered in the general journal before the posting is made, it is corrected by drawing a line through the error, such as an inappropriate account title or incorrect amount, and writing the correct account title or correct amount above the error. For example, the entry below was journalized but not posted.

July 14	Cash	375
	Accounts Receivable.......................................	375
	To record payment from customers.	

The amount of the entry is determined to be incorrect; it should have been $425. The entry is corrected as follows:

		425
July 14	Cash	~~375~~
		425
	Accounts Receivable.......................................	~~375~~
	To record payment from customers.	

If the error was not discovered until after the posting had taken place and the error was in the *amount* posted, it would be corrected in a similar fashion in the ledger account. However, if the error involves the wrong account, then a correcting journal entry is required. For example, assume that the acquisition of office equipment for cash was incorrectly recorded as a credit to Accounts Payable, as seen below.

Jan. 26	Office Equipment...	218
	Accounts Payable..	218
	To record the acquisition of office equipment.	

To correct this error the following entry is needed:

Jan. 31	Accounts Payable...	218
	Cash	218
	To correct an error in the entry of Jan. 26 in which office equipment purchased for cash was erroneously recorded as an acquisition on account.	

Some Minor Points

■ When recording entries in the journals or postings to the ledgers, dollar signs are not used.

■ Commas to indicate thousands of dollars and decimal points to indicate cents are omitted because the rule lines accomplish the purpose served by these items.

■ For even-dollar amounts, the cents column may be left blank, or zeros or dashes may be used.

■ When financial reports are prepared, dollar signs are always used. They are placed only before the first amount at the top of each column of figures and also before amounts representing subtotals and totals.

■ Commas and decimal points are required on financial statements prepared on unruled paper.

REVIEW OF THE STEPS IN THE ACCOUNTING PROCESS

At this point, it's a good idea for you to review the steps involved in the accounting process:

1. First, the business entity enters into a transaction with a second party. A business document, such as a sales invoice, is prepared. This business document provides evidence that a transaction has in fact transpired. The transaction is analyzed and journalized in the general journal.

2. At frequent intervals the entries in the general journal are posted to the accounts in the general ledger.

3. Typically, at the end of each month, the balances of the general ledger accounts are determined and a trial balance is prepared.

4. The financial statements are then prepared from the information contained in the trial balance—first the income statement, followed by the statement of retained earnings, and finally the balance sheet.

You should keep clearly in mind that the ultimate objective of the accounting system is to prepare the financial statements. The objective is not the accounting system. Some students become so captivated by the logic of the accounting system that the system itself dominates their attention and activity. Do not fall into this trap. The chairman of the board of directors of General Motors could care less if the system is on the back of an envelope, a pen-and-ink system, or a computer system; or if two-column or three-column journals are used and if accounts are balanced daily or weekly. What is of concern to him is that *the system provides a timely, efficient method that will result in the preparation of financial statements that will reflect fairly the results of operations and the financial position* (the income statement and balance sheet) of General Motors *for the period of time specified.*

CHAPTER SUMMARY

The objective of general financial accounting activity is to prepare the balance sheet, the statement of retained earnings, and the income statement. This objective is achieved through the ***pen-and-ink–double-entry accounting system.*** The pen-and-ink system is actually used by small business entities. Large business entities use high-speed computer techniques to handle massive quantities of data, but they are based on the basic concepts of the pen-and-ink system.

The basic building block of any accounting system is the account. For each individual asset, liability, stockholders' equity, revenue, and expense item encountered in an entity's financial activities, an account is established. An account consists of three elements: the account title, a location to record increases in the account, and a location to record decreases in the account. Accounts used by business entities appear in balance column form. However, **T-accounts,** which are representative of the actual accounts, are used by accountants and students when analyzing accounting problems.

All the accounts that appear in the financial statements of a business entity are contained in a book called the **general ledger.** Certain general ledger accounts, such as Accounts Receivable, require that a separate book be maintained listing the individual subparts that constitute the whole. The separate book containing the individual accounts is called a **subsidiary ledger,** whereas the related general ledger account is referred to as the **control account.**

Financial transactions increase or decrease specific general ledger accounts. These increases or decreases in the accounts are recorded with the use of the arbitrary **rules of debits and credits.** Debits refer to the left side of any account, and credits refer to the right side. Since each financial transaction consists of two parts in the double-entry accounting system, for every account debited there must be another account (or accounts) credited. Debits must always equal credits.

Since we have arbitrarily decided that debits will be used to increase asset accounts, it follows that credits must be used to increase liability and stockholders' equity (including revenue) accounts. This is so because the basic accounting equation, **Assets = Liabilities + Stockholders' Equity,** must always remain in balance. If debits increase asset accounts, then credits must decrease asset accounts. It then follows that debits must decrease liability and stockholders' equity (including expense and dividends) accounts.

For any specific account the sum of the increases will either exceed or be less than the sum of the decreases. The result is the **account balance.** If the sum of the debits exceeds the sum of the credits, the account is said to have a **debit balance.** Conversely, when credits exceed debits, a **credit balance** results. The typical balance of an account is called its **normal balance** and is *determined by whichever, the debit or the credit, causes the account to increase.*

Thus, *assets, expenses, and dividends accounts have normal debit balances, whereas liabilities, stockholders' equity, and revenue accounts have normal credit balances.*

The accounts are arranged in the general ledger in the order that they would appear in the financial statements, balance sheet accounts first, followed by income statement accounts. Balance sheet accounts are grouped together according to the following classifications: **current assets, noncurrent assets, current liabilities, long-term liabilities,** and **stockholders' equity.** These classifications will appear as headings on balance sheets. The income statement accounts are listed in the general ledger with the revenue accounts appearing first, followed by the expense accounts.

The recordkeeping process is greatly facilitated when the accounts are numbered. The system of numbered accounts for any business entity is called its **chart of accounts.**

The recordkeeping process begins with the recording of business transactions in a book of original entry called a **journal.** Transactions are listed in the journal in chronological order. Periodically the journal-entry debits and credits are transferred to the appropriate general ledger accounts. This process is referred to as **posting.** After the last entries are journalized and posted, a **trial balance** is prepared, typically at the end of every month. The trial balance simply lists all the balances of the general journal ledger accounts and totals all accounts having debit balances and all accounts having credit balances. The sum of the debits in the trial balance must equal the sum of the credits.

Upon completion of the trial balance, the financial statements are prepared.

IMPORTANT TERMS USED IN THIS CHAPTER

Book of original entry The record used by accountants to initially enter transactions. It is called a *journal.* Transactions are recorded as they occur chronologically. (page 74)

Chart of accounts The system of numbered general ledger accounts for an economic entity. (page 59)

Control account A general ledger account, the detail of which is maintained in another book called a *subsidiary ledger.* (page 55)

Credit The right side of an account, which reflects increases to liability, stockholders' equity, and revenue accounts and decreases to asset, expense, and dividends accounts. (page 60)

Debit The left side of an account, which reflects increases to asset, expense, and dividends accounts and decreases to liability, stockholders' equity, and revenue accounts. (page 60)

Dividends The account used to record the distribution of assets, usually cash, to the stockholders. (page 59)

Footing The addition of a column of figures. (page 54)

Journal A book of original entry listing financial transactions affecting general ledger accounts in chronological order in terms of their debit and credit amounts. (page 74)

Journalizing The process of recording financial transactions in a journal. (page 75)

Ledger A book containing the individual accounts of a business entity. (page 55)

Normal balance The typical debit or credit balances found in the individual ledger accounts. (page 65)

Posting The act of transferring the debit and credit entries in a journal to the appropriate ledger accounts. (page 76)

Subsidiary ledger A book containing the detailed information of a general ledger account called a control account. (page 55)

Trial balance A schedule reflecting the balances of the individual general ledger accounts. (page 71)

QUESTIONS

1. One of the most important things to understand about an accounting system is that the system itself is not the most important thing. Explain.

2. What is the difference between an *account* and a *ledger?*

3. What is the purpose of *journals* and how do they relate to *ledgers?*

4. Explain the meaning of the terms *debit* and *credit.*

5. What are the rules of debit and credit for the balance sheet and income statement accounts?

6. Debits and credits are used to increase and decrease accounts. How is it possible for one of these items, say, debits, to be able to both increase and decrease accounts?

7. What are normal balances? How are they determined?

8. What type of errors could cause a trial balance not to balance?

9. What purpose does the trial balance serve?

10. A trial balance may be in balance but the accounts may be incorrect. How is this possible?

11. How are business transactions entered in the general journal?

12. What is a *T-account?*

13. Of what purpose is a chart of accounts?

14. Listed below are several accounts. Assuming that the business entity has experienced substantial activity during the year, indicate for each account whether or not it will have debit entries and/or credit entries, and the normal balance.

   a. Cash
   b. Interest Expense
   c. Fees Earned
   d. Accounts Payable
   e. Capital Stock
   f. Office Equipment
   g. Accounts Receivable
   h. Rent Expense

15. Cash deposited in a bank is reflected as a debit in the ledger account Cash. However, the bank refers to this transaction as "We have credited your account." Explain this apparent inconsistency.

16. In reviewing the accounts listed in a trial balance it is observed that Accounts Receivable has a $50 credit balance and yet the trial balance balances. Explain.

17. Listed below are the total debits and credits from three trial balances that do not balance. For each case, indicate the type of error you would initially attempt to locate.

	Debit Total	Credit Total
a.	$18,700	$18,600
b.	13,470	13,230
c.	87,614	87,974

18. A number of events common to the accounting function of a business entity are presented below. Prepare a list of these events as they would occur in their logical order.

   a. Determining ledger account balances
   b. Analyzing the transaction
   c. Preparing a balance sheet
   d. Preparing a trial balance
   e. Occurrence of a business transaction
   f. Posting from the journal to the ledger
   g. Preparing a business document
   h. Preparing an income statement
   i. Journalizing transactions
   j. Preparing a statement of retained earnings

19. A business entity performed services in the amount of $450 for a customer. The entry was recorded in the general journal as a debit to Accounts Receivable and a credit to Revenue in the amount of $540. How will this error be discovered?

20. Listed below are several errors. For each error, determine if the trial balance totals would be equal or unequal.

   a. The Able Company paid $1,400 for office supplies. The transaction was recorded as a debit to Office Equipment and a credit to Cash for $1,400.
   b. The Baker Company collected $275 from an account receivable. The entry was recorded as a debit to Cash for $275 and a credit to Accounts Receivable of $257.
   c. Charlie Company purchased office supplies on account in the amount of $400. The entry was not recorded.

d. Dog Company entered a $50 debit balance in the Accounts Receivable account in the general ledger as $50 in the credit column on the trial balance.

e. Easy Company recorded rental of office equipment of $150 as a debit to Office Equipment and a credit to Cash.

EXERCISES

**Exercise 2-1
Identifying and
journalizing transactions
found in ledger accounts**

Rapid Delivery, Inc., is a corporation that commenced operations in November, 1988, offering a package delivery service to local businesses. The first eight transactions of the corporation are listed below in T-accounts. From the information given, prepare the general journal entries that were originally made.

Cash					Accounts Payable			
(1)	7,250	(3)	1,050	(8)	2,500	(2)	1,490
(7)	1,200	(4)	1,720			(4)	5,000
		(6)	1,400				
		(8)	2,500				

Accounts Receivable					Capital Stock		
(5)	3,600	(7)	1,200			(1)	7,250

Office Supplies on Hand			Delivery Fees Earned		
(3)	1,050			(5)	3,600

Office Equipment			Salary Expense		
(2)	1,490		(6)	1,400	

Truck		
(4)	6,720	

**Exercise 2-2
Journalizing transactions**

The American Company completed the following transactions for the month of December, 1988. Record the transactions in a general journal.

Dec. 3   Billed customers for consulting fees, $2,700.
      7   Acquired office supplies on account, $300.
    13   Paid rent for the month, $360.
    15   Paid salaries, $950.
    21   Received $1,350 from customers billed on Dec. 3.
    28   Acquired office equipment, $1,000, paying $250 in cash and the remainder on account.

**Exercise 2-3
Preparing a trial balance**

The accounts of the Atlanta Moving & Storage Company are arranged in alphabetical order as listed below. All accounts have a normal balance. Prepare a trial balance as of Dec. 31, 1988, listing the accounts in the proper order.

Accounts Payable...............	$ 2,170	Retained Earnings.............	$28,950
Accounts Receivable...........	2,670	Salaries Expense................	26,200
Building......................	30,000	Salaries Payable	1,520
Capital Stock.................	20,000	Storage Fees Earned............	16,700
Cash	1,350	Trucks	25,000
Land.........................	10,350	Utilities Expense..............	1,070
Moving Fees Earned	27,300		

(Check figure: Total of trial balance = $96,640)

Exercise 2-4
Preparing a corrected trial balance

Presented below is the Nov. 30, 1988, trial balance of Acme Plumbing. Unfortunately, the trial balance does not balance.

ACME PLUMBING
Trial Balance
November 30, 1988

Cash	$ 2,670	
Accounts Receivable	8,460	
Plumbing Supplies on Hand	1,350	
Plumbing Equipment	6,720	
Accounts Payable..........................		$ 3,120
Salaries Payable		590
Capital Stock.............................		10,000
Retained Earnings	2,120	
Plumbing Revenues........................		47,300
Salary Expense	38,100	
Rent Expense	3,600	
Telephone Expense	680	
Totals	$63,700	$61,010

After reviewing the general journal entries and the general ledger accounts, you discover the following:

1. The total credits in the accounts payable ledger account were $16,750. The debit totaled $13,530.
2. In transferring the balance in the Plumbing Supplies on Hand account, the first two digits were transposed.
3. An entry found in the general journal for a $40 debit to Telephone Expense and a credit to Accounts Payable for a like amount were not posted to the general ledger accounts.
4. A credit to Accounts Receivable for $150 was not posted to the general ledger. The corresponding debit to cash for $150 was posted correctly.

Prepare a corrected trial balance

(Check figure: Total of trial balance = $63,270)

Exercise 2-5
Describing the effects of errors on the trial balance

Several errors were made in the records of the National Company for the month of March, 1988. For each of the errors listed below, (a) indicate whether or not the trial balance will balance; (b) if the trial balance does not balance, identify the debit or credit column as being the larger amount; and (c) tell the most likely reason for the error's discovery.

1. National performed certain services for the American Company amounting to $125. The general journal entry was recorded as a debit to Accounts Receivable and a credit to Revenues for Services Rendered of $152.
2. The acquisition of shop supplies for $40 was posted to the general ledger accounts as a debit to Shop Supplies for $50 and a credit to Cash of $40.

3. Office supplies acquired on account for $180 were recorded in the journal as a debit to Office Equipment and a credit to Accounts Payable.
4. The general ledger account Accounts Payable had total debits of $350 and total credits of $480. The balance of Accounts Payable in the trial balance was $110.

Exercise 2-6
Identifying the sources of debits and credits to various accounts

As you become more familiar with the relationship between business transactions and the accounting system, you should see that the accounts are increased and decreased by numerous repetitive transactions. And you should see that individual accounts are usually increased or decreased by very common transactions. For example, we have seen that Cash is increased by debits, and the most common sources of those debits are investments by owners, cash received when services are rendered, and collections of accounts receivable.

For the accounts listed below, identify the most common reasons for increasing or decreasing the account balances by listing those reasons under the column heading "Sources of Debits" or "Sources of Credits."

Account	Sources of Debits	Sources of Credits
Cash	_____	_____
Accounts Receivable	_____	_____
Supplies on Hand	_____	_____
Accounts Payable	_____	_____

PROBLEMS: SET A

Problem A2-1
Recording transactions in T-accounts and preparing a trial balance

On Oct. 1, 1988, Mary Novak received notice from the State of California that her application for a corporate charter was approved. Upon receiving the notice, Mary opened an electrical contracting service to be known as Marquette Electric, Inc. During the month of October, the following transactions were completed:

Oct. 1   Mary Novak and three other stockholders invested a total of $6,500 in the new business.

2   A new truck costing $9,300 was acquired. A down payment of $2,300 was made in cash, and a note payable was given for the remainder.

5   Electrical equipment in the amount of $1,125 and electrical supplies in the amount of $430 were acquired on account.

9   Received $1,460 cash from Locke Publishing Company for electrical work completed this date.

12   Acquired $320 of electrical supplies, paying cash.

14   Electrical work at Ricci Lone Star Printing, Inc., was completed. A bill amounting to $3,070 was submitted.

15   Payment was made in full for the electrical equipment acquired on Oct. 5.

17   Collected $2,070 from Ricci Lone Star Printing, Inc.

23   Paid the first installment of the note payable, $1,050. Of this total, $50 represents interest expense.

26   Received an invoice in the amount of $375 for repairs to the truck.

28   Paid utilities, $80.

30   Paid wages in the amount of $850.

31   Paid dividends amounting to $1,000.

Required

1. Record the transactions directly into T-accounts by entering the appropriate debits and credits.

The following accounts will need to be established: Cash; Accounts Receivable; Electrical Supplies on Hand; Electrical Equipment; Truck; Notes Payable; Accounts Payable; Capital Stock; Dividends; Electrical Contracting Fees Earned; Wages Expense; Truck Repair Expense; Utilities Expense; Interest Expense. The date of the transaction should be used to identify each transaction.

2. After the transactions have been recorded in the T-accounts, prepare a trial balance.

(Check figure: Total of trial balance = $17,835)

Problem A2-2
Journalizing and posting transactions and preparing a trial balance

Berkeley Sanitation, Inc., was organized by Karen Hanson and several other individuals on Nov. 1, 1988, for the purpose of collecting and disposing of garbage. The following transactions were completed during the first month of operations:

Nov. 3   Deposited $14,500 cash from stockholders in a new account at Golden Bear National Bank.

4   Acquired a used garbage truck for $8,700, paying $2,700 in cash and issuing a $6,000 note payable to Hill Used Trucks.

5   Acquired office equipment, $1,670, and office supplies, $580, on account from Landis Office Supply Company.

6   Collected garbage in the Oakland Hills subdivision and submitted bills to residents for service, $1,830.

7   Paid Landis Office Supply for office supplies acquired on Nov. 5.

10   Paid rent for the month on office building, $1,250.

11   Paid salaries to employees, $1,500.

14   Received payments from residents of Oakland Hills subdivision, $770.

15   Acquired office supplies from Purcell Office Supplies, Inc., for $365 on account.

17   Received a $2,150 check from Golden Gate Industrial Park for services rendered this date.

21   Paid the telephone bill, $90.

24   Billed Windy Circle subdivision residents $2,675 for services rendered.

26   Paid $1,560 to Hill Used Trucks, $1,500 being a reduction in the note payable and $60 interest expense.

30   Paid $500 dividends to stockholders.

Required

1. Prepare general journal entries for the transactions listed above.
2. Post the general journal entries to the general ledger accounts using the following account numbers:

Account Number	Account	Account Number	Account
10	Cash	30	Capital Stock
11	Accounts Receivable	31	Dividends
12	Office Supplies on Hand	40	Garbage Collection Fees
13	Office Equipment	51	Salaries Expense
14	Truck	52	Rent Expense
20	Notes Payable	53	Telephone Expense
21	Accounts Payable	54	Interest Expense

3. Prepare a trial balance as of Nov. 30, 1988.

(Check figure: Trial balance = $27,690)

Problem A2-3
Preparing a classified balance sheet

Listed below are the balance sheet accounts of Jim Hill Corporation as of Jan. 31, 1988:

Capital Stock	$200,000	Accounts Receivable	$50,000
Building	160,000	Equipment Note Payable	50,000
Equipment	150,000	Salaries Payable	30,000
Mortgage Payable	108,000	Notes Payable	20,000
Inventory	81,000	Cash	15,000
Land	80,000	Federal Taxes Payable	5,000
Accounts Payable	71,000	Prepaid Advertising	4,000
Retained Earnings.	58,000	Supplies on Hand	2,000

CA

Notes payable are due July 1, 1988, and the equipment note payable is due Nov. 1, 1992.

Required

From this information, prepare a balance sheet classifying the accounts as current assets, noncurrent assets, current liabilities, long-term liabilities, or stockholders' equity.

(Check figure: Total Assets = $542,000)

Problem A2-4
Preparing journal entries from comparative balance sheets and an income statement

The comparative balance sheets for July 1 and July 31, 1988, together with the July, 1988, income statement, for Central Valley Moving Corporation are presented below.

CENTRAL VALLEY MOVING CORPORATION
Comparative Balance Sheets

	July, 1988			July, 1988	
	1	**31**		**1**	**31**
Assets			**Liabilities and Stockholders' Equity**		
Cash	$ 982	$ 4,883	Liabilities:		
Accounts Receivable.	2,016	1,510	Accounts Payable	$ 1,926	$ 1,724
Supplies on Hand	735	821	Taxes Payable	300	50
Prepaid Rent	360	240	Total Liabilities	$ 2,226	$ 1,774
Moving Truck	10,500	10,500			
			Stockholders' Equity:		
			Capital Stock	$ 6,000	$ 6,000
			Retained Earnings.	6,367	10,180
			Total Stockholders' Equity	$12,367	$16,180
			Total Liabilities and Stockholders'		
Total Assets	$14,593	$17,954	Equity	$14,593	$17,954

CENTRAL VALLEY MOVING CORPORATION
Income Statement
For the Month Ended July 31, 1988

Revenues:		
Moving Fees Earned		$5,625
Expenses:		
Salaries Expense	$1,450	
Insurance Expense	125	
Utilities Expense	117	
Rent Expense	120	
Total Expenses		1,812
Net Income		$3,813

Central Valley Moving acquires all goods and services on account except for salaries, which are paid in cash on paydays. Moving fees are made 20% on account, 80% for cash.

| **Required** | Prepare general journal entries, without explanations, which will reflect the transactions that transpired during the month of July. (*Hint:* You will find it helpful to use T-accounts for Accounts Receivable, Accounts Payable, and Cash.) |

Problem A2-5
Correcting a trial balance

Jim Landis and Ted Purcell operate a forklift repair service under the corporate name of Northridge Repair Service. The trial balance for Apr. 30, 1988 (presented below), prepared by their bookkeeper, Jack Smith, does not balance.

NORTHRIDGE REPAIR SERVICE
Trial Balance
April 30, 1988

Cash	$ 1,104	
Accounts Receivable	2,846	
Repair Supplies on Hand	664	
Prepaid Advertising	400	
Repair Equipment	4,468	
Notes Payable		$ 1,300
Accounts Payable		1,954
Capital Stock		2,000
Retained Earnings		1,400
Dividends		1,000
Repair Revenues		6,510
Salaries Expense	2,930	
Advertising Expense	122	
Telephone	99	
Totals	$12,633	$13,164

A review of Mr. Smith's work reveals the following information:

a. Credits to the general ledger account Accounts Payable were underfooted by $600.
b. Repair revenues are overstated in the ledger account by $400.
c. A credit posting for Repair Revenues from the general journal in the amount of $636 is missing.
d. Repair supplies acquired in the amount of $174 have been incorrectly posted to the Repair Equipment account.
e. An account receivable for $98 was incorrectly added as $89 when computing the balance of the Accounts Receivable account.
f. A debit posting from the general journal for $52 is missing from the Advertising Expense account.
g. A credit posting of $150 to Notes Payable should have been made to Accounts Payable.
h. A debit posting of $340 to Repair Supplies on Hand was incorrectly posted as $34.

| **Required** | Prepare a corrected trial balance. |

(Check figure: Trial balance totals $14,000)

Problem A2-6
Journalizing and posting
transactions; preparing a
trial balance and financial
statements

The balance sheet for Frank Flynn Financial Consultant as of Feb. 1, 1988, appears below:

FRANK FLYNN FINANCIAL CONSULTANT
Balance Sheet
February 1, 1988

Assets		Liabilities and Stockholders' Equity		
Assets:		Liabilities:		
Cash	$ 3,926	Notes Payable		$ 1,000
Accounts Receivable .	1,857	Accounts Payable.............		4,013
Prepaid Insurance....	400	Total Liabilities..................		$ 5,013
Office Supplies on				
Hand.............	612	Stockholders' Equity:		
Office Equipment	4,210	Capital Stock........	$10,000	
Automobiles	9,578	Retained Earnings ...	5,570	
		Total Stockholders' Equity........		15,570
		Total Liabilities and Stockholders'		
Total Assets	$20,583	Equity.........................		$20,583

During the month of February 1988, the transactions listed below took place.

Feb. 1   Bought office supplies on account from the Klein Office Supply Company, $526.
    3   Paid $1,021 to Owen Supplies, Inc., for office supplies acquired on account in January.
    4   Billed clients $1,400 for financial consulting.
    9   Paid $175 for advertising in the *St. Louis Evening News* for the month of February.
   11   Collected $715 on accounts receivable.
   12   Bought office equipment for cash from Ulness Equipment Company, $375.
   15   Paid salaries, $850.
   18   Acquired an automobile for use in the business for $9,000. A note payable for $7,000 was issued to Carter Motor Company, and $2,000 was paid in cash.
   19   Provided financial advice to the Ryan Corporation, receiving $950 cash.
   22   Paid rent for the month, $415.
   25   Received cash payments of $1,310 on accounts receivable.
   26   Paid dividends $1,000.
   29   Paid salaries, $875.

Required

1. Enter the amounts from the Feb. 1, 1988, balance sheet into the appropriate general ledger accounts using the following account numbers:

Account Number	Account	Account Number	Account
110	Cash	160	Automobiles
120	Accounts Receivable	210	Notes Payable
130	Prepaid Insurance	220	Accounts Payable
140	Office Supplies on Hand	310	Capital Stock
150	Office Equipment	320	Retained Earnings

2. Prepare general journal entries for the above transactions.
3. Post the entries to the general ledger using page 18 as the general journal page reference and the following additional account numbers:

Account Number	Account	Account Number	Account
330	Dividends	520	Advertising Expense
410	Financial Consulting Fees	530	Rent Expense
510	Salaries Expense		

4. Prepare a trial balance as of Feb. 29, 1988.

(Check figure: Trial balance totals $29,438)

5. Prepare an income statement, a statement of retained earnings, and a balance sheet.

PROBLEMS: SET B

Problem B2-1
Recording transactions in T-accounts and preparing a trial balance

Lance Walters and several other businessmen organized Walters Stock Brokers, Inc., on Dec. 1, 1988. During the month of December the following transactions occurred:

Dec.	2	Issued capital stock to the stockholders for $5,750 and deposited that amount in the Third National Bank of Jackson.
	3	Acquired $600 of office supplies on account from the Yazoo Office Supply Company.
	5	Bought a building for $15,000, paying $2,250 cash and financing the $12,750 difference by a mortgage payable to the Third National Bank.
	6	Bought office equipment on account from Oxford-Starkville Furniture Company, $2,500.
	7	Received, in cash, commissions of $1,200 for stock transactions completed for clients.
	14	Paid amount due to Yazoo Office Supply Company.
	17	Received an invoice from the Cotton White Telephone Company—Yellow Pages Division for advertising, $245. Record this as advertising expense.
	19	Billed clients for commissions on stock transactions amounting to $3,650.
	20	Paid employees $1,750 salaries.
	24	Received $1,375 from clients billed on the 19th.
	29	Paid telephone bill, $115.
	30	Paid one-half amount due to the Oxford-Starkville Furniture Company.

Required

1. Record the transactions directly into T-accounts, entering the appropriate debits and credits. Use the dates of the transactions to identify each transaction.

Establish the following T-accounts: Cash; Accounts Receivable; Office Supplies on Hand; Office Equipment; Building; Accounts Payable; Mortgage Payable; Capital Stock; Commissions Earned; Salaries Expense; Advertising Expense; Telephone Expense.

2. Prepare a trial balance as of Dec. 31, 1988.

(Check figure: trial balance totals $24,845)

Problem B2-2
Journalizing and posting transactions and preparing a trial balance

Pension Consultants, Inc., was incorporated on Apr. 1, 1988, in the State of Michigan with the objective of providing actuarial services to companies having pension plans. The following transactions reflect the activity of the new company for the month of April:

Apr.	1	Issued capital stock in the amount of $15,000 to stockholders. Deposited cash received in the Freedom National Bank of Detroit.
	2	Acquired computer equipment for $75,000. The equipment was financed by a $10,000 down payment and a $65,000, 12% note payable due to Dearborn Electronics Company.

5	Office equipment in the amount of $4,214 and office supplies in the amount of $383 were acquired on account from Ann Arbor Office Equipment Company.
8	Paid city of Detroit $223 for a business license.
10	Received a check from Lansing Metals, Inc., in the amount of $2,617 for consulting services rendered.
11	Paid Ann Arbor Office Equipment Company for the office supplies.
15	Paid employees $2,108.
17	Billed Royal Oak Construction $9,315 for services.
19	Bought $415 of office supplies from Grosse Pointe Supply Company on account.
20	Received an invoice from the *Detroit Evening News* amounting to $287 for advertising.
23	Received $5,216 from Royal Oak Construction.
25	A check in the amount of $3,117 was received from Lincoln Park Medical Supply Company for services rendered.
29	Paid $3,500 dividends to stockholders.

Required

1. Prepare general journal entries for the transactions listed above.
2. Using the following list of accounts and account numbers, post the general journal entries to the ledger accounts.

Account Number	Account	Account Number	Account
110	Cash	310	Capital Stock
120	Accounts Receivable	320	Dividends
130	Office Supplies on Hand	410	Consulting Fees Earned
140	Office Equipment	510	Salaries Expense
150	Computer Equipment	520	License Fee Expense
210	Notes Payable	530	Advertising Expense
220	Accounts Payable		

3. Prepare a trial balance.

(Check figure: Trial balance totals $99,965)

Problem B2-3
Preparing a classified balance sheet

The accounts listed below were taken from the general ledger of Revon Johnson Corporation on Oct. 31, 1988.

Accounts Payable..............	$52,500	Mortgage Payable..............	$75,000
Accounts Receivable...........	27,000	Notes Payable (due Feb. 1,	
Building.....................	90,000	1989).......................	7,500
Capital Stock.................	70,000	Notes Receivable	15,000
Cash	4,500	Prepaid Rent.................	3,000
Equipment....................	45,000	Retained Earnings	30,500
Inventory....................	30,000	Salaries Payable	22,500
Land........................	37,500	Supplies on Hand.............	6,000

Required

Prepare a balance sheet classifying the accounts as current assets, noncurrent assets, current liabilities, long-term liabilities, and stockholders' equity.

(Check figure: Total Assets = $258,000)

Problem B2-4
Preparing journal entries from comparative income statements

Seminole Corporation acquires all its goods and services on open account with the exception of salaries. Payments are made only after appropriate billings are received and accounts payable established. For revenues earned, Seminole has historically received 25% of the total directly in cash and 75% billed as accounts receivable.

The trial balances of Seminole Corporation for the months ended July 31, 1988, and Aug. 31, 1988, are presented below.

	July, 1988		August, 1988	
Cash	$ 240		$2,340	
Accounts Receivable.....................	510		300	
Office Supplies on Hand..................	120		210	
Office Equipment........................	1,230		1,350	
Accounts Payable........................		$ 180		$ 90
Capital Stock...........................		100		100
Retained Earnings.......................		500		500
Dividends	390		420	
Revenues Earned........................		2,400		4,800
Salaries Expense........................	630		720	
Utilities Expense	60		150	
Totals.................................	$3,180	$3,180	$5,490	$5,490

Required

Prepare general journal entries that reflect the transactions that occurred during the month of August, 1988. Do not record the general journal entry explanations. You will need to establish T-accounts for Accounts Receivable, Accounts Payable, and Cash to determine the collection of accounts receivable and the payment of accounts payable.

Problem B2-5
Correcting a trial balance

The trial balance of Lehigh Valley Steel Corporation for May, 1988, does not balance. It was prepared by Eugene Grace, an inexperienced bookkeeper. The trial balance is presented below.

Cash	$ 425	
Accounts Receivable	1,813	
Supplies on Hand.........................	826	
Equipment................................	6,015	
Accounts Payable.........................		$ 726
Salaries Payable		250
Capital Stock.............................		3,000
Retained Earnings		2,953
Dividends.................................		1,000
Revenues		4,326
Salaries Expense	975	
Rent Expense	300	
Utilities Expense..........................	83	
Totals	$10,437	$13,255

When recomputing the balances of each of the general ledger accounts, the following two errors were revealed:

a. Utilities expense was overfooted by $18.

b. The total debits in the Cash account amounted to $1,976 and the credits totaled $1,651. Upon reviewing the process of transferring the amounts in the ledger accounts to the trial balance and reviewing the trial balance, the following errors were discovered:

c. The credit column in the trial balance was incorrectly footed.

d. The balance in the accounts receivable general ledger of $1,831 was transferred as $1,813 to the trial balance.

   Retracing the postings from the general journal to the general ledger disclosed several more errors:

e. A credit posting to Accounts Receivable in the amount of $470 should have been $47.

f. A credit posting to Accounts Payable of $372 was missing.

g. A credit of $127 was posted to Accounts Payable rather than the correct amount of $217.

h. A credit posting to Revenue in the amount of $43 was missing.

| **Required** | Prepare a corrected trial balance. |

(Check figure: Trial balance totals $11,760)

Problem B2-6
Journalizing and posting transactions; preparing a trial balance and financial statements

Keystone Corporation has been in existence for several years. Presented below is the June 1, 1988, trial balance, together with the account numbers.

1	Cash	$ 5,961	
2	Accounts Receivable	6,504	
3	Office Supplies on Hand	1,863	
4	Office Equipment	13,161	
5	Accounts Payable		$ 5,394
6	Capital Stock		20,000
7	Retained Earnings		2,095
8	Dividends	-0-	
9	Revenues Earned		-0-
10	Salaries Expense	-0-	
11	Rent Expense	-0-	
12	Utilities Expense	-0-	
	Totals	$27,489	$27,489

During the month of June, the following transactions were completed:

June 2	Bought office equipment on account from Lander Office Supply Company, $4,155.
4	Paid Mayflower Furniture Company $2,694 for office equipment acquired in May.
5	Received $1,041 from customers for services rendered on this date.
7	Bought $2,217 of office supplies on account from Bethlehem Supply Company.
8	Received $4,458 from customers billed in previous months.
10	Paid rent for month, $1,050.
15	Paid salaries, $1,278.
16	Billed customers $4,593 for services rendered.
20	Paid on account to Liberty Hurricane Company $2,763 for office supplies purchased in May.
23	Paid utilities, $126.
26	Billed customers $2,922 for services rendered.
29	Received cash of $3,981 from customers previously billed.
30	Paid dividends to stockholders, $3,000.

| **Required** | 1. Enter the June 1, 1988, trial balance amounts into the appropriate general ledger accounts.
2. Prepare general journal entries for the transactions for the month of June. |

3. Post the transactions to the general ledger. (Use the general journal page number 7 as the posting reference.)
4. Prepare a trial balance.

(Check figure: Trial balance totals $36,960)

5. Prepare an income statement, a statement of retained earnings, and a balance sheet.

DECISION PROBLEM

Preparing financial statements

On Apr. 1, 1988, the National Football League granted a franchise to Nick Miggans and several other Baltimore businesspeople to establish a professional football team to be called the Baltimore Badboys, Inc. The group contributed $10,000 and received 1,000 shares of capital stock. Additional capital was obtained by means of a $20,000, 5-year note payable issued to the Chesapeake Sienna Alumni Club, a group of football afficionados.

The newly established corporation acquired used training equipment on May 15 from the Bethlehem Bulldogs for $6,300, paying $1,800 cash and financing the remainder by means of an additional note payable to the Bulldogs, the 1987 Superbowl champs, due in October, 1989.

During the 1988 season, the owners of the franchise worked diligently to establish a team. They hired a coaching staff, purchased player contracts for 43 professional athletes, rented a stadium and training facilities, and performed a myriad of other activities associated with professional sports. But no accounting records were kept. At the close of the season (the Badboys finished with a 6 – 10 record), the owners want to know how well the franchise did financially, and they come to you for help.

From the checkbook you are able to determine that deposits of $107,500 were made from Apr. 1 to Dec. 31. These consisted of the $10,000 capital stock and $20,000 note payable mentioned above, plus $47,500 admission fees and $30,000 TV revenues from NBS for television rights. The total of the checks written amounts to $81,500, consisting of $16,350 for training camp expenses, $42,115 for salaries, $3,621 for cleaning expenses, $4,000 for rent expense, $6,000 for player equipment, the $1,800 to the Bethlehem Bulldogs, $6,614 for advertising, and $1,000 in dividends.

In addition to the above, you find that the last payment from NBS for $5,000 for televising the Dec. 28 game with the Daytona Daiseys has not yet been received. And the Badboys have unpaid items totaling $1,016, representing $516 salaries, and $500 cleaning expenses.

Required

Prepare an income statement, a statement of retained earnings, and a balance sheet. (Hint: Establish a T-account for each account needed. Analyze the information in the form of business transactions, recording them directly into the T-accounts.)

(Check figure: Total Assets = $43,300)

Periodic Procedures: Adjusting the Accounts

After studying this chapter you should understand the following:

- The distinction between *external* and *internal* transactions
- Why certain accounts require adjustments at the end of an accounting period
- What a *contra-asset account* is
- Why the net income of a business entity is not a precise amount
- The purpose of an adjusted trial balance and how to prepare one
- The various steps involved in the accounting process
- What we mean by *classified financial statements*
- The *cash basis* and the *accrual basis* of accounting
- The *revenue-recognition principle* and the *matching concept*

It may come as a surprise to you that the basic elements of the accounting model are not precisely measured on the financial statements of a business enterprise. Only after completing all the business transactions over the *entire life* of a business entity can the exact amount of assets, revenue, expenses, and net income be determined. But that's utterly impractical.

Accounting is not an exact science

To see what we mean, consider a company having a building acquired at a cost of $400,000 on Jan. 1, 1964, when the company first started operations. At that time the company estimated that the building would have a 40-year life, and would be replaced by a new building on Jan. 1, 2004. But 25 years later, Jan. 1, 1989, the building proves to be dysfunctional — meaning that for whatever reason it no longer serves its original purpose — and a new building is acquired on that date.

At this early point in your accounting education we think you can already see intuitively that the cost of the original building must be assigned to the expense of doing business over the period of time that the building was in use. Very simply, on Jan. 1, 1964, the yearly building expense for the next 40 years was *estimated* at $10,000 per year ($400,000 ÷ 40 years). But since the building was replaced in 1989, the *actual* yearly expense turned out to be $16,000 per year ($400,000 ÷ 25 years). The precise amount of the yearly building expense can be determined only after the full life of the building.

Accountants must use estimates

**FIGURE 3-1
A Comparison of the
Estimated vs. Actual
Useful Life of a Building**

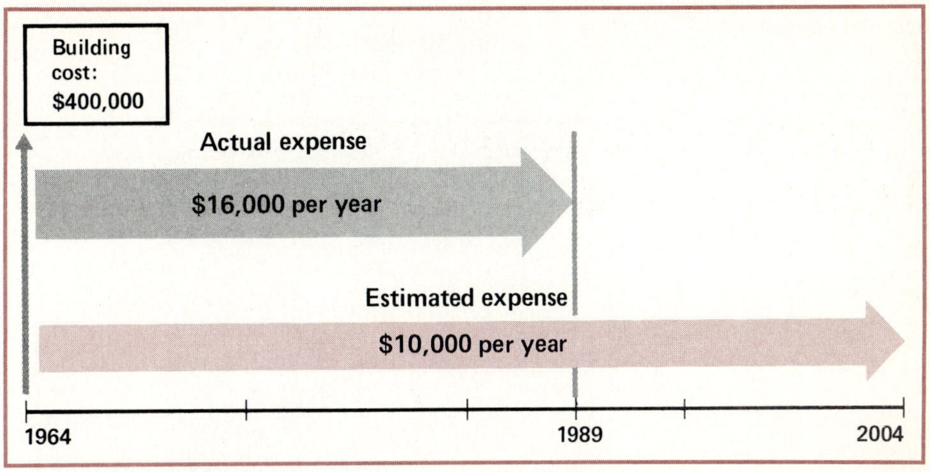

Building
cost:
$400,000

Actual expense

$16,000 per year

Estimated expense

$10,000 per year

1964   1989   2004

*Annual expense is
estimated in 1964 at the
beginning of the asset's life*

*The actual yearly expense
is determined only at the
end of the asset's life*

*Most business entities
remain in business as far
into the future as can
reasonably be projected*

*Financial statements are
prepared monthly,
quarterly, and yearly*

*Financial statements reflect
fairly, not precisely, the
financial position and
results of operations of
business entities*

*External transactions are
between a business entity
and second parties*

Of course, anyone interested in the affairs of a business entity cannot wait until the entity completes all the business transactions over its entire life before receiving financial reports on its financial position and results of operations. It is true that some business entities cease operations after several years, but most remain in business decade after decade and will continue to remain in business as far into the future as can reasonably be projected. This is the basis of the *going concern* concept discussed in Chapter 1.

To provide timely information in financial statements, accountants break the life of business entities into time frames. At the end of each time frame, accountants prepare financial statements. These time frames are referred to as *accounting periods* and are typically a year, a quarter, or a month in length. Parties external to the entity do not receive monthly statements; they do not need such frequent reporting. The contrast between annual and quarterly reports is illustrated in the financial statements shown on page 98.

Notice that the quarterly report is a highly condensed version of the income statement. Sometimes a highly condensed version of the balance sheet is also given. It is the annual report that offers complete financial information to external parties. Although financial statements cannot be regarded as precise, they do reflect fairly the financial position and results of operations for the accounting periods indicated. Business decisions are made with the reliance that financial statements fairly represent what they are supposed to represent. We use the term *fairly* to mean that the financial statements reflect the underlying economic events and transactions within an acceptable range of accuracy; much of the study of accounting has to do with what we mean by "fairly."

One of the advantages of recognizing the life of a business entity as a series of regular, successive accounting periods is *comparability.* Comparing between business activities of the current period and those of similar past periods makes it possible to judge how the business performed. Has revenue increased? Have expenses decreased? Has net income improved? Has the entity's financial position been strengthened? These are typical questions that can be answered by comparing financial statements of successive accounting periods.

You will find that preparing financial statements at the end of accounting periods does present some problems. The types of transactions you have learned to record in the accounting records in the first two chapters represent exchange transactions between a business entity and *second parties* — parties external to the entity. We refer to these as *external transactions.*

**Financial Statements for
External Parties**

Annual reports

MOON SERVICE COMPANY
Income Statement
Year Ended December 31, 1989

Revenue:
Fees Earned		$700,000
Investment Income......		240,000
Total Revenue......		$940,000

Expenses:
Salaries......	$250,000	
Rent Expense	50,000	
Advertising Expense	80,000	
Total Expenses		380,000

Net Income $560,000

MOON SERVICE COMPANY
Balance Sheet
December 31, 1989

Assets

Current Assets:
Cash..................	$ 40,000
Accounts Receivable	160,000
Supplies on Hand.......	10,000
Total Current Assets	$210,000

Noncurrent Assets:
Truck..................	30,000

Total Assets $240,000

Liabilities and Stockholders' Equity

Liabilities

Current Liabilities:
Note Payable	$ 20,000
Accounts Payable	30,000
Total Current Liabilities ...	$ 50,000

Stockholders' Equity

Capital Stock	$100,000
Retained Earnings........	90,000
Total Stockholders' Equity .	$190,000

Total Liabilities and
Stockholders' Equity $240,000

Quarterly report

MOON SERVICE COMPANY
Income Statement
Quarter Ended December 31, 1989

Revenue	$150,000
Expenses.................	98,500
Net Income	$ 51,500

Consider, for example, an external transaction made on Oct. 1 of the current year for a $1,200, 12-month insurance policy. On that date prepaid insurance would be recorded as an asset measured at $1,200. But 3 months later, on Dec. 31, only 9 months of insurance coverage remain, while 3 months of insurance expense has been incurred. The financial statements prepared at the end of the accounting period *must* reflect these shifts in asset and expense values; the statement must show the following:

1. All assets owned

2. All liabilities owed

3. All revenue earned

4. All expenses incurred

FIGURE 3-2
Adjusting Entry: Prepaid Insurance Becomes Insurance Expense

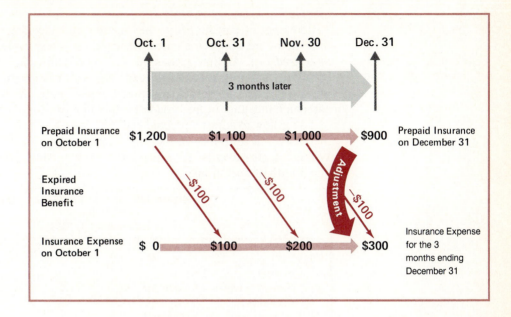

Adjusting entries are internal transactions

To meet this objective, some of the accounts must be *adjusted.* The adjustment is accomplished by means of a general journal entry called an *adjusting entry.* This is referred to as an *internal transaction.*

Figure 3-2 shows the values that should be reflected on the financial statements for Prepaid Insurance and Insurance Expense on Oct. 1 and Dec. 31. Insurance for 12 months was paid for in advance; insurance was "consumed" for 3 months; and 9 months of insurance not yet consumed, a future economic benefit, remain. At $100 per month, this would mean that $900 should be the amount of Prepaid Insurance reported on the balance sheet. Further, because 3 months of economic benefits have been received, at $100 per month, $300 of Insurance Expense should be reported on the income statement. Thus, on Dec. 31, an *adjusting entry* is needed that will reduce Prepaid Insurance by $300 and increase Insurance Expense by a like amount.

TYPES OF ADJUSTING ENTRIES

There are two broad classifications of adjusting entries:

Deferrals and accruals are two types of adjusting entries

1. One classification includes adjustments to certain external transactions previously recorded. These transactions reflect cash received or paid for goods or services to be provided in the future. We will call these *deferrals.*

2. The other classification of adjusting entries includes revenue already earned and expenses already incurred for which no transaction as yet has been recorded. These we will call *accruals.*

Every adjusting entry affects both the income statement and the balance sheet.

Deferrals

Within the broad classification of deferrals there are three types of adjusting entries: *prepaid expenses, unearned revenue,* and *depreciation.*

Prepaid Expenses

Items that are paid for before they are used are called prepaid expenses. At the time these items are acquired a cost is incurred. This cost represents an asset and is an **unexpired cost.** As time passes the asset is consumed in part or in total and the consumed amount becomes an expense, which is an **expired cost.** Examples of prepaid expenses are prepaid insurance, prepaid rent, office supplies on hand, repair parts on hand, and, in the broadest sense, buildings and office equipment.

An asset is an unexpired cost
An expense is an expired cost

To see how to adjust a prepaid expense, as well as how to make the other adjustments we will introduce in the following pages, consider the trial balance of The Wilma Adams Advertising Agency, shown below, which is prepared at the end of the first month of operations.

THE WILMA ADAMS ADVERTISING AGENCY
Trial Balance
November 30, 1989

Line			
	Cash	$ 244	
(a)	Note Receivable, 12% due Apr. 30	1,500	
	Accounts Receivable	1,251	
(b)	Advertising Supplies on Hand	386	
(c)	Prepaid Rent	450	
(d)	Office Equipment	3,600	
	Accounts Payable		$ 572
(e)	Unearned Advertising Revenue		600
	Capital Stock		2,000
	Retained Earnings		1,500
(f)	Dividends	150	
	Advertising Revenue		3,706
(g)	Salary Expense	725	
	Utilities Expense	47	
	Miscellaneous Expense	25	
	Totals	$8,378	$8,378

On Nov. 1, rent at $150 per month for 3 months was paid in advance by the advertising agency and recorded in the general journal by the following entry:

Nov. 1 Prepaid Rent 450
      Cash 450
      To record payment of rent in advance for November, December, and January at $150 per month.

At the end of November the advertising agency has received the benefit of occupying space for 1 month and has the right to occupancy for 2 additional months. The accounting record—that is, the Prepaid Rent [the line designated (c)] as seen in the Nov. 30 trial balance—does not reflect this situation. An adjusting entry is required. One month's expired cost, $150, must be recorded as Rent Expense, and 2 months' unexpired costs must remain on the balance sheet as Prepaid Rent of $300. The adjusting entry would be recorded as follows:

Rent Expense adjusting entry

Nov. 30 Rent Expense 150
      Prepaid Rent... 150
      To record rent expense.

In essence, $150 has been transferred from the Prepaid Rent account to the Rent Expense account, as can be seen by the posted T-accounts:

	Asset				Expense	
	Prepaid Rent				**Rent Expense**	
Nov. 1	450	Nov. 30	150	Nov. 30	150	
Bal.	300					

Notice that the balance in the Prepaid Rent account after the posting of the adjusting entry is $300.

Advertising Supplies on Hand represents another type of prepaid expense. Notice the line designated (b) on The Wilma Adams Advertising Agency trial balance. As of Nov. 30, the trial balance indicates that there is $386 of advertising supplies on hand. These supplies were acquired on Nov. 8 and recorded in the general journal by the following entry:

The advertising supplies were acquired on Nov. 8, but that's not what is on hand at Nov. 30

Nov. 8   Advertising Supplies on Hand   386
              Cash   386
              To record acquisition of advertising supplies.

These supplies represent an asset worth $386 to the agency on Nov. 8. But as the agency uses advertising supplies during the month, the asset is reduced and an expense, Advertising Supplies Used, is incurred. Can you see that no purpose would be served by recording Advertising Supplies Used as an expense each time supplies are consumed? To do so would require extensive bookkeeping efforts with no benefit, since the financial statements are not needed until *the end of the month.* But you should realize that at the end of the month an adjusting entry for the supplies is required to properly reflect the amount consumed—*the expense incurred*—and the amount of supplies remaining—*the value of supplies on hand.* The values to be recorded in the financial statements by means of adjusting the accounts are determined by counting (taking an inventory of) the advertising supplies remaining on hand at the end of the month. By subtracting the supplies on hand at the end of the month from the supplies acquired during the month (plus the supplies on hand at the beginning of the month, if any), the amount of supplies used can be determined.

For example, if the amount of supplies on hand at the end of the month as revealed by the count is $133, then $253 of advertising supplies must have been used during the month, as seen in the following analysis:

Advertising Supplies	
On hand, Nov. 1	$ 0
Acquired, Nov. 8	386
Available	$386
On hand, Nov. 30	133
Used	$253

From this information the appropriate adjusting entry required would be recorded as follows:

The adjusting entry reduces the asset, Advertising Supplies on Hand, and increases the expense, Advertising Supplies Used, to reflect the situation on Nov. 30

Nov. 30   Advertising Supplies Used   253
                 Advertising Supplies on Hand..............................   253
             To record advertising supplies used.

The debit to Advertising Supplies Used establishes in the accounts the fact that a $253 expense has been incurred. The credit to Advertising Supplies on Hand reduces the asset from $386 to $133, the value of the asset at month-end.

Posting the adjusting entry to the ledger accounts would affect the accounts as shown in the following T-accounts:

The T-accounts reflect the transfer of $253 of used advertising supplies from the asset account to the expense account

Asset		Expense	
Advertising Supplies on Hand		**Advertising Supplies Used**	
Nov. 1 386	Nov. 30 253	Nov. 30 253	
Bal. 133			

Unearned Revenue

Unearned revenue is adjusted in much the same way we adjust prepaid expenses. The difference lies only in the accounts involved: Liability and revenue accounts are adjusted rather than asset and expense accounts.

To see what we mean, look at the account Unearned Advertising Revenue of $600 [designated line (e)] on the trial balance of the advertising agency (page 100). This represents a $600 payment made to the agency by a client in advance of the advertising services yet to be rendered. The payment was made on Nov. 1 for 6 months of weekly advertising to be placed in local newspapers. As of Nov. 1, The Wilma Adams Advertising Agency has received an asset, Cash, for $600; and incurred an obligation, which accountants refer to as a liability, Unearned Advertising Revenue, to perform a service in the amount of $600 for the client. As the weeks go by and the ads are placed in the newspaper, the obligation is reduced and revenue is earned. Since financial statements are needed as of Nov. 30, an adjusting entry is required on that date to properly reflect all revenue earned during the month and all liabilities owed at month-end. After all, $100 of the $600 paid by the client was indeed spent for the cost of newspaper ads during the month of November. Thus, the agency earned that $100 during November, leaving $500 in Unearned Revenue as of the end of the month. The appropriate adjusting entry reducing the liability Unearned Advertising Revenue by $100 ($600 ÷ 6 months) and recording the Advertising Revenue of $100 is illustrated as follows:

The advertising revenue adjusting entry reduces the liability, Unearned Advertising Revenue, and increases the revenue account, Advertising Revenue

Nov. 30   Unearned Advertising Revenue.................................   100
                 Advertising Revenue   100
             To record advertising revenue earned $100.

Posting the adjusting entry to the ledger accounts is illustrated in the following T-accounts:

These T-accounts show the transfer of $100 from the liability account to the revenue account

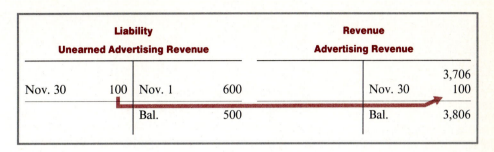

	Liability			Revenue	
	Unearned Advertising Revenue			Advertising Revenue	
					3,706
Nov. 30	100	Nov. 1	600	Nov. 30	100
		Bal.	500	Bal.	3,806

Depreciation

The cost of such noncurrent assets as buildings, equipment, and vehicles must be allocated as an expense over the periods of time these assets are expected to be used by the company owning them. This expense is called ***depreciation.***

Allocating the cost of buildings and equipment over their useful lives is called depreciation

To illustrate the adjustment necessary to reflect the expiration of fixed assets, refer again to The Wilma Adams Advertising Agency trial balance. Office equipment in the amount of $3,600 was acquired on Nov. 1 [see line (d)]. The equipment is estimated to have a 10-year life, after which it will be considered worthless. Depreciation expense is determined by allocating the $3,600 over 10 years, or $360 per year. One month's depreciation would then be $30 ($360 ÷ 12), and the adjusting entry would be:

A depreciation adjusting entry reduces an asset by using the Accumulated Depreciation account

```
Nov. 30   Depreciation Expense .........................................   30
                Accumulated Depreciation: Office Equipment..................        30
              To record 1 month's depreciation
```

The ledger accounts would reflect the following:

The recording of $30 depreciation expense is illustrated in these T-accounts

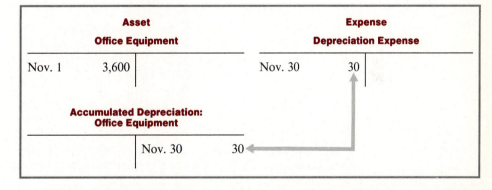

	Asset			Expense	
	Office Equipment			Depreciation Expense	
Nov. 1	3,600		Nov. 30	30	
	Accumulated Depreciation: Office Equipment				
		Nov. 30	30		

Unlike the adjustments made for prepaid assets, when the depreciation adjusting entry is recorded, the fixed asset is not directly reduced. Rather, the account ***Accumulated Depreciation*** is used. This account is a ***contra account,*** specifically a ***contra-asset account.*** By the term *contra account* we mean an account that has a balance opposite the normal balance. We would expect an asset account to have a debit balance, but a contra-asset account has a credit balance. Thus, a contra-asset account reduces assets—the Accumulated Depreciation account reduces the noncurrent asset accounts. A contra-liability account would have a debit balance.

A contra-asset account has a credit balance

The book value of a depreciable asset is the difference between its cost and its related accumulated depreciation

On the balance sheet, both the Office Equipment account and the Accumulated Depreciation: Office Equipment account would appear. The difference between these two accounts ($3,570) is called the ***book value*** of the asset. It is the value that is recorded in the "firm's books," and it would appear on the balance sheet like this:

Office Equipment	$3,600
Less: Accumulated Depreciation	30
	$3,570

The reason we use a contra-asset account is to preserve the original cost of the fixed asset. Users of the financial statements can then compare the depreciation recorded to date—that is, the accumulated depreciation—with the original cost found in the asset account. This comparison provides the user with information as to the relative age of the assets. For example, assume that a balance sheet were prepared 7 years from the date The Wilma Adams Advertising Agency started business. The Accumulated Depreciation account would have a balance of $2,520 ($3,600 × $\frac{7}{10}$) and would appear on the Oct. 1 balance sheet 7 years hence as follows:

Office Equipment	$3,600
Less: Accumulated Depreciation	2,520
	$1,080

The book value of $1,080, when compared to the cost, would inform investors that the office equipment is nearing the end of its useful life and that the company may need to replace the asset in the near future.

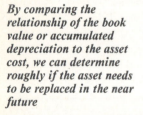

By comparing the relationship of the book value or accumulated depreciation to the asset cost, we can determine roughly if the asset needs to be replaced in the near future

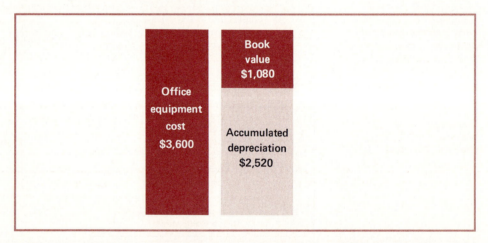

The general ledger account Accumulated Depreciation: Office Equipment would accumulate depreciation of $30 per month for 84 months (7 years × 12 months) as seen below:

Accumulated Depreciation: Office Equipment		
	Nov. 30, 1989	30
	Dec. 31, 1989	30
	Jan. 31, 1990	30
	Sept. 30, 1996	30
	Oct. 31, 1996	30
	Bal.	2,520

Accruals

Accrual adjusting entries record revenues earned and expenses incurred

Adjustments for revenue already earned and expenses already incurred but for which no transaction has been recorded are called *accruals.* We will consider two types of adjusting entries as examples of accruals: salaries and interest.

Salaries

Expenses are paid in one of three ways:

1. In advance of the benefits they provide, like the deferrals discussed earlier
2. During the accounting period when the benefits are received — for example, the telephone bill
3. After their benefits have already been received

Accrual adjusting entries are made at period-end

The most recognizable business expenses not paid for until after their benefits have been received are salaries and wages. No one is paid until his or her services have been provided — not the President of the United States, not the production-line workers at General Motors, not your instructor, and not you.

Employees earn their salary or wages every hour of the day and every day of the week. However, for practical reasons, employees are paid after they have provided their services, periodically — weekly, biweekly, or monthly. When these payments are made before the end of the accounting period, the expense is recorded by a journal entry debiting Salaries Expense and crediting Cash. A problem occurs when the last day of the accounting period is not the day on which employees are paid — that is, when it is not a payday. In this case the employees have performed a service that represents an expense to the company. The company in turn has a liability to the employees for these services. The financial statements must reflect both the *expense incurred* and the *liability owed.* You can see that an adjusting entry is required.

Referring again to The Wilma Adams Advertising Agency, notice that Salary Expense amounts to $725 [designated line (g)] on the trial balance dated Nov. 30, 1989. This represents the sum of two biweekly payments, one made on Friday, Nov. 10, and one on Friday, Nov. 24, as shown in the following calendar for the month of November:

NOVEMBER						
Working Days					**Weekend**	
Mon.	**Tues.**	**Wed.**	**Thurs.**	**Fri.**	**Sat.**	**Sun.**
		1	2	3	4	5
6	7	8	9	*PAYDAY* *$350*	11	12
13	14	15	16	17	18	19
20	21	22	23	*PAYDAY* *$375*	25	26
27	28	29	30	**DECEMBER** 1	2	3
4	5	6	7	*PAYDAY* *$400*	9	10

During the last week of November there are four additional workdays prior to the end of the month. The next scheduled payday is not until Friday, Dec. 8. Assume that salaries accrue at a rate of $40 a day. Thus, $160 ($40 × 4 days) of additional Salary Expense must be recorded in the general journal on Nov. 30 to properly reflect all the expenses incurred during the month of November. Further, the advertising agency has, as of Nov. 30, a liability of $160 for unpaid salaries that must also be recorded. The adjusting entry to accrue the $160 would be recorded as follows:

Salaries adjusting entry increases an expense, Salary Expense, and records a liability, Salaries Payable

Nov. 30	Salary Expense	160	
	Salaries Payable		160
	To record accrual of salaries, $160.		

After the adjusting entry is recorded, Salary Expense will total $885, representing the proper expense for the month—salaries already paid, $725; plus salaries to be paid, $160. Salaries Payable will be $160, which is the liability as of Nov. 30. The effect of the adjusting entry is illustrated in the T-accounts as follows:

These T-accounts reflect the recording of the accrued salaries adjusting entry

Expense		Liability	
Salary Expense		**Salaries Payable**	
Nov. 10	350	Nov. 30	160
Nov. 24	375		
Nov. 30	160		
Bal.	885		

Care must be taken when the Dec. 8 payroll is recorded. If the entry is made in the usual manner—that is, a debit to Salary Expense and a credit to Cash—Salary Expense for December would be overstated by $160. Assuming that the Dec. 8 payroll amounts to $400, the appropriate entry for the date would be recorded as follows:

Dec. 8	Salaries Payable..	160	
	Salary Expense...	240	
	Cash..		400
	To record payment of salaries.		

When the Dec. 8 entry is made, Salaries Payable must be debited because that liability was paid. Salary Expense is debited for $240, representing the expense incurred for the 6 working days in December (6 days × $40). The November calendar should help you in understanding this entry. The $400 paid to employees on Dec. 8 consists of $160 paid for work done in November and $240 for work done in December.

Interest

Like salaries, interest is earned, or incurred, day by day. However, accountants do not record it until after it is paid. Thus, if the accounting period ends before the interest is paid, an adjusting entry is required. This adjusting entry will record the amount of the interest income (or interest expense, in the case of borrowed funds) incurred during the period and the corresponding asset for the interest receivable (or liability for the interest payable).

To see how this works, consider the 12% note receivable due to The Wilma Adams Advertising Agency on Apr. 30 [see line (a)]. The note was issued on Nov. 1, 1989, and will be repaid 6 months later, on April 30, 1990. The interest income incurred on this note during the month of November is calculated according to the following formula:

Interest calculation

$$\text{Interest} = \text{principal} \times \text{rate} \times \text{time}$$
$$= \$1{,}500 \times 12\% \text{ per year} \times \tfrac{1}{12} \text{ year}$$
$$= \$1{,}500 \times \frac{.12}{\text{year}} \times \frac{1 \text{ year}}{12}$$
$$= \$15$$

The adjusting entry to record the interest income incurred in November is presented below:

Interest income adjusting entry

Nov. 30	Interest Receivable	15	
	Interest Income		15
	To record interest income for the month of November.		

If Wilma Adams had issued a 12% note payable rather than the note receivable, the adjusting entry would be as follows:

Interest expense adjusting entry

Nov. 30	Interest Expense	15	
	Interest Payable		15
	To record interest expense for the month of November.		

IMPROPER ADJUSTING ENTRY

The Securities and Exchange Commission reported on April 5, 1984, that as a result of their investigation of Alpex Computer Corporation's financial statements for the year ended December 31, 1981, they found that the statements were materially false and misleading. Among other improprieties the SEC discovered that Alpex had improperly recorded as income $81,314 of accrued interest on worthless notes receivable. As a result of the improper recording of the item, Alpex's revenues were overstated by 40%; operating losses were understated by 85%; and net income was overstated by 13%.

Source: Securities and Exchange Commission, *Accounting and Auditing Enforcement Release No. 27,* Apr. 5, 1984.

The purpose of the interest income accrual adjusting entry is to properly match revenue earned to the appropriate accounting period. Apparently Alpex Computer Corporation has used this simple adjusting entry to significantly increase revenues on its 1981 income statement.

THE ADJUSTED TRIAL BALANCE

The adjusted trial balance is prepared after the adjusting entries are made

After the adjusting entries are recorded and posted, a second trial balance is prepared. We call this second trial balance the **adjusted trial balance.** The first trial balance is called the **unadjusted trial balance.** Both trial balances of The Wilma Adams Advertising Agency are presented below. Notice that the adjustments are inserted between the two trial balances to show how the unadjusted trial balance was "adjusted" in determining the adjusted trial balance.

THE WILMA ADAMS ADVERTISING AGENCY					
	Unadjusted Trial Balance Nov. 30, 1989		Adjustments	Adjusted Trial Balance Nov. 30, 1989	
Cash	$ 244			$ 244	
Note Receivable, 12% due Apr. 30	1,500			1,500	
Interest Receivable			+ 15 (a)	15	
Accounts Receivable	1,251			1,251	
Advertising Supplies on Hand	386		−253 (b)	133	
Prepaid Rent	450		−150 (c)	300	
Office Equipment	3,600			3,600	
Accumulated Depreciation: Office Equipment			+ 30 (d)		$ 30
Accounts Payable		$ 572			572
Salaries Payable			+160 (g)		160
Unearned Advertising Revenue		600	−100 (e)		500
Capital Stock		2,000			2,000
Retained Earnings		1,500			1,500
Dividends	150			150	
Advertising Revenue		3,706	+100 (e)		3,806
Interest Income			+ 15 (a)		15
Salary Expense	725		+160 (g)	885	
Rent Expense			+150 (c)	150	
Advertising Supplies Used			+253 (b)	253	
Depreciation Expense			+ 30 (d)	30	
Utilities Expense	47			47	
Miscellaneous Expense	25			25	
Totals	$8,378	$8,378		$8,583	$8,583

The financial statements are prepared directly from the adjusted trial balance. We prepare the income statement first because the net income figure is needed when we prepare the statement of retained earnings. The statement of retained earnings then provides the ending retained earnings balance, which we need for the balance sheet. The income statement is relatively easy to prepare once the adjusted trial balance is prepared, as can be seen from the illustration on page 109.

THE WILMA ADAMS ADVERTISING AGENCY

Adjusted Trial Balance November 30, 1989			Income Statement Month Ended November 30, 1989		
Cash	$ 244		Revenue:		
Capital Stock		$2,000	Advertising Revenue		$3,806
Retained Earnings		1,500	Interest Income		15
Dividends	150		Total Revenue...............		$3,821
Advertising Revenue........		3,806	Operating Expenses:		
Interest Income		15	Salary Expense	$885	
Salary Expense	885		Rent Expense	150	
Rent Expense	150		Advertising Supplies Used ..	253	
Advertising Supplies Used	253		Depreciation Expense......	30	
Depreciation Expense........	30		Utilities Expense	47	
Utilities Expense	47		Miscellaneous Expense.....	25	
Miscellaneous Expense.......	25		Total Operating Expenses.....		1,390
Totals....................	$8,583	$8,583	Net Income		$2,431

On the statement of retained earnings we simply add the net income of $2,431 to the beginning balance in the Retained Earnings account, and subtract the dividends of $150 [line (f), unadjusted trial balance] to arrive at the ending retained earnings balance. There were no additional capital stock investments during November by The Wilma Adams Advertising Agency. The statement of retained earnings would appear as follows:

THE WILMA ADAMS ADVERTISING AGENCY
Statement of Retained Earnings
Month Ended November 30, 1989

Retained Earnings, Nov. 1, 1989...		$1,500
Net Income	$2,431	
Less: Dividends...	150	2,281
Retained Earnings, Nov. 30, 1989..		$3,781

Finally, the balance sheet is prepared using again the adjusted trial balance, as illustrated on page 110.

THE ACCOUNTING PROCESS REVIEWED

Financial statements are the ultimate objective of accounting

The ultimate objective of financial accounting is to prepare financial statements that represent meaningfully and fairly the results of operations of a business entity over a period of time and its financial position at a point in time. The process we have described in this chapter and the preceding chapter is a practical means of achieving that objective. The steps involved in the financial accounting process are shown in Figure 3-3 on pages 110–111.

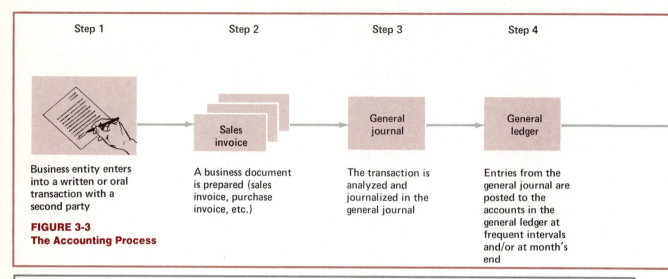

FIGURE 3-3
The Accounting Process

Step 1	Step 2	Step 3	Step 4
Business entity enters into a written or oral transaction with a second party	A business document is prepared (sales invoice, purchase invoice, etc.)	The transaction is analyzed and journalized in the general journal	Entries from the general journal are posted to the accounts in the general ledger at frequent intervals and/or at month's end

THE WILMA ADAMS ADVERTISING AGENCY

Adjusted Trial Balance
November 30, 1989

Cash	$ 244	
Notes Receivable, 12% due Apr. 30	1,500	
Interest Receivable	15	
Accounts Receivable	1,251	
Advertising Supplies on Hand	133	
Prepaid Rent	300	
Office Equipment	3,600	
Accumulated Depreciation: Office Equipment		$ 30
Accounts Payable		572
Salaries Payable		160
Unearned Advertising Revenue		500
Capital Stock		2,000
Retained Earnings		1,500
Dividends	150	
Advertising Revenue		3,806
Miscellaneous Expense	25	
Totals	$8,583	$8,583

Balance Sheet
November 30, 1989

Assets

Current Assets:

Cash	$ 244	
Notes Receivable, 12% due Apr. 30	1,500	
Interest Receivable	15	
Accounts Receivable	1,251	
Advertising Supplies on Hand	133	
Prepaid Rent	300	
Total Current Assets		$3,443

Noncurrent Assets:

Office Equipment	$3,600	
Less: Accumulated Depreciation: Office Equipment	30	
Total Noncurrent Assets		3,570
Total Assets		$7,013

Liabilities

Current Liabilities:

Accounts Payable	$ 572	
Salaries Payable	160	
Unearned Advertising Revenue	500	
Total Liabilities		$1,232

Stockholders' Equity

Capital Stock	$2,000	
Retained Earnings	3,781	
Total Stockholders' Equity		5,781
Total Liabilities and Stockholders' Equity		$7,013

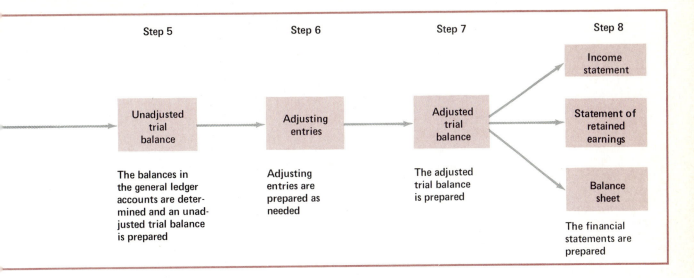

Step 5	Step 6	Step 7	Step 8

Unadjusted trial balance → Adjusting entries → Adjusted trial balance → Income statement / Statement of retained earnings / Balance sheet

The balances in the general ledger accounts are determined and an unadjusted trial balance is prepared

Adjusting entries are prepared as needed

The adjusted trial balance is prepared

The financial statements are prepared

FORM AND CONTENT OF FINANCIAL STATEMENTS

Classified financial statements are very useful

Financial statements become more useful when their basic elements—the individual asset accounts, liability accounts, revenue accounts, and expense accounts—are grouped meaningfully. Until now, we have presented only simple financial statements containing relatively few items. With so few items we did not need to present **classified financial statements**—*financial statements with like accounts grouped together.* People who use financial statements find the classification of the assets and liabilities into common groupings very helpful when analyzing and comparing financial statements for lending and investment decisions.

Users of financial statements can readily determine the profitability and solvency of a business entity by studying the relationship between significant asset and liability groupings on the balance sheet as well as the relationships between revenue and expense groupings on the income statement. These useful groupings enable the user to compare financial statements of different companies. Can you appreciate the difficulty statement users would have if each company were to use its own system of classification?

The form and content of financial statements evolved over time and continues to evolve in response to changing business practices. What was acceptable presentation in the early 1960s may not be acceptable today. Within the broad framework of financial statement classification, individual business entities will attempt to give a clear, meaningful, and fair presentation of their results of operations and financial position.

The Balance Sheet

Typically, assets on the balance sheet are classified into five major groupings: (1) current assets, (2) investments, (3) property, plant, and equipment, (4) intangibles, and (5) other assets.

Liabilities generally are classified into two groups: (1) current liabilities and (2) long-term liabilities. Stockholders' equity is classified into three groups: (1) capital stock, (2) additional paid-in capital, and (3) retained earnings.

The balance sheet of the Hillsborough Retail Store, presented on pages 112–113, illustrates these classifications, each of which is discussed in the following sections.

HILLSBOROUGH RETAIL STORE
Balance Sheet
December 31, 1989

Assets

A classified balance sheet lists the current asset accounts first

Current Assets:

Cash	$ 2,356	
Marketable Securities	6,200	
Notes Receivable	1,500	
Accounts Receivable	8,217	
Merchandise Inventory	29,114	
Prepaid Expenses	1,623	
Total Current Assets		$ 49,010

Investments:

Bonds	$ 3,500	
Stocks	7,250	
Total Investments		10,750

Property, Plant, and Equipment:

Land		$10,700	
Buildings	$60,250		

These are contra-asset accounts

Less:	Accumulated Depreciation	13,175	47,075
Equipment	$42,500		
Less:	Accumulated Depreciation	10,600	31,900
	Total Property, Plant, and Equipment		89,675

Intangibles:

Goodwill	$ 2,500	
Patents	1,525	
Total Intangibles		4,025
Total Assets		$153,460

Liabilities and Stockholders' Equity

Liabilities

Liabilities are classified as either current or long-term

Current Liabilities:

Notes Payable	$ 7,000	
Accounts Payable	13,426	
Salaries Payable	2,137	
Federal Income Taxes Payable	4,281	
Unearned Revenue	3,148	
Total Current Liabilities		$29,992

Long-Term Liabilities:

Mortgage Payable, $7\frac{1}{4}$%	$45,170	
Bonds Payable, $8\frac{3}{8}$%, due May 1, 1996	20,000	
Total Long-Term Liabilities		65,170
Total Liabilities		$ 95,162

(continued)

The stockholders' equity section

Stockholders' Equity

Capital Stock:
    Common stock, $1 par value, authorized 15,000 shares, issued and outstanding 2,000 shares..................... $ 2,000
Additional Paid-in Capital:
    Paid-in capital in excess of par value....................   25,600
Retained Earnings..   30,698
    Total Stockholders' Equity..   58,298

Total Liabilities and Stockholders' Equity............................. $153,460

Assets

Current Assets Current assets are assets that are *expected to be converted into cash within a year or the normal operation cycle, whichever is longer.* The ***operating cycle*** is the average length of time between the purchase of merchandise inventory and the realization of cash from the sale of the merchandise inventory. It consists of three phases:

The operating cycle consists of three phases

1. The purchase of merchandise inventory
2. The sale of the merchandise inventory on account
3. The collection of cash from the accounts receivable

FIGURE 3-4
The Operating Cycle

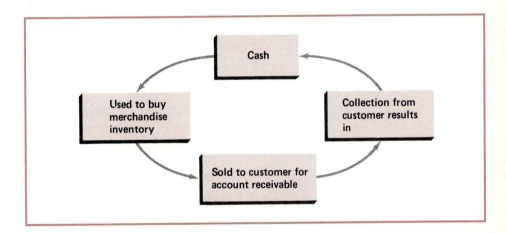

For some entities, such as a grocery store, this period of time — the operating cycle — is only a few weeks. For others, it may extend over a number of years — examples are the distillery industry (it takes years for some liquors to mature into their flavors) and the lumber industry (there are many years between seedling and timber). Most businesses find, however, that their operating cycles are several months in duration, and if not, then commonly less than a year.

    Current assets include Cash, Marketable Securities, Notes Receivable, Accounts Receivable, Merchandise Inventory, and Prepaid Expenses. These assets will be converted into cash during the operating cycle.

    Current assets are listed on the balance sheet in order of their *liquidity.* By the term liquidity we mean the nearness to cash. The most liquid asset is *Cash.* As assets move through the operating cycle from Merchandise Inventory to Accounts Receivable to Cash, they become more liquid.

Marketable Securities are classified as current assets because management intends to dispose of them within the year. U.S. Treasury bills, certificates of deposit, and common stocks of other business entities are typical examples. Companies will invest in marketable securities because they have excess cash available for short periods of time — 30, 60, or 90 days. These financial instruments will provide the company with a rate of return that is not available when cash is held in checking accounts.

Notes Receivable expected to be collected within the year are current assets. Notes receivable commonly originate when a customer cannot pay his or her account receivable when it becomes due. The note, which bears interest, is a more formal agreement than the account receivable. It is a written promise to pay a certain amount on some certain future date.

Merchandise Inventory is the product or products acquired by companies from various suppliers that the companies plan to resell to their customers.

Prepaid Expenses consist of Prepaid Rent, Prepaid Insurance, and Supplies on Hand. These items are not typically shown separately but are included in total under the caption Prepaid Expenses since, even in total, they are not generally large in amount. Prepaid Expenses represent current assets because if they were not already owned, the business entity would be required to expend current assets to obtain them. They will be consumed during the operating cycle and become expenses.

Investments   Investments are distinguished from marketable securities in that management does not intend to convert investments into cash within the year. Bonds, stocks, and real estate are typical assets classified under the Investment caption.

Property, Plant, and Equipment   Tangible, long-lived assets that are used in the production or sale of inventory or in the providing of services are classified as plant and equipment. Land, Buildings, and Equipment are the most common plant and equipment accounts. Land does not wear out; consequently, no depreciation is recorded for land.

Buildings and equipment, on the other hand, do wear out, having limited lives, and their cost must be allocated over the period of time they provide usefulness. This, as you already know, is called *depreciation*. **Accumulated Depreciation** (a contra asset) is reflected under the plant and equipment classification as a subtraction from the related Building or Equipment account.

Intangibles   Intangible assets represent legal rights or certain economic relationships that provide their owners with future economic benefits. Goodwill, patents, franchises, and copyrights are common examples. Intangible assets do not have physical substance.

Other Assets   Occasionally, a business entity will have an asset that cannot be classified within one of the other four classifications. In this situation the classification **Other Assets** is used.

Liabilities

Current Liabilities   Obligations that require the use of current assets for their payment are classified as current liabilities. Thus, they represent liabilities that will be paid within an operating cycle or a year, whichever is longer. Common current liabilities are Notes Payable, Accounts Payable, Salaries Payable, and Taxes Payable.

Unearned Revenue is advance payments received from customers. These payments represent an obligation to provide future goods or services and are consequently also classified as current liabilities. They may be listed as Advances from Customers, Unearned Revenue (as in the Hillsborough Retail Store illustration), or Prepaid Income. Rent received by property owners in advance and payments received by publishers for magazine subscriptions are two examples of unearned revenue.

Long-Term Liabilities Simply stated, liabilities that are not current liabilities are long-term liabilities. They represent obligations that will be paid in the future, later than 1 year after the date on the balance sheet. Mortgages Payable and Bonds Payable are the two most common examples.

Stockholders' Equity

Stockholders' equity represents the stockholders' interest in the business. Sometimes you may see the term *Owners' Equity* used. This term is broader in nature than stockholders' equity, and it is used to cover equity ownership in all three forms of business organization: proprietorships, partnerships, and corporations. But we are concerned now only with corporations, so we will postpone a discussion of proprietorships and partnerships until Chapter 11.

Capital Stock Look back at the Hillsborough Retail Store example in the stockholders' equity section. Common stock is listed there with information about its par value, the number of shares authorized, issued, and outstanding. Here is what has happened. Before the Hillsborough Retail Store began operating, the stockholders submitted an application for authority to incorporate to the state. The state approved the application, allowing Hillsborough Retail Store to issue up to 15,000 shares of *common stock* having a par value of $1. This par value is an arbitrary figure and in no way represents the amount the stock will sell for. For now just accept that it provides a little protection of capital for the creditors of the corporation. We will discuss the nature of corporations in all the detail you want in Chapter 11.

Hillsborough Retail Store, upon receiving approval from the state, issued 2,000 shares of stock to its stockholders and did so at $13.80 per share, which brings us to the next stockholder's equity account.

Additional Paid-in Capital When the $27,600 cash (2,000 shares $\times$ $13.80 per share) was received from the stockholders, of course Cash was increased. And the Common Stock account was increased by $2,000 (2,000 shares $\times$ $1 par value), because the state said that if we have $1-par-value common stock, we must have a general ledger account on our books called Common Stock, $1 par value, equal to $2,000. The rest goes to an account called Paid-in Capital in excess of par and is $25,600. That should be enough of an explanation for now. We will continue to use the account Capital Stock until you return to this topic later.

Retained Earnings Retained Earnings is just what the account title indicates. It is the earnings of the corporation from the very first day the doors were opened until today that have not been paid out to stockholders in the form of dividends. It is the earnings that are retained in the business. *Please,* do not think that retained earnings is cash. It is not. There is no relationship between retained earnings and cash. Retained earnings is a concept—it is all the revenue the company ever earned less all the expenses the company incurred, less all the dividends the company ever paid.

PART TWO The Accounting System
Cash vs. Accrual Accounting

116

The Income Statement

A classified income statement for the Hillsborough Retail Store appears below.

HILLSBOROUGH RETAIL STORE
Income Statement
For the Year Ended December 31, 1987

Sales...			$429,480
Cost of Merchandise Sold		253,170	
Gross Profit on Sales			$176,310
Operating Expenses:			
Selling Expenses:			
Sales Commissions............................	$26,321		
Sales Salaries	9,407		
Advertising Expense...........................	3,500		
Insurance Expense	1,250		
Depreciation Expense	1,600		
Total Selling Expenses		$ 42,078	
General and Administrative Expenses:			
Executive Salaries	$52,900		
Clerical Salaries..............................	11,250		
Insurance Expense	450		
Office Supplies Expense.......................	926		
Taxes Expense................................	4,083		
Depreciation Expense	2,750		
Total General and Administrative Expenses		72,359	
Total Operating Expenses..			114,437
Net Income			$ 61,873

Three major classifications are found on the Hillsborough Retail Store income statement: (1) sales, (2) cost of merchandise sold, and (3) operating expenses. Operating expenses consist of selling expenses and general and administrative expenses.

Sales and cost of merchandise sold will be discussed in detail in Chapter 5.

The operating expenses deal with selling expenses and general administrative expenses. If an expense is related to the selling effort, it is classified as a selling expense. If not, it is a general and administrative expense.

CASH VS. ACCRUAL ACCOUNTING

At this point you must be made aware of the distinction between accounting on a cash basis and accounting using an accrual basis. The income statement of the Hillsborough Retail Store is prepared under the accrual basis, as are all income statements prepared in accordance with generally accepted accounting principles.

In *cash-basis* accounting, a revenue is reported on the income statement only if that revenue was in fact received in the form of cash. The same goes for expenses on the income statement; an expense is reported only if it was indeed disbursed in cash. Thus, net income under the cash basis would simply represent the difference between cash receipts and cash disbursements. If the cash basis of accounting were used, none of the adjustments discussed in this chapter would be necessary.

CHAPTER 3 Periodic Procedures: Adjusting the Accounts
Cash vs. Accrual Accounting

117

The accounting profession has determined that financial statements prepared under *the cash basis of accounting* do not *fairly represent the results of operations or the financial position of a business entity.* A company using the cash basis could easily increase its net income by encouraging its customers to pay their bills early. Net income could also be significantly increased if the company delayed payment of its own bills. This is referred to as *profit manipulation.* The cash basis of accounting is therefore not part of generally accepted accounting principles.

Cash-basis accounting is subject to profit manipulation

Generally accepted accounting principles require that financial statements be prepared under the *accrual basis* of accounting. The accrual basis is based on two concepts: the revenue-recognition principle and the matching concept.

According to the *revenue-recognition principle,* revenue is reported in the financial statements *in the accounting period in which it is earned, not in the accounting period when the cash representing that revenue is received.* For example, a department store sells a shirt to a credit account customer on Dec. 28. The revenue representing the sale of that shirt is recognized on that date — not when the customer pays for the shirt, which may be sometime later in January or February.

According to the *matching concept,* all expenses associated with the generation of revenue must be matched against that revenue in the same period that the revenue was earned. The sale of the shirt in the example above would require that the cost of the shirt, the salaries of the sales people, the depreciation on the display counter, and all the other expenses associated with the sale of the shirt must be expensed when the shirt is sold, whether those expenses were paid for or not.

The following example will help explain the difference between the cash basis and the accrual basis of accounting, as well as clarify what we mean by the revenue-recognition principle and the matching concept.

Assume that the Brown Company entered into a contract on Jan. 18, 1989, with the Green Company to supply Green with a machine for an agreed price of $1,000.

On Feb. 21, 1989, Brown purchases the machine from a wholesaler for $800 on account.

Brown delivers the machine to Green on Mar. 16, 1989, payment to Brown to be made on account.

Green pays Brown $1,000 on Apr. 30, 1989.

Brown pays the wholesaler $800 on May 15, 1989.

Brown's transactions are summarized in Figure 3-5.

FIGURE 3-5
A Summary of Brown's Transactions

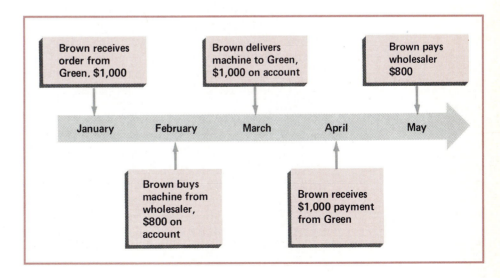

PART TWO   The Accounting System
Cash vs. Accrual Accounting

118

Under the cash basis of accounting, Brown's net income for each of the 5 months would be determined as follows:

Cash basis

	January	February	March	April	May
Revenue	$0	$0	$0	$1,000	$ 0
Expenses	0	0	0	0	800
Net Income	$0	$0	$0	$1,000	$(800)

The accrual basis of accounting would report net income for each of the 5 months according to the following table:

Accrual basis

	January	February	March	April	May
Revenue	$0	$0	$1,000	$0	$0
Expenses	0	0	(800)	0	0
Net Income	$0	$0	$ 200	$0	$0

It is the accrual basis that best provides the statement user with information concerning future cash flows and that consequently represents fairly the results of operations. In January an ***agreement to sell*** a machine was made between Brown and Green. This agreement does not constitute a sale, since performance has not been made by either party. Brown must provide the machine and Green must accept it before a sale is effected.

The purchase of the machine by Brown for $800 in February represents the acquisition of an asset, Merchandise Inventory. At this point it is not an expense, since it has not yet been delivered to Green.

Income is earned in March because:

1. Revenue is recognized by the delivery of the machine—a sale is made; and

2. An expense is incurred, the machine is sold, and it becomes an expense on the income statement—Cost of Merchandise Sold—to be matched against the sale made this period.

The collection of the $1,000 account receivable in April represents the increase in one asset, Cash, and the reduction of a second, Accounts Receivable.

The payment of $800 in May represents the reduction of Cash and the reduction of a current liability.

Under the cash basis, revenue of $1,000 is not recognized until actually received in April, and expenses of $800 are not recorded until actually paid in May. Clearly, the evidence exists in March that can provide the basis for reporting the economic substance of the transaction to those interested in such information. A legal sale has in fact been made. The subsequent receipt from the sale and payment to the wholesaler follow as a normal consequence that *can be predicted at the point of sale.*

Profit manipulation is difficult under the accrual basis, where there are established criteria for recognizing both revenue and expenses. These criteria specify the time when revenue and expenses are to be recognized; it cannot be manipulated.

CHAPTER SUMMARY

Creditors, potential owners, and other parties outside a business entity are, of course, concerned about its financial resources, its obligations, and the results of its activities. These parties do not have direct access to the accounting records of the entity. Nevertheless, they need to be informed in a timely and regular manner of the economic activity of the business entity.

The life of a business entity is divided into time frames—months, quarters, and years—called *accounting periods.* Accountants prepare financial statements at the end of each time frame—that is, at the end of each month, each quarter, and each year.

The *balance sheet* reports the status as of the close of business on the *last day of a time frame;* the *income statement* reports the activity *during the period of time covered by the time frame.*

A business entity needs and buys assets such as buildings and equipment that are used during many years, covering many accounting periods. Only after an asset was no longer useful would a business entity know exactly how long it served and how to allocate its cost precisely over each of the accounting periods during its useful life. But it is highly impractical to wait for the end of an asset's useful life to account precisely for its cost during each accounting period. The practical solution is to estimate how long it will be useful, and to allocate its total cost over each of the accounting periods of its life—a process called *depreciation,* resulting in an expense called *Depreciation Expense.* Because the calculation of Depreciation Expense depends on an estimate, it is only an approximation of the actual expense. And because Depreciation Expense is not precise, neither is the net income calculated and reported during an accounting period.

During an accounting period a business entity makes exchanges with second parties (buyers, sellers, lenders). These exchanges are called *external transactions.* The economic result of an external transaction is recorded during the accounting period in which it was made even though the actual result may not occur until a later period. That is, the accounts debited or credited by some external transactions may not reflect the actual situation at the end of the accounting period. For example, some assets acquired during a period may have been consumed before the end of that period; interest income may have been earned but not yet received on money loaned; or salary expense may have been incurred for salaries earned by employees but not yet paid. Nevertheless, the financial statements prepared at the end of the accounting period must reflect the following:

1. All assets owned
2. All liabilities owed
3. All revenue earned
4. All expenses incurred

To meet this objective, certain amounts must be increased or decreased by means of adjusting entries in the general journal—an *internal transaction*—as of the last day of the accounting period.

There are two basic types of adjusting entries: *deferrals,* which require adjustment because the goods and/or services already paid for in full may not have been completely consumed at period-end; and *accruals,* which represent revenue earned and expenses incurred for which no transaction has been recorded during the period.

Prepaid Expenses, Unearned Revenue, and Depreciation are deferrals.

At the moment an asset is acquired, it is represented as a *prepaid expense*—an unexpired cost. A Prepaid Expense becomes an expired cost—representing an expense—as the asset is consumed over time.

Similarly, when ***Unearned Revenue*** is received, it is represented as a liability. As services are performed or goods are delivered in fulfillment of the Unearned Revenue, the liability is reduced and revenue is represented as earned.

The expenses for buildings and equipment are similar to Prepaid Expenses. Over time, as they are used, they become expired costs—represented as ***Depreciation Expenses.*** But, unlike Prepaid Expenses, the Building and Equipment accounts are not reduced directly as the expense is recorded. Rather, a ***contra-asset*** account called ***Accumulated Depreciation*** is increased. The use of the contra-asset account maintains the Building or Equipment account at its original cost, which provides useful information to statement users.

Salary Expense, Interest Expense, Interest Revenue, and the counterparts of these items—Salaries Payable, Interest Payable, and Interest Receivable—are examples of accruals. These accounts are accrued over time although payment is made or received on specific dates. When the financial statements are prepared on dates other than the date of a payment or a receipt, the accruals must be measured and recorded by adjusting entries to present fairly the results of operations and the financial position.

After all the adjusting entries are, first, recorded in the general journal and, next, posted to each of the appropriate general ledger accounts, then an ***adjusted trial balance*** can be prepared. The adjusted trial balance is used to prepare the financial statements.

If each of these types of accounts—asset accounts, liability accounts, revenue accounts, and expense accounts—is grouped in some meaningful way, they will provide the basis for easily preparing useful financial statements. Such financial statements are referred to as ***classified financial statements.***

The balance sheet is classified into the following groupings:

1. Five major asset groupings:
   a. Current assets
   b. Long-term investments
   c. Property, plant, and equipment
   d. Intangibles
   e. Other assets

2. Two major liability groupings
   a. Current liabilities
   b. Long-term liabilities

3. Stockholders' equity accounts
   a. Capital stock
   b. Additional paid-in capital
   c. Retained earnings

The income statement classifications consist of the following:

1. Revenue
2. Cost of merchandise sold
3. Operating expenses
   a. Selling expenses
   b. General and administrative expenses

Generally accepted accounting principles require that financial statements be prepared using the ***accrual basis of accounting*** rather than the ***cash basis.*** The underlying concept of the accrual basis of accounting is the ***revenue-recognition principle:*** Revenue must be reflected on the financial statements in the accounting period in which it is earned. Furthermore, expenses must be also reflected on the financial statements in the accounting period in which they are incurred, and they must be matched against revenue earned. This is called the ***matching concept.***

IMPORTANT TERMS USED IN THIS CHAPTER

Accounting period The length of time for which financial activities are reported on the income statement. An accounting period is typically 1 year. However, income statements are also prepared quarterly, thus covering accounting periods of 3 months' duration. (page 97)

Accrual-basis accounting The generally accepted accounting principle requiring that revenue be recorded when earned and that expenses be recorded when incurred. (page 117)

Accruals Expenses that are incurred and whose benefits have been consumed, but that have not yet been paid for; also revenue that is earned and whose benefits have been received but for which payment has not been received. (page 99)

Accumulated Depreciation A balance sheet account that is shown as a deduction from the related Building or Equipment account. It is a contra asset and accumulates the depreciation taken on the asset over its useful life. (page 103)

Additional paid-in-capital The difference between the cash amount received when issuing stock and the stock's par value. (page 115)

Adjusted trial balance A trial balance prepared after all adjusting entries have been made. (page 108)

Adjusting entries The entries made at the end of an accounting period to reflect internal changes during the period in all expenses and liabilities incurred, revenue earned, and assets owned. (page 99)

Book value The difference between the amount shown in a specific fixed asset account and its accumulated depreciation. (page 103)

Capital stock A stockholder's equity account representing the measurement of the par value of the total number of shares of common stock that are outstanding. (page 115)

Cash-basis accounting The accounting system that records revenue only upon the receipt of cash and records expenses only upon payment. It is not a generally accepted accounting principle. (page 116)

Contra account An account with a balance opposite the normal balance. A contra-asset account, for example, has a credit balance, whereas an asset account has a debit balance. (page 103)

Current assets Assets that are expected to be converted into cash within a year or within the normal operating cycle, whichever is longer. (page 113)

Current liabilities Obligations requiring the use of current assets for their liquidation or payment. (page 114)

Depreciation The cost of a fixed asset (other than land) that is allocated over the period of time for which benefits are received from the fixed asset. (page 103)

Expired cost An expense representing the amount of an asset that is considered to have been used up over a period of time. (page 100)

External transactions Exchange transactions between the business entity and parties outside the entity. (page 97)

Intangibles Legal rights or certain economic relationships that provide their owners with future economic benefits. (page 114)

Internal transactions Adjusting entries made by a business entity to reflect more accurately the status of the accounts at the end of a period. (page 99)

Long-term investments Bonds, stocks, and real estate that a business entity owns and does not intend to sell for cash within the year. (page 114)

Long-term liabilities Obligations that will be paid at some future time beyond 1 year from the balance sheet. (page 115)

Matching concept The generally accepted accounting principle that requires that expenses incurred for providing a product or service during an accounting period be matched against revenue earned by that product or service during the same accounting period. (page 117)

Operating cycle The time between the purchase of merchandise inventory and the realization of cash from the sale of that merchandise inventory. (page 113)

Prepaid expenses Expenses that are paid for before they are used; consequently they are classified as current assets. (page 100)

Retained earnings The lifetime earnings of a corporation less the lifetime dividends. (page 115)

Revenue-recognition principle The generally accepted accounting principle requiring that revenue be reflected on the income statement in the period in which it is earned. (page 117)

Time-period principle The generally accepted accounting principle that requires that the economic life of a business entity be divided into time frames called *accounting periods* and that financial statements be prepared at the end of these time frames. (page 97)

Unearned revenue The liability incurred for cash received in advance of goods or services rendered. (page 102)

Unexpired cost That part of the cost of an asset representing the economic benefit it has not yet provided or its services not yet consumed. (page 100)

QUESTIONS

1. There are two types of business transactions, *external* transactions and *internal* transactions. How do they differ?

2. At the end of an accounting period, certain accounts are adjusted. Why?

3. What is the meaning of the term *unexpired cost? Expired cost?*

4. Explain the difference between *deferrals* and *accruals* as classifications of adjusting entries.

5. "The net income of a business entity is determined by measuring the amount of revenue generated and subtracting the expenses incurred, appropriately measured. As a consequence the resulting difference, net income, is a precise measure of operating performance for the period under consideration." Comment.

6. What is the nature of the account Accumulated Depreciation?

7. If a company fails to accrue salaries at the end of a month, what will be the effect of this omission on the financial statements?

8. Give examples of three unexpired costs and three related expired costs.

9. If rent is paid monthly in advance on the first day of each month, there is an advantage in debiting rent expense when payment is made. Explain this advantage.

10. Consider a new account that has not been discussed in the chapter, called *Prepaid Income.* What is the nature of this account, and how should it be classified?

11. Explain the difference between *marketable securities* and *investments.*

12. Why are *classified financial statements* prepared?

13. What are *current assets?* What are *current liabilities?*

14. What is an *operating cycle?*

15. The cash basis of accounting is not considered to be a generally accepted accounting principle. Explain why not.

16. What is the *matching concept?*

17. Explain the *revenue-recognition principle.*

18. What are the steps involved in the accounting process?

EXERCISES

Exercise 3-1
Preparing adjusting entries

Paydays at Atlas Corporation are on alternate Fridays, the last one being Oct. 20, 1989. Atlas has 32 employees who earn $7.50 per hour. All employees work 8 hours per day, 5 days per week.

Prepare the adjusting entry to record the accrual of salaries for the year ended Tuesday, Oct. 31, 1989, and the entry required on Friday, Nov. 3, when the employees are paid.

Exercise 3-2
Analyzing accounts, determining the missing item

This exercise is designed to test your ability to analyze an account. For each of the four independent cases listed below, determine the amount indicated.

a. During the year, $3,600 of supplies were acquired. At the beginning of the year, $600 of supplies were on hand; while $1,400 was the balance at year-end. Determine the amount of supplies used during the year.

(Check figure: $2,800)

b. At year-end the count of supplies on hand amounted to $1,800. Supplies acquired during the year were $7,200, and supplies used were $7,800. Determine the amount of supplies that were on hand at the beginning of the year.

(Check figure: $2,400)

c. During the year, $10,800 of supplies were consumed. The beginning balance of the supplies on hand amounted to $2,400, while the ending balance was $2,000 more. Determine the amount of supplies acquired during the year.

(Check figure: $12,800)

d. Supplies acquired during the year amounted to $45,000. The ending balance of supplies was one-half that of the beginning balance, and the supplies consumed during the year amounted to twice the beginning balance. Determine the ending balance.

(Check figure: $15,000)

Exercise 3-3
Preparing adjusting entries

Prepare the appropriate adjusting entry required at the end of the month indicated.

a. The McHill-Graw Company paid $4,575 rent in advance on July 1, 1989, for the months of July, August, and September. Determine the July 31 adjusting entry.

b. Prentice Corporation issued a $500,000 note payable to the New York Downhome Bank, receiving cash in that amount on Nov. 1, 1989. The note is a 180-day, 12% note due on Apr. 30, 1990, together with the interest. Determine the adjusting entry for the Prentice Corporation on Dec. 31, 1989.

c. The New York Privates received $4,200,000 in advance ticket sales by May 1, 1989, representing sales of 35,000 season tickets at $12 each for 10 home games. By Oct. 31, 1989, the

Privates were undefeated and had played nine games, six of which were home games. Determine the adjusting entry to record the revenue earned for the six home games as of Oct. 31, 1989.

d. Row-VanHarper acquired an electronic typesetter on Oct. 1, 1989, for $18,000. The machine has an estimated life of 15 years, after which it will be worthless. Determine the adjusting entry to record depreciation on the machine as of Dec. 31, 1989.

Exercise 3-4
Finding the effects of errors

Errors of omission are common in our daily lives; we simply forget to do something. If a business entity fails to record the year-end adjusting entries, that is an error of omission. Using the following chart, indicate the effect of five errors of omission on each of the financial statement classifications listed. If, as a result of the omission, a classification is overstated, indicate this by placing a (+) in the appropriate space. An understatement is to be indicated by a (−). If the omission has no effect on the classification, place (0) in the appropriate space.

	Effect of Omission				
	a	b	c	d	e
Revenue					
Expenses					
Net Income					
Current Assets					
Noncurrent Assets					
Current Liabilities					
Long-Term Liabilities					
Stockholders' Equity					

a. Office Supplies on Hand was not reduced to reflect office supplies used.
b. Interest income on notes receivable was not accrued.
c. Depreciation was not recorded.
d. Salaries were not accrued.
e. Unearned Revenue was not reduced to reflect revenue earned.

Exercise 3-5
Preparing adjusting entries

A count of office supplies on hand for the *Tampa Times, St. Pete Press,* and *Clearwater Clarion* on Dec. 31, 1988, amounted to $4,500 for each company. On Jan. 1, 1989, the $4,500 is reflected on each company's books as follows:

	Tampa Times	St. Pete Press	Clearwater Clarion
Office Supplies Used	-0-	$4,500	-0-
Office Supplies on Hand	$4,500	-0-	$4,500

Supplies in the amount of $17,300 were acquired by each company during 1989. The *Tampa Times* debited Office Supplies on Hand, but the other two newspaper company's debited Office Supplies Used.

On Dec. 31, 1989, all three companies had $3,700 of supplies remaining.
Prepare the appropriate adjusting entries for each company.

Exercise 3-6
Determining missing items

Panhandle Pots & Pans Company maintains its records in accordance with generally accepted accounting principles and makes all sales transactions and acquisitions of supplies on account. For the following two items determine the amount indicated.

a. During the year the Accounts Receivable account increased by $5,200 and sales amounted to $16,800. What were the cash collections?

(Check figure: $11,600)

b. Supplies on Hand decreased by $600 during the year. Supplies used for the year amounted to $2,000. Accounts Payable for supplies increased by $200. What were the cash payments for supplies? (Hint: First calculate supplies acquired on account, then calculate the cash payments.)

(Check figure: $1,200)

PROBLEMS: SET A

Problem A3-1
Preparing adjusting entries

The California Corporation ends its accounting year on Dec. 31. Presented below is information pertaining to California's 1989 year-end activities.

a. On Mar. 31, 1989, California Corporation received $7,200 for advertising services to be performed by California evenly over the next 24 months. The amount was recorded as Unearned Advertising Revenue.

b. A balance of $3,700 was reflected in the Office Supplies on Hand account on Dec. 31, 1989. A count of the office supplies on Dec. 31 amounts to $1,430.   *2370*

c. Depreciation on machinery amounts to $7,500 for the year.

d. Rent in the amount of $4,800 was paid in advance on Oct. 1, 1989, and recorded as Prepaid Rent. The payment was for a 12-month period.

e. Salaries in the amount of $7,400 were earned by employees as of Sunday, Dec. 31, 1989, but not paid since the biweekly payday is on Friday, Jan. 5, 1990.

Required

For each item listed above, record in a general journal the appropriate adjusting entry.

Problem A3-2
Preparing adjusting entries

Presented below are a number of independent situations requiring adjusting entries. Analyze each item carefully and prepare the appropriate adjusting journal entry, assuming that the accounting year ends Dec. 31, 1989, unless otherwise indicated.

a. The Prepaid Rent account of the Allentown Company had a balance of $4,200 on Jan. 1, 1989. This balance represents the remaining future service of a 1-year lease paid in advance for the rental of company autos. The lease was dated June 1, 1988. A new lease was written on June 1, 1989, calling for a 10% increase in the monthly rent. A check was written in the amount equal to 12 months' rent paid in advance on June 4, 1989.

b. Bethlehem Realty pays its employees every Friday. This year May 31 is a Wednesday. Pay rates for the 11 employees are as follows:

Employees	Daily Rate
4	$50 *200*
3	$55 *165*
4	$60 *240* *605* *1815*

All 11 employees worked Monday, Tuesday, and Wednesday. The accounting year ends May 31, 1989.

c. The Carbondale Company sells a monthly magazine for $1.75 per copy. During the course of the year 1989, 94,400 two-year subscriptions were sold. As of the first of the year Unearned Magazine Revenue had a balance of $631,800. At year-end it is determined that the liability to provide future magazines amounts to $2,548,800. When subscriptions are received, the liability account is credited.

d. The Dunmore Company has an insurance policy covering its building, which was acquired on Oct. 1, 1986. At that time Dunmore paid $1,620 in advance for the 3-year policy. The policy was renewed on Oct. 1, 1989, for an additional 3 years at a cost of $1,800, which was paid on that date. The company's policy is to debit Prepaid Insurance when insurance is paid for in advance.

e. A drill press costing $140,000 was acquired by the Easton Drilling Company on Apr. 1, 1989. It is anticipated that the drill press will be used for 25 years; consequently the annual depreciation is $5,600.

f. On Oct. 1, 1989, the Factoryville Company borrowed from one of its customers $14,000 to be repaid in 6 months together with 10% interest (interest is expressed at the annual rate).

g. Repair parts in the amount of $16,093 were acquired during the year 1989 by the Germantown Company. At Dec. 31, 1989, a physical count of the repair parts totaled $3,245. The balance in the account on Jan. 1, 1989, was $4,180. When repair parts are acquired, it is the company's policy to debit Repair Parts on Hand.

Problem A3-3
Journalizing and posting entries and preparing a trial balance

Presented below is the unadjusted trial balance of Orange Ball Express Corporation, a freight-hauling company. It was prepared from the general ledger on Dec. 31, 1989.

ORANGE BALL EXPRESS CORPORATION
Unadjusted Trial Balance
December 31, 1989

Cash	$ 3,090	
Notes Receivable	4,000	
Interest Receivable	-0-	
Accounts Receivable	10,150	
Prepaid Equipment Rentals	3,600	
Repair Parts on Hand	24,860	
Land	10,000	
Building	90,000	
Accumulated Depreciation: Building		$ 30,000
Trucks	28,500	
Accumulated Depreciation: Trucks		14,250
Accounts Payable		6,360
Salaries Payable		-0-
Capital Stock		40,000
Retained Earnings		9,940
Transportation Revenues		131,950
Interest Income		-0-
Salary Expense	54,600	
Rent Expense	-0-	
Repair Parts Used	-0-	
Depreciation Expense: Trucks	-0-	
Depreciation Expense: Building	-0-	
Utilities Expense	3,700	
Totals	$232,500	$232,500

Required

1. Prepare adjusting journal entries for each of the following items:

a. The Prepaid Equipment Rentals represents rent paid in advance for certain transportation equipment. The rent was paid on July 1, 1989, for 15 months in advance.

b. The note receivable is dated Apr. 1, 1989. It is a 12% note and is due on Sept. 1, 1990.

c. Depreciation expense for the trucks is determined to be $5,700. Building depreciation is computed at $2,250.

d. The count of the Repair Parts on Hand at Dec. 31, 1989, amounts to $6,360.

e. Utility bills in the amount of $135 are unpaid on Dec. 31, 1989.

f. Salaries in the amount of $2,540 have accrued by Dec. 31, 1989.

2. For each account found in the adjusted trial balance, establish a general ledger account. Enter the amount found in the unadjusted trial balance into the general ledger account. Post the adjusting entries and compute the adjusted balances.
3. Prepare an adjusted trial balance.

(Check figure: Totals = $243,485)

Problem A3-4
Journalizing and posting adjusting entries; preparing an adjusted trial balance and financial statements

The unadjusted trial balance for the year ended June 30, 1989, for Scranton Storage Company appears below.

SCRANTON STORAGE COMPANY
Unadjusted Trial Balance
June 30, 1989

Cash	$ 1,570	
Accounts Receivable	2,630	
Office Supplies on Hand	950	
Land	15,540	
Buildings	65,400	
Accumulated Depreciation: Buildings		$ 15,000
Equipment	12,500	
Accumulated Depreciation: Equipment		5,000
Accounts Payable		3,210
Note Payable		20,000
Capital Stock		30,000
Retained Earnings		12,440
Storage Revenue		75,700
Salary Expense	57,650	
Telephone Expense	2,910	
Interest Expense	2,200	
Totals	$161,350	$161,350

Required

1. For each item found in the unadjusted trial balance, establish a general ledger account.
2. Additional information is presented below. From this information, prepare the necessary adjusting entries, establishing new general ledger accounts as needed.
   a. Depreciation for the year amounts to $1,500 for the buildings and $1,000 for the equipment.
   b. Accrued salaries in the amount of $950 have not been paid as of June 30.
   c. A count of the office supplies on June 30 amounts to $165.
   d. A telephone bill in the amount of $97 remains unpaid and unrecorded on June 30.
   e. Included in the Storage Revenue account is $2,500 representing storage revenues for July, 1989, paid for in advance. (You must reduce the Storage Revenue account and establish a liability account Unearned Storage Revenue.)
   f. The interest rate on the note payable is 12% per year. The note is due on Oct. 1, 1991. Note that $2,200 of interest expense has been paid in 1989.
3. Prepare an adjusted trial balance.

(Check figure: Trial balance totals = $165,097)

4. Prepare an income statement and a classified balance sheet properly dated for the Scranton Storage Company. Do not prepare a statement of retained earnings.

Problem A3-5
Preparing adjusting entries from unadjusted and adjusted trial balances

The unadjusted and adjusted trial balances of Southland Corporation are presented below.

	Unadjusted		Adjusted	
SOUTHLAND CORPORATION				
Trial Balances				
December 31, 1989				
Cash	$ 1,540		$ 1,540	
Notes Receivable	1,000		1,000	
Interest Receivable....................	-0-		100	
Accounts Receivable	3,710		3,960	
Prepaid Advertising	1,800		1,200	
Supplies on Hand......................	2,740		1,680	
Land	20,000		20,000	
Building	130,000		130,000	
Accumulated Depreciation: Building.....		$ 25,000		$ 28,000
Furniture	15,000		15,000	
Accumulated Depreciation: Furniture....		5,000		6,000
Accounts Payable......................		2,670		2,800
Interest Payable		-0-		300
Salaries Payable		-0-		650
Unearned Revenue		-0-		900
Mortgage Payable......................		40,000		40,000
Capital Stock.........................		50,000		50,000
Retained Earnings		34,130		34,130
Dividends.............................	6,000		6,000	
Revenue..............................		187,300		186,650
Interest Income.......................	-0-			100
Salary Expense	147,900		148,550	
Advertising Expense	10,700		11,300	
Supplies Used	3,710		4,770	
Depreciation: Building	-0-		3,000	
Depreciation: Furniture	-0-		1,000	
Utilities Expense......................	-0-		130	
Interest Expense	-0-		300	
Totals	$344,100	$344,100	$349,530	$349,530

Required

The year-end adjusting entries can be determined by comparing the two trial balances. By this method record the adjusting journal entries made on Dec. 31, 1989.

Problem A3-6
Preparing a classified balance sheet

An alphabetical list of accounts for the Bennett Corporation is presented below.

Accounts Payable.............	$ 1,700		Bonds Payable	$ 70,000
Accounts Receivable.........	2,500		Buildings	175,000
Accrued Interest on Notes			Capital Stock	300,000
Payable....................	500		Cash	3,500
Accumulated Depreciation:			Common Stock: General	
Building....................	24,000		Motors.....................	2,700
Accumulated Depreciation:			Depreciation Expense.........	26,000
Equipment	125,000		Equipment	477,500
Advances to Employees	1,000		Federal Income Taxes Payable .	16,500
Advertising Expense	400		Goodwill	5,000

Hellertown City Bonds........	$ 3,300	Notes Receivable.............	$ 2,000
Interest Income	700	Patents.....................	12,500
Land.......................	10,000	Prepaid Rent.................	3,500
Land Held for Future		Retained Earnings...........	105,600
Plant Site..................	15,000	Salaries Payable	1,500
Marketable Securities	3,200	Sales	426,500
Merchandise Inventory........	31,500	Supplies on Hand	1,200
Mortgage Payable.............	95,000	Unearned Revenue	1,600
Notes Payable: Current........	8,000		

Required	Prepare a classified balance sheet.

(Check figure: Total Assets = $600,400)

PROBLEMS: SET B

Problem B3-1
Preparing adjusting entries

The following information is available at Dec. 31, 1989, concerning the activities of the Pearson Corporation for the year:
a. Recorded in the Unearned Leasing Revenue account is $2,400 of revenue that has been earned as of Dec. 31, 1989.
b. Annual depreciation on office equipment amounts to $13,750.
c. The corporation acquired a 2-year insurance policy on Oct. 1 for $1,200, paid in advance on that date. As of Dec. 31, the $1,200 remains in the Prepaid Insurance account.
d. The general ledger account Shop Supplies on Hand shows a debit balance of $3,670. A physical count of the shop supplies results in an amount of $825.
e. Accrued salaries for the last 3 days in 1989 amount to $2,650.

Required	Record the appropriate general journal adjusting entries.

Problem B3-2
Preparing adjusting entries

For each of the independent items below, prepare adjusting journal entries for the accounting year ended Dec. 31, 1989, unless otherwise indicated.
a. The Atlanta Corporation sells magazines on a subscription basis. On Apr. 1, 1989, cash in the amount of $1,800 was received for magazine subscriptions for the next 36 months. The corporation made a credit to a liability account when the cash was received.
b. Boston Corporation had a $400 balance in its Prepaid Insurance account on Jan. 1, 1989, from a 3-year insurance policy acquired on Sept. 1, 1986. On Apr. 1, 1989, the corporation acquired a second policy, paying $1,680 in advance for the 2-year policy. The first policy was renewed on Sept. 1, 1989, for an additional 3 years by a payment of $2,160. The corporation records insurance in the prepaid account.
c. Cincinnati, Inc., has a $30,000, 12% note payable due to the First State Bank on Mar. 30, 1990. The money was borrowed on Oct. 2, 1989. (Unless stated otherwise, interest is always expressed at the annual rate.)
d. The Dallas Company rents its Infomax computers from the manufacturer. On July 1, 1987, the company paid the manufacturer $1,200 in advance for the computers it will rent for 2 years. On July 1, 1989, Dallas Company renewed the rental agreement, paying $1,320 in advance for an additional 2 years. The company records rent paid in advance in an asset account.
e. Erie Corporation had a balance of $1,617 in its Office Supplies on Hand account on Jan. 1, 1989. During the year acquisition of office supplies were made totaling $3,603 and recorded in the asset account. A count of the office supplies on Dec. 31, 1989, revealed that $526 remained on hand.
f. The employees of Frankfort Corporation are paid every Friday. The company employs 34 individuals, who are paid according to the following union scale:

Union Scale Classification	Per-Hour Rate	Number of Employees
A	$11.50	3
B	9.75	8
C	8.00	12
D	4.25	11

All 34 employees worked 8 hours each day Monday through Wednesday Oct. 31, 1989. The accounting year ends on Oct. 31, 1989.

g. Galvaston Company acquired a new machine on Sept. 1, 1989, at a cost of $54,000. The machine has an estimated 15-year useful life, thus the annual depreciation is $3,600.

Problem B3-3
Journalizing and posting adjusting entries and preparing a trial balance

The unadjusted trial balance presented below was prepared from the general ledger accounts of the Rogers Pest Control Company on Dec. 31, 1989.

ROGERS PEST CONTROL COMPANY
Unadjusted Trial Balance
December 31, 1989

Cash	$ 3,710	
Accounts Receivable	4,150	
Prepaid Advertising	1,800	
Pest Control Supplies on Hand	25,725	
Land	9,000	
Building	38,700	
Accumulated Depreciation: Building		$ 10,500
Trucks	26,500	
Accumulated Depreciation: Trucks		11,300
Accounts Payable		2,160
Salaries Payable		-0-
Unearned Pest Control Revenue		-0-
Capital Stock		20,000
Retained Earnings		29,145
Dividends	3,000	
Pest Control Revenue		127,400
Salary Expense	87,500	
Pest Control Supplies Used	-0-	
Advertising Expense	-0-	
Maintenance Expense	320	
Depreciation Expense: Building	-0-	
Depreciation Expense: Trucks	-0-	
Miscellaneous Expense	100	
Totals	$200,505	$200,505

Required

1. From the following information, prepare adjusting journal entries:

a. Included in the Pest Control Revenues is $735 representing an advance payment by the City Convention Center to exterminate termites from their building during remodeling in January, 1990.

b. On Dec. 28, 1989, Rogers Pest Control Company services the Elks Club. The fee of $85 has not yet been recorded.

c. Accrued salaries on Dec. 31,1989, amount to $925.

d. A bill in the amount of $135 for maintenance has been received but has not been recorded.

e. Depr. exp. for the building and trucks amounts to $1,500 and $1,900, respectively.

f. Pest Control Supplies on Hand on Dec. 31, 1989, amounts to $2,340.

g. The balance in the Prepaid Advertising account represents a payment made on Oct. 1, 1989, for 12 months of advertising in the *Big Town Daily News.*

2. Establish a ledger for each account found in the trial balance, record the amounts from the unadjusted trial balance, post the adjusting entries, and determine the ending balances.

3. Prepare an adjusted trial balance as of Dec. 31, 1989.

(Check figure: Trial balance totals = $205,050)

Problem B3-4
Journalizing and posting adjusting entries; preparing an adjusted trial balance and financial statements

The unadjusted trial balance of Golden Age Retirement Home for the year ended July 31, 1989, appears below.

GOLDEN AGE RETIREMENT HOME		
Unadjusted Trial Balance		
July 31, 1989		
Cash	$ 2,615	
Accounts Receivable...........................	12,075	
Prepaid Insurance	900	
Land..	25,000	
Retirement Home	250,000	
Accumulated Depreciation: Retirement Home..........		$ 31,250
Retirement Home Furniture.....................	80,000	
Accumulated Depreciation: Retirement Home Furniture........		12,500
Accounts Payable		940
Mortgage Payable		130,000
Capital Stock		100,000
Retained Earnings.............................		157,470
Dividends	46,000	
Retirement Home Revenues.....................		375,400
Salary Expense................................	281,300	
Supplies Used.................................	16,260	
Linen Expense	41,500	
Laundry Expense..............................	36,700	
Interest Expense..............................	14,300	
Utilities Expense	910	
Totals..	$807,560	$807,560

Required

1. For each item in the trial balance, open a general ledger account.

2. From the information presented below, prepare adjusting entries and post them to the general ledger accounts. Establish new accounts as needed.

   a. Accrued salaries as of July 31, 1989, amount to $1,260.

   b. The Prepaid Insurance represents 6 month's insurance paid in advance on Apr. 1, 1989.

   c. Supplies used during the year amounts to $14,710. (Notice that the company chose to record acquisitions of supplies as an expense rather than an asset.)

   d. Unearned Revenue in the amount of $1,625 is included in Retirement Home Revenues.

   e. Interest Expense for the mortgage in the amount of $1,300 has accrued on July 31, 1989.

   f. Depreciation for the year amounts to $6,250 for the Retirement Home and $5,350 for the Retirement Home Furniture.

3. Prepare an adjusted trial balance as of July 31, 1989.

(Check figure: Trial balance totals = $821,720)

4. Prepare an income statement for the year ended July 31, 1989, and a classified balance sheet as of July 31, 1989. Do not prepare a statement of retained earnings.

**Problem B3-5
Preparing adjusting
entries from unadjusted
and adjusted trial balances**

Presented below are the unadjusted and adjusted trial balance of TeleView Cable Corporation as of December 31, 1989. By comparing the two trial balances, determine the adjustments that were made to the accounts and prepare adjusting journal entries for each. You may omit the journal explanations.

TELEVIEW CABLE CORPORATION
Trial Balances
December 31, 1989

	Unadjusted		Adjusted	
Cash	$ 1,570		$ 1,570	
Accounts Receivable	4,070		4,610	
Prepaid Rent.......................	600		450	
Supplies on Hand....................	1,340		205	
Land	20,000		20,000	
Building	175,000		175,000	
Accumulated Depreciation: Building.....		$ 25,000		$ 26,500
Equipment.........................	51,000		51,000	
Accumulated Depreciation: Equipment ..		18,700		19,900
Accounts Payable....................		1,420		1,420
Salaries Payable		-0-		670
Interest Payable		-0-		400
Unearned Revenue		-0-		1,750
Mortgage Payable...................		40,000		40,000
Capital Stock......................		50,000		50,000
Retained Earnings		45,240		45,240
Dividends..........................	12,000		12,000	
Revenues..........................		265,340		264,130
Salary Expense	175,720		176,390	
Rent Expense	-0-		150	
Supplies Used	-0-		1,135	
Depreciation Expense: Building	-0-		1,500	
Depreciation Expense: Equipment	-0-		1,200	
Interest Expense	4,400		4,800	
Totals	$445,700	$445,700	$450,010	$450,010

**Problem B3-6
Preparing a classified
balance sheet**

The list of accounts presented below for the Pam Pinellas Company is in alphabetical order. From this list, prepare a classified balance sheet dated Dec. 31, 1989.

Accounts Payable..............	$13,200	Investment in Municipal Bonds .	$ 12,300
Accounts Receivable...........	36,500	Investment in Real Estate.......	8,400
Accum. Depr.: Building	19,100	Land.........................	14,500
Accum. Depr.: Equipment......	26,300	Marketable Securities	13,500
Advertising Expense	13,400	Merchandise Inventory.........	22,700
Buildings	83,200	Mortg. Payable Dec., 2012......	58,300
Capital Stock..................	50,000	Net Income, 1989	72,300
Cash	8,000	Notes Payable Due 1990	10,000
Copyrights...................	7,500	Notes Receivable	5,500
Depreciation Expense..........	27,300	Patents......................	10,000
Equipment....................	97,500	Prepaid Advertising...........	3,600
Equip. Notes Payable Due 1995.	40,000	Ret. Earnings, Dec. 31, 1989....	97,900
Federal Income Taxes Payable ..	9,200	Salaries Payable	5,700
Franchise Cost	6,300	Sales	362,500
Goodwill	12,200	Unearned Revenue	12,000

(Check figure: Total Assets = $296,300)

DECISION PROBLEM

Analyzing data and preparing an income statement

Joe Soilfree operates a dry-cleaning establishment in Cleveland, Ohio. Mr. Soilfree maintains his accounting records on a cash basis but adjusts the records to the accrual basis at the end of the accounting year. Early in the year the company's accountant retired. As a consequence, Mr. Soilfree requests that you prepare an income statement on the accrual basis for the Soilfree Dry Cleaning Company for the year ended Dec. 31, 1989. You are provided with the information presented below:

a. Cash receipts for the year totaled $611,845. Washing and pressing amounted to $372,420 and dry cleaning $179,250. Commencing on Oct. 1, 1989, Mr. Soilfree initiated a plan whereby customers could pay a fixed amount every 3 months and Soilfree would provide unlimited dry cleaning, washing, and pressing. The fee for this service was $75, to be paid at the beginning of the 3-month contract.

An analysis of the contracts reveals that 123 customers paid for this service on Oct. 1, 187 on Nov. 1, and 215 on Dec. 1. The total amount received for the unlimited service is included in the cash receipts. Mr. Soilfree asserts that three-fifths of the unlimited service is washing and pressing, and two-fifths is dry cleanings.

Also included in the cash receipts were the following: $12,250 for alterations, a $7,500 bank loan, and $1,050 from a note receivable the Soilfree Dry Cleaning Company had at the beginning of the year.

b. Cash payments for the year amounted to $566,020, and are summarized below:

Salaries	$175,500	Office equipment	$ 25,000
Cleaning supplies (record as an expense)	126,350	Dividends	125,000
		Utilities	950
Insurance (record as asset)	720	Delivery truck	12,500
Payment to banks (see *f*)	100,000		

c. Salaries in the amount of $1,650 remain unpaid at the end of the year.

d. The cleaning supplies on hand increased by $11,020 from Jan. 1 to Dec. 31, 1989. Unpaid bills for cleaning supplies amounted to $4,250 at year-end.

e. The $720 expenditure for insurance represents the renewal of a 2-year insurance policy at $30 per month. The old rate was $25 per month. The policy was renewed on Apr. 1, 1989, when the old policy expired.

f. Outstanding bank loans required payments of $100,000 during the year. Of this total, $65,000 represents interest. The $7,500 bank loan was dated Dec. 1, 1989. It is a 12% loan that must be repaid in full on June 1, 1990.

g. Depreciation on the building, which is owned by the company, is estimated to be $2,500 per year. Depreciation on the office equipment and delivery trucks is estimated to be $21,000 and $1,000, respectively.

Required

1. From this information, prepare general journal entries to summarize the year's activities.

2. Prepare an income statement for the year ended Dec. 31, 1989.

(Check figure: Net Income = $200,270)

CHAPTER 4

Periodic Procedures: Closing the Accounts and the Worksheet

After studying this chapter, you should be able to:

- Identify which accounts are closed at the end of an accounting period and explain why
- Prepare *closing entries*
- Prepare a *worksheet*
- Use a worksheet to prepare *interim financial statements*
- Prepare a *post-closing trial balance*
- Explain why *reversing entries* are used

The accounting process we have described thus far would be adequate for only the smallest of business entities. That is, for a small business like the ones in the examples in the preceding chapters, we could prepare financial statements directly from the adjusted trial balance at the end of each accounting period — monthly, quarterly, and annually. Due to the relatively few accounts, no additional period-end accounting procedures would be required.

Additional periodic procedures are necessary

For most business entities, however, additional periodic procedures are necessary. As the number of accounts increases, it becomes more difficult to prepare the financial statements and commence a new accounting period without the aid of these additional accounting procedures. Consider for a moment the problem of a company that recorded Salaries Expense in the general ledger totaling $65,000 for the entire year 1989. During the month of January, 1990, salaries of $6,000 are incurred. In preparing financial statements for January, 1990, we can see that salaries *should be* reported at $6,000. But without some way of identifying the end of the 1989 accounting period and the start of the 1990 period, the journalization of the 1990 salaries would result in a $6,000 posting to the Salaries Expense account in the general ledger, as illustrated below:

This account is not correct because it shows salaries expense for both 1989 and 1990

Salary Expense		
Jan.–Dec. 1989	65,000	
Jan. 1990	6,000	

The result is that in the general ledger, salaries would be reflected at $71,000, representing the total from 1989 plus the first month of 1990.

We must find a way to identify clearly the 1989 salaries and distinguish them from the 1990 salaries. What we need to show is that:

The Salary Expense account for 1989 should show only 1989 salaries

and the 1990 Salary Expense account should show only 1990 salaries

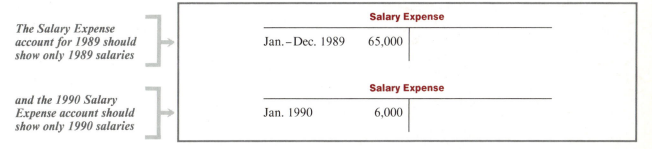

Salary Expense	
Jan.–Dec. 1989	65,000

Salary Expense	
Jan. 1990	6,000

The procedure used in accounting to solve this problem is called the ***closing process,*** which we will discuss and explain in the first half of this chapter.

The greater the number of transactions a company has, the greater the risk that errors can occur at any point where data are recorded—in recording the journal entries, posting from the journals to the ledger, or adjusting the accounts. Not only does a large number of transactions increase the risk of error, but so does the frequency with which the accounts are used. That is, larger companies must prepare financial statements more frequently, usually on a monthly basis, than smaller companies. Thus, a company that prepares financial statements more frequently suffers a greater risk of error in its reporting.

To help deal with the possibility of error, accountants use a tool called a ***worksheet.*** The worksheet helps in four ways:

1. It organizes the process of preparing the financial statements.

2. It reduces the possibility of introducing errors in that process.

3. It aids in discovering errors that do occur.

4. It provides monthly statements without the formal adjusting and closing process.

In the second half of this chapter, we will introduce the worksheet and explain how to use it.

THE CLOSING PROCESS

To prepare you for what's coming up in this chapter, we will begin by briefly reviewing and expanding on two things introduced earlier: the accounts used to prepare balance sheets—balance sheet accounts—and the accounts used to prepare income statements—income statement accounts.

Balance sheet accounts represent an account balance at a particular point in time

Balance sheet accounts represent the balance of an asset, liability, or stockholders' equity account *at a particular point in time.* For example, business transactions cause increases and decreases in the Cash account regularly throughout the accounting period. But the balance in a Cash account represents the amount of cash on hand at the time the balance is calculated. Balance sheet accounts are sometimes called ***permanent accounts*** or ***real accounts*** because, once established, they will generally remain on the books for many years.

Income statement accounts accumulate amounts for particular periods of time

Income statement accounts, which comprise *revenue accounts* and *expense accounts,* represent accumulations of revenue and expenses *during a particular period of time.* For example, a Salary Expense account represents the total salary expense incurred between the start of the accounting period and date of the income statement. When we discuss salary expense, we must specify not only the amount of the expense but also the time period during which those salaries were incurred. Are the salaries for the month? The quarter? The year 1989? The year 1990? Because revenue accounts and expense accounts reflect activity only for the period of time they cover, both of these income statement accounts are sometimes referred to as **temporary accounts,** or as **nominal accounts.** *Temporary* describes the nature of these accounts: They exist for only one accounting period. These accounts will show increases over time; they cannot show decreases.

Income statement accounts only increase during the year; they do not decrease

Deriving the Retained Earnings Account from the Revenue and Expense Accounts

If we were to rely solely on what we have learned thus far to prepare financial statements, our work would be more difficult than it need be. We would have two problems:

1. At the end of a period the Retained Earnings account would reflect a beginning-of-period balance while all other balance sheet accounts would reflect period-end balances. That's because we do not record anything in the Retained Earnings account. We use the revenue and expense accounts instead. What we must do is get the Retained Earnings account to show an end-of-period balance.

2. The balances in the revenue and expense accounts would not be for the latest accounting period (for example, the year 1989), but rather would be cumulative balances, starting from when the company first commenced operations. That is, revenue and expense account balances, as we now know them, *are not period-end balances, but cumulative balances.* We have to find some way of getting the accounts to show totals for only a single period.

The closing process transfers revenue and expense accounts back to the Retained Earnings account

The closing process is a procedure whereby the revenue and expense accounts are "transferred" back to the Retained Earnings account. This procedure makes it simpler to end one accounting period and start another. The closing process solves the two problems.

Each revenue and expense account is "closed out" at the end of an accounting period. *By* **closed out** *we simply mean that at period-end the account is reduced to a zero balance.* If we do that for each of the revenue and expense accounts, then the amount we close out will be a total for the period, for each account, not a cumulative total. A zero balance at the end of one accounting period means, of course, that the account starts with a zero balance at the beginning of the next period.

After closing, all revenue and expense accounts will have a zero balance

Now, an obvious question is, What do we do with the closed-out balances from each of the revenue and expense accounts? The answer is: We transfer them to the Retained Earnings account. In doing that, we accomplish the other objective: transferring the period-end balances from each of the revenue and expense accounts to the Retained Earnings account, yielding a Retained Earnings account that reflects period-end balances.

That's the basic idea behind the closing process. We'll now show you in a step-by-step sequence how it works, using the Graf's Wallpapering and Decorating Service adjusted trial balance, shown at the top of the facing page.

GRAF'S WALLPAPERING AND DECORATING SERVICE
Adjusted Trial Balance
December 31, 1989

Cash.........................	$ 1,250		⎫
Notes Receivable..............	2,500		⎪
Accounts Receivable	3,375		⎪
Prepaid Advertising Supplies ...	1,625		⎪
Prepaid Rent	1,750		**Balance**
Equipment	16,250		**Sheet**
Accumulated Depreciation.....		$ 7,500	**Accounts**
Salaries Payable...............		500	⎪
Notes Payable		6,250	⎪
Accounts Payable		1,125	⎪
Capital Stock		10,000	⎪
Retained Earnings.............		16,250	⎭

Dividends Account with Debit Balance {Dividends.................... 42,500 } **Dividends Account**

Revenue Accounts with Credit Balances

Wallpapering Revenue.........	62,500	⎫
Decorating Revenue...........	38,750	
Interest Income...............	250	

Expense Accounts with Debit Balances

Salary Expense................	56,250	**Income**
Depreciation Expense	3,750	**Statement**
Rent Expense.................	3,750	**Accounts**
Wallpaper Supplies Used.......	8,375	
Utilities Expense	1,125	
Interest Expense	625	

Totals	$143,125	$143,125

Closing the Expense Accounts

In the adjusted trial balance for Graf's Wallpapering and Decorating Service, there are six expense accounts, and, as we already learned, expense accounts accumulate debit balances. The six expense accounts are: Salary Expense, Depreciation Expense, Rent Expense, Wallpaper Supplies Used, Utilities Expense, and Interest Expense.

Expense accounts are closed by credits equal to the account's debit balance

An expense account is closed by "crediting" it for an amount equal to the debit balance. This results in a zero balance, or to be more consistent and precise, a zero debit balance. Remember: *A zero balance is our objective in closing an expense account at the end of a period.*

But what do we do with the debit balance that was in the expense account before we credited it?

Expense and Revenue Summary is an account that aids in the closing process

For the closing process, we must establish a temporary account called ***Expense and Revenue Summary*** (or ***Income Summary,*** or ***Profit and Loss Summary***). It is so called because it contains a record of the expenses, or debit balances, for the period, and, as we shall see, also the revenue or credit balances for the period.

The sum of the debit balances is recorded as a debit in Expense and Revenue Summary.

The closing entry recorded in the general journal for Graf's Wallpapering and Decorating Service to close the expense accounts would appear as follows:

Closing the income statement accounts with debit balances by debiting the Expense and Revenue Summary account

1989
Dec. 31 Expense and Revenue Summary 73,875
   Salary Expense 56,250
   Depreciation Expense 3,750
   Rent Expense 3,750
   Wallpaper Supplies Used 8,375
   Utilities Expense 1,125
   Interest Expense 625
  To close the expense accounts.

After posting the closing entry to the general ledger, each expense account will have a zero balance. The sum of the debit balances of the expense accounts is transferred to the Expense and Revenue Summary account as a debit. The effect of the closing process on the expense accounts is illustrated in the diagram below.

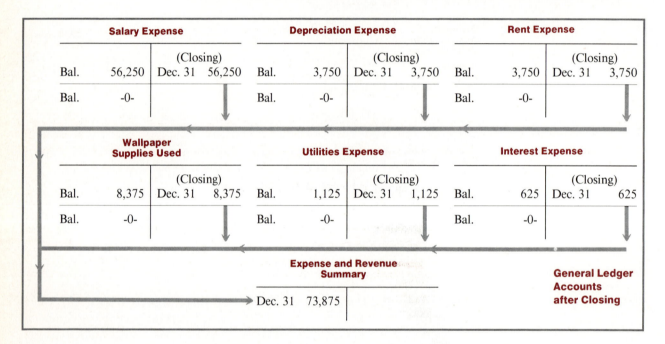

Closing the Revenue Accounts

Graf's Wallpapering and Decorating Service has three revenue accounts which, of course, have credit balances: Wallpapering Revenue, Decorating Revenue, and Interest Income. A revenue account is closed by debiting it by an amount equal to its credit balance. The result, of course, is a zero balance, or more correctly, a zero credit balance.

Revenue accounts are closed by debits equal to the account's credit balance

Each credit balance to be closed is recorded in the general journal for Graf's as follows:

To close the revenue accounts we must debit each revenue account and credit the Expense and Revenue Summary

1989
Dec. 31 Wallpapering Revenue 62,500
  Decorating Revenue 38,750
  Interest Income 250
   Expense and Revenue Summary 101,500
  To close the revenue accounts.

The sum of the three credit balances is transferred as a credit entry to the Expense and Revenue Summary. This is illustrated below.

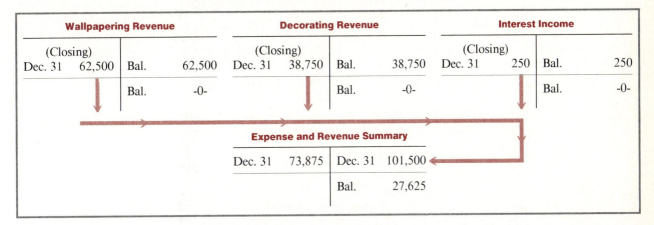

Wallpapering Revenue				**Decorating Revenue**				**Interest Income**		
(Closing)				(Closing)				(Closing)		
Dec. 31	62,500	Bal.	62,500	Dec. 31	38,750	Bal.	38,750	Dec. 31	250	Bal.	250
		Bal.	-0-			Bal.	-0-			Bal.	-0-

Expense and Revenue Summary

Dec. 31	73,875	Dec. 31	101,500
		Bal.	27,625

After all the debit and credit balances have been transferred to the Expense and Revenue Summary, each expense and revenue account is left with a zero balance ready to accumulate the next accounting period's debits and credits.

Closing the Expense and Revenue Summary

The Expense and Revenue Summary is now just that—a summary. The ***summary balance*** is the difference between the sum of the transferred debits—the expenses—and the sum of the transferred credits—the revenue—which is the net income for the period. In this case, the credit balance is $27,625, or the income for the period. If the debits had exceeded the credits, a net loss would have resulted (expenses would have been larger than revenue).

The balance in the Expense and Revenue Summary account—the $27,625 net income—is now transferred to the Retained Earnings account by a closing entry. This will increase the Retained Earnings account by the amount of the net income and reduce the Expense and Revenue Summary to a zero balance. Now (1) the Retained Earnings account reflects the effects of its component revenue and expense accounts, *and* (2) all revenue and expense accounts from this accounting period have zero balances. Our objective has been accomplished.

A third closing entry transfers the balance in the Expense and Revenue Summary to the Retained Earnings account

The general journal entry closing the Expense and Revenue Summary and the effect of posting this entry to the general ledger Retained Earnings account for Graf's Wallpapering and Decorating Service are illustrated as follows:

```
1989
Dec. 31   Expense and Revenue Summary ..........................  27,625
               Retained Earnings ....................................        27,625
          To close the expense and revenue summary account.
```

Expense and Revenue Summary				**Retained Earnings**		
Dec. 31	73,875	Dec. 31	101,500		Bal.	26,250
(Closing)					(Closing)	
Dec. 31	27,625	Bal.	27,625		Dec. 31	27,625
		Bal.	-0-			

The last closing entry transfers the Dividends account balance to the Retained Earnings account

One more step is needed to complete the closing process: We need to close out the Dividends account. The Dividends account is used whenever the owner of a business entity distributes funds to stockholders. Dividends are not expenses. For this reason the Dividends account is not closed when the expense accounts are closed to the Expense and Revenue Summary. Instead, dividends are reductions in the retained earnings of the business, just as are expenses. Also, dividends accumulate over time just as expenses do.

So for the same two reasons we closed the expense and revenue accounts—to reflect the ending Retained Earnings balance and to have a zero balance in the temporary accounts—we also close the Dividends account. This is accomplished by the following general journal entry:

```
1989
Dec. 31   Retained Earnings ......................................  42,500
                Dividends ........................................              42,500
            To close the dividends account.
```

The Retained Earnings account will reflect the ending balance after the Dividends debit has been closed, shown as follows:

Dividends		Retained Earnings		
Bal. 42,500	(Closing) Dec. 31 42,500	(Closing) Dec. 31 42,500	Bal. 26,250	Beginning Retained Earnings Balance
Bal. -0-			(Closing) Dec. 31 27,625	
			Bal. 11,375	Ending Retained Earnings Balance

With the closing of the Dividends account, the closing process is completed: All expense and revenue accounts and the Dividends account have a zero balance, and the Retained Earnings account reflects the period-end balance.

THE WORKSHEET

Worksheets are extremely important and helpful, but they are not part of the permanent accounting records of a business entity.

Records such as the general journal, the general ledger, and the financial statements are permanent. These records require that they be permanent, so they are maintained in a durable state, by use of ink in a manual system or by printed or typed material in an electronic or mechanical system.

Worksheets are prepared in pencil; they are not part of the permanent accounting records

Worksheets are prepared in pencil so that any detected errors can be easily erased and corrected prior to preparing the period-end financial statements, which are permanent. Accountants prepare worksheets to help organize the period-end accounting procedures in a logical manner.

In the process of recording in the journal and posting in the ledgers, and in adjusting and closing entries, it is not uncommon to make mistakes. To avoid the possibility of advancing those mistakes to the permanent records, it makes sense to first prepare a trial run of the period procedures. The worksheet provides this trial run.

After the worksheet is prepared, it is examined for errors. Any errors found are corrected. It is then an easy matter to prepare the formal—and permanent—financial statements from the corrected, error-free worksheet. Also, because of the way the worksheet is organized, it makes the adjusting and closing processes more straightforward and easier to do.

In the worksheet there are five column headings, each embracing a pair of debit–credit columns, as shown below:

Unadjusted Trial Balance		Adjustments		Adjusted Trial Balance		Income Statement		Balance Sheet	
Debit	Credit	Debit	Credit	Debit	Credit	Debit	Credit	Debit	Credit

Unadjusted Trial Balance Columns

The unadjusted trial balance is entered on the first pair of columns on the worksheet

After all external transactions during the accounting period have been recorded in the general journal and posted to the general ledger, the unadjusted trial balance is prepared and entered on the first pair of columns on the worksheet.

To demonstrate how to use the worksheet, we'll begin with the unadjusted trial balance of the Royal Company, shown in the worksheet below.

The unadjusted trial balance is recorded on a worksheet

ROYAL COMPANY
Worksheet
Month Ended October 31, 1989

Accounts	Unadjusted Trial Balance		Adjust
	Debit	Credit	Debit
Cash	1,960		
Accounts Receivable	3,080		
Prepaid Rent	2,520		
Office Supplies on Hand	420		
Office Equipment	7,000		
Accounts Payable		2,100	
Unearned Revenue		1,190	
Capital Stock		5,000	
Retained Earnings		4,450	
Dividends	840		
Revenue		7,840	
Salary Expense	4,620		
Utilities Expense	140		
Totals	20,580	20,580	

The Royal Company started its first operations on Oct. 1, 1989. At the end of October, in addition to what we see in the unadjusted trial balance, we also know the following facts:

1. Royal's rent is $280 per month.

2. The value of Office Supplies on Hand is $280.

3. A machine purchased and installed on the first of October is depreciated at the rate of $210 per month.

4. Revenue in the amount of $560 has been earned but not yet recorded, since cash was not received.

5. Unearned Revenue of $420, recorded earlier in the month, has been earned.

6. Salaries in the amount of $350 are owed to Royal's employees.

Adjustments Columns

Adjustments are entered in the second pair of columns on the worksheet

You may have already gotten the idea that for accounts requiring adjustments, the adjustments are not entered into the general journal. Rather, the adjustments are entered on the worksheet in the second pair of columns, labeled Adjustments.

ROYAL COMPANY
Worksheet
Month Ended October 31, 1989

Accounts	Unadjusted Trial Balance		Adjustments		Adjusted Trial Bal
	Debit	Credit	Debit	Credit	Debit
Cash	1,960				1,960
Accounts Receivable	3,080		(d) 560		3,640
Prepaid Rent	2,520			(a) 280	2,240
Office Supplies on Hand	420			(b) 140	280
Office Equipment	7,000				
Accounts Payable		2,100			
Unearned Revenue		1,190	(e) 420		
Capital Stock		5,000			
Retained Earnings		4,450			
Dividends	840				
Revenue		7,840		(d) 560	
				(e) 420	
Salary Expense	4,620		(f) 350		
Utilities Expense	140				
Totals	20,580	20,580			
Rent Expense			(a) 280		
Office Supplies Used			(b) 140		
Depreciation Expense			(c) 210		
Accumulated Depreciation				(c) 210	
Salaries Payable				(f) 350	
Totals			1,960	1,960	

Rent of $280 has expired. This amount is deducted from Prepaid Rent . . .

. . . and the account Rent Expense is inserted on the worksheet

Now, let's see how adjustments are handled on the worksheet. We will consider how to make adjustments for the six items already introduced. Refer to the worksheet on page 142 as you go through the steps.

1. The $2,520 Prepaid Rent on the unadjusted trial balance represents rent paid in advance on Oct. 1, 1989, for the next 9 months (Royal's rent is $280 per month) ending June 30, 1990. Since the month of October has expired, we must recognize 1 month's rent expense and reduce the prepaid rent by $280.

   The first step in making this adjustment: On the worksheet enter $280 in the credit column under Adjustments and opposite the Prepaid Rent account.

   The second step: Subtract $280 credit adjustment from the $2,520 debit balance in the unadjusted trial balance. The result yields a $2,240 debit balance remaining, which will be reflected in the adjusted trial balance column for Prepaid Rent. (To focus on one thing at a time — in this case, how and what to record in the adjustments column — we will forego discussion of this step and the adjusted trial balance as we proceed through the following items, confining our explanation mostly to the adjustments columns. We will return to the adjusted trial balance as the next topic in explaining how to use the worksheet.)

   The third step: The debit portion of the adjustment is to recognize $280 Rent Expense. But this account, Rent Expense, does not appear on the unadjusted trial balance. We must introduce a Rent Expense account to the worksheet. Once we do that, we can enter opposite Rent Expense and under Adjustments a $280 debit, as shown in the illustration.

   The fourth step: We have just made one adjustment. Soon, we will have made a number of adjustments in the adjustments column. Remember that one of the purposes of the worksheet is to help us analyze and review all the adjustments for the period, to examine the adjustments for errors (if it turns out that the period-end balance doesn't balance), and to correct them. To do that, we will need some way of quickly and easily identifying the corresponding pairs of debits and credits comprising each adjustment. Thus, we *key* with a reference letter the debit and credit entries that comprise an adjustment. To identify the adjustments originating with the unadjusted Prepaid Rent account, see in the illustration that we use the letter *a* to designate the credit component, the $280 credit adjustment to Prepaid Rent, as well as the debit component, the corresponding $280 debit adjustment to Rent Expense. This letter *a* identifies the debit and credit adjustments that comprise the adjustment to the Prepaid Rent account at the end of the period.

The debit and credit portions of an adjusting entry are identified on a worksheet by a reference letter

2. A count of the office supplies on hand on the last day of the month reveals that the value of the supplies on hand at the end of the month is $280. Since the Office Supplies on Hand account had a $420 debit balance on the first of the month, we will need an adjustment of $140. On the worksheet under the adjustments column, a $140 credit is entered for the Office Supplies on Hand account. This $140 credit adjustment results in a $280 debit balance, as shown under the adjusted trial balance column, at the end of the period for the Office Supplies on Hand account.

   Since office supplies were used during the month and since there was no Office Supplies Used account listed in the unadjusted trial balance, we must introduce that account. The $140 expense is then recognized on the worksheet by entering a $140 debit under the adjustments column opposite the newly introduced Office Supplies Used account. The credit and debit are both keyed with *b* to identify this adjustment.

Office supplies of $140 are consumed. The Office Supplies Used account must be inserted on the worksheet.

For the depreciation of $210, both the Depreciation Expense and the Accumulated Depreciation accounts must be added

3. Depreciation for the month amounts to $210. However, notice that neither the expense account, Depreciation Expense, nor the contra-asset account, Accumulated Depreciation, appears on the unadjusted trial balance. Because both accounts are needed to account for—that is, *adjust*—the $210 depreciation, we simply introduce them on the worksheet. Under the adjustments column opposite the newly introduced Depreciation Expense account we enter a $210 debit, and corresponding to that, we enter a $210 credit under the adjustments column opposite the newly introduced Accumulated Depreciation account. The letter *c* identifies the debit and the credit corresponding to the depreciation adjustment. (Note: Because this is the first month of the first year of operations, there are no prior-years' activities. Specifically, depreciation is not reflected in an Accumulated Depreciation account. In subsequent periods, the account Accumulated Depreciation will, of course, have a balance.)

4. At the end of the month, $560 of revenue was earned but has not been recorded. For this adjustment, keyed with *d*, we must record a $560 debit opposite Accounts Receivable and a corresponding $560 credit opposite Revenue.

5. Unearned revenue recorded previously in the month in the amount of $420 was earned by the end of the month. The adjustment for this is that a $420 debit is entered for the Unearned Revenue account and a $420 credit is entered for Revenue, each entry keyed *e*. Note that there are two adjustments for Revenue: *d*, $560 credit from Accounts Receivable, and *e*, $420 credit from Unearned Revenue.

6. Accrued salaries on Oct. 31, 1989, amount to $350. By now you should be able to make this adjustment quickly and easily. For the Salary Expense account, enter a $350 debit under the adjustments column; and introduce a new account, Salaries Payable, for which you enter a $350 credit, all of which is keyed *f*.

After the last adjustment has been entered on the worksheet, caution dictates that we check our work at this point before we proceed to the next column. The debit column is totaled and the credit column is totaled. If the sum of the debits equals the sum of the credits, we may proceed. If not, then there is an error somewhere in the adjustments column.

We have seen that there are cases when accounts must be introduced into the worksheet when making adjustments. After you have prepared several worksheets and become more familiar with the adjusting process, you will learn to anticipate the need for additional accounts and what accounts you will need. You will then be able to allow sufficient space in appropriate places on the worksheet for these accounts.

It might be helpful to consider that there are two ways of looking at the entries in the adjustments column: (1) there are those adjustments made to the trial balance accounts already recorded in the first column of the worksheet (see the top of the adjustments column); and (2) there are those adjustments to accounts that are not on the worksheet and that have to be introduced (see the bottom of the adjustments column).

Adjusted Trial Balance Columns

The adjusted trial balance reflects the adjustments to the unadjusted trial balance

The adjusted trial balance column is, like all the headings on the worksheet, exactly what it says it is. The "adjusted" column reflects "adjustments" to the "unadjusted" column.

For each account, the unadjusted trial balance debits and the adjustments debits are added and the sum is recorded in the debit column of the adjusted trial balance.

For example, Accounts Receivable has a $3,080 debit in the unadjusted trial balance. This debit is added to the $560 debit adjustment, and the result is the $3,640 debit in the adjusted trial balance. Of course, the same is done for the credits for each account. For accounts that are newly introduced on the worksheet, the adjusted balances — the adjustment debits and credits — are simply carried over into the adjusted trial balance columns.

The first thing we do with the adjusted trial balance is the same thing we just did with the adjustments: We add up all the debits and add up all the credits. If the sum of the debits equals the sum of the credits, then we can be assured that we have not made any arithmetic errors in the amounts in the adjusted trial balance columns. If it turns out that the sums don't balance — aren't equal — then we have some work to do: We must look for the error or errors and correct them. Once we are assured that the sums of the adjusted debits and credits are equal, the adjusted trial balance is ready for us to use in preparing the worksheet income statement and balance sheets, which are the next sequence of worksheet columns.

The worksheet for Royal Company below has been extended to the point where it illustrates the progress to the adjusted trial balance from the preceding columns.

If you have already observed something about the totals of the columns, you are beginning to think like an accountant: The total of the adjusted debits is $21,700,

ROYAL COMPANY
Worksheet
Month Ended October 31, 1989

Accounts	Unadjusted Trial Balance		Adjustments		Adjusted Trial Balance		Income State
	Debit	Credit	Debit	Credit	Debit	Credit	
Cash	1,960				1,960		
Accounts Receivable	3,080		(d) 560		3,640		
Prepaid Rent	2,520			(a) 280	2,240		
Office Supplies on Hand	420			(b) 140	280		
Office Equipment	7,000				7,000		
Accounts Payable		2,100				2,100	
Unearned Revenue		1,190	(e) 420			770	
Capital Stock		5,000				5,000	
Retained Earnings		4,450				4,450	
Dividends	840				840		
Revenue		7,840		(d) 560		8,820	
				(e) 420			
Salary Expense	4,620		(f) 350		4,970		
Utilities Expense	140				140		
Totals	20,580	20,580					
Rent Expense			(a) 280		280		
Office Supplies Used			(b) 140		140		
Depreciation Expense			(c) 210		210		
Accumulated Depreciation				(c) 210		210	
Salaries Payable				(f) 350		350	
Totals			1,960	1,960	21,700	21,700	

which is *not* equal to the sum of the totals of the unadjusted debits and the adjustments debits ($20,580 + $1,960 = $22,540). Of course, the same is true for the credits: The credit total of the third column does not equal the sum of the totals of the credits of the first two columns.

If you already understand why, then you are beginning to think like a keen accountant. The reason for the apparent inconsistency can be explained as follows: While debits in the adjustments column may be added to debits in the unadjusted trial balance column in arriving at the total debits in the adjusted trial balance column—as with the salary expense ($4,620 Dr. + $350 Dr. = $4,970 Dr.)—debits in the adjustments column *may also be subtracted* from credits in the unadjusted trial balance column in arriving at the credit balance in the adjusted trial balance. Unearned revenue provides an example on the Royal Company worksheet—$1,190 Cr. − $420 Dr. = $770 Cr. Of course, the same is true when dealing with the credit adjustment—Office Supplies on Hand ($420 Dr. − $140 Cr. = $280 Dr.).

Income Statement and Balance Sheet Columns

Income statement accounts from the adjusted trial balance are transferred to the income statement columns

The next step in using the worksheet is to separate the adjusted trial balance into income statement account balances and balance sheet account balances. The procedure is simply to transfer from the adjusted trial balance columns each debit and credit balance to its proper place in the income statement columns and each debit and credit balance to its proper place in the balance sheet columns. How well you do that depends, of course, on how well you know which are income statement accounts and which are balance sheet accounts. (Refer to the worksheet on the facing page as you proceed through the following discussion.)

Balance sheet accounts are transferred to the balance sheet columns

For example, Cash is a balance sheet account; therefore, we carry the $1,960 debit from the adjusted trial balance forward to the balance sheet debit column. Accounts Receivable is also a balance sheet account, so of course we carry the $3,640 adjusted trial balance debit balance forward to the balance sheet debit column. Revenue and Salary Expense are both income statement accounts; thus the $8,820 Adjusted Revenue credit is carried forward as an income statement credit, and the $4,970 Salary Expense debit is carried forward as a debit on the income statement.

As always, attention to detail is very important. Carrying an account balance forward to the wrong column is a common error, as you will soon discover. Carrying the Salaries Payable balance to the income statement credit column is perhaps the most common student error. This is so because of the location of Salaries Payable on the worksheet. It is not found near the other balance sheet accounts because it was added to the bottom of the worksheet by the Salaries adjusting entry; it is located with the income statement accounts. The tendency is to carry the balance to the income statement credit column, because most of the other accounts in this section of the worksheet are carried there. It is a simple, inadvertent error, but it is nevertheless an error.

After all items from the adjusted trial balance have been carried forward to their proper places, each income statement column is totaled and each balance sheet column is totaled.

The total of the income statement credit column (in this example there is only one income statement credit) is $8,820. The total of the income statement debits is $5,740. The income statement credits exceed the income statement debits by $3,080, which is the *net income* for the month. If the debit column had exceeded the credit column, a *net loss* would have been the result.

The balance sheet debits add up to $15,960. Balance sheet credits add up to $12,880. Balance sheet debits exceed balance sheet credits by $3,080, which is the net

	ROYAL COMPANY Worksheet Month Ended October 31, 1989											
	Unadjusted Trial Balance		Adjustments		Adjusted Trial Balance		Income Statement		Balance Sheet	
Accounts	**Debit**	**Credit**	**Debit**	**Credit**	**Debit**	**Credit**	**Debit**	**Credit**	**Debit**	**Credit**
Cash	1,960				1,960				1,960	
Accounts Receivable	3,080		(d) 560		3,640				3,640	
Prepaid Rent	2,520			(a) 280	2,240				2,240	
Office Supplies on Hand	420			(b) 140	280				280	
Office Equipment	7,000				7,000				7,000	
Accounts Payable		2,100				2,100				2,100
Unearned Revenue		1,190	(e) 420			770				770
Capital Stock		5,000				5,000				5,000
Retained Earnings		4,450				4,450				4,450
Dividends	840				840				840	
Revenue		7,840		(d) 560						
				(e) 420		8,820		8,820		
Salary Expense	4,620		(f) 350		4,970		4,970			
Utilities Expense	140				140		140			
Totals	20,580	20,580								
Rent Expense			(a) 280		280		280			
Office Supplies Used			(b) 140		140		140			
Depreciation Expense			(c) 210		210		210			
Accumulated Depreciation				(c) 210		210				210
Salaries Payable				(f) 350		350				350
Totals			1,960	1,960	21,700	21,700	5,740	8,820	15,960	12,880
Net Income							3,080			3,080
Totals							8,820	8,820	15,960	15,960

income. The balance sheet cannot balance until net income is added to the Retained Earnings account. Remember, the Retained Earnings account reflects the *beginning* rather than the *ending* balance. Net income must be added (and dividends subtracted) to arrive at the ending Retained Earnings balance.

If the net income (or loss) determined from the totals of the income statement column debits and credits turns out to be different from the net income (or loss) determined from the totals of the balance sheet column debits and credits, then you can be sure the worksheet contains one or more errors.

But if the net income (or loss) determined from the income statement columns turns out to be the same as the net income (or loss) determined from the balance sheet columns, can you be sure that there are no errors in the worksheet? The answer is no. For example, if Salaries Payable had been incorrectly entered as an income statement credit item rather than a balance sheet credit item, the affected parts of the worksheet would appear as shown at the top of the next page.

The worksheet may "balance" but still contain an error

Accounts	Unadjusted Trial Balance		Income Statement		Balance Sheet	
	Debit	Credit	Debit	Credit	Debit	Credit
Cash					1,960	
Salaries Payable				350		
			5,740	9,170	15,960	12,530
Net Income			3,430			3,430
			9,170	9,170	15,960	15,960

Because this is in the wrong place

this is wrong

Caution: *This net income is wrong because the Salaries Payable credit balance was entered incorrectly in the income statement credit column*

Although Salaries Payable was entered in the wrong place, Net Income is $3,430 as determined by both the income statement columns and the balance sheet columns arithmetic. But $3,430 is not the correct income, because the total credits on both the income statement column and the balance sheet column are wrong. The error would most likely be discovered when we prepare the income statement. We would, hopefully, recognize that Salaries Payable should not be classified as a revenue item.

Preparing the Financial Statements

The income statement is prepared first

Keep in mind that the sole purpose of preparing the worksheet is to aid in the preparation of the financial statements. If worksheets didn't serve this purpose, we wouldn't use them. Once a worksheet is prepared, it is easy to prepare the financial statements. The income statement is prepared from the information contained on the worksheet in the income statement columns; for our example, it appears as follows:

ROYAL COMPANY
Income Statement
Month Ended October 31, 1989

Revenue		$8,820
Expenses:		
Salary Expense	$4,970	
Utilities Expense	140	
Rent Expense	280	
Office Supplies Used	140	
Depreciation Expense	210	
Total Expenses		5,740
Net Income		$3,080

Next, the ending stockholders' equity must be determined which may be part of the balance sheet

The balance sheet is prepared in a similar manner. Remember, however, that the worksheet contains the *beginning* Retained Earnings balance, which must be adjusted by the net income and dividends to arrive at the ending Retained Earnings balance. So the *ending* Retained Earnings balance is computed like this: $4,450 beginning balance + $3,080 net income − $840 dividends = $6,690 ending balance.

ROYAL COMPANY
Balance Sheet
October 31, 1989

Assets			Liabilities and Stockholders' Equity		
Current Assets:			Current Liabilities:		
Cash	$1,960		Accounts Payable	$2,100	
Accounts Receivable	3,640		Salaries Payable	350	
Prepaid Rent	2,240		Unearned Revenue	770	
Office Supplies on Hand	280		Total Current Liabilities		$ 3,220
Total Current Assets		$ 8,120			
			Stockholders' Equity:		
Plant and Equipment:			Capital Stock	$5,000	
Office Equipment	$7,000		Retained Earnings	6,690	
Less: Accumulated Depreciation	210		Total Stockholders' Equity		11,690
Total Plant and Equipment		6,790			
			Total Liabilities and Stockholders'		
Total Assets		$14,910	Equity		$14,910

Journalizing the Adjusting and Closing Entries

Adjusting and closing entries may be recorded in the general journal and general ledger either at the end of each month, each quarter, or at the end of the year, depending on the company's policy. The most common period to formally adjust and close the accounts is annually. If it is a company's policy to formally adjust and close at the end of each year, then after the worksheet is completed and financial statements are prepared at the end of each month or quarter, no further periodic procedures are needed. The adjusting and closing entries are not journalized and consequently not posted.

The adjusting and closing entries may be recorded at the end of each month, each quarter, or at year-end

But at year-end, after the worksheet is completed and the financial statements are prepared, the adjusting and closing entries are formally journalized. For adjusting entries this involves merely recording in the general journal information contained in the adjustments columns of the worksheet. Once the adjusting entries are journalized, they are then posted to the general ledger accounts.

Let's see how this works for the Royal Company. After Royal's financial statements have been prepared for the period ended Oct. 31, 1989, the adjusting entries are entered in the general journal as shown on page 150.

The adjusting entries are then posted to the general ledger, as can be seen in the Royal Company general ledger illustrated on page 151.

Closing Entries

The closing entries are also prepared from the information contained on the worksheet. By using the income statement debit and credit columns on the worksheet and the amount of the Dividends in the debit balance sheet column, the closing entries can be prepared.

In the worksheet, the accounts shown in the income statement debit column, all of which are expenses, are credited in the general ledger to reduce them to a zero balance. The expense accounts are now ready for the next accounting period. The total of the debit column, $5,740, which is the total of the expenses, is now debited to the Expense and Revenue Summary account, which as you recall is a new account established just to facilitate the closing process.

Each account in the income statement credit column (in this example there is only one account) is credited to reduce it to a zero balance so that the revenue accounts are

Adjusting Entries
Adjusting entries are prepared from the worksheet.

ROYAL COMPANY
General Journal

Page 12

Date	Account Titles and Explanation	Post. Ref.	Debit	Credit
Oct. 31	Rent Expense		2 8 0	
	Prepaid Rent			2 8 0
	To adjust prepaid rent and recognize			
	rent expense for the month.			
31	Office Supplies Used		1 4 0	
	Office Supplies on Hand			1 4 0
	To adjust office supplies on hand and			
	recognize office supplies used for the			
	month.			
31	Depreciation Expense		2 1 0	
	Accumulated Depreciation			2 1 0
	To record depreciation expense for			
	the month.			
31	Accounts Receivable		5 6 0	
	Revenue			5 6 0
	To record revenue earned but not			
	collected at end of month.			
31	Unearned Revenue		4 2 0	
	Revenue			4 2 0
	To adjust unearned revenue and to			
	recognize revenue earned for the			
	month.			
31	Salary Expense		3 5 0	
	Salaries Payable			3 5 0
	To record accrued salaries at the end			
	of the month.			

ready to be used for the next accounting period. And the Expense and Revenue Summary account is credited for the total of the credit income statement column, $8,820 — the total revenue.

The Expense and Revenue Summary account will now have a credit balance of $3,080 — the net income ($8,820 Cr. − $5,740 Dr.) for the month. The net income is transferred to the Retained Earnings account by a debit of $3,080 to the Expense and Revenue Summary account (reducing this account to a zero balance) and a credit to the Retained Earnings account.

Finally, the Dividends are transferred to the Retained Earnings account by a debit to the Retained Earnings account of $840 and a corresponding credit to the Dividends account (reducing the Dividends account to a zero balance).

ROYAL COMPANY
General Ledger

Cash				
Bal.	1,960			

Unearned Revenue				
GJ 12	420	Bal.	1,190	
		Bal.	770	

Rent Expense				
GJ 12	280	GJ 13	280	

Capital Stock				
		Bal.	5,000	

Accounts Receivable				
Bal.	3,080			
GJ 12	560			
Bal.	3,640			

Retained Earnings				
		Bal.	4,450	
GJ 13	840	GJ 13	3,080	
		Bal.	6,690	

Office Supplies Used				
GJ 12	140	GJ 13	140	

Prepaid Rent				
Bal.	2,520	GJ 12	280	
Bal.	2,240			

Dividends				
Bal.	840	GJ 13	840	

Depreciation Expense				
GJ 12	210	GJ 13	210	

Office Supplies on Hand				
Bal.	420	GJ 12	140	
Bal.	280			

Revenue				
		Bal.	7,840	
		GJ 12	560	
		GJ 12	420	
GJ 13	8,820		8,820	

Accumulated Depreciation				
		GJ 12	210	

Office Equipment				
Bal.	7,000			

Salary Expense				
Bal.	4,620			
GJ 12	350			
	4,970	GJ 13	4,970	

Salaries Payable				
		GJ 12	350	

Accounts Payable				
		Bal.	2,100	

Utilities Expense				
Bal.	140	GJ 13	140	

Expense and Revenue Summary				
GJ 13	5,740	GJ 13	8,820	
GJ 13	3,080		3,080	

The general ledger after the adjusting and closing entries have been posted.

The closing entries of the Royal Company are presented in the general journal shown below.

ROYAL COMPANY General Journal						Page 13
Date	**Description**	**Post. Ref.**	**Debit**		**Credit**	
1987 Oct. 31	Expense and Revenue Summary		5740			
	Salary Expense				4970	
	Utilities Expense				140	
	Rent Expense				280	
	Office Supplies Used				140	
	Depreciation Expense				210	
	To close the expense accounts.					
31	Revenue		8820			
	Expense and Revenue					
	Summary				8820	
	To close the revenue accounts.					
31	Expense and Revenue Summary		3080			
	Retained Earnings				3080	
	To close the expense and revenue summary.					
31	Retained Earnings		840			
	Dividends				840	
	To close dividends account.					

Post-Closing Trial Balance

We need a final joint check on the adjusting and closing process. This check is the *post-closing trial balance.* A post-closing trial balance contains only asset, liability,

ROYAL COMPANY Post-Closing Trial Balance October 31, 1989		
Cash	$ 1,960	
Accounts Receivable	3,640	
Prepaid Rent	2,240	
Office Supplies on Hand	280	
Office Equipment	7,000	
Accumulated Depreciation		$ 210
Accounts Payable		2,100
Salaries Payable		350
Unearned Revenue		770
Capital Stock		5,000
Retained Earnings		6,690
Totals	$15,120	$15,120

and stockholders' equity accounts because all revenue, expense, and Dividends accounts *have been closed,* their balances having been transferred to the Retained Earnings account. As the name implies, a post-closing trial balance is prepared from the general ledger after the adjusting and closing entries have been posted. Presented at the bottom of the facing page is the Oct. 31, 1989, post-closing trial balance of the Royal Company.

Interim Statements

Monthly and quarterly financial statements are called interim statements

A principal advantage of the worksheet is that we can prepare financial statements from it directly, and without having to formally adjust and close the general ledger accounts. We may wish to do this for interim periods. By the term *interim periods* we mean the accounting periods contained within the annual accounting period — monthly and quarterly accounting periods, as illustrated in the following diagram:

	Accounting Periods						
	Jan.	**Feb.**	**Mar.**	**Apr.**	**May**	**Nov.**	**Dec.**
Monthly	First month	Second month	Third month	Fourth month	Fifth month	Eleventh month	Twelfth month
Quarterly		First quarter			Second quarter		Fourth quarter
Annual				Year			

Financial statements can be and are prepared informally from the worksheet on a monthly or quarterly basis. Such statements are called *interim statements.*

For the first month of the year the monthly interim financial statements are prepared directly from the worksheet, just as we described in the previous sections. But the adjusting and closing entries *are not journalized.* At the end of the second month another worksheet is prepared. The adjustments on this second worksheet must be recorded *cumulatively* for the 2 months. For example, since the Royal Company started operations on Oct. 1, 1989, the adjustments on the worksheet as of Oct. 31 represent *only 1 month's activity.*

For the second worksheet, which would be dated Nov. 30, 1989, *2 months'* activity would be reflected by the worksheet adjustments. For example, the Prepaid Rent adjustment for Nov. 30, 1989, would appear as follows:

	ROYAL COMPANY **Worksheet** **Two Months Ended November 30, 1989**										
	Unadjusted Trial Balance		**Adjustments**		**Adjusted Trial Balance**		**Income Statement**		**Balance Sheet**	
Accounts	**Debit**	**Credit**	**Debit**	**Credit**	**Debit**	**Credit**	**Debit**	**Credit**	**Debit**	**Credit**
Prepaid Rent	2,520			(*a*) 560	1,960				1,960	
Rent Expense			(*a*) 560		560		560			

Worksheet adjustments are cumulative

Rent Expense is recorded as a $560 debit, representing *2 months'* expense. When the income statement is prepared for the month of November, it will represent financial activity for the 2-month period. In order to prepare an income statement solely for the month of November, the income statement items from the month of October must be subtracted from the income statement items for the 2-month period ended Nov. 30, 1989, as illustrated below.

	From the Nov. 30 Worksheet Representing 2 Months	From the Oct. 31 Worksheet Representing 1 Month	Income Statement for the Month of November
Revenue......................................	$19,740	$8,820	$10,920
Expenses:			
Salary Expense	$10,500	$4,970	$ 5,530
Utilities Expense.............................	350	140	210
Rent Expense	560	280	280
Office Supplies Used	490	140	350
Depreciation Expense	420	210	210
Total Expense...........................	$12,320	$5,740	$ 6,580
Net Income	$ 7,420	$3,080	$ 4,340

The balance sheet can be prepared directly from the Nov. 30 worksheet since balance sheet accounts, by their nature, are cumulative anyway.

Quarterly interim income statements are prepared by adding together the monthly income statements comprising the quarter, except the first quarter. Can you see why? At the end of the first quarter the worksheet prepared at that time will reflect 3 months' activity — the quarter's activity. So the figures on the first-quarter worksheet are used for the first-quarter interim income statements.

A company may elect to adjust and close its accounts monthly if it so wishes. But if the company elects to adjust and close its accounts only at the end of the yearly accounting period, the worksheet can be used to provide the necessary information for the preparation of the interim financial statements.

ACCOUNTING POLICY AND ADJUSTING ENTRIES

Let's return for a moment to the Royal example (page 141) and the account Prepaid Rent. Royal made an advance cash payment for 9 months' rent. We have already described that transaction in academic terms as an external transaction that will provide future economic benefits, and we recorded it in the asset account.

The mirror image of this transaction is the payment received from Royal by the business entity renting the building — or office space or whatever — to Royal. This business entity has incurred an obligation that must be fulfilled over the next 9 months. If we were this company, we would record this obligation in a liability account called Unearned Rental Revenue.

On either side of this event — one side is paying for the rent in advance, the other side is receiving rent in advance — the economic substance of the transaction does, in fact, represent an asset (rental fees paid for) and a liability (rental services owed for fees received).

We have used balance sheet accounts to record either side of the transaction (Prepaid Rent or Unearned Rental Revenue). These accounts must be adjusted as each month passes and monthly financial statements are prepared. Royal's Prepaid Rent account will be reduced and the Rent Expense account increased as service is received; the building owner's Unearned Rental Revenue account will be reduced and the Rental Revenue account will be increased as it "delivers" the monthly rental service. The financial statements will reflect the expense incurred or revenue earned, and the remaining future economic benefit or future obligation.

But what would happen if Royal had elected to record the $2,250 advance rental payment for 9 months' rent in the Rent Expense account rather than the Prepaid Rent account? Would there be economic calamity? Would the FASB expel Royal from the business community? Of course not. No one really cares how Royal elects to record its transactions *so long as its financial statements reflect the economic substance of the transactions.* That is why adjusting entries are made: to adjust the accounts so that the financial statements prepared from the accounts—or as we now know, from the worksheet—do in fact reflect the economic substance of the multitude of transactions the business entity entered into during the accounting period.

The question that should now be asked is, *Why?* Why record rent paid in advance as an expense? Here's why. Let's assume that Royal has an accounting year of Oct. 1 to Sept. 30. And that Royal *does not* prepare monthly adjusting and closing entries. Instead, Royal prepares cumulative adjustments on the various monthly worksheets and prepares financial statements directly from those worksheets.

At the end of the first month an adjusting entry is needed on the worksheet that will reduce the Rent Expense from $2,520 to $280—1 month's rent. The entry must also establish the asset account Prepaid Rent to reflect 8 months' future economic benefit — $2,240. The entry would appear on the worksheet as follows:

	Unadjusted Trial Balance		Adjustments		Adjusted Trial Balance	
ROYAL COMPANY **Worksheet** **Month Ended October 31, 1989**						
Accounts	**Debit**	**Credit**	**Debit**	**Credit**	**Debit**	**Credit**
Prepaid Rent			(*a*) 2,240		2,240	
Rent Expense	2,520			(*a*) 2,240	280	

Now, compare the *adjusted trial balance* above with the one on page 147. Prepaid Rent ($2,240) and Rent Expense ($280) are the same in both cases. Thus, the financial statements will reflect the economic substance of the transaction.

Let's move 9 months down the road. Can you see that no adjusting entry is required? As of June 30, Rent Expense for the year is $2,520 and no Prepaid Rent exists. This may be the reason Royal elected to record the transaction initially in an expense account. They know that by the time the year is over—assuming that the rental agreement is not renewed—no *formal* adjusting entry will be required. Remember that we assumed Royal adjusts and closes the books only at year-end.

Transactions may be recorded initially in expense or revenue accounts

You can see now that *there may be occasions where a business entity may elect to record a transaction in an expense account rather than an asset account. And, the mirror image of the transaction may be recorded in a revenue account rather than a liability account.* This is an *accounting policy decision.* Once the decision is made, the accountant will then follow the policy in recording the transaction and make the appropriate adjusting entry based on that policy decision.

In the following two sections, we will show through examples how the accounting policy selected determines the way accounts are adjusted.

Asset vs. Expense Classification

Acquisition of certain assets may be recorded as expenses, then later be adjusted

On Oct. 1, 1989, the Cannon Company acquires a 3-year insurance policy for $1,200 paid in advance. Cannon will record this transaction in one of two ways, depending on which of two possible accounting policies it follows. The $1,200 payment may initially be recorded either as an asset or as an expense; both possibilities are illustrated as follows:

Date	. . . an Asset	Initial Entry Recorded as . . . . . . or as		. . . an Expense	
1989	Prepaid Insurance	1,200		Insurance Expense	1,200	
	Cash		1,200	Cash		1,200

When an insurance policy is acquired, it can be recorded as either an asset or an expense . . .

Financial statements are to be prepared on Dec. 31, 1989. At $1,200 for 3 years, the cost of insurance comes out to $33.33 per month. On Dec. 31, 3 months' insurance has been consumed, or

$$\text{Insurance expense} = \$33.33 \text{ per month} \times 3 \text{ months} = \$100$$

leaving 33 months' insurance remaining, or

$$\text{Prepaid insurance} = \$1,200 - (\$33.33 \text{ per month} \times 3 \text{ months}) = \$1,100$$

on Dec. 31.

Prepaid Insurance must reflect a $1,100 debit balance and Insurance Expense must be stated at $100. To arrive at these debit balances, an adjusting entry is required. The appropriate adjustment depends on how the initial transaction was recorded. Presented below in general journal entry form are the required adjusting entries.

. . . so long as the appropriate adjusting entry is made.

Date	Adjusting Entry Required If Initial Entry Recorded as . . . . . . an Asset		. . . or as	. . . an Expense	
1989					
Dec. 31	Insurance Expense	100		Prepaid Insurance	1,100	
	Prepaid Insurance		100	Insurance Expense		1,100

The effect of the adjusting entries on the general ledger accounts is illustrated below for both accounting policies.

	General Ledger Accounts after Adjusting Entry If Initial Entry Recorded as . . .		
	. . . an Asset	. . . or as	. . . an Expense
	Prepaid Insurance		**Prepaid Insurance**
10/1/89 1,200	12/31/89 Adj. 100	12/31/89 Adj. 1,100	
12/31/89 1,100			
	Insurance Expense		**Insurance Expense**
12/31/89 Adj. 100		10/1/89 1,200	12/31/89 Adj. 1,100
		12/31/89 Bal. 100	

Liability vs. Revenue Classification

The Morrow Company received a check on July 1, 1989, for $1,600, representing 2 years' rent paid in advance. At this date, Morrow may record a credit in that amount for either Unearned Rental Revenue or Rental Revenue, depending on its accounting policy, as follows:

When cash is received for rent paid in advance, the entry can be recorded as a liability or as revenue . . .

Date	. . . a Liability	Initial Entry Recorded as . . . . . . or as	. . . a Revenue	
1989				
July 1	Cash. 1,600		Cash. 1,600	
	Unearned Rental Revenue .	1,600	Rental Revenue	1,600

On Dec. 31, 1989, financial statements are required. At $1,600 for 2 years, the revenue from rentals will be $66.67 per month. On Dec. 31, 6 months' rental revenue has been earned, or

$$\text{Rental revenue} = \$66.67 \text{ per month} \times 6 \text{ months} = \$400$$

leaving 18 months' unearned rental revenue remaining, or

$$\text{Unearned rental revenue} = \$1,600 - (\$66.67 \text{ per mo.} \times 6 \text{ mos.}) = \$1,200$$

On Dec. 31 Unearned Rental Revenue must reflect a $1,200 credit balance and Rental Revenue must be stated at $400. The adjusting entries required to achieve these balances are presented as follows:

. . . so long as the appropriate adjusting entry is made.

Date	. . . a Liability	Adjusting Entry Required If Initial Entry Recorded as . . . . . . or as	. . . a Revenue	
1989				
Dec. 31	Unearned Rental Revenue. 400		Rental Revenue 1,200	
	Rental Revenue	400	Unearned Rental Revenue. .	1,200

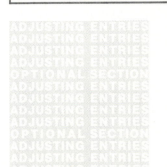

Illustrated below are the general ledger accounts after the appropriate adjusting entries have been made.

		General Ledger Accounts after Adjusting Entry If Initial Entry Recorded as . . .		
	. . . a Liability	. . . or as	. . . a Revenue	

Unearned Rental Revenue (as a Liability)

12/31/89 Adj.	400	7/1/89	1,600
		12/31/89 Bal.	1,200

Unearned Rental Revenue (as a Revenue)

12/31/89 Adj.	1,200

Rental Revenue (as a Liability)

12/31/89 Adj.	400

Rental Revenue (as a Revenue)

12/31/89 Adj.	1,200	7/1/89	1,600
		12/31/89 Bal.	400

REVERSING ENTRIES

In the preceding two examples we have seen how the choice of an accounting policy affects the manner in which adjusting entries are recorded. Recording the advance payment for insurance in the Insurance Expense account requires an adjusting entry that establishes the Prepaid Insurance account at year-end and reduces the Insurance Expense account to an amount actually consumed. Likewise, when rent payments are received in advance and recorded as Rental Revenue, the appropriate adjustment at year-end is to establish the Unearned Rental Revenue account and reduce the Rental Revenue to the amount actually earned.

The policy of recording entries in income statement accounts (Insurance Expense and Rental Revenue, for example) that require year-end adjustments presents a bookkeeping problem in subsequent accounting periods.

Refer back to the Cannon example (page 156) of the $1,200 insurance policy acquired on Oct. 1, 1989. Now look ahead to 1990 and assume that Cannon buys a second policy on Apr. 1 for $800. It's a 1-year policy. How will this be recorded? Let's assume that the accounting policy is to use income statement accounts; thus the entry will be:

```
1990
Apr. 1  Insurance Expense........................................... 800
             Cash...................................................         800
```

But wait a minute: Where is the unconsumed insurance from the first policy—the Prepaid Insurance? It's in the Prepaid Insurance account, having been transferred there by the Dec. 31 adjusting entry. Further, the Insurance Expense account for 1989 has been closed out by the Dec. 31 closing entry. The ledger accounts on Apr. 1, 1990, accordingly would appear as follows:

Prepaid Insurance			Insurance Expense			
12/31/89	1,100		10/1/89	1,200	12/31/89 Adj.	1,100
			12/31/89 Bal.	100	12/31/89 Closing	100
			1/1/90 Bal.	-0-		
			4/1/90	800		

We now have our eggs in two baskets; they should be in one. We have $1,100 in Prepaid Insurance and $800 in Insurance Expense. What needs to be done is to *transfer* the $1,100 from the Prepaid Insurance account to the Insurance Expense account because it is the Cannon Company's accounting policy to record insurance in the Insurance Expense account. The general journal entry required to accomplish this would be as follows:

```
1990
Jan. 1   Insurance Expense...........................................   1,100
               Prepaid Insurance .......................................          1,100
```

Reversing entries are exactly the opposite of adjusting entries

Compare this entry to the adjusting entry recorded on page 156, where the insurance was initially recorded as an expense. It is exactly the opposite, the *reverse.* For this reason it is called a ***reversing entry.***

Reversing entries are prepared as of the first day of a new accounting period. The entry to reverse the Morrow Company's Dec. 31 adjusting entry (assuming that the Rental Revenue account was used to record the initial receipt of the $1,600 rent, paid in advance, as on page 157) would be:

```
1990
Jan. 1   Unearned Rental Revenue ..................................   1,200
               Rental Revenue..........................................          1,200
         To reverse Dec. 31, 1989, adjusting entry.
```

Reversing entries maintain internal accounting consistency . . .

We can generalize from these two examples. Whenever a company elects to record a transaction initially in an income statement account, and that transaction must later be adjusted, then the adjusting entry must be reversed. This is done *to achieve internal accounting consistency.*

. . . and simplify the recordkeeping process

There is a second reason for reversing entries. Reversing entries are made *to simplify the recordkeeping process.* We can illustrate this by using salaries as an example. Let's assume that Salary Expense is $500 per day; that Dec. 31, 1989, is on Wednesday; and that the usual payday is on Friday. This would mean that on Dec. 31, $1,500 in salaries has been earned but not yet paid. Thus, the adjusting entry for this accrual is $1,500 and would be recorded as follows:

```
1989
Dec. 31  Salary Expense ............................................   1,500
               Salaries Payable .......................................          1,500
         To record adjustment for accrual of salaries.
```

Prior to this accrual, from Jan. 1, 1989, to Dec. 26, Salary Expense amounted to $127,700. The general ledger accounts Salary Expense and Salaries Payable would appear as follows after the adjusting entry was posted:

General Ledger

Salary Expense				Salaries Payable		
1/1/89–12/26/89					12/31/89	
	127,700				Adj.	1,500
12/31/89						
Adj.	1,500					
12/31/89						
Bal.	129,200					

Salary Expense for the entire year would then be closed by the following closing entry:

1989
Dec. 31   Expense and Revenue Summary 129,200
                    Salary Expense   129,200
              To close the Salary Expense account.

Posting the closing entry as a credit to the Salary Expense account in the general ledger would result in a zero balance in that account.

Salary Expense			
1/1/89–12/26/89	127,700		
12/31/89 Adj.	1,500		
12/31/89 Bal.	129,200	12/31/89 Closing	129,200
Bal.	-0-		

Thus far there are no problems in the way things were handled in 1989. Now here comes the problem of the adjusting entry needing to be reversed to start the new year 1990.

On Friday, Jan. 2, 1990, $2,500 ($500 × 5) is paid to the employees for their week's service. For each of the past 51 weeks the bookkeeper or the computer has recorded the payroll entry in the following manner:

The first payroll entry in a new year requires special consideration

Salary Expense 2,500
    Cash   2,500
To record salaries paid.

For each of the past 51 weeks, that entry has been correct.

Unfortunately, if the entry is recorded in the same manner on Jan. 2, 1990, it will be incorrect. The $2,500 does not represent Salary Expense for the year 1990. Only $1,000 is Salary Expense for 1990; $1,500 is Salary Expense from 1989, as you can see in the following diagram:

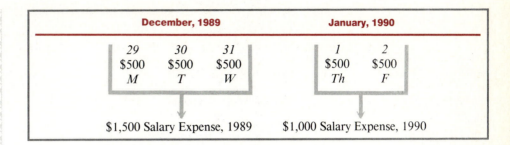

December, 1989			January, 1990	
29	30	31	1	2
$500	$500	$500	$500	$500
M	T	W	Th	F

$1,500 Salary Expense, 1989 $1,000 Salary Expense, 1990

There are two ways to solve this accounting problem.

First, the accountant could make the Jan. 2, 1990, entry for the bookkeeper or the computer. The entry required is:

We could record the first payroll entry in a new year like this . . .

1990
Jan. 2   Salaries Payable (1989)...................................... 1,500
         Salary Expense (1990) 1,000
            Cash... 2,500
         To record salary expense paid for 1990 and pay accrued salaries payable from 1989.

Second, a reversing entry could be made as of Jan. 1, 1990. The accrued salaries adjusting entry of Dec. 31, 1989, is reversed as follows:

. . . or we could record a reversing entry

1990
Jan. 1   Salaries Payable 1,500
            Salary Expense.. 1,500
         To reverse salary adjusting entry of Dec. 31, 1989.

The ledger accounts, after the reversing entries are posted, would appear as presented below:

Salary Expense				Salaries Payable			
	127,700			1/1/89		12/31/89	
12/31/89				Reversing	1,500	Adj.	1,500
Adj.	1,500						
						Bal.	-0-
12/31/89		12/31/89					
Bal.	129,200	Closing	129,200				
		1/1/90					
		Reversing	1,500				

Notice that the liability account — Salaries Payable — now has a zero balance and that the expense account — Salary Expense — has a $1,500 *credit* balance. The credit in the Salary Expense account is in *anticipation* of the $2,500 debit to be received when the payroll entry of Jan. 2 is made. Now the bookkeeper or the computer can make the Jan. 2 payroll entry in exactly the same way as the entry for each of the other 51 weeks. That is, the Jan. 2, 1990, payroll entry can be made as follows:

The use of a reversing entry enables us to record the payroll entry just as we have done in the past

1990
Jan. 2 Salary Expense... 2,500
        Cash.. 2,500
      To record salaries paid.

Posting this entry to the Salary Expense account, which has been adjusted and closed in 1989 and reversed for $1,500 in 1990, results in a $1,000 debit balance for the year 1990, as shown below:

Salary Expense			
	127,700		
12/31/89 Adj.	1,500		
12/31/89 Bal.	129,200	12/31/89 Closing	129,200
1/2/90	2,500	1/1/90 Reversing	1,500
1/2/90 Bal.	1,000		

THE CASE OF AN ACCOUNTANT'S BLIND TRUST

In 1973 a stock loan company called MESCO Broker Services, Inc., was organized in New York City. The company was 70 to 80% owned by Mesirow & Company, which was located in Chicago. The president of MESCO engaged the services of an accountant on a part-time basis to prepare the books of original entry, post to the general ledger, make adjusting entries, and prepare the financial statements that were sent to Mesirow & Company.

From the inception of MESCO, the company president began taking salary advances. When the salary advances became excessive, Mesirow officials in Chicago insisted that the practice be stopped and that the advances be treated as a loan to be repaid promptly. In August, 1975, the accountant discovered that the president had again taken an advance. The president assured the accountant that the advance would be repaid. Consequently, the accountant recorded the advance as a prepaid expense which was covered by not issuing a paycheck to the president the next pay period.

Shortly thereafter the accountant discovered that the president was again taking advances. The president assured the accountant that they would be repaid. As the accountant discovered the advances in the check book, he would record them as advances in the cash payments journal but cancel them out by a month-end adjusting entry showing the advances as deposits in transit. On the first business day of the following month a reversing entry was made to reestablish the advance account. By this means the advances were not disclosed on the financial statements that were sent to Mesirow in Chicago.

By the end of March, 1976, the advances had accumulated to $22,400. Since MESCO's fiscal year-end was Mar. 31, the cash shortage had to be covered. The president accomplished this by borrowing $2,400 from the accountant and $20,000 from two individuals in the stock loan business. The $20,000 was repaid by 12 installments from MESCO by charging the payments to "Stock Loan Fees," a regular expense account. The president repaid the accountant $1,000. (The remaining $1,400 was never repaid.)

Commencing in November, 1977, the president began writing checks for fictitious disbursements, entering a fictitious payee on the check stub. The accountant covered these checks by reflecting a transfer of funds between various bank accounts, thus overstating MESCO's cash balance.

Just before the Mar. 31, 1978, year-end the president showed the accountant a deposit slip for $55,000 to cover the missing funds. The deposit slip was a forgery, but when this was discovered the president was missing.

Source: Securities Exchange Act of 1934, Release No. 21135, July 12, 1984.

The MESCO case illustrates the use of reversing entries to hide improper cash advances. The case also illustrates the need for healthy skepticism when dealing with unusual requests from corporate executives.

From this example we can generalize: If a company elects to use reversing entries, then *all accrual adjusting entries must be reversed.* In addition to the Salary Expense/ Salaries Payable accrual adjusting entry, we have encountered two other common accruals: the Interest Expense/Interest Payable and the Interest Income/Interest Receivable adjustments. *Accrual adjusting entries are reversed to simplify the record-keeping process.*

A simple way to determine when a reversing entry must be made is this: If the adjusting entry increases a balance sheet account, then that adjusting entry must be reversed. Look at the first adjusting entry we discussed. It's the one dealing with insurance. When insurance was recorded as an expense, the adjusting entry (see page 156) increased the Prepaid Insurance account. And so it was with the second adjusting entry (see page 157). When rental revenue was recorded in a revenue account, the adjusting entry increased the Unearned Revenue account. And when we discussed payroll, the adjusting entry (page 160) increased the Salaries Payable account. All of these accounts—Prepaid Insurance, Unearned Revenue, and Salaries Payable—are balance sheet accounts.

THE ACCOUNTING PROCESS REVIEWED

You must be continually aware that the ultimate objective of financial accounting is to prepare financial statements that represent meaningfully and fairly the results of operations of a business entity over a period of time and its financial position at a point in time. The process we have described in this chapter and the preceding two chapters is a practical means of achieving that objective. The steps involved in the financial accounting process are shown in Figure 4-1 on pages 164 and 165.

CHAPTER SUMMARY

Balance sheet and income statement accounts differ in their basic nature. ***Balance sheet accounts***—sometimes called ***permanent accounts*** or ***real accounts***—represent the balance of an account *at a particular point in time.* ***Income statement accounts***— sometimes called ***temporary accounts*** or ***nominal accounts***—represent accumulations of revenue and expenses *during a particular period of time.*

The income statement accounts—revenue and expenses—and also the Dividends account are extensions of the balance sheet Retained Earnings account. They represent increases and decreases to the Retained Earnings account, but we do not record these increases and decreases directly in the Retained Earnings account. Instead we use the revenue, expenses, and Dividends accounts because we need the information they contain to prepare the income statement, to determine net income or loss, and to prepare the statement of retained earnings.

Balance sheet accounts can increase or decrease from one accounting period to another, but income statement accounts can only increase.

The use of ***closing entries*** solves two problems for us:

1. Closing entries transfer the revenue, expense, and dividends accounts back to the Retained Earnings account. This enables us to determine the balance of the Retained Earnings account at the end of the accounting period.
2. Closing entries reduce to a zero balance all revenue, expense, and dividends accounts. This enables us to accumulate data in these temporary accounts for

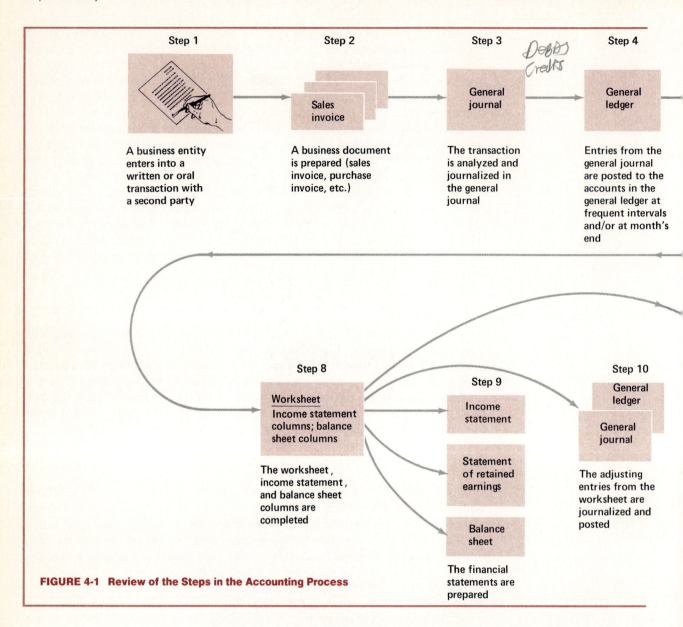

FIGURE 4-1 Review of the Steps in the Accounting Process

the next accounting period. These new accumulations will reflect data *just for the new period.* No data from previous periods will be included, since the accounts started at a zero balance.

Expense accounts are closed by crediting each expense account for an amount equal to the balance in the account. We make the corresponding debit, which will be equal to the sum of the expenses, to a new account, which we call *Expense and Revenue Summary.*

Similarly, we close the revenue accounts by debiting each revenue account for an amount equal to the balance in the account. The corresponding credit for the sum of the revenue accounts is made to the Expense and Revenue Summary.

The balance in the Expense and Revenue Summary, which is the *net income* or *net loss* for the period, is then transferred to the Retained Earnings account by debiting

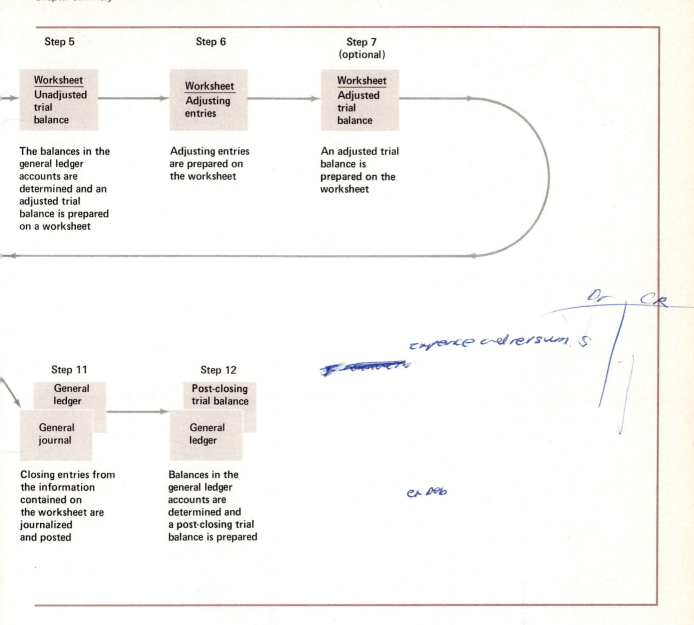

Step 5

Worksheet
Unadjusted
trial
balance

The balances in the
general ledger
accounts are
determined and an
adjusted trial
balance is prepared
on a worksheet

Step 6

Worksheet
Adjusting
entries

Adjusting entries
are prepared on
the worksheet

Step 7
(optional)

Worksheet
Adjusted
trial
balance

An adjusted trial
balance is
prepared on the
worksheet

Step 11

General
ledger

General
journal

Closing entries from
the information
contained on
the worksheet are
journalized
and posted

Step 12

Post-closing
trial balance

General
ledger

Balances in the
general ledger
accounts are
determined and
a post-closing trial
balance is prepared

(in the case where net income exists; crediting in the case of a net loss situation) Expense and Revenue Summary and crediting the Retained Earnings account.

Finally, we close the Retained Earnings account by a credit to that account. A debit for a like amount transfers the dividends to the Retained Earnings account. Now the Retained Earnings account will reflect the ending balance, the beginning Retained Earnings balance having been increased by the net income—or decreased by a net loss—and decreased by dividends.

The ***worksheet,*** which is prepared in pencil, is a tool used by an accountant to organize the adjustments to the accounts and to simplify the process of preparing the monthly, quarterly, and yearly financial statements. The worksheet is used to make adjustments in the trial balance. From the resulting ***adjusted trial balance,*** the interim and year-end income statement and balance sheet can be prepared.

Monthly income statements are obtained from the worksheet by simply subtracting the accumulated amounts in the most recent worksheet income statement columns from the accumulated amounts up through the prior month. The difference represents the current month's income statement because the adjustments made on the worksheet are cumulative from the beginning of the year.

Quarterly income statements are prepared by adding together three monthly income statements representing that particular quarter.

A *post-closing trial balance* is prepared after the closing entries have been journalized and posted. The post-closing trial balance contains only balance sheet accounts and is a final check on the adjusting and closing process.

Reversing entries are easy to make. We simply reverse the *appropriate* adjusting entry. The difficulty is knowing which adjusting entry is appropriate. The following rule should help: *If the adjusting entry increases a balance sheet account, it must be reversed.*

IMPORTANT TERMS USED IN THIS CHAPTER

Accounting policy A business entity's decision on the manner in which accounting alternatives are handled. The decision to record rent paid in advance in the nominal account Rent Expense rather than in the real account Prepaid Rent is an accounting policy decision. (page 154)

Adjusted trial balance A list of the general ledger accounts after their respective amounts have been updated by the adjustments. The adjusted trial balance is usually prepared on the worksheet. (page 144)

Adjustments Internal transactions prepared by business entities to bring the accounts up to date prior to the preparation of the financial statements. (page 142)

Balance sheet accounts Asset, Liability, and Stockholders' Equity accounts. These accounts represent the amount of the particular account at a point in time. They are also called *permanent accounts* or *real accounts.* (page 135)

Closing entries Internal transactions recorded by business entities to clear all income statement accounts to a zero balance at the end of an accounting period and to transfer these balances to the Retained Earnings account. (page 136)

Expense and Revenue Summary An account used to simplify the closing process. Income statement accounts are first closed to the Expense and Revenue Summary account, which in turn is closed to the Retained Earnings account. This account is also called the *Income Summary* account. (page 137)

Income statement accounts Revenue and Expense accounts. These accounts are extensions of the Retained Earnings account and accumulate data for a month, a quarter, or a year, but no longer. They are also called *nominal accounts* or *temporary accounts.* (page 136)

Interim statements Financial statements prepared on a monthly or quarterly basis directly from the worksheet. (page 153)

Post-closing trial balance A list of the general ledger accounts after the adjusting and closing entries have been journalized and posted. Only balance sheet accounts will contain balances in a post-closing trial balance. (page 152)

Reversing entries Journal entries that are exactly the opposite of adjusting entries. Where adjusting entries debit an account, the reversing entry will credit that account for the same amount. Reversing entries are used to simplify the record-keeping process and to maintain internal accounting consistency. (page 158)

Unadjusted trial balance A list of the general ledger accounts after all external transactions have been recorded and posted but prior to consideration for adjustments. (page 141)

Worksheet A multi-column paper used by accountants to organize the period-end accounting procedures in a logical manner. (page 140)

QUESTIONS

1. What is the difference between *adjusting the accounts* and *closing the books?*

2. Why is a *post-closing trial balance* prepared?

3. Explain why the Revenue, Expense, and Dividends accounts are called *temporary* or *nominal* accounts.

4. Why are closing entries necessary?

5. What is the difference between the *Expense and Revenue Summary* account and the *Income Summary* account? How are these accounts used?

6. What purpose does the worksheet serve?

7. If the total debits from the unadjusted trial balance are added to the total debits from the adjustments column on a worksheet, the result will be the total debits for the adjusted trial balance. Comment.

8. Depreciation Expense does not appear on an unadjusted trial balance on a worksheet, yet an adjustment requires that depreciation be recorded. How is this situation handled?

9. It is not necessary to prepare an adjusted trial balance on a worksheet. Comment.

10. Explain why some companies may not journalize in the general journal adjustments entered on the worksheet.

11. By using a worksheet accountants are assured that all errors will be found, since a worksheet must balance. Comment.

12. A balance sheet cannot be prepared directly from the information contained in the balance sheet columns of a worksheet. Why not?

13. The income statement debit column on a worksheet will not equal the income statement credit column. Nor will the balance sheet debit column equal the balance sheet credit column. Why not?

14. What advantage does the worksheet offer an accountant when preparing interim financial statements?

15. How does a worksheet facilitate the year-end procedures of journalizing the adjusting and closing entries?

16. Are reversing entries required?

17. A business entity's accounting policy determines how its adjusting entries are made. Explain.

18. What are reversing entries? Why are they necessary?

19. If a company uses reversing entries, how does it determine which adjusting entries to reverse?

20. Summarize briefly the various steps in the accounting process.

EXERCISES

Exercise 4-1
Preparing closing entries

From the information in the Hamlet Company's adjusted trial balance presented below, prepare the appropriate year-end closing entries.

HAMLET COMPANY
Adjusted Trial Balance
December 31, 1989

Cash	$ 1,656	
Accounts Receivable	3,723	
Prepaid Rent	800	
Moving Van	14,500	
Accumulated Depreciation		$ 4,500
Accounts Payable		1,207
Salaries Payable		924
Capital Stock		4,000
Retained Earnings		5,982
Dividends	18,000	
Moving Service Revenue		60,508
Packing Service Revenue		15,009
Salary Expense	40,300	
Gasoline Expense	11,194	
Rent Expense	200	
Depreciation Expense	1,500	
Miscellaneous Expense	257	
Total	$92,130	$92,130

Exercise 4-2
Preparing closing entries

The income statement of the Scranton Corporation is presented below:

SCRANTON CORPORATION
Income Statement
For the Year Ended May 31, 1989

Revenue:		
Mine Consulting Fees Earned		$86,300
Interest Income		9,200
Total Revenue		$95,500
Expenses:		
Salary Expense	$53,400	
Research Expense	24,100	
Depreciation Expense	8,500	
Rent Expense	1,400	
Utilities Expense	950	
Total Expenses		88,350
Net Income		$ 7,150

Dividends in the amount of $4,000 were paid to stockholders during the year. The corporation closes its books annually on May 31. Prepare the year-end closing entries.

Exercise 4-3
Completing a worksheet

A number of figures are missing from the worksheet presented below. However, there is sufficient information for you to determine the missing figures. Complete the worksheet by supplying the missing figures. *(Check figure: Net Income = $9)*

Accounts	Unadjusted Trial Balance Debit	Unadjusted Trial Balance Credit	Adjustments Debit	Adjustments Credit	Income Statement Debit	Income Statement Credit	Balance Sheet Debit	Balance Sheet Credit
Cash							4	
Accounts Receivable							6	
Prepaid Insurance	7							
Supplies on Hand				1			5	
Equipment	15							
Accumulated Depreciation								8
Accounts Payable		2						
Salaries Payable								
Unearned Revenue		8						
Capital Stock		5						
Retained Earnings								7
Dividends							3	
Revenue				4		28		
Salary Expense			2		12			
Insurance Expense			3					
Supplies Used					1			
Depreciation Expense			2					
Utilities Expense	1							
Net Income								

Exercise 4-4
Preparing a worksheet

The following accounts are found in the Nov. 30, 1989, Babcock Corporation general ledger:

Accounts Payable..................	$ 5·	Insurance Expense.................	$ 3
Accounts Receivable...............	5	Office Equipment..................	25
Accumulated Depreciation	13	Prepaid Advertising................	7
Capital Stock	10	Retained Earnings.................	8
Cash	3	Salary Expense....................	15
Commissions Earned	33	Supplies on Hand	11
Dividends	2	Unearned Commissions............	4
Entertainment Expense	2		

Information pertaining to the Nov. 30, 1989, year-end adjustments is as follows:

Accrued Salaries....................	$1	Advertising Expense	$3
Depreciation	4	Supplies on Hand...................	5
Commissions Earned (for which cash has already been received)......	2		

From this information, prepare and complete a worksheet.

(Check figure: Net Income = $1)

Exercise 4-5
Preparing an interim income statement

The income statement columns from the April and May, 1989, worksheets of the General Corporation are presented below. Using this information, prepare the May, 1989, income statement.

(Check figure: Net Income = $2,350)

GENERAL CORPORATION
Worksheet Income Statement Columns

	April 1989		May 1989	
Commercial Revenue......................		$16,500		$22,000
Residential Revenue......................		10,000		14,500
Salary Expense...........................	$18,400		$23,500	
Travel Expense	3,100		4,300	
Depreciation Expense.....................	2,000		2,500	
Supplies Used............................	1,800		2,300	
Advertising Expense......................	400		750	
	$25,700	$26,500	$33,350	$36,500
Net Income...............................	800		3,150	
	$26,500	$26,500	$36,500	$36,500

Exercise 4-6
Preparing adjusting and reversing entries

The following three transactions occurred during the 1989 fiscal year:

Apr. 1   Twelve months of insurance was acquired for $600.
May 1   Cash was received in the amount of $1,800 for commissions to be earned evenly over the next 18 months.
Aug. 1   Store supplies in the amount of $1,650 were acquired. On Dec. 31, $280 of the store supplies remain unused. There was no beginning balance.

Record the appropriate Dec. 31, 1989, adjusting entry for each of these transactions assuming:

a. First, that the transactions were recorded in balance sheet accounts; then
b. That the transactions were recorded initially in income statement accounts.

Exercise 4-7
Identifying reversing entries

Six adjusting entries are presented below. Identify which of the six will require reversing.

				Number
1989				
Dec. 31	Prepaid Advertising	1,470		1
	Advertising Expense		1,470	
	To record unexpired advertising at year-end.			
31	Revenue	2,730		2
	Unearned Revenue		2,730	
	To record liability for unearned revenue at year-end.			
31	Depreciation Expense	1,500		3
	Accumulated Depreciation		1,500	
	To record depreciation for the year.			
31	Interest Receivable	1,260		4
	Interest Income		1,260	
	To record accrued interest.			

31	Office Supplies Used	1,840	5
	Office Supplies on Hand		1,840
	To record office supplies used during the period.		
31	Salary Expense	1,230	6
	Salaries Payable		1,230
	To record accrued salaries.		

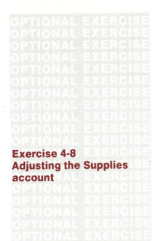

Exercise 4-8
Adjusting the Supplies account

At the start of the current year, American, Continental, and National Companies all had $6,700 of office supplies on hand. The three companies have different accounting procedures for recording supplies. American and National show this beginning balance in the Supplies on Hand account, but Continental reflects the beginning balance in the Supplies Used account. American debits the account Supplies on Hand when supplies are acquired, while Continental and National follow the policy of debiting Supplies Used upon the acquisition of supplies. All three companies acquired a total of $36,740 of supplies at various times throughout the year, and all three have $2,730 of supplies on hand at the end of the year.

Prepare the appropriate adjusting entry for each company.

PROBLEMS: SET A

Problem A4-1
Preparing closing entries

Bill's Barricades, Inc., provides wooden barricades to local construction and paving companies during road construction or repairing activities. The following list of accounts was obtained from the Dec. 31, 1989, adjusted trial balance:

Accounts Payable.............	$ 4,715	Interest Income	$ 3,700
Accounts Receivable..........	9,370	Interest Payable	150
Accumulated Depreciation:		Interest Receivable............	300
Barricades	60,000	Land........................	50,000
Accumulated Depreciation:		Miscellaneous Expense........	515
Building....................	30,000	Mortgage Payable.............	193,000
Barricade Rental Revenue.....	157,640	Notes Payable................	18,000
Barricades	145,000	Notes Receivable.............	24,000
Building....................	240,000	Prepaid Insurance	1,800
Capital Stock	100,000	Retained Earnings, Jan. 1,	
Cash	3,650	1989	48,475
Depreciation Expense:		Salaries Expense..............	97,525
Barricades	12,500	Salaries Payable	1,795
Depreciation Expense: Building	6,000	Supplies on Hand	2,015
Dividends	25,000	Supplies Used................	3,765
Insurance Expense...........	600	Telephone Expense	1,060
Interest Expense.............	1,800	Utilities Expense	1,705

Required Prepare the appropriate year-end closing entries.

(Check figure: Retained Earnings, Dec. 31, 1989 = $59,345)

Problem A4-2
Preparing a worksheet

Gator State Airlines Corporation has just completed its first year of operations. Its unadjusted trial balance is presented below.

GATOR STATE AIRLINES CORPORATION Unadjusted Trial Balance October 31, 1989		
Cash	$ 930	
Accounts Receivable	1,820	
Prepaid Advertising	1,040	
Prepaid Rent	1,400	
Repair Parts on Hand	2,550	
Aircraft	5,000	
Notes Payable		$ 3,000
Unearned Passenger Revenue		2,600
Capital Stock		2,000
Retained Earnings		2,440
Dividends	10,000	
Passenger Revenue		22,000
Freight Revenue		20,000
Salary Expense	27,800	
Insurance Expense	1,000	
Miscellaneous Expense	500	
Totals	$52,040	$52,040

Five adjustments are needed at year-end. Information pertaining to these adjustments is as follows:

a. Eighty percent of the Prepaid Rent is applicable to the year commencing Nov. 1, 1988.
b. Repair parts remaining on hand on the last day of October amount to $720.
c. Accrued salaries amount to $750 on Oct. 31.
d. One-half of the Unearned Passenger Revenue is earned as of Oct. 31, 1989.
e. The aircraft is estimated to have a 10-year life; no residual value is anticipated.

Required

1. Enter the unadjusted trial balance on a worksheet.
2. Record the adjustments on the worksheet.
3. Complete the worksheet.

(Check figure: Net Income = $9,800)

Problem A4-3
Completing a worksheet

A number of amounts are missing from the Dec. 31, 1989, worksheet for Wanderlust Travel Agency. From the information in the worksheet, determine the missing amounts.

(Check figure: Net Income = $720)

WANDERLUST TRAVEL AGENCY
Worksheet
December 31, 1989

Accounts	Unadjusted Trial Balance		Adjustment		Income Statement		Balance Sheet	
	Debit	Credit	Debit	Credit	Debit	Credit	Debit	Credit
Cash	850						850	
Accounts Receivable	1,210						1,305	
Prepaid Insurance				120			360	
Office Supplies on Hand	615						180	
Office Equipment	3,600						3,600	
Accum. Depr.: Office Equipment		900						1,350
Building	45,000						45,000	
Accum. Depr.: Building		10,000		500				
Land	15,000						15,000	
Accounts Payable		725						725
Revenue Received in Advance		170						65
Mortgage Payable		35,000						
Capital Stock								10,000
Retained Earnings		16,560						
Dividends							10,000	
Revenue						63,450		
Salary Expense	57,300							
Advertising Expense					1,200			
Telephone Expense	900							
Miscellaneous Expense					450			
Insurance Expense								
Office Supplies Used								
Depr. Expense: Office Equipment								
Depr. Expense: Building								
Salaries Payable								1,375
Net Income								

Problem A4-4
Preparing a worksheet,
financial statements,
adjusting and closing
entries

The unadjusted trial balance of West Coast Surveyors, Inc., taken from the general ledger on Dec. 31, 1989, is presented below.

Cash	$ 2,305	
Accounts Receivable.....................................	8,710	
Prepaid Insurance	2,760	
Engineering Supplies on Hand	3,525	
Prepaid Rent...	2,500	
Survey Trucks	27,500	
Accum. Depr.: Survey Trucks.............................		$ 9,250
Building...	126,300	
Accum. Depr.: Building..................................		32,170
Land..	42,500	
Accounts Payable		6,100
Unearned Survey Fees		2,000
Mortgage Payable		120,000
Capital Stock		20,000
Retained Earnings.......................................		23,355
Dividends	37,000	
Survey Revenue...		175,035
Engineering Consulting Revenue...........................		27,300
Salary Expense..	143,400	
Truck Repair Expense	1,515	
Telephone Expense.......................................	1,250	
Interest Expense...	12,795	
Professional Development Expense.........................	1,000	
Utilities Expense	2,150	
Totals	$415,210	$415,210

Additional Data

Presented below is information pertaining to the year-end adjustments:

a. Insurance for 24 months was acquired on Mar. 1, 1989.

b. Depreciation for the year is estimated to be $2,100 for the survey truck and $7,210 for the building.

c. Engineering supplies in the amount of $1,315 remain on hand at year-end.

d. Office equipment was leased on July 1, 1989. A 1-year lease was paid in advance at that time.

e. Salaries in the amount of $7,215 are accrued at year-end.

f. Unearned survey fees of $500 have been earned by year-end.

g. Interest on the mortgage of $860 has accrued as of Dec. 31.

Required

1. Record the unadjusted trial balance on the appropriate columns of a worksheet.
2. Prepare the appropriate adjustments on the worksheet and complete the worksheet.
3. Prepare the financial statements.
4. Journalize the adjusting and closing entries.

(Check figure: Net Income = $18,730)

**Problem A4-5
Completing the
accounting cycle**

After several years of interning at Healthy Hospital, Drs. Ache, Pain, and Complain agree to combine their respective talents and form a professional corporation. The following transactions occurred in June, 1989, the first month of the new medical practice:

June 1 The corporation was able to acquire financing from a medical supply company for medical equipment valued at $25,000 and medical supplies amounting to $5,000. A note payable due in 5 years in the amount of $30,000 and bearing 12% interest was signed by the corporation for the equipment and supplies.

A local bank agreed to lend the corporation $50,000 as a mortgage on land valued at $16,000 and a building at $73,250. Drs. Ache, Pain, and Complain contributed $42,750 cash (receiving capital stock in exchange) to provide for the additional financing necessary on the land and the building and to provide for a $3,500 cash balance.

4 A check in the amount of $300 was issued to Solid Insurance Company for 6 months' insurance on the building and contents. The debit is to be recorded as prepaid insurance.

8 Deposited cash receipts totaling $4,320 for medical services performed during the first week.

11 Paid salaries, $2,100.

14 Acquired additional medical supplies on account, $1,510. Medical supplies are to be recorded in an asset account.

17 Billed patients $3,630 for medical services rendered.

20 Received $3,600 from various patients for medical service to be performed from June 1 to November 30 (6 months). The credit is to be recorded in the Unearned Medical Revenue account.

22 Collected $1,975 from patients billed on June 17.

27 Paid $710 for medical supplies acquired on June 14.

28 Paid utilities bill, $135.

29 Paid $1,500 dividends.

30 Paid $300 due on the mortgage. Of this amount, $250 represents interest expense.

Additional Data

Information pertaining to adjustments necessary at the end of the month is presented below:

a. Depreciation on the medical equipment and the office building for the month amounts to $1,200 and $750, respectively.

b. Medical supplies on hand at the end of the month amounts to $4,870.

c. The Prepaid Insurance account is to be adjusted to reflect 1 month's insurance expired.

d. Accrued salaries on June 30 amount to $325.

e. The Medical Revenue account is to be adjusted for the amount of unearned medical revenue earned during the month.

f. Interest expense in the amount of $300 has accrued on the note payable.

Required

1. Record the transactions for the month of June in a general journal.
2. Post the transactions to the general ledger T-accounts.
3. Prepare an unadjusted trial balance on a worksheet.

4. Complete the worksheet, prepare the adjusting entries, and post the adjustments.
5. Prepare the financial statements.   *(Check figure: Net Income = $1,800)*
6. Prepare the closing entries and a post-closing trial balance.

Problem A4-6
Preparing adjusting entries

The Jan. 1, 1989, trial balance presented below of Oldtimer Retirement Home, Inc., was prepared after the reversing entries were made but before any of the 1989 transactions were recorded. Companies do not prepare this type of trial balance; we are using it here to develop your understanding of adjusting and reversing entries.

The retirement home was acquired on July 1, 1986, and has an estimated useful life of 40 years. An insurance policy was acquired on the same date, covering the building and its contents. At that time the entire 3-year premium was paid in advance.

No office supplies were acquired during 1988. The balance in the Office Supplies on Hand account on Jan. 1, 1989, represents one-third of the amount on hand at the same date 1 year previous.

OLDTIMERS RETIREMENT HOME, INC. Trial Balance January 1, 1989		
Cash	$ 11,740	
Accounts Receivable	10,600	
Prepaid Insurance	2,000	
Office Supplies on Hand	1,500	
Retirement Home	240,000	
Accum. Depr.: Retirement Home		$ 15,000
Accounts Payable		3,740
Mortgage Payable		193,420
Capital Stock		25,000
Retained Earnings		27,940
Revenue		2,640
Salaries Expense		2,200
Linen Supplies Used	4,600	
Interest Expense		500
Totals	$270,440	$270,440

Required

Oldtimer Retirement Home made seven adjusting entries on Dec. 31, 1988. From the information presented, record these entries in general journal form without journal explanations.

Problem A4-7
Preparing adjusting and reversing entries

a. The One-O-One Parachute Jumping School received a $1,500 advance payment for jump training for the months of December, January, and February on Nov. 30, 1989. In addition, the school acquired $3,750 of office supplies on Jan. 15, 1989, the day the school first opened for business. At Dec. 31, 1989, only $1,200 of the supplies remained.
b. Accrued salaries amounted to $1,350 on Dec. 31, 1989. The salaries were paid on Friday, Jan. 3, 1990, and amounted to $2,940.

Required

1. Prepare the appropriate Dec. 31 adjusting entries for the unearned revenue and office supplies and the Jan. 1, 1990, reversing entries (if appropriate), assuming that the initial entry to record the unearned revenue and the supplies was entered in a real account.
2. Repeat the above entries assuming that the initial entries were recorded in nominal accounts. You may omit the journal explanations.

3. Prepare, without explanation, the Jan. 3, 1990, entry to pay the salaries, assuming first that a Jan. 1, 1990, reversing entry was made; then assuming that no reversing entry was made.

PROBLEMS: SET B

Problem B4-1
Preparing closing entries

The general ledger accounts of the Allentown Automobile Body Repair Company are presented below in descending order by amount. The balances have been determined after all the adjustments for the year ended Dec. 31, 1989, have been made.

Auto Repair Revenue	$116,000	Repair Parts on Hand	$2,968
Building	92,000	Notes Payable	2,800
Salary Expense	62,660	Office Supplies Used	2,404
Mortgage Payable	49,900	Cash	2,040
Capital Stock	30,000	Entertainment Expense	1,656
Accum. Depr.: Building	29,600	Prepaid Insurance	1,260
Accounts Receivable	28,400	Utilities Expense	1,232
Retained Earnings, Jan. 1, 1989	21,688	Salaries Payable	1,100
Land	20,000	Depr. Expense: Building	860
Dividends	20,000	Office Supplies on Hand	652
Office Equipment	10,800	Depr. Expense: Office	
Accounts Payable	10,160	Equipment	500
Notes Receivable	8,240	Telephone Expense	496
Repair Parts Used	5,408	Interest Income	440
Accum. Depr.: Office		Miscellaneous Expense	328
Equipment	3,600	Interest Expense	100
Advertising Expense	3,284		

Required

Using the appropriate accounts, prepare the Dec. 31, 1989, year-end closing entries.

(Check figure: Retained Earnings, Dec. 31, 1989 = $39,200)

Problem B4-2
Preparing closing entries

Presented below is the Dec. 31, 1989, unadjusted trial balance of Golden State Advertising Agency.

GOLDEN STATE ADVERTISING AGENCY Worksheet December 31, 1989		
Cash	$ 2,580	
Commissions Receivable	4,260	
Prepaid Insurance	1,440	
Office Supplies on Hand	1,605	
Office Equipment	9,525	
Accum. Depr.: Office Equipment		$ 3,075
Accounts Payable		1,515
Capital Stock		10,000
Retained Earnings		8,630
Dividends	28,500	
Commissions Earned		60,555
Office Salaries Expense	29,145	
Rent Expense	3,600	
Advertising Expense	1,875	
Telephone Expense	1,245	
Totals	$83,775	$83,775

The following information is available pertaining to the year-end adjustments:

a. A physical count of the office supplies on hand at year-end amounts to $555.
b. Insurance in the amount of $360 has expired.
c. Depreciation of the office equipment for the year is estimated to be $2,025.
d. Office salaries accrued on Dec. 31, 1989, amounted to $645.
e. Commissions in the amount of $3,570 have been earned at year-end but have not been received nor recorded.

| **Required** | Enter the unadjusted trial balance on a worksheet, record the required adjustments, and complete the worksheet. *(Check figure: Net Income = $24,180)* |

Problem B4-3
Completing a worksheet

The Dec. 31, 1989, year-end worksheet for the Apex Auto Repair Company is presented below. A number of amounts are missing from the worksheet. From the information on the worksheet, determine the missing amounts. *(Check figure: Net Income = $24,380)*

APEX AUTO REPAIR COMPANY
Worksheet
December 31, 1989

Accounts	Unadjusted Trial Balance Debit	Unadjusted Trial Balance Credit	Adjustments Debit	Adjustments Credit	Income Statement Debit	Income Statement Credit	Balance Sheet Debit	Balance Sheet Credit
Cash							3,150	
Accounts Receivable							2,170	
Prepaid Rent				600			300	
Auto Parts on Hand	1,620							
Repair Equipment	4,075						4,075	
Accum. Depr.: Repair Equip.		2,230						2,745
Office Equipment	2,600						2,600	
Accum. Depr.: Office Equip.		650						
Accounts Payable								1,315
Unearned Repair Revenue			105					105
Capital Stock		2,000						2,000
Retained Earnings		1,000						1,000
Dividends	20,355						20,355	
Repair Revenue						45,165		
Insurance Expense	700							
Office Salaries Expense					12,870			
Advertising Expense	1,800							
Utilities Expense					1,325			
Tax Expense					1,570			
Rent Expense								
Auto Parts Used			1,080					
Depr. Expense: Repair Equipment								
Depr. Expense: Office Equipment			325					
Office Salaries Payable								670
Net Income								

Problem B4-4
**Preparing a worksheet,
financial statement,
adjusting, closing, and
reversing entries**

The following unadjusted trial balance of the Green Mountain Service Company was taken from the general ledger on Dec. 31, 1989, the last day of the accounting year:

Cash	$ 1,685	
Notes Receivable	3,000	
Accounts Receivable.	5,170	
Prepaid Insurance	2,400	
Prepaid Rent ($70 per month)	2,520	
Office Supplies on Hand	3,710	
Office Equipment	18,375	
Accum. Depr.: Office Equipment.		$ 4,180
Notes Payable.		2,000
Accounts Payable		2,165
Unearned Service Revenue		3,650
Common Stock		10,000
Retained Earnings.		17,000
Dividends	26,240	
Revenues from Services		83,255
Salary Expense.	47,050	
Advertising Expense	6,200	
Travel Expense.	3,720	
Utilities Expense	2,180	
Totals	$122,250	$122,250

Additional Data
The following information is available on year-end adjustments:

a. Interest accrued in the Note Receivable account amounts to $150.
b. Rent for 36 months was paid in advance on Aug. 31, 1989.
c. Office Supplies Used during the year amounted to $2,105.
d. Depreciation Expense is estimated to be $1,150 for the year.
e. Interest on Notes Payable in the amount of $50 has accrued.
f. One-half of the Unearned Service Revenue has been earned during the year.
g. Salaries in the amount of $2,170 are accrued at year-end.
h. Insurance for 24 months was acquired on July 1, 1989.

Required

1. Enter the unadjusted trial balance on a worksheet.
2. Record the appropriate adjusting entries on the worksheet and complete the worksheet.
3. Prepare the financial statements.
4. Journalize the adjusting and closing entries.

(Check figure: Net Income = $19,725)

**Problem B4-5
The complete accounting
cycle**

Abagail Adams established an advertising agency on Nov. 1, 1989. During the month of November, the following transactions occurred:

Nov. 1   Ms. Adams contributed the following assets to the business entity entitled Adams Advertising Agency: Cash, $15,000; Building, $60,000; Land, $10,000; and Office Equipment, $15,000. The land and building were subject to a $55,000 mortgage payable. Capital stock in the amount of $45,000 was issued.

4   Paid the Smokey Insurance Company $1,560 for a 2-year insurance policy on the building and equipment. Use the Prepaid Insurance account to record the debit.

7   Acquired advertising supplies on account, $2,650.

10   Performed advertising services for clients in the amount of $16,200 and billed accordingly.

13   Paid salaries, $7,310.

16   Paid rent for the month, $250.

19   Received $6,000 from clients for advertising services to be performed equally in November, December, and January.

22   Collected $4,100 of accounts receivable.

25   Paid one-half of accounts payable incurred for office supplies acquired on Nov. 7.

28   Paid telephone bill for November, $55.

30   A $5,000 dividend was paid.

Additional Data

The following information pertaining to month-end adjustments is available:

a. The building has an estimated life of 40 years; no residual value is to be considered.
b. The office equipment has an estimated life of 10 years; no residual value is to be considered.
c. One month of prepaid insurance has expired.
d. Advertising supplies on hand on Nov. 30 amounts to $915.
e. Accrued salaries at the end of the month amount to $3,075.
f. The unearned advertising account must be adjusted — see transaction dated Nov. 19.

Required

1. Record the transactions in a general journal.
2. Post the transactions to the general ledger T-accounts.
3. Prepare an unadjusted trial balance on a worksheet.
4. Complete the worksheet.
5. Prepare the financial statements.
6. Journalize monthly adjusting entries and closing entries, and post the general ledger.
7. Prepare a post-closing trial balance.

(Check figure: Net Income = $5,460)

Problem B4-6
Preparing adjusting entries

The Jan. 1, 1989, trial balance of the Brandon Cleaning Company is presented below. The Jan. 1 reversing entries have been recorded in the accounts, but no external entries have yet been made. Companies do not prepare this type of trial balance; we are using it only to reinforce the concepts of adjusting and reversing entries. Brandon Cleaners began operations on July 1, 1988. At that time a 2-year contract was signed with Tampa Advertising Agency to provide monthly advertising in the local newspapers, radio, and television stations. The 2-year fee was paid in advance.

BRANDON CLEANING COMPANY Trial Balance January 1, 1989		
Cash	$ 700	
Accounts Receivable	1,000	
Prepaid Advertising	1,800	
Office Equipment	3,140	
Accum. Depr.: Office Equipment		$ 500
Accounts Payable		1,600
Capital Stock		2,000
Retained Earnings		1,940
Cleaning Revenue		1,500
Salaries Expense		1,000
Office Supplies Used	1,200	
Rent Expense	500	
Interest Income	200	
Totals	$8,540	$8,540

Required

Seven adjusting entries were made on Dec. 31, 1988. By reviewing carefully the Jan. 1, 1989, trial balance, you will be able to identify these adjustments. Record the adjustments; you may omit the entry explanations.

Problem B4-7
Preparing adjusting and reversing entries

The Boston Company acquired office supplies for cash in the amount of $650 on July 1, 1989. A count of the office supplies on hand on Dec. 31, 1989, amounted to $225. On Nov. 1 of the same year the company received a check in the amount of $1,250 from the New York Company for fees paid in advance for services to be rendered over the next 5 months commencing with the month of November. As of Dec. 31, 1989, the Boston Company had accrued salaries in the amount of $1,355. Salaries are paid on Jan. 5, 1990, in the amount of $2,400.

Required

1. Record the Dec. 31 adjusting entries for the office supplies, unearned revenues, and salaries. For the first two, assume that the initial transaction was first recorded in a real account, then assume that the initial transaction was recorded in a nominal account.
2. After you record the adjusting entries, record the Jan. 1, 1990, reversing entries for the office supplies and the unearned revenues, where appropriate.
3. Finally, record the payment of the salaries on Jan. 5, 1990, assuming first that a reversing entry was not made, then assuming that a reversing entry was made.

You may omit journal explanations for all your entries.

DECISION PROBLEM

As a loan officer of the First National Bank of St. Louis, your first appointment on Jan. 5, 1989, is with Mr. and Mrs. Dunwoody. The Dunwoodys own and operate a travel agency in downtown St. Louis and wish to obtain a $50,000 loan from your bank to expand the business to two other locations.

Preliminary investigations appear favorable for the loan. All that remains is to examine the financial data from the travel agency and, if that is satisfactory, the loan will be approved. Your bank has a responsibility to invest its resources prudently, and as a consequence has established the following tests that must be satisfied before any loan can be granted:

a. The current assets must be twice the current liabilities.

b. Long-term debt may never exceed 60% of year-end total assets.

c. Net income must be greater than 15% of revenues.

d. Net income must exceed 10% of year-end total assets.

The Dunwoodys arrive promptly at 9:00 a.m. and after brief pleasantries provide you with a neatly typed financial statement derived from their check book. In addition to

---

DUNWOODY TRAVEL AGENCY
Financial Statement
December 31, 1988

Cash Receipts:

Cash at Start of Business, Jan. 1, 1984.	-0-
Capital Stock Issued to Mr. and Mrs. Dunwoody, Jan. 1, 1984	$ 5,000
Cash Received from Travel Agency Fees, Jan. 1, 1984 – Dec. 31, 1988	750,000
Note Payable Received July 1, 1988, Due June 30, 1989	10,000
Mortgage Payable Received Jan. 1, 1984	100,000
Total Cash Taken into the Business	$865,000

Cash Expenditures:

For Salaries	$550,000
Land	40,000
Building	120,000
Office Equipment	30,000
Dividends Paid	50,000
Reduction of Mortgage	3,000
Interest on Mortgage	9,000
Interest on Note, $100 Due on Jan. 1, 1989.	500
Advertising, of Which $1,000 Applies to 1989.	16,000
Supplies, of Which $250 Are on Hand on Dec. 31, 1988	7,750
Insurance	9,000
Utilities.	6,000
Total Cash Spent by the Business	$841,250
Cash at End of Business, Dec. 31, 1989.	$ 23,750

the financial statement, you determine that the travel agency owes $100 interest on the Note Payable and $1,000 for office supplies as of Dec. 31, 1988, and has receivables from clients amounting to $5,000 as of the same date.

You inform the Dunwoodys that you cannot give them a decision until you have had time to review the financial information they have provided. You will call them tomorrow with your decision.

The Dunwoodys have not maintained adequate accounting records. What you must do is to convert their records into a proper set of financial statements before you can apply the four tests. You can assume that revenues and expenses are earned and incurred evenly over the 5-year time period. You can also assume that depreciation on the building would be $3,000 per year and on the equipment $2,000 per year.

Required

1. Prepare an income statement for the 5-year period and an income statement for 1988.
2. Prepare a statement of retained earnings.
3. Prepare a balance sheet.
4. Compute values for the four tests and determine if the loan should be granted.

Accounting for Merchandise

After you have studied
this chapter, you
should be able to:

- Calculate the *cost of goods sold* of a merchandising concern
- Explain how a worksheet for a merchandising firm differs from a worksheet for a service business
- Prepare closing entries for a merchandising firm
- Explain the difference between the periodic and perpetual inventory systems

Thus far, we have explained what the accounting process is and how it works: It begins with an economic entity's business transactions (sometimes referred to as external transactions) and ends with the financial statements that depict the entity's financial activity during a period and its financial status at the end of that period. The financial statements prepared by an economic entity can be either formal or informal. *Informal* financial statements covering monthly and quarterly accounting periods are prepared for internal use to help management determine if it is achieving its objectives. *Formal* financial statements are prepared annually; external users can examine them to see how well the entity is performing.

To illustrate the steps of the accounting process, we used in our examples economic entities that are *business,* as opposed to *nonprofit,* entities. Not only did we use business entities, but we used a particular type, a *service* firm whose business activity is to provide, or sell, a service. Real estate agencies, advertising agencies, law firms, and self-employed individuals providing tennis instruction are all examples of service businesses. It is easier to introduce the basic ideas of the accounting process using service entities as examples.

Retailers and wholesalers are merchandising firms that buy and sell products

You are now prepared to understand how the accounting process works for *merchandising firms* (also called *trading firms*), whose business activity is to buy and sell products, either at the *retail* level (the shop from which you, the consumer, buy the product) or at the *wholesale* level (the firm from which the retail shop buys what it sells). The relationship between the merchandising firms and the manufacturer and final consumer is depicted in Figure 5-1.

FIGURE 5-1
Relationship between Merchandising Firms, Manufacturer, and Final Consumer

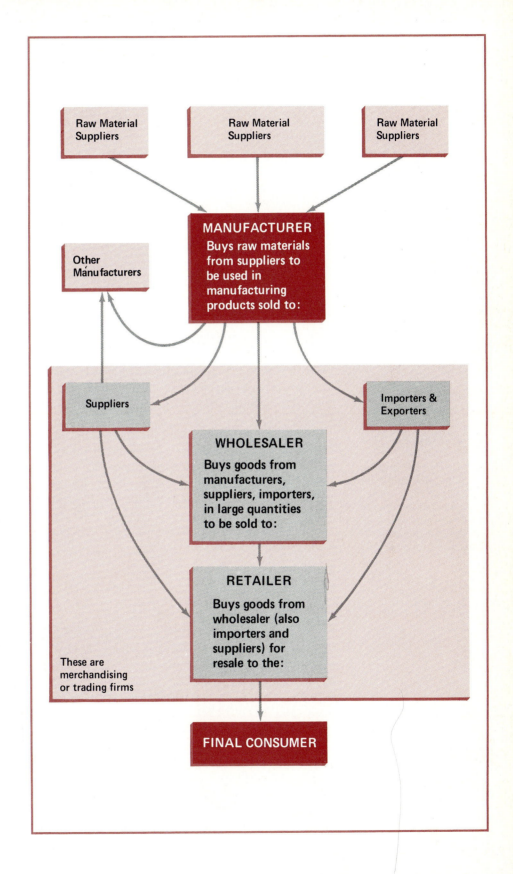

Let's compare and contrast the income statements of a service firm, Mollie's Motel, and a merchandising concern, Sam's Store:

A service firm:

MOLLIE'S MOTEL
Income Statement

Revenue:		
Room Rentals		$36,000
Expenses:		
Salary Expense	$21,000	
Depreciation Expense	4,000	
Cleaning Expense	2,000	
Repairs Expense	1,500	
Linen Used	500	
Total Expenses		29,000
Net Income		$ 7,000

A merchandising concern:

SAM'S STORE
Income Statement

Sales		$120,000
Cost of Goods Sold		80,000
Gross Profit		$ 40,000
Operating Expenses:		
Salary Expense	$25,000	
Depreciation Expense	7,000	
Delivery Expense	3,000	
Insurance Expense	500	
Total Operating Expenses		35,500
Net Income		$ 4,500

The net income for the service company, Mollie's Motel, is simply the difference between revenue earned and total expenses incurred.

For a merchandising concern there are two types of expenses: the cost of goods sold and the operating expenses. The cost of goods sold is the expense of the merchandise sold for the period. And the operating expenses are all the other expenses necessary to run the business.

The net income of a merchandising concern is determined by subtracting the cost of goods sold from sales to calculate gross profit, and then subtracting the operating expenses from the gross profit to calculate the net income

To determine the net income for a merchandising concern, the cost of goods sold is subtracted from the revenue represented by the sale of that merchandise; the difference is **gross profit** (also called **gross margin**). A service concern does not have gross profit because it does not sell merchandise. From gross profit the operating expenses are deducted to determine the net income. The merchandising concern's operating expenses are similar to the service concern's expenses.

This chapter deals with accounting for a merchandising concern, particularly how to measure the cost of goods sold.

THE INCOME STATEMENT OF A MERCHANDISING CONCERN

The income statement of Micro Discount Supply Company at the top of the facing page illustrates how a merchandising firm's income statement is organized. Refer to it as we explain some of the basic details within it. The Micro Discount Supply Company buys microcomputer hardware and software directly from manufacturing companies and sells by direct mail to its customers nationwide.

A merchandising firm's income statement has three distinct sections

The Micro Discount Supply income statement, like every merchandising firm's income statement, comprises three distinct sections: sales, cost of goods sold, and operating expenses. Some merchandising firms may segregate operating expenses into two subsections—selling expenses and general and administrative expenses. Selling expenses consist of those expenses related to the marketing function, such as sales salaries or commissions, delivery expenses, and depreciation on store equipment. General and administrative expenses include all other expenses.

The sales section

The cost of goods sold section

The operating expenses section

	MICRO DISCOUNT SUPPLY COMPANY Income Statement Year Ended December 31, 1989			
(a)	Gross Sales			$177,750
(b)	Less: Sales Returns and Allowances		$ 2,325	
(c)	Sales Discounts		2,700	(5,025)
	Net Sales			$172,725
	Cost of Goods Sold:			
(d)	Inventory, Jan. 1, 1989			$ 19,050
(e)	Purchases	$127,875		
(f)	Less: Purchase Returns and Allowances	$ 855		
(g)	Purchase Discounts	2,025	(2,880)	
(h)	Plus: Freight-In		2,955	
(i)	Net Purchases		127,950	
(j)	Cost of Goods Available for Sale		$147,000	
(k)	Less: Inventory, Dec. 31, 1989		23,025	
(l)	Cost of Goods Sold			123,975
(m)	Gross Profit			$ 48,750
	Operating Expenses:			
	Salary Expense		$ 27,375	
	Advertising Expense		6,255	
	Rent Expense		2,700	
	Depreciation Expense: Store Equipment		1,125	
	Insurance Expense		750	
	Store Supplies Used		1,920	
	Total Operating Expenses			40,125
	Net Income			$ 8,625

The Sales Section

The primary objective of a merchandising concern is the same as for any business entity: to earn a profit. For a merchandising firm to earn a profit, the amount of its sales revenue must exceed the sum of its cost of goods sold and its operating expenses.

Merchandise, like services, can be paid in full with cash at the time of the purchase. This is commonly referred to as a *cash sale.* Or, the seller can agree to accept payment at some time after delivery of the merchandise. This is referred to as a *sale on account.* A cash sale is one where the merchandise is paid for by cash or check on the same day that the merchandise is sold. A sale on account occurs when the merchandise is sold with a promise to pay later.

Sales are made either for cash or on account

A cash sale would be recorded in the general journal as shown below:

```
Cash ..................................   42,750
    Sales ...........................              42,750
To record cash sale of merchandise.
```

Cash sales and credit sales add up to total sales

Sales made on account would be recorded in the general journal as follows:

Accounts Receivable	135,000	
Sales...........................		135,000
To record sale of merchandise on account.		

If we were to look into the general journal for the Micro Discount Supply Company, we would see that these two entries add up to total sales of $177,750 as shown on the income statement [line (*a*)]. Of course, we would find hundreds of entries made during the course of the business year, but the total of these hundreds of entries would reflect cash sales of $42,750 and credit sales of $135,000.

Sales Returns and Allowances

After purchasing an item, a customer may find it defective in some way — perhaps it malfunctions, or was identified as the wrong size or the wrong color. The customer returns the item to the seller (the merchandising firm), which acknowledges receipt of the returned item — a transaction that essentially negates the original sale.

Perhaps the defective item is not totally useless (it's merely the wrong color, let's say). As an alternative to returning it, the customer may be allowed to keep it and pay a reduced price, or a part of the original purchase price may be refunded. This allowance on price (also referred to as a ***price concession***) helps to avoid the costs of freight, and perhaps storage, which the merchandising firm incurs in accepting returned items.

In either case, the amount of the return or the allowance can be recorded as an entry in the general journal by simply debiting Sales and crediting Cash or Accounts Receivable. But that's not the way it is generally done. First we'll explain why not; then we'll show how returns and allowances are accounted for.

Merchandise returned because it is defective or the wrong color or size is a common problem of all merchandising concerns

The owners of a merchandising firm will want to know how much merchandise is being returned and why. Is it being returned because it is defective in some way? Merchandise *is* returned for this reason; indeed, a certain amount of returns should be expected in the normal course of business. But returns should not represent a significant percentage of sales.

Are there more than expected returns? Is the merchandise being returned because of some failure that is within the control of management? If so, the failure should be corrected. The signal that management action is needed is returns that exceed expected levels.

Sales Returns and Allowances is a contra-revenue account and has a debit balance

How efficiently that signal reaches management depends on the way in which returns and allowances are accounted for. Representing returns and allowances in the general journal by debiting Sales (as suggested earlier) provides no helpful information about the level of returns. To provide information on returns and allowances, a separate account, Sales Returns and Allowances, is established in the general ledger. This is a ***contra-revenue account,*** which, as you should remember from our discussion in Chapter 3, will have a balance opposite that of a revenue account: The contra-revenue account ***Sales Returns and Allowances has a debit balance.***

When merchandise is returned, this transaction is recorded in this contra account by the following general journal entry:

Sales Returns and Allowances..............	2,325	
Cash (or Accounts Receivable).........		2,325
To record returned merchandise.		

MATTEL, INC., 1971 SALES

Prior to 1971 Mattel, Inc., had recorded half a decade of record sales and earnings, and the company had projected another record year for 1971. The company's fiscal year-end was January 31, by which time management was aware that the projections would not be met; they had miscalculated the market for "Hot Wheels" and "Sizzlers." In order to reflect a sixth straight year of record sales, Mattel's management, among other things, recorded falsely $14.7 million of sales which resulted in overstating the 1971 pretax earnings by $7.8 million.

Sales are recognized under generally accepted accounting principles when the seller has completed all the obligations to the buyer and the risk of ownership has transferred to the buyer.

Mattel recorded sales to 35 customers using 156 invoices under a procedure referred to by Mattel as the "bill and hold" program. This program was a practice where the customer agrees to buy goods but the seller holds the goods until the buyer requests them. In the past Mattel had a limited number of these transactions, all evidenced by written agreement and the physi-

cal segregation of the inventory items. Under the January 1971 "bill and hold" program, the merchandise was not shipped by January 31 nor was it physically segregated from Mattel's inventory; the customer did not have to pay for the merchandise until the goods were received and could cancel the order at any time prior to receipt; the risks of ownership remained with Mattel; and in many cases the invoices were prepared without consultation with or participation of the customer.

All the "bill and hold" invoices were recorded in the last 11 days of January 1971.

Since Mattel had adjusted its inventory records to account for the "bill and hold" sales of January 1971, even though the merchandise was not shipped, problems developed in inventory control. The inventory records were unreliable; employees could not tell how much inventory was on hand or whether an order was a fiscal 1972 sale or a 1971 "bill and hold" item.

To compensate for these difficulties Mattel reversed the "bill and hold" sales on its books in May 1972 for $6.3 million of "bill and hold" sales of January 1971 and $6.6

million fiscal 1972 sales. When this reversing entry was recorded in the Accounts Receivable control account, the subsidiary accounts receivable accounts, and the Sales account, another problem was created. The general ledger sales account reflected negative sales for the month of May. To cover the negative sales figure Mattel recorded $11.1 million of fictitious sales, which were posted to its Accounts Receivable account and the Sales account but not to the subsidiary ledgers. Of course that resulted in a difference of $11.1 million between the control account and the subsidiary ledgers. The schedule of accounts receivable for the months May to August all showed a reconciling item of $11.1 million called "May Shipping." By September 1971 normal sales were sufficient to absorb the cancellation of the $11.1 million in fictitious sales and the remaining "bill and hold" sales.

Source: Securities Exchange Act of 1934, Release No. 17878, *Accounting Series Release No. 292,* June 22, 1981.

The Mattel case illustrates the chain of problems that can develop when a company attempts to "adjust" sales figures to reflect higher earnings.

Again, if we were to look into the general ledger account, we would see that there were a number of returns and allowances during the year and that the $2,325 is the sum of such transactions. The Sales Returns and Allowances are shown on line (*b*) of the Micro Discount Supply Company income statement.

Sales Discounts

Sales Discounts is also a contra-revenue account and has a debit balance

In a sales transaction, the seller and buyer agree to an exchange. The seller agrees to exchange merchandise in return for a specified payment. The exchange agreement — that is, the terms of the sale — will require payment, generally in the form of cash, at either the point of sale or some future date.

Payment in cash at the time of the sale represents no problems for the seller (the merchandising firm) or the accountant. Payment on account represents work for the accountant, and generally represents a disadvantage for the merchandising firm. Before we explain that, you need to know a few things about the timing of a future payment, how it is specified on the bill, and how it is recorded in the ledger accounts.

The arrangement between the seller and the buyer of merchandise concerning the method of payment is usually expressed on the *sales invoice* — the bill. This arrangement is referred to as the *credit terms* of the sale. One common arrangement is to require that the bill be paid 10 days after the end of the month in which the sale was made. This is expressed on the sales invoice as:

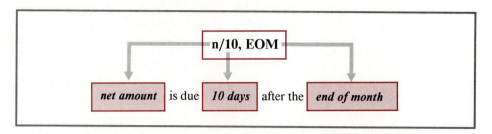

The **net amount** is the cost of the merchandise less any discounts or other price reductions allowed by the seller. It is the amount that the buyer must pay.

Another common credit term is to require payment 30 days after the sale, as evidenced by the date on the sales invoice. The term *n/30* is used to express this arrangement:

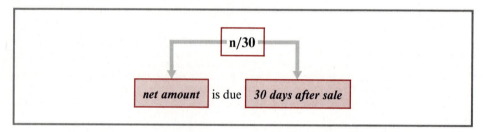

Selling merchandise on account has an obvious disadvantage: The seller has already delivered the merchandise but must wait a period of time before cash is received in payment. While waiting for payment, the seller has salaries to pay, new merchandise to acquire, and other obligations that must be paid for. It is in the seller's interest to encourage the buyer to pay promptly. The seller will offer a **cash discount** (a sales discount) if the bill is paid within a specified period of time. For example, it is common practice to offer a 2% discount off the price of the merchandise if it is paid in full within 10 days from the date of the sale. And, of course, if it isn't paid for within 10 days, then it must be paid for within 30 days from the date of the sale. These terms are represented on the sales invoice as:

Sales discounts encourage early payment

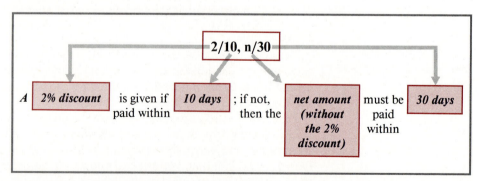

The discount and the period it will be offered are established by the seller. A seller might offer terms 3/10, n/30, meaning a 3% discount if paid within 10 days of the invoice date, or payable in full within 30 days.

To illustrate the accounting for sales discounts, assume that all Micro Discount Supply's credit sales, $135,000, are subject to the credit terms 2/10, n/30, and that all customers on account pay within the 10-day discount period. The entry in the general journal representing the amount of discounts allowed, or *sales discounts,* would be calculated by $135,000 \times 2\%$, or:

$$\text{Sales discounts} = \$2,700$$

[See line (*c*) of the Micro Discount income statement on page 187.] And, of course, that discount means that of the $135,000 receivable, only $132,300 ($135,000 − $2,700) in cash is collected.

The entry would appear in the general journal as follows:

Cash	132,300	
Sales Discounts	2,700	
Accounts Receivable		135,000

To record collection of accounts receivable subject to 2/10, n/30 credit terms.

The sales section of an income statement lists the revenue account Sales and the two contra-revenue accounts, Sales Returns and Allowances and Sales Discounts

Sales Discounts, like Sales Returns and Allowances, is a **contra-revenue account,** and as such it also has a **debit balance.** Both accounts are subtracted from gross sales to arrive at net sales. Sales Discounts and Sales Returns and Allowances accounts represent concessions on the sales price given to the buyer, and as such reduce the seller's revenue. Let's look again at the sales section of the Micro Discount Supply Company income statement to reinforce what we have just explained:

Gross Sales		$177,750
Less: Sales Returns and Allowances	$2,325	
Sales Discounts	2,700	5,025
Net Sales		$172,725

Trade Discounts

In certain industries some manufacturers and suppliers provide catelogs of their merchandise to their customers. As Figure 5-1 shows, retailers, as well as wholesalers, buy merchandise from manufacturers, suppliers, and importers; wholesalers sell it to retailers; retailers sell it to consumers. We are primarily concerned here about what happens at the manufacturer and supplier level and how it affects the sale at the level between the *retailer,* which we have been referring to as the merchandising firm, and the *consumer,* whom we have referred to as the customer. And what happens is that the manufacturer or supplier may publish a catalog with prices that the retailer can charge its customers. The prices in these catalogs are referred to as **suggested retail prices** or **manufacturer's suggested list prices.** The catalogs do not show the prices the retailers pay. Instead, the catalogs show the discount, commonly referred to as the **trade discount** or the **chain discount** — the amount the retailers deduct from the price listed in the catalog to determine their cost (the price they pay to the manufacturer or supplier). These catalogs and this type of pricing and discounting are common practices in the jewelry and auto-parts industries.

Trade discounts are a means of changing the prices of catalog items

Because these catalogs are expensive to produce, manufacturers and suppliers do not want to revise and publish new catalogs every time they change the prices they charge to retailers. Instead, they keep the manufacturer's suggested list price published in the catalog, but change the trade discount. This is done by simply mailing to the retailers a list of changes in the discount terms. Manufacturers and suppliers may also use trade discounts to make price differentials for several different classes of customers or for different quantities ordered.

Now, let's see what a trade discount or a chain discount is and how it works.

If you look in an auto-parts catalog, you might find the listed price for a carburetor (a necessary part of the system that feeds fuel to the engine) as follows:

$$\$100, \ 40\text{-}10\text{-}5$$

$100 is the manufacturer's suggested price to the customer.

The retailer figures out the price it pays to the manufacturer in the following way:

A trade discount provides different levels of discount, making it easy to change the price of a product

Suggested list price	$100.00
Less: *40%* trade discount.	40.00
	$ 60.00
Less: *10%* trade discount.	6.00
	$ 54.00
Less: *5%* trade discount.	2.70
Price retailer pays manufacturer or supplier	$ 51.30

Thus, the retailer pays $51.30, which is the equivalent of a total discount of $48.70 off the manufacturer's suggested list price. The manufacturer or supplier will record this sale at $51.30. The retailer will record the acquisition of the merchandise at $51.30, and will in turn sell the merchandise to the customer for $100, or less if he or she so desires.

A manufacturer or supplier who wishes to change the discounted price of a given item — that is, the price he or she receives for it — will change the trade discount. For example, the manufacturer may increase the price by reducing the discount to 40-10 from 40-10-5. Thus the discounted price is effectively increased to $54.00 from $51.30. A manufacturer or supplier may sell directly to retailers at a discount of 40 or 40-10, but the terms to wholesalers might be 40-10-5.

The Cost of Goods Sold Section

The accounting concept of matching requires that the cost incurred in providing goods and services for sale must be matched against the revenue generated by those goods or services in the accounting period they are sold

To determine the net income for any business entity, whether a service business or a merchandising business, you must understand the concept of *matching.* According to this basic principle, the costs incurred in providing goods and services for sale must be matched against the revenue generated by these goods or services in the accounting period they are sold. For example, in the case of a service business — say, Acme Home Cleaning Service — the cost of providing the home-cleaning service to Mrs. Jones may be the $50 wages paid by Acme to their two employees. These wages would be *matched* against the $75 revenue — the fee charged Mrs. Jones — that the expenditure of the labor was able to generate. The idea of matching for a merchandising business proceeds along the same lines. If Tastegood Donuts sells you a dozen creme-filled donuts for $1, the price that Tastegood paid for the donuts — say, $0.50 — must be matched against the $1 revenue generated.

For a merchandising firm the cost of the products that the firm offers for sale constitutes a major expenditure. The matching concept requires that only those products sold during an accounting period be matched against the revenue earned. This significant expense is called the ***cost of goods sold.*** The amount of product not sold — the product on hand at the end of an accounting period — is called the ***ending inventory.*** Of course, the inventory that is on hand at the end of one accounting period is on hand at the beginning of the next accounting period. In this case it is called ***beginning inventory.***

Because cost of goods sold represents the largest expense on the income statement, it deserves special attention. It is placed on the income statement immediately following the revenue section — as illustrated in the case of the Micro Discount Supply Company — so that it can be matched directly with that revenue. The cost of goods sold section represents, or accounts for, all the costs that were incurred to provide the products that were sold during the accounting period. Very briefly, the cost of goods sold is determined by adding together beginning inventory and purchases. This results in the goods that are available for sale. The amount of goods not sold — the ending inventory — is subtracted from the goods that could have been sold — the cost of goods available for sale — to determine what has been sold — the cost of goods sold. Now for the detail.

Beginning Inventory

To calculate the cost of goods sold, we begin with the inventory on hand at the start of the accounting period. This year's beginning inventory is simply last year's ending inventory, which was determined by a physical count of each item comprising the inventory at the close of the last business day of the year. The beginning inventory of the Micro Discount Supply Company amounts to $19,050 [line (*d*) on the income statement]. (This process of taking the inventory count and determining its value will be discussed in detail in Chapter 9.)

Purchases

The second item we need to calculate cost of goods sold is the cost of the purchases. We use the term ***purchases*** in accounting to refer to merchandise that is bought for one purpose — to be resold.

Purchases refer only to merchandise acquired to be resold

We have exercised great care in the previous chapters to avoid the use of the word *purchases* for this very reason. Office supplies, prepaid insurance, buildings, repair parts, and automobiles are all ***acquired.*** Only merchandise held for resale is ***purchased.*** Thus, the general ledger account Purchases records only the inventory obtained during the year for resale.

Like Sales, Purchases may be for cash or on account. The following entry in the general journal illustrates the recording of cash purchases for the Micro Discount Supply Company:

Purchases	26,625	
Cash.............................		26,625
To record cash purchases.		

Purchases on account are recorded in the general journal in the following manner:

Purchases	101,250	
Accounts Payable		101,250
To record purchases on account.		

The sum of the cash purchases and purchases on account is $127,875 — the total Purchases [line (*e*)] by Micro Discount for the year 1989. Remember, each of these entries represents the total of hundreds of entries made during the year.

Purchase Returns and Allowances

Before we proceed to this next item, return for a moment to Sales Returns and Allowances. Remember that a merchandising firm — that is, a seller — accepts returns of merchandise (found to be defective for whatever reason) and provides a place in its accounting system to record and account for these sales returns and allowances.

Now, let's look at the other side of this situation. As a purchaser, there is likelihood that you may have to return a certain part of your purchases because of some kind of defect. *Sales returns and allowances* to the seller are at the same time *purchase returns and allowances* to the buyer. Therefore, buyers, such as merchandising firms, must provide a place in their accounting systems to record and account for purchase returns and allowances.

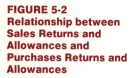

Purchase Returns and Allowances is a contra-expense account and as such has a credit balance

A general ledger account, **Purchase Returns and Allowances,** is established to accumulate this information for management (of a merchandising firm) to review. It provides the same kind of signals to management as the information on Sales Returns and Allowances. Management should expect a normal amount of Purchase Returns and Allowances. But, if the amount suddenly becomes excessive, that indicates to management that its purchasing system and the merchandise need to be examined and analyzed. The relationship of Sales Returns and Allowances and Purchase Returns and Allowances is shown in Figure 5-2.

Purchase Returns and Allowances are recorded in the same way as Sales Returns and Allowances. The summary entry for recording Purchase Returns and Allowances for the Micro Discount Supply Company is as follows:

Cash (or Accounts Payable)   855
    Purchase Returns and Allowances.   855
To record merchandise returned to the seller.

Purchase Returns and Allowances represent transactions in which merchandise is "returned" to the seller and the amount of the price of that merchandise is "returned" to the buyer. Therefore, the amount of Purchase Returns and Allowances appears on

FIGURE 5-2
Relationship between Sales Returns and Allowances and Purchases Returns and Allowances

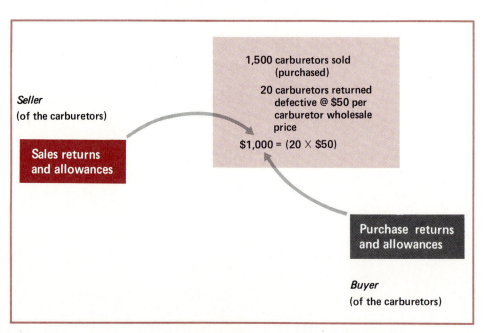

the income statement as a subtraction from Purchases. For our example, this is shown as $855 [line ($f$)] subtracted from Purchases in Micro Discount's income statement.

Purchase Discounts

Purchase Discounts is also a contra-expense account

A seller's sales discounts are at the same time the buyer's purchase discounts. To see how a buyer accounts for and reports purchase discounts on an income statement, let's look back at Micro Discount's purchases on account of $101,250 and assume that the seller's terms are

$$2/10, \text{ n}/30$$

By now we know this means that the seller will accept, as payment in full, 2% less than the amount payable if it is paid within 10 days from the invoice date, or the full amount payable within 30 days. Let's assume that this amount is paid within 10 days, which means that Micro Discount's purchase discount is: 2% × $101,250, or

$$.02 \times \$101,250 = \$2,025$$

and that the amount paid to the seller is:

$$\$101,250 - \$2,025 = \$99,225$$

This is recorded in the general journal as

Accounts Payable.	101,250	
Purchase Discounts.		2,025
Cash		99,225

To record payment of accounts subject to credit terms of 2/10, n/30.

Since a purchase discount represents the part of the total purchase amount that does not have to be paid, it is subtracted from total purchases, as shown [line (g)] on Micro Discount's income statement.

Freight-In

Thus far, we have discussed some of the basic relationships in an economic transaction between a seller (manufacturer, wholesaler, supplier) and a buyer (retailer or other wholesaler) of merchandise. But we haven't yet discussed a very important relationship, a physical relationship: How will the merchandise be transported from seller to buyer, and who will pay the cost of transportation?

FOB shipping point means that the seller will pay the freight to the shipping point

Generally, the terms of the sale will specify who pays the cost of transportation, commonly referred to as the *freight charges.* The term *FOB shipping point* means that the seller agrees to place the merchandise on trucks, railroad cars, or other transportation units *free on board*—at no cost to the buyer—at the shipping point. The cost of transportation from the shipping point to wherever the buyer wants the merchandise delivered is paid for by the buyer. As a convenience, the seller may prepay the freight and simply add the cost to the amount of the invoice for the merchandise purchased by the buyer.

The transportation cost, or freight charged, is usually referred to as *freight-in* by the buyer. A separate account, Freight-In, is established in the general ledger to accumulate these costs.

Although the freight charges are indeed a necessary cost that must be incurred along with the purchase cost, they are segregated from the Purchases account for one specific reason. The Freight-In account provides information to management about the specific costs incurred for transportation. Management uses this information to determine what its transportation needs are, whether or not it is getting its money's worth from its transportation expenses, and whether or not it should buy or lease transportation equipment.

The general journal entry summarizing the total FOB shipping point freight charges paid by Micro Discount Supply Company during the year is as follows:

```
Freight-In.......................................................  2,955
    Cash ........................................................           2,955
To record freight charges on merchandise purchased.
```

Freight-in is a cost that must be incurred in buying merchandise and is shown [line (*h*)] on Micro Discount's income statement as $2,955.

FOB destination means that the seller will pay the freight to the point of destination

When the seller agrees to pay the cost of transportation, that agreement is referred to as **FOB destination.** FOB destination specifies that the seller will place the merchandise free on board the transportation unit from the shipping point to its destination. There is no freight cost to the buyer. (Of course, you will be safe in assuming that a seller who agrees to FOB destination has already raised the price of the merchandise to cover the cost of transporting it.)

By this point, perhaps you already realize that the amount paid for merchandise — Purchases — does not represent, or fully account for, the value of that merchandise — that is, Net Purchases.

To determine the value of Net Purchases:

1. Add the amount of Purchase Returns and Allowances and the amount of Purchase Discounts.

2. Subtract the sum of Purchase Returns and Allowances and Purchase Discounts from the amount of Purchases.

3. After that subtraction, add the Freight-In costs.

4. The result of that simple arithmetic is Net Purchases.

Net Purchases represents the cost of the merchandise purchased, including all associated costs. Net Purchases [line (*i*)] for the Micro Discount Supply Company is determined as follows:

Purchases		$127,875
Less: Purchase Returns and Allowances	$ 855	
Purchase Discounts	2,025	(2,880)
Plus: Freight-In		2,955
Net Purchases		$127,950

Cost of Goods Available for Sale

All the merchandise purchased during the accounting period, as well as all the merchandise in inventory at the beginning of the period, represents the total amount of merchandise that could possibly be sold during the period. This is called the **cost of goods available for sale.** It is the sum of the cost of the merchandise on hand when the period started — the beginning inventory — and the cost of merchandise purchased during the period — net purchases. Cost of goods available for sale for Micro Discount Supply amounts to $147,000 [line (*j*)] determined as follows:

Beginning Inventory plus Net Purchases equal Goods Available for Sale

Inventory, Jan. 1, 1989	$ 19,050
Net Purchases	127,950
Cost of Goods Available for Sale.	$147,000

Ending Inventory

Of course, a firm will not have sold all its purchases and inventory during an accounting period. The nature of a merchandising business requires that there always be some stock immediately available for sale. After the close of business on the last business day of the year, the amount of merchandise on hand is determined by a physical count of the various items of merchandise in stock at the time. The cost of the ending inventory is then determined by multiplying the unit price of each item by the item quantities and accumulating the total. For example, assume that the count of boxes of $9\frac{1}{2} \times 11$ paper was 27 and the count of So Simple word processing software totaled 9. The unit price paid for each item, assume, was $39.25 and $179.85, respectively. The total cost of these items would be determined as follows:

Item	Quantity	Unit Price Paid	Cost
Boxes of $9\frac{1}{2} \times 11$ paper	27	$ 39.25	$1,059.75
So Simple word processing software	9	179.85	1,618.65
Total cost			$2,678.40

The cost of the entire inventory is calculated in exactly the same manner. A typical merchandising firm could have several thousand items in stock at year-end, so you can see that the process of taking inventory is no small task.

The cost of the ending inventory, determined as described above, for Micro Discount Supply Company, is $23,025 [line (k)]. The ending inventory represents the cost of the merchandise that has not been sold.

Cost of Goods Sold

One of the most important bits of information reported on an income statement of a merchandising concern is gross profit. This figure is used by people who work with financial statements to study the relationship between sales and merchandise sold. To determine gross profit, the cost of goods sold for the period is matched against net sales for the same period. That, of course, brings us to the final item in this discussion of the components of the cost of goods sold section on an income statement — the cost of goods sold.

Goods available for sale less the ending inventory equals the cost of goods sold

The cost of the merchandise sold during a period is determined by subtracting from the cost of the goods available for sale the cost of the goods that were *not* sold. Or, what amounts to the same thing, cost of goods sold is the cost of goods available for sale less the ending inventory. The $123,975 cost of goods sold [line (l)] for the Micro Discount Supply Company is calculated as follows:

Cost of Goods Available for Sale.	$147,000
Less: Inventory, Dec. 31, 1989	23,025
Cost of Goods Sold	$123,975

To help you obtain a better grasp of this concept, consider the following example.

Assume that a sidewalk apple vendor starts the day with 2 apples on hand. During the day he purchases 7 additional apples. So he has a total of 9 apples available for sale. At the end of the day, 3 apples remain unsold. Six apples then must have been sold ($2 + 7 - 3 = 6$).

Beginning Inventory	2 apples
Plus: Purchases	7 apples
Total Goods Available for Sale	9 apples
Less: Ending Inventory	3 apples
Total Goods Sold	6 apples

Converting this to money terms, assume that the 2 apples of beginning inventory cost $0.12 each and the purchases for the day cost $0.15 each. The cost of goods sold would be determined as follows:

Beginning Inventory (2 apples × $0.12)	$0.24
Purchases (7 apples × $0.15)	1.05
Goods Available for Sale	$1.29
Less: Ending Inventory (3 apples × $0.15)	0.45
Cost of Goods Sold	$0.84

PERIODIC PROCEDURES OF A MERCHANDISING CONCERN

The period-end procedures of a merchandising firm follow the same sequence of steps as a service company:

1. External transactions are recorded in the general journal.

2. The amounts in the general journal are posted to the appropriate general ledger accounts.

3. The trial balance is prepared on the worksheet.

4. Adjustments are entered on the worksheet.

5. The adjusted trial balance is completed on the worksheet.

6. The financial statements are prepared.

Closing, adjusting, and reversing entries are all procedures that a merchandising firm must do periodically, just like a service firm. The types of accounts that are common to both a merchandising business and a service business are recorded and treated in exactly the same way. The accounts that are particular solely to a merchandising business, such as the Inventory account (a service business does not have inventory, hence has no Inventory account), represent new accounts to you, and we must explain how they are treated. Let's look at how the accounts particular to a merchandising firm are treated, using the worksheet on page 200 for the Micro Discount Supply Company dated Dec. 31, 1989.

On this worksheet, we have not included the adjusted trial balance columns. Accountants, like other people, don't want to do any more work than necessary, so they proceed directly from the adjustments to the income statement and balance sheet columns. After some practice, you should be able to do the same. So, you may as well start now.

Three adjustments were made as of Dec. 31, 1989.

(a) Depreciation Expense: Store Equipment of $1,125 was recorded.

(b) Store Supplies on Hand was adjusted to reflect $1,920 Store Supplies Used.

(c) Salaries Accrued were $1,875.

The trial balance columns and the adjustments columns are treated in exactly the same way for both service businesses and merchandising businesses. On the worksheet, the distinction between the two is the way the balances in the accounts that distinguish merchandising firms from service firms are carried over to the income statement and the balance sheet columns. These accounts are shown in the shaded areas on Micro Discount's worksheet.

The accounts dealing with sales and purchases, which are income statement accounts, are carried over to the income statement columns in the same manner as any revenue or expense account would be extended, whether for a merchandising firm or service firm. The accounts that pertain to revenue and expenses are illustrated in the large shaded area on the Micro Discount Supply Company worksheet on page 200.

The Inventory Account on the Worksheet

All accounts on the trial balance, except the Inventory and Retained Earnings accounts, have period-end balances

Before we proceed to the Inventory account, let's revisit briefly the Retained Earnings account. We will review why the Retained Earnings account is a beginning balance on the period-end trial balance in the worksheet and how it is closed. And that review will serve as the basis for introducing the Inventory account, which also represents a beginning balance. (All accounts shown on the unadjusted trial balance, except the Retained Earnings and Inventory accounts, reflect their end-of-period balances.)

As you may remember, the revenue accounts, the expense accounts, and the Dividends account are all *part of* the Retained Earnings account. As revenue is earned, the Retained Earnings account is increased. As expenses are incurred and dividends are made, the Retained Earnings account is decreased. The Revenue, Expense, and Dividends accounts, although part of the Retained Earnings account, are kept separate from the Retained Earnings account until the end of the accounting period. The reason for keeping separate accounts for revenue, expenses, and dividends is to provide information for the preparation of the income statement and the statement of retained earnings.

The Retained Earnings account is brought up to date by the closing entries

At the end of the accounting period, after the adjusting entries are recorded in the general journal and posted to the ledger account, the Revenue, Expense, and Dividends account balances are transferred to the Retained Earnings account by means of the closing entries. This serves two purposes. First, the Revenue, Expense, and Dividends accounts are reduced to a zero balance — ready to receive transactions for the new accounting period. And second, the Retained Earnings account is brought up to date; it now has a balance that reflects the *end-of-period* position.

There is a parallel between the way the Retained Earnings and Inventory accounts are handled. Like the Retained Earnings account, the Inventory account represents a beginning balance on the period-end trial balance. That means that although there were many transactions that caused changes in inventory during an accounting period, those changes were not recorded in the Inventory account. The balance we see

	MICRO DISCOUNT SUPPLY COMPANY Worksheet December 31, 1989							
	Unadjusted Trial Balance		Adjustments		Income Statement		Balance Sheet	
Accounts	**Debit**	**Credit**	**Debit**	**Credit**	**Debit**	**Credit**	**Debit**	**Credit**
Cash	17,550						17,550	
Inventory*	19,050				19,050	23,025	23,025	
Store Supplies on Hand	2,625			(b) 1,920			705	
Store Equipment	11,250						11,250	
Accumulated								
Depreciation:								
Store Equipment		2,250		(a) 1,125				3,375
Notes Payable		4,500						4,500
Common Stock		20,000						20,000
Retained Earnings*		18,655						18,655
Dividends	4,500						4,500	
Sales		177,750				177,750		
Sales Returns and								
Allowances	2,325				2,325			
Sales Discounts	2,700				2,700			
Purchases	127,875				127,875			
Purchase Returns and								
Allowances		855				855		
Purchase Discounts		2,025				2,025		
Freight-In	2,955				2,955			
Salary Expense	25,500		(c) 1,875		27,375			
Advertising Expense	6,255				6,255			
Rent Expense	2,700				2,700			
Insurance Expense	750				750			
	226,035	226,035						
Depreciation Expense:								
Store Equipment			(a) 1,125		1,125			
Store Supplies Used			(b) 1,920		1,920			
Salaries Payable				(c) 1,875				1,875
			4,920	4,920	195,030	203,655	57,030	48,405
Net Income					8,625			8,625
					203,655	203,655	57,030	57,030

* All accounts shown on the adjusted trial balance, except the Retained Earnings and Inventory accounts, reflect end-of-period balances.

recorded in the Inventory account at the end of the period is the same balance that was recorded at the beginning of the period.

Of course, merchandise is purchased during the period. A reasonable question is: Where is that merchandise accounted for, if not in the Inventory account? The answer is that it is accounted for in the Purchases account, which does indeed change as a result of these transactions during the accounting period.

So, there are two basic ideas you must keep in mind as you proceed through this section:

1. *The Inventory account does not change during an accounting period.*

2. *Merchandise purchased during the period is recorded in the Purchases account, which, in effect, represents changes in inventory.*

The Inventory account is also brought up to date by the closing entries

The ending Inventory balance is obtained in the accounting records via the closing process, just like the ending Retained Earnings balance. To provide the information required for the closing entries, as well as the information for preparing the income statement and balance sheet, both the beginning and ending Inventory balances are reflected on the worksheet. The amount of the ending inventory is determined by physically counting the entire inventory, as we have previously explained.

The Jan. 1, 1989, beginning inventory—$19,050 in the Micro Discount Supply Company worksheet—is carried over as a debit balance in the income statement (illustrated on the worksheet by the small shaded area). Carrying the Inventory balance to the debit column of the income statement is similar to carrying Purchases or Salary Expense to the debit column under the income statement. That is, the beginning inventory is similar to an expense incurred during the period. This period's beginning inventory was last period's ending inventory, the inventory that was not sold last period. It remains on hand to be sold this period and once sold must be considered as part of the total cost of goods sold—an expense to be matched against this period's revenue.

The beginning inventory is like an expense for the period

The ending inventory is an asset

The ending inventory, $23,025 (which Micro Discount has determined by a physical count), is entered in *both* the income statement credit column and the balance sheet debit column. The ending inventory represents those purchases acquired during the year that have not been sold. The ending inventory will be sold next year and, therefore, should not be considered as an expense of the current period. The ending inventory must be subtracted from the total merchandise that is available for sale to determine the proper expense for the current period—the cost of goods sold. That is why the ending inventory is entered as a credit on the worksheet income statement columns: It reflects a reduction of the expenses. Debits *increase* expenses; credits *decrease* expenses. Refer again to the Micro Discount income statement (page 187), specifically the cost of goods sold section. Line (k)—the ending inventory—is subtracted from line (j)—the cost of goods available for sale—to determine line (l), the cost of goods sold. This income statement was prepared from the information contained on the Micro Discount worksheet. Refer to the boxed information in the shaded areas on the worksheet to see the cost of goods sold accounts on the worksheet.

The ending Inventory debit balance of $23,025 on the worksheet balance sheet represents the cost of the inventory on hand at the end of the current period. It is an asset that will become an expense when it is sold. But on Dec. 31, 1989, it is not sold and must be reported on the balance sheet as an asset.

Closing Entries for a Merchandising Concern

Remember in Chapter 4 how we used the worksheet as an aid in preparing the closing entries for a service business? Well, we follow the same basic procedures in using the worksheet of a merchandising business to help us prepare its closing entries.

The closing process

With a service business we first closed all the expense accounts. Remember, in the last chapter we did not yet know about the contra-revenue accounts, Sales Returns and Allowances and Sales Discounts, nor about the contra-expense accounts, Purchase Returns and Allowances and Purchase Discounts.

First close all income statement accounts with a debit balance

It will now be easier for you to first close all income statement accounts with debit balances. On the Micro Discount worksheet these are found in the debit column under the income statement heading. Notice that the total of this column is $195,030. That will be the amount that must be debited to the Expense and Revenue Summary account. Also notice that in addition to the Purchases account, both Sales Returns and Allowances and Sales Discounts have debit balances, as does the *Beginning Inventory.* Here is the first closing entry:

1989
Dec. 31   Expense and Revenue Summary 195,030
                  Inventory...   19,050
                  Sales Returns and Allowances   2,325
                  Sales Discounts   2,700
                  Purchases   127,875
                  Freight-In   2,955
                  Salary Expense.....................................   27,375
                  Advertising Expense   6,255
                  Rent Expense.......................................   2,700
                  Insurance Expense...................................   750
                  Depreciation Expense: Store Equipment   1,125
                  Store Supplies Used   1,920
          To close income statement accounts having debit balances
          including beginning inventory.

Now, what has this accomplished? Well, first of all, the Purchases account, the Sales Returns and Allowances account, the Sales Discounts account, and the Freight-In account are all "zeroed out."

Second, the cost of the beginning inventory is eliminated from the Inventory general ledger account, which now looks like this:

Inventory			
1989			
Bal. 1/1	19,050	Closing 12/31	19,050

The second closing entry is to close all income statement accounts having a credit balance. (With a service business we closed all revenue accounts, but back in Chapter 4 we did not have Purchase Returns and Allowances, Purchase Discounts, and Ending Inventory.) The second closing entry is shown below:

Next, close income statement accounts with credit balances

1989
Dec. 31   Inventory..   23,025
          Sales...   177,750
          Purchase Returns and Allowances......................   855
          Purchase Discounts..................................   2,025
                  Expense and Revenue Summary   203,655
          To close income statement accounts having credit balances
          and to establish ending inventory.

The credit of $203,655 to the Expense and Revenue Summary is the total of the credit income statement column on the worksheet. We have closed all the remaining income statement accounts, including our new accounts, Purchase Returns and Allowances and Purchase Discounts. And we have established the ending inventory. Look at the Inventory account now:

Inventory			
1989			
Bal. 1/1	19,050	Closing 12/31	19,050
Closing 12/31	23,025		

The account now reflects the ending balance.

Remember that we are now dealing with a corporation. So to complete the closing process we will close the Expense and Revenue Summary account to the Retained Earnings account as follows:

Dec. 31	Expense and Revenue Summary.............................	8,625	
	Retained Earnings		8,625
	To close the Expense and Revenue Summary account.		

And finally we will close the Dividends account.

Dec. 31	Retained Earnings	4,500	
	Dividends...		4,500
	To close the Dividends account.		

PERIODIC AND PERPETUAL INVENTORY SYSTEMS

What we have been describing is a system of gathering information about merchandise inventory and presenting that information on financial statements. This information tells the reader how much merchandise is still on hand at the end of the accounting period and how much merchandise was sold. This system we call the *periodic inventory system.* This particular system has a major disadvantage: We do not know how much merchandise is on hand unless we count it, and we cannot prepare an income statement without knowing the ending merchandise inventory. (We can estimate the ending merchandise inventory using techniques to be explained in Chapter 9, after you have more experience dealing with inventory problems.) There is another inventory system that can tell us how much inventory is on hand without counting the merchandise; this system we call the *perpetual inventory system.* Let's first review the periodic inventory system and then describe the perpetual system.

Periodic Inventory System

When merchandise inventory (notice that we use the terms merchandise and inventory to describe items a wholesaler or retailer buys to resell to others—sometimes we use both terms together, a common redundant expression in accounting) is acquired, an account called Purchases is debited for the cost of the merchandise. If freight charges were incurred, an account called Freight-In is debited. And if some of the merchandise is later returned, an account called Purchase Returns and Allowances is credited. If the merchandise was subject to a cash discount for early payment of the account payable, an account called Purchase Discounts is credited when payment is made. The total cost of all the units available is determined by adding beginning merchandise inventory to the purchases and freight-in and subtracting the returns and allowances and discounts. The cost of goods sold is determined by subtracting the ending inventory (which we must count) from the total cost of all units available.

Perpetual Inventory System

The perpetual inventory system keeps a running balance of the amount of inventory on hand

With a perpetual inventory system the business keeps an up-to-date record of inventory units; in particular cases, inventory costs are kept up to date as well. The most common type of perpetual inventory systems keeps track of only the number of units on hand. Many large department and discount stores have cash registers that record the stock number of each item purchased by each customer. These records are then used to determine how many units are on hand at a given time. Management can then reorder on a timely basis to ensure that there is always enough product on the shelves.

Perpetual systems that regularly record both the number of units and the cost of each unit are used mainly by businesses that handle a low volume of high-value articles. For example, an automobile dealership maintains a perpetual inventory system, recording inventory units and the cost of each unit. A drugstore may not. For a drugstore to use a perpetual units and cost system, it would have to keep track of thousands of different products; when one bottle of mouthwash is sold, a record would have to be made of its stock number (brand and size) and its cost (the drug store could have purchased it at any one of a half-dozen different amounts). When the perpetual inventory system is used, the cost of each unit purchased is recorded directly into the Merchandise Inventory account. The Purchases account is not used. When freight charges are incurred, they too are entered directly into the Merchandise Inventory account. The Freight-In account is not used. The same goes for returns and discounts: They are entered as credits to the Merchandise Inventory account and not to Purchase Returns and Allowances nor to Purchase Discounts. When a sale of merchandise is made, an account called Cost of Goods Sold is debited for the cost of the merchandise and the Merchandise Inventory account is credited. By this means the perpetual inventory system can tell us at any time the cost of goods sold and the cost of the units still on hand—the ending inventory. Let's return to the Micro Discount Supply Company as an example to contrast the entries made under a periodic system and under a perpetual system. Remember that Micro Discount had a beginning inventory of $19,050; purchases of $127,875, of which $26,625 were cash purchases; returns of $855; discounts of $2,025; freight charges of $2,955; an ending inventory of $23,025; and the cost of goods sold amounted to $123,975. The general journal entries to record these transactions under both the periodic and perpetual inventory systems would be as at the top of page 205.

Note: The cost of goods sold is the same under either system, $123,975. It is reflected on line (*l*), page 187 in the Micro Discount income statement, which was prepared using the periodic system. And the same amount is now determined under the perpetual system. It is the $127,875 acquisitions, less the $855 returns and the $2,025 discount, plus the $2,955 freight, less the $125,650 cost of merchandise sold (this figure was not given in the Micro Discount example using the periodic system, since it was not needed), plus the $1,675 cost of returned merchandise (this figure was also not given in the periodic system, since it was on hand when the inventory was counted).

Periodic Inventory System			**Perpetual Inventory System**		
Purchases......................	127,875		Inventory......................	127,875	
Accounts Payable.............		101,250	Accounts Payable.............		101,250
Cash		26,625	Cash		26,625
To record the acquisition of merchandise for cash and on account.			To record the acquisition of merchandise for cash and on account.		
Cash	855		Cash	855	
Purchase Returns and			Inventory....................		855
Allowances		855	To record mdse. returned to seller.		
To record mdse. returned to seller.					
Accounts Payable.................	101,250		Accounts Payable.................	101,250	
Purchase Discounts...........		2,025	Inventory....................		2,025
Cash		99,225	Cash		99,225
To record payment of accounts subject to credit terms of 2/10, n/30.			To record payment of accounts subject to credit terms of 2/10, n/30.		
Freight-In.......................	2,955		Inventory......................	2,955	
Cash		2,955	Cash		2,955
To record freight charges on merchandise purchased.			To record freight charges on merchandise purchased.		
Cash	42,750		Cash	42,750	
Accounts Receivable.............	135,000		Accounts Receivable.............	135,000	
Sales		177,750	Sales		177,750
To record sale of merchandise for cash and on account.			To record sale of merchandise for cash and on account.		
Note: No entry is made under the periodic system.			Cost of Goods Sold	125,650	
			Inventory....................		125,650
			To record cost of merchandise sold.		
Sales Returns and Allowances......	2,325		Sales Returns and Allowances......	2,325	
Cash		2,325	Cash		2,325
To record return of mdse. sold.			To record return of mdse. sold.		
Note: No entry is made under the periodic system.			Inventory......................	1,675	
			Cost of Goods Sold		1,675
			To record cost of mdse. returned.		

Now let's take a look at the inventory ledger accounts (see page 206) under each system. There is a difference: Under the periodic system the Inventory account is *static* — it does not change until the closing entries are made. But under the perpetual system the Inventory account is *dynamic* — it changes every time the inventory changes. Please be aware that under the perpetual inventory system we still have to count the ending inventory to ensure the accuracy of our records.

As you study the two methods, notice the following:

1. The perpetual inventory system uses no Purchases account. It records all purchases directly in the Inventory account.

The periodic system uses a Purchases account.

2. The perpetual inventory system records merchandise returned to suppliers by directly reducing the Inventory account.

The periodic inventory system uses a Purchase Returns account.

Periodic Inventory Account					Perpetual Inventory Account				
1989					1989				
Bal. 1/1	19,050	Closing	19,050		Bal. 1/1	19,050	Returns	855	
Closing	23,025				Purchases	127,875	Discount	2,025	
					Freight	2,955	Cost of Sales	125,650	
					Returns	1,675			
1990					1990				
Bal. 1/1	23,025				Bal. 1/1	23,025			

3. The perpetual inventory system records cost of goods sold and reduces inventory when merchandise is sold.

The periodic system calculates cost of goods sold based on the inventory remaining on hand at the end of the period and records cost of goods sold through the closing process.

4. The perpetual inventory system records customer returns by reducing Cost of Goods Sold and increasing the Inventory account.

The periodic system requires no inventory entry; the merchandise is merely returned to stock.

5. The cost of goods sold and the inventory amounts are readily available at any time under the perpetual inventory system.

Cost of goods sold and inventory amounts are usually not available until they are calculated at year-end under the periodic system.

CHAPTER SUMMARY

A merchandising firm sells a product, not a service. The cost of that product, which is referred to as the *cost of goods sold,* is matched against the *net sales* to determine the *gross profit* made on that product. To determine net income, operating expenses are subtracted from the gross profit.

To account for the revenue of a merchandising firm, we have to consider several things that do not exist for the revenue of a service business. The revenue section of an income statement for a merchandising firm contains a Sales revenue account and also two contra-revenue accounts—*Sales Returns and Allowances* and *Sales Discounts.*

To calculate cost of goods sold we have to consider the accounts for *Beginning Inventory* and *Ending Inventory; Purchases,* the two contra accounts *Purchase Returns and Allowances* and *Purchase Discounts;* and *Freight-In.* The sum of beginning inventory and net purchases during the period is equivalent to goods available for sale. Ending inventory is subtracted from goods available for sale to determine the cost of goods sold.

Two types of sales discounts the accountant must be concerned with are as follows:

1. A discount used to encourage a buyer to pay a sale on account promptly. This is a *cash discount,* which is available only if the bill is paid within a specified period.
2. A *trade discount,* or *chain discount,* which is the amount a buyer (wholesaler or retailer) takes off the *list* price of an item to determine the price he or she pays.

A merchandising firm's periodic accounting procedures are not significantly different from those of a service entity. The revenue and expense accounts particular to a merchandising firm are represented in the trial balance on a worksheet just as are any business entity's expense or revenue accounts.

Only the Inventory account is handled differently on a worksheet. The beginning inventory is carried over to the income statement debit column. The ending inventory is placed in both the credit income statement column and the debit balance sheet column.

The beginning inventory is eliminated by the closing entry that credits the beginning inventory. At the same time, Sales Returns and Allowances, Sales Discounts, Purchases, and Freight-In are closed out with all other expense accounts by credits. The corresponding debit is to the Expense and Revenue Summary. The ending inventory is established in the closing entry that debits Ending Inventory, Sales, Purchase Returns and Allowances, and Purchase Discounts. The corresponding credit is to the Expense and Revenue Summary.

Two inventory systems exist that enable companies to determine their ending inventories and the cost of goods sold. The *periodic inventory system* requires the company to count the ending inventory. Then, by adding the beginning inventory together with the net purchases (purchases less purchase returns and allowances and purchase discounts plus freight-in) and subtracting the ending inventory, the cost of goods sold is determined. The *perpetual inventory system* records the purchase, returns, freight charges, and cost of the merchandise sold directly in the Inventory account, thus producing an up-to-date record of the inventory on hand and the cost of the goods sold.

IMPORTANT TERMS USED IN THIS CHAPTER

Cost of goods sold A calculation that determines the amount of merchandise that is sold during a period. It is reflected as a separate section of a merchandising firm's income statement. (page 192)

FOB destination Terms expressed in a sales contract with respect to shipping merchandise, specifying that the seller is obligated to pay for the freight cost to the buyer's location. (page 196)

FOB shipping point Terms expressed in a sales contract specifying that the buyer is obligated to pay for the freight cost of shipping merchandise from the seller's location. (page 195)

Freight-In A general ledger account used to accumulate the cost of transporting merchandise. *Transportation-In* is another title commonly used for this account. (page 195)

Gross profit The difference between net sales and cost of goods sold. (page 186.)

Inventory Merchandise purchased by a merchandising firm for resale but not yet sold. (page 192)

Periodic inventory system A system of determining the ending inventory and the cost of goods sold at the end of a period of time by counting the units on hand. (page 203)

Perpetual inventory system A system for keeping an up-to-date record of the cost of inventory on hand and the cost of goods sold. (page 204)

Purchase Discounts A general ledger account used to record the reduction from the purchase price that is allowed if payment is made within a specified period of time. (page 195)

Purchase Returns and Allowances A general ledger account used to accumulate the cost of merchandise returned to the seller as well as the amount of a concession granted by the seller for unsatisfactory goods. (page 194)

Purchases A general ledger account used to accumulate the cost of merchandise purchased during the period for resale. (page 193)

Sales A general ledger account used to accumulate the revenue earned from the sale of merchandise. (page 187)

Sales Discounts A general ledger account used to accumulate the amount allowed as a reduction from the sales price when the invoice is paid within a specified period. (page 189)

Sales Returns and Allowances A general ledger account used to accumulate the cost of merchandise returned by the buyer as well as the amount of a concession granted to the buyer for unsatisfactory goods. (page 188)

Trade discounts Deduction allowed to wholesalers and retailers from the price of merchandise listed in catalogs. Also called *chain discounts.* (page 191)

QUESTIONS

1. Income statements are all the same; an income statement from a service company will look just like an income statement from a merchandising concern. Comment.

2. The term *gross profit* appears on the income statement of a merchandising concern. What does this term mean?

3. Often, when merchandise is sold on account, a *cash discount* is given when the bill is paid. Why?

4. What is the purpose of the account *Sales Returns and Allowances?*

5. The account Sales Returns and Allowances is like the following accounts: Sales Discounts, Purchase Returns and Allowances, Purchase Discounts, and Accumulated Depreciation. Explain.

6. Sales agreements often contain terms such as *n/30, EOM; 2/10, n/30;* and *2/10, 1/30, n/60.* What do these terms mean?

7. What is a *trade discount?* How does it differ from a cash discount?

8. Hamlet Company acquired merchandise costing $4,500. The sales agreement called for a 20-10-5 trade discount and a cash discount of 3/10, n/30. If the invoice is paid within 10 days, how much will the merchandise cost?

9. An important figure on an income statement is the *cost of goods sold*. How is this figure determined?

10. Why is *freight-in* considered part of the cost of goods sold?

11. When a trial balance is prepared for a merchandising concern, it includes the *beginning*, not the *ending inventory*. Explain how the worksheet is used to provide the appropriate inventories for the income statement.

12. What do the terms *FOB shipping point* and *FOB destination* mean?

13. How do the closing entries of a merchandising concern differ from the closing entries of a service-type company?

14. The *periodic inventory system* has certain disadvantages. What are they?

15. The Inventory account under the periodic inventory system is a static account, much like the Retained Earnings account. Explain this comment.

16. The Inventory account under the *perpetual inventory system* is a dynamic account. Explain.

17. How does the perpetual inventory system handle the sales of merchandise? The return of merchandise sold?

18. Why don't corporations simply credit the Purchases account when merchandise is returned under the periodic inventory system, rather than crediting the Purchase Returns and Allowances account?

19. The account Freight-In is a nominal account. Where is this account found on an income statement?

20. Both the buyer and the seller are affected when merchandise is returned. How does each record the transaction under a periodic inventory system?

EXERCISES

Exercise 5-1
Calculating Cost of Goods Sold

Using the information presented below, determine the amount of the Cost of Goods Sold.

Purchases	$20	Freight-In	$4
Ending Inventory	15	Purchase Discounts	2
Beginning Inventory..............	10	Purchase Returns and Allowances....	1

(Check figure: Cost of Goods Sold = $16)

Exercise 5-2
Computing missing items

In the five following tabulations several items are missing (these missing items are indicated by a dash). You are to compute the missing items and complete the tabulations.

	1	2	3	4	5
Sales	—	200	100	400	—
Beginning Inventory	100	—	20	120	—
Purchases	—	220	70	—	260
Goods Available for Sale	340	—	—	—	300
Ending Inventory	—	180	—	80	80
Cost of Goods Sold	280	—	65	440	—
Gross Profit	320	20	—	—	80

Exercise 5-3
Preparing closing entries

The following accounts appeared in the general ledger of the Emerson Company at the end of the year:

Sales..........................	$360	Dividends.......................	$45
Purchases	195	Freight-In......................	40
Capital Stock..................	100	Purchase Returns and Allowances ..	35
Inventory, Jan. 1..............	105	Cash...........................	30
Accounts Receivable	60	Accounts Payable...............	25
Inventory, Dec. 31	55	Insurance Expense	20
Retained Earnings	50	Salaries Payable...............	15
Salaries Expense	50	Sales Discounts................	10

Using this information, prepare the year-end closing entries dated Dec. 31.

Exercise 5-4
Computing the advantage of borrowing to pay an invoice within the discount period

Dalton Enterprises received an invoice from Big Rock Gravel Company for $3,500 on May 1, 1989. The terms of the invoice were 3/10, n/30, meaning that the invoice must be paid by May 11 if the discount is to be taken. But Dalton will not have the funds available on May 11 to pay the invoice. Dalton can, however, borrow the necessary funds from the United National Federal First Bank of Cutter City at a rate of 12% per year.

If Dalton were to borrow the necessary funds for 20 days (Dalton has a large account receivable that will be collected on May 31; these funds will be used to pay the loan), would Dalton save any money by borrowing the necessary funds on May 11 to pay the invoice within the discount period? How much would they save?

(Check figure: Savings = $82.37)

Exercise 5-5
Computing trade and cash discounts

Alpha Auto Parts purchased $5,400 of auto parts from the Beta Mfg. Company. The invoice had the following trade discount: 40-10-5. In addition, a 2% cash discount is available if the invoice is paid within the discount period. If the invoice is paid before the cash discount expires, how much will Alpha pay Beta?

(Check figure: $2,714.80)

Exercise 5-6
Preparing a simple worksheet

Presented below is an abbreviated worksheet for the Empire Corporation for the year ended Dec. 31, 1989.

Accounts	Income Statement		Balance Sheet	
	Debit	**Credit**	**Debit**	**Credit**
Inventory				
All other accounts	60	80	25	30

Complete the worksheet; the beginning and ending inventories were $25 and $40, respectively.

(Check figure: Net Income = $35)

Exercise 5-7
Preparing a worksheet

The unadjusted trial balance of the Weston Company as of Dec. 31, 1989, appears below:

WESTON COMPANY
Unadjusted Trial Balance
December 31, 1989

Cash.	$ 10	
Accounts Receivable	30	
Inventory, Jan. 1, 1989	100	
Shop Supplies on Hand	40	
Shop Equipment	130	
Accumulated Depreciation		$ 30
Accounts Payable		20
Capital Stock		100
Retained Earnings.		80
Dividends.	25	
Sales. .		395
Sales Returns and Allowances	35	
Purchases	185	
Purchase Discounts.		15
Freight-In	20	
Salary Expense.	60	
Insurance Expense	5	
Totals. . .	$640	$640

Additional Information
a. Accrued salaries at year-end amount to $15.
b. Shop Supplies on Hand at year-end amount to $5.
c. Depreciation on the Shop Equipment is $10.
d. The Dec. 31 Inventory amounts to $20.

Prepare a worksheet.

(Check figure: $35 loss)

Exercise 5-8
Recording journal entries for returns

The General Sales Company uses the periodic inventory system. During the month of March, the following transactions occurred:

Mar. 3 Purchased inventory on account, $2,350.
     9 Returned $250 of inventory purchased on the 3d.
    12 Sold inventory on account for $1,600.
    17 Inventory sold for $175 on the 12th is returned.

Prepare the general journal entries for the four dates.

Exercise 5-9
Calculating purchases

Presented below are selected data from the general ledger of the General Toy Corporation. Using this information, determine the purchases for the period.

Beginning Inventory	$ 27,500	Purchase Discounts	$5,500
Cost of Goods Sold	100,000	Purchase Returns and	
Ending Inventory	17,700	Allowances	3,500
Freight-In.	4,200		

(Check figure: Purchases = $95,000)

Exercise 5-10
Computing ending inventory

The Jameson Company has sustained a fire loss at their warehouse. Information obtained from the company records reveals the following:

Beginning Inventory	$17,300	Purchase Discounts	$2,650
Cost of Goods Sold	73,150	Purchase Returns and	
Freight-In	1,700	Allowances	3,100
Purchases	95,200		

From this information, calculate the value of the ending inventory so that Jameson may file an insurance claim for the loss.

(Check figure: Ending Inventory = $35,300)

Exercise 5-11
Recording inventory transactions under the periodic and perpetual systems

The Thomas Company opened its store on May 1, 1989. During the month of May, the following transactions occurred:

May 2 Purchased merchandise on account from the Corner Supply Store, $37,500.
  9 Sold merchandise to Alfred Jones on account, $16,250. The merchandise cost $11,300.
  14 Returned merchandise costing $4,550 to the Corner Supply Store.
  21 Merchandise costing $2,050 was returned by Alfred Jones. The merchandise was sold for $2,730.

Prepare general journal entries for the above transactions, first using the periodic inventory system and then using the perpetual inventory system.

PROBLEMS: SET A

Problem A5-1
Preparing journal entries

The Fletcher Corporation, which uses the periodic inventory system, had the following transactions during the month of May, 1989:

May 3 Sold merchandise on account, $2,100; credit terms 2/10, 1/20, n/60.
  8 Purchased office equipment on account, $5,500; credit terms 2/10, n/30.
  9 Sold office supplies for cash at cost, $350, as an accommodation to Easy Rider Cattle Company.
  10 Received amount due from the May 3 sale.
  11 Purchased merchandise inventory on account, $4,500; credit terms 3/10, n/30.
  12 Returned for credit $1,100 of defective merchandise acquired on May 11.
  14 Purchased $2,570 of merchandise inventory for cash.
  15 Paid for the merchandise acquired on May 11 less the return of May 12.
  17 Paid for the office equipment purchased on May 8.
  18 Sold merchandise on account, $6,500; credit terms 3/10, 1/20, n/60.
  21 Sold merchandise for cash, $2,350.
  23 Paid cash, $3,750, for merchandise, plus an additional $175 for freight charges.
  29 Received payment due from the sale of May 18.
  30 The customer from the May 18 sale returned $600 of merchandise that he claimed was defective. Seattle Cattle Company paid the customer the amount due.

Required Record these transactions in a general journal.

**Problem A5-2
Calculating ending
inventory**

Tim Wilson, the controller of the Atlas Corporation, wants to know the approximate value of the inventory on hand as of July 31, 1989. The corporation uses the periodic inventory system, and the last time that the inventory was counted was on Dec. 31, 1988, at which time the value was $165,900. Mr. Wilson will not count the inventory on July 31, 1989, but will use the following procedures to estimate the value of the ending inventory:

1. The amount of net sales will be determined.
2. The gross profit will be estimated by multiplying the net sales by 45%.
3. The cost of goods sold will be estimated by subtracting the gross profit from the net sales.
4. The cost of goods available for sale will be determined.
5. The ending inventory will be estimated by subtracting the cost of goods sold from the cost of goods available for sale.

Mr. Wilson has gathered the following data from the general ledger accounts as of July 31, 1989:

Sales...............	$1,785,200	Sales Returns and	
Sales Discounts..........	31,500	Allowances...........	$19,300
Purchase Discounts........	15,700	Purchase Returns and	
Freight-In............	10,500	Allowances..........	4,900
Purchases............	879,300		

Required   Determine the value of the ending inventory.

(Check figure: Ending Inventory = $81,180)

**Problem A5-3
Preparing a worksheet
and closing entries**

The Blue Ridge Corporation's unadjusted trial balance for the year ended Sept. 30, 1989, is presented below:

THE BLUE RIDGE CORPORATION Unadjusted Trial Balance September 30, 1989		
Cash..	$ 1,750	
Accounts Receivable........................	3,530	
Inventory..................................	25,700	
Prepaid Rent..............................	4,800	
Store Supplies on Hand....................	2,860	
Store Equipment..........................	33,400	
Accum. Depr.: Store Equipment...........		$ 6,250
Accounts Payable.........................		2,250
Capital Stock.............................		40,000
Retained Earnings.........................		23,750
Dividends................................	25,000	
Sales....................................		175,670
Sales Returns and Allowances.............	1,280	
Sales Discounts..........................	2,340	
Purchases...............................	98,100	
Purchase Returns and Allowances.........		720
Purchase Discounts.......................		1,020
Freight-In...............................	2,030	
Salary Expense...........................	41,300	
Advertising Expense......................	6,300	
Utilities Expense.........................	1,270	
Totals....................................	$249,660	$249,660

On the last business day of the year, Sept. 30, 1989, the inventory was counted and it amounted to $19,450.

Additional Information

a. Depreciation on the store equipment amounted to $1,750.
b. At year-end the amount of Store Supplies on Hand amounted to $915.
c. Salaries in the amount of $860 were accrued on Sept. 30, 1989.
d. One-half of the prepaid rent had expired by the last day of the year.

Required

1. Prepare, without the adjusted trial balance columns, a worksheet for the year ended Sept. 30, 1989.
2. Record the appropriate general journal entries to close the accounts for the year ended Sept. 30, 1989.

(Check figure: Net Income = $11,585)

Problem A5-4
Preparing a worksheet, financial statements, adjusting, and closing entries

Listed below are the accounts of the Turner Corporation as of the last day of the business year, June 30, 1989.

Accounts Payable	$ 2,300	Accounts Receivable	$ 4,700
Accumulated Depreciation:		Accumulated Depreciation:	
Office Equipment	7,500	Office Building	15,000
Capital Stock	35,000	Cash	3,500
Dividends	20,000	Freight-In	4,400
Insurance Expense	4,900	Inventory, July 1, 1988	35,600
Land	28,000	Notes Payable	4,500
Mortgage Payable	55,000	Office Building	65,000
Office Equipment	25,000	Office Supplies on Hand	1,700
Prepaid Advertising	2,000	Purchases	135,000
Purchase Discounts	8,500	Purchase Returns and	
Retained Earnings	43,000	Allowances	7,600
Sales Discounts	17,500	Sales	249,700
Salaries Expense	62,500	Sales Returns and Allowances	12,000
Travel Expense	6,300		

The inventory was counted at the close of business on June 30, 1989, and amounted to $26,900.

Additional Data

a. Depreciation amounted to $2,100 and $2,850 for the office equipment and the office building, respectively.
b. The office supplies remaining on hand on the last day of the year amounted to $300.
c. One-half of the advertising expired during the year.
d. Accrued salaries were $1,300 at year-end.

Required

1. Prepare a worksheet for the year ended June 30, 1989.
2. Prepare the financial statements.
3. Prepare the adjusting and closing entries in a general journal.

(Check figure: Net Income = $5,850)

Problem A5-5
Preparing journal entries from comparative trial balances

Presented at the top of page 215 are two trial balances of the GuessWhat Corporation. The trial balances reflect business activities ending Oct. 31 and Nov. 30, 1989.

	October		November	
Cash.....................................	$ 250		$ 700	
Accounts Receivable	1,800		2,200	
Inventory	9,300		9,300	
Prepaid Insurance........................	1,200		950	
Office Supplies on Hand	900		400	
Office Equipment	6,200		6,200	
Accum. Depr.: Office Equipment		$ 2,700		$ 2,750
Office Building	28,500		28,500	
Accum. Depr.: Office Building.............		8,250		9,500
Land	5,000		5,000	
Accounts Payable		2,100		1,800
Salaries Payable..........................		900		1,300
Unearned Revenue........................		3,200		2,000
Capital Stock............................		15,000		15,000
Retained Earnings		5,000		5,000
Dividends...............................	2,000		2,700	
Sales....................................		55,650		66,700
Sales Returns and Allowances	1,300		1,450	
Sales Discounts..........................	700		950	
Purchases	25,300		32,700	
Purchase Returns and Allowances		900		1,250
Purchase Discounts		450		550
Freight-In...............................	1,800		1,950	
Salary Expense	6,700		7,600	
Insurance Expense	400		650	
Office Supplies Used	700		1,200	
Depreciation Expense: Office Equipment......................	600		650	
Depreciation Expense: Office Building	1,500		2,750	
Totals	$94,150	$94,150	$105,850	$105,850

Required

Prepare the general journal entries that will summarize the external and internal transactions for the month of November. Assume that the adjusting entries are recorded monthly, and that all purchases and sales are made on account. You may record the entries without the explanations. (Hint: Record sales on account first, then the collection of the sales—don't forget the unearned revenues—then do the same with the purchases.)

**Problem A5-6
Preparing journal entries under the periodic and perpetual inventory systems**

During the course of business activity, The Great East India Company had the following transactions:

Nov. 1   Purchased merchandise on account from the London Tea Company, $26,000, credit terms, 2/10, n/30.

3   Purchased for cash merchandise from Holland Exports, $15,000.

6   Sold merchandise to Boston Redskins, Inc., on account, credit terms 3/10, n/30, $6,500. The inventory cost $4,800.

9   Returned defective merchandise amounting to $1,500 to the London Tea Company.

10   Received amount due from Boston Redskins, Inc.

10   Paid the London Tea Company the amount due.

Nov. 14   Sold merchandise to Portland Company, trade terms 40-10-5, credit terms 3/10, n/30, $5,000. The inventory cost $2,000.

16   Portland returned goods that were sold to them for $1,000 (cost $250) before considering the trade and cash discounts.

23   Portland paid the amount due.

<table>
<tr><td>**Required**</td><td>1. Prepare the general journal entries to record the transactions assuming that a periodic inventory system is used.

2. Prepare the general journal entries to record the transactions assuming that a perpetual inventory system is used.

3. Assuming that the beginning inventory amounted to $21,500, first prepare the general ledger inventory account under first the perpetual inventory system. Then, using the amount of the ending inventory determined under this system, prepare the general ledger inventory account under the periodic inventory system.</td></tr>
</table>

(Check figure: Ending Inventory = $54,450)

Problem A5-7
Preparing a classified
income statement

The income statement accounts of the Seahawk Corporation for the year ended Dec. 31, 1989, are presented below. They are in descending order.

Sales	$345,000	Sales Returns and Allowances...	$2,900
Purchases.....................	180,600	Purchase Discounts	2,800
Inventory, Jan. 1, 1989.........	42,300	Office Supplies Used	2,700
Salaries Expense...............	38,900	Purchase Ret. and Allow........	2,300
Inventory, Dec. 31, 1989	33,700	Depreciation Expense	2,100
Advertising Expense	9,200	Entertainment Expense.........	1,800
Rent Expense	4,800	Telephone Expense	1,400
Freight-In....................	3,700	Utilities Expense...............	1,100
Sales Discount	3,300	Insurance Expense.............	900

Required

Prepare an income statement with three distinct sections: Sales, Cost of Goods Sold, and Operating Expenses. Divide the operating expenses into two sections: Selling, and General and Administrative. Include in the last classification the telephone and utilities expenses.

(Check figure: Net Income = $88,100)

PROBLEMS: SET B

Problem B5-1
Preparing journal entries

The Macho Tire Corporation uses the periodic inventory system. During the month of February, 1989, the corporation had the following transactions:

Feb. 2   Purchased merchandise inventory on account, credit terms 2/10, n/30, $3,500.

4   Paid $4,200 cash for inventory purchased, $300 of which was for freight.

5   Purchased office supplies on account, $1,900, credit terms 2/10, n/30.

7   Sold merchandise on account, 3/10, 1/20, n/60, $2,400.

9   Returned for credit $700 of merchandise acquired on Feb. 2.

10   Purchased merchandise inventory on account, credit terms 2/10, n/30, $5,500.

11   Paid for the inventory purchased on Feb. 2 less the return of Feb. 9 and the appropriate discount.

14   Paid for the office supplies acquired on Feb. 5.

16   Sold merchandise for cash, $4,600.

18   Received returned merchandise of $400 from the sales transaction of Feb. 7.

19   Paid for inventory purchased on Feb. 10.

21   Received payment for merchandise sold on Feb. 7.

25   Returned defective inventory amounting to $600 to the vendor from the Feb. 10 transaction, receiving cash.

Feb. 28   Purchased office equipment on account, credit terms 2/10, n/30, $2,500.

28   Sold office supplies costing $500 for cash to a competitor as an accommodation.

> **Required**

Record these transactions in a general journal.

**Problem B5-2
Calculating ending
inventory and net income**

Diversified Wholesaler, Inc., completed its first-quarter 1989 operations on Mar. 31. An income statement as of that date is desired, but the value of the ending inventory is not known since a physical count was not taken. Of course, an income statement cannot be prepared without knowing the value of the ending inventory. However, the ending inventory can be estimated by using the following procedure.

By analyzing previous year's income statements, a relationship between the net sales and the gross profit can be determined. For Diversified Wholesalers, Inc., this relationship is 42% (that is, gross profit is 42% of the sales figure). If this 42% factor is multiplied by the net sales figure for the first quarter of 1989, the resulting figure will approximate the gross profit figure for the quarter. Subtracting the gross profit from the net sales provides an estimate of the cost of goods sold. Since the cost of goods available for sale can be computed from the accounting records, all that remains to determine the ending inventory is to subtract the cost of those goods sold from the cost of those goods that were available for sale.

The following information is available from the corporation's records:

Advertising Expense	$ 40,800	Purchase Discounts	$ 9,870
Delivery Expense	34,300	Purchase Ret. and Allow.	3,215
Depreciation Expense	12,000	Salaries Expense	126,315
Freight-In	6,800	Sales	750,000
Inventory, Jan. 1, 1989	98,720	Sales Discounts	14,300
Purchases	478,825	Sales Returns and Allowances	9,400

> **Required**

Using this procedure to find the ending inventory, prepare an income statement for the first quarter of 1989 for Diversified Wholesalers, Inc.

(Check figure: Net Income = $91,631)

**Problem B5-3
Preparing a worksheet
and closing entries**

The unadjusted trial balance of the Caldwell Company as of Mar. 31, 1989, is presented below:

Cash	$ 1,200	
Accounts Receivable	3,090	
Inventory	27,400	
Prepaid Insurance	1,800	
Office Supplies on Hand	3,750	
Office Equipment	8,640	
Accum. Depr.: Office Equipment		$ 2,050
Accounts Payable		6,070
Capital Stock		30,000
Retained Earnings		14,710
Dividends	24,000	
Sales		147,430
Sales Returns and Allowances	1,910	
Sales Discounts	2,620	
Purchases	84,210	
Purchase Returns and Allowances		1,370
Purchase Discounts		2,050
Freight-In	2,390	
Salary Expense	36,340	
Advertising Expense	2,730	
Rent Expenses	3,600	
Totals	$203,680	$203,680

Sept. 16   Purchased merchandise on account, $20,000, from Downtown Supply Company under the following trade terms: 40-15-5. In addition, credit terms of 2/10, n/30 are available.

     21   Returned $4,000 of goods acquired from Downtown Supply. (The $4,000 amount does not consider either the trade or the cash discount.)

     24   Paid Downtown Supply the amount due.

Required

1. Prepare general journal entries to record the transactions, first using the periodic inventory system and then using the perpetual inventory system.
2. The beginning inventory amounted to $13,750. First prepare the general ledger inventory account under the perpetual inventory system. Using the ending inventory determined by the perpetual system, prepare the inventory account under the periodic system.

(Check figure: Ending Inventory = $76,634)

Problem B5-7
Preparing a classified income statement

A number of selected accounts appear below from the June 30, 1989, year-end trial balance of Altoona Pullman Coaches, Inc.

Sales	$426,100		Freight-In......................	$7,650
Purchases.....................	289,560		Purchase Returns and	
Capital Stock..................	125,000		Allowances	5,610
Inventory, July 1, 1988.........	60,520		Sales Returns and Allowances...	5,470
Salary Expense:			Purchase Discounts	4,760
Selling......................	58,720		Accounts Receivable	3,800
Inventory, June 30, 1989	55,700		Research and Development	
Entertainment and Travel			Expense	2,400
Expense	17,900		Office Supplies Used	1,960
Salary Expense:			Rent Expense	1,400
Administrative	10,000		Utilities Expense...............	1,200
Depreciation Expense	10,500		Telephone Expense	760
Sales Discounts................	8,320		Miscellaneous Expense	720

Required

Prepare an income statement classified like the Micro Discount Supply Company example in the text. The statement should have three distinct sections: a section for Sales, a section for Cost of Goods Sold, and a section for Operating Expenses. The operating expenses should be split into Selling and General and Administrative Expenses. Only the Salary Expense: Administrative, the Utilities Expense, and the Miscellaneous Expense should be in the last classification.

(Check figure: Net Income = $15,090)

DECISION PROBLEM

The general manager of the Austin Division of Texas Supplies and Materials has just received the financial statements for the division for the year ended Dec. 31, 1989. He is most concerned because he had anticipated the division's net income to be about $130,000 and the actual figure is just over $90,000. The general manager assigns you the task of determining the cause of the difference and provides you with a 118-page computer printout of the division's activity.

You find on the first summary page the following:

```
**********************************************************
TEXAS SUPPLIES AND MATERIALS DATE:    1/17/90  PAGE 1 OF 118

DIVISION 012 (AUSTIN)          TIME:    14:30:17

SUMMARY INCOME STATEMENT       PERIOD: 1/1/89 TO 12/31/89


**********************************************************

SALES                          $2,496,986

COST OF GOODS SOLD             (1,977,654)

OPERATING EXPENSES             (  427,018)

NET INCOME                     $   92,314


**********************************************************
```

Based on past experience, you know that the net income should be about $5\frac{1}{4}\%$ of sales. Contained on page 17 of the report is the following:

```
**********************************************************

TEXAS SUPPLIES AND MATERIALS DATE:   1/17/90 PAGE 17 OF 118

DIVISION 012 (AUSTIN)          TIME:    14:30:53

COST OF GOODS SOLD             PERIOD: 1/1/89 TO 12/31/89


**********************************************************

INVENTORY: JAN 1                                 $   547,026

PURCHASES                           $1,978,315

PURCHASE RETURNS        $79,133

PURCHASE DISCOUNTS       18,719      (97,852)

FREIGHT-IN                           42,117

NET PURCHASES                                      1,922,580

GOODS AVAILABLE                                  $2,469,606

INVENTORY: DEC 31                                   491,952

COST OF GOODS SOLD                               $1,977,654


**********************************************************
```

A review of the past year's activity reveals that purchase returns usually average about 3.8% to 4.2% of purchases, and purchase discounts from vendors are a constant 3%. The division never buys materials from Dec. 15 to the following Jan. 15 because of the holiday season.

Required	1. What can you identify as the problem with the Austin Division? 2. How much should net income be? Show supporting computations. 3. How would you suggest the problem be solved?

CHAPTER 6

Internal Control and Data Processing

When you have completed this chapter, you should be able to:

- Discuss the nature of an internal control system
- Describe the problems inherent in developing a system of internal control
- Explain why a system of internal control is important
- Explain the purpose of special journals and how to use them
- Explain the posting process of a business entity using special journals
- Describe the relationship between subsidiary and control accounts

"But Mr. Wilson was our most trusted employee," lamented the office manager after the embezzlement was discovered. "Better I should have assigned someone I didn't trust to the funds transfers section, and then I would have watched him like a hawk. Mr. Wilson never even took a day's vacation, such a nice gentleman he was, how could he do this to me?"

An all too familiar scene to those of us in accounting. Look in your local newspaper for the next several months and you will see a similar situation reported. Would we let someone we didn't trust handle our money? And Mr. Wilson never took a vacation. Of course not! If he had, someone else would have had to handle his responsibilities and they would have discovered his "unique" methods of transferring company funds. Mr. Wilson would have been caught. The problem here is that the company evidently did not have any method of providing certain checks and balances in its operations that would discourage this particular fraud. In short, there was no system of *internal control.* That's what this chapter is all about, a discussion of procedures, techniques, and practices designed to provide a dependable and efficient accounting system that will help management plan and control the company's business activities as well as safeguard the company's resources. And part of a dependable and efficient accounting system is the method of processing mass amounts of data, the topic of the last sections of the chapter.

INTERNAL CONTROL

An internal control system can not completely prevent fraud. It can, however, make the perpetration of fraud very difficult

One of the very first things we need to realize about any internal control system, no matter how tightly it is designed, is that it cannot be made 100% foolproof. That's why casualty insurance is carried on company assets, and that's why fidelity bonds are carried on employees who handle company funds. But an internal control system can be so designed to make it difficult for one person to perpetrate a fraud. Several dishonest employees will have to coordinate activities (collusion) to do their despicable deeds.

Two types of internal controls are *accounting controls* and *administrative controls.* While we will be most concerned with accounting controls, a brief mention of administrative controls is necessary.

Administrative controls deal with the efficiency of an organization

Administrative controls are the procedures and methods that are concerned mainly with the operational efficiency of the organization and compliance with the organization's policies. They include such things as time-and-motion studies, performance reports, statistical analyses, and various directives such as requiring company executives to have annual medical examinations. Administrative controls are important to any organization, but accountants are more concerned with controls that affect the reliability of the financial statements and that safeguard the company's resources.

Accounting controls deal with procedures, techniques, and practices that protect a company's assets and provide reliable financial statements

Accounting controls are the procedures, techniques, and practices intended to protect the company's resources and provide for reliable financial statements. We can organize our discussion of internal accounting controls by looking at personnel controls, record controls, and checks and balances.

Personnel Controls

In the selection, training, and assignment of personnel there are several basic considerations needed to develop a strong system of internal control. These considerations are: employee competence, duty assignments, employee responsibility and authority, accountability, and custodianship.

It is essential that employees have the necessary talent, intelligence, and training for their assigned duties

■ *Employee competence*   The organization must make an effort to assure that employees are very carefully selected and that they have the necessary talents, intelligence, and training for the duties assigned to them. And it is equally important that these employees be properly supervised as they perform their duties. Talent and intelligence are wasted if the employee has not been adequately trained to perform assigned tasks. The most important assignment a supervisor has is to train people with the view of having them reach their highest potential within the organization.

A system of internal control must be designed so that responsibility for actions are clearly identified

■ *Assignment of responsibility*   Let's picture an accounts receivable section of a large department store; say that we have about 10 employees assigned to this section. A phone call comes to you from an irate customer complaining about an error in her account. As manager of this section you need to discuss the error with the individual who made the error. Now errors are going to happen; we can't avoid that fact of life. But we can attempt to prevent the same error from happening again. And we have an opportunity to help someone learn from the error. Remember what good old Fra Pacioli once said (page 78): If you don't do anything, you aren't going to make any mistakes; and if you don't make any mistakes, you will not learn. So you ask the group who committed the error, and if the group is like most other groups, 10 fingers will point to 10 different people. The point is that the system must be designed so the responsibility can be pinpointed without question. The group should have been organized so that each employee was assigned a group of customer account numbers over which he or she had responsibility.

■ *Division of work*   Back to Mr. Wilson again. What may have happened was that Mr. Wilson was assigned the responsibilities of depositing customer checks in the bank and also maintaining the accounts receivable records. How easy for him — he just pockets some customer checks and marks their accounts paid with the collections from the next customer or two. As long as he knows where he is in his "system," he can continue this indefinitely. If this was what Mr. Wilson did, we could have prevented it from happening by having someone else handle the responsibility of depositing the checks or maintaining the accounts receivable records. Employee assignments should be divided so that related operations are not performed by the same individual. Where this is the case, it takes several employees conspiring to commit fraud.

Employee assignments should be divided so that related operations are not performed by the same individual

■ *Rotation of duties*   Rotating the individual assignments within the work unit will serve several purposes. First, it gives the employees training in many of the different areas of the unit, thus providing them with a bigger picture of the unit's role in the organization. Second, it enhances the value of employees, enabling them to understand, appreciate, and perform each other's work should the need arise. Third, it strengthens the system, since departures from standard operating procedures will be discovered when another employee performs the assignment. Fourth, it provides a broader background for the employees, serving as a basis for future promotion.

Rotating employee assignments is essential for training and control

The organization should have a policy that all employees be required to take annual leave. Clearly, such a policy would benefit employees; it can also benefit the firm. How we wish that Mr. Wilson had taken vacations!

Records Controls

Sometimes the activities in records controls may overlap the activities in personnel controls; generally, that's okay. Its just another way of looking at the overall problem of controls. We are going to classify records control into three parts: custodianship, adequacy, and documentation.

■ *Custodianship*   Someone within the firm has to be assigned the responsibility of collecting cash receipts and depositing the cash in the bank. Someone must also be responsible for the company's small tools, parts, and vehicles. If the individual responsible for the tools and parts were also the individual who maintained the records on the tools and parts inventory, a potential would exist for that individual to supply himself and his friends with all the tools and parts they need at company expense. Some fringe benefit! The point is that the individual assigned the custodianship of the firm's resources must not have access to the records pertaining to those resources. The individual assigned the responsibility of maintaining the accounts receivable records must not have any access to cash; those preparing the payroll records must not be able to draw checks from the payroll cash account.

Custodianship of assets and record control must be kept separate

■ *Adequacy*   In order to provide control over the firm's resources as well as to provide timely, accurate, and reliable information to management, adequate records must be maintained. As a matter of fact, all publicly held corporations in the United States are required by law (the Foreign Corrupt Practices Act) to maintain adequate records to assure that the corporation's resources are what and

Adequate records include a chart of accounts, control and subsidiary records, and prenumbered paper forms as well as appropriate recordkeeping equipment

WHEN E. F. HUTTON KITES, PEOPLE LOSE

Check kiting is the process of covering a shortage in cash by writing a check on one cash account and depositing the check in another cash account. The deposit is reflected in the second cash account but the withdrawal is not recorded on the first account. Since it may take several days for the check to be processed by the banking system, the cash shortage can be covered. Accountants generally look for check kiting by requesting that two bank statements be mailed directly from the bank to the accountant: one at month's end and another, called a "cutoff statement," 10 days later. All interbank transfers reflected on the second statement are then traced and verified to determine their validity.

The following information was extracted

from an article in the May 2, 1985, business section of the Tampa Tribune:

E. F. Hutton pleaded guilty to 2,000 federal felony charges and was fined $2.75 million in a check kiting scheme that may have involved a total of $10 billion. An estimated 400 banks lost "tens of millions of dollars" in interest payments on money that did not exist. The checks were written on funds of distant banks before money was deposited in those banks to cover the checks. About 10 to 25 people were involved in the scheme and the Justice Department stated that other firms may be doing the same thing.

The 2,000 felony charges represent 2,000 separate counts of mail and wire fraud—each charge representing a single check. The checks were worth $4.349 billion. Each charge drew a fine of $1,000 and

the additional $750,000 levy was to defray the costs of the government investigation.

The Justice Department stated that between July 1, 1980, and February 28, 1982, E. F. Hutton drew against uncollected funds, with daily overdrafts sometimes exceeding $250 million.

The 1981 transactions with the United Virginia Bank in Alexandra, Va., illustrates how the scheme worked. Day after day E. F. Hutton owed the bank about $9 million. Each day new checks were deposited to cover the previous day's checks—but the bank never got the money, only more checks.

Reprinted by permission of the Tampa Tribune-Times.

where the corporation says they are. The law requires that a system of internal control must be adequate to assure that the management of the corporation has knowledge of all the entity's business transactions and has approved them. Adequate records include a chart of accounts, control accounts and the related subsidiary records, and prenumbered sequential paper forms such as sales orders and checks.

The company's recordkeeping equipment—cash registers, check protectors, bookkeeping machines, and computer hardware and software—must all be adequate to provide the safeguards necessary to achieve proper control as well as to provide timely, accurate, and reliable information to management.

All business transactions must be adequately documented

■ **Documentation** This is another aspect of having adequate records. Each function within the organization must **document** its activity with adequate records. Take the sales function, for example. Documentation includes the *purchase order* from a company wishing to buy our product, the *credit approval* from our firm's credit department, the *sales invoice,* the *shipping invoice* marked "shipped," the *accounts receivable subsidiary ledger account* for the customer, and whatever other documents, properly authorized with appropriate signatures, are necessary to verify that an order was authorized, filled, sent, received, and paid for. In other words, adequate **documentation** must exist to trace and verify each transaction the corporation enters into from beginning to end. In accounting lingo this is considered to be an "adequate audit trail."

Checks and Balances

The last aspect of internal control we will consider is that of checks and balances. Any good system must provide for a continual review of the recordkeeping functions and the verification of resources. Our discussion is organized into three parts: reconciliations, internal auditing, and external auditing.

Reconciliations are made periodically between a company's assets and the related records

■ *Reconciliations*   Every month the company will receive from the bank a statement of the amount of cash the company has on deposit at the bank. The company must then compare the amount reflected on the bank statement with the amount in the general ledger Cash account. This is called a *reconciliation.* Any differences must be explained. We will see how to do this in the next chapter. The Accounts Receivable Control account must be reconciled with the accounts receivable subsidiary ledger (the individual accounts receivable accounts). We will see how to do this in the next section of this chapter. The Inventory account (in a perpetual inventory system) must be reconciled with the physical count of the inventory. And so it goes for all the company's resources. The records are compared with the actual resources to verify that the resource exists and to know how much of it there is.

■ *Internal auditing*   Internal auditing is usually associated with large corporations, but many of the functions of internal auditing departments of large corporations can be carried out by small companies. Basically, the function of the internal audit is to review the organization's activities to discover errors or irregularities, to determine if procedures and policies are being followed, and to uncover inefficiency.

■ *External auditing*   Before providing an opinion on a company's financial statements, the CPA must review the company's system of internal control. This outside review offers the company an impartial check of the company's system and often results in many suggestions for improvement.

DATA PROCESSING

Part of a system of good internal control is having adequate records. The system we have developed in the first four chapters has adequate records to handle only the smallest of companies. We need to expand the recordkeeping system to handle a much larger mass of business activities. We need to study data processing.

The accounting process we have presented up to this point should work well enough for business entities, service or merchandising, that do not have many trans-

THE E.S.M. AUDIT

"He was bright, charming, and personable, which makes it all the harder to understand," said Howard Groveman, the national director of accounting and auditing for Alexander Grant & Co., about Jose Gomez, a partner involved in an alleged bribery in the alleged E.S.M. fraud. Mr. Gomez was one of the youngest partners in the firm's history.

The E.S.M. Government Securities alleged fraud triggered a panic that resulted in the temporary closing of four score and ten Ohio Saving & Loan institutions. Jose Gomez was the Alexander Grant partner in charge of the E.S.M. audit. E.S.M. had a negative net worth of $300 million in March, 1985, when it collapsed.

The Securities and Exchange Commission charged Mr. Gomez with accepting $125,000 in payments from E.S.M. for approving false E.S.M. financial statements.

The internal controls of the large CPA firm require that the local office managing partner appoint an "engagement partner" to oversee a specific audit. The engagement partner then recommends a manager and an audit team to perform the engagement. Thus, there should be three responsible individuals for an audit engagement: the audit manager, the engagement partner, and the local office managing partner. This is the internal control feature of separation of duties. But in the E.S.M. case Mr. Gomez was the managing partner of the Fort Lauderdale, Florida, office, the engagement partner, and he acted as the manager.

Source: "The Lesson of E.S.M." by Jeffery A. Trachtenberg, *FORBES,* May 6, 1985, p. 128.

The internal control features you studied in this section of the chapter apply not only to business entities but to the CPA firms that audit those business entities.

actions or many customers or suppliers. Any transaction, no matter how simple or complex, can be handled by this process. Any *number* of transactions can also be handled, *given an unlimited amount of time*. However, time is limited and expensive, and most business entities have many transactions. Consequently, business entities have developed accounting systems to perform the accounting process. These systems are basically tailor-made for each business entity and range from simple manual accounting systems to expensive and complex electronic systems.

The accounting process you have learned about so far is, basically, the simple manual accounting system, and is illustrated in Figure 6-1. Electronic accounting systems are computer-based and sophisticated, often using the latest and largest of computers and peripheral equipment. The type of system a business entity needs depends on how easily its various types of business transactions can be classified into like groups. For example, a manual system may group together all sales on account for recording. An electronic system may batch all daily customer billings together to update customer files, update inventory stocks, send bills to customers, and compute the amount of the Accounts Receivable balance. All transactions within each group are handled in the same manner.

An electronic accounting system is based on the same principles as a manual accounting system, and it does the same work a manual system does. The difference, of course, is that the electronic system can handle many, many more transactions than a manual system, and can do all of them very much faster. A lot faster!

Within the last decade the microcomputer has played an important part in data processing for many small to medium-size companies. Software packages have been developed for the accounting activity that enable companies to process large amounts of data and generate financial statements for a very reasonable cost.

Accounting textbooks use the basic manual data processing system to describe how transactions are analyzed, classified, and summarized, resulting in the final accounting product—the financial statements. But you should appreciate that even

FIGURE 6-1 Manual Accounting System

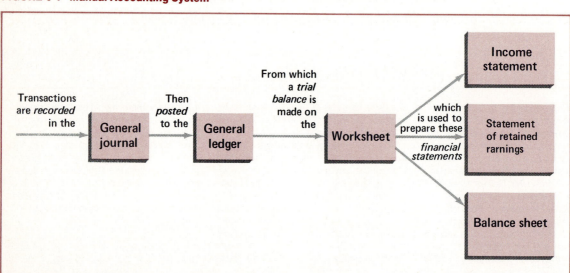

the smallest of firms is today using some electronic systems. And you should also appreciate that the electronic systems are based on the concepts you have learned, and will learn, about a manual system.

Most transactions can be classified into four groups: buying and selling merchandise on account; paying and receiving cash

To begin our discussion of a manual system, let's consider a merchandising firm's transactions. Although an entity engages in many transactions in the normal course of doing its business, almost all of them can be classified in one of four major groups. For example, a merchandising firm sells merchandise on account, purchases merchandise for resale on account, receives cash, and pays cash. For each of these distinct activities a *special journal* is designed. A special journal is a *book of original entry* — a book where transactions are first recorded — designed to record only one class of business transactions. The four most common special journals are the *sales journal,* the *cash receipts journal,* the *purchases journal,* and the *cash payments journal.* The general journal is used only to record transactions that cannot be recorded in one of the special journals.

The Sales Journal

Only sales on account are recorded in the sales journal

The sales journal is a book of original entry designed to handle only one type of transaction: the sale of merchandise on credit. This transaction requires a debit to Accounts Receivable and a credit to Sales. No other transaction should be recorded in the sales journal. A cash sale, for example, should not be recorded in the sales journal; it should be recorded in the cash receipts journal. The sales journal is a single-column journal, as can be seen in The Jones Company sales journal illustrated in Exhibit 6-1. This is because only one money column is needed — the amount debited to Accounts Receivable is also the amount credited to Sales.

Cash sales are recorded in the cash receipts journal

EXHIBIT 6-1

	THE JONES COMPANY			
	Sales Journal			Page 16
Date	**Account Debited**	**Invoice No.**	**Post. Ref.**	**Amount**
1989				
Aug. 4	Sally Hamm	418	✓	100
6	John Davis	419	✓	85
7	Tom Adams	420	✓	20
15	Linda Jones	421	✓	90
18	Nancy Kantz	422	✓	200
21	William Lennord	423	✓	450
27	Robert Grafton	424	✓	80
30	Ann Knox	425	✓	180
Total				1,205
				(1130/4100)

The evidence of each sale is a *sales invoice,* which lists the date of the sale, the customer's name, the credit terms, the amount of the sale, and the invoice number. The sales invoice representing the sale to Linda Jones would look like this:

THE JONES COMPANY
1531 Fletcher Avenue
Tampa, Florida 33620

Invoice No. _____ 421 _____

Invoice Date _____ Aug. 15, 1989 _____

Sold to: Linda Jones _____

Terms _____ 2/10, n/30 _____

3116 Second Street _____

Shipped Via _____ Customer pick-up _____

Brandon, FL 33511 _____

Date Shipped _____ Aug. 15, 1989 _____

Quantity	Description		Unit Price	Amount
8	13EL7	Fans	$7.50	$60.00
24	20AQ1	Belts	1.25	30.00
				$90.00

A copy of the sales invoice provides the authority and the information to record the transaction in the sales journal.

Notice that the sales journal does not require a description or explanation for a transaction. Because only one type of transaction is recorded, it is obvious what that transaction is—a sale of merchandise on account.

The invoice number provides a reference to the sales invoice. Thus, if any additional information or a review of the original information is needed, the sales invoice can be located by its invoice number.

At the end of each month the total sales on account from the sales journal is posted to the general ledger as a single debit to the Accounts Receivable account and a single credit to the Sales account. In Exhibit 6-1, this is represented by:

$$\underline{\underline{\$1,205}}$$
$$(1130/4100)$$

where $1,205 = the total of all the sales on account for the month
         1130 = the company's account number for Accounts Receivable
         4100 = the account number for Sales

Of course, the left/right order of the account numbers indicates that $1,205 is debited to Accounts Receivable (that is, to the account whose reference number is on the left of the slash mark) and $1,205 is credited to Sales (to the account whose number is on the right of the slash).

In this simple illustration, eight sales transactions were recorded but only one posting was required. In a more realistic business situation, there would be several hundred sales transactions during a month's time. No matter how many transactions there are, only one posting is required. This is the advantage provided by the sales journal in the posting process.

Let's look at the debit side of this entry—Accounts Receivable. We might see a disadvantage in relying solely on the sales journal. The Accounts Receivable account informs management of the amount of total credit outstanding to its customers. The account does not provide any information on the credit of individual customers. Management must know on a daily basis the credit status of the individual customers. Has anyone exceeded his or her credit limit? If so, can additional credit be granted? How long is the account overdue? Answers to these and other related questions are vital to a well-managed company.

The Subsidiary Ledger and the Control Account

Information on the credit of individual customers is recorded in a ***subsidiary ledger,*** which is separate from the general ledger and in which a separate account is maintained for each individual customer. These customer accounts are alphabetized.

The alphabetized ***accounts receivable ledger*** is a subsidiary ledger of the Accounts Receivable account in the general ledger. The Accounts Receivable account in the general ledger is called the ***control account.*** A subsidiary ledger should be established for any general ledger account comprising many individual accounts. For example, if a business entity had 20 different cash accounts, a subsidiary ledger would be established where each of the individual cash accounts could be found, and the general ledger account Cash would be a control account. Subsidiary ledgers are most commonly used for accounts receivable, accounts payable, and equipment.

A subsidiary ledger may contain only 10 or fewer accounts or as many as 10,000 accounts. Figure 6-2 below illustrates the relationship between each of five

The accounts receivable ledger is a subsidiary ledger

FIGURE 6-2
The Jones Company
The relationship between general and subsidiary ledgers.

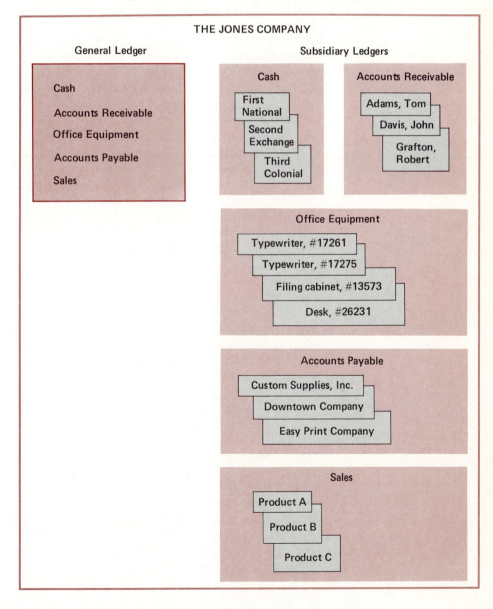

possible general ledger control accounts and the subsidiary ledgers for each control account.

Where there are many individual accounts in a subsidiary ledger, it would be impossible to list each one on a trial balance. However, we don't have to deal with this impossibility because of the control account. The control account reflects the total of the balances of all the individual subsidiary ledger accounts. It takes the place of these numerous accounts in the trial balance.

Let's return to our illustration of the sales journal (page 229) to demonstrate more fully the relationship between the subsidiary ledger and the control account. When The Jones Company makes a sale, such as the $100 credit sale to Sally Hamm on Aug. 4, two things happen: (1) The sale is recorded in the sales journal, and (2) it is also posted as a debit in Sally's Accounts Receivable account in the subsidiary ledger. The fact that the posting has been made is indicated by the check mark (✓) in the posting reference column of the sales journal.

Exhibit 6-2 on the facing page illustrates the process of posting from the sales journal to the subsidiary ledger. The subsidiary ledger is posted every day credit sales are made; the general ledger is posted only on the last day of the month.

Let's take a closer look at the posting process. The Aug. 4 entry in the sales journal represents a sale on account to Sally Hamm for $100. On the date of this transaction a debit is posted to the Accounts Receivable subsidiary account of Sally Hamm. In this subsidiary ledger account the *S16* refers to page 16 of the sales journal, identifying the source of the information recorded. The (✓) in the sales journal indicates that the information it identifies has been posted to the subsidiary ledger.

At the end of the month the total amount of the sales on account, $1,205, is posted to the general ledger accounts. Note that a posting reference, S16, is placed in the control account to identify the source of the information posted.

Before the trial balance is prepared at the end of the month, all the debit balances in the accounts receivable subsidiary ledger are totaled to see if the total agrees with the debit balance in the control account (Accounts Receivable in the general ledger). If no errors occurred, the two will balance.

The Cash Receipts Journal

The cash receipts journal is a multi-column journal

The special journal used to record transactions in which cash is received is called the ***cash receipts journal.*** Unlike the single-column sales journal, the cash receipts journal contains many columns. There is only one source for data recorded in the sales journal—sales on account—so one column is sufficient. But cash is received from many different sources. Therefore, in the cash receipts journal, a column is needed to record each source of the cash. However, only one column is needed to record the receipt of cash.

Collection of receivables and cash sales are the two most common sources of cash

In designing a cash receipts journal, each business entity must consider all its sources of cash. The two most common regular sources of cash are the collection of accounts receivable and cash sales. Thus, a credit column is established for each of these accounts: Accounts Receivable and Sales. Although there are other sources of cash, they do not occur regularly. So, they are lumped together in one column labeled Sundry Accounts Credit. Nevertheless, for any source that produces more than a few cash transactions each month, a column should be established. The cash receipts journal of The Jones Company is illustrated in Exhibit 6-3 at the top of page 234.

Cash sales are recorded in the cash receipts journal by entering the amount of the cash received in the cash debit and the sales credit columns. For example, the amount entered typically represents the total of each day's cash sales as indicated by cash-reg-

EXHIBIT 6-2 Posting from the Sales Journal to the Subsidiary Ledger and General Ledger
The subsidiary ledger is posted daily; the general ledger, monthly.

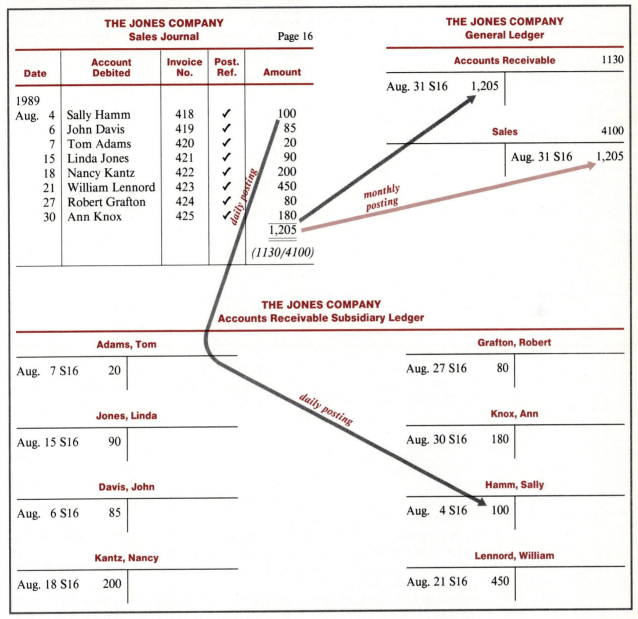

ister tapes. Exhibit 6-3 illustrates three cash sales entries — Aug. 3, Aug. 15, and Aug. 21. Each of these daily totals represent numerous cash sales transactions during the day indicated.

The total of the sales credit column in the cash receipts journal, $1,200 in Exhibit 6-3, is the total cash sales for the month. This amount is posted to the credit column of the Sales account in the general ledger. Thus, a large number of sales transactions have been recorded in the general ledger account by only one posting.

EXHIBIT 6-3

<table>
<thead>
<tr><th colspan="10" style="text-align:center">THE JONES COMPANY
Cash Receipts Journal   Page 9</th></tr>
<tr><th>Date</th><th>Account
Credited</th><th>Explanation</th><th>Post.
Ref.</th><th>Sundry
Accounts
Cr.</th><th>Accounts
Receivable
Cr.</th><th>Sales
Cr.</th><th>Sales
Disc.
Dr.</th><th>Cash
Dr.</th></tr>
</thead>
<tbody>
<tr><td>1989
Aug. 3</td><td></td><td>Cash sales</td><td>—</td><td></td><td></td><td>500</td><td></td><td>500</td></tr>
<tr><td>5</td><td>Common Stock</td><td>Issue common stock</td><td>3100</td><td>1,000</td><td></td><td></td><td></td><td>1,000</td></tr>
<tr><td>11</td><td>Sally Hamm</td><td>Invoice, 8/4 less 2%</td><td>✓</td><td></td><td>100</td><td></td><td>2</td><td>98</td></tr>
<tr><td>15</td><td></td><td>Cash sales</td><td>—</td><td></td><td></td><td>300</td><td></td><td>300</td></tr>
<tr><td>17</td><td>John Davis</td><td>Invoice, 8/6 partial</td><td>✓</td><td></td><td>45</td><td></td><td></td><td>45</td></tr>
<tr><td>20</td><td>Notes Payable</td><td>Bank loan</td><td>2110</td><td>600</td><td></td><td></td><td></td><td>600</td></tr>
<tr><td>21</td><td></td><td>Cash sales</td><td>—</td><td></td><td></td><td>400</td><td></td><td>400</td></tr>
<tr><td>22</td><td>Nancy Kantz</td><td>Invoice, 8/18 less 2%</td><td>✓</td><td></td><td>200</td><td></td><td>4</td><td>196</td></tr>
<tr><td>30</td><td>Tom Adams</td><td>Invoice, 8/7</td><td>✓</td><td></td><td>20</td><td></td><td></td><td>20</td></tr>
<tr><td></td><td></td><td></td><td></td><td>1,600</td><td>365</td><td>1,200</td><td>6</td><td>3,159</td></tr>
<tr><td></td><td></td><td></td><td></td><td>(—)</td><td>(1130)</td><td>(4100)</td><td>(4110)</td><td>(1110)</td></tr>
</tbody>
</table>

Recall our discussion on sales discounts earlier in Chapter 5. When credit terms are granted and the customer pays the bill within the discount period, a sales discount is given. The general journal entry to record a collection of an account receivable within the discount period would be as follows:

Cash 98
Sales Discount 2
    Accounts Receivable 100
To record collection of accounts receivable subject to 2/10, n/30 credit terms.

To record this in the cash receipts journal, two debit money columns are needed: one for cash and one for sales discount.

For example, The Jones Company made a sale on account in the amount of $100 to Sally Hamm on Aug. 4, as reported in the sales journal back in Exhibit 6-1 (page 229). Sally paid in full on August 11, as indicated in the third line of the cash receipts journal (Exhibit 6-3). Therefore, $100 credit is entered for Sally in the accounts receivable column of the cash receipts journal. And, because she paid her bill within 10 days (assuming 2/10, n/30), she gets a discount of 2% (of $100), or $2, which is entered as a debit in the sales discount column.

Notice the check mark (✓) in the posting reference column after the account of Sally Hamm. This indicates that the $100 credit was posted to her Accounts Receivable account in the subsidiary ledger. As with the sales journal, the subsidiary ledger accounts are posted each day.

The total of the accounts receivable column in the cash receipts journal is posted as a credit to the Accounts Receivable Control account in the general ledger at the end of the month. In our example, the total was $365. Therefore, a credit of $365 is posted to the Accounts Receivable Control account on the last day of the month. To indicate that this has been posted, the Accounts Receivable Control account number (1130) is placed under the accounts receivable credit column.

The sundry accounts column is used to handle all sources of cash other than cash sales and collections of receivables

Sources of cash other than cash sales or collections of accounts receivable are entered in the sundry accounts credit column. Two such examples are shown in Exhibit 6-3. On Aug. 5, stockholders invested an additional $1,000 in the business; and on Aug. 20, the company borrowed $600 from the bank by issuing a note payable. In each case the general ledger account title must be entered under the caption Account Credited. At the end of the month the amounts found in the sundry column are posted to their respective general ledger accounts. The account numbers of these accounts are entered in the posting reference column to evidence that the posting has been done.

The amounts within each column of the cash receipts journal are added — or as accountants say, *footed* — at the end of the month. The totals of the credit columns are then added together, or *crossfooted.* Similarly, the debit columns are crossfooted. The purpose of the crossfooting is to prove the equality of the debits and credits. In our example, the crossfooting of the column totals from the cash receipts journal of Exhibit 6-3 appears as follows:

Sundry Accounts Cr.		Accounts Receivable Cr.		Sales Cr.				Sales Discounts Dr.		Cash Dr.
$1,600	+	$365	+	$1,200	=	$3,165	=	$6	+	$3,159

Upon the assurance that the debits and credits in the cash receipts journal are equal, the totals of each of the columns are posted to their respective accounts in the general ledger. The posting is evidenced in the cash receipts journal by annotating under each column total the number that identifies it in the general ledger.

In the sundry accounts credit column, two entries appear. These entries must be posted individually to the general ledger accounts Common Stock and Notes Payable, and the identifying account numbers for each must be entered in the posting reference column.

The total of the sundry accounts credit column is used only in crossfooting to prove equality of the debits and credits. The total, of course, is not posted because it is a combination of several accounts. This total provides no useful information; it is used simply to aid in proving the equality of the debits and credits. Consequently, no account number is placed under the column total. Instead, the symbol (—) is placed under the column to show that it has been considered in the crossfooting.

Presented in Exhibit 6-4 at the top of the next page are the accounts of the general ledger and the accounts receivable subsidiary ledger after both the sales journal and the cash receipts journal have been posted.

Notice that the source of each of the postings is referenced by the journal page numbers. The posting from the sales journal page 16 is referenced as S16, while the posting from the cash receipts journal page 9 is referenced as CR9.

EXHIBIT 6-4

THE JONES COMPANY — General Ledger		THE JONES COMPANY — Accounts Receivable Subsidiary Ledger	

THE JONES COMPANY
General Ledger

Cash   1110

| Aug. 31 CR9 | 3,159 | | |

Accounts Receivable   1130

| Aug. 31 S16 | 1,205 | Aug. 31 CR9 | 365 |

Notes Payable   2110

| | | Aug. 20 CR9 | 600 |

Common Stock   3100

| | | Aug. 5 CR9 | 1,000 |

Sales   4100

| | | Aug. 31 S16 | 1,205 |
| | | 31 CR9 | 1,200 |

Sales Discounts   4110

| Aug. 31 CR9 | 6 | | |

THE JONES COMPANY
Accounts Receivable Subsidiary Ledger

Adams, Tom

| Aug. 7 S16 | 20 | Aug. 30 CR9 | 20 |

Davis, John

| Aug. 6 S16 | 85 | Aug. 17 CR9 | 45 |

Grafton, Robert

| Aug. 27 S16 | 80 | | |

Hamm, Sally

| Aug. 4 S16 | 100 | Aug. 11 CR9 | 100 |

Jones, Linda

| Aug. 15 S16 | 90 | | |

Kantz, Nancy

| Aug. 18 S16 | 200 | Aug. 22 CR9 | 200 |

Knox, Ann

| Aug. 30 S16 | 180 | | |

Lennord, William

| Aug. 21 S16 | 450 | | |

The Purchases Journal

Only purchases on account are recorded in the purchases journal

Like the sales journal, the ***purchases journal*** is a book of original entry designed to record just one type of business transaction — the purchase of merchandise on account. It is a one-column journal in which each entry is a debit to Purchases and a credit to Accounts Payable. This single-column journal is illustrated in Exhibit 6-5.

Each transaction is recorded in the purchases journal by entering the date of the transaction, the vendor's (creditor's) name, the date of the invoice, and the amount of the purchase. The vendor's accounts are posted each day to their accounts payable in the subsidiary ledger. For example, see the posting of the Easy Print Company account of Aug. 2 in Exhibit 6-5. The procedure is much the same as posting from the sales journal to the subsidiary and general ledgers. The purchases journal page number P11 is recorded as a posting reference in the subsidiary ledger account of the Easy Print Company as the source of authority for the posting.

At the end of the month the purchases journal is footed and the total is posted as a debit to Purchases and also as a credit to Accounts Payable in the general ledger. The account numbers of these two accounts — 5100 and 2120, respectively — are annotated under the total of the amount column, indicating that the total has been posted

EXHIBIT 6-5

THE JONES COMPANY
Purchases Journal   Page 11

Date	Account Credited	Invoice Date	Post. Ref.	Amount
1989				
Aug. 2	Easy Print Company	8/2	✓	275
9	Federal Company	8/6	✓	150
14	Custom Supplies, Inc.	8/10	✓	100
19	Downtown Company	8/19	✓	320
22	Federal Company	8/21	✓	15
24	Great Goods, Inc.	8/20	✓	255
				1,115
				(5100/2120)

monthly posting

daily posting

THE JONES COMPANY
General Ledger

Accounts Payable   2120

Aug. 31 P11	1,115	

Purchases   5100

Aug. 31 P11	1,115	

THE JONES COMPANY
Accounts Payable Subsidiary Ledger

Custom Supplies, Inc.

	Aug. 14 P11	100

Downtown Company

	Aug. 19 P11	320

Easy Print Company

	Aug. 2 P11	275

Federal Company

	Aug. 9 P11	150
	Aug. 22 P11	15

Great Goods, Inc.

	Aug. 24 P11	255

to both accounts. The journal page number is recorded as a posting reference in the general ledger account as authority for the posting.

The Cash Payments Journal

The cash payments journal is a multi-column journal

The payment of cash is recorded in the *cash payments journal.* A cash payments journal is structured in much the same way as a cash receipts journal. Because cash is paid out for at least several different purposes, each many times during a month, there are at least several columns in a cash payments journal. Accounts Payable, Purchases, and Sundry are column headings for the typical debits recorded; Purchase Discounts and Cash are the column headings for recording the credits. The cash payments journal of The Jones Company is illustrated in Exhibit 6-6 below.

You are most likely aware that a business entity does not make cash payments in currency, but rather by check. The reason, of course, is that payment by check provides security and control—that is, it provides information that the payments were paid and were received by the payee, as well as a record of the payment amounts, dates paid, and related information. Thus, the format of a cash payments journal differs from a cash receipts journal in one respect: Rather than having a column for explaining the nature of cash received, it has a column for simply recording the number of the check used for the cash payment. Of course, should it be necessary to know the nature of the payment, that information can be found for that check in the checkbook records.

There is one exception to the rule that cash payments must be made in check, not currency: Petty cash payments, of course, are made in currency. The reason is practicability and expediency. We'll discuss petty cash disbursements in Chapter 7.

Each cash payment is posted from the cash payments journal to the appropriate general and subsidiary ledger accounts in the same way that each cash receipt was posted from the cash receipts journal. Transactions with vendors are posted each day to appropriate accounts in the accounts payable subsidiary ledger. When a transaction is posted from the journal to the subsidiary ledger, a check mark (✓) is entered in the posting reference column. In Exhibit 6-6 the check marks for the entries to Federal Company, Easy Print Company, and Custom Supplies serve as examples that each has been posted.

EXHIBIT 6-6

		THE JONES COMPANY						
		Cash Payments Journal						Page 24
Date	**Check No.**	**Account Debited**	**Post. Ref.**	**Sundry Accounts Dr.**	**Accounts Payable Dr.**	**Purchases Dr.**	**Purchase Discounts Cr.**	**Cash Cr.**
1989								
Aug. 3	316	Rent Expense	5400	175				175
9	317	Purchases	—			135		135
11	318	Federal Company	✓		150		3	147
16	319	Salary Expense	5200	200				200
17	320	Easy Print Co.	✓		175			175
22	321	Purchases	—			400		400
24	322	Custom Supplies	✓		100		2	98
26	323	Freight-In	5120	10				10
				385	425	535	5	1,340
				(—)	(2120)	(5100)	(5115)	(1110)

At the end of the month, each individual entry in the sundry accounts debit column is posted to its appropriate account in the general ledger. Instead of a check mark, the account number of the general ledger account is entered in the posting reference column of the cash payments journal to indicate that the transaction has been posted. Examples of these cash payments are Rent Expense, Salary Expense, and Freight-In, as shown in the sundry accounts debit column in Exhibit 6-6.

The cash payments journal is footed and crossfooted to prove the equality of the debits and credits, as was done for the cash receipts journal. Finally, the totals of the columns to be posted in the general ledger are posted in their respective accounts, and to indicate that this had been done, the account numbers are entered under the column totals of the cash payments journal.

The General Journal

Only a few transactions will now be recorded in the general journal

With these four special journals, relatively few transactions are recorded in the general journal. Only transactions that do not involve cash receipts or cash payments, or the purchase or sale of merchandise on credit, are entered as original entries in the general journal. *Adjusting, closing,* and *reversing* entries are examples of such entries.

Two transactions that must be recorded in the general journal are illustrated below. The first, dated Aug. 20, is the acquisition of office equipment on account. This entry cannot be recorded in the purchases journal because that journal records only *purchases of merchandise* on account.

The second transaction is the return of items previously sold to a customer. Because this entry involves neither cash nor a purchase nor a sale, the only place for this entry is in the general journal.

Since the acquisition of office equipment on account is not a **purchase,** *it must be recorded in the general journal*

	General Journal			Page 3
Date	**Account Titles and Explanation**	**Post. Ref.**	**Debit**	**Credit**
Aug. 20	Office Equipment Accounts Payable To record the acquisition of office equipment from Tate Office Supplies Company, terms 3/10, n/30.	1210 2120/✔	575	575
23	Sales Returns and Allowances Accounts Receivable To record the return of items previously sold to Linda Jones on account.	4120 1130/✔	50	50

We post the general journal entries to the appropriate general ledger accounts just as we always have. Evidence that an entry from the journal was posted to the general ledger is signified by the number of the general ledger accounts marked opposite the account posted in the posting reference column. Note in the two general journal entries above that the general ledger accounts—Office Equipment (1210), Accounts Payable (2120), Sales Returns and Allowances (4120), and Accounts Receivable (1130)—have been posted to the general ledger accounts. Also notice that the subsidiary ledger accounts—Tate Office Supplies Company (Accounts Payable) and Linda Jones (Accounts Receivable)—have also been posted. The postings are evidenced by the check marks (✔) after the account numbers in the posting reference column.

EXHIBIT 6-7 General and Subsidiary Ledgers after Posting

THE JONES COMPANY
General Ledger

Cash 1110

Debit		Credit	
Aug. 31 CR9	3,159	Aug. 31 CP24	1,340
Bal.	1,819		

Accounts Receivable 1130

Debit		Credit	
Aug. 31 S16	1,205	Aug. 23 G3	50
		31 CR9	365
Bal.	790		

Office Equipment 1210

Debit		Credit	
Aug. 20 G3	575		

Notes Payable 2110

Debit		Credit	
		Aug. 20 CR9	600

Accounts Payable 2120

Debit		Credit	
Aug. 31 CP24	425	Aug. 20 G3	575
		31 P11	1,115
		Bal.	1,265

Common Stock 3100

Debit		Credit	
		Aug. 5 CR9	1,000

Sales 4100

Debit		Credit	
		Aug. 31 S16	1,205
		31 CR9	1,200
		Bal.	2,405

Sales Discounts 4110

Debit		Credit	
Aug. 31 CR9	6		

Sales Returns and Allowances 4120

Debit		Credit	
Aug. 23 G3	50		

Purchases 5100

Debit		Credit	
Aug. 31 P11	1,115		
31 CP24	535		
Bal.	1,650		

Purchase Discounts 5115

Debit		Credit	
		Aug. 31 CP24	5

Freight-In 5120

Debit		Credit	
Aug. 26 CP24	10		

Salary Expense 5200

Debit		Credit	
Aug. 16 CP24	200		

Rent Expense 5400

Debit		Credit	
Aug. 3 CP24	175		

THE JONES COMPANY
Subsidiary Ledgers

Accounts Receivable

Adams, Tom

| Aug. 7 S16 | 20 | Aug. 30 CR9 | 20 |
| Bal. | 0 | | |

Davis, John

| Aug. 6 S16 | 85 | Aug. 17 CR9 | 45 |
| Bal. | 40 | | |

Grafton, Robert

| Aug. 27 S16 | 80 | | |

Hamm, Sally

| Aug. 4 S16 | 100 | Aug. 11 CR9 | 100 |
| Bal. | 0 | | |

Jones, Linda

| Aug. 15 S16 | 90 | Aug. 23 G3 | 50 |
| Bal. | 40 | | |

Kantz, Nancy

| Aug. 18 S16 | 200 | Aug. 22 CR9 | 200 |
| Bal. | 0 | | |

Knox, Ann

| Aug. 21 S16 | 180 | | |

Lennord, William

| Aug. 31 S16 | 450 | | |
| Bal. | 450 | | |

Accounts Payable

Custom Supplies, Inc.

| Aug. 24 CP24 | 100 | Aug. 14 P11 | 100 |
| | | Bal. | 0 |

Great Goods, Inc.

| | | Aug. 24 P11 | 255 |

Downtown Company

| | | Aug. 19 P11 | 320 |

Tate Office Supplies Co.

| | | Aug. 20 G3 | 575 |

Easy Print Company

| Aug. 17 CP24 | 175 | Aug. 2 P11 | 275 |
| | | Bal. | 100 |

Federal Company

Aug. 11 CP24	150	Aug. 9 P11	150
		Aug. 22 P11	15
		Bal.	15

THE JONES COMPANY
Schedule of Accounts Receivable
August 31, 1989

Davis, John	$ 40
Grafton, Robert	80
Jones, Linda	40
Knox, Ann	180
Lennord, William	450
Total	$790

THE JONES COMPANY
Schedule of Accounts Payable
August 31, 1989

Downtown Company	$ 320
Easy Print Company	100
Federal Company	15
Great Goods, Inc.	255
Tate Office Supplies Company	575
Total	$1,265

Proving the Control Accounts

Exhibit 6-7 (pages 240–241) shows the general ledger and subsidiary ledger for The Jones Company after all the journals have been posted at the end of the month. A trial balance (see Exhibit 6-8) is prepared from the general ledger to test that the sum of its debits equals the sum of its credits. In Exhibit 6-8 the sum of the debits, $5,275, equals the sum of the credits, $5,275. Before continuing with the period-end procedures—preparing the adjusting entries, the closing entries, and the financial statements—we prepare a **schedule** (list) of the subsidiary ledgers to prove that the total of the accounts in a subsidiary ledger equals the balance in the control account. Schedules of accounts receivable and accounts payable appear at the bottom of Exhibit 6-7. The schedule of accounts receivable does not include the accounts of Tom Adams, Sally Hamm, or Nancy Kantz. They all have zero balances, and consequently do not owe The Jones Company anything on the last day of the month. Likewise, in the schedule of accounts payable the Custom Suppliers, Inc., account, which has a zero balance, is not listed.

A schedule of accounts receivable or accounts payable is a list of all the balances in the subsidiary ledger accounts

EXHIBIT 6-8

THE JONES COMPANY
Trial Balance
August 31, 1989

	Debit	Credit
Cash	$1,819	
Accounts Receivable	790	
Office Equipment	575	
Notes Payable		$ 600
Accounts Payable		1,265
Common Stock		1,000
Sales		2,405
Sales Discounts	6	
Sales Returns and Allowances	50	
Purchases	1,650	
Purchase Discounts		5
Freight-In	10	
Salary Expense	200	
Rent Expense	175	
Totals	$5,275	$5,275

The schedule of accounts receivable amounts to $790, which is the balance found in the Accounts Receivable general ledger account. The subsidiary ledger and control accounts are in agreement. The same is true for the $1,265 total of the accounts payable subsidiary ledger and its control account.

With the proving of the control accounts we have described the last of the new things we need to do in our expanded accounting system. Our manual accounting system now includes five journals, subsidiary ledgers, and the worksheet, and is illustrated in Figure 6-3.

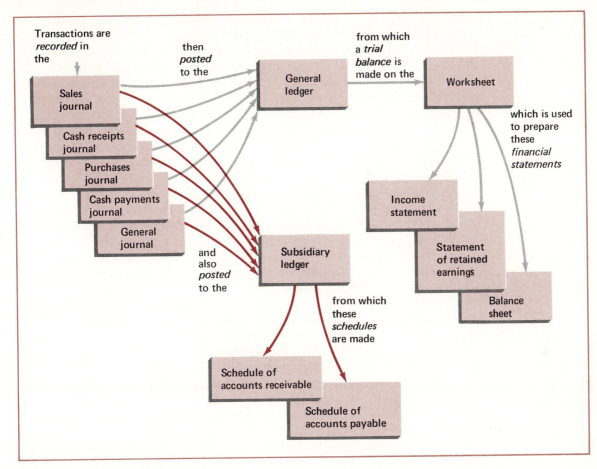

FIGURE 6-3 The Accounting System

CHAPTER SUMMARY

A system of internal control contains procedures, techniques, and practices to provide a dependable, efficient accounting system that will help management plan and control the company's business activities as well as safeguard its resources. There are two types of internal controls: ***accounting controls*** and ***administrative controls.*** Accounting controls protect the company's resources and provide for reliable financial statements; administrative controls are concerned with the operational efficiency of the organization and compliance with its policies.

Accounting controls are ***personnel controls, record controls,*** and ***checks and balances.*** Personnel controls are concerned with employee competence, assignment of responsibilities, division of work, and rotation of duties. The organization should select and train employees who have the necessary talents and intelligence for the duties assigned. And the employees should be assigned duties that are clearly identifiable so that responsibility can be pinpointed. It is important to divide employee assignments so that related operations are not performed by the same individual. Employees should be rotated among the duty assignments. This affects not only training but system control as well, since each employee will realize that at any time someone else may be reassigned to perform his or her duties.

Records controls consist of custodianship, adequacy, and documentation. The employee assigned the responsibility of custodianship of certain resources should never be allowed to have access to the records pertaining to those resources. Records and the recordkeeping equipment should be adequate to provide timely, accurate, and reliable information. And each function within the organization must provide properly documented evidence to verify that it fulfills an appropriate business activity and has been approved at all stages of the transaction.

Checks and balances consist of reconciliations, internal auditing, and external auditing. Reconciliations are required periodically to compare the actual resources to company records to see that the resources in fact do exist and that their proper value is reflected on the company books. The internal auditing function will review the organization's activities to discover errors or irregularities, to determine if company procedures and policies are being followed, and to uncover inefficiencies. The external audit performed by a certified public accountant provides an impartial review of the company records and may result in suggestions for improvement.

Each business activity can be represented in a special journal that is part of a system of internal control. Moreover, a special journal saves time in recording many of the same kinds of business transactions.

There are four types of special journals. The *sales journal* is designed to record all sales of merchandise on account; the *purchases journal* records merchandise bought on account. All transactions involving cash receipts are recorded in the *cash receipts journal;* and all transactions involving cash payments are recorded in the *cash payments journal.* Sales journals and purchases journals are typically one-column journals. The amount of the Accounts Receivable debit is identical to the amount of the Sales credit; similarly, the Purchases debit is identical to the Accounts Payable credit. The cash receipts and the cash payments journals are multi-column journals that are typically tailor-made for the business entity using them.

Transactions that cannot be handled in one of the special journals must be recorded in the general journal.

Posting the special journals to the general ledger accounts involves posting only the column totals to the appropriate account. However, postings from the special journals must also be made to the individual subsidiary ledger accounts in the case of accounts receivable and accounts payable.

IMPORTANT TERMS USED IN THIS CHAPTER

Accounting controls The procedures, techniques, and practices that will protect the company's resources and provide for reliable financial statements. (page 224)

Administrative controls The procedures and methods that are concerned mainly with the operational efficiency of the organization and compliance with its policies. (page 224.)

Cash payments journal A book of original entry designed for recording those transactions involving expenditures of cash. (page 238)

Cash receipts journal A book of original entry designed only for recording business transactions involving receipt of cash. (page 232)

Control account A general ledger account, such as Accounts Receivable, which is supported by a subsidiary ledger containing the detail of the control account. (page 231)

Documentation The providing of adequate records to trace and verify each transaction from its beginning to its end. (page 226)

Internal auditing The function of reviewing the organization's activities to discover errors or irregularities, to determine if the procedures and policies of the company are being followed, and to uncover inefficiencies. (page 227)

Internal control The procedures, techniques, and practices designed to provide a dependable efficient accounting system that will help management plan and control the company's activities as well as safeguard the company's resources. (page 224)

Purchases journal A book of original entry used only to record purchases on account. (page 236)

Sales journal A book of original entry used only to record sales on account. (page 229)

Special journals Books of original entry designed to record only one class of business transactions. (page 229)

Subsidiary ledger A group of accounts, such as the accounts payable subsidiary ledger, which provide the detail of a general ledger control account, in this case Accounts Payable. (page 231)

QUESTIONS

1. Two types of internal controls exist. What are they? Explain each.

2. A company with a strong system of internal control will never have to worry about fraud. Evaluate this statement.

3. What is internal control?

4. Describe the factors an internal control system must consider regarding personnel.

5. Custodianship, adequacy, and documentation are all part of records control; describe each of these functions.

6. In any good system of internal control, checks and balances exist. List and describe three such checks and balances.

7. Internal auditing has the same objectives as external auditing. Evaluate this statement.

8. The Wilson Company bills its customers monthly and receives payments the following month by check. The receptionist opens the daily mail, makes a list of the checks, and gives this list to the bookkeeper, then the receptionist deposits the checks in the bank. At the end of the month a bank statement is sent by the bank to the office manager, who reconciles the bank's balance with the cash reflected on the bookkeeper's general ledger Cash account. Evaluate this system.

9. Explain the relationship that exists between a *control account* and its *subsidiary ledger*.

10. What is the purpose of establishing special journals when any transaction, no matter how complex, can be entered in the general journal?

11. The sales journal and the cash receipts journal are posted once a month to the general ledger, yet the individual entries contained in those journals affecting Accounts Receivable are posted daily to the subsidiary ledger. Explain.

12. The general journal is not needed when companies use special journals. Evaluate this statement.

13. The sales journal of the Welker Company has 326 entries for the month of October. How many posting entries must be made to the sales account for the month of October, assuming that no cash sales were made? Under the same assumption, how many postings must be made to the accounts receivable subsidiary ledger?

14. What purpose do the posting references have in the journals and ledgers?

15. What do the terms *foot* and *crossfoot* mean? Why is it necessary to crossfoot the cash payments journal?

EXERCISES

Exercise 6-1
Analyzing internal control

Wentworth Wholesale Company follows the policy of having material handlers reorder inventory items when they notice that the item is in short supply.
　　Comment on this practice.

Exercise 6-2
Analyzing internal control

As the new office manager of the Eastside Branch of Stardust Sales Company, you receive a phone call from a very disturbed customer. It seems that the customer claims he paid his bill for $157.54 more than 2 months ago, yet for the past 2 months he has received an invoice for that amount from your office. As you investigate the complaint you discover that the office procedure is for Mr. Todsen, the assistant office manager, to receive all daily receipts and deposit them in the bank. His wife, who is the office bookkeeper, records the receipts directly from the bank deposit slips.
　　What action should you now take?

Exercise 6-3
Analyzing internal control

The Houston Development Company is expanding very rapidly. The current computer operator has just received a promotion and is being transferred to the Dallas branch office. As a result, a bright young graduate from the University of Houston's excellent computer science department is hired, given the operating manual to read over the weekend, and will commence duties on the following Monday.
　　Comment on this practice.

Exercise 6-4
Analyzing internal control

Fair Price Food Store has nine checkers ringing up customer sales. All nine checkers work out of a central cash register containing one cash drawer.
　　Comment on this practice.

Exercise 6-5
Analyzing internal control

At the Titas Company a large new mainframe computer was just installed. The company has terminals in each department where individuals have complete access to the mainframe. This being the case, management is considering eliminating the computer department.
　　Comment on this practice.

Exercise 6-6
Identifying the appropriate journal

Ten transactions are listed below. For each transaction, indicate which of the five basic journals should be used to record the transaction. Use the following symbols for the basic journals:

Journal	Symbol
Cash Receipts	CR
Cash Payments	CP
Sales	S
Purchases	P
General	G

a. Payment of account payable.
b. Sales on account.
c. Adjusting entry for office supplies.
d. Collection of accounts receivable.
e. Receipt of office equipment from the owner of the business; the equipment is to be used in the business.
f. Acquisition of inventory on account.
g. Cash sales.
h. Return of inventory previously purchased but not yet paid for.
i. Acquisition of office supplies on account.
j. Acquisition of inventory for cash.

Exercise 6-7
Discovering errors

Engle Enterprise has several errors in their accounting system. They request your help in explaining how the system will eventually (if at all) uncover these errors.

a. A posting of $456 appears in the general ledger account, Accounts Receivable. However, the total of the accounts receivable column in the cash receipts journal is correctly footed (added) to $546.
b. The total of the purchases journal amounts to $26,350. It is posted as a debit to Purchases and a credit to Accounts Payable as $26,530.
c. A sales invoice of $575 is entered in the sales journal as $755.
d. The accounts payable column of the cash payments journal is incorrectly totaled to $15,678. It should be $15,876.

Exercise 6-8
Identifying the sources of debits and credits

This exercise is designed to test your knowledge of the relationship between the journals and the accounts. For each of the accounts listed, indicate the journal source of the most common debit and credit entries.

Accounts	Journal Source Debit	Journal Source Credit
Cash	Cash Receipts	_____
Accounts Receivable	_____	_____
Prepaid Rent	_____	_____
Accounts Payable	_____	_____
Sales	_____	_____
Sales Returns and Allowances	_____	_____
Sales Discounts	_____	_____
Purchases	_____	_____
Purchase Returns and Allowances	_____	_____
Purchase Discounts	_____	_____
Salaries Expense	_____	_____

Exercise 6-9
Completing the journals and posting to the ledger

The sales and cash receipts journals of the James Company for the first month of operations, July, 1989, are presented below:

Sales Journal				Page 7
Date	**Account Debited**	**Invoice Number**	**Post. Ref.**	**Amount**
July 5	Sally Anderson	1001		450
8	Albert Baines	1002		700
11	Nancy Carlson	1003		560
17	Sam Dunlap	1004		975
21	John Eastman	1005		400

Cash Receipts Journal								Page 5
Date	**Account Credited**	**Post. Ref.**	**Explanation**	**Sundry Accounts Credit**	**Accounts Receivable Credit**	**Sales Credit**	**Sales Discount Debit**	**Cash Debit**
July 3			Cash sales			400		400
10	Sally Anderson		Invoice no. 1001, less 2%		450		9	441
14	Notes Payable		Issue note payable	500				500
19	Albert Baines		Invoice no. 1002		700			700
23	John Eastman		Invoice no. 1005, less 2%		400		8	392
27			Cash sales			750		750
30	Capital Stock		Issue capital stock	675				675

Notice that the journals have not been footed, crossfooted, or posted to the ledger accounts. Complete the journals and post to the general and subsidiary ledger accounts using the following account numbers:

Account	Number	Account	Number
Cash	101	Capital Stock	310
Accounts Receivable	110	Sales	410
Notes Payable	220	Sales Discounts	420

Exercise 6-10
Determining cash sales

Samson Company has the following debit and credit totals for selected accounts:

Accounts	Debit	Credit
Cash	$1,600	$600
Accounts Receivable	3,200	?
Sales Returns and Allowances	100	-0-
Sales Discounts	180	-0-

Cash and Accounts Receivable had balances of $400 and $600, respectively, at the beginning of the period. You are able to determine that included in the cash debits is $200 from the sale of certain equipment. Credit sales amounted to $2,600. Accounts Receivable has an ending balance of $2,000.

From this information, compute the amount of cash sales made during the period.

(Check figure: $80)

PROBLEMS: SET A

Problem A6-1
Analyzing internal control

Mr. Bumble operates a retail store in a certain town to which we will assign no fictitious name. For the first time in many years, Mrs. Corney failed to report to work. Her responsibilities include maintaining the general and subsidiary ledgers as well as handling all cash receipts. Mr. Bumble himself controls all cash disbursements. Late in the morning of Mrs. Corney's most unusual absence, a Mr. Sowerberry, the parochial undertaker, appeared at the Bumble establishment to acquire material for his business. Since Mrs. Corney was unavailable, Mr. Bumble processed the order. As Mr. Bumble removed Mr. Sowerberry's subsidiary accounts receivable ledger card, Mr. Bumble remarked that Mr. Sowerberry had made only a partial payment on his last invoice. This astounded Mr. Sowerberry, and he informed Mr. Bumble that he had indeed paid the invoice in full by check delivered himself to Mrs. Corney on Thursday last. Perplexed Mr. Bumble asks young Oliver to review the accounts receivable subsidiary ledger. After several hours Oliver reports back to Mr. Bumble that most customers are current on their accounts but that many had made two or more payments on individual invoices.

| *Required* |

Explain the possible reason for the partial payments being posted to the accounts.

Problem A6-2
Analyzing internal control

Several items of inventory were missing from the Appomattox Warehouse on Dec. 31, 1989. The inventory records reflected that the items had been placed in stock and had not yet been sold. But a careful count of the inventory on the last day of the year revealed that the items were nowhere to be found. The items, while small in size, were rather expensive, ranging from $750 to $2,200 each. Bob Lee, the company general manager, requests the warehouse supervisor, Jim Longstreet, to describe the operating procedures followed at the warehouse.

Longstreet reports that as merchandise is received it is counted by George Pickett, who then completes the Count Form and forwards it together with the supplier's invoice to Jubal Early in the purchasing department. Jubal prepares a purchase order from this information, and compares the order with the Request for Inventory Form (a form prepared by the retail stores and sent directly to the vendors). If a difference exists in the amount received and the amount requested, Jubal calls George Pickett to reaffirm the count. If the count is confirmed, the purchase order is signed by Jubal and sent to the payment department, where Joe Johnston prepares a check to be mailed to the supplier.

Merchandise is removed from stock only when a Send Inventory Form is received. These forms are prepared by the salespeople in the retail outlets of the company and are processed daily.

| *Required* |

Evaluate the procedures used by this company to control its inventory.

Problem A6-3
Recording transactions in sales, purchases, and general journals; posting to general and subsidiary ledgers

Transactions relating to the purchase and sales of merchandise during the month of January, 1989, for the Bulldog Company appear below:

Jan. 3   Purchased mdse. in the amount of $6,700 from Gator, Inc.; invoice dated Jan. 2.

   4   Sold to the War Eagle Company merchandise amounting to $3,550; invoice no. 342.

   6   Returned $300 of merchandise acquired from Gator, Inc.

   9   Purchased from Wildcat Enterprises $10,250 of merchandise; invoice dated Jan. 9.

   11   Sold merchandise to Rebel, Inc., on invoice no. 343 amounting to $3,750.

   14   Purchased $7,350 of merchandise from the Tide Company; invoice dated Jan. 12.

   17   Received $400 of merchandise returned by the War Eagle Company.

   22   Sold to the Maroon Bulldog $22,500 of merchandise on invoice no. 344.

   25   Purchased $5,700 of merchandise from Tiger, Ltd.; invoice dated Jan. 24.

   29   Merchandise was sold to Rebel, Inc., amounting to $11,200; invoice no. 345.

   30   Purchased $15,000 of mdse. from Tide Company; invoice dated Jan. 29.

Required

1. Using a single-column purchases journal, a cash payments journal similar to those illustrated in the text, and a general journal, record the transactions.
2. Foot the purchases journal; foot and crossfoot the cash payments journal.
3. Post to the general ledger accounts and the accounts payable subsidiary ledger. Use the following account numbers for posting references:

Cash	101	Purchase Returns and Allowances . .	552
Office Equipment	161	Freight-In	553
Accounts Payable	201	Advertising Expense	610
Purchases	550	Salary Expense	640
Purchase Discounts	551		

Use page number 42 for the purchases journal, 73 for the cash payments journal, and 16 for the general journal.
4. Prove the control account for Accounts Payable by preparing a schedule of accounts payable.

(Check figure: Accounts Payable balance = $2,208)

Problem A6-7
Comprehensive problem

(Note: This problem is to be used as a mini-practice set.)
At the close of business on Aug. 31, 1989, the Thomas Biddle Store had the following account balances: Cash, $2,000; Inventory, $4,500; Store Equipment, $5,000; Accumulated Depreciation: Store Equipment, $100, Capital Stock, $5,000; and Retained Earnings, $6,400.

The Thomas Biddle Store buys and sells merchandise on account under 2/10, n/30 credit terms. During the month of September, 1989, the following transactions took place:

Sept. 1   Capital stock in the amount of $1,500 was issued.

       2   Purchased $1,950 merchandise on account from Otto Products, Inc.; invoice date Sept. 1.

       2   Paid freight charges of $180 in cash; check no. 418.

       3   Sold to William Lancaster merchandise on account, $800; invoice no. 136.

       5   Returned $700 defective merchandise to Otto Products, Inc.

       7   Purchased an additional $700 of merchandise from Otto Products, Inc., on account; invoice dated this date.

       8   Sold $1,650 of merchandise to Tony Mundale on account; invoice no. 137.

       8   Received amount due from William Lancaster.

     10   Cash sales, $2,310.

     11   Issued check no. 419 to Otto Products for amount due from Sept. 2 purchase (note the returned merchandise on Sept. 5).

     12   Sold to William Lancaster $900 of merchandise on account; invoice no. 138.

     13   Purchased from Nance Wholesale merchandise costing $2,200; invoice date Sept. 12.

     15   Purchased $320 merchandise for cash from Pearson Supply Company. Issued check no. 420.

     15   Purchased from Pearson Supply Company $1,400 of merchandise on account; invoice dated Sept. 14.

     15   Purchased from Pearson Supply Company $400 of store supplies on account; invoice dated Sept. 15.

     16   Sold $1,700 of merchandise to William Lancaster on account; invoice no. 139.

     17   Received amount due from Tony Mundale.

     18   Paid salaries, $645. Issued check no. 421.

     19   Paid Otto Products, Inc., amount due from Sept. 7 purchase. Issued check no. 422.

     21   Sold to Terri Keller $500 of merchandise on account; invoice no. 140.

     21   Issued check no. 423 for $400 dividend.

     22   Purchased $500 merchandise on account from Otto Products, Inc.; invoice dated Sept. 22.

Sept. 22   Paid Nance Wholesale amount due. Issued check no. 424.
    26   Received payment from Terri Keller for amount due.
    28   William Lancaster returned defective merchandise amounting to $200 that he had acquired on Sept. 3. He paid for this merchandise on Sept. 8.
    28   Purchased on account from Pearson Supply Company merchandise costing $2,750; invoice dated Sept. 27.
    29   Sold Tony Mundale (invoice no. 141) $2,450 merchandise on account.
    30   Received payment from William Lancaster for merchandise sold on invoice no. 139.

Required

1. Record the September transactions in the appropriate journal, using single-column sales and purchases journals, multi-column cash receipts and payments journals, and a general journal.
2. Foot and crossfoot the journals.
3. Using the following account and journal page numbers, post the general and subsidiary ledgers:

Account	Number	Account	Number	Journal	Page Numbers
Cash	110	Sales Returns and		Sales	14
Accounts Receivable	120	Allowances	430	Cash Receipts	21
Inventory	130	Purchases	510	Purchases	32
Store Supplies on Hand	140	Purchase Discounts	520	Cash Payments	9
Store Equipment	150	Purchase Returns and		General	4
Accumulated Depreciation:		Allowances	530		
Store Equipment	155	Freight-In	540		
Accounts Payable	210	Salary Expense	610		
Salaries Payable	220	Store Supplies Used	620		
Capital Stock	310	Depreciation Expense: Store			
Retained Earnings	320	Equipment	630		
Dividends	330	Expense and Revenue			
Sales	410	Summary	800		
Sales Discounts	420				

4. Prepare an unadjusted trial balance on a worksheet and record the following adjustments on the worksheet:
    a. Store Supplies Used, $150.   **c.** Accrued Salaries, $75.
    b. Depreciation Expense: Store Equipment, $50.   **d.** Ending Inventory, $4,000.
    Complete the worksheet.
5. Record adjusting and closing entries in the general journal and post to the general ledger.
6. Prepare schedules of accounts receivable and accounts payable.

(Check figure: Net loss = $596)

PROBLEMS: SET B

Problem B6-1
Evaluating internal control

Upon graduating from State University, you are employed by Devoe Industries as an administrative assistant. Your first assignment is to visit the company's Gluck Division, located in Portland, Maine, in order to evaluate their system of internal control.

    Gluck is mailed directly from the Portland plant to customers throughout the Northeast. All sales are made on 30-day credit. Sales invoices are typed and posted to the accounts receivable accounts by Ms. Hansen, who performs this task from 8:00 a.m. to 9:00 a.m. each day prior to opening the office for the business day. From 9:00 a.m. to 5:00 p.m. Ms. Hansen serves as the receptionist. The mail arrives at 10:30 a.m. and is received by Ms. Hansen, who opens the mail, removes the payments together with the number 2 copy of the sales invoice returned by the customer. She puts the payments in her desk drawer with the rest of the week's receipts and locks the drawer. All other mail is given to the plant manager's secretary, Ms. Whipple.

Ms. Hansen comes into the office on Saturday morning to post the receipts to the accounts receivable ledger and the Cash account, and prepares the receipts for the weekly deposit, which is made on Monday morning at 10:00 a.m. The sales invoices are placed on Ms. Whipple's desk for her to file during the week.

Once a month Ms. Hansen receives the bank statement from the Exchange Bank of Portland, and she reconciles the bank statement with the cash balance in the company's general ledger. She also, once a month, bills the customers.

| **Required** | Evaluate the system of internal control, providing suggestions for its improvement. |

**Problem B6-2
Developing a system of
internal control**

Mike Linebacker, a professional football player for the St. Louis Blues, owns a bar in State College, Pennsylvania, called the Nittany Lion Drinking Establishment. The bar caters to the Penn State student body, selling mostly Blue and White beer on tap and some mixed drinks. In the past Mike has had problems with some dishonest employees. Some would sell drinks without ringing up the sale and pocket the price of the drink. On one occasion an employee even brought in his own cash register so the customers could see him ring up the drinks. He would keep the money in his cash register and return to Mike the money in Mike's cash register.

| **Required** | Provide some suggestions to develop a system of internal control for Mike's bar. Mike is an absentee owner, visiting State College only once or twice a month. |

**Problem B6-3
Recording transactions in
sales, purchases, and
general journals; posting
to the general and
subsidiary ledgers**

The Deacon Corporation had the following transactions relating to the purchase and sale of merchandise during its first month of operation, July, 1989:

July 2 Purchased merchandise from Holland Company, $4,500; invoice dated July 1.
   4   Purchased merchandise from French Imports, $6,000; dated July 4.
   5   Sold merchandise to Alpha Company for $3,000; invoice no. 101.
   9   Returned $500 of merchandise to the Holland Company; the merchandise was the wrong color.
   12 Purchased $13,550 of merchandise from the German Export Group; invoice dated July 10.
   13 Received merchandise amounting to $300 returned by the Alpha Company; the merchandise was defective.
   18 Sold to the New York Company merchandise amounting to $7,500; invoice no. 102.
   23 Sold $5,000 on merchandise to Texas, Inc.; invoice no. 103.
   26 Purchased $21,000 of merchandise from the Canton Company; invoice dated July 25.
   29 Sold $750 of merchandise to Alpha Company, invoice no. 104.

| **Required** | 1. Using a single-column sales journal, a single-column purchases journal, and a general journal, record the transactions listed above. |

2. Post to the general and subsidiary ledger accounts. Use the following general ledger account numbers:

Accounts Receivable..............	120	Sales Returns and Allowances........	610
Accounts Payable	240	Purchases.......................	700
Sales..........................	600	Purchase Returns and Allowances..	710

Use page number 1 for the sales journal, page number 2 for the purchases journal, and page number 3 for the general journal.

**Problem B6-4
Recording transactions in the cash receipts and cash payments journals**

The cash transactions for the month of November, 1989, for Tellson and Company are described below. The company uses multi-column cash receipts and cash payments journals as described in the chapter.

Nov.	1	Acquired office furniture, $5,300.
	2	Purchased merchandise from Lorry, Inc., $4,500.
	4	Paid freight charges of the merchandise purchased from Lorry, Inc., $250.
	6	Sold merchandise for cash, $2,100.
	8	Paid Manette Company invoice of $5,000 less 2% discount.
	10	Acquired a delivery truck from Antoine Motors, paying a down payment of $4,000 and issuing a note payable for $10,500.
	10	Cash sales of merchandise amounted to $3,200.
	12	Paid rent on the office for the month of November, $1,250.
	13	Received payment from Cruncher Company for merchandise, $4,500 less 3% discount.
	14	Mr. Tellson invested an additional $5,000 in the business, receiving capital stock.
	15	Paid semimonthly salaries amounting to $15,000.
	18	Paid Pross Company invoice of $6,500 less 2% discount.
	20	Purchased merchandise, $2,100.
	22	Paid General Telephone Company $350.
	23	Received $7,500 from the Shooter's Hill Bank on note payable due 6 months hence.
	25	Paid Defrage Company $2,000 on a past-due invoice.
	26	Cash sales of merchandise, $5,100.
	28	Received payment from Sydney Carton, $4,000 less a 3% discount.
	29	Received payment from Charles Darnay, $5,500. The payment is made past the discount date.
	30	Paid semimonthly salaries amounting to $15,000.

Required

Record the transactions in the cash receipts and cash payments journals. Foot and crossfoot the journals.

(Check figures: Total cash receipts and cash payments: $36,645 and $61,020, respectively)

**Problem B6-5
Preparing entries and posting; sales, cash receipts, and general journals**

The Danko Company completed the following transactions relating to sales and collection of cash during the month of August, 1989. All credit sales have terms of 2/10, n/30, and invoices are dated the transaction date.

Aug.	2	Issued $1,000 capital stock.
	3	Sold, on invoice no. 717, $900 of merchandise to G. Peters on account.
	5	Sold to R. Otto merchandise on account amounting to $1,600; invoice no. 718.
	9	Sold to J. Moon on credit $2,100 of merchandise; invoice no. 719.
	10	Received payment from G. Peters.
	13	Borrowed $2,500 from the First National Bank on a 10% note payable due in 1 year.
	17	Received amount due from R. Otto.
	17	J. Moon returned $300 of defective merchandise from Aug. 9 sale.
	19	Sold to G. Peters on account merchandise in the amount of $3,200; invoice no. 720.
	19	Received amount due from J. Moon.
	22	Sold merchandise on account to J. Moon, $800; invoice no. 721.
	25	G. Peters returned as defective $400 of merchandise sold on Aug. 3.

Aug. 25   Sold on account to R. Otto merchandise in the amount of $1,500; invoice no. 722.

     30   Cash sales, $900.

Required

1. Record the transactions in the appropriate journal. Use a single-column sales journal, a cash receipts journal similar to the one illustrated in the text, and a general journal.
2. Total the sales and cash receipts journals; crossfoot the cash receipts journal.
3. Using the following account and journal page numbers, post to the general and accounts receivable ledgers.

Account	No.	Journal	Page No.
Cash	10	Sales	27
Accounts Receivable	11	Cash Receipts	19
Notes Payable	20	General	8
Capital Stock	30		
Sales	50		
Sales Discounts	51		
Sales Returns and Allowances	52		

4. Prepare a schedule of accounts receivable as of the end of the month to prove the balance in the Accounts Receivable Control account.

(Check figure: Accounts Receivable balance = $5,108)

Problem B6-6
Preparing entries and posting; purchases, cash receipts, and general journals

Listed below are the transactions completed by the Taylor Supply Company for the month of October, 1989, relating to purchases and cash payments. Assume all merchandise purchased for credit have terms of 2/10, n/30.

Oct. 1   Purchased $2,600 of merchandise from the Scranton Merchandise Corporation on account; invoice dated Oct. 1.

     1   Merchandise on account in the amount of $3,500 was acquired from Quentin Wholesale; invoice dated Oct. 1.

     4   Paid Quentin Wholesale amount due by issuing check no. 125.

     5   Returned defective merchandise to Scranton Merchandise Corporation for credit, $250.

     8   Issued check no. 126 in the amount of $1,200 for salary expense.

     8   Issued check no. 127 for $500 dividends.

     10   Purchased from Scranton Merchandise Corporation $1,750 merchandise on account; invoice dated Oct. 8.

     10   Paid Scranton Merchandise Corporation amount due from Oct. 1 purchase. Issued check no. 128.

     14   Purchased merchandise on account from Thomas, Inc., $800, invoice dated this date. Freight charges on this merchandise amounted to $55. Issued check no. 129 in payment of freight.

     15   Returned $1,350 of defective merchandise acquired from Quentin Wholesale on Oct. 1. Taylor debited Quentin's account.

     18   Issued check no. 130 to Scranton Merchandise Corporation for amount due.

     19   Purchased on account $4,250 of merchandise from Quentin Wholesale; invoice dated this date.

     21   Issued check no. 131 for $170 cash purchases.

     26   Issued check no. 132 for partial payment of $2,500 of merchandise acquired on Oct. 19.

Required

1. Record the transactions in a single-column purchases journal, a cash payments journal, or the general journal.

2. Total the purchases and cash payments journals. Crossfoot the cash payments journal.
3. Using the posting reference numbers below post to the general and accounts payable ledgers:

Account	No.	Journal	Page No.
Cash	110	Purchases	71
Accounts Payable	210	Cash Payments	56
Dividends	320	General	24
Purchases	510		
Purchase Discounts	520		
Purchase Returns and Allowances	530		
Freight-In	540		
Salary Expense	610		

4. Prepare a schedule of accounts payable outstanding as of Oct. 31, 1989, to prove the Accounts Payable Control account.

(Check figure: Accounts Payable balance = $1,227)

**Problem B6-7
Comprehensive problem**

(Note: This problem is to be used as a mini-practice set.)
The following transactions were completed by the Mary Whitehall Company during the month of June, 1989:

June 1   Received $2,500 cash from the First National Bank; issued a note payable for that amount due in 60 days.

1   Purchased office supplies of $1,000 cash. Issued check no. 118.

2   Sold merchandise on account to Mary Berstein and Tom Adams; $1,200 and $2,700 respectively.

3   Purchased merchandise from the Xact Supply Company on account amounting to $1,000, invoice dated June 2.

5   Mary Berstein returned merchandise acquired on June 2, $300.

6   Sold merchandise on account of Lucy Carter, $950.

9   Paid Xact Supply amount due. Issued check no. 119.

10   Sold $200 of office supplies on hand for cash to a competitor as an accommodation.

12   Received payments from Tom Adams and Mary Berstein.

13   Purchased on account merchandise costing $1,750 from Tyler Commercial Company.

14   Sold merchandise on account to Norma Elder, $1,300.

15   Cash sales, $850.

15   Paid salaries, $500. Issued check no. 120.

19   Sold merchandise on account to John Davis, $3,200.

19   Purchased from Xact Supply Company $250 of merchandise.

19   Paid Tyler Commercial amount due. Issued check no. 121.

20   Received payment due from Lucy Carter.

21   Returned to Tyler Commercial for credit defective merchandise costing $1,000. The merchandise was paid for on June 19.

21   Sold merchandise on account to Nancy Foxworth, $250.

23   Purchased $2,100 of merchandise on account from Tyler Commercial.

25   Received $600 partial payment from Norma Elder.

25   Purchased office equipment on account from Vitenwyk Corporation, $500.

26   Sold Mary Berstein merchandise on account, $2,150.

26   Mary Whitehall invested $1,000 cash in the company, receiving capital stock.

29   Purchased merchandise costing $1,350 on account from Villanson and Company.

30   Issued check no. 122 for cash purchases amounting to $500.

30   Mary Berstein paid amount due.

| *Required* | 1. Using single-column sales and purchases journals, a cash receipts and a cash payments journal, and a general journal, record the transactions listed above. |

1. Using single-column sales and purchases journals, a cash receipts and a cash payments journal, and a general journal, record the transactions listed above.
2. Foot and crossfoot the journals.
3. Post to the general and subsidiary ledgers, using the following account numbers for posting references:

Cash	110	Retained Earnings	320
Accounts Receivable	120	Sales	410
Inventory	130	Sales Returns and Allowances	420
Office Supplies on Hand	140	Sales Discounts	430
Office Equipment	150	Purchases	510
Accumulated Depreciation: Office		Purchase Returns and Allowances	520
Equipment	155	Purchase Discounts	530
Accounts Payable	210	Salary Expense	610
Notes Payable	220	Office Supplies Used	620
Capital Stock	310	Depreciation: Office Equipment	630

Use the following page numbers for the journal posting references:

Sales	32	Cash Payments	41
Cash Receipts	17	General	9
Purchases	21		

The beginning inventory is $7,000. To balance this, place a $5,000 credit in Capital Stock, and a $2,000 credit in Retained Earnings as a beginning balance. Ending inventory amounts to $7,500. Assume that all credit sales and purchases are under 2/10, n/30 terms. The first sales invoice is no. 624.

4. Prepare an unadjusted trial balance on a worksheet and record the following adjustments on the worksheet: **a.** Supplies Used, $250; **b.** Depreciation: Office Equipment, $50. Complete the worksheet.
5. Record adjusting and closing entries in the general journal and post to the general ledger.
6. Prepare a schedule of accounts receivable and accounts payable.

(Check figure: Net income = $5,970)

DECISION PROBLEM

You have been appointed the athletic director of Big Time University. Big Time has just completed a new facility for its basketball program. The Hoops Hood, as the new facility is called, has a capacity of 25,578 seats. Since the Big Time Bruisers have always been a national powerhouse in basketball, near capacity crowds can be expected in the new facility.

Your responsibility is to design a system of internal control to assure the university that all monies for the basketball games are collected and accounted for. Season tickets are sold at $40 to students (about 7,500 are expected to be sold), at $90 to faculty (about 500), at $140 to Blue Jacket Club Members (about 9,300), and at $180 to White Jacket Club Members (about 1,500). The remaining tickets are sold on a game-by-game basis at the Hoops Hood box office and at the four gates on game nights. The remaining tickets sell for $6 each.

This year's schedule includes 12 home games.

| *Required* | Design a system for distributing, accounting for, and controlling the tickets and controlling cash receipts. |

FINANCIAL STATEMENTS:

Florida Steel Corporation

Contained in the following six pages are the financial statements of Florida Steel Corporation, a company listed on the New York Stock Exchange. Ernst and Whinney, an international certified public accounting firm, audited the statements, and their report is found on the last page. Florida Steel's statements were selected because they are relatively free from complicated accounting issues, yet illustrate the principles of accounting and disclosure discussed in the book.

Included with the financial statements are three pages of disclosures entitled *Notes to Financial Statements.* These are an integral part of the statements. Notice in particular that the first note, *Note A,* is a summary of significant accounting policies as required by generally accepted accounting principles.

STATEMENTS OF FINANCIAL POSITION

FLORIDA STEEL CORPORATION AND SUBSIDIARIES

	September 30	
	1986	**1985**
ASSETS		
CURRENT ASSETS		
Cash and cash equivalents	$ 1,862,971	$ 2,182,529
Accounts receivable, less allowance for possible		
losses (1986—$650,000 and 1985—$600,000)	41,964,829	36,355,893
Inventories	42,080,013	46,548,892
Prepaid expenses	575,260	510,421
Recoverable income taxes	59,067	66,932
TOTAL CURRENT ASSETS	**86,542,140**	**85,664,667**
INVESTMENTS	**8,941,880**	**6,641,880**
PLANT AND EQUIPMENT		
Land	3,181,204	2,711,098
Buildings and improvements	17,936,482	17,561,922
Machinery and equipment	170,780,988	163,468,845
Construction in progress (estimated cost to		
complete: 1986—$8,636,000; 1985—$4,174,000)	1,856,057	2,116,800
	193,754,731	185,858,665
Less allowances for depreciation	72,925,813	66,730,516
	120,828,918	**119,128,149**
OTHER ASSETS	**204,522**	**196,081**
	$216,517,460	**$211,630,777**
LIABILITIES AND SHAREHOLDERS' EQUITY		
CURRENT LIABILITIES		
Trade accounts payable	$ 23,077,928	$ 20,289,321
Salaries, wages and employee benefits	9,085,756	7,775,014
Other current liabilities	2,198,801	2,167,582
Federal and state income taxes	9,766,242	876,382
Current maturities of long-term borrowings	3,641,400	308,000
Short-term borrowings	2,000,000	
TOTAL CURRENT LIABILITIES	**49,770,127**	**31,416,299**
LONG-TERM BORROWINGS	**23,559,046**	**52,700,446**
DEFERRED INCOME TAXES	**35,140,000**	**32,030,000**
SHAREHOLDERS' EQUITY		
Common Stock, par value $1.00 per share—		
authorized: 25,000,000 shares		
issued and outstanding: 1986—6,021,902 shares		
and 1985—5,985,949 shares	6,021,902	5,985,949
Capital in excess of par	3,938,450	3,254,918
Reinvested earnings	98,087,935	86,243,165
TOTAL SHAREHOLDERS' EQUITY	**108,048,287**	**95,484,032**
	$216,517,460	**$211,630,777**

See notes to financial statements.

STATEMENTS OF OPERATIONS

FLORIDA STEEL CORPORATION AND SUBSIDIARIES

| | Year Ended September 30 | | |
	1986	1985	1984
NET SALES	$319,324,037	$287,985,316	$286,108,096
OTHER INCOME	1,430,367	28,232	5,405,922
	320,754,404	288,013,548	291,514,018
COSTS AND EXPENSES			
Cost of sales, excluding depreciation	260,569,625	245,424,541	250,135,673
Selling and administrative	17,023,297	15,580,045	14,757,008
Depreciation	10,349,046	9,269,699	9,166,917
Interest expense	4,449,175	5,657,851	6,429,822
	292,391,143	275,932,136	280,489,420
INCOME BEFORE INCOME TAXES	28,363,261	12,081,412	11,024,598
INCOME TAXES	12,970,000	4,340,000	4,363,000
NET INCOME	$ 15,393,261	$ 7,741,412	$ 6,661,598
NET INCOME PER SHARE	$2.56	$1.30	$1.12

See notes to financial statements.

STATEMENTS OF SHAREHOLDERS' EQUITY

FLORIDA STEEL CORPORATION AND SUBSIDIARIES

	Common Stock	Capital in Excess of Par	Reinvested Earnings
BALANCES AT OCTOBER 1, 1983	$5,965,185	$2,510,714	$76,615,086
Net income for 1984			6,661,598
Cash dividends ($.40 per share)			(2,386,075)
Compensation under employee stock plans	9,678	434,320	
BALANCES AT SEPTEMBER 30, 1984	5,974,863	2,945,034	80,890,609
Net income for 1985			7,741,412
Cash dividends ($.40 per share)			(2,388,856)
Compensation under employee stock plans	11,086	309,884	
BALANCES AT SEPTEMBER 30, 1985	5,985,949	3,254,918	86,243,165
Net income for 1986			15,393,261
Cash dividends ($.59 per share)			(3,548,491)
Compensation under employee stock plans	35,953	683,532	
BALANCES AT SEPTEMBER 30, 1986	$6,021,902	$3,938,450	$98,087,935

See notes to financial statements.

STATEMENTS OF CHANGES IN FINANCIAL POSITION

FLORIDA STEEL CORPORATION AND SUBSIDIARIES

| | Year Ended September 30 | | |
	1986	1985	1984
SOURCE OF WORKING CAPITAL			
From operations:			
Net income	$15,393,261	$ 7,741,412	$ 6,661,598
Charges not requiring funds in the current period:			
Depreciation	10,349,046	9,269,699	9,166,917
Deferred income taxes	3,110,000	3,503,000	3,952,000
TOTAL FROM OPERATIONS	**28,852,307**	**20,514,111**	**19,780,515**
Additional long-term borrowings	5,592,989	10,000,000	7,500,000
Proceeds from sale of plant and equipment, less gains included in net income	284,033	1,061,119	2,120,354
Compensation under employee stock plans	719,485	320,970	443,998
Reduction of noncurrent notes receivable		1,066,667	291,916
Other items, net	(8,441)	(313,208)	310,078
	35,440,373	**32,649,659**	**30,446,861**
APPLICATION OF WORKING CAPITAL			
Reduction of long-term borrowings	34,734,389	8,844,554	14,308,000
Cash dividends	3,548,491	2,388,856	2,386,075
Plant and equipment additions	8,084,747	17,253,132	11,472,892
Non-current assets of acquired subsidiaries	6,549,101		
	52,916,728	**28,486,542**	**28,166,967**
WORKING CAPITAL INCREASE (DECREASE)	**(17,476,355)**	**4,163,117**	**2,279,894**
Beginning working capital	54,248,368	50,085,251	47,805,357
ENDING WORKING CAPITAL	**$36,772,013**	**$54,248,368**	**$50,085,251**
CHANGES IN COMPONENTS OF WORKING CAPITAL			
Increase (decrease) in working capital assets:			
Cash and cash equivalents	$ (319,558)	$ (5,157,590)	$ 6,138,562
Accounts receivable	5,608,936	(2,116,124)	1,371,839
Inventories	(4,468,879)	11,264,254	2,427,661
Prepaid expenses	64,839	282,058	(45,749)
Recoverable income taxes	(7,865)	(210,558)	(10,522,510)
	877,473	**4,062,040**	**(630,197)**
Increase (decrease) in working capital liabilities:			
Trade accounts payable	2,788,607	(338,547)	683,893
Salaries, wages and employee benefits	1,310,742	1,474,363	49,535
Other current liabilities	31,219	235,007	(70,250)
Federal and state income taxes	8,889,860	528,100	(573,269)
Current maturities of long-term borrowings	3,333,400		
Short-term borrowings	2,000,000	(2,000,000)	(3,000,000)
	18,353,828	**(101,077)**	**(2,910,091)**
WORKING CAPITAL INCREASE (DECREASE)	**($17,476,355)**	**$ 4,163,117**	**$ 2,279,894**

See notes to financial statements.

NOTES TO CONSOLIDATED FINANCIAL STATEMENTS
FLORIDA STEEL CORPORATION AND SUBSIDIARIES

NOTE A—SUMMARY OF SIGNIFICANT ACCOUNTING POLICIES

Principles of Consolidation: The consolidated financial statements include the accounts of the Company and its wholly-owned subsidiaries. All significant intercompany accounts and transactions have been eliminated in consolidation.

Business Segment: The Company is engaged in the manufacture, fabrication and marketing of steel products primarily for use in construction and industrial markets.

Contract Revenue: Sales under contracts are recognized as deliveries of materials are made. Included in trade accounts receivable at September 30, 1986, and 1985, are receivables amounting to approximately $13,280,000 and $12,291,000, respectively, arising from the delivery of fabricated products sold under both short- and long-term contracts.

Inventories: Inventories are stated at the lower of cost (determined principally by use of the last-in, first-out method) or market.

Investments: Investments are stated at the lower of cost or market and are comprised of properties held for resale.

Plant and Equipment: Plant and equipment are stated on the basis of cost. Major renewals and betterments are capitalized and depreciated over their estimated useful lives. Maintenance and repairs are charged against operations as incurred. Upon retirement or other disposition of plant and equipment, the cost and related allowances for depreciation are removed from the accounts and any resulting gain or loss is reflected in operations.

Plant start-up and other preoperating costs of new facilities are charged against operations as incurred.

For financial reporting purposes, the Company provides for depreciation of plant and equipment using the straight-line method over the estimated useful lives of 10 to 30 years for buildings and improvements and 3 to 18 years for machinery and equipment.

Income Taxes: The provision for income taxes is based on financial statement income and, therefore, includes deferred income taxes on transactions reported in different periods for income tax purposes.

The Company uses the flow-through method of recognizing investment tax credits.

Pension Plans: The Company has pension plans covering substantially all employees. Pension cost represents normal cost and amortization of prior service costs principally over 30 years. The Company's policy is to fund accrued pension costs currently.

Net Income Per Share: Net income per share is based on the Company's average number of shares of Common Stock outstanding during each year (6,010,360 in 1986, 5,972,351 in 1985, and 5,965,264 in 1984).

NOTE B—INVENTORIES

| | September 30 | |
	1986	1985
Finished goods	$26,638,289	$28,677,972
Work in process	3,677,827	6,271,498
Raw materials and operating supplies	11,763,897	11,599,422
	$42,080,013	**$46,548,892**

If the first-in, first-out (FIFO) method of inventory accounting had been used by the Company, inventories would have been $6,171,061 and $7,137,605 higher than reported at September 30, 1986 and 1985, respectively.

During 1986 inventory quantities were reduced resulting in the liquidation of LIFO inventory quantities carried at higher costs prevailing in prior years compared with the cost of 1986 purchases. The effect of this liquidation decreased net income for 1986 approximately $70,000. During 1985 and 1984 inventory quantities were reduced resulting in the liquidation of LIFO inventory quantities carried at lower costs prevailing in prior years as compared with the cost of 1985 and 1984 purchases. The effect of the liquidations increased net income for 1985 and 1984 by approximately $100,000 and $1,089,000, respectively. The liquidations for 1985 and 1984 resulted from the sale of production facilities and are included in other income (see Note G).

NOTE C—BORROWINGS
Long-term borrowings consist of the following:

| | September 30 | |
	1986	1985
Credit agreement	$ 4,000,000	$33,000,000
Term loan	10,000,000	10,000,000
Industrial revenue bonds	13,200,446	10,008,446
	27,200,446	53,008,446
Less current maturities	3,641,400	308,000
	$23,559,046	**$52,700,446**

Effective December 31, 1985, the Company amended the credit agreement with a bank whereby the Company may borrow a maximum of $60,000,000 on a revolving-credit basis to December 31, 1988, and a term-loan basis for an additional five years. The interest rates are the prime rate during the revolving-credit period, and ¼ of 1% above the prime rate during the term period. Alternative interest rates, which may at times be less than prime, are available at the Company's discretion. A fee is also payable at a rate ranging from ¼ to ⅜ of 1% per annum on the unused portion of the commitment. The Company has agreed to maintain average compensating balances, which are usually satisfied by balances maintained for normal business operations.

On March 7, 1985, the Company borrowed $10,000,000 from a bank on a term-loan basis for four years at an interest rate of 12.1%. Semi-annual payments in the amount of $1,666,700 begin October, 1986.

The Company has borrowed $13,200,446 through industrial revenue bonds issued to construct facilities in Jackson, Tennessee; Charlotte, North Carolina; Jacksonville, Florida; and Tampa, Florida. The interest rates on these bonds range from 60% to 63% of the prime rate.

The credit agreement, term-loan and industrial revenue bonds contain certain restrictive provisions which relate principally to the payment of cash dividends, acquisition of fixed assets, and incurrence of indebtedness, and which require the maintenance of minimum net current assets to net current liabilities of no less than 1.7 to 1.0 and interest-bearing indebtedness to not exceed 50% of the sum of net worth plus interest-bearing indebtedness. The amount of reinvested earnings available for dividends, per the agreements, was approximately $10,608,000 at September 30, 1986. Similar restrictions existed in the prior year.

Aggregate maturities of long-term borrowings for the four years subsequent to September 30, 1987, are as follows: 1988—$4,403,900; 1989—$5,216,200; 1990—$2,083,000; and 1991—$3,280,000.

As of September 30, 1986, the Company had available additional borrowing capacity of $79,000,000, which includes $56,000,000 on a revolving-credit basis.

NOTES TO CONSOLIDATED FINANCIAL STATEMENTS—CONTINUED

FLORIDA STEEL CORPORATION AND SUBSIDIARIES

NOTE D—INCOME TAXES

The provisions for income taxes are comprised of the following amounts:

	1986	1985	1984
Currently payable			
Federal	$ 9,704,000	$ 590,000	$ 298,000
State	156,000	247,000	113,000
	$ 9,860,000	$ 837,000	$ 411,000
Deferred:			
Federal	1,760,000	2,853,000	3,952,000
State	1,350,000	650,000	
	3,110,000	3,503,000	3,952,000
	$12,970,000	**$4,340,000**	**$4,363,000**

A reconciliation of the difference between the effective income tax rate for each year and the statutory Federal income tax rate follows:

	1986	1985	1984
Tax provision at statutory rates	$13,047,000	$5,559,000	$5,071,000
State income taxes, net of Federal income tax effect	813,000	351,000	61,000
Investment and other tax credits, net	(681,000)	(1,559,000)	(432,000)
Lower tax rates on long-term capital gains			(445,000)
Other items, net	(209,000)	(11,000)	108,000
	$12,970,000	**$4,340,000**	**$4,363,000**

The sources of timing differences on which deferred income taxes have been provided and the related income tax effect follow:

	1986	1985	1984
Depreciation	$ 1,036,000	$5,631,000	$5,043,000
Adjustments for Internal Revenue Service examination		(194,000)	
Accruals not currently deductible for income tax purposes	(2,026,000)		
Investment and other tax credits, including utilization of net operating losses	3,957,000	(1,589,000)	(1,331,000)
Other items, net	143,000	(345,000)	240,000
Total deferred income taxes provided	**$ 3,110,000**	**$3,503,000**	**$3,952,000**

During 1986, 1985, and 1984, income taxes were reduced by approximately $18,000, $144,000, and $426,000, respectively, resulting from an additional tax benefit related to the vesting of shares under a restricted stock plan (see Note F). During 1985, $194,000 was reclassified from deferred income taxes to Federal and state income taxes payable as a result of Internal Revenue Service examinations of 1983 and 1984 Federal income tax returns.

NOTE E—EMPLOYEE BENEFIT PLANS

Total pension expense for 1986, 1985, and 1984 was $2,659,000, $2,506,000, and $2,136,000, respectively. Accumulated plan benefit information, as estimated by consulting actuaries, and plan net assets available for benefits are as follows:

	October 1	
	1985	1984
Actuarial present value of accumulated plan benefits:		
Vested	$19,482,000	$17,273,000
Nonvested	3,370,000	3,195,000
	$22,852,000	**$20,468,000**
Plan net assets available for benefits	**$24,569,000**	**$20,470,000**
Assumed rates of return used to determine accumulated plan benefits:		
Active participants	8.0%	8.0%
Inactive participants	12.6%	12.6%

Pension costs have been determined in accordance with Accounting Principles Board Opinion No. 8. The Company has not determined the impact on pension costs of the recently issued FASB Statement 87, which must be adopted by fiscal 1988.

The Company also has a voluntary savings plan available to substantially all of its employees. Under this plan, the Company contributes amounts based upon a percentage of the savings paid into the plan by employees. Costs under this plan were $654,000, $574,000, and $551,000 for 1986, 1985, and 1984, respectively.

NOTE F—EMPLOYEE STOCK PLANS

The Company has a restricted stock plan and has reserved 600,000 shares of Common Stock for the purpose of paying incentive compensation to certain officers and key employees based upon the economic performance of the Company. The plan, as administered by the Executive Compensation Committee of the Board of Directors (composed solely of non-management directors), provides that the total fair market value of the aggregate shares transferred annually under the plan shall not exceed 7% of the Company's net income for such year. However, any stock transferred under the plan shall be forfeited if the participant leaves the employ of the Company within five years from the date of the grant. A participant may request up to 25% of any awards in cash in lieu of stock. Charges to earnings for grants made under the plan amounted to $801,000 and $563,000 for the years ended September 30, 1986 and 1985. No awards were made in 1984. During 1986, 1985, and 1984, 19,834, 30,660 and 49,600 shares, respectively, vested to participants of the plan. Capital in excess of par was increased by $18,000, $144,000, and $426,000 for 1986, 1985, and 1984, respectively, resulting from an additional tax benefit related to the vesting of the shares.

Effective January 1, 1983, the Company converted its Tax Reduction Act Stock Ownership Plan (TRASOP) to a payroll-based Employee Stock Ownership Plan (PAYSOP). The PAYSOP provides additional retirement benefits to eligible employees, including employees who participate in the restricted stock plan. Contributions to the PAYSOP are made by the Company in either cash or the Company's Common Stock in an amount equal to one-half of 1% of each eligible employee's annual gross compensation paid. A supplemental contribution is made in an amount equal to 4% of the plan year gross compensation paid for each first-year eligible employee, excluding participants in the restricted stock plan. Cash contributions are to be invested in the Company's Common Stock which is to be held in trust for the benefit of the participants. The 4% supplemental contribution amount is vested at the rate of 20% for each year of participation. The remainder of the annual contribution is fully vested at all times.

The Company has provided for contributions to the PAYSOP in 1986, 1985, and 1984 of $201,000, $332,000, and $308,000, respectively. Income tax expense has been reduced in 1986, 1985, and 1984 by $229,000, $227,000, and $216,000, respectively, for the additional tax credits earned by contributing to the plan.

NOTES TO CONSOLIDATED FINANCIAL STATEMENTS—CONTINUED
FLORIDA STEEL CORPORATION AND SUBSIDIARIES

NOTE G—OTHER INCOME

Other income for 1986 includes a $917,000 gain on the sale of excess land at the Fort Lauderdale, Florida, Reinforcing Steel Fabricating Plant which resulted in a net gain after taxes of $660,000 ($.11 per share).

Other income for 1985 includes a $870,000 gain on sale of a production facility. The Company sold the Miami Structural Steel Fabricating Plant on March 1, 1985, and recognized a net gain after taxes of $515,000 ($.09 per share). The $870,000 includes $186,000 resulting from liquidation of this facility's LIFO inventories carried at lower costs prevailing in prior years as compared with the cost of 1985 purchases. The $870,000 gain was offset by charges of $450,000 for disposal of certain equipment and $1,100,000 for the writeoff of a note receivable deemed partially uncollectible. The note receivable was part of the proceeds from the sale of a production facility in 1983.

Other income for 1984 includes $5,257,000 of gains on the sale of two production facilities. The Company sold the Tampa Miscellaneous Fabricating Plant on February 29, 1984, and the Tampa Steel Service Center on March 1, 1984, and recognized a net gain after taxes of $2,823,000 ($.47 per share). The $5,257,000 includes $1,873,000 resulting from liquidation of these facilities' LIFO inventories carried at lower costs prevailing in prior years as compared with the cost of 1984 purchases. Additionally, the Company recognized a charge of $401,000 ($.07 per share) for disposal of certain equipment.

NOTE H—ACQUISITIONS OF SUBSIDIARIES

The Company purchased all of the outstanding common stock of Stafford Rail Products, Inc. on March 3, 1986, and Atlas Steel and Wire Corporation on September 19, 1986, for cash of approximately $4,700,000. The acquisitions have been accounted for as purchases with the purchase prices assigned to the net assets based on the fair value of the assets and liabilities at the dates of acquisition. Their results of operations have been consolidated with those of the Company since the dates of acquisition.

The following unaudited pro forma combined results of operations for the years ended September 30, 1986 and 1985, give effect to the acquisitions as though they had occurred on October 1, 1984.

	1986	1985
Net Sales	$339,510,000	$317,123,000
Income before Extraordinary Item	$ 15,527,000	$ 7,974,000
Net Income	$ 16,032,000	$ 7,974,000
Net Income per Share	$ 2.67	$ 1.34

Pro forma information does not purport to be indicative of the results that actually would have been obtained if the combined operations had been conducted during the periods presented and is not intended to be a projection of future results.

NOTE I—LITIGATION AND CONTINGENCIES

The Company is defending various claims and legal actions which are common to its operations. This includes a suit in the Commonwealth of Puerto Rico against the Company and others for alleged violations of Puerto Rican anti-dumping statutes asking damages in excess of $5,000,000. While it is not feasible to predict or determine the ultimate outcome of these matters, none of them, in the opinion of management, will have a material effect on the Company's financial position or results of operations.

Board of Directors and Shareholders
Florida Steel Corporation
Tampa, Florida

Report of Certified Public Accountants

We have examined the statements of financial position of Florida Steel Corporation as of September 30, 1986 and 1985, and the related statements of operations, shareholders' equity, and changes in financial position for each of the three years in the period ended September 30, 1986. Our examinations were made in accordance with generally accepted auditing standards and, accordingly, included such tests of the accounting records and such other auditing procedures as we considered necessary in the circumstances.

In our opinion, the financial statements referred to above present fairly the financial position of Florida Steel Corporation at September 30, 1986 and 1985, and the results of its operations and changes in its financial position for each of the three years in the period ended September 30, 1986, in conformity with generally accepted accounting principles applied on a consistent basis.

Ernst + Whinney

Tampa, Florida
October 24, 1986

Accounting for Assets, Current Liabilities, and Related Revenue and Expenses

By now you know that the resources a company uses in its operations are called assets. You have already had some experience in recording assets, adjusting asset accounts, and placing them on simple financial statements. In Part Three we will take a close look at the major assets found on the balance sheets of most businesses.

As assets are used up they become expenses. You will learn how to measure the amount of an asset that has been used up and how to transfer these amounts to expense accounts.

Cash and marketable securities are

said to be the most liquid assets because they can be readily used to buy things that the business needs in its operations. You will learn the elaborate internal control measures that a business must take to ensure that cash is not stolen or misused. These measures are a part of the internal control system you have already studied.

When a company sells something on credit or loans someone money, it has a right to receive future payment. You will learn about the two major types of receivables — accounts receivable and notes receivable. And as you learn about accounts and notes receivable you will also learn about their mirror image, accounts and notes payable. You will also learn how to account for receivables that we expect not to collect — our bad debts.

Merchandise inventory is perhaps the most important asset for most businesses. It is this asset that is sold to earn revenues. You already know one way to calculate cost of goods sold expense. In Chapter 9 you will learn four different methods that may be used to determine the amounts assigned to ending inventory and cost of goods sold. You will also learn how you can estimate the amount of inventory when you can't count it because it has been stolen or destroyed.

The long-lived assets that a company has may be tangible or intangible. You will learn how to calculate the cost of these assets and how to allocate their costs to expense accounts.

Cash and Marketable Securities

ACCOUNTING FOR CASH

The Nature of Cash

For accounting purposes, "cash" represents more than money in the form of paper currency and coins that we use in simple, everyday financial transactions. The accountant's "cash" appearing on the balance sheet includes money in other forms as well, although not all other forms. For example, many people consider savings accounts, travelers' checks, checking accounts, money orders, U.S. government savings bonds, and postage stamps to be money. Not all of these, however, are cash. *Cash,* as the term is used by accountants, means:

Accountant's definition of cash

1. A current asset on deposit in a bank that can be withdrawn immediately and used for any business purpose, *or*

2. A current asset that a bank will readily accept for deposit

According to the accountant's definition, cash includes: paper currency and coins; the money in checking accounts; a check written on a checking account (also called a *demand deposit account*); the money in certain savings accounts (the money in some types of savings accounts cannot be withdrawn without penalty); money orders (a form of check usually issued at a bank, post office, or convenience store); and travelers' checks (a form of check requiring the user to sign at the time the check is issued and again at the time it is used to pay for something).

Cash does not include postage stamps, U.S. government savings bonds, or promissory notes (which are simply formal IOUs), whether from individuals or companies. None of these forms of money is considered cash, because they cannot be deposited directly in a bank account. Nor is money held in a special bank account that can be used for only one purpose, such as to retire long-term debt or pay retirement benefits. This money would not be represented as cash on the balance sheet because its use is restricted. Management could not legally use it to pay employees for their services or to purchase merchandise. Items not included in Cash do appear elsewhere on the balance sheet, under such headings as Temporary Investments, Prepaid Postage, or Long-Term Investments.

Internal Control over Cash

Cash, in any form, can be converted to its simplest, most acceptable form—commonly referred to as *money,* which everyone wants. Because it is so easily convertible into money, everyone wants cash in any form. And because everyone wants it, it must be protected.

If not protected or controlled, cash in the form of money may be lost to pilfering; cash in other forms may be lost in enormous sums to clever schemes of theft. Of course, cash is also lost through honest mistakes. For these reasons the cash flowing through an economic entity must be protected or controlled.

Internal control of cash In Chapter 6 you learned about the system of internal control. In this chapter we will see how this system can be used to protect the company's cash. We will focus on two parts of the system:

1. *Custodianship,* in this case the controls used to protect the currency, coins, checks, and other physical forms that cash may take; and

2. *Other records controls,* in this case the various recordkeeping controls that assure the ready availability of reliable information about the flow of cash in all forms. (This information includes the reasons why cash is received and the purposes for which it is spent.)

In even the smallest merchandising firm, you can readily observe an example of the most basic form of internal control of the cash system—the *cash register.* A cash register provides physical control—protection for cash in its physical form—as well as recordkeeping control—gathering information about where cash has come from. A cash register makes an instant record of cash received, provides a receipt for the customer, and serves as a place to temporarily secure the cash received. The record of money received is a copy of the customer's receipt. It is preserved on a paper tape (or sometimes a magnetic tape) locked in the cash register, and is used to verify that the amount of money received by a sales clerk is the same amount that is placed in the cash register.

Cash registers and company safes are not as secure as a bank vault. Cash received during the day should not be kept at the business overnight. To minimize opportunities for theft, it should be deposited in the firm's checking account each day.

Cash registers and safes are obvious controls over cash. Other controls are not so obvious. For example, the cash receipts journal and the cash payments journal are used to provide recordkeeping control and to make cash theft schemes more difficult to carry out. In all but the smallest businesses these journals make it possible to isolate the handling and recording of the inflow of cash from writing checks and recording the outflow of cash to pay bills. This separation makes it difficult for the theft of cash between its being received and deposited in a checking account and the writing of checks on that account to go undetected.

In very small firms with only a few employees, it is not always possible to have one person in charge of recording cash inflows and another handling cash outflows. In these businesses it is best for the owner or manager to perform as many of the cash-related chores as possible.

Other internal controls over cash include:

- Using checks to pay for all expenditures

- Requiring written authorization, called a *voucher,* before any check can be issued

- Requiring the signatures of two or more of the firm's managers on all checks greater than a certain amount

- Reconciling the monthly bank statement, performed by someone who doesn't ordinarily handle cash

- Using a carefully controlled fund, called a *petty cash fund,* for payments in small amounts that make a check impractical or unacceptable

The Voucher System

As you know, an internal control system extends beyond cash; it includes physical and recordkeeping controls over all the assets of the business. One part of this system assures that appropriate planned acquisitions are made, received in good condition, billed at correct amounts, and paid for on time. In a small business, the owner is usually involved directly in each of these activities. Thus, in safeguarding his or her interests, the owner effects an informal system of internal control.

However, owners of large businesses cannot be closely involved in all the activities of the business. The activities are organized into many separate functions, and different groups of employees are delegated the authority to perform each function. For example, one group of employees orders goods and services, another group receives and inspects them, a third group decides the proper amount and timing of payment, and still another group actually writes and mails the checks. In large firms it is necessary to have a formal system of internal control to assure that the activity of incurring obligations (acquiring goods and services) is separated from the activity of paying for them. Of course, the purpose of separating these activities is to have different individuals performing them. Nevertheless, there must be a written form of communication (what to pay, how much, when, etc.) linking the various activities of the employees, to allow management to control and monitor what goes on. This is what the voucher system is all about. In the following paragraphs the voucher system is briefly explained (see also Figure 7-1).

In a large organization the authority to acquire goods and services is centralized in one department called the *purchasing department.* No other department within the organization is allowed to acquire goods and services. With the purchasing function centralized, not only is control achieved, but volume purchasing for many departments will result in reduced costs.

When a particular department needs goods and/or services, it must request the purchasing department to acquire them — it does so on a form called a *purchase requisition.*

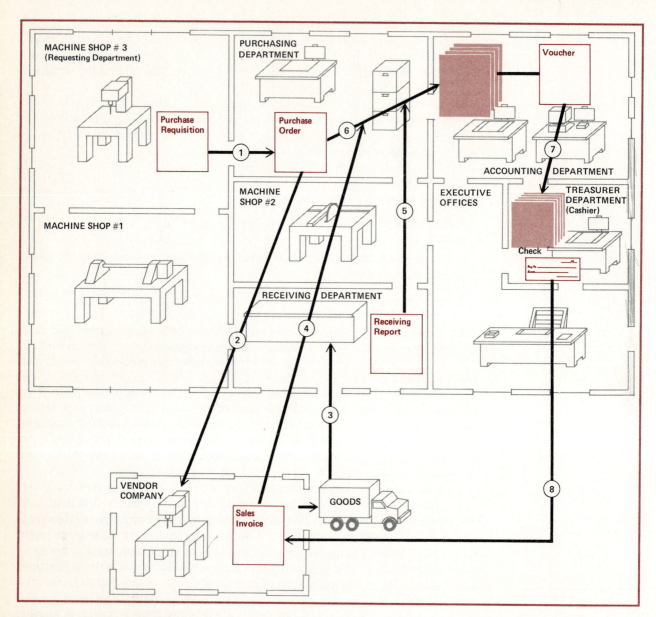

FIGURE 7-1 The Voucher System

The numbers represent the sequential documentation flow:

   1. A purchasing requisition is prepared and sent to the purchasing department.
   2. A purchase order is mailed to a vendor.
   3. The vendor ships the goods to the receiving department.
   4. The vendor mails a sales invoice to the purchasing department.
   5. The receiving department checks the goods and sends a receiving report to the purchasing department.
   6. All documents are sent to the accounting department for review.
   7. A voucher authorizing payment is prepared and sent to the cashier.
   8. A check is issued and mailed to the vendor.

Upon receiving the purchase requisition the purchasing department verifies that the requested items are authorized and (after combining similar requests from other departments) prepares a ***purchase order.*** The purchase order is mailed to a vendor (a company that supplies the requested goods and/or services).

The vendor in turn sends the goods or provides the services and mails a ***sales invoice*** to the requesting company. If goods are sent, they arrive at the receiving department, where they are checked to be sure they are in good condition and are what was requested. A ***receiving report*** is prepared.

All the documentation is forwarded to the accounting department: the purchase requisition, the purchase order, the sales invoice, and the receiving report. The accounting department verifies the arithmetic accuracy, checks authorized signatures, prepares a ***voucher*** (attaching the documents to it), and records the activity in a ***voucher register.*** The voucher register is similar to the cash payments journal.

Finally, the voucher is sent to the cashier for payment, and the information concerning the payment is entered in the ***check register.***

Bank Reconciliation

Checks written to employees, vendors, and others are presented to your bank for payment. Your bank sends you a bank statement, usually once each month, which summarizes your checks that have been presented for payment as well as your deposits and service charges for the period. Exhibit 7-1 on page 274 shows what a typical monthly bank statement looks like. Notice that the check numbers and amounts of all checks processed by the bank during the month are shown. Deposits and service charges are identified by the date they were added or deducted from your account.

It is not at all uncommon to find that the ending balance in the monthly statement compiled by the bank does not agree with the ending balance that appears in the checkbook. When this happens, someone in the business must determine the reasons for the difference between the two ending balances. A complete and satisfactory explanation of the differences between the bank's records and the company's is called a ***reconciliation.***

Some differences may be expected routinely every month. For example, the amount of checks written by the business but not received by the bank before it prepares the monthly bank statement will appear as a deduction in the checkbook but not in the bank's records. Similarly, deposits mailed but not yet received by the bank will appear in the business's records but not on the bank's monthly statement.

Other differences may result from errors or embezzlement by an employee. The bank may have incorrectly deducted the amount of a check, or the business may have entered an amount incorrectly in its checkbook. An employee may have stolen a blank check, forged it, and cashed it. Since the check was never entered in the checkbook, a difference will exist between the bank balance and the checkbook balance.

Bank reconciliations are an important part of the internal control system. They help us locate errors in the recordkeeping system and assist us in discovering employee schemes to defraud the company. The bank reconciliation should always be prepared by an individual who is not involved with preparing and approving vouchers or writing checks. We want an *independent* party verifying that the work of the other employees was accurate and proper.

EXHIBIT 7-1

MERCHANTS NATIONAL BANK

Direct Inquiries to:
Merchants National Bank of Texas
PO Box 35907
Temple, Texas   76501
(817) 555-4444

Statement Date
11/30/89

Account Number
1098674399

ROBERT LAMB MEAT MARKET
478 Hill Street
Temple, Texas   76501

Balance Last Statement	Deposits and Credits		Checks and Debits		Balance This Statement
	No.	Total Amount	No.	Total Amount	
3,993.62	7	4,925.54	15	3,458.36	5,460.80

Date	Amount Credited	Description
11/2	1,385.56	Deposit
11/7	347.78	Deposit
11/9	1,244.56	Deposit
11/13	527.91	Deposit
11/18	876.30	Deposit
11/24	462.87	Deposit
11/29	80.56	Deposit

Checks:

Date	Check No.	Amount	Date	Check No.	Amount
11/2	1862	188.95	11/2	1875	222.77
11/4	1876	160.73	11/5	1884	88.33
11/7	1896	100.00	11/9	1899	275.75
11/10	1900	25.79	11/10	1901	341.07
11/14	1902	890.50	11/17	1903	84.19
11/19	1905	308.61	11/22	1906	170.87
11/26	1907	400.80	11/30	1909	178.64

Other Debits:

Date	Amount	Description
11/30	21.36	Service charge

MEMBER FDIC

NOTICE: SEE REVERSE SIDE FOR INFORMATION.

Most businesses use the bank-and-books-to-correct-cash reconciliation to trace the differences between the bank statement and checking account. This method allows us to show corrections needed in the checkbook (and accounting records) and still derive a correct ending cash balance. Using the Nelson Company as an example, we will illustrate how to reconcile both the ending balance on the bank statement and the ending balance in the checkbook to the same correct cash balance.

NELSON COMPANY
Bank Reconciliation:
Bank-and-Books-to-Correct-Cash Method

John Norton, an accountant employed by the Nelson Company, is responsible for preparing the monthly bank reconciliation. The bank statement showed an ending balance for Nov. 30, 1989, of $34,173.80, whereas the checkbook balance was $30,388.60. The idea with this method is to adjust each of the balances to reflect the correct end-of-month balance, and in doing so, to reconcile the two with one another. Adjusting the bank balance begins with the ending balance from the bank statement; adjusting the checkbook balance begins with the ending balance in the checkbook. Each is adjusted independently; the resulting corrected balance for each should be identical.

The reconciliation process disclosed the following items. After reading each, refer to Exhibit 7-2 (page 276) to see how it appears on the reconciliation.

1. In comparing the checkbook stubs with the canceled checks, John discovered that 15 checks totaling $5,854.80 had not yet been processed by the bank. The $5,854.80 must be deducted from the $34,173.80 balance reported by the bank, since Nelson Company no longer has control over this amount of cash. From Nelson's point of view the cash is spent; only the mechanical process of presenting the checks to Nelson's bank remains.

2. Cash in the amount of $1,970 was deposited in the night depository on Nov. 30 and did not appear on the bank statement, since it was processed by the bank on Dec. 2. This $1,970 must be added to the ending balance, since it is cash that was still at Nelson's disposal on Nov. 30. A correct Nov. 30 cash balance must include this amount.

3. An error was discovered in the checkbook. In comparing the canceled checks with the check stubs, John noticed that check no. 1140, written in the amount of $120, had been deducted from the checkbook as $210. The checkbook balance is incorrect. It is too low by the amount of $90 ($210 − $120). This error must be corrected by adding $90 to the Nov. 30 checkbook balance.

4. A bank error was also found in comparing canceled checks with check stubs. The bank had deducted check no. 1131 from Nelson's account as $346. The actual amount of the check was $364. The bank should be notified at once so that its records can be corrected. In order for the correct cash balance to be derived on the bank reconciliation, the $18 error ($364 − $346) must be deducted from the balance according to the bank.

5. A check stamped NOT SUFFICIENT FUNDS (NSF) was returned with the bank statement. T. Burkitt, a customer, had given Nelson the check to pay for merchandise. Nelson thought that Burkitt's check was cash at the time it was received. The bank clearing process revealed that it was in fact nothing more than a written promise to pay cash. Nelson has less cash than the checkbook balance represents. So Burkitt's check for $182.60 must be deducted from the balance shown in Nelson's checkbook to reflect the correct cash balance. Until Nelson collects from Burkitt, the check represents not cash but simply an IOU.

6. The November bank statement shows a $25.00 service charge. Bank service charges are fees levied by the bank for printing and processing the company's checks, returning NSF checks, and providing other banking services. These service charges have not been deducted from Nelson's checkbook because the amount was unknown until the bank statement was received. This deduction must appear on the reconciliation in calculating the correct cash balance.

Since no other errors or differences can be detected, the 11/30/89 balances and adjustments are totaled, each total producing a correct ending cash balance of $30,271. This amount should appear as Cash in Bank on Nelson's balance sheet on Nov. 30, 1989, despite the fact that it appears neither in Nelson's checkbook nor on the Nov. 30 bank statement. Exhibit 7-2 shows how the completed reconciliation would appear.

EXHIBIT 7-2 Bank Reconciliation
Bank and book balances reconciled to correct cash amount.

NELSON COMPANY
Bank Reconciliation
November 30, 1989

Balance per bank statement, 11/30/89		$34,173.80	Balance per checkbook, 11/30/89		$30,388.60
Add:			Add:		
Deposits in transit on 11/30/89		1,970.00	Check no. 1140 for $120 deducted from checkbook as $210		90.00
Total		$36,143.80	Total		$30,478.60
Deduct:			Deduct:		
Checks outstanding on 11/30/89	$5,854.80		NSF check of Burkitt	$182.60	
Check no. 1131 for $364 deducted from account as $346	18.00	(5,872.80)	Bank service fees	25.00	(207.60)
Correct ending balance, 11/30/1989		$30,271.00	Correct ending balance, 11/30/1989		$30,271.00

If correct amounts are identical after all adjustments have been made, your reconciliation is complete.

Recording Unrecorded Transactions and Correcting Errors

As you have just seen, the reconciliation process often uncovers transactions that by their nature haven't been recorded in the checkbook records, as well as errors in some of the transactions that have been recorded. From the Nelson Company reconciliation, an example of a typical unrecorded transaction is the check in the amount of $182.60 that was returned because it wasn't represented by sufficient cash in the checking account of the individual who wrote it (T. Burkitt). All unrecorded transactions and errors detected — whether uncovered in the bank balance reconciliation or the firm's checkbook balance reconciliation — must be accounted for and recorded in the bank's records as well as in the firm's accounting records. The firm is responsible for correcting errors and recording corrections and unrecorded transactions in its records; the bank is responsible for the same in its records.

The company must analyze each adjustment in the checkbook section of the reconciliation and determine which accounts are correct and which are in error. There are few general rules for deciding how unrecorded transactions and errors should be recorded in the accounting records; each adjustment must be considered independently. Let's analyze the adjustments, which are typical, shown for the Nelson Company in the preceding illustration.

Adjustment

Check no. 1140 for $120 erroneously deducted from the checkbook as $210...... $90

Correcting an error in recording a check

Analysis When this transaction was originally recorded in a journal, some account was debited for $210 and Cash was credited for $210. We must discover which account was debited so we can correct it. Inspection of the book of original journal entry (cash payments journal or general journal) will reveal which account was debited for a greater amount than it should have been. Assume that the account was Advertising Expense. We have determined by inspecting the original journal entry, then, that too much Advertising Expense was recorded and that too much was deducted from Cash.

Correcting Entry

Cash 90
    Advertising Expense 90
To correct an error in recording check no. 1140 ($210 − $120 = $90).

Adjustment

NSF check of T. Burkitt $182.60

Recording an NSF check

Analysis When the check was received from Burkitt, Nelson debited Cash and credited another account, let's say Sales. The book of original entry (cash receipts journal or general journal) will show the credit to the Sales account. The only account in error in the original entry is Cash, since a sale was made and recorded in the correct amount. The problem is that cash was not received from the customer; the check represents not cash but an IOU. Proper recording of this transaction will involve debiting Accounts Receivable to record the IOU from the customer, and crediting Cash, reducing it by the amount of Burkitt's check, which turned out not to represent cash after all.

Correcting Entry

Accounts Receivable: T. Burkitt	182.60	
Cash		182.60

To record an NSF check received with the November bank statement.

Adjustment

Bank service fees $25.00

Recording bank service fees

Analysis Since the amount of bank service charges may vary with the number of checks processed and the number and types of other services a firm uses, Nelson first learned the amount of the bank service charges for November by seeing the amount on the bank statement. Nelson must record the fees by debiting an expense and reducing cash.

Correcting Entry

Bank Service Charge Expense	25.00	
Cash		25.00

To record November bank service charge.

One fact you should have noticed from the above examples: When a correction or unrecorded transaction requires that an amount must be *added* to the checkbook balance on the reconciliation, there is a corresponding entry that includes a *debit (increase) to Cash* in the same amount. Similarly, for adjustments requiring a *deduction* from the checkbook balance on the reconciliation, there is a corresponding general journal entry requiring *a credit (decrease) to Cash.*

Petty Cash

Most cash payments made by businesses are in the form of checks. The fact that each check must be individually prepared and signed provides a measure of control over the outflow of cash. The canceled checks provide proof that payment was made.

Reason for petty cash fund

However, in spite of these advantages, there are instances where payment by check is impractical. In these instances, payment is made in the form of currency and coin. A small amount of currency and coin set aside for this purpose is called a *petty cash fund.* Examples of proper uses of petty cash include payment of taxi fare for an employee to deliver personally and immediately business documents across town, payment for delivery charges on a part for a typewriter that was shipped collect, and purchase of a small number of postage stamps.

Setting up a petty cash fund

The petty cash fund is established by transferring a small amount of cash from the checking account, say, $50, in the form of currency, to a person who is designated to be responsible for it—the *petty cashier.* This person may be a receptionist, a secretary, a bookkeeper, or any employee considered responsible and reliable and in a position to disburse it effectively. The petty cash fund is set up by a check made payable to Petty Cash. The petty cashier then cashes this check and keeps the money in a container he or she is responsible for safeguarding.

The accounting entry to establish the petty cash fund is as follows:

LOOSE CASH CONTROLS RESULT IN EMBEZZLEMENT

Hermetite Corp. manufactures hermetic seals, an electrical component, for sale to the electronics industry. The company's stock is owned by the public. Hermetite's size may be judged by its sales and income. Sales and income for 1980 were approximately $11 million and $500,000, respectively. During 1981 the company earned about $500,000 on $9.5 million of sales.

Hermetite doesn't know exactly when Samson Gilman, the bookkeeper and office manager, began to embezzle from the company; but it was determined that between September 1975 and October 1980, he stole approximately $240,000. In 1978 his theft was about 34% of Hermetite's income before income taxes!

How can a trusted employee steal from a relatively large company over an extended period of time? We need only look at Hermetite's internal controls over cash to see how Gilman perpetrated his fraud.

Gilman obtained blank Hermetite checks and made them payable to a local bank. He "signed" the checks using a signature plate embossed with the company president's signature. He endorsed and cashed the checks at the local bank. Gilman has the cash as easy as this! Now to cover up the theft to avoid detection.

Since Gilman kept the company books, he simply did not record the fake checks in the cash payments journal—but he did include the amount in the totals of the journal columns. (That takes care of the credit to Cash.) The fake purchase reports that he made out resulted in a debit to Raw Materials Purchases. (Now both the debit and credit are "buried" in the books.)

Gilman would have been caught, however, if someone else had reconciled the bank statement with the cash account each month. The checks endorsed by Gilman would have raised the suspicions of even

the office boy. Unfortunately for Hermetite, another of Samson Gilman's duties was to reconcile the bank account. It was a very easy matter for him to destroy the incriminating checks before anyone learned of them.

Hermetite's lack of meaningful internal controls enabled Gilman to steal virtually at will. He had complete control over the blank company checks, facsimile signature plates, check-writing machines, journals, bank statements, and canceled checks. Moreover, Gilman personally prepared Hermetite's cash payments journal, corporate checks, bank reconciliations, and forms used to input data into the data processing system that compiled the general ledger and other records.

Source: Securities Exchange Act of 1934 Release No. 18976, Administrative Proceeding File No. 3-6162, Aug. 18, 1982.

Hermetite should have been aware of Gilman's theft long before he had the opportunity to steal as much as he did. The CPA who audited Hermetite's financial statements each year should have noticed the lax control over cash and informed the company management of the problems. If more rigorous procedures had been established, perhaps Mr. Gilman would not have been tempted to embezzle funds.

Based on what you have learned about internal control in Chapters 6 and 7, what controls can you suggest to Hermetite to ensure that the new bookkeeper does not repeat Gilman's theft?

Petty Cash..	50	
Cash...		50

To establish a petty cash fund.

This entry transfers cash from a cash-in-bank (checking) account to a cash-on-hand account. The total cash of the business remains unchanged.

Petty cash voucher explained

Just as for payments by check, payments from the petty cash fund can be made only with authorization in writing. This written authorization is also a voucher, although it is much simpler than the one we discussed at the beginning of the chapter, and may look something like this:

PANDORA CORP.
Petty Cash Disbursement Voucher

Date _December 28, 1989_   Voucher No. _____ 104 _____

Amount of Payment $ ___ 14.35 _____

Reason for Payment ___ To pay for office machine part _____

_received on C.O.D. shipment_____

Signature of Person Receiving Payment ___ M. Quintal _____

Approved by ___ Isaac Martin _____

Usually the petty cashier fills out the voucher and has the person requesting the cash sign it. The petty cashier then files the voucher in the petty cash container and disburses money from the container in the amount of the voucher. The total of the money and the amounts represented by the vouchers must at all times equal the original total of the petty cash fund. That is, the petty cashier must have either the money or approved vouchers showing what it was used for.

Petty cash disbursement vouchers are similar to the vouchers used in the voucher system described earlier. Both vouchers are written authorizations to pay cash. Petty cash vouchers differ in that they are usually not recorded in a formal register.

Replenishing the petty cash fund

When the money in the petty cash fund is running low, the petty cashier will present the vouchers to the manager at a higher level of responsibility who has the authority to replenish it.

Assume that the following vouchers were presented for reimbursement:

Petty Cash Voucher Number	Reason for Disbursement	Amount
101	Paid messenger to deliver package	$ 5.25
102	Purchased postage stamps	1.50
103	Purchased office supplies	6.40
104	Paid for office machine part which was shipped COD	14.35
105	Purchased office supplies	4.40
	Total	$31.90

A check would be made out to Petty Cash for $31.90 and the various expenses represented by each of the vouchers would be recorded. The following entry would be made:

Delivery Expense	5.25	
Office Supplies Expense	10.80	
Postage Expense	1.50	
Repairs Expense	14.35	
Cash		31.90

To replenish petty cash fund and record expenses.

The replenishment entry made no debit to Petty Cash since we did not increase the petty cash fund. The petty cash fund asset shows a total of $50 before and after the reimbursement. Before reimbursement the asset Petty Cash was, of course, overstated by $31.90, because some of the money had been spent. The replenishment entry formally records the disbursements of money for expenses that have already taken place. The petty cashier now has $50 in money in the cash box and no paid vouchers. The process of petty cash outlays and fund reimbursement can begin again.

The asset Petty Cash is debited only when the fund is originally established or when it is increased. Expenses are debited when the fund is replenished. The fund is replenished whenever it is running low and at the end of the accounting cycle. When cash is running low, replenishment is necessary to ensure that an adequate amount is always on hand to meet day-to-day petty cash needs. At the end of the accounting cycle, replenishment is necessary to record all previously unrecorded expenses in accordance with the matching principle.

Cash Over and Short

Treatment of small mistakes in cash

In spite of the safeguards designed to control the inflows and outflows of money, small mistakes do occur. For example, assume that in the previous petty cash fund illustration the petty cash vouchers total $31.90 and the currency and coins in the petty cash box total $16.70. The petty cash fund, which should total $50, now totals only $48.60 ($31.90 + $16.70). The $1.40 shortage in the petty cash fund was due to a petty cashier mistake — probably paying out more than a petty cash voucher authorized.

The entry to replenish the petty cash fund must also record the cash shortage:

Delivery Expense	5.25	
Office Supplies Expense	10.80	
Postage Expense	1.50	
Repairs Expense	14.35	
Cash Over and Short	1.40	
Cash		33.30

To replenish a petty cash fund, record expenses and a $1.40 cash shortage.

The Cash Over and Short account was debited for $1.40 to record the shortage. If there has been an overage, the same account would be credited for the amount of the overage. If Cash Over and Short has a debit balance at the end of the accounting period, it would be reported as a Miscellaneous Expense on the income statement. A credit balance in the account would be reported as Miscellaneous Income.

The Cash Over and Short account is also used when the money in a cash register drawer (say, $530) does not total to the same amount that is recorded on the cash register tape (say, $528). In this case the entry to record the cash sales must also record the cash overage or shortage:

Cash	530	
Sales		528
Cash Over and Short		2

To record cash sales for the day and a cash overage of $2.

Management will monitor the amount and frequency of cash overages and shortages from a particular petty cash fund or cash register. Frequent overages and shortages may indicate that employees are being careless. Repeated shortages may mean that employees are stealing.

ACCOUNTING FOR MARKETABLE SECURITIES

The Nature of Marketable Securities

Many businesses experience widely fluctuating cash balances during the year. During some seasons of the year, most of their cash may be invested in merchandise inventory; during other seasons most of the goods may be sold, inventory may be low, and there will be a surplus of cash in the company's checking account. A toy manufacturer, for example, probably has an overabundance of cash during the fall months when the Christmas season shipments have been completed and payments are received from customers. This abundance of cash will be needed later next spring and summer when the company will again invest in the toys for the following Christmas.

Surplus cash is the cash that is not needed for the current day-to-day operation of the business. What should a company do with a temporary cash surplus? One alternative would be to leave the funds in the checking account until needed. A better option would be to use this extra cash in some way to earn a return. If the surplus cash can be put to work for a short time, any profit earned will be more than if the cash is left idle in a checking account that earns little or no interest. The investments that a company makes with a temporary cash surplus are called *marketable securities,* or *temporary investments.*

To be classified as a marketable security, or temporary investment, on the balance sheet, two tests must be met:

Marketable security classification tests

1. Management must intend to hold the investment for a short time, usually less than 1 year.

2. The investment must be readily marketable; i.e., management must be able to sell the investment very quickly.

The Composition of Marketable Securities

Bonds, stocks, and short-term notes issued by corporations and by the U.S. government are common types of securities that may be purchased and held for short periods.

Bonds are issued by corporations as a way of borrowing money. By acquiring a bond you are really lending cash to the corporation selling it. Once purchased, bonds may be traded on the securities exchanges just as stocks are. Bond prices are quoted on the securities exchanges as a percentage of their maturity value. A $1,000 bond quoted at 100 would sell for 100% of its maturity value, or $1,000. The same bond quoted at 96 would sell for 96% of its maturity value, or $960. No matter what you pay for a bond, you will receive the maturity value ($1,000) at the end of the bond's life. The income from a bond is the interest paid to the investor — the lender — for the use of his or her cash. Of course, management will purchase bonds of companies in sound financial condition to minimize the risk of not receiving interest when it is due.

Stock is a document that represents evidence of ownership, or a share of ownership, in another company. Individuals and corporations may readily invest in a share of ownership through a broker who buys it at a stock exchange such as the New York Stock Exchange or the American Stock Exchange. Stock prices are quoted in dollars per share of stock. A stock quoted at $12\frac{1}{2}$ would sell for $12.50 per share; one quoted at $378\frac{3}{4}$ would sell for $378.75 per share. By purchasing shares of stock, management hopes to profit by receiving dividends or by selling the stock for more than its original cost. Management will, of course, be very careful to buy a relatively safe stock, because the cash invested will be needed in a short time. Investing in speculative, high-risk stocks could result in a loss of a significant part of the cash used in the investment — the price of these shares could quickly decline considerably below the original purchase price.

Management may also elect to purchase bonds and stocks as long-term investments. These investments ordinarily involve the use of cash that will not be needed in the future. Long-term investments are not included as marketable securities; we will discuss this more fully in Chapter 14.

Accounting for Temporary Investments in Bonds

When bonds are purchased, they are recorded in the Marketable Securities account at the cost of the bond. As interest is earned, it is recorded as Interest Income. When the bonds are sold, any difference between the selling price and the cost is recorded in the journal as a gain or loss. These procedures are demonstrated in the Moana Mower Company illustration that follows.

MOANA MOWER COMPANY

Purchase of temporary bond investment

Transaction On Oct. 1, 1989, the Moana Mower Company purchased from a broker 100 South Seas Telephone bonds, each of the $1,000 bonds paying 8% annual interest. The $100,000 (100 bonds × $1,000 each) cost includes all brokerage fees related to the transaction. The bonds pay interest semiannually on Sept. 30 and on Mar. 31.

Analysis Moana Mower's management invested some extra cash in South Seas Telephone bonds. Management intends to hold the bonds and earn interest until the cash is needed the following spring.

Journal Entry

```
1989
Oct. 1   Marketable Securities...............................   100,000
             Cash.........................................              100,000
         To record the purchase of one hundred $1,000 South Seas
         Telephone bonds bearing interest at 8% annually.
```

Accrual of interest earned on bonds

Adjustment By Dec. 31, 1989, Moana's year-end interest for 3 months has been earned. Three months' interest would be calculated as follows:

$$(.08)(\$100,000)(\tfrac{3}{12}) = \$2,000$$

Analysis Since 3 months' interest was earned in 1989 but will not be received until Mar. 31, 1990, it must be recorded on Dec. 31, 1989, the accounting year-end, by means of an adjusting entry.

Adjusting Entry

```
1989
Dec. 31  Interest Receivable ....................................   2,000
             Interest Income.....................................            2,000
         To record 3 months' interest earned on a temporary investment
         in bonds.
```

Cash interest received on bonds

Transaction On Mar. 31, 1990, Moana received $4,000 for 6 months' interest on the South Seas Telephone Bonds:

$$(.08)(\$100,000)(\tfrac{6}{12}) = \$4,000$$

Analysis Moana received $2,000 in interest that was earned in 1989 and $2,000 that was earned in 1990. The amount earned in 1989 has already been recorded as income; the receivable remains to be collected. The amount earned in 1990 must be recorded as income.

Journal Entry

```
1990
Mar. 31  Cash ..............................................   4,000
             Interest Receivable....................................            2,000
             Interest Income.....................................            2,000
         To record receipt of 6 months' interest on South Seas Telephone
         bonds.
```

Sale of temporary bond investment

Transaction On Apr. 1, 1990, Moana sold the South Seas Telephone bonds for $100,500.

Analysis Moana needs the cash to pay for salaries, purchases of inventory, advertising, and other operating expenses. A broker sold the bonds on one of the security exchanges.

Journal Entry

1990
Apr. 1 Cash 100,500
       Marketable Securities 100,000
       Gain on Sale of Marketable Securities............... 500
      To record the sale of one hundred $1,000 South Seas Telephone bonds.

Moana Mower management used $100,000 of surplus cash to earn $4,500—$4,000 interest plus $500 increase in value of the bonds—during the 6-month period. Had the funds been left in the checking account, they would have produced little or no income for the company.

Accounting for Temporary Investments in Stock

Stock purchased as a temporary investment is recorded in the journal at cost, including all brokerage fees. Dividends, which are not guaranteed, are recorded as Dividend Income when distributed to shareholders. A marketable security sold for more than its original cost results in a gain. If sold for less than original cost, it results in a loss.

Entries to record these types of transactions are shown in the following illustration.

FLETCHER FENCE COMPANY

Purchase of temporary stock investment

Transaction Fletcher Fence Company purchased 1,000 shares of Millward Motor Co. stock on Dec. 1, 1989, when the stock was selling for $38 per share. A $1,900 commission was paid to a broker to handle the transaction.

Analysis Fletcher Fence decided to invest some seasonally idle cash in a relatively safe stock. Millward Motors stock has a stable market price, and the company has consistently paid each year a $4 dividend on each share. A stockbroker was contacted who purchased the shares on the New York Stock Exchange in Fletcher's behalf. The total cost of the shares is calculated as shown below:

$$(1{,}000 \text{ shares})(\$38 \text{ per share}) + \$1{,}900 \text{ (commission)} = \$38{,}000 + \$1{,}900$$
$$= \$39{,}900$$

Journal Entry

1989
Dec. 1 Marketable Securities..................................... 39,900
      Cash 39,900
      To record the purchase of 1,000 shares of Millward Motor Company stock.

Cash dividend received on stock investment

Transaction On Jan. 15, 1990, Millward declared and paid its quarterly dividend — $1 per share.

Analysis Fletcher Fence received $1,000 from Millward Motors. Note that Fletcher does not accrue dividends at the accounting year-end in the same way that Moana Mower accrued interest in the previous illustration. Dividends are not earned with the passage of time as interest is. Millward Motors is not obligated to pay its owners dividends. It makes that evaluation four times a year. A firm is obligated to its bondholders to pay interest at set times.

Journal Entry

```
1990
Jan. 15  Cash .......................................... 1,000
              Dividend Income............................         1,000
         To record dividend received from Millward Motors.
```

Sale of temporary stock investment

Transaction On Mar. 30, 1990, Fletcher sold the Millward stock for $43.50 per share and paid a broker $2,000 to handle the transaction.

Analysis Since Fletcher needed the cash for its day-to-day operations, the Millward stock was sold. A broker's commission must be paid when stock is sold, just as when stock is purchased. The amount received is as follows:

Selling price	$ 43.50 per share
Number of shares sold	1,000 shares
Total	$43,500
Less: Broker's commission	2,000
Net cash received	$41,500

The net cash received of $41,500 less the cost of $39,900 yields a gain of $1,600.

Journal Entry

```
1990
Mar. 30  Cash ........................................... 41,500
              Marketable Securities ............................         39,900
              Gain on Sale of Marketable Securities...............          1,600
         To record the sale of Millward Motors Company stock.
```

Like any asset, the value of stock changes with time. But, unlike most other assets, the change in value of stock, can be determined easily — the prices of shares of stock are quoted continuously. This value is reliable as an unbiased measure because it is set by many buyers and sellers trading stock on the stock exchange. At what value is the stock to be reported on a balance sheet at the end of an accounting period?

Temporary investments on balance sheet at lower of cost or market

Generally accepted accounting principles dictate that temporary investments in stock be shown on the balance sheet at either the original cost or the market value, whichever is lower. Thus on Dec. 31, 1989, if the Millward stock had been selling for $37 per share, Fletcher would have shown Marketable Securities at $37,000 and recorded a $2,900 loss. This value is less than the original cost — the idea behind reporting the lower value is to show a more conservative financial picture to the readers of Fletcher's financial statement.

Fletcher would prepare the following entry to record the loss:

```
1989
Dec. 31   Loss to Reduce Marketable Securities to Market Value..........  2,900
               Allowance to Reduce Marketable Securities to Market Value         2,900
          To reduce marketable securities to market value, which is lower
          than cost
```

The loss would be shown on the income statement as a nonoperating loss. The allowance account would be shown as a contra asset deducted from Marketable Securities.

Fletcher's Dec. 31, 1989, balance sheet, then, would have shown the following:

Marketable Securities (cost)	$39,900	
Less: Allowance to Reduce Marketable Securities to Market Value.	(2,900)	$37,000

If the value of stock has increased above the original cost, the stock is shown on the balance sheet at original cost. No gain is recognized until the stock is sold. Again, this rule against showing increases in value presents a conservative financial picture to the statement readers.

You should have a good grasp of why we feel that lower-of-cost-or-market procedures are important. We will leave a complete discussion of the complex rules governing the application of this technique to a more advanced accounting course.

BALANCE SHEET CLASSIFICATIONS

Current assets, the first category of accounts appearing in the asset section of any balance sheet, includes all assets that will be converted into cash or used up in the operation of the business during the next year. The current asset accounts are arranged in order of liquidity — first is the asset most readily converted into cash and last is the asset least readily converted into cash. The top of this list is, of course, Cash, followed by Marketable Securities. Various types of receivables would appear next. A listing of typical current assets in order of liquidity follows:

Current Assets:

Cash

Marketable Securities

Less: Allowance to Reduce Marketable Securities to Market Value

Notes Receivable

Accounts Receivable

Less: Allowance for Uncollectible Accounts

Other Receivables

Merchandise Inventory

Supplies Inventory

Prepaid Assets

Receivables and Inventories will be discussed in detail in the next two chapters.

CHAPTER SUMMARY

To the accountant, cash means a current asset on deposit in a bank that can be withdrawn immediately and used for any business purpose, or a current asset that a bank will readily accept for deposit. Cash includes paper currency and coins, checking accounts, certain savings accounts, money orders, and travelers' checks.

Because cash is the most liquid and most readily acceptable asset, it is universally desirable. For that reason, special internal controls must be established to protect it from theft. Among the safeguards are *cash registers, printed receipts, safes, separate recording of cash receipts and cash payments,* a *voucher system* to control cash payments, *reconciliation of bank statements,* and *petty cash funds.*

A voucher system requires that all expenditures be authorized, that all goods and services received be inspected and reported, and that the proper amount be paid to the vendor in a timely fashion. The voucher system works like this: A department needing goods or services prepares a *purchase requisition,* which is sent to the purchasing department. In turn the purchasing department prepares and mails to the vendor a *purchase order.* The vendor fills the order, ships the goods, and provides a *sales invoice.* The goods are received by the receiving department and are inspected. A *receiving report* is sent to the purchasing department. All the documents are then forwarded to the accounting department for review and approval. Upon approval, a check is authorized and issued by the cashier and the check is mailed to the vendor.

Bank reconciliations are prepared to explain the differences between the cash balance shown on the bank statement and the cash amount in the company's checkbook. An important part of the system of internal control, bank reconciliations help locate errors made by the company and by the bank. The *bank-and-books-to-correct-cash* reconciliation method is the technique used by most businesses. The reconciliation will reveal unrecorded transactions, which will have to be corrected by making an entry in the general journal.

Where it is impractical to issue checks for small amounts of cash, most businesses establish a *petty cash fund.* A responsible person is designated in charge of the fund and will disburse funds only with written authorization in the form of a *petty cash disbursement voucher.* The fund is established by transferring money from the corporate checking account to the petty cash fund. It is replenished by issuing a check on the corporate checking account for the amount of petty cash disbursements evidenced by the authorized vouchers.

When a business has cash that is temporarily in excess of its operating needs, the company will invest this excess cash in *marketable securities.* Marketable securities are bonds, stocks, and short-term notes issued by corporations and governmental units. Income is earned by the instruments in the form of interest, dividends, and by selling the securities for more than the price paid for them.

When a classified balance sheet is prepared, the current assets are listed in order of liquidity.

IMPORTANT TERMS USED IN THIS CHAPTER

Bank reconciliation An analysis of the differences between the ending cash balance as reported by the bank and the ending cash balance as recorded in the company's records. (page 273)

Bond A security issued, or sold, by a corporation as a means of borrowing money, which means that a bond is really a loan from the bondholder. (page 282)

Cash All money on deposit in banks that can be obtained immediately and used at the discretion of the management of the company, and all items on hand that will be accepted by a bank for deposit. (page 269)

Current assets All assets that will be converted into cash or used up in the operation of the business during the next year. The current asset accounts are usually the first category in the asset section of a balance sheet. (page 286)

Deposit in transit Cash sent to the bank — sent through the mail or placed in a night depository — for deposit but not received in time to be included in the ending balance and listed on the bank statement. (page 275)

Dividend A corporation's earnings distributed in the form of cash or other assets, to its shareholders. (page 285)

Internal control The system of safeguards intended to protect assets from theft and to ensure proper financial recordkeeping. (page 270)

Marketable securities Investments that can be readily sold and that management intends to keep for less than 1 year. Also known as *temporary investments* or *short-term investments.* (page 281)

NSF check (Not Sufficient Funds check) A check presented for payment to the bank and rejected because the depositor's account does not contain sufficient cash to represent the amount of the check. (page 275)

Petty cash fund A small amount of cash used for payments when a check is impractical. The contents of the fund must always total the same amount. The fund may contain cash or cash and paid vouchers. (page 278)

Purchase order A business document that reaches outside the firm — an external business document — recognized as having the power and authority to specify an order for goods or services to suppliers and vendors and the commitment to pay for them. (page 273)

Purchase requisition An internal business document, that is, a document that originates and remains within the firm, specifying goods or services needed and requesting the firm to acquire them. (page 271)

Receiving report An internal business document to indicate the quantity and condition of goods or services that have been received. (page 273)

Sales invoice A business document prepared by the vendor, or supplier, itemizing the goods or services ordered and delivered. The sales invoice usually constitutes a request for payment. (page 273)

Stock A certificate issued by a corporation, representing the share of ownership in it. (page 284)

Vendor A seller of goods or services. (page 273)

Voucher A written authorization to pay. Vouchers usually contain the name of the individual or company to be paid, the amount of the payment, the reason for the payment, a signature authorizing payment, and the accounts to be debited or credited as a result of the payment. (page 273)

Voucher system The system used by a business to ensure that all expenditures are authorized; that the goods or services ordered are received; and that only the goods or services received are paid for, and within a time period that allows the firm to take advantage of cash discounts. (page 271)

QUESTIONS

1. Explain why a travelers' check for $1,000 is cash according to the accountant's definition, whereas a U.S. government savings bond is not cash.

2. List at least six internal controls over cash that would be used by a large department store.

3. Separation of duties is a common internal control technique. Separation of duties may not be possible in a small business with only a few employees. Explain how a small business may attempt to compensate for not having many employees.

4. What internal control system assures that appropriate planned acquisitions are made, received in good condition, billed at correct amounts, and paid for on time?

5. What is the purpose of each of the business documents listed below?

   a. Purchase requisition   **c.** Sales invoice
   b. Purchase order   **d.** Receiving report

6. In which business department is each of the following documents prepared?

   a. Purchase requisition   **d.** Voucher
   b. Purchase order   **e.** Check
   c. Receiving report

7. Why do businesses prepare bank reconciliations?

8. What are outstanding checks? Why are they subtracted from the bank statement cash balance on bank reconciliations?

9. A company received a check with its bank statement marked "NSF." What is an NSF check? How will it appear on a bank-and-books-to-correct-cash reconciliation?

10. Which of the following items on a bank reconciliation require the company to make a journal entry?

   Outstanding checks   Deposits in transit
   Bank service fees   NSF checks
   Checkbook errors   Bank errors

11. What are petty cash funds? Why are they used?

12. "The contents of a $50 petty cash fund must always equal $50 even if $38 has been paid from it." Explain what is meant by this statement.

13. How are petty cash vouchers like vouchers used in the voucher system? How do they differ?

14. Where will Cash Over and Short appear on an income statement? Explain.

15. What two tests must an investment meet in order to be classified as a marketable security?

16. Why do companies purchase marketable securities?

17. A company purchased a bond maturing in 20 years. Can this bond be classified as a marketable security? Explain.

18. What rule is used to determine the order of current assets on a balance sheet?

EXERCISES

Exercise 7-1
Determining the items to include in Cash

Tahiti Nursery's balance sheet shows cash in the amount of $25,344. The following items were used in arriving at this amount:

Currency and coin on hand	$ 322.20
Postage stamps on hand	31.80
Checking account balance	23,040.00
Petty cash fund balance	150.00
U.S. government savings bond	300.00
Passbook savings account at Fiji Savings	1,350.00
Travelers' checks received from customers	60.00
A promissory note from John Sumner, a customer	90.00

What is the correct amount of cash that Tahiti Nursery should report on its balance sheet?

(Check figure: Correct cash = $24,922.20)

Exercise 7-2
Evaluating bank reconciliation items

A bank reconciliation is being prepared that reconciles the bank and book balances to the correct cash balance. Indicate the proper treatment for each of the items below by placing an "X" in the appropriate column(s) on your solution paper.

	Add to Bank Balance	Deduct from Bank Balance	Add to Book Balance	Deduct from Book Balance
Outstanding checks	_____	_____	_____	_____
Bank service charges	_____	_____	_____	_____
A check for $36 entered in the checkbook as $63	_____	_____	_____	_____
Deposits in transit	_____	_____	_____	_____
A customer's NSF check returned with the bank statement	_____	_____	_____	_____

Exercise 7-3
Explaining entries made from a bank reconciliation

Roger Byam prepared the following journal entries based on items on the May, 1989, bank reconciliation:

	1989			
a.	May 31	Bank Service Charge Expense	80	
		Cash		80
b.	31	Accounts Receivable: R. Lamb	75	
		Cash		75
c.	31	Cash	92	
		Supplies Expense		92

Explain the type of adjustment on the bank reconciliation that would have resulted in each of the entries.

Exercise 7-4
Recording petty cash reimbursement

On June 1, 1989, Williams Co. established a $75 petty cash fund. On June 30, the petty cash box contained the following petty cash disbursement vouchers:

Voucher Number	Purpose of Disbursement	Amount of Disbursement
101	Office Supplies	$10.50
102	Postage	4.50
103	Merchandise	15.00
104	Computer Floppy Disks	27.00
105	Freight-In	4.50

The petty cash box also contained $12.00 in currency and coins.

Prepare the appropriate entries to establish the petty cash fund on June 1 and to reimburse the fund on June 30.

(Check figure: June 30 entry includes a $63 credit to Cash)

Exercise 7-5
Calculating interest earned on temporary bond investments)

Fryer Co. purchased a $30,000 Nelson, Inc., bond on May 1, 1989. The bond pays 9% interest on Apr. 30 and Oct. 31 each year. Calculate the amount of interest income from this temporary investment that would appear on Fryer's Dec. 31, 1989, income statement.

(Check figure: Interest income for 1989 = $1,800)

Exercise 7-6
Recording temporary investments in stock

Montague Music invests seasonally idle cash in common stock. Prepare journal entries to record the following transactions relating to Montague's marketable securities during 1989:

June 1	Purchased 600 shares of Hector Computer, Inc., stock for $51 per share. A broker's commission of $1,200 was paid.
30	Received a cash dividend of $0.90 per share.
Sept. 1	Sold 150 shares for $8,700 less a broker's commission of $300.
Dec. 31	The market value of the stock was $43 per share. If the lower-of-cost-or-market method is used, at what amount should the marketable securities appear on the balance sheet?

(Check figure: Gain on sale = $450)

Exercise 7-7
Preparing the current asset section of a balance sheet

Duke Art Supply has the following assets on Dec. 31, 1989:

Building......................	$ 71,200	Accum. Depr.: Trucks	$ 5,120
Office Supplies	5,200	Cash in Checking Account.....	46,560
Cash on Hand................	1,760	Merchandise Inventory........	394,240
Accounts Receivable..........	131,200	Accum. Depr.: Trucks	10,400
Prepaid Insurance	3,040	Marketable Securities	5,280
Trucks	31,120		

Select the current asset accounts from the list above and prepare the current assets section of Duke's balance sheet in good form.

(Check figure: Total current assets = $587,200)

PROBLEMS: SET A

Problem A7-1
Preparing a bank reconciliation

You have been assigned the task of preparing the Feb. 28, 1989, bank reconciliation for Resolution Hardware. During the process of completing the reconciliation you discover the following facts:

a. The balance in the checkbook on Feb. 28, 1989, was $3,837.95.

b. Checks written prior to Feb. 28 that have not yet cleared the bank total $1,585.25.

Required	1. Prepare all entries needed on the above dates. (Include any appropriate closing entries.) 2. How much interest income will Quintal Trailers show on its income statement for the year ended Sept. 30, 1990?

(Check figure: 1990 interest income = $3,600)

PROBLEMS: SET B

Problem B7-1
Preparing a bank reconciliation

As an accountant for the Dutch East India Company, one of your responsibilities is to prepare the monthly bank reconciliation. In preparing to complete the Nov. 30, 1989, reconciliation, you have assembled the following facts:

a. The balance on the Nov. 30 bank statement was $16,427.33.
b. The balance in the checkbook on Nov 30 was $11,019.81.
c. Check no. 5102 was deducted in the checkbook as $663.24. The actual amount of the check was $636.24
d. A deposit of $2,216.42 was placed in the night depository on Nov. 30. The deposit was not recorded by the bank until Dec. 1, so it does not appear on the November bank statement.
e. Bank service charges for the month total $35.25. This charge has not been deducted in the checkbook.
f. Checks written prior to Nov. 30 that have not yet cleared the bank total $7,632.19.

Required	Prepare a reconciliation of bank and book balances to the correct cash amount.

(Check figure: Correct cash = $11,011.56)

Problem B7-2
Preparing a bank reconciliation

The following bank reconciliation was prepared by the accountant for Brunswick Cleaners:

BRUNSWICK CLEANERS
Bank Reconciliation
January 31, 1989

Balance per bank statement, Jan. 31, 1989		$ 6,704.22
Add: Deposits in transit		317.84
Deduct: Outstanding checks		(1,391.50)
Correct cash balance, Jan. 31, 1989		$ 5,630.56
Balance per checkbook, Jan. 31, 1989		$ 5,641.37
Add:		
Check no. 619 for $18.51 was deducted in the checkbook as $185.10. The check was issued to pay for changing the oil in the delivery truck		166.59
Deduct:		
Bank service charge for January	$ 15.25	
Check no. 640 for $155 was deducted in the checkbook and entered in the financial records as $15.50. The check was issued to pay for cleaning fluid	139.50	
NSF check from customer: John Davit	22.65	(177.40)
Correct cash balance		$ 5,630.56

Required	Prepare journal entries for Brunswick Cleaners that would be indicated as a result of the January bank reconciliation.

(Check figure: Cash is credited for a net of $10.81 in the journal entry or entries)

128450

**Problem B7-3
Preparing a bank
reconciliation and journal
entries**

William Elphinstone owns and operates a real estate office. You have been hired to prepare a reconciliation of Elphinstone's cash balance on the bank statement with the amount that appears in his company books. You are also to determine the correct cash amount. Elphinstone provides you with the following information:

PALMIRA NATIONAL BANK
Palmira, NY

Elphinstone Real Estate
4130 Vista Drive
Palmira, NY

Statement Date: May 31, 1989

Balance Last Statement	Deposits and Credits		Checks and Debits		Balance This Statement
	No.	Total Amount	No.	Total Amount	
1,936.60	4	11,673.58	12	8,689.62	4,920.56

Date	Amount Credited	Description
5/3	2,355.98	Deposit
5/15	4,461.28	Deposit
5/22	2,856.32	Deposit
5/25	2,000.00	Deposit

Checks:

Date	Check No.	Amount	Date	Check No.	Amount
5/4	2376	286.80	5/19	2489	511.64
5/7	2484	123.00	5/21	2490	957.75
5/8	2486	1,388.55	5/25	2491	848.32
5/10	2487	2,477.00	5/29	2492	1,821.64
5/17	2488	109.22			

Other Debits:

Date	Amount	Description
5/31	40.00	Safe deposit box rental (1 year)
5/31	75.70	NSF check (R. Prado)
5/31	50.00	Monthly service charge

**From Cash Receipts Journal
(All cash receipts are deposited):**

Date	Cash (Dr.)
5/5	2,355.98
5/15	4,461.28
5/22	2,856.32
5/25	2,000.00
5/31	859.12
Total	12,532.70

Depit Trans

**From Cash Payments Journal
(All cash payments are made by check):**

Date	Check No.	Cash (Cr.)
5/5	2484	213.00
5/6	2485	616.20
5/7	2486	1,388.55
5/7	2487	2,477.00
5/12	2488	109.22
5/15	2489	511.64
5/18	2490	957.75
5/21	2491	848.32
5/23	2492	1,821.64
5/25	2493	11.76
5/28	2494	556.24
5/31	2495	47.80
Total		9,559.12

outstanding

From the General Ledger:

Date	Explanation	P/R	Dr.	Cr.	Balance
Apr. 31	Balance	✓			1,601.30
May 31		C/R-2	12,532.70		14,134.00
May 31		C/P-5		9,559.12	4,574.88

a. In reviewing the April bank statement, you discover that check no. 2370 ($48.50) and check no. 2376 ($286.80) were outstanding on Apr. 30.

b. The $40 charge for the safe deposit box rental was incorrect. Elphinstone had applied for a safe deposit box but canceled the order when none were available.

c. Check no. 2484 was written to pay for an advertisement in the local newspaper. An incorrect amount was entered in the checkbook and cash payments journal. The correct amount, $123.00, appears on the check.

d. The bank returned a customer's check marked NSF. Elphinstone believes that he will collect from R. Pardo, the customer.

Required

1. Prepare a bank reconciliation that reconciles Elphinstone's bank statement balance and his cash book balance to a correct cash balance.

2. Prepare any journal entries needed on Elphinstone's books as indicated by the reconciliation.

(Check figure: Correct cash balance = $4,539.18)

Problem B7-4
Reimbursing a petty cash fund that has been misused

Toddler, Inc., has a $100 petty cash fund that is kept by Thelma Spendthrift. When Spendthrift failed to report to work for several days, Toddler investigated. Spendthrift's roommate said that Thelma had moved to Los Angeles to work in the movies. The Toddler internal audit department decided that an audit of Thelma's petty cash box would be appropriate. The petty cash box contained the following:

Sales invoices. Merchandise was sold to customers and the cash put in the petty cash fund........	$8,722.16
A receipt for mailing a package by Express Mail	21.15
Invoices for merchandise paid for out of petty cash.......................................	733.22
A receipt for a package that arrived postage due	5.78
An IOU from the Toddler company president ..	50.00
Currency and coin	12.01

Required

1. In what ways did Thelma Spendthrift misuse the petty cash fund?

2. Prepare a schedule showing the amount of cash that should be in Thelma's petty cash box.

3. Prepare the entry required to reimburse the petty cash fund. The $100 fund is to be the responsibility of Selma Safeman. (Hint: You will need to record the purchases and sales that Thelma processed through petty cash.)

(Check figure: Cash that should be in the petty cash box = $8,012.01)

Problem B7-5
Recording temporary investments in bonds

On Jan. 1, 1989, Hallet Co. adopted a policy of investing seasonally idle cash in corporate bonds. The 1989 and 1990 transactions relating to these investments are shown below:

1989

Jan. 1   Hallet purchased twenty-five $1,000 bonds of Chase, Inc. The cost of the 12% bonds including brokerage fees was $25,000. The bonds pay interest semiannually on June 30 and Dec. 31.

June 30	Received the semiannual interest.
July 1	Sold five of the Chase bonds for $5,375 net of brokerage fees and commissions.
Dec. 31	Received the semiannual interest.
31	Closed all temporary accounts relating to the bond investment.
1990	
Jan. 1	Sold the remainder of the Chase, Inc., bonds for $19,400 net of brokerage fees and commissions.

Required

Prepare journal entries to record the transactions and events listed above. Your entries should be supported by clearly labeled calculations.

(Check figure: Total interest earned during 1989 = $2,700)

Problem B7-6
Recording temporary investments in stock

Cole Appliances, Inc., routinely invests seasonally idle cash in common stocks. The following transactions took place during 1989:

Jan. 1	Cole purchased 2,500 shares of Dependable Steel Co. for $4 per share. A $256 commission was paid to the broker who handled the purchase.
Feb. 16	Cole bought 650 shares of Liberty Publishing Co. for $18 per share. A broker's commission of $130 was paid on the transaction.
Mar. 31	Received a quarterly dividend of $0.40 per share on the Liberty stock.
May 18	Two hundred fifty shares of Liberty stock were sold; $4,625 cash was received after all brokerage commission was paid.
June 30	Received a $0.40 per share quarterly dividend on the Liberty stock and a $0.30 per share semiannual dividend on the Dependable stock.
Sept. 30	Received a $0.40 per share quarterly dividend on the Liberty stock.
Nov. 8	Eight hundred shares of the Dependable stock were sold for $6 per share. A commission of $0.50 per share must be deducted from the sales price in determining the amount received by Cole.
Dec. 31	A $0.30 per share dividend was received on the Dependable stock. No fourth-quarter dividend was received on the Liberty stock.
31	Entries were made to close all temporary accounts.

Required

1. Prepare journal entries to record the transactions and events listed above. Your entries should be supported by clearly labeled calculations.
2. Assume that on Dec. 31, 1989, the market price of the Dependable stock was $3.90 per share; the market price of the Liberty stock was $17.60 per share. At what amount will the marketable securities appear on the Dec. 31, 1989, balance sheet? Explain.

(Check figure: Total dividend income during 1989 = $1,840)

Problem B7-7
Recording temporary investments in bonds

Bounty Bay Co. invests seasonally idle cash in corporate bonds. The following transactions and events relate to these investments. (Assume that Bounty Bay's fiscal year ends on Aug. 31.)

1988	
May 1	Purchased fifteen $1,000 Burma Imports Company bonds. The bonds pay 15% interest on Apr. 30 and Oct. 31. The $15,000 cost includes all brokerage fees and commissions.
July 1	Purchased ten $1,000 bonds of Sewell Enterprises. These bonds pay 18% interest on June 30 and Dec. 31 each year. The $10,000 cost includes all brokerage fees and commissions.
Aug. 31	Wilson accrued interest on the Burma Imports and Sewell Enterprises bonds.
Oct. 31	Received the semiannual interest on the Burma Imports bonds.
Nov. 1	Sold five of the Burma Imports bonds. The net cash proceeds from the sale were $4,887.
Dec. 31	Received the semiannual interest on the Sewell Enterprises bonds.

1989

Jan.	1	Sold five of the Sewell bonds. The net cash proceeds from the sale were $5,725.
Apr.	30	Received the semiannual interest on the Burma Imports bonds.
June	30	Received the semiannual interest on the Sewell bonds.
July	1	Sold the five remaining Sewell bonds; $5,315 was received after all commissions and fees were deducted.
Aug.	31	Bounty Bay accrued all appropriate interest.

Required

1. Prepare all entries needed at the above dates. (Include any appropriate closing entries.)
2. How much interest income will Bounty Bay show on its income statement for the year ended Aug. 31, 1989?

(Check figure: 1989 interest income = $2,675)

DECISION PROBLEM

As a management trainee of the Omega Construction Company, you have been assigned to the field office of the Sunbelt Truss and Lumber Division of the company on Nov. 30, 1989, to review their financial activities. In addition to your other responsibilities, you are requested to review the petty cash fund.

Sunbelt has a plant and office building located in Orangetown that serves the western half of the state. Recently a consortium of residential builders began construction in Sunshine City, located in the southeastern section of the state. In response to this large demand, Sunbelt established a production facility consisting of a large, open-sided shed, two large saws, an assembly line to join the pre-cut 2″ × 4″s and 2″ × 6″s into trusses and a press to straighten the trusses. A crew of 10 to 12 men operate the production facility. Located next to the shed is a trailer that serves as a field office for the production foreman and a part-time high school student who does routine clerical work and typing.

A petty cash fund of $500 was established on Oct. 18, 1989, and is the responsibility of Rocky Strongarm, the production foreman. A review of the cash payments journal in the Orangetown office has revealed that the petty cash fund has not been replenished since it was established. This is the reason you have been requested to review the fund while you are at the field office.

The petty cash fund is physically located in a tin security box locked in Mr. Strongarm's desk. A count of the cash in the security box, which you make in Mr. Strongarm's presence, amounts to $350. Several documents are also contained in the security box. These documents reveal the following information:

1. A special order received at the field office required the immediate acquisition of $750 of 2″ × 6″s from Orangetown Lumber Company. When the lumber arrived on Oct. 23, the driver insisted on cash payment, which was made from the petty cash fund.

2. Tony Martini, the no. 2 sawman, failed to make his October and November car payments. He asked Mr. Strongarm to loan him $500 until Jan. 15. Mr. Strongarm agreed, advancing him the money from petty cash on Nov. 15 but stating on a note, signed by Mr. Martini, that 18% interest would be charged.

3. One of the documents was a receipt in the amount of $700 dated Nov. 1, 1989, from Southeastern County Home Builders for an IBM typewriter, serial number 731057. A call to your supervisor, Mr. William E. Johnson, Regional Manager of Omega Construction Company, reveals that the typewriter is one of two assigned to the field office. You find only one in the field office, and it has serial number 731131. Company records reveal that the typewriter cost $1,250 and has accumulated depreciation of $550 as of Nov. 1, 1989.

4. American Homes purchased $1,500 of trusses on job order no. 3235. Due to unfortunate financial difficulties experienced by American Homes in recent years, they are a COD customer. The job order reveals that Mr. Strongarm received fifteen $100 bills from American Homes on Oct. 19, 1989. Your supervisor informs you in the telephone conversation mentioned in 3 above that job no. 3235 is still open and no entry is in the cash receipts book for the $1,500.

5. Appearing on the stationery of SunCoast Travel Agency is the following note: "Marybeth arrived at noon today with the $750 cash. Hope you and the Mrs. enjoy your trip. If you have any other travel plans in the near future, please call me."

   The part-time high-school clerk/typist is named Marybeth. She informs you that Mr. Strongarm instructed her to take $750 from petty cash to SunCoast Travel.

6. A notation on a purchase order from Seaview Builders reveals that Seaview paid Mr. Strongarm $650 cash on Nov. 1, 1989, for trusses for a Cape Cod model to be constructed in late December. No such receipt has been recorded in the cash receipts book per your supervisor at the Orangetown office.

7. A dining room table was acquired from Green Mountain Boys Furniture Company for $450. A call to the furniture company reveals that the furniture was delivered to Mrs. Strongarm at her residence. The driver of the delivery truck was instructed to go to the field office for payment. There Mr. Strongarm paid him $450 from a tin box.

8. Joe Weeks, the assistant production foreman, received $300 from the petty cash fund for the weekly period Oct. 23 to Oct. 30. In the telephone conversation mentioned above, your supervisor informs you that Mr. Weeks' pay check was not issued at the Orangetown office because his time card was lost. Mr. Strongarm was instructed to pay Mr. Weeks from the petty cash fund. Mr. Weeks' payroll records reveals that $300 is the correct amount.

Required

Write a memo to your supervisor explaining the problems found with the petty cash fund and providing suggestions for improvement. Include in your memo a schedule that will reconcile the petty cash fund and suggested general journal entries assuming the fund is *not* replenished.

CHAPTER 8

Receivables and Payables

Some of the things you will learn by studying this chapter are:

- What is meant by an *account receivable* and an *uncollectible account*
- Why the direct write-off method violates the matching concept
- What is meant by the *Allowance for Uncollectible Accounts* and *Bad Debts Expense*
- How to use the *percentage of credit sales method* and the *aging of receivables method* to calculate Bad Debts Expense
- What a *promissory note* is
- The difference between *interest-bearing* and *non-interest bearing* notes
- How to calculate the proceeds from a discounted note and prepare the journal entries associated with the discounting process
- Why accounting for current liabilities is important
- How we account for estimated and contingent liabilities

Your ability to borrow money enables you to enjoy many of the things our society makes available. Very few people would own their own homes if they could not borrow money. Nor would many of us have cars, furniture, or a multitude of goods and services (including college educations) without being able to borrow money from various stores, banks, or other sources. In fact, the operation of our national and international economies depends on the extension of credit. Without it, or if its cost is too high, goods and services cannot be paid for; plants close, and people are unemployed. The vast majority of our businesses purchase inventories and acquire plant and equipment by incurring liabilities. We, as individuals, have far more purchasing potential when credit is available. Our aggregate purchasing potential has enabled business and industrial firms to expand to the size where large-scale production is possible, thus reducing the costs of goods and services. Extending credit to business entities has provided them with the resources necessary to build plants and acquire or manufacture inventories that we demand.

Extending credit means that someone has provided and someone else has obtained goods or services. It also means that someone has received an asset—a *receivable*—for the goods or services provided. And it means that someone else has incurred a liability—a *payable*—for the goods or services received. These receivables and payables must be properly accounted for. An unrecorded receivable usually means an unrecorded revenue. An unrecorded liability results in an unrecorded expense. In either case the measurement of net income will be incorrect.

Extending credit to customers is not without risk. Some customers will not pay the amounts owed, and that requires the accountant to estimate the amount that will not be paid and to record the appropriate expense in the year the sale was made. That's what accounting for uncollectibles is all about, and it is covered in the first section of this chapter.

Credit can be extended by means of accepting promissory notes for accounts receivables. These notes provide for the payment of interest for the length of time the credit is extended. The second section of this chapter is concerned with these accounting matters.

The last section of the chapter is concerned with those types of liabilities that may or may not exist. Not only that, but we may or may not know the amount owed.

ACCOUNTS RECEIVABLE AND ACCOUNTS PAYABLE

Purchasers, either individuals or large organizations, usually don't give a stack of cash money to the accounting department of the seller the moment they receive the goods or services ordered. Nor do they pay at that precise moment with cash in the form of a check. They pay later, *after* having received the goods or services.

There are two reasons for credit purchases: (1) Buyers need goods and services that they can't (or may prefer not to) pay for immediately—e.g., it would be inconvenient to pay each truck driver as soon as a shipment of goods is unloaded—and (2) sellers can sell more through credit sales than if they were to insist on immediate cash payments. And this brings us to accounts receivable and accounts payable.

To an accountant, a credit sale is an *account receivable,* which is also called an *open account* or a *trade receivable.* In a credit sale, the seller and buyer enter into a contract, written or oral, in which the buyer agrees to pay the seller for all goods and services purchased within a specified time—typically 30, 60, or 90 days—after the buyer is billed. From the time the seller records the sale until the time the cash is collected, the seller has a claim against the buyer for the value of the goods or services delivered. This claim is carried in the seller's records as an account receivable and in the buyer's records as an account payable. Figure 8-1 shows this credit sales process.

Accounts receivable are claims against customers for goods or services sold on credit

Sales on account are recorded in the sales journal and then posted to the general ledger Account Receivable and the subsidiary ledger Account Receivable for each individual customer. Remember from your study of the sales journal in Chapter 6 that the column total of the sales journal is posted to the general ledger and each individual sale is posted to the subsidiary ledger. Thus, when you look at the balance sheet for any accounting period, you will see one line listing Accounts Receivable, which might be in the amount of, say, $57,385. That amount, of course, is the sum of perhaps thousands of individual accounts receivable, all recorded in individual ledger accounts. These ledger accounts might be recorded in the form of hand-printed notations on ledger sheets, or in the more modern medium on a computer memory device. The total of all the Accounts Receivable ledger accounts in the subsidiary ledger and the total of the Accounts Receivable account in the general

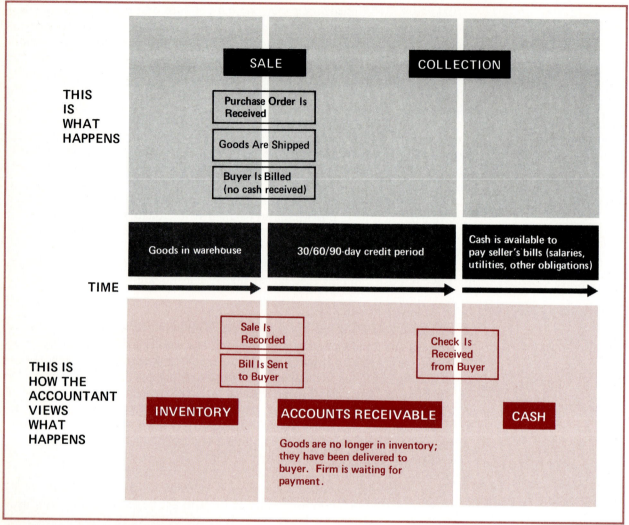

FIGURE 8-1 The Credit Sales Process
The credit sales process involves selling goods, shipping them to customers, and waiting to receive cash. The accountant sees this as a flow from inventory to accounts receivable and finally to cash.

ledger must, of course, agree at all times. The same procedure is used for purchases on account. They are recorded in the purchases journal and posted to the Accounts Payable control and subsidiary accounts.

As an example, consider the following, Reluctant Company made a sale of $500 to T. Heggen on account. The entry to record this sale in general journal form[1] is as follows:

The entry to record a sale on account

1989			
Dec. 30	Accounts Receivable: T. Heggen	500	
	Sales.		500
	To record sale on account.		

---

[1] All our journal entries in the examples throughout the rest of the book are in general journal form even though the entry may actually be made in a special journal. This will make illustrations much easier, because we won't have to construct special journals each time we make an entry.

All of Reluctant's accounts receivable on Dec. 31, 1989, are listed in the reconciliation below. This schedule proves that the total of the accounts receivable in the subsidiary ledger equals the balance of the Accounts Receivable Control account in the general ledger.

The total of the subsidiary ledger Accounts Receivable must equal the total of the general ledger Accounts Receivable

---

RELUCTANT COMPANY
Reconciliation of General and Subsidiary Accounts Receivable Ledgers
December 31, 1989

Accounts Receivable general ledger account balance		$2,830
Subsidiary ledger Accounts Receivable:		
D. Carmack	$420	
F. Grindle	150	
T. Heggen	500	
H. Hollingsworth	810	
R. Luttrell	120	
S. Marcus	405	
J. Oswald	175	
A Wright	250	
Total		$2,830

When T. Heggen paid his account on Jan. 5, 1990, the following entry was made in the general journal:

The entry to record a payment on account

```
1990
Jan. 5   Cash ................................................... 500
              Accounts Receivable: T. Heggen ...........         500
```

The accounting process for accounts receivable is shown in Figure 8-2. This illustration assumes that the accounting year (fiscal year) ends before the account receivable is collected.

Accounting for Uncollectible Accounts

Any business firm will carefully evaluate a customer's current financial condition and credit history before selling to that customer on account. In spite of the care taken before granting credit, there occasionally will be those customers who, for whatever reasons, cannot or will not pay their accounts.

How does the accountant treat an account receivable that is not paid and in all probability will never be paid? To understand how to represent in the accounting records an account receivable that will not be paid, consider the following:

1. The firm used resources in providing the goods or services sold on account.

2. Revenue was recorded at the time of the sale.

3. Goods or services were delivered.

4. Until those goods or services are paid for, the amount of the unpaid bill is much like a loan to the buyer.

5. The seller may give up hope that the buyer will pay, but the seller does not simply forget about the costs represented in the value of goods or services delivered and not paid for.

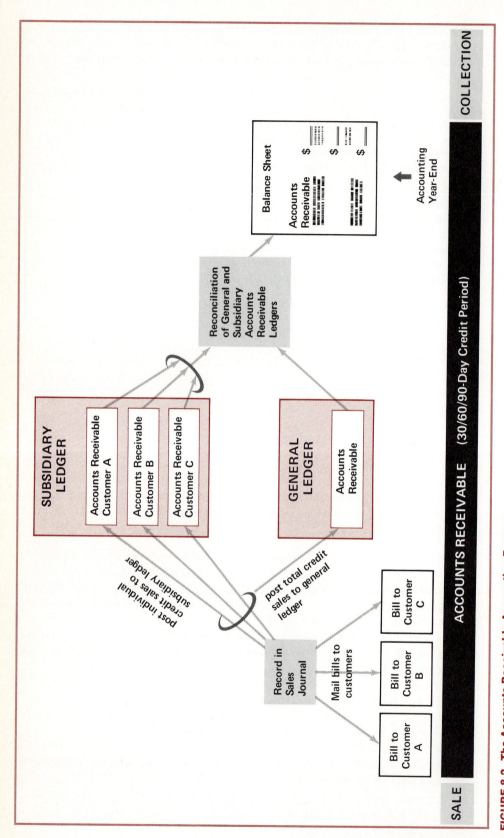

FIGURE 8-2 The Accounts Receivable Accounting Process

When a credit sale is made, it is recorded in the sales journal and posted to the general and subsidiary accounts receivable ledger accounts. At the end of the period, general and subsidiary ledgers are reconciled. Accounts Receivable appears as a single amount on the balance sheet.

All that adds up to a ***bad debt,*** which is regarded as a cost of doing business, or more specifically, as a cost of granting credit to do business. The amount that will not be collected is usually called ***uncollectible accounts expense*** or ***bad debts expense.***

The two most common ways of accounting for bad debts expense are: (1) the direct write-off method, in which the accountant recognizes bad debts expense when a specific customer's account is determined to be uncollectible; and (2) the percentage of credit sales and the aging of receivables methods, in which the accountant estimates total uncollectible accounts and records bad debts expense before knowing which specific customer's accounts will be uncollectible.

Direct Write-Off Method

As an example of the direct write-off method, assume that during 1989, Yarby, Inc., made sales on account to several thousand customers. One of them, J. Billings, declared bankruptcy, having no cash available to satisfy creditors' demands. Upon learning of Billings' bankruptcy, Yarby determined that Billings' account was uncollectible and at the same time recognized it as a bad debts expense: Yarby, Inc., made the following entry to write off Billings' account:

The entry to write off an account using the direct write-off method

1989			
Feb. 20	Bad Debts Expense	290	
	Accounts Receivable: J. Billings		290
	To write off account of J. Billings that is uncollectible.		

Bad Debts Expense will appear as an operating expense on Yarby's income statement. The credit will be posted to Yarby's Accounts Receivable general ledger account and to the Accounts Receivable: J. Billings subsidiary ledger account. The write-off effectively removes Billings' account receivable from our books; it now has a zero balance.

Direct write-off violates matching and distorts Accounts Receivable

Accounting theory limits the use of the direct write-off method because of two major objections to it: (1) It violates the matching principle and (2) it distorts the amount of Accounts Receivable on the balance sheet. The violation of the matching principle distorts what is reported on the income statement. Remember: According to the matching principle, the expenses incurred in earning revenue during a period of time should be matched with the revenue earned during that period.

For example, assume that a sale on account is made in 1989. This sale is recorded as an Account Receivable and a 1989 revenue. This revenue appears on the 1989 income statement. Now, assume that 1990 comes along but not the customer's payment. It is 1 year later and the company has not yet been paid. The company finally gives up hope that payment will ever be received. The account is declared uncollectible and becomes Bad Debts Expense. The Sales Revenue appeared on the 1989 income statement. Some of the expenses—that Bad Debt Expense—that contributed to 1989 income appear on the 1990 income statement, not on the 1989 income statement. The result of this mismatching is that both 1989 and 1990 incomes are distorted.

Continuing with our example, let us turn to the other major objection to the direct write-off method: that it distorts Accounts Receivable on the balance sheet. If, in 1989, the company reasonably expects to collect all the accounts, there is no distortion. However, the company knows that some accounts will later prove uncollectible. Failure to recognize this fact and to estimate these uncollectibles blissfully implies that every cent of every sale on account will be received in payment. Thus, the direct write-off method will result in a 1989 balance sheet Accounts Receivable amount that is greater than the amount that the company expects to collect.

Direct write-off method is simple and accurate

The direct write-off method offers two advantages—it is simple and accurate. It is simple because the company does not have to develop a means of estimating uncollectibles—no estimate is needed. It is accurate because no estimation errors are made—there are no estimates.

Publicly held companies must abide by generally accepted accounting principles, so they cannot use the direct write-off method. Owners of small businesses often ignore the major objections to the direct write-off method and use it because it is so simple to apply. The Internal Revenue Service also allows its use on income tax returns.

Percentage of Credit Sales Method

Percentage of credit sales method estimates uncollectible accounts

Unlike the direct write-off method, the percentage of credit sales method records bad debts expense before we know which specific customers' accounts will be uncollectible. The percentage of credit sales method requires that an estimate of uncollectibles be made at the end of each year by multiplying sales made on credit by a percentage. The percentage reflects management's estimate of the portion of the current year's credit sales that will ultimately prove uncollectible.

Management makes this estimate by examining the past experience of its collections, as well as the collection experience of similar companies having similar credit-granting policies. For example:

Steuben, Inc., had total sales of $2,800,000 during 1989; $300,000 were cash sales and $2,500,000 were on credit. Steuben's management determined that approximately $1\frac{1}{2}$% of the total credit sales would eventually prove uncollectible. That is, at the end of 1989, management estimates that $1\frac{1}{2}$% of all the credit sales made during 1989 will never be collected.

Based on this estimate, the amount of the 1989 bad debts expense is calculated as follows:

Total sales..	$2,800,000
Less: Cash sales	−300,000
Credit sales..	$2,500,000
Bad debts percentage, $1\frac{1}{2}$%, or	×.015
1989 Bad debts expense...	$ 37,500

The following is the adjusting entry to record this estimate:

The entry to record an estimate of bad debts expense using the percentage of credit sales method

1989			
Dec. 31	Bad Debts Expense	37,500	
	Allowance for Uncollectible Accounts....................		37,500
	To record an estimate of the 1989 credit sales that are expected to be uncollectible.		

Bad Debts Expense is classified on the income statement as an operating expense—it's a cost of doing business. Allowance for Uncollectible Accounts is a contra account to the current asset Accounts Receivable. Remember: A contra asset is an asset account with a negative (credit) balance. It is subtracted from another asset account—in this case, Accounts Receivable.

In the direct write-off method our debit was to Bad Debts Expense and our credit was to Accounts Receivable. Why did we credit a contra account in the percentage of credit sales method rather than crediting Accounts Receivable? The contra asset, Allowance for Uncollectible Accounts, is used for two reasons. First, use of this

The Allowance for Uncollectible Accounts is used: (1) To show the reader the portion of receivables we expect not to collect

account allows the balance sheet to show the total accounts receivable and the portion of this total that the company expects not to collect. If Steuben collects none of the $2,500,000 credit sales by the end of 1989, Accounts Receivable is disclosed on the 1989 balance sheet as follows:

Accounts Receivable...................................	$2,500,000	
Less: Allowance for Uncollectible Accounts	(37,500)	$2,462,500

If we had credited Accounts Receivable, only the $2,462,500 amount could be disclosed. The balance sheet reader needs to know what part of the accounts receivable probably won't be collected.

(2) Because we can't credit Accounts Receivable subsidiary ledger accounts

A second, and more practical, reason that a contra asset was used is that it is impossible to properly post the credit to Accounts Receivable. Remember, whenever this account is debited or credited, we must post the amount to the general ledger account and to the subsidiary ledger account(s). At the time we estimate our bad debts we know the total amount of our uncollectibles, but we don't know which specific customers will not pay. We can't post to subsidiary ledger accounts because we don't know whose account to post. We use Allowance for Uncollectible Accounts until we determine which customers' accounts are bad.

For example, on Jan. 15, 1990, Steuben, Inc., determined that the $1,230 account of L. Wilkes could not be collected. The following entry is made to write off the account:

Entry to write off a customer's account when bad debts were estimated

1990			
Jan. 15	Allowance for Uncollectible Accounts	1,230	
	Accounts Receivable: L. Wilkes..........................		1,230
	To write off the account of L. Wilkes that is determined to be uncollectible.		

Now we can post the credit to the Accounts Receivable general ledger account and to L. Wilkes' Accounts Receivable subsidiary ledger account. Notice that no expense is recorded when the account is written off. The expense was estimated in advance as part of the $37,500 Bad Debts Expense calculated and recorded in the general journal on Dec. 31, 1989.

The sequence of events thus far is this:

The percentage of credit sales procedure

1. Credit sales for the year are totaled.

2. Based on past experience, a percentage of the credit sales that will not be collected is estimated.

3. At the end of the year the amount of bad debts expense is calculated and recorded in the general journal by a debit to Bad Debts Expense and a credit to Allowance for Uncollectible Accounts. Notice that we have recorded the sales revenue and the bad debts expense in the same year—good matching.

4. Later, as an individual customer hasn't paid and it is determined that he or she won't pay, that customer's account is written off, reduced to zero, by debiting (reducing) the Allowance for Uncollectible Accounts, and by crediting (reducing) Accounts Receivable in both the general ledger and the subsidiary ledger.

There are cases where a particular account is identified and written off as uncollectible, and then that customer finally pays up. To follow the accounting procedures in this kind of case, let's continue with our example.

On Jan. 20, 1990, Steuben, Inc., wrote off D. Roberts' $475 account, which was believed to be uncollectible. On Jan. 31, a check was received from Roberts to pay the account in full. The following journal entries are necessary to record these events:

Entries:
(1) To write off a customer's account

1990
Jan. 20   Allowance for Uncollectible Accounts. 475
            Accounts Receivable: D. Roberts. 475
            To write off uncollectible account of D. Roberts.

(2) To reinstate the account

  31   Accounts Receivable: D. Roberts. 475
            Allowance for Uncollectible Accounts 475
            To reinstate D. Roberts account previously written off.

(3) To record receipt of payment

  31   Cash 475
            Accounts Receivable: D. Roberts. 475
            To record payment of account in full.

The entry on Jan. 31 to reinstate Roberts' account does just that — it restores his account to where it was before the Jan. 20 write-off entry. Roberts' account is reinstated in Steuben's general and subsidiary ledgers, showing that it is no longer considered a write-off; rather it is a paid-up account. The subsidiary ledger accounts provide a credit history for each customer. Reinstating Roberts' account puts his credit history in a favorable position for him to ask for credit again in the future.

Let's return for a moment to the Allowance for Uncollectible Accounts, or the **Allowance for Bad Debts,** as it is sometimes called. Remember: We estimated, based on an accurate picture of past credit experience, that $37,500 in Accounts Receivable would not be paid. If Roberts just paid his $475; what does that payment do to our estimate of uncollectibles? It does nothing. A total of $37,500 will eventually still not be paid. Instead of Roberts, someone else, not yet identified, will turn out to be a nonpaying culprit.

Aging of Receivables Method

The aging of receivables method estimates uncollectible amounts

Like the percentage of credit sales method, the aging of receivables method of determining the amount of receivables that will not be collected involves recording bad debts expense before we know which specific customers' accounts will be uncollectible. It is more accurate than the percentage of credit sales method, but it requires a bit more work.

Instead of looking at the total credit sales made during a period, this method looks at how old an account receivable is at the end of a period. The older a particular account receivable is, the greater the likelihood that it will never be collected. For accounts receivable that are just past due, there is less certainty that they will not be collected.

The *aging of receivables method* entails performing three steps at the end of each period:

The aging of receivables procedure

1. Receivables are grouped by age. For example, a 2-month-past-due $10,000 account receivable and a 2-month-old $50 receivable are grouped together, while a 1-year, $1,000 receivable and a $100, year-old receivable are grouped together.

2. A percentage reflecting an estimate of how much will never be collected is applied to the total amount of receivables in each age group—perhaps 5% of the fresh (2-month-old) receivables is estimated to be uncollectible. This means that of the $10,050 total ($10,000 + $50), $502.50 (.05 × $10,050) is expected not to be collected. For the year-old receivables, let's say that 90% is estimated to be uncollectible. Of the $1,100 ($1,000 + $100) of receivables in this group, $990 (.90 × $1,100) are expected to be bad.

3. And finally, the amounts of the uncollectibles for each age group are added to get the total amount of uncollectibles estimated for the period. In our simple example, $502.50 + $990.00 = $1,492.50 total uncollectibles.

The estimates for the percentages to apply in each age group are determined from past experience, and generally in much the same way as the estimates for the percentage of credit sales method.

The example that appears below will illustrate the aging of receivables technique. Mulholland Company began operations on Jan. 1, 1989. On Dec. 31, 1989, the following aging schedule was prepared:

Accounts Receivable Aging Schedule **December 31, 1989**					
Customer's Name	**Not Yet Due**	**1–30 Days Past Due**	**31–60 Days Past Due**	**61–90 Days Past Due**	**Over 90 Days Past Due**
Brauge, F.	$ 250				
Carney, L.	348				
Dolan, T.			$ 615		
Farnsworth, L.					$ 100
Garrity, G.				$ 78	
Keith, J.		$ 198			
Youngquist, P.		491			
Vanessi, T.	90				
Totals	$160,000	$45,000	$14,000	$2,500	$1,000

An aging schedule groups accounts by how old they are

Based on this schedule and after carefully considering the collection experience of similar companies in the industry, Mulholland's management then prepared the following estimate of uncollectible accounts:

1989 estimate of uncollectible accounts based on the aging of receivables method

Estimate of Uncollectible Accounts **December 31, 1989**			
Age Category	**Amount in the Age Category**	**Percentage Expected to Be Uncollectible**	**Amount Expected to Be Uncollectible**
Not yet due	$160,000	2%	$3,200
1–30 days past due	45,000	5	2,250
31–60 days past due	14,000	15	2,100
61–90 days past due	2,500	40	1,000
Over 90 days past due	1,000	80	800
Totals	$222,500		$9,350

Since this is Mulholland's first year of operations, the following entry would be prepared to record Bad Debts Expense for 1989:

The entry to record an estimate of Bad Debts Expense using the aging of receivables method

```
1989
Dec. 31   Bad Debts Expense............................................  9,350
                Allowance for Uncollectible Accounts.....................        9,350
          To record bad debts expense for 1989.
```

During 1990, a number of individual accounts remained uncollected for so long that Mulholland finally gave up expecting them to be paid. Mulholland identified each account, declared it to be uncollectible, and wrote it off. The total amount written off for these uncollectible accounts was $7,150. The Allowance for Uncollectible Accounts was estimated to be $9,350. Thus, the difference between the allowance originally estimated and the write-offs, $9,350 − $7,150, leaves $2,200 remaining in the allowance account from 1989. We still expect $2,200 in 1989 receivables to be uncollectible, but we still haven't identified the individual customers' accounts.

As of Dec. 31, 1990, new credit sales have been added to Accounts Receivable and collections and write-offs have been deducted; write-offs have been deducted from Allowance for Uncollectibles but 1990 Bad Debts Expense has not yet been added. The accounts, then, have the following balances:

Accounts Receivable	$394,000
Allowance for Uncollectible Accounts	(2,200)

At the end of 1990, another schedule of 1990 Accounts Receivable grouped by age is prepared. The following estimate of uncollectible accounts is then made:

1990 estimate of uncollectible accounts using the aging of receivables method

Estimate of Uncollectible Accounts December 31, 1990			
Age Category	**Amount in the Age Category**	**Percentage Expected to Be Uncollectible**	**Amount Expected to Be Uncollectible**
Not yet due	$298,000	2%	$ 5,960
1–30 days past due	64,000	5	3,200
31–60 days past due	25,000	15	3,750
61–90 days past due	4,500	40	1,800
Over 90 days past due	2,500	80	2,000
Totals	$394,000		$16,710

The balance of Allowance for Uncollectible Accounts must be deducted when calculating Bad Debts Expense using the aging of receivables method

We have estimated that $16,710 of accounts receivable on hand on Dec. 31, 1990, will be uncollectible. Some of these are carried over from 1989 and were provided for in the bad debts entry on Dec. 31, 1989. To be specific, the $2,200 balance in the allowance account applies to 1989 receivables. We don't want to record this $2,200 as Bad Debts Expense *again*—we already took care of this amount in 1989. We must deduct this amount, then, in calculating our 1990 Bad Debts Expense, as the following calculation shows:

Bad Debts Expense for 1990:
    Total accounts estimated to be uncollectible on Dec. 31, 1990 . . . . $16,710
    Less: Balance in Allowance for Uncollectible Accounts before 1990 Bad
         Debts Expense is recorded 2,200

Bad debts provision needed in 1990. . . . . $14,510

The following general journal entry is made:

1990
Dec. 31   Bad Debts Expense   14,510
               Allowance for Uncollectible Accounts.   14,510
               To record bad debts expense for 1990.

The Allowance for Uncollectible Accounts appears in the general ledger as follows:

The Allowance for Uncollectible Accounts showing 1989 and 1990 transactions

Allowance for Uncollectible Accounts			
Total of specific accounts written off during 1990	7,150	1989 provision for uncollectible accounts	9,350
Total debits	7,150	Total credits	9,350
		Balance 12/31/90 before 1990 bad debts are recorded	2,200
		1990 provision for uncollectible accounts	14,510
		Balance 12/31/90 after 1990 bad debts are recorded	16,710

Sometimes the Allowance for Uncollectible Accounts account may have a debit balance. This happens when we have written off more accounts than we estimated would go bad. When this happens the aging of receivables method requires that we add enough to the allowance account to produce the credit balance that the aging schedule indicates it should have. For example, assume in our previous illustration that the Allowance for Uncollectible Accounts had a *debit* balance of $1,000 (we wrote off $10,350 of uncollectibles instead of $7,150). The calculation of bad debts expense would be as follows:

Bad Debts Expense for 1990:
    Total accounts estimated to be uncollectible on Dec. 31, 1990 . . . . $16,710
    Add: Debit balance in Allowance for Uncollectible Accounts before 1990 Bad
         Debts Expense is recorded 1,000

Bad debts provision needed in 1990. . . . . $17,710

The Allowance for Uncollectible Accounts would end up with a credit balance of $16,710 ($1,000 debit + $17,710 credit = $16,710 credit). This is exactly the amount that the aging schedule predicts will be uncollectible.

Remember, the aging schedule tells you the balance you will need in the allowance account. If the allowance already has a credit balance, deduct the credit balance from the aging schedule amount to derive bad debts expense. If the allowance has a debit balance, add the debit balance to the aging schedule amount to derive bad debts expense.

Inaccurate Estimates

The objectives of accounting for uncollectibles are: (1) to determine, as accurately as possible, the amount of accounts that will indeed be collected; and (2) to match the expense associated with not collecting, Bad Debts Expense, with the revenue that it helped to generate.

The direct write-off method accomplishes the first objective but ignores the second. The percentage of credit sales and the aging of receivables methods attempt to fulfill both objectives. In making this attempt these methods use estimates of future uncollectibles. Like any prediction of future events, these estimates are sometimes inaccurate. We adjust for—correct—the inaccurate estimates periodically (say, every 2 years or every 5 years). The accounting department of the company will be asked to do an analysis of the company's collections and write-offs to determine the amount that should be in the Allowance for Uncollectible Accounts. The techniques they use in making this determination are beyond the scope of this text. While we won't focus on how the analysis is made, we will discuss how the adjustment is recorded. Let's look at an example to see how the adjustment is made.

The accounting department prepares an analysis to calculate the error in estimating Bad Debts Expense

Schaffer Co. has used the percentage of credit sales method to estimate bad debts for the past 5 years. On Dec. 31, 1989, *after* Bad Debts Expense has been recorded for 1989, the receivables, allowance, and expense accounts have the following balances:

Accounts Receivable	$612,300
Allowance for Uncollectible Accounts	12,200
Bad Debts Expense (1989)	5,000

Schaffer's accounting department conducted an analysis which showed that a total of $14,800 is expected to be uncollectible. Schaffer has accumulated an inaccuracy—an error—in its estimated bad debts over the last 5 years of $2,600 ($14,800 − $12,200). In fact, Schaffer's Bad Debts Expense has been too low by a total of $2,600 over the 5 years:

Amount needed in Allowance for Uncollectible Accts. on Dec. 31, 1989	$ 14,800
Less: Amount actually in Allowance for Uncollectible Accts. on Dec. 31, 1989	(12,200)
Amount by which allowance must be increased (decreased)	$ 2,600

Inaccurate estimates are corrected by adjusting the current year's Bad Debts Expense and by correcting the balance of the Allowance for Uncollectible Accounts. Schaffer needs to increase the allowance account and increase the expense account by making the following journal entry:

The entry to correct inaccurate estimate of Bad Debts Expense

1989			
Dec. 31	Bad Debts Expense (1989)	2,600	
	Allowance for Uncollectible Accounts		2,600
	To correct for inaccurate estimates in bad debts over the past 5 years.		

If Schaffer's estimated bad debts has been too high, the expense would have been credited and the allowance debited.

Account balances before and after the correcting entry are:

	Balance before Correction	Balance after Correction
Accounts Receivable	$612,300	$612,300
Allowance for Uncollectible Accounts...............	12,200	14,800
Bad Debts Expense (1989)	5,000	7,600

1989 Bad Debts Expense now contains $5,000 that applies directly to 1989 credit sales and $2,600 that is a correction of inaccurate estimates over the past 5 years. Generally accepted accounting principles require that we correct errors in estimates in this way even though we introduce some mismatching—the $2,600 is shown as a 1989 expense even though it applies to 1985, 1986, 1987, 1988, and 1989.

Schaffer's management will adjust the percentage applied to each year's credit sales in the future to calculate a more accurate estimate of uncollectibles. Instead of

W. T. GRANT BANKRUPTCY—CREDIT POLICY A CONTRIBUTING FACTOR

By Stanley H. Slom

When W. T. Grant Co. went into bankruptcy on Oct. 2, 1975, the giant retailer's downfall was widely regarded as a classic example of a company that overreached itself and failed to attract a large and loyal clientele.

Now as a court-appointed trustee probes into the reasons for the biggest retailing failure in history, another picture of Grant is beginning to emerge from thousands of pages of testimony by former executives and other employees. It shows a company that was suffering from a host of internal problems and lacking budget and credit controls.

John E. Sundman, Grant's senior vice-president and treasurer, described credit controls as a disaster area. Before he joined Grant, consumer credit was approved at the store level, he said, and the rejection rate was 20%. That responsibility was transferred to headquarters in October 1974,

and rejections of consumer applications soared to 80%.

Mr. Sundman gave an illustration of Grant's credit reputation before he joined the company. "My son-in-law, who was an officer in the Army post (Fort Monmouth, N.J.) at that time, told me that it was common knowledge among the enlisted men that the best way to furnish a house when they moved to a new post was to get it on credit from Grant, because they were fairly confident that they wouldn't have to pay for it if they didn't want to," he said.

In fact, Grant headquarters encouraged the stores to promote consumer credit even though it was costing the company somewhere between 15% and 19% of its sales, he said. As of the year ended Jan. 30, 1975, Grant's sales were $1.7 billion.

Mr. Sundman said that prior to Feb. 1, 1975, he couldn't rely with confidence upon any credit information figures coming out of

Grant's stores in the Southeast. There was, he said, improper reporting of delinquent customer accounts, and often merchandise was repossessed without the delinquent customer's account being credited or the merchandise entered on the store records.

Also, he said, important information was lacking concerning the aging of accounts receivable throughout the Grant chain. Aging is the amount of time an account is unpaid. At one point, he said he found that someone had changed the time of writing off bad debts, which averaged $2 million a month, to nine months from six months.

Based on the information he had, Mr. Sundman said, he reached the conclusion that Grant's profit for the year ended Jan. 31, 1974—the period in which the bad-debts time was lengthened—had been overstated to make the company look better.

Source: The Wall Street Journal, Feb. 4, 1977, p. 6.

Someone in the W. T. Grant organization was "improving" profits by $2 million per month by delaying the write-off of uncollectible accounts. You know that the entry to write off an account usually does not affect bad debts expense or any revenue accounts; how, then, did the delay benefit Grant? We can only guess exactly how the delay helped. The most likely explanation goes something like this:

Since Grant was using the aging of receivables method, bad debts could have been manipulated by changing the aging categories—some accounts could thereby be moved from a category with a high percentage of uncollectibility to a category with a lower percentage of uncollectibility. Thus, the monthly estimate of bad debts expense would be lower and net income would be higher—by $2 million per month—than it would have been if the receivables had been aged properly.

Comments about the Preceding Entries

June 19 The assumption was made that the $10,000 note was for a sale/purchase transaction. If the note had been for payment of an account, Bailey would have credited Accounts Receivable and Canappa would have debited Accounts Payable. No interest is recorded on the note until it is earned or incurred (until the note has been held for a period of time). Interest accrues as time passes.

July 31 Since Bailey's and Canappa's fiscal years end July 31, interest accrued through that day, $105, is recorded. Interest Receivable or Interest Payable, $105, appears along with Notes Receivable or Notes Payable, $10,000, under current assets or current liabilities on the July 31 balance sheet. The Interest Receivable or Interest Payable account is carried forward into the next accounting year, when it will be collected/paid. Interest Income or Interest Expense, $105, would be shown under Other Income or Other Expenses on the income statement for the year ended July 31, 1989.

Aug. 18 The full amount of the principal and interest was collected/paid. The remaining $45 ($10,000 × .09 × $\frac{18}{360}$) interest accrued was recorded. Notice that 42 days of interest, $105, accrued before July 31; and 18 days of interest, $45, after July 31. The full interest was collected/paid on Aug. 18.

Sometimes money can be saved by borrowing money

It may surprise you to know that money can be saved by borrowing money. If merchandise is sold with credit terms including a cash discount for early payment, a wise decision if cash were not available on the day before the discount expired would be to borrow money to pay the invoice within the discount period rather than letting the discount lapse and paying the bill in full on the due date.

Refer back to the Sally Canappa situation. Assume that Canappa purchased goods from Bailey on June 9 costing $10,204 under credit terms of 2/10, n/30. Canappa would be entitled to a $204 discount ($10,204 × 2%) if the invoice is paid by June 19. The invoice must be paid within 30 days. But Canappa does not have $10,000 ($10,204 − $204) on June 19, 10 days from the invoice date, so Canappa borrows that amount from the bank (not Bailey as in the previous example) on June 19 at 9% for 60 days. We have seen that the interest on this note for 60 days amounts to $150 ($10,000 × 9% × $\frac{60}{360}$), which is $54 less than the $204 discount.

By paying the invoice on time with money borrowed from the bank and repaying the bank 60 days later, Canappa was able to save $54.

Dishonored Notes

A note that is not paid at maturity is a dishonored note

A note that is not paid at maturity is a **dishonored note.** When a note passes its maturity date but has not been paid, the note becomes dishonored and the holder transfers the record of it to Accounts Receivable. For example, assume that the Costello Co. received a $2,000, 6% note due in 90 days from Ludlow, Inc., in payment of a past-due account receivable. At maturity, Ludlow failed to pay the $2,000 plus $30 interest due.

Day 1	Notes Receivable..	2,000
	Accounts Receivable: Ludlow	2,000
	To record receipt of $2,000, 6%, 90-day note in settlement of an account receivable.	
Day 90	Accounts Receivable.......................................	2,030
	Interest Income	30
	Notes Receivable..	2,000
	To record interest earned ($2,000 × .06 × $\frac{90}{360}$) and dishonoring of note by Ludlow.	

Costello recorded the $30 interest earned even though Ludlow did not pay. Costello has allowed Ludlow the use of the $2,000 for 90 days and is entitled to the $30 interest charge for the 90 days of credit extended to Ludlow. Costello's claim on day 90 is $2,030, not just the $2,000 face value of the note. Interest will continue to accrue on the past-due receivable. Some state laws allow the rate to increase to the maximum legal limit. The longer the maker of the note delays paying, the more he or she will owe the payee of the note.

The probability of collecting Ludlow's account receivable may be very low. This fact should be considered by Costello's management in calculating the estimate of Bad Debts Expense at the end of the current year.

Non-Interest-Bearing Notes

Maturity value of non-interest-bearing notes includes principal and interest

A ***non-interest-bearing promissory note*** contains all of the characteristics of an interest-bearing note except that the maturity value includes principal *and* interest. It would be accurate to say that these notes *include* interest in the face of the note. The holder of a non-interest-bearing note does earn interest. The interest is *included* in the amount written on the face of the note *rather than added* to the face value of the note.

Assume that Insignia, Inc., received a note from Doug Dowdy to settle a $5,000 account receivable. Insignia agreed to accept from Dowdy a note for $5,200 maturing in 6 months. An illustration of this type of note appears below.

Non-Interest-Bearing Note
This non-interest-bearing note is for $5,200 — $5,000 principal; $200 interest.

__$5,200__	Tedium, Maine	January 1, 1989
__six months__	**after date** __I__	**promise to pay to**
the order of	Insignia, Inc.	
Five Thousand Two Hundred and 00/100 -		**dollars**
for value received.		
Payable at Apathy National Bank.		
		__Doug Dowdy__

The $200 above the amount of the $5,000 account represents the interest that will be paid to Insignia for having to wait 6 months to receive payment. On the day Insignia receives the note, no interest has been earned. Insignia will earn the interest as the 6-month period passes.

Insignia and Dowdy would prepare the following entries for the note:

Entries to record:
(1) Issuance and receipt of non-interest-bearing note

```
1989
Jan.  1  Notes Receivable .....  5,200          Accounts Receivable:
             Accounts                               Insignia............  5,000
             Receivable: payable                Discount of Notes
             Dowdy .........            5,000      Payable.............    200
             Discount on                               Notes Payable ....          5,200
             Notes                               To record issuance of
             Receivable ......          200      $5,200, 6-month note
         To record receipt of                    in settlement of $5,000
         $5,200, 6-month note                    account.
         in settlement of $5,000
         account.
```

(2) Accrual of interest for the full term of the note	June 30 Discount on Notes
	     Receivable 200
	       Interest Income. . . 200
	   To record interest
	   earned on Dowdy note.
		Interest Expense 200
		     Discount on Notes
		       Payable. 200
		   To record interest
		   incurred on note issued
		   to Insignia.

(3) Collection and payment of note at maturity	30 Cash. 5,200
	     Notes
	       Receivable 5,200
	   To record receipt of
	   payment on Dowdy
	   note.
		Notes Payable 5,200
		     Cash 5,200
		   To record payment to
		   Insignia on note due
		   this date.

Discount on Notes Receivable/Payable is a contra account showing the unearned interest on the non-interest-bearing note

Discount on Notes Receivable/Payable reflects the *unearned* interest on the note. It is a contra-current asset/liability account which is shown as a deduction from the notes on the balance sheet.

If Insignia/Dowdy's fiscal year had ended during the 6-month period, say, Mar. 31, the amount of interest earned as of the last day of the year would have been transferred from the discount account to the interest account. On the date the note is due, the remainder of the amount in the discount account would be transferred to Interest. This process is illustrated below:

The discount is transferred to Interest as it is earned or incurred over time

Jan. 1		Mar. 31		June 30	
$5,200	Note	$5,200	Note	$5,200	Note
(200)	Discount	(100)	Discount	-0-	Discount
$5,000	Note (net)	$5,100	Note (net)	$5,200	Note (net)
$ -0-	Interest	$ 100	Interest	$ 100	Interest (Jan. 1 – Mar. 31)
				$ 100	Interest (Apr. 1 – June 30)

Notice that as the amount of the discount decreases, the amount of interest increases. The $5,000 was earned or incurred when Insignia sold merchandise to Dowdy on account sometime before Jan. 1; the $200 interest was earned/incurred as the 6-month period passed — $100 over the first 3 months and $100 over the last 3 months. By June 30, then, the entire $5,200 was earned/incurred.

Discounting Notes Receivable

"Selling" a note receivable to a bank is called discounting the note

A holder of a note who needs cash before the note matures may take the note to a bank, which **discounts** it. This simply means that the bank "buys" the note from the holder, paying the holder an amount of cash that is normally less than the maturity value of the note, and then collects the maturity value from the maker at the maturity date. The difference between the amount that the payee receives from the bank and the maturity value of the note is the bank's fee for discounting the note. In effect, this difference is the interest the bank will earn instead of the payee.

The bank calculates its fee for accepting the note from the holder, the **discount,** by applying a discount rate to the maturity value of the note. This **discount rate** is really an interest rate charged by the bank for holding the note for the remainder of its life.

Notes may be discounted with recourse or without recourse

What happens if the maker of the note fails to pay the bank at maturity? If the note was discounted **with recourse,** the bank will demand payment from the original payee. Discounting with recourse means that the bank requires the payee on the note to agree to pay the amount of the note if the maker won't pay it at maturity. If the note was discounted **without recourse,** the bank is stuck with the loss, unable to commit the original payee to pay the amount the maker fails to pay. So you can be sure that almost no bank discounts without recourse.

Both interest-bearing and non-interest-bearing notes may be discounted. We will demonstrate the calculations and entries associated with discounting interest-bearing notes. Discounting non-interest-bearing notes will be left for a more advanced accounting course.

Calculating the Proceeds upon Discounting an Interest-Bearing Note

When discounting an interest-bearing note, the following formula can be used to calculate the amount of cash received—commonly referred to as the *proceeds:*

Formula for calculating the amount of cash received when a note is discounted

$$\text{Proceeds} = \left(\begin{array}{c} \textbf{maturity value} \\ \textbf{of note} \end{array} - \begin{array}{c} \textbf{discount} \\ \textbf{amount} \end{array} \right)$$

$$\begin{array}{c} \textbf{Discount} \\ \textbf{amount} \end{array} = \left(\begin{array}{c} \textbf{maturity value} \\ \textbf{of note} \end{array} \times \begin{array}{c} \textbf{discount} \\ \textbf{rate} \end{array} \times \begin{array}{c} \textbf{time remaining} \\ \textbf{until maturity} \end{array} \right)$$

Therefore,

$$\textbf{Proceeds equals} = \left(\begin{array}{c} \textbf{maturity} \\ \textbf{value} \end{array} \right) - \left(\begin{array}{c} \textbf{maturity} \\ \textbf{value} \end{array} \times \begin{array}{c} \textbf{discount} \\ \textbf{rate} \end{array} \times \begin{array}{c} \textbf{time remaining} \\ \textbf{until maturity} \end{array} \right)$$

Vanessi Co. received a 6-month, 6%, $5,000 note from LeSuer, Inc., on Jan. 1, 1989. Vanessi discounted the note with recourse at the Limbo National Bank on May 1, 1989. Limbo charged a 7% discount rate. The maturity value of the note and the proceeds received by Vanessi are calculated as follows:

Maturity value of the note:	
Face value	$5,000
Add: Interest for life of note ($5,000 × .06 × $\frac{180}{360}$)	150
Maturity value	$5,150

Proceeds of the discounting:	
Maturity value	$5,150.00
Less: Discount charged by Limbo ($5,150 × .07 × $\frac{60}{360}$)	(60.08)
Proceeds received by Vanessi	$5,089.92

Recording the Discounting of an Interest-Bearing Note

Vanessi's entries related to this note would be as follows:

Entries to record:
(1) Receipt of note

1989				
Jan.	1	Notes Receivable	5,000.00	
		Sales		5,000.00
		To record sale to LeSuer, Inc., and receipt of 6-month, 6% note.		

(2) Accrual of interest earned as of discounting date	May 1	Interest Receivable		100.00	
		Interest Income			100.00
		To accrue the interest earned from the day the note was received until it was discounted ($5,000 $\times$ .06 $\times$ $\frac{120}{360}$).			

(3) The proceeds received, financing fee, and contingent obligation	May 1	Cash..		5,089.92	
		Financing Expense		10.08	
		Interest Receivable			100.00
		Notes Receivable Discounted......................			5,000.00
		To record discounting of LeSuer, Inc., note with recourse at Limbo Bank. Financing fee ($10.08) equals face value ($5,000) plus interest earned to date ($100) less proceeds ($5,089.92).			

(4) Removal of note and contingent obligation when maker pays bank at maturity	June 30	Notes Receivable Discounted.........................		5,000.00	
		Notes Receivable.................................			5,000.00
		To remove the LeSuer note from the books. The maker paid the bank at maturity.			

Before the note was discounted, that is, up through Apr. 30, Vanessi accrued and recorded the interest that had been earned at the original 6% interest rate. This entry is exactly the same type of entry as is made at the end of the company's fiscal year to accrue interest earned.

The May 1 entry to record the discounting of the note contains two items that need special attention and explanation. First, the Financing Expense ($10.08) amounts to the difference between what Vanessi would have gotten if the principal plus the full amount of interest earned to date had been paid ($5,100) and the amount actually received ($5,089.92). The Financing Expense, $5,100 − $5,089.92 = $10.08, eventually appears on Vanessi's income statement in the other income and expense category.

Noted Receivable Discounted is a contra asset representing a contingent obligation

Second, since the note was discounted with recourse, the Notes Receivable Discounted account was credited to reflect the fact that Vanessi has a ***contingent obligation,*** a potential responsibility, to pay the note if LeSuer fails to settle with the bank at maturity. If the note had been discounted without recourse, the credit would simply have been to Notes Receivable.

Immediately following the discounting, Vanessi has two accounts in its books:

1. Notes Receivable .... $5,000   Debit balance

2. Notes Receivable Discounted................ ($5,000)   Credit balance

Both of these accounts would appear under current assets on a balance sheet prepared at this time. Notes Receivable Discounted is a contra account to Notes Receivable.

You should take care not to confuse Notes Receivable Discounted with Discount on Notes Receivable. Notes Receivable Discounted is a contra asset indicating a contingent obligation. Discount on Notes Receivable is a contra asset reflecting the unearned interest included in the face amount of a non-interest-bearing note.

Discounting an Interest-Bearing Note: Maker Dishonors

Let's do a second illustration of the discounting process to ensure that you are familiar with the calculations and entries. In this example the maker of the note will not pay the bank at maturity. Pay close attention to the entries used to record this fact.

Dolan Company received an $8,000, 9% note from Steuben, Inc. The 120-day note was received on Oct. 31 and discounted at the Monotony Bank on Dec. 30, 1989, with recourse. The bank's discount rate was 10%.

1989			
Oct. 31	Notes Receivable..	8,000.00	
	Accounts Receivable: Steuben		8,000.00
	To record receipt of a 120-day, 9% note from Steuben in settlement of an open account.		
Dec. 30	Interest Receivable	120.00	
	Interest Income		120.00
	To accrue interest earned for 60 days ($8,000 × .09 × $\frac{60}{360}$).		
30	Cash..	8,102.67	
	Financing Expense	17.33	
	Interest Receivable		120.00
	Notes Receivable Discounted.......................		8,000.00
	To record discounting Steuben note at Monotony Bank with recourse.		

Computations	
Proceeds:	
Face value	$ 8,000.00
Add: Total interest during life of note ($8,000 × .09 × $\frac{120}{360}$).............	240.00
Maturity value	$ 8,240.00
Less: Discount ($8,240 × .10 × $\frac{60}{360}$)	(137.33)
Total proceeds..	$ 8,102.67
Financing expense:	
Face value	$ 8,000.00
Add: Interest earned to date ($8,000 × .09 × $\frac{60}{360}$)	120.00
Less: Proceeds...	(8,102.67)
Total financing expense..	$ 17.33

(handwritten note: who cares!!!)

Entries made when the maker dishonors his or her discounted note

1990			
Feb. 28	Accounts Receivable: Steuben	8,240	
	Cash..		8,240
	To record payment to Monotony Bank to settle Steuben's note plus interest. Steuben dishonored the note.		
28	Notes Receivable Discounted...............................	8,000	
	Notes Receivable		8,000
	To remove Steuben's note and the associated contingent obligation.		

Notice that Dolan was required to pay the bank $8,240, the same amount that Steuben should have paid. Also observe that Dolan removed the $8,000 note and the contingent obligation from the records. The claim that Dolan has against Steuben now amounts to $8,240, which is carried as an account receivable.

Receivables from Officers and Owners

*Receivables from officers
and owners should be
separately disclosed on the
balance sheet*

Occasionally a business firm will lend available cash to its owners or to its managers who need loans for their personal use. After all, if a firm has surplus cash and is expected to put it to use earning income, it can accomplish this by making interest-earning loans to its owners and managers. In some cases these loans are represented by formal instruments, such as promissory notes; in other cases, they exist only in the form of verbal agreements. Most accountants believe that while these agreements may be entirely proper, it is best to identify such receivables separately on the balance sheet—specifying them as loans to owners, managers, or officers of the firm. This disclosure will highlight the fact that the business has entered into a transaction with a party who is closely related to it. Readers of the balance sheet will then be fully informed of the loan and may investigate the circumstances surrounding the transaction if they so desire.

External Credit: Credit Card Sales

*External credit is used
when a company accepts
VISA, MasterCard, and
similar charge cards*

Most retailers today make sales to customers accepting credit cards such as VISA, MasterCard, American Express, and Diners Card. Each of these credit cards represents credit provided by an organization external to the customer and retailer. Thus, this form of credit is sometimes referred to as ***external credit.***

A customer making a purchase through use of a credit card signs a standard form agreeing to pay to the credit card company the amount of the sale. The retailer sends this form to the credit card company, which in turn pays the amount of the credit sale to the retailer.

The credit card company charges the retailer a fee for providing credit to the customer. The fee is commonly a percentage of the amount of credit—the sales price of the product or service—provided. For this fee, the credit card company not only provides the credit, but in doing so, assumes the costs of providing credit—credit investigation, recordkeeping, billing, and bad debt losses.

The following is an example showing how a retailer using the external credit of a credit card company records its transactions.

Buckeye Stores has an agreement with Plastic Money Charge cards which provides that Buckeye will remit charge tickets to Plastic Money and receive cash within 10 days. Plastic Money will charge Buckeye 8% of the gross sales for which it provides credit for this service. On Aug. 1, 1989, Buckeye had charge sales of $10,000 and made the following journal entry:

*Entries to record:
(1) Sales on external credit
cards*

1989			
Aug. 1	Receivable from Plastic Money...............................	9,200	
	Financing Expense..	800	
	Sales		10,000

To record sales less financing expense of $800 ($10,000 × .08) remitted to Plastic Money for reimbursement.

The following entry would be made to record the receipt of cash from Plastic Money:

*(2) Collection from credit
card company*

1989			
Aug. 5	Cash	9,200	
	Receivable from Plastic Money..........................		9,200

To record cash received from credit card company.

ACCOUNTING FOR ESTIMATED AND CONTINGENT LIABILITIES

Warranties

We may find that there are certain liabilities that we know exist at the time financial statements are prepared but unfortunately we do not know the amount of these liabilities. An example of this type of liability is the obligation incurred when goods are sold with warranties. Appliances are typically sold with the guarantee that in the event of a malfunction within a reasonable period of time after acquisition, the seller will repair the appliance at no cost to the buyer.

Some liabilities exist but we don't know how much they are. We have to estimate the amounts

Our job here is to estimate the amount of the liability and reflect this on the balance sheet. When we estimate the liability we are, of course, also estimating the related expense that will be reflected on the income statement. The expense is incurred in the period the sale of the appliance was made, not in a subsequent period when the repairs are performed. This is the basis of the matching principle.

When the repairs are made, the liability is eliminated. Let's see how this works. Assume Coal Township Appliance Company sold 400 appliances during the year 1989. From past experience they can estimate that 10% of the appliances will prove to be defective. They also estimate that the typical repair will cost $20. During 1989, 15 appliances require service calls at a total cost of $315. In 1990, 27 additional service calls are made at a total cost of $490. Coal Township Appliance Company would make these entries in 1989:

1989			
Various	Warranty Expense	315	
dates	Cash, Parts, Labor		315
	To record expenditures amounting to $315 for repair services on 15 appliances that were sold in 1989.		

1989			
Dec. 31	Warranty Expense	500	
	Estimated Liability under Warranty Obligations		500
	To record estimated liability under warranty obligations for repair services to be performed on appliances sold in 1989 (400 appliances sold × 10% = 40 appliances estimated to be repaired; 40 − 15 repaired in 1989 = 25 appliances sold in 1989 that are estimated will be repaired in 1990 at $20 each = $500).		

The income statement prepared for the year ended Dec. 31, 1989, would reflect warranty expenses in the amount of $815 matched against appliance sale revenues. Expenditures in 1989 amounted to $315 on 15 actual repairs, which are recorded as 1989 expenses. In addition it is estimated that 25 more repairs must be made [(400 × 10%) − 15], at an estimated cost of $500 (25 × $20), and this amount is also expensed in 1989, resulting in a total of $815.

The Dec. 31, 1989, balance sheet would show the estimated liability of $500 representing the estimate of the obligation for future repair services that relate to 1989 sales. In 1990 the entry to record the expenditure of $490 relating to the 27 actual appliances serviced that were from 1989 sales would be:

1990			
Various			
dates	Estimated Liability under Warranty Obligations	490	
	Cash, Parts, Labor		490
	To record expenditures amounting to $490 relating to 1989 sales.		

At this point the balance in the liability account is a $10 credit. If the company had perfect knowledge, the liability would have been established for $490, the estimate made at the end of 1989. But no one possesses perfect knowledge; hence, actual experience will differ from the estimate and a debit or credit balance in the liability account will result. No adjustment of the liability account is required unless a trend develops where it becomes obvious that the estimate is either too high or too low. A revision of the estimating process is then in order.

Premiums

A very similar situation occurs when companies offer premiums to stimulate sales of certain products. You all have seen the cereal companies offer dishes, knives, plates, and other prizes when you send in a certain number of cereal box tops and perhaps some money. This is an advertising tool to increase the sale of the product. The accounting for the advertising expense or promotional expense is just like that for the warranties. The expense of the advertising must be recorded in the year the product was sold, but not all the box tops will be returned in that year. So the accountant must estimate the amount of premium claims that are outstanding at year-end. And this amount is recorded as an estimated liability on the balance sheet.

For example, assume that in 1989 General Food Store offers their customers a coupon for every $10 of grocery purchases. The coupons can be exchanged for a dish of the customer's choice, on a basis of one coupon plus $1 for one dish. Past experience indicates that 80% of the coupons will be redeemed. During 1989 General Food Store purchased 25,000 dishes at an average cost of $1.40 per dish and 22,000 coupons were redeemed. The entries to record the acquisition of the dishes and the redemption of the coupons would appear as follows:

1989	Inventory of Dishes (25,000 × $1.40).........................	35,000	
	Accounts Payable		35,000
	To record the acquisition of 25,000 dishes at $1.40 each.		
	Advertising Expense...	8,800	
	Cash...	22,000	
	Inventory of Dishes (22,000 × $1.40).....................		30,800
	To record the redemption of 22,000 coupons for dishes.		

If total sales for the year amounted to $300,000, General Food Store would have to estimate the amount of coupons that remain outstanding at the end of the year. This estimate would be determined by considering that, based on sales of $300,000, there would be 30,000 coupons ($300,000 ÷ $10) issued during the year and that 24,000 would be redeemed (30,000)(.8). Since 22,000 have already been turned in, that would leave 2,000 outstanding, so the Dec. 31, 1989, journal entry would be:

1989			
Dec. 31	Advertising Expense...	800	
	Estimated Liability for Coupons Outstanding..................		800
	To record the estimated liability for coupons outstanding [($1.40 − $1.00) × 2,000].		

Contingencies

Certain current liabilities are indefinite as to existence and amount. These are referred to as *contingent liabilities.* Some future event must take place (or not take place) that will determine if the liability will require payment and the amount of such a payment. Examples of such liabilities are litigation, expropriation, and accommodation endorsement of indebtedness of others. Litigation refers to lawsuits in progress. Expropriation is the act of a country taking control of businesses operating within its jurisdiction. An accommodation endorsement is the co-signing of a note for someone to provide the creditor with additional security. If the maker of the note fails to pay the note, the co-signer must.

Accounting for contingent liabilities requires a decision to be made regarding the chance or likelihood of the specific future event taking place. This "likelihood" is classified into three categories: *probable, reasonably possible,* and *remote.*

Only in the case of a contingency classified as probable will we record a liability and the corresponding loss. Even if the liability is classified as probable, the amount of the loss must be capable of reasonable estimation before the entry can be recorded.

To illustrate, assume that Phills Phosphate Company operates a branch in Bartow, Florida. A recent lower-level court decision has awarded an employee $100,000 in an injury damage suit. Although the company will appeal the ruling, legal counsel is of the opinion that it is *probable* the company will lose the appeal. The entry to record the contingent liability is:

A contingent liability is recorded

Loss Due to Litigation	100,000	
Contingent Liability for Litigation		100,000

To record loss in period sustained and to establish contingent liability in the amount of $100,000.

If the contingent liability is classified as reasonably possible or if it is probable but the amount cannot be estimated, a footnote to the financial statements is prepared describing the contingency. If the contingent liability is classified as remote, in most cases no accounting is necessary. Remember that only *material* contingent items would be reported on the financial statements or disclosed in the footnotes.

PAYROLL ACCOUNTING

One of the more significant obligations of most business entities is the cost of labor. For many companies this cost approaches 50% of the company's total operating costs. The burden of accounting for labor costs, as many of us are aware, is increased by federal, state, and local legislation regarding payrolls. Our employers must pay taxes on their total payroll, and they must withhold taxes from our pay and remit these taxes to the proper authorities. Payroll records must be maintained, and various periodic reports must be submitted to appropriate governmental bodies at the times requested by these bodies. All of this increases considerably our employer's cost of labor and the related cost of recording payroll information.

A complete description of accounting for payroll is beyond the scope of this text, however, a discussion of payables would not be complete without a brief exposure to this important topic.

Unfortunately for us, the amount we receive from our employer each payday (**take-home pay**) is not the same as we have earned (**gross pay**). That is because several deductions are subtracted from our gross pay to arrive at our net pay. For the most part these deductions are required by law or union contracts. Other deductions for such items as medical and life insurance, U.S. savings bonds, and stock purchase plans may have been authorized by many of us. The deductions required by law are federal income taxes, Social Security taxes, state and city income taxes where applicable, and state unemployment compensation tax on employees, where applicable.

Federal Income Taxes

The federal government requires our employers to act as tax-collecting agents for the receipt of employees' income taxes. Employers are required to compute the amount of income taxes to be withheld from each employee and to collect and deposit that amount to the account of the federal government. This pay-as-you-go system assures the government that the majority of taxes due will be collected in a timely manner.

The amount that is deducted from our gross earnings for federal income taxes is dependent on the amount of our gross earnings for the pay period and the number of allowances we claim. An allowance for each dependent is deducted from our estimated annual earnings in determining the amount of federal income taxes to be withheld for the pay period. The amount of the allowance is determined by Congress and may change from time to time; in 1987 it was $1,900, in 1989 it will be $2,000.

The amount of taxes withheld from our salary is calculated such that given our pay rate and allowances, the total withheld during the year will approximately equal our tax liability at the end of the year.

Federal Insurance Contributions Act (FICA)

The funds necessary to provide monthly retirement payments and Medicare benefits for qualified retired workers are obtained by payroll deductions authorized by the Federal Insurance Contributions Act (FICA). The retirement and medical benefits are provided for qualified workers under the provisions of the Social Security Act. Retirement benefits are based on the age at retirement and the average earnings of the retiree.

Funds required to operate the Social Security programs are collected by the employer through the means of withholding contributions by each employee from the employee's gross earnings. The FICA taxes are contributed at a rate specified by Congress on a certain level of employee earnings, again specified by congress. For example, current rates are 7.15% on the first $43,800 of earned wages.

Recording the Payroll

To illustrate the recording of the current liability for payroll, assume that the employees of the Pulver Company of Scranton, Pennsylvania, had gross earnings of $75,000 for the pay period May 1 to May 15, 1989. No employee earned over $43,800. Income taxes withheld amount to $15,000, and there was $3,000 withheld for medical insurance policies with the Keystone Insurance Company. The following general journal entry would be recorded by the Pulver Company:

Salary Expense	75,000	
Federal Income Taxes Withheld		15,000
FICA Taxes Payable ($75,000 × 7.15%)		5,363
Payable to Keystone Insurance Company		3,000
Salaries Payable		51,637

To record the May 15 payroll.

Employer Payroll Taxes

What has been discussed so far about payrolls has been limited to the amounts that have been withheld from us. Our employer is also subject to payroll taxes. These taxes are based on the amount of gross earnings up to prescribed limits earned by the employees of our employer. These taxes represent an operating expense of doing business.

FICA Taxes

The amount that we contribute to the Social Security program is matched by our employer. The FICA tax expense and corresponding liability for our employer is determined by multiplying the total amount of wages subject to the FICA tax by the appropriate tax rate.

Federal and State Unemployment Tax Act

Unemployment funds are provided by the Social Security system under a joint federal-state program. These funds are administered by the state governments and are used for the relief of those qualified persons who are temporarily unemployed. The FUTA (Federal Unemployment Tax Act) and the State Unemployment Tax are levied on the employers and are not deducted from the employee's gross earnings. (Some states do require an employee contribution.) Congress again sets the rates and base amounts for these taxes. Currently these rates are 6.2% on the first $7,000 of wages for the Federal tax. The employer may reduce the Federal tax by contributions to the State tax up to 5.4%. Thus, a total tax of 6.2% is levied, with .8% going to the federal government for approving the state programs and for paying a portion of the state's administrative expenses. The state's portion, 5.4%, is used to pay unemployment compensation.

Recording Payroll Taxes

Using the Pulver Company example, the following entry illustrates the recording of payroll taxes for the pay period ending May 15, 1989 (assume that $50,000 is subject to the unemployment compensation taxes):

Payroll Tax Expense...	8,463.50	
FICA Taxes Payable ($75,000 × 7.15%)......................		5,362.50
Federal Unemployment Taxes Payable ($50,000 × .8%)		400.00
State Unemployment Taxes Payable ($50,000 × 5.4%)		2,700.00

To record the payroll taxes for the May 15 payroll.

RECEIVABLES AND PAYABLES ON THE BALANCE SHEET

The partial balance sheet illustrated below shows the disclosure of all receivables and payables discussed in this chapter.

TURNDALE COMPANY
Partial Balance Sheet
December 31, 1989

Assets

Current Assets:

Cash		$ 30,000
Marketable Securities		5,000
Receivable from Credit Card Company		130,200
Notes Receivable	$25,000	
Less: Discount on Notes Receivable	(1,200)	
Notes Receivable Discounted	(4,000)	19,800
Accounts Receivable	$62,000	
Less: Allowance for Uncollectible		
Accounts	(2,635)	59,365
Receivable from Officers		2,500
Interest Receivable		1,435

Liabilities

Current Liabilities:

Notes Payable	$15,000	
Less: Discount on Notes Payable	(700)	$ 14,300
Accounts Payable		120,000
Interest Payable		550
Estimated Liability under Warranty Obligations		4,500
Payable to Customers		1,850
Salaries Payable		8,600
Federal Income Taxes Withheld		1,400
FICA Taxes Payable		920
Federal Taxes Payable		100
State Taxes Payable		540

CHAPTER SUMMARY

When customers buy on credit, the seller's accounting records show this transaction as an account receivable, commonly referred to as an *open account*. An *account receivable* indicates the buyer's agreement to pay the seller for goods or services purchased. The buyer would call this an account payable. Accounts receivable that are not expected to be collected after a reasonable length of time are recognized by the seller as *bad debts expense*—one of the costs of providing credit to customers.

The *direct write-off method* delays the recognition of a bad debts expense until a specific account is identified as uncollectible. This method is not in accord with good accounting practice because it does not properly match expenses and revenues and because it distorts the measurement of the amount of Accounts Receivable. The *percentage of credit sales method* and the *aging of receivables method* both estimate

Bad Debts Expense prior to identifying a specific uncollectible account. These methods do a better job of matching and of measuring Accounts Receivable. Errors resulting from inaccurate estimates are corrected in future periods based on analyses by the firm's accounting department.

Estimates of accounts receivable that won't be collected are recorded by debiting Bad Debts Expense and crediting Allowance for Uncollectible Accounts. A specific customer's account is written off by debiting Allowance for Uncollectible Accounts and crediting Accounts Receivable. If a customer later pays an account that was written off, the account is reinstated by debiting Accounts Receivable and crediting Allowance for Uncollectible Accounts; payment is then recorded by debiting Cash and crediting Accounts Receivable.

Accounts Receivable and Allowance for Uncollectible Accounts are classified as current assets on the firm's balance sheet. A customer's account receivable with a credit balance is reported as a current liability for the firm.

Promissory notes—recorded as notes receivable—are often used as a way of offering credit when a sale is made or as a way of formally extending the length of the credit period when an account receivable is past due. Promissory notes are written promises to pay. The promise may specify a face amount—the *principal*—and interest separately payable. Or the promise may specify only a face amount that includes principal and interest, payable together.

Promissory notes may be held until maturity or they may be discounted at a bank prior to maturity. When a note is *discounted with recourse,* and if the maker fails to pay at maturity, then the payee is responsible for paying the bank at maturity. A note *discounted without recourse* carries no such obligation.

When the maker of a note fails to pay at maturity, the payee changes the account from a note receivable to an account receivable and, of course, continues to try to collect.

Interest income is recognized on notes as it is earned. Journal entries are made to formally record the interest income earned either when a note is discounted, when an income statement is prepared, or at the maturity date of the note. In many cases part of the interest earned may be recognized at more than one of these dates.

Receivables from officers and owners—a firm's loans to its officers or owners—are identified on the balance sheet separately from other receivables. This is done to inform readers that transactions have occurred between the business and individuals closely related to it.

Many retailers rely on *external credit*—credit card plans—to provide credit for their sales. The credit card company normally charges a fee that is a percentage of the sales price for providing credit for the retailer.

Estimated liabilities, such as product warranties and premiums, and *contingent liabilities,* such as litigation, are examples of liabilities and their related expenses that must be estimated and recorded. We classify contingent liabilities as probable, reasonably possible, or remote in order to determine the appropriate accounting treatment.

Payrolls represent a significant expense and liability for a business. In determining employees' net take-home pay deductions are subtracted from their gross pay. The deductions are of two types: those required by law or contract and those that are voluntary. *Deductions required by law* are federal income taxes withheld, Federal Insurance Contributions Act withholdings, state and city income taxes where appropriate, and union dues where appropriate. *Voluntary deductions* are those the employee authorizes the employer to withhold from his or her gross earnings, such as health insurance premiums and U.S. savings bonds payments. In addition to the

6. When bad debts expense is estimated, a contra asset, Allowance for Uncollectible Accounts, is credited. Why isn't Accounts Receivable credited instead?

7. Under what circumstances is it necessary to reinstate a customer's account?

8. What is the purpose of aging receivables?

9. When the aging of receivables method is used, why is it necessary to consider the balance in Allowance for Uncollectible Accounts in determining the current Bad Debts Expense?

10. Lewis Co.'s accounting department determined that over the past 5 years Bad Debts Expense has been too high by $4,200. What will Lewis do to correct this error in estimating?

11. Wash Engines, Inc., has several customers' accounts with credit balances. What things could have occurred to cause these credit balances?

12. What is the difference between an account receivable and a note receivable?

13. Why might a company rather hold a note receivable from a customer than an account receivable?

14. What is a dishonored note receivable?

15. Is it true that no interest is earned when a non-interest-bearing note is held?

16. What does the balance of Discount on Notes Receivable represent? Where does this account appear on a balance sheet?

17. Rulco, Inc., can discount a customer's note at the bank "with recourse" or "without recourse." What is the difference between these two? Which will Rulco prefer?

18. Tower Co. discounted a customer's note receivable with recourse. How is the contingent obligation on this note shown on the balance sheet?

19. What special treatment is given receivables from officers and owners of a company? Why is this special treatment necessary?

20. Why is accounting for current liabilities important?

21. When notes are discounted, a liability is recorded for the face value of the note and cash is increased by the proceeds. How is the difference between the proceeds and the face value of the note accounted for?

22. Explain why year-end adjusting entries are needed for estimated liabilities such as warranties.

23. What is a contingent liability?

24. How are the three classes of contingent liabilities accounted for?

25. What are the most common deductions from gross earnings in computing *net pay*?

26. How does an employer determine the amount of federal income taxes to withhold from an employee?

27. How does an employer determine the amount of FICA taxes to withhold from an employee?

28. Describe the various employer payroll taxes.

EXERCISES

Exercise 8-1
Determining and recording bad debts expense using the percentage of credit sales method

Younquist Privies, Inc., uses the percentage of credit sales method to estimate uncollectible accounts. During 1989 Younquist's sales totaled $750,000; 93% of this amount was on credit. Younquist's management estimates that about $1\frac{1}{4}$% of credit sales will eventually prove uncollectible. Prepare the journal entry to record Bad Debts Expense for 1989.

(Check figure: Estimated Bad Debts Expense = $8,719)

Exercise 8-2
Calculating bad debts expense using the percentage of credit sales method and the direct write-off method

During the 2 years that Wilkes Barber Supplies has been in business, credit sales have amounted to $350,000 in year 1 and $470,000 in year 2. Wilkes Barber Supplies wrote off customer accounts amounting to $4,950 in year 1 and $7,040 in year 2. Calculate Wilkes Bad Debts Expense for each year assuming that:

a. The percentage of credit sales method is used and management estimates that 2.4% of credit sales will prove uncollectible.
b. The direct write-off method is used.

Which method is considered preferable? Why?

(Check figure: Year 2 Bad Debts Expense using percentage of credit sales = $11,280)

Exercise 8-3
Writing off an uncollectible account; reinstating the account when the customer pays

Williamson Grain Co. sold $4,600 of wheat to Bagels, Ltd., during 1988. When Bagels had not paid by Oct. 5, 1989, Williamson decided to write off the account as uncollectible. On Nov. 2, 1989, a check arrived from Bagels paying the account in full. Prepare the entries to write off the account, to reinstate the account, and to record the receipt of the $4,600. Williamson uses the percentage of credit sales method to account for uncollectible accounts.

Exercise 8-4
Determining bad debts expense by analyzing Allowance for Uncollectible Accounts

Turndale Tea Co. uses the percentage of credit sales method to estimate uncollectible accounts. On Jan. 1, 1989, the Allowance for Uncollectible Accounts had a credit balance of $7,200. During 1989 customer accounts amounting to $6,100 were written off as uncollectible. The balance of the allowance account on Dec. 31, 1989, was $9,320 after the entry to record Bad Debts Expense had been posted. Calculate the amount that was recorded as Bad Debts Expense for the year.   *(Check figure: Bad Debts Expense for 1989 = $8,220)*

Exercise 8-5
Recording transactions related to interest-bearing note

During 1989 Ringgold Manufacturing entered into the following transactions with Keith Furniture Sales:

June 15	Ringgold received a $36,000, 10%, 90-day note from Keith for an assortment of patio furniture.
30	Ringgold's accounting year ends.
Sept. 13	Ringgold's receives payment in full from Keith.

Prepare the proper journal entry for Ringgold on each of the three dates. Show supporting calculations.   *(Check figure: Interest income recorded on June 30 = $150)*

Exercise 8-6
Calculating the proceeds upon discounting a note

Garrity Wholesale Flowers accepted a $25,000 note from a customer in settlement of a past-due account receivable. The 120-day note bears interest at 12%. Needing cash desperately, Garrity immediately took the note to Ennu Island Bank and discounted it with recourse. The bank charged a 15% discount rate.

Calculate the proceeds—the amount of cash that Garrity received upon discounting the note.   *(Check figure: Cash proceeds received by Garrity = $24,700)*

Exercise 8-7
Journal entries for an interest-bearing and a discounted note

On Dec. 1, 1988, Moulton Motors, Inc., issued a promissory note to the Great Pacific National Bank in the amount of $950,000. The note is a 6-month note and bears interest at the rate of 15%. Prepare general journal entries for the issuance of the note, the Dec. 31, 1988, adjustment, and the May 30, 1989, payment, assuming that:

a. The bank pays Moulton Motors $950,000 on Dec. 1, 1988, and collects the face of the note plus interest on May 30, 1988.

b. The bank discounts the note on Dec. 1, 1988, subtracting the total 6 months' interest from the face of the note, and collects the $950,000 borrowed funds on May 30, 1989.

(Check figure: Interest Expense, May 30 = $59,375)

Exercise 8-8
Determining the number of days to borrow money so that discount isn't lost

Thompson is a little short of cash. He just acquired equipment for his property on Marvin Gardens for $60,000 with credit terms of 2/10, n/30. Thompson can borrow funds from the Naval Exchange Bank at 9%. For how long a period could Thompson borrow funds from the bank such that the interest on the borrowed funds does not exceed the purchase discount? (Assume a 360-day year.)

(Check figure: 82 days)

Exercise 8-9
Estimating product warranties

Between Jan. 1, 1988, and Dec. 31, 1988, Pulver Appliance Company of Scranton sold 4,800 washers and dryers. The appliances are sold under an 18-month warranty plan whereby the company will repair any appliance it sells at no cost to the customer for the first 18 months of service. Repair costs are estimated to be $20 per unit, and 7% of the units are estimated to require repairs. During 1988, 216 units were repaired at a cost of $4,698. An additional 103 units were repaired in 1989 at a cost of $2,083 before the warranties expired.

Record a single entry to summarize the repairs made in 1988, record the Dec. 31 adjusting entry to recognize the remaining liability at that date, and finally record a single entry to summarize the repairs made in 1989.

(Check figure: Estimated liability on Dec. 31 = $2,400)

Exercise 8-10
Accounting for contingent liabilities

Peoples Utility of Pennsylvania operates a nuclear power plant on an island in the Lehigh River. During the month of April, 1989, a series of human errors caused the cooling system to malfunction and the nuclear fuel core to overheat as a result. Damage to the fuel core, if any, cannot be determined until the reactor cools down and is safe to inspect, a process that may take several months. Peoples Utility has a year-end of Apr. 30. The power plant is insured for $300,000,000, has a book value of $375,000,000 and a fair value of $780,000,000.

a. Assuming that it is probable that the plant is so damaged that it will never operate again, what accounting treatment is required?

b. Assuming that it is reasonably possible that some damage occurred, what accounting treatment is required?

Exercise 8-11
Preparing payroll entry

The data presented below have been selected from the records of Pauley Corporation for the May 15 payroll:

Gross Earnings	$50,000	Federal Income Taxes Withheld .	$10,000
FICA Tax Withheld	4,000	Union Dues Withheld	500

Using this information, prepare, without explanation, the general journal entry to record the payroll.

(Check figure: Salaries Payable = $35,500)

Exercise 8-12
Recording payroll tax expense

During the month of November, 1989, the payroll of Kalinka Shopfitters, Inc., amounts to $100,000. Of this amount, three-fourths was not subject to state and federal unemployment taxes and one-fourth was not subject to the FICA tax. Assuming that the state unemployment tax rate is 2.1%, the federal unemployment tax rate is .8%, and the FICA tax rate is 8%, prepare, without explanation, the general journal entry to record the employer payroll taxes for the month of November.

(Check figure: Payroll Tax Expense = $6,725)

PROBLEMS: SET A

**Problem A8-1
Calculating bad debts
expense using direct
write-off, percentage of
credit sales, and aging of
receivables**

The following facts relate to Farnsworth Farm Equipment Company:

a. Jan. 1, 1989, balance of Allowance for Uncollectible Accounts = $4,720 (credit).
b. Total of customer accounts written off during 1989 = $3,370.
c. Total sales during 1989 = $450,000; 80% of sales are on credit.

| **Required** |

Calculate Farnsworth's Bad Debts Expense for 1989:

1. Assuming that the direct write-off method is used.
2. Assuming that the percentage of credit sales method is used; Hunter uses $2\frac{3}{4}$% to estimate.
3. Assuming that the aging of receivables method is used. An aging schedule shows that accounts totaling $8,760 are estimated to be uncollectible.

(Check figure: Bad Debts Expense using percentage of credit sales = $9,900)

**Problem A8-2
Recording transactions
relating to Accounts
Receivable and bad debts**

Selected transactions of Stefanowski Security Co. for the years 1988 and 1989 are shown below:

1988

Jan.–Dec.	Total cash sales were $450,000; total credit sales were $1,500,000. (Prepare a summary entry.)
Jan.–Dec.	Collections on accounts amounted to $1,240,000. (Prepare a summary entry.)
Dec. 31	Stefanowski estimated that uncollectible accounts would amount to about $2\frac{1}{4}$% of credit sales.

1989

Jan. 20	Stefanowski wrote off the $720 account of Samantha Shiftless as uncollectible.
Mar. 4	The $4,060 account of D. Ed Beat was written off as uncollectible.
Apr. 30	A check was received from Samantha Shiftless in full settlement of her account $720.
Jan.–Dec.	Various other individual accounts amounting to $31,040 were written off.
Jan.–Dec.	Total sales were $1,950,000. Of these, 12% were for cash; the remaining sales were on account.
Jan.–Dec.	Total other cash collections were $1,803,000.
Dec. 31	Stefanowski estimated Bad Debts Expense for 1989 using the same percentage as in the prior year.

| **Required** |

1. Prepare general journal entries to record the transactions above. Calculations should be included as part of your journal entry explanation where appropriate.
2. Calculate the balance of Accounts Receivable and Allowance for Uncollectible Accounts on Dec. 31, 1989.

(Check figure: Bad Debts Expense for 1988 = $33,750)

Problem A8-3
Preparing an aging schedule and entries to record bad debts expense

Olson Office Supply has the following uncollected accounts receivable on June 30, 1989:

Customer Name	Amount	Collection Status
N. Julian	$1,360	Not yet due
J. Cleland	400	20 days past due
R. Hennessy	1,800	51 days past due
O. Juarez	840	Not yet due
T. Barnard	870	63 days past due
T. Fay	760	105 days past due
J. Upchurch	1,820	Not yet due
J. Earnhardt	1,020	Not yet due
R. Henry	400	35 days past due
D. Clayton	1,200	30 days past due
J. Durham	500	Not yet due
H. Perry	180	45 days past due
R. Rasco	2,700	Not yet due
F. Connell	1,720	74 days past due
H. Kinnan	890	Not yet due
B. Humphries	430	95 days past due
J. Davis	1,080	29 days past due

Olson uses an aging schedule to prepare an estimate of uncollectible accounts for the year. Estimates of the percentage uncollectible in each category follow:

Not yet due .... 2%   61–90 days past due 40%
1–30 days past due............... 6%   Over 90 days past due 80%
31–60 days past due 15%

Required

1. Prepare an aging schedule and an estimate of the total amount expected to be uncollectible. (Round to nearest whole dollar.)
2. Prepare an adjusting entry to record Bad Debts Expense on June 30, 1989, assuming that the Allowance for Uncollectible Accounts has a credit balance before adjustment of $950.
3. Prepare an adjusting entry to record Bad Debts Expense on June 30, 1989, assuming the Allowance for Uncollectible Accounts has a debit balance before adjustment of $540.

(Check figure: Balance of Allowance for Uncollectible Accounts after adjustment = $2,689)

Problem A8-4
Recording entries relating to interest-bearing and non-interest-bearing notes

Costello Fixture, Inc., has an account receivable from Handy Stop Co. in the amount of $6,000. Since Handy is temporarily short of cash, it proposes to give Costello a 90-day note to settle the account. Costello agrees, and the note is signed on Mar. 31, 1989. Costello's accounting year ends on Apr. 30. Handy pays the note on June 30, 1989.

Required

1. Prepare Costello's journal entries on Mar. 31, Apr. 30, and June 30, assuming that Handy gave Costello a $6,000 note bearing 12% interest. Show supporting calculations.
2. Prepare Costello's journal entries on Mar. 31, Apr. 30, and June 30, assuming that Handy gave Costello a $6,180 non-interest-bearing note. Show supporting calculations.

(Check figure: Interest income recorded on Apr. 30 for each note = $60)

Problem A8-5
Calculating proceeds from discounting three notes

On June 1, 1989, Insignia Binocular, Inc., discounted the three notes described below at the Plains National Bank. The bank charged an 18% discount rate on each note.

Note A: A $6,000, 60-day, 12% note received May 1, 1989
Note B: A $20,000, 6-month, 18% note maturing in 4 months
Note C: A $30,000, 1-year, 15% note received on June 1, 1989

Required	Calculate the amount of cash that would be received by Insignia from discounting each of the three notes. Your calculations should be clearly labeled.

(Check figure: Cash received from discounting Note A = $6,028.20)

**Problem A8-6
Recording the receipt,
discounting, and payment
of a dishonored note**

Dowdy Distributors experienced the following transactions relating to a note receivable:

July 1, 1988   Received a $36,000 note from Odessa Lamps in payment of an overdue account. The note bears interest at 10% and matures in 9 months.

Jan. 1, 1989   After holding the note for 6 months, Dowdy discounted it at the Fairfax Bank with recourse. The bank charged an 15% discount rate.

Apr. 1, 1989   Dowdy received notice from the bank that Odessa failed to pay the note when due. Dowdy paid the maturity value of the note to Fairfax Bank.

Required	Prepare the appropriate journal entries relating to each of the transactions above. Show clearly labeled calculations to support your entries. Dowdy's accounting year ends on June 30.

(Check figure: Proceeds from discounting the note = $37,248.75)

**Problem A8-7
Recording transactions
relating to notes receivable**

Freeman Equipment Company sells forklifts to wholesalers, retailers, and manufacturers. These machines are normally sold on 60-day open accounts, but occasionally Freeman will accept a longer-term note. The transactions below relate to three such notes that were received in 1989:

Feb. 1   Freeman received a 12-month, 18%, $12,000 note from Pilgrim Foods in exchange for a forklift with a total retail price of $12,000.

May 1   Freeman sold Bellaire Battery Co. two forklifts with a total sales price of $30,000. Bellaire gave Freeman a 9-month, non-interest-bearing note for $33,375.

1   Freeman discounted the Pilgrim Foods note at the Liberty Bank with recourse. The bank charged a discount rate of 20%.

Aug. 1   Freeman sold Du-Gro Chemical Company a forklift for $24,000. Du-Gro gave Freeman a 6-month, 10% note.

Dec. 31   Freeman discounted the Du-Gro note at the Franklin Finance Company without recourse. Franklin charged a 12% discount rate.

31   Freeman's accounting year ends.

Required	1. Prepare the appropriate journal entries to record each of the transactions above. Show supporting calculations as part of your journal entry explanations. 2. Prepare Freeman's Dec. 31, 1989, balance sheet disclosure that relates to Notes Receivable. 3. What is the total interest earned during 1989 by Freeman on these three notes?

(Check figure: Interest earned during 1989 = $4,540)

**Problem A8-8
Recording accounts
receivable and external
credit card transactions**

Steuben's Sportswear sells a full line of ladies clothing. Steuben sells to customers for cash, on a 30-day Steuben's charge account, or through two national credit cards: Passport and Mister Charge. Steuben remits charge tickets to the national credit card companies weekly. Passport assesses a fee of 6% of gross sales, while Mister Charge charges 8% of gross sales. Both credit card companies remit cash to Steuben within 10 days.

Steuben has the following sales and collections during January , 1989:

	Jan. 1–7	Jan. 8–14	Jan. 15–21	Jan. 22–31
Cash sales	$ 500	$ 840	$1,050	$ 620
Steuben's charge sales	800	1,260	3,080	2,460
Passport sales	2,000	2,900	2,600	1,000
Mister Charge sales	1,300	2,200	1,600	2,400
Collected on Steuben's accounts		690	1,480	1,830
Collected from Passport		1,880	2,726	2,444
Collected from Mister Charge		1,196	2,024	1,472

On Jan. 31, Steuben provided for estimated uncollectible accounts using the percentage of credit sales method. Steuben estimates that 2% of credit sales will prove uncollectible.

Required

1. Prepare summary entries to record sales and collections for *each* of the 4 weeks.
2. Prepare the entry to record Bad Debts Expense on Jan. 31.
3. What receivable amounts will appear on the Jan. 31, 1989, balance sheet?

(Check figure: Bad Debts Expense = $152)

**Problem A8-9
Determining correct
balance sheet disclosures
of receivables accounts**

Morton, Inc, reports the following receivables on its tentative Sept. 30, 1989, balance sheet:

Accounts Receivable....................................	$ 87,900	
Less: Allowance for Uncollectibles	(1,978)	$ 85,922
Receivable from Credit Card Companies		142,700
Interest Receivable.......................................		1,625
Notes Receivable.......................................	$ 41,450	
Less: Discount on Notes Receivable	(4,050)	
Notes Receivable Discounted............................	(11,000)	26,400
Net Receivables		$256,647

Upon investigation you discover the following additional facts:

a. The balance of Accounts Receivable includes customer accounts of $800 with credit balances and a receivable from the president of Marlin in the amount of $2,000.
b. Notes Receivable includes all notes, some of which have been discounted. Notes totaling $8,250 were discounted with recourse and $2,750 without recourse.
c. The $11,000 Notes Receivable Discounted includes all notes discounted—with and without recourse.

Required

1. Determine the current balance that should be disclosed for each one of the accounts on the balance sheet shown above. Add any accounts that you believe are necessary.
2. Prepare a corrected receivables section for the Sept. 30, 1989, balance sheet.

(Check figure: Gross Accounts Receivable from Trade Customers = $86,700)

**Problem A8-10
Current liabilities on the
balance sheet**

The following information is available on Dec. 31, 1989, concerning Limbo Island Manufacturing Company's liabilities:

a. Accounts Payable total $215,300.
b. The company received a check in the amount of $14,500 from Mannion, Inc., as an advance payment on job no. 1436, which will be completed late in March, 1989.
c. Limbo Island Manufacturing Appliance Division sells direct to customers and the appliances carry a 24-month warranty; 62,000 appliances were sold in 1989. The company

estimates that 8% of the appliances sold will require repairs, which will average $20 per unit. During 1989, 2,070 units that had been sold in 1989 were repaired under warranty.

d. Salaries and wages unpaid as of Dec. 31, 1989, amounted to $14,430.

e. Limbo Island Manufacturing received notice on Dec. 21, 1989, that Garner Oil was placed in bankruptcy. Limbo Island had endorsed as a guarantor a $15,000 note payable issued by Garner Oil to the Houston Drilling Supply Company.

f. Two notes payable were outstanding as of the last day of the year. The first was a note issued to the Exchange Bank in the amount of $30,000. The note, which was issued on Mar. 1, 1989, and will mature on Feb. 28, 1990, bears interest at a rate of 12%. Limbo Island received $30,000 from the Exchange Bank on Mar. 1, 1989.

The second note was issued to Rayburn Trust on Oct. 1, 1989. This $50,000 note will mature on Mar. 30, 1990, and has an interest rate of 14%. Limbo Island received $46,500 on the day the note was issued.

Required

Prepare the current liabilities section of Limbo Island Manufacturing Company's balance sheet as of Dec. 31, 1988.

(Check figure: Total Current Liabilities = $398,280)

**Problem A8-11
Preparing entries for
promotional campaign**

Sales have been lagging for Johnson Soap Company, and as a result the company adopted a promotion campaign in 1988. For its lead product, Lyndon Lime Soap Powder, the company will give each customer a coupon for every box purchased. The coupons can be exchanged for a series of gifts described on the boxes by sending in five coupons for each gift. The company estimates that 60% of the coupons will be redeemed.

For the year 1988, Johnson Soap purchased 15,000 gifts at an average cost of $1.80 each. During the year the company sold 150,000 boxes of Lyndon Lime Soap Powder at $4.25 per box; 57,000 coupons were redeemed. In 1989, sales of the soap powder amounted to 182,000 boxes at $4.30 per box; 72,500 coupons were redeemed, including some coupons from 1988. The company purchased an additional 13,000 gifts at $1.80 each.

Required

Prepare general journal entries for the years 1988 and 1989 relating to the promotion campaign.

(Check figure: Estimated liability for coupons outstanding 1989 = $25,092)

**Problem A8-12
Preparing payroll entries
for a 3-month period**

Presented below are data relating to the monthly payrolls of South Seas Publications for the second quarter of 1989:

	April	May	June
Total salaries paid	$93,500	$95,200	$91,700
Salaries subject to FICA tax	92,700	64,300	49,800
Salaries subject to unemployment taxes	36,900	19,600	8,400

Federal income taxes withheld from all employees amount to 25% of the total salaries paid. The FICA tax rate is 7%; the federal and state unemployment tax rates are .8% and 2.3%, respectively.

South Seas Publications remits to the Internal Revenue Service on the third day following the end of the month payment for federal income taxes and all FICA taxes due. On the same day payment is made to the State of Hawaii for the state unemployment tax due. The federal unemployment tax is paid in January.

Required

1. Prepare, without explanations, the general journal entries to record the payroll and related taxes for the months of April, May, and June. (Round your answers to the nearest whole dollar.)

Problem B8-10
Current liabilities on a
balance sheet

Juneau Corporation obtained the following information relating to its liabilities for the year ended Sept. 30, 1989:

a. The corporation received $12,750 from the Alaska Snowshoe Company on Sept. 1, 1989, for consulting services to be rendered from Sept. 1 to Nov. 30, 1989.

b. Salaries in the amount of $3,750 have accrued by Sept. 30, 1989.

c. In addition to its consulting activities, the Juneau Corporation sells a product that carries a 24-month warranty. During the period Oct. 1, 1988, to Sept. 30, 1989, 15,000 units were sold. Repairs were made on 615 units in 1989. It is estimated that 7% of the units sold will require repairs at an average cost of $16 each.

d. Accounts payable at year-end amounted to $23,760.

e. The Fairbanks National Bank notified Juneau Corporation that a note in the amount of $7,000 issued by the Spenard Company was past due. Juneau Corporation had co-signed the note as an accommodation for the Spenard Company.

f. A note payable to the Fort Richardson Chemical Exchange Bank in the amount of $50,000 was issued on July 1, 1989. On that date the corporation received $44,000 from the bank. The note matures on Jan. 1, 1990.

g. Another note payable to the Richardson Chemical Exchange Bank in the amount of $25,000 was issued on Jan. 1, 1987. The note is due on Jan. 1, 1990, together with 12% interest.

Required

Prepare the current liabilities section of the Juneau Corporation's balance sheet as of Sept. 30, 1989.

(Check figure: Total Current Liabilities = $124,220)

Problem B8-11
Preparing entries for a
promotional campaign

Phoenix Mills Company began a promotional campaign on Jan. 1, 1989, to promote the sales of their line of breakfast cereals, which includes Wheat Wams, Barley Bangs, and O.K. Oats. One of the major features of the campaign is that customers buying the cereal products will be able to obtain a valuable set of original Yuma glassware by sending to Phoenix Mills $10 and five box tops from any of the three cereals. The advertising consultant advises Phoenix Mills that for every 10,000 boxes of cereal sold, 650 box tops will be returned.

For the years 1989 and 1990 the following transactions relating to the campaign occurred:

1989
a. Purchased 5,000 sets of glasses from Yuma Glass Company at $18.75 per set. An asset account, Promotional Glassware Inventory, was debited and Accounts Payable was credited.
b. Sold 400,000 boxes of the three types of cereal for an average price of $3.75 per box.
c. Customers returned 23,000 box tops together with the proper amount of cash. Phoenix Mills distributed the appropriate number of sets of glassware. The account Promotional Expense is used to record the related expense.
d. The year-end adjusting entry was recorded to reflect the estimated expense.
1990
e. Acquired 5,700 sets of glassware on account from Yuma Glass Company at $18.75 per set.
f. 500,000 boxes of cereal were sold at an average price of $3.90.
g. Customers returned 29,000 box tops and paid the appropriate amount for the glassware. The company issued the proper number of sets of glassware to the customers.
h. Recorded the appropriate year-end adjusting entry.

Required

Prepare the general journal entries relating to the transactions listed above.

(Check figure: Estimated liability for promotional campaign, 1990 = $11,375)

Problem B8-12
Preparing payroll entries
for a 3-month period

The employees of Abbott Homes, Inc., are paid monthly on the last day of the month. The data presented below reflect activity concerning the payroll for the third quarter of 1989:

Month	Total Salaries Paid	Salaries Subject to FICA Taxes	Salaries Subject to Unemployment Compensation Taxes
July	$248,000	$248,000	$190,000
August	261,000	235,000	130,000
September	255,000	187,000	98,000

Income taxes are withheld at a rate of 25% on all salaries. A 7% FICA tax applies to earnings up to a maximum of $40,000, and federal and state unemployment taxes are applied at rates of .8% and 2.7%, respectively, on earnings up to $7,000. Remittances are made to the Internal Revenue Service and the State Unemployment Agency on the third day following the end of the month. The federal unemployment tax is paid in January.

Required

1. Prepare, without explanations, the general journal entries to record the payroll and related taxes for the months of July, August, and September.
2. In June total salaries amounted to $230,000, all of which was subject to FICA taxes and $195,000 of which was subject to unemployment taxes. Using this information and the information contained in the chart above, prepare the general journal entries, without explanation, to record the remittances made relating to the payroll taxes for the months of July, August, and September.

(Check figure: Total remittance for July = $94,965)

DECISION PROBLEM

As a staff assistant assigned to the office of Mr. Important, vice president of Corporate Giant, Inc., you are asked to help determine why profits for the Some-What-Less-Than-Medium Division have been declining for the past several years. While other staff assistants are working on such areas as inventories and payrolls, your assignment deals with Accounts Receivable and the related bad debts accounts. Mr. Important informs you that he is concerned by the increase in the amount of bad debts since early 1982.

While at the division's headquarters, located in Averagetown, USA, you discover the following:

1. The credit department's computer printout of its customer list reveals that the division has retained over 95% of its customers since 1982 and that well over 90% of these customers are in good standing. The small number of customers who are behind in their payments represent some customers that the credit department is sure will pay within the next 60 days, and a few accounts that will be written off. The potential write-off is insignificant in amount.

2. A review of the division's operating manual reveals that all mail, including remittances by customers, is received in a section called Incoming. One employee in Incoming, Eric Walker, records the remittances by use of an IBM PC

and provides three lists of the daily remittances. The first list is sent to Accounting, the second list to Finance, and the third list is retained in Incoming. The remittances are sent with the list to Finance.

3. A visit to the accounting department reveals that the accounts receivable clerk is Miss Sandy Walker. She has the responsibility for recording from sales invoices the increases to the customer accounts; and from the second copy of Incoming's remittance list, the payments from customers.

   Miss Walker informs you that most customers make several payments on each invoice. A review of several accounts confirms her statement.

4. In the finance department, Mr. Jones receives the remittances and compares them with the Incoming list. From this information the daily deposit is made to The Averagetown Local Bank. At month's end Mrs. Sanders of the finance department prepares the bank reconciliation.

5. The billing department sends statements of account to the customers on a 30-day cycle. This requires that a full-time employee, Betty Walker White, devote more than 75% of her time to this activity.

6. Write-off of bad debts is initiated and approved only at the officer level. Specifically, John Walker, the division assistant manager, sends to the accounting department on a monthly basis any accounts authorized to be written off.

7. Checks for the division can be written only by the treasurer or the assistant treasurer. While reviewing several months of cancelled checks from the division's six bank accounts, you discover that at the end of each month there are always numerous interbank transfers. All of these interbank transfer checks are signed by the assistant treasurer, Mrs. Mary Walker.

8. From concern over its employees' civil rights, the company dropped its nepotism rules on Jan. 1, 1981.

| **Required** | Provide a possible explanation for the declining division profits since 1982. Fully explain what you think is happening at the division.

Accounting for Merchandise Inventory

Merchandise inventory is finished goods held for sale by retailers and wholesalers. Completed goods held for sale by manufacturers is called *finished goods inventory.* Since accounting for merchandise inventory and finished goods inventory is the same, we will use the term merchandise inventory to refer to both in this chapter.

Some goods are purchased in finished condition, ready to sell—no work is performed on them before they are sold. For example, retailers such as hardware stores purchase hammers and nails, and screwdrivers and screws, all of which are immediately ready for resale. Another example is shirts and blouses that your local clothing shop buys and places on the shelves for immediate resale.

Other goods are purchased that require some minor finishing or assembly before they are ready for sale. Examples are bicycles that are shipped unassembled and put together by your local bicycle shop and that are then ready for sale, and some furniture that must be assembled before it is sold. Since such finishing activities are minor, goods such as these are included in merchandise inventory.

There are firms that purchase raw materials that require considerable work to convert into finished products. For example, a furniture manufacturer buys wood, plastic, glue, nails, and other raw materials and converts them into tables, desks, and bookcases. The wood, plastic, glue, and nails are *raw materials inventory.* The completed—except perhaps for minor assembly—tables, desks, and bookcases are merchandise inventory, or finished goods inventory.

To be included in merchandise inventory the finished goods must be held for sale. Thus, the same assets represented by one firm as merchandise inventory may be considered differently by another firm. Consider this simple example: Byron Office Supply Company has desks and file cabinets in its warehouses ready for sale—these are assets that Byron represents as merchandise inventory. The Paynter Plumbing Supply Company buys some of these desks and file cabinets—these assets are represented by Paynter's accountants as office equipment, because that's what they are. Paynter "consumes" desks and file cabinets; it doesn't sell them. Paynter's sells pipes, valves, bathtubs, and sinks—these things are Paynter's merchandise inventory.

Any good, whether it is iron ore or vacant lots or toy trains, if it is a finished good and held ready for sale, is the merchandise inventory of the firm owning it.

In this chapter, we are going to be concerned only with merchandise that is completely finished or that requires only minor assembly. That will keep manufacturing costs out of our discussion of accounting for merchandise inventory. (We'll take those up in our companion text, *Managerial Accounting,* when you will be prepared for it.) Accounting for merchandise inventory involves two problems:

1. Determining the total cost of inventory acquired

2. Allocating those costs between the goods that were sold (cost of goods sold) and those that remain (ending inventory)

DETERMINING THE COST OF MERCHANDISE PURCHASED

General rule for finding the cost of merchandise

The following is a general rule for determining the cost of merchandise:

The cost of merchandise includes the invoice price and all reasonable and necessary costs incurred in getting it to a condition and place where it is ready for sale.

This rule means that the merchandise inventory's cost includes not only its invoice price but also the costs of freight, insurance during shipment, handling, and storage —all reasonable costs incurred in getting the asset to the point where it becomes merchandise inventory on the shelf ready for the consumer to purchase. Most firms have many different products on their shelves for sale. Yet some of the costs, such as fire insurance, handling, and storage, represent costs that cover all merchandise. In reality, a firm's accounting system does not carefully trace each of these costs to each item in inventory. To do so would prove unnecessarily expensive in comparison to the value of the information obtained. For example, to apply the cost rule literally would mean that the salary of a receiving clerk in a department store must be divided among all the various items of inventory in proportion to the time spent unloading each one. The cost of allocating the clerk's salary, typically around $15,000 per year, among $5,000,000 of inventory, would contribute little to the profitability of the department store. Nor would it provide relevant information on the income statement.

Nevertheless, all of the basic costs are accounted for in one way or another; some are accounted for very carefully, as we shall see.

Invoice Price

The first thing we have to consider in determining the cost of inventory is the price paid to the seller for it. The amount paid is often less than the price listed in the seller's catalog. In other words, the seller has ***discounted*** the catalog (or list) price. Sellers offer three different types of discounts: trade discounts, quantity discounts, and cash discounts (purchase discounts).

Trade Discounts

You learned in Chapter 5 that *trade discounts* are deductions allowed to wholesalers and retailers from the price of merchandise listed in catalogs. Trade discounts may be specified as a single percentage or a chain of percentages. The following example will remind you how trade discounts work. Winston Wholesale sells to retailers at a 20-20 trade discount. If the total list price of the merchandise purchased is $100,000, the price after trade discounts is calculated as follows:

Total list price	$100,000
Less 20% (.2 × $100,000)	(20,000)
Total after first 20%	$ 80,000
Less 20% (.2 × $80,000)	(16,000)
Price after trade discounts.	$ 64,000

If you're still unsure about your understanding of trade discounts, review pages in Chapter 5.

Quantity Discounts

Quantity discounts reduce the price for customers buying large quantities

To customers buying a large quantity of the same item, a wholesaler may offer not only a trade discount but also a quantity discount. Usually, the manufacturer or wholesaler includes in his or her catalog or price list this additional *quantity discount* and the quantity at which it becomes applicable.

The invoice price on the customer's bill is the list price less the trade discount and any quantity discounts. For example, DeVriess Sports World receives a 20% trade discount on purchases from Wynn Wholesale Sporting Goods. Wynn also offers an additional 5% quantity discount if a gross (12 dozen) of softballs is purchased. The invoice price of 15 dozen softballs at a list price of $40 per dozen is:

Calculation of invoice price with trade and quantity discounts

List price, 15 dozen @ $40.	$600
Less: Trade discount (.20 × $600).	(120)
Subtotal	$480
Less: Quantity discount (.05 × $480).	(24)
Invoice price	$456

DeVriess would prepare the following entry to record the purchase:

Purchases	456	
Accounts Payable		456

To record the purchase of 15 dozen softballs on account.

Cash Discounts

Cash discounts are offered to encourage customers to pay quickly

The purpose of *cash discounts* is to encourage buyers to pay for their purchases in a short period of time. As we already explained in Chapter 5, these discounts are usually expressed by abbreviations such as 2/10, n/30. This means that the buyer may deduct 2% from the invoice price if payment is made within 10 days of receiving the invoice, or that the net invoice price is due in full within 30 days.

In the preceding example, if DeVriess were offered terms of 2/10, n/30, he could deduct an additional $9.12 [(.02)($456)] — if he pays within 10 days of the invoice date. DeVriess may choose to record the purchase in one of two ways — at the gross invoice price, $456, or at the net invoice price, $446.88 ($456.00 − $9.12). Let's look closely at these two alternatives, the gross method and the net method.

The Gross Method If DeVriess elects to use the gross method, he would make the following entry on the date of purchase:

Purchases.. 456.00
    Accounts Payable.. 456.00
To record the purchase of merchandise.

If DeVriess pays within 10 days, he receives the $9.12 discount and records the payment like this:

Accounts Payable.. 456.00
    Purchase Discounts.. 9.12
    Cash... 446.88
To record cash payment within the discount period.

If DeVriess fails to pay within the 10-day period, no discount is recorded. Accounts Payable would be debited and Cash credited for $456.

Remember, the Purchase Discounts account is deducted from Purchases when we prepare the cost of goods sold section of the income statement.

The Net Method If DeVriess had followed the net method rather than the gross method, he would have recorded the purchase initially at the list price less trade, quantity, *and cash discounts* — $446.88. The *anticipated* cash discount is deducted; remember, DeVriess must pay within 10 days to be entitled to this discount.

Here are the purchase and payment entries assuming that DeVriess takes advantage of the cash discount:

On the date of the purchase:
Purchases.. 446.88
    Accounts Payable.. 446.88
To record purchase of merchandise.

On the date of payment 9 days later:
Accounts Payable.. 446.88
    Cash... 446.88
To record payment within the discount period.

If DeVriess fails to pay within the 10-day discount period, he must pay the full $456, but Accounts Payable has a balance of only $446.88. When he pays the $446.88, DeVriess no longer owes Wynn Wholesale, so he simply eliminates the account payable with a debit equal to the balance in the account. He credits Cash for the amount of the payment. The $9.12 difference is recorded in a new account called

Purchase Discounts Lost. Here is DeVriess' entry if he *does not* pay within the discount period:

Accounts Payable...	446.88	
Purchase Discounts Lost	9.12	
Cash		456.00

To record payment of account after the discount period has expired.

This new account, Purchase Discounts Lost, is a red flag to management, indicating a failure in the company's operating procedure to take all discounts allowed. Purchase Discounts Lost is not used in the calculation of cost of goods sold. Since it is really an interest charge for waiting to pay for the merchandise, Purchase Discounts Lost is shown on the income statement as a nonoperating expense, just as Interest Expense would be.

The partial income statements on page 356 will illustrate the *location* of Purchase Discounts and Purchase Discounts Lost. These statements are for two different companies—a single company will use *either* the gross *or* the net method but not both.

Purchase Returns and Allowances

When merchandise is received, it is routinely inspected by the purchaser to ensure that it is of the quality ordered and not defective. Merchandise that does not pass this inspection is returned to the seller and an entry like the following is made in the buyer's general journal:

Buyer's entry to record returned merchandise

Nov. 15	Accounts Payable..	588	
	Purchase Returns and Allowances		588
	To record the return of 20 defective units of merchandise.		

Purchase Returns and Allowances is a contra account that is deducted from Purchases in calculating cost of goods sold on the income statement.

The amount of the debit to Accounts Payable and the credit to Purchase Returns and Allowances is determined by whether the gross or the net method has been used to record purchases. If the gross method has been used, the amount in the entry will be before cash discounts. If the net method has been used, the amount in the entry will be after cash discounts.

Freight-In

If the buyer of merchandise is required to pay the cost of transporting that merchandise, the transportation cost becomes a part of the total inventory cost. The transportation cost is charged to a Freight-In account and is added to the cost of merchandise purchased in determining total cost in the cost of goods sold section of the income statement. The entry to record a $38 payment for freight would look like this:

Entry to record freight paid by the buyer

June 25	Freight-In	38	
	Cash..		38
	To record payment of shipping costs on merchandise purchased.		

THE COST OF GOODS SOLD SECTION

Two steps are required to calculate the cost of goods sold as shown on the income statement:

1. Find the cost of *all* the merchandise that the company had available for sale during the period.

2. Subtract from it the cost of the merchandise that was not sold at the end of the period.

An example of this calculation is shown at the top of page 357.

The key to this calculation is, of course, the cost of merchandise inventory at the end of the period. We know how to calculate the net cost of merchandise purchased. The merchandise inventory at the beginning of the period is merely the preceding period's ending inventory. Thus, the purpose of this chapter is to determine the costs represented by merchandise inventory at the end of the period so that we can report the cost of goods sold during the period and have the beginning inventory for the next period.

GROSS PRICE METHOD COMPANY Partial Income Statement		
Sales		$10,000
Cost of Goods Sold:		
Merchandise Inventory (beginning)		$ 4,000
Add: Purchases......... $3,200		
Deduct: Purchase Discounts............. (64)		
Net Purchases....................	3,136	
Goods Available for Sale	$ 7,136	
Less: Merchandise Inventory (ending)	(2,500)	
Cost of Goods Sold		(4,636)
Gross Profit on Sales		$ 5,364
Operating Expenses:		
Selling Expenses.................	$ 850	
General and Administrative Expenses	614	
Total Operating Expenses.............		(1,464)
Income from Primary Operations.............		$ 3,900
Other Income and Expenses:		
Interest Expense		(1,380)
Net Income		$ 2,520

NET PRICE METHOD COMPANY Partial Income Statement		
Sales.....................................		$26,000
Cost of Goods Sold:		
Merchandise Inventory (beginning)....................		$ 9,000
Add: Purchases		6,800
Goods Available for Sale		$15,800
Less: Merchandise Inventory (ending).......................		(8,300)
Cost of Goods Sold....................		(7,500)
Gross Profit on Sales.........................		$18,500
Operating Expenses:		
Selling Expenses................	$ 2,200	
General and Administrative Expenses	1,400	
Total Operating Expenses.............		(3,600)
Income from Primary Operations		$14,900
Other Income and Expenses:		
Interest Expense................	$ 1,380	
Purchase Discounts Lost	510	
Total Other Expenses................		(1,890)
Net Income...........................		$13,010

Observe that Freight-In is added to Purchases while Purchase Discounts and Purchase Returns are subtracted

FULLER, INC. Schedule of Cost of Goods Sold Month Ended March 31, 1989		
Merchandise Inventory, Mar. 1.		$ 74,200
Add: Merchandise Purchased during March:		
Purchases	$184,500	
+ Freight-In	5,100	
− Purchase Discounts	(3,500)	
− Purchase Returns and Allowances	(7,600)	
Net Cost of Merchandise Purchased		178,500
Goods Available for Sale during March		$252,700
Less: Merchandise Inventory, Mar. 31		(87,100)
Cost of Goods Sold Expense		$165,600

DETERMINING ENDING INVENTORY — PHYSICAL UNITS

To determine the cost represented in ending inventory, you must: (1) measure, or count, the number of physical units of merchandise owned by the firm, that is, the units available for sale but not yet sold; and (2) then determine the total cost represented by those unsold units.

As we shall see, the number of units to be physically counted in inventory include:

Physical units included in ending inventory

1. The units in the firm's warehouses, stockrooms, shelves, and even in the windows and showcases for display

2. The units ordered and owned by the firm, but not yet received

3. The units that may be on their way to a customer or sales agent but are still owned by the firm

4. The units in the hands of a sales agent but still owned by the firm

All businesses that own inventory should count it at least once each year. Even firms with sophisticated computer systems or complex hand-kept records of each item entering and leaving the firm need to count the inventory to be sure that no recordkeeping errors were made and to discover the amount of any inventory stolen or spoiled.

The Physical Count

A reliable ending inventory cost depends on an accurate count of all the merchandise in inventory. The best way to do that is through a visual inspection and a physical count of all the mechandise not sold at the end of the period. Teams of employees are assigned to count all units on the shelves, in the stockrooms, and in other storage areas. Their count totals are entered on tally sheets similar to the one shown on page 358. Note that no costs are entered on the tally sheet at the time of the physical count. The costs are supplied later by the accounting department. To ensure the accuracy of the total inventory, the original counter's totals are checked and verified on a random basis by another counter.

The physical count covers the units found on the firm's premises. But as we began to explain, that's only one part of measuring the physical units for the purposes of ending inventory. There may also be units owned by the firm but not available on the

There are several things to observe from these calculations:

The total number of units purchased during the month was 500 units; the total number sold was 280. That means 280 units ÷ 500 units, or 56% of all units purchased, physically "flowed" through the firm.

Now let's take a look at what we mean by *cost flow*. The total cost for all the units was $1,000; the cost of goods sold, as we saw, was $460. That means, based on the total cost of all goods purchased, there was a cost flow of $460 ÷ $1,000 or 46% of total costs through the firm.

Here is a case where the flow of physical units and the flow of costs are certainly and clearly not the same. The reason should also be clear: the pattern of rising prices for each subsequent batch of units during the month. The lower unit costs from purchases at the beginning of the month were charged to the cost of the units sold. That left the higher unit costs from the purchases toward the end of the month to be assigned to the units in the ending inventory.

Weighted Average (WA)

Before we look at the weighted average inventory method, let's see how a weighted average differs from a simple average. Consider the following greatly simplified example:

Moon's Office Supplies purchased one desk for $40 and later bought 10 more identical ones for $1,500 ($150 each). The simple average cost would be:

$$\frac{\text{Unit cost in each batch purchased}}{\text{Number of batches purchased}} = \frac{\$40 + \$150}{2} = \frac{\$190}{2} = \$95 \text{ simple average cost per unit}$$

The size of the two batches purchased was clearly different, but the simple average calculation considered them to be the same. Thus the simple average gives us an inaccurate cost per unit of $95. We know that this cost is not accurate because the simple average cost per unit, $95, multiplied by the number of units, 11, equals $1,045 — not the $1,540 ($40 + $1,500) that we know to be the total cost.

The weighted average cost takes into consideration not only the cost per unit in each batch but also the number of units purchased at each cost. More weight is given to the second batch than the first — in fact, 10 times more weight, since 10 times more units were purchased. Moon's weighted average cost would be:

$$\frac{\text{Total cost for all units purchased}}{\text{Total number of units purchased}} = \frac{\$1,540}{11} = \$140 \text{ weighted average cost per unit}$$

Weighted average assigns the same per-unit costs to goods sold and goods unsold

A weighted average weights each batch purchased by including the total cost of the batch and the number of units in the batch. Less weight is given to smaller and/or lower-cost batches than to larger and/or higher-cost batches. The weighted average gives us an accurate average cost per unit, since $140 weighted average cost per unit × 11 units = $1,540.

In the weighted average inventory method, the cost of each unit of inventory is considered to be the weighted average cost of all goods available for sale during the period. This means that the weighted average cost per unit is used to calculate cost of goods sold, as well as the cost of ending inventory.

Lenox Company's cost of goods sold and the cost of ending inventory using the weighted average method would be determined as follows:

$$\text{Weighted average cost per unit of goods available} = \frac{\text{total cost of all units available for sale}}{\text{total units available for sale}}$$

$$\text{Weighted average cost} = \frac{\$1,000}{500 \text{ units}}$$

$$= \$2.00 \text{ per unit}$$

Lenox's weighted average cost of goods sold

Cost of goods sold using weighted average:

$2.00 per unit × 280 units sold = \$560 **Cost of goods sold**

Lenox's weighted average ending inventory

Ending inventory cost using weighted average:

$2.00 per unit × 220 units left unsold = \$440 **Ending inventory**

Last In, First Out (LIFO)

LIFO:
(1) Last costs go to Cost of Goods Sold
(2) First costs go to Ending Inventory

The last-in, first-out method assigns costs in reverse order to that of the FIFO method. *With LIFO, as the name implies, the last costs incurred are assigned to Cost of Goods Sold and the earlier costs are assigned to Ending Inventory.*

Lenox Company cost calculations under LIFO are shown below:

LIFO Cost of Goods Sold Expense	Units Sold	×	Unit Cost	=	Total Cost
From Jan. 27 purchase............................	50	×	$3.00	=	$150.00
From Jan. 20 purchase............................	100	×	2.50	=	250.00
From Jan. 18 purchase............................	130	×	2.00	=	260.00
LIFO cost of goods sold	280	units			$660.00

Lenox's LIFO cost of goods sold

LIFO Ending Inventory	Units Unsold	×	Unit Cost	=	Total Cost
From Jan. 5 purchase.............................	50	×	$1.00	=	$ 50.00
From Jan. 12 purchase............................	100	×	1.50	=	150.00
From Jan. 18 purchase............................	70	×	2.00	=	140.00
LIFO ending inventory............................	220	units			$340.00

Lenox's LIFO ending inventory

Of course, by this point, you have noticed that there are startling differences for costs of goods sold and costs of ending inventory among the three methods. Let's cover the final inventory cost method, and then we'll explain which methods will yield the most representative inventory costs for various situations.

Specific Identification (SI)

The specific identification method is based on the assumption that each unit purchased, sold, or in inventory has its own identity, that it is separate and distinguishable from any other unit. If this is possible, then certainly it is simple enough to specify the particular cost of each unit. Each unit sold or remaining in inventory is identified, and its specific unit cost is used in calculating cost of goods sold or ending inventory cost.

Specific identification is used when each unit is clearly different

Of course, the specific identification method does not work for large volumes of identical, low-cost items. This method is appropriate for companies that handle a relatively low volume of physical units, each having a high cost. Of course, each unit must be clearly different from the others, as would be the case with original oil paintings, antiques, diamonds, and automobiles.

The specific identification method is *not* appropriate where each unit is the same in appearance but is differentiated from other units through serial numbers, such as the same model of washers, refrigerators, or televisions.

Specific identification: Cost flows and physical flows are the same

Of course, it is highly unlikely that the situation for Lenox as described in Exhibit 9-1 would be suitable for the specific identification method. Nevertheless, let's assume that it is suitable, for the purpose of demonstrating how to calculate cost of goods sold and ending inventory cost using this method.

For purposes of this illustration of specific identification, the units and costs shown below were selected arbitrarily. Management in a real-world situation would be required to trace each unit to the purchase invoice to determine the unit cost. You should have noticed that unlike the other three methods, the specific identification method has no regular cost flow pattern.

Specific Identification Cost of Goods Sold

	Units Sold	×	Unit Cost	=	Total Cost
From Jan. 5 purchase	30	×	$1.00	=	$ 30.00
From Jan. 12 purchase	60	×	1.50	=	90.00
From Jan. 18 purchase	130	×	2.00	=	260.00
From Jan. 20 purchase	60	×	2.50	=	150.00
From Jan. 27 purchase	0	×	3.00	=	0
Specific identification cost of goods sold	280	units			$530.00

Lenox's specific identification cost of goods sold

Specific Identification Ending Inventory

	Units Unsold	×	Unit Cost	=	Total Cost
From Jan. 5 purchase	20	×	$1.00	=	$ 20.00
From Jan. 12 purchase	40	×	1.50	=	60.00
From Jan. 18 purchase	70	×	2.00	=	140.00
From Jan. 20 purchase	40	×	2.50	=	100.00
From Jan. 27 purchase	50	×	3.00	=	150.00
Specific identification ending inventory	220	units			$470.00

Lenox's specific identification ending inventory

A Shortcut

In each of the four methods illustrated, the total 500 units and the total $1,000 cost were accounted for. That is, using each method, we showed that all of the units and all of the cost were included either in cost of goods sold or in ending inventory. This fact is summarized below:

	FIFO		Weighted Average		LIFO		Specific Identification	
	Units	$	Units	$	Units	$	Units	$
Cost of goods sold.......	280	460	280	560	280	660	280	530
Ending inventory	220	540	220	440	220	340	220	470
Total goods available	500	1,000	500	1,000	500	1,000	500	1,000

Cost of goods sold = cost of goods available less cost (FIFO, WA, LIFO, SI) of ending inventory

Since we know the total costs of all units on hand during the period, it is possible to calculate ending inventory cost and then determine cost of goods sold by subtracting it from the total cost of all goods available. Likewise, we could calculate cost of goods sold and then determine ending inventory by subtracting it from the total cost of all goods available. For example, assume that only ending inventory costs were calculated for Lenox Company. The cost of goods sold could be determined by simply subtracting ending inventory costs from total cost, as follows:

	FIFO	Weighted Average	LIFO	Specific Identification
Total cost of goods available	$1,000	$1,000	$1,000	$1,000
Computed ending inventory cost	−540	−440	−340	−470
Assumed cost of goods sold	$ 460	$ 560	$ 660	$ 530

This shortcut approach is the way that cost of goods sold is calculated in real businesses. The FIFO, weighted average, LIFO, and specific identification methods are really ending inventory methods. Now you realize that once we find the ending inventory, using one of these methods, cost of goods sold may be determined by a simple subtraction of ending inventory from total cost of goods available.

You will understand the inventory methods better at first if you calculate the ending inventory and cost of goods sold amounts separately. Then, you can check your answers by adding the two to see if you get the total cost of goods available.

Before we go any further, look at Figure 9-2 (pages 366–367) for one more illustration of how these four cost flow methods work.

Comparing Inventory Cost Methods

You should have observed thus far that for the same number of units sold, each method yields a different cost of goods sold. That means that for the same selling price per unit, each method provides a different profit. This fact is shown in the table on page 369 comparing different gross profits under the four different methods for calculating ending inventory and cost of goods sold. In each case, we assume that the selling price is $5.00 per unit for each of the 280 units sold during January.

FIGURE 9-2
Four Inventory Cost Flow Methods
Assumptions: The company has five identical units. The units were acquired in the order shown—the $2 unit first, the $4 unit second, etc. The cost of each unit is shown on the unit. Three units are sold; two units are left.

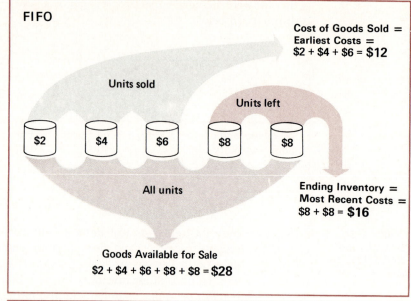

FIFO

Units sold

Units left

$2 $4 $6 $8 $8

All units

Cost of Goods Sold = Earliest Costs = $2 + $4 + $6 = **$12**

Ending Inventory = Most Recent Costs = $8 + $8 = **$16**

Goods Available for Sale
$2 + $4 + $6 + $8 + $8 = **$28**

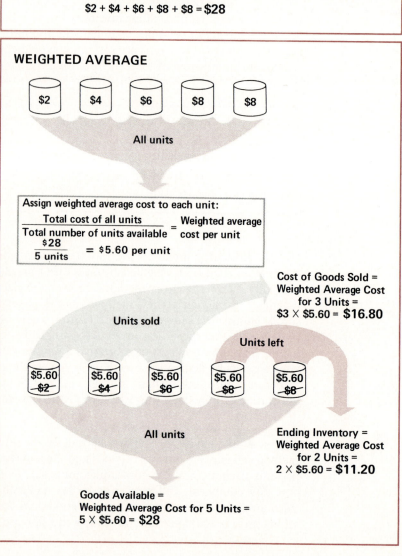

WEIGHTED AVERAGE

$2 $4 $6 $8 $8

All units

Assign weighted average cost to each unit:

$$\frac{\text{Total cost of all units}}{\text{Total number of units available}} = \frac{\text{Weighted average}}{\text{cost per unit}}$$

$$\frac{\$28}{5 \text{ units}} = \$5.60 \text{ per unit}$$

Units sold

Units left

$5.60 ~~$2~~ $5.60 ~~$4~~ $5.60 ~~$6~~ $5.60 ~~$8~~ $5.60 ~~$8~~

All units

Cost of Goods Sold = Weighted Average Cost for 3 Units = $3 × $5.60 = **$16.80**

Ending Inventory = Weighted Average Cost for 2 Units = 2 × $5.60 = **$11.20**

Goods Available = Weighted Average Cost for 5 Units = 5 × $5.60 = **$28**

The flows in these diagrams are intended to show cost flows, not physical flows— remember that the units are identical, so physical flow is not important.

Cost of Goods Sold plus Ending Inventory equals Cost of Goods Available ($28) for each method.

Cost of Ending Inventory is: FIFO = Most Recent Costs; Weighted Average = Weighted Average Cost per Unit × Number of Units Unsold; LIFO = Earliest Costs; Specific Identification = Actual Cost of Physical Units Left.

Cost of Goods Sold is: FIFO = Earliest Costs; Weighted Average = Weighted Average Cost per Unit × Number of Units Sold; LIFO = Most Recent Costs; Specific Identification = Actual Cost of Physical Units Sold.

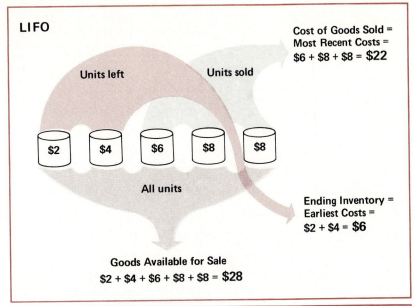

LIFO

Units left   Units sold

$2 $4 $6 $8 $8

All units

Cost of Goods Sold =
Most Recent Costs =
$6 + $8 + $8 = **$22**

Ending Inventory =
Earliest Costs =
$2 + $4 = **$6**

Goods Available for Sale
$2 + $4 + $6 + $8 + $8 = **$28**

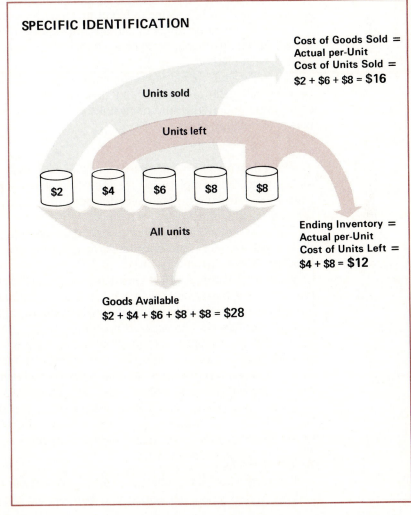

SPECIFIC IDENTIFICATION

Units sold

Units left

$2 $4 $6 $8 $8

All units

Cost of Goods Sold =
Actual per-Unit
Cost of Units Sold =
$2 + $6 + $8 = **$16**

Ending Inventory =
Actual per-Unit
Cost of Units Left =
$4 + $8 = **$12**

Goods Available
$2 + $4 + $6 + $8 + $8 = **$28**

	FIFO	Weighted Average	LIFO	Specific Identification
LENOX COMPANY Gross Profits under Four Inventory Methods Month Ended January 31, 1989				
Sales (280 × $5)	$1,400	$1,400	$1,400	$1,400
Cost of goods sold:				
1/1/89 inventory	0	0	0	0
Purchases............................	$1,000	$1,000	$1,000	$1,000
Goods available for sale	$1,000	$1,000	$1,000	$1,000
1/31/89 inventory	540	440	340	470
Cost of goods sold	$ 460	$ 560	$ 660	$ 530
Gross Profit..........................	$ 940	$ 840	$ 740	$ 870

Each inventory method yields a different gross profit

Depending on which inventory cost method Lenox uses, the company can show profits ranging from $740 to $940. Yet in each case sales and purchases are exactly the same. The only difference lies in the method used to calculate ending inventory costs.

Why are so many different inventory cost methods available? Why is it possible to report the *same* events, using different methods, and produce different results?

These questions are difficult, perhaps impossible, to answer satisfactorily. Nevertheless, let's try to answer them by examining some of the advantages and disadvantages of each method.

The underlying characteristics of each method are shown in Exhibit 9-2 (facing page) as well as the advantages and disadvantages that we are about to discuss. An assumption underlying our conclusions is that inventory costs are rising; that is, a period of inflation exists.

FIFO

The ending inventory calculated using the FIFO method contains the more recent, highest costs. That implies that the units sold were assigned the older, lower costs. Thus FIFO calculates the highest ending inventory costs and the lowest cost of goods sold among the three inventory methods.

Ending inventory is reported as a current asset on the balance sheet. If you believe that the balance sheet should report the most recent costs possible, you would use the FIFO method for inventory costs.

FIFO advantages

The main advantage of FIFO is that it is a simple method to use. Also, for most merchandising businesses, the flow of costs approximates the flow of physical units. Some business people believe that this logical relationship between cost and physical flow is important in choosing an inventory method. Accounting theory, you remember, does not emphasize the flow relationship, so this advantage is largely a personal one for those business people who feel it is important.

FIFO disadvantages

The disadvantages of FIFO are that it does not match current costs with current revenue, certainly not as well as does LIFO. (Remember: Using FIFO, the cost of goods sold is based on older, hence usually lower, unit costs.) In periods of rapidly rising prices, this mismatch will produce an artificially high income, causing the firm to pay higher income taxes than if the LIFO method were used.

Weighted Average

This method considers that each unit of inventory of a particular type is identical and can be sold for the same price, and therefore has equal economic significance to the firm. Units having equal economic significance should be assigned equal costs. The weighted average method assigns an equal cost to each unit, sold or unsold, unlike the FIFO or LIFO method.

EXHIBIT 9-2   Characteristics of Four Inventory Costing Methods

	FIFO	Weighted Average	LIFO	Specific Identification
Ending inventory costs	The more recent unit costs are assigned to the units not sold—those in ending inventory.	The same unit costs—the weighted average cost per unit—are assigned to units not sold and to units sold.	The earliest unit costs are assigned to the units not sold—those in ending inventory.	The actual per-unit cost of each unit unsold is assigned to ending inventory.
Cost of goods sold	Earliest unit costs are assigned to units sold—those in cost of goods sold expense.	The same unit costs—the weighted average cost per unit—are assigned to units sold and unsold.	The more recent unit costs are assigned to the units sold—those in cost of goods sold expense.	The actual per-unit cost of each unit sold is assigned to cost of goods sold expense.
Advantages (strengths)	1. Simple method to use 2. Yields ending inventory amount on the balance sheet comprising more current costs than if weighted average or LIFO is used 3. Produces cost flow approximating physical flow better than weighted average or LIFO	1. Assigns equal unit cost to each unit of inventory 2. Does not produce widely fluctuating profits when inventory costs are fluctuating as FIFO and LIFO do	1. Matches more recent costs with current revenue better than FIFO or weighted average 2. Yields the lowest income, thus the lowest income tax obligation during periods of inflation	1. Simple method to use 2. Cost flows and physical flows are the same 3. Matches each unit cost with the revenue it helped produce
Disadvantages (weaknesses)	1. Does not match recent costs with current revenue as well as LIFO does 2. Yields a higher taxable income than LIFO or weighted average during periods of inflation	1. Does not match recent costs with current revenue as well as LIFO does 2. Does not produce an ending inventory amount containing costs that are as recent as under FIFO	1. Does not produce an ending inventory amount containing costs that are as recent as under FIFO or weighted average 2. Complicated to use by a firm with many products	1. Use is limited to those firms having small quantity of high-cost, unique goods

Weighted average advantages

An advantage of the weighted average method is that it produces costs of goods sold, and thus profits, that fluctuate less sharply than FIFO and LIFO. A substantial increase or decrease in inventory cost will cause FIFO and LIFO incomes suddenly to increase or decrease. Weighted average will combine these new costs with old costs in calculating the average cost per unit. Charging these average unit costs to cost of goods sold will result in a less dramatic change in income.

*Weighted average
disadvantages*

Disadvantages of the weighted average method are: (1) It fails to match current costs with curent revenue as well as LIFO does; and (2) it does not produce an ending inventory cost that approximates current inventory costs as well as FIFO.

LIFO

LIFO advantages

One advantage of LIFO is that it matches most recent costs with most current revenue. (Remember that under LIFO the costs of the units most recently purchased are assigned to cost of goods sold.) Because of this better matching, LIFO provides a better measure of income than either FIFO or weighted average.

Furthermore, in periods of rising costs LIFO produces a lower income than the income calculated by either FIFO or weighted average. The Lenox Company illustration (page 368) clearly shows this. Why would a company want to show a lower income? The lower a firm's taxable income, the lower the income taxes the firm has to pay. The Internal Revenue Service requires that if a company adopts LIFO, it must use LIFO for both income statement reporting and for the income tax return. In the 1970s many corporations switched to the LIFO method of calculating ending inventory and cost of goods sold to gain this income tax advantage.

LIFO disadvantages

The disadvantages of LIFO are: (1) It may be rather complicated to implement in companies having a large number of different types of inventory; and (2) it may result in very old and currently unrealistic ending inventory costs, and thus, an unrealistic measure of current assets on the balance sheet.

Specific Identification

The specific identification cost method matches specific costs of identified units with specific revenue earned by selling those units. Thus, the cost flows follow exactly the physical flow of goods through the firm.

This method would be impractical for companies with extremely large numbers of units of inventory and undesirable for companies dealing in units that are not clearly different from each other. Because it is not based on orderly patterns of costs flowing through the accounts, there is no point in comparing it with the other cost flow methods.

Consistency of Inventory Method

*Consistency requires using
the same inventory method
each year*

The *consistency* principle of accounting requires that the same accounting method should be applied from period to period. This means that when a company selects an inventory method, such as FIFO, it must use that method each year. The method used is disclosed in the footnotes to the financial statements or as a parenthetical note alongside the merchandise inventory on the balance sheet. Readers of the income statement and the balance sheet will be able to follow trends in cost of goods sold and ending inventory costs over a period of time, because they will know that any change in income or asset valuation will be caused by a change in actual costs, not by a change in the method of determining inventory costs.

The consistency principle doesn't prohibit a firm from ever changing accounting methods. A firm can change methods if it has a good reason to do so. The effects of the change on income and asset measurement are disclosed in the financial statement footnotes.

LOWER OF COST OR MARKET

There may be cases where there is plenty of an item in inventory but the demand for it suddenly falls off. Two things will then happen:

1. At the wholesale or supplier level, the replacement cost of those items will decline. This replacement cost is what we will call the ***market price of inventory.***

2. At the level of merchandising firm, the selling price will have to be lowered to get rid of—that is, to be competitive in selling—what remains in inventory.

Thus the firm is caught in a squeeze between lower selling price and higher inventory cost.

The firm's inventory isn't valued at the lower replacement cost because it hasn't bought any at that price. Indeed, it is loaded with inventory purchased at the older, higher price, which is the cost of that inventory.

Further, since the firm must sell it at a lower selling price, the company's ability to generate the normal gross profit on its sales is impaired—its cost of goods sold will be at the old, higher costs while its sales will be at the new, lower selling price. Such a loss in profit is measurable. The loss—and the reduction in the inventory's value—should be recognized in the period when the drop in replacement cost—the event causing the loss—occurs, not in a later period when the items are sold.

NO FREE LIFO

Everybody knows that LIFO inventory accounting helps minimize the effect of inflation on an income statement by using the most recent inventory cost. The latest additions to inventory (last in), with the highest costs, are counted as being the first shipped (first out). This eliminates the lag effect of the more traditional first-in, first-out method in which oldest costs are matched first against most recent prices, thus inflating earnings continuously until prices stop rising.

But there is a price for having a more realistic income statement, à la LIFO: an increasingly less realistic balance sheet. It works like this: Usually, when a company switches from FIFO to LIFO, its existing stock of raw materials, work in progress and finished goods stay on the books at costs prevalent at the time of the switch, which is generally much less than their current value. The difference between that ever older stock of goods with its frozen values and current market value is the "LIFO cushion." That cushion can grow in periods of rising prices as inventory grows—the difference between this year's larger stock of goods and last year's then becomes another layer of the cushion. But the cushion doesn't show on the balance sheet, thus owners' equity is understated.

When a company pares inventory and cuts into the cushion, it gets a major and misleading shot in the arm from matching frozen older costs against current prices. That's what a number of oil companies have been doing since last year [1981]. But until that happens the LIFO cushion is not transferred to owners' equity.

Just how distorted those equity figures can be for a company with a lot of capital tied up in inventory was underscored recently in a survey of the chemical industry done by Norman Weinger of Oppenheimer & CO., the brokerage house. Weinger calculated that Union Carbide's net worth was understated by about 18% just because of its aging LIFO cushion.

The LIFO news is not all bad, of course. A big LIFO cushion can be a very pleasant surprise for stockholders. According to Weinger, many steel companies' LIFO cushions equal or exceed the companies' total stock market value. National Steel's LIFO cushion at the end of 1981 totaled $742 million—towering over its recent market value of $322 million.

What happens now that inflation is slowing down? To the extent that it continues to slow, the LIFO cushions will cease growing; but they'll still be there—unless real deflation sets in. But here's another complication: This year, with so many companies cutting inventories, a good part of those cushions are helping to pad earnings, making them look better than they are. That's the fascinating thing about accounting: The more you strive to make it reflect the real world, the more complex it becomes.

***

Source: FORBES, Dec. 6, 1982, pages 168, 171.

A growing company is going to have a growing amount of ending inventory each year. The greater quantities of inventory will be necessary for the company to meet increased customer demands. When using LIFO, these greater and greater quantities of ending inventory build upon one another much like a layer cake. The oldest costs are in the bottom layer, with newer and newer costs added each year. If these old costs were to appear on the income statement, they would be matched with recent, much higher selling prices, yielding abnormally high profit margins. The difference between these lower costs and more recent higher inventory costs is called a "LIFO cushion" in the article you have just read. A strike, an interrupted source of inventory supply, a decrease in demand for the company's products, or some other situation might cause a company to use up its LIFO cushion by reducing the quantity of its ending inventory. The result is to show much higher profits on the income statement—and a much higher tax bill due to the IRS.

The lower-of-cost-or-market method measures the drop in the replacement cost of inventory

The loss in value resulting from a reduction in the replacement cost of inventory is calculated by the **lower-of-cost-or-market** method, simply called **LCM**. LCM is calculated by comparing inventory cost, as determined by one of the methods discussed earlier in the chapter, with market, which is the current replacement cost of the goods. LCM can be applied to each item of inventory, to various subgroupings of inventory, or to the inventory as a whole, as is shown below:

Inventory Item No.	Description	Quantity	Cost (FIFO)	Market (Replacement Cost)	LCM Item by Item
101	Hose	10	$ 20	$ 18	$ 18
102	Bracket	40	40	42	40
103	Clamp	5	20	15	15
206	Motor	100	125	100	100
208	Mount	60	180	165	165
210	Generator	250	188	208	188
Totals			$573	$548	$526

The LCM item-by-item column amounts are determined by comparing the cost and market for each item and choosing the lower of the two in each case — the cost is lower for items no. 102 and no. 210; market is lower for all the others. These LCM item-by-item amounts are totaled and this amount, $526, is used to calculate the loss as follows:

LCM item by item

Cost (FIFO). $573
LCM (item by item)   526
Loss. . . . . $ 47

The loss in value can be estimated also by comparing the total cost of all the inventory with the total market of all the inventory:

LCM total inventory basis

Cost (FIFO). $573
LCM (total inventory).   548
Loss. . . . . $ 25

A firm will choose the one of these methods — item by item, or total inventory — that is easiest for it to use. Either method of estimating the loss is acceptable, provided that it is used consistently from period to period.

Conservatism means we use the methods that are least likely to overstate assets and income

The principle of **conservatism** is the justification for the LCM rule. Conservatism in accounting means that we should choose accounting methods that are least likely to overstate assets and income. Valuing inventory at cost when its replacement cost is lower overstates the asset Merchandise Inventory. Thus, we apply the conservatism principle and use LCM to reduce Inventory to a more realistic amount and, at the same time, recognize the loss in value that has occurred.

We have demonstrated the basic idea behind LCM. For further consideration of the more complex refinements of this technique, consult a more advanced accounting text.

ESTIMATING INVENTORY AMOUNTS

There may be situations where it is inconvenient or impossible to count inventory for the purpose of preparing an income statement. For most firms, the time and expense involved in counting inventory once each month would make it too costly to prepare monthly income statements. Also, a catastrophe, such as a fire, could destroy inventory, making it impossible to count. Thus, it would be impossible to prepare a meaningful income statement—we wouldn't know how much of the inventory purchased had been sold before the fire and how much had been destroyed. To overcome these problems, two methods have been devised as ways of estimating ending inventory without actually taking a physical count: the *gross profit method* and the *retail inventory method.*

Gross Profit Method

The *gross profit method* relies on the relationship among sales, cost of goods sold, and gross profit to derive an estimate of ending inventory cost. The following illustration demonstrates how this method works.

A partial income statement (we have left out operating expenses and income taxes) for the year 1988 for Colonist Company follows:

COLONIST COMPANY Partial Income Statement Year Ended December 31, 1988			
Sales		$100,000	100%
Cost of Goods Sold:			
Beginning Inventory	$16,000		
Purchases	74,000		
Goods Available for Sale	$90,000		
Ending Inventory	10,000	80,000	80%
Gross Profit on Sales		$ 20,000	20%

On Apr. 4, 1989, the Colonist Company warehouse was completely destroyed by fire. The accounting records were stored in a fireproof vault, making available the information about sales revenue, beginning inventory cost, and purchases for the period Jan. 1–Apr. 4, 1989.

We have added percentages on the 1988 Colonist income statement so that you can see the relationship among sales, cost of goods sold, and gross profit. Cost of goods sold is 80% of sales ($80,000 ÷ $100,000), and gross profit is 20% of sales

($20,000 ÷ $100,000). There were no changes in inventory costs or selling prices that would have altered these percentages during the first part of 1989. We assume, then, that the same percentage relationships existed until the date of the fire. The salvaged 1989 accounting records provide these data:

Sales (Jan. 1–Apr. 4, 1989)	$24,000
Purchases (Jan. 1–Apr. 4, 1989)	16,200
Beginning Inventory (Jan. 1, 1989)	10,000

Ending inventory can be calculated as follows:

Goods available for sale:		
Beginning inventory (known) (Jan. 1)		$10,000
Purchases (known) (Jan. 1–Apr. 4)		16,200
Goods available for sale		$26,200
Less: Cost of goods sold:		
Sales (known) (Jan. 1–Apr. 4)	$24,000	
×Cost of goods sold % (estimated)	80%	19,200
Estimated ending inventory, Apr. 4, 1989		$ 7,000

You should be aware of two things when you consider using the gross profit method:

To use the gross profit method we must know sales, a gross profit %, beginning inventory, and purchases

1. Accounting records are normally protected against fire and theft. So it is not unrealistic to expect that sales, beginning inventory, and purchases figures would be available.

2. Percentages expressing the relationship between past gross profit and sales, and cost of goods sold and sales, should not be used blindly. Consideration should always be given to modifying these percentages to reflect any recent changes in costs or selling prices.

Retail Inventory Method

The retail inventory method estimates ending inventory by relying on the relationship between the cost of inventory and its selling price

The *retail inventory method* is based on the percentage relationship between the cost of inventory and its selling price. As its name implies, this method was developed for use by retail establishments to estimate ending inventory cost.

You will need to understand three terms to follow how to use this method:

1. *Original markup*   The amount added to the cost of merchandise to arrive at its original selling price

2. *Additional markup*   An addition to the original selling price yielding an even higher selling price

3. *Markdown*   A deduction from the original selling price resulting in a lower selling price

	Cost	Retail
FAIRBURN FASHIONS		
Calculation of Ending Inventory		
Using Retail Inventory Method		
June 30, 1989		
Beginning inventory..	$ 38,000	$ 51,000
Purchases (net)	92,500	115,000
Additional markups..		10,000
Markdowns		(2,000)
Total cost and selling price of goods available	$130,500	$174,000
Less: Sales (net)		(114,000)
Ending inventory at retail		$ 60,000
×Cost-to-retail ratio ($130,500 ÷ $174,000)...............		75%
Ending inventory at cost		$ 45,000

For all goods available for sale during the period, Fairburn first accumulated the total cost, $130,500, and the total selling price, $174,000, of all goods available during the period. These amounts were used to compute a *cost-to-retail ratio,* which is the ratio of the cost of goods available to the selling price of goods available ($130,500 ÷ $174,000 = 75%). This ratio simply states that the cost of the goods on hand was 75% of their retail selling price.

Next, actual sales *at the retail price* are deducted from the total selling price of all goods available for sale.

This calculation yields an ending inventory at its retail selling value.

Ending inventory at cost is derived by multiplying ending inventory at retail by the cost-to-retail ratio.

We have used the retail inventory method to estimate the cost of ending inventory. In actual practice the retail inventory method may be used to estimate ending inventory at lower-of-cost-or-market or at replacement cost, depending on how the markups and markdowns are treated in the computation. Further modifications are required if an estimate of LIFO ending inventory is desired. The complexities of these applications are beyond the scope of an introductory text.

INVENTORY ERRORS

Errors can happen in the process of calculating ending inventory costs. After all, it is a complex process that includes counting inventory, determining which units to include or exclude based on FOB and consignment terms, and applying one of the cost flow methods.

To understand how an error in the calculation of ending inventory cost affects the income statement, consider the illustration at the top of page 376.

Note that an error in ending inventory for year 1 also affects the next year because the ending inventory cost in year 1 becomes the beginning inventory cost for year 2. If the ending inventory cost of year 2 is correct, there will be no additional effect on year 3 because the beginning inventory for year 3 will be correct. Thus the impact of the error is confined to a 2-year period, and the error is said to *self-correct* or *counterbal-*

Under identical starting, operating, and ending conditions, each method will produce a different gross profit. The inventory method chosen must be used consistently year after year unless a change in method can be justified. When there is a change in inventory method, it must be disclosed on the financial statements.

If the demand for an item falls off at the retail level, the value of the inventory of those items will similarly decline. And at the wholesale level, their replacement cost will also decline. When this happens, the problem is what to use as inventory "cost" —the actual cost already paid? Or the current replacement cost (also referred to as *market cost*)? A solution to this problem is *lower of cost* (actual cost paid) *or market* (current replacement cost), or *LCM.* LCM recognizes a loss in the period in which the value of the inventory declined, not in the period in which the inventory is sold.

When a physical count of inventory is inconvenient, impractical, or impossible, the cost of ending inventory may be estimated by the *gross profit method* or the *retail inventory method.*

An error in the ending inventory of one year will automatically cause an error in the beginning inventory of the next period. Errors in ending inventory amounts are said to be *self-correcting,* or *counterbalancing,* over a 2-year period.

Any of the four methods of determining ending inventory cost may be applied in a *perpetual* or a *periodic* inventory system. Under a complete perpetual inventory system both the cost and the number of units on hand are known at all times. In a periodic system the ending inventory is determined by physical count and costs are assigned based on this count. The periodic system determines ending inventory only at the end of a period.

IMPORTANT TERMS USED IN THIS CHAPTER

CHAPTER SUMMARY

Additional markup The incremental increase in price above the original selling price of inventory. (page 374)

Cash discount A reduction in the invoice price for paying cash within a specified period. The payment terms are abbreviated in the general form 2/10, n/30, where 2/10 means 2% discount if paid within 10 days and n/30 means that the total invoice price is due within 30 days if no discount is taken. Any terms may be specified. (page 353)

Consignment An arrangement in which one business, the consignee, sells goods owned by another business, the consignor. At no time does the consignee own the goods. The consignee receives a commission for selling the consignor's goods and has a responsibility for caring for them while they are in his or her possession. (page 358)

Consistency principle The assumption that the accounting methods used in a current time period have already been used in past periods and will continue to be used in future periods. (page 370)

Finished goods inventory The name that manufacturers use for merchandise inventory. (page 351)

First in, first out (FIFO) The method of accounting for inventory costs that assumes that the first, or earliest, costs incurred are the first costs that will be charged to Cost of Goods Sold Expense and the most recent costs will be assigned to Ending Inventory. (page 361)

FOB destination Terms of shipping inventory that specify: (1) that the seller pays the freight to the point of destination; and (2) that title, the ownership, to the inventory passes from the seller to the buyer at the destination point. (page 358)

FOB shipping point Terms of shipping inventory that specify: (1) that the seller does not pay the freight beyond the shipping point; and (2) that title passes from the seller to the buyer at the shipping point. The shipping point is usually considered to be the seller's place of business. (page 358)

Freight-in Transportation cost paid by the buyer. (page 355)

Gross method A method of recording purchases on credit at the gross invoice price—after trade and quantity discounts but before cash discounts. When cash discounts are taken, Purchase Discounts is credited for the amount of the discount. (page 354)

Gross profit method A method of estimating the cost of inventory based on past records of sales, cost of goods sold, and gross profit and the relationships among these amounts. (page 373)

Last in, first out (LIFO) The method of accounting for inventory costs that assumes that the most recent costs incurred are the first costs that will be charged to Cost of Goods Sold Expense, and the first costs, and oldest costs, will be assigned to Ending Inventory. (page 363)

Lower of cost or market (LCM) A comparison of the cost of inventory with the replacement cost of the same inventory to determine if there has been a loss in the value of inventory that should be recorded. When replacement cost is lower than cost, a loss is recorded. (page 370)

Markdown The incremental decrease in the selling price below the original selling price. (page 374)

Merchandise inventory Goods held for sale. In manufacturing concerns, merchandise inventory is usually called finished goods inventory. (page 351)

Net method A method of recording purchases on credit at the net invoice price anticipating that cash discounts will be taken. If the cash discount is not taken, Purchase Discounts Lost is debited at the time of payment. (page 354)

Original markup The amount by which the original selling price exceeds its purchase price. See also *additional markup.* (page 374)

Periodic inventory method A system of determining the ending inventory units, ending inventory cost, and cost of goods sold at the end of a period of time. (page 377)

Perpetual inventory method A system for keeping an up-to-date record of the cost of inventory on hand and the cost of goods sold. (page 377)

Quantity discount A reduction in the list price for purchasing a large number of units. (page 353)

Retail inventory method A system for estimating the cost of ending inventory based on the relationship between the retail price of goods available for sale and the cost of those same goods. (page 374)

Specific identification The method of accounting for inventory costs that identifies each specific unit of inventory and its cost. When the inventory is sold, its cost is assigned to Cost of Goods Sold; otherwise the cost remains in Ending Inventory. This method can be used only in those instances where each item is clearly different from the others. (page 363)

Trade discount A variable reduction in the listed selling price; the reduction allowed is at the discretion of the seller. Hence, a way of adjusting the price for different classes of customers. (page 353)

Weighted average method The method of accounting for inventory costs that assigns the same cost to each unit sold and each unit remaining in inventory. The weighted average cost for each unit equals the total cost of goods available for sale divided by the total number of units available for sale. (page 362)

QUESTIONS

1. How is raw materials inventory different from merchandise inventory?

2. Are dump trucks merchandise inventory? Explain.

3. Conner Co. has an account called Purchase Discounts on its books. Is Conner using the gross or net method of recording purchases? Explain.

4. Howard Co. received a trade discount, a quantity discount, and a cash discount on merchandise recently purchased. Howard uses the net method of recording purchases. Which of these discounts will be recorded in a separate account? Explain.

5. Where do Purchase Discounts and Purchase Discounts Lost appear on a company's income statement? Will a single company have both of these accounts on the same income statement? Explain.

6. Lee Co. buys all of its inventory FOB shipping point, whereas Key Co. buys all of its inventory FOB destination. Which company will have a Freight-In account? Explain.

7. Should goods out on consignment be included in ending inventory? Explain.

8. FIFO, LIFO, and weighted average are said to be inventory cost flow assumptions. Does cost flow differ from physical flow? Explain.

9. Which inventory method has the same cost flow and physical flow? Explain why.

10. List the strengths, or advantages, of the FIFO inventory method.

11. Merchandise inventory may be purchased at several different prices during a period and yet the weighted average method assigns the same amount to each unit in ending inventory. What is the justification for this weighted average procedure?

12. List the strengths, or advantages, of the LIFO inventory method.

13. The consistency principle means that the same accounting principles (or methods) used this period were also used last period. Does this mean that once a company decides to use FIFO, it can never switch to LIFO or weighted average?

14. How are *cost* and *market* determined in the lower-of-cost-or-market application?

15. What are two methods of determining an estimated ending inventory amount? Under what circumstances might a company want to estimate ending inventory?

16. When the gross profit method is used, two assumptions are made. What are they?

17. What estimation method makes use of a cost-to-retail ratio? How is this ratio calculated?

18. Why does an error in the ending inventory of year 1 also cause an error in year 2 income?

19. Errors in ending inventory are said to be *self-correcting*. Explain what this means.

20. What is the primary difference between a periodic inventory system and a perpetual inventory system?

EXERCISES

Exercise 9-1
Calculating the cost of inventory purchased by using trade, quantity, and cash discounts

On Apr. 1, Rabbitt Co. purchased 300 tires from the Radial Tire Co. The tires have a list price in Radial's catalog of $45 each. Radial allows a 25-10 trade discount and a quantity discount of 2% on orders of 100 or more tires. The terms of the purchase are 3/15, n/45. Rabbitt paid for the order on Apr. 12. What was the cost of the tires to Rabbitt?

(Check figure: Net cost of inventory = $8,662.34)

Exercise 9-2
Recording the purchase of and payment for goods using the gross method

On Oct. 1, Harding, Inc., purchased 50 beds from Hickory Furniture Manufacturing for $70 each. Terms of the purchase were 2/10, n/30; there were no trade or quantity discounts. Harding uses the *gross method* of recording purchases.

a. Assuming that Harding paid on Oct. 9, prepare entries for Oct. 1 and Oct. 9.
b. Assuming that Harding paid on Oct. 31, prepare entries for Oct. 1 and Oct. 31.

(Check figure: Purchase Discount recorded on Oct. 9 = $70)

Exercise 9-3
Recording the purchase of and payment for goods using the net method

On June 1, Stillwell Stores purchased 45 toasters from Carmody Electric Products for $4.75 each. There are no trade or quantity discounts offered, but a cash discount is available with terms of 3/10, n/30. Stillwell uses the *net method* of recording purchases.

a. Assuming that Stillwell paid on June 5, prepare entries for June 1 and June 5.
b. Assuming that Stillwell paid on June 28, prepare entries for June 1 and June 28.

(Check figure: Purchase Discounts Lost recorded on June 28 = $6.42)

Exercise 9-4
Preparing the cost of goods sold section of an income statement

The following information was taken from the records of Grubnecker, Inc., on Dec. 31, 1989:

Merchandise Inventory, Jan. 1, 1989	$ 52,000
Purchase Discounts	7,150
Purchases	343,500
Freight-In	29,700
Merchandise Inventory, Dec. 31, 1989	72,300
Purchase Returns and Allowances	21,600

Calculate the Cost of Goods Sold for the year ended Dec. 31, 1989.

(Check figure: Cost of Goods Sold = $324,150)

Exercise 9-5
Determining the number of physical units in ending inventory

Wynn Wholesale Supply is in the process of determining the number of physical units that should be in ending merchandise inventory. Using the information below, calculate the proper total physical units in ending inventory. Give a reason for omitting any item that you do not believe should be included in ending inventory.

Disposition	Number of Units
In stockroom	47,500
In shipment from suppliers (purchased FOB shipping point)	3,600
In shipment from suppliers (purchased FOB destination)	16,200
Out on consignment	12,750
On loading platform awaiting shipment to customers (legal title has not yet passed to customers)	2,250
In on consignment	1,900
In shipment to customers (merchandise was sold FOB shipping point)	4,150

(Check figure: 66,100 units in ending inventory)

Exercise 9-6
Calculating the ending inventory and cost of goods sold using periodic FIFO, LIFO, and weighted average

Philip Francis Queeg, president of Queeg's Ball Bearings, Tucson, Arizona, wants you to prepare a comparison of ending inventory and cost of goods sold using three different periodic inventory methods. Data from the company's records follow:

	Units	Purchase Price per Unit
Beginning Inventory	25	$ 6.00
Mar. 5 purchase	70	9.00
Mar. 14 purchase	140	10.00
Mar. 25 purchase	120	12.00
75 units were on hand at the end of March.		

Calculate the amount of Ending Inventory and Cost of Goods Sold using periodic FIFO, weighted average, and LIFO.

(Check figure: Cost of Goods Sold using FIFO = $2,720)

Exercise 9-7
Using the gross profit method to estimate inventory lost

Fuller Furniture lost all of its inventory in a recent tornado. Since the company uses the periodic inventory method, there is no record of exactly how much inventory was on hand at the time of the disaster. The controller asks you to provide an estimate of the amount that was on hand. The following information is available:

Purchases (net) $390,000
Sales 580,000
Beginning inventory 90,000
Gross profit % for the prior period 30%

(Check figure: Estimated inventory on hand = $74,000)

Exercise 9-8
Using the retail inventory method to estimate ending inventory

Maryk Men's Apparel wants to determine its approximate quarterly income without going to the expense and bother of counting ending inventory. The following information has been gathered for the quarter:

	Cost	Retail
Sales.....................................	—	$295,000
Beginning inventory.......................	$ 50,000	74,000
Additional markups	—	12,000
Purchases (net)...........................	215,200	270,000
Markdowns...............................	—	5,000

Prepare an estimate of Maryk's gross profit for the quarter. (Use the retail inventory method to determine ending inventory.)

(Check figure: Estimated gross profit = $72,136)

Exercise 9-9
Calculating the effects of inventory errors on income of 2 years

Langhorne's Lighting Supplies sells light fixtures. At the end of 1988, the bookkeeper omitted some units from ending inventory. The units were out on consignment. The cost of the fixtures omitted was $9,000. The error was discovered on Dec. 31, 1989. Income statements prepared *before* the error was discovered follow:

LANGHORNE'S LIGHTING SUPPLIES
Income Statements
Years Ended December 31

	1988		1989	
Sales...		$80,000		$145,000
Cost of Goods Sold:				
Beginning Inventory.....................	$12,000		$16,000	
Purchases	41,000		73,000	
Goods Available for Sale................	$53,000		$89,000	
Ending Inventory	16,000	37,000	24,000	65,000
Gross Profit...........................		$43,000		$ 80,000
Operating Expenses.....................		17,000		31,000
Net Income.............................		$26,000		$ 49,000

Ending inventory on Dec. 31, 1989, was correct. What effect will the bookkeeper's error have on 1988 and 1989 income? Prepare calculations to support your answer.

(Check figure: 1989 income is overstated by $9,000)

Exercise 9-10
Calculating ending inventory and cost of goods sold using perpetual LIFO

Duke Sammis Sales provides you with the following purchases and sales data:

Date	Description	Units	Cost Each	Total Cost
Dec. 1	Purchase	12	$22	$ 264
8	Purchase	18	24	432
14	Sale	10		
22	Purchase	20	26	520
31	Sale	24		
Total cost of goods available				$1,216

Calculate Cost of Goods Sold and Ending Inventory using perpetual FIFO and perpetual LIFO.

(Check figure: Cost of Goods Sold using LIFO = $856)

PROBLEMS: SET A

Problem A9-1
Calculating the cost of inventory using the gross method

Winston's Watercraft made three purchases of inventory during its first month of operations:

Mar. 5   Purchased 12 canoes from New City Boats. New City gave Winston a 30% trade discount and terms of 3/20, n/30. The list price per canoe was $250. The inventory was shipped FOB destination; the total freight bill was $104. Winston paid for the inventory on Mar. 23.

7   Purchased 4 fiberglas fishing boats listing for $860 each from Whopper Craft. Whopper gave Winston a 40-10 trade discount and terms of 3/20, n/60. The boats were sent FOB shipping point and arrived at the store on Mar. 20. The freight on the shipment was $125. Winston paid Whopper on Apr. 15.

10   Purchased 3 speedboats from Pro-Ski Boats. The boats listed for $6,500 each. Winston received a 20% trade discount, a 4% quantity discount, and terms of 2/15, n/30. The boats, shipped FOB shipping point, were received on July 20. Freight charges amounted to $315. Winston paid Pro-Ski on Apr. 19.

Required   Assuming that Winston uses the gross method of recording purchases, prepare clearly labeled schedules showing the calculation of the cost of (1) the canoes, (2) the fishing boats, and (3) the speedboats. Assume that the cash discount period begins on the purchase date; i.e., Mar. 5, Mar. 7, and Mar. 10. Note: Journal entries are not required.

(Check figure: Cost of the speedboats = $15,291.00)

Problem A9-2
Preparing entries to record purchases under the gross and net methods

Acres Art Supplies made the following purchases and payments during the month of November, 1989:

Nov. 3   Purchased assorted paints and brushes from Rainbow Supplies for $7,200. Terms of the purchase were 2/10, n/30.

     6   Purchased easels and canvases from Art Goods, Inc. Terms of the purchases were 3/15, n/45. The gross invoice amount was $2,200.

   12   Acres paid Rainbow for the Nov. 3 purchase.

   30   Acres paid Art Goods for the easels and canvases.

Required

Assuming that the discount period begins on the date of purchase, prepare entries to record Acres' November purchases and payments using (1) the gross method of recording purchases; (2) the net method of recording purchases. Supporting calculations should included as part of your journal entry explanations.

(Check figure: Purchase Discounts Lost using the net method = $66.00)

Problem A9-3
Calculating ending inventory and cost of goods sold using FIFO, LIFO, and weighted average

Carmody Company began business in June. The following purchases were made during the month:

Date	Units	Cost per Unit	Total Cost
June 3	30	$7.00	$210
10	40	7.20	288
14	90	7.40	666
24	40	7.60	304
28	20	7.80	156

Carmody's stock clerk reported that 75 units were on hand at the end of the month.

Required

Calculate the ending inventory and cost of goods sold under the periodic FIFO, LIFO, and weighted average methods. Do not use the shortcut. (Round the weighted average cost per unit to the nearest cent.)

(Check figure: Ending Inventory using the weighted average method = $553.50)

Problem A9-4
Calculating ending inventory and cost of goods sold using FIFO, LIFO, and weighted average

Porteous Power Tools received the following schedules from the purchasing department manager and the marketing director:

PORTEOUS POWER TOOLS		
Summary of Purchasing Activity		
Quarter Ended March 31, 1989		

Date	Description	Units	Cost per Unit
Jan. 1	Inventory on hand	8,800	$ 9.60
Jan. 10	Purchase	2,000	9.90
Jan. 12	Return of defective units	500	9.90
Feb. 18	Purchase	3,000	10.20
Feb. 21	Purchase	6,000	10.50
Feb. 28	Purchase	1,500	10.40
Mar. 14	Purchase	4,500	10.80
Mar. 28	Return of defective units	800	10.80

PORTEOUS POWER TOOLS
Summary of Sales
Quarter Ended March 31, 1989

Period Covered	Description	Units	Sales Price per Unit
Jan. 1–15	Sales	2,300	$24.00
Jan. 1–15	Customer returns	30	24.00
Jan. 16–31	Sales	4,200	24.60
Jan. 16–31	Customer returns	20	24.60
Feb. 1–15	Sales	2,100	25.00
Feb. 16–28	Sales	1,400	25.50
Feb. 16–28	Customer returns	50	25.50
Mar. 1–31	Sales	4,000	25.60

Required

Compute the ending inventory and cost of goods sold for Porteous Power Tools for the first quarter of 1989 under the periodic FIFO, LIFO, and weighted average methods. Use the shortcut. Round the weighted average cost per unit to the nearest cent.

(Check figure: Ending Inventory using the periodic LIFO method = $102,390)

Problem A9-5
Applying LCM on an item-by-item basis, and to inventory as a whole

Pluto's Paint Store uses lower of cost or market to value ending inventory. The following inventory summary was prepared on Oct. 31, Pluto's year-end:

Inventory Group	Stock Number	Quantity	Cost (FIFO)	Market (Replacement Cost)
Paint	A401	40 cases	$1,600	$1,525
	A415	10 cases	450	400
	A420	45 cases	2,340	2,400
Brushes	B101	10 cases	135	145
	B115	50 cases	945	963
	B117	20 cases	194	205
	B119	5 cases	64	44
Ladders	C940	20 each	446	400
	C945	100 each	2,560	2,300
	C948	3 each	90	99

Required

Calculate the amount of inventory that Pluto should disclose on the Oct. 31 balance sheet assuming that lower of cost or market is applied:

1. On an item-by-item basis
2. To the inventory as a whole

(Check figure: LCM applied on an item-by-item basis = $8,373)

Problem A9-6
Using the gross profit method to estimate inventory lost in a storm

On Dec. 13, 1944, a typhoon destroyed much of the inventory of the USS Caine Company. The company managed to salvage only $920 of merchandise. The insurance adjuster needs to have an estimate of the total inventory on hand at the time of the storm in order to pay Caine Company for its losses. The company manager has put together the following information:

USS CAINE COMPANY
Income Statement
Year Ended June 30, 1944

Sales (net)...		$320,000
Cost of Goods Sold:		
Merchandise Inventory, July 1, 1943	$ 23,100	
Purchases (net)...	201,300	
Goods Available for Sale	$224,400	
Merchandise Inventory, June 30, 1944....................	32,400	192,000
Gross Profit on Sales		$128,000
Operating Expenses..		51,000
Net Income		$ 77,000
Sales (July 1, 1944, through Dec. 13, 1944)............................		$ 97,000
Purchases (July 1, 1944, through Dec. 13, 1944)........................		65,000

Required

Calculate the amount of inventory Caine Company lost in the storm.

(Check figure: Cost of inventory lost = $38,280)

Problem A9-7
Using the retail inventory method to estimate inventory; preparing an income statement and a balance sheet

Willie Keith, owner of Keith's Camera, is considering selling a part of the business to Marie Minott. Marie has asked to see an up-to-date set of financial statements. Willie is upset because his fiscal year doesn't end for another 2 months and he believes it will be expensive and time-consuming to count physical inventory. You volunteer to help Willie in the preparation of his financial statements. You suggest that the retail inventory method be used to estimate ending inventory. Willie provides the information shown below:

KEITH'S CAMERA
Adjusted Trial Balance
April 30, 1989

	Debit	Credit
Cash	$ 48,000	
Merchandise Inventory, July 1, 1988	25,500	
Supplies on Hand	2,400	
Store Fixtures...	96,000	
Accumulated Depreciation: Store Fixtures.....................		$ 25,200
Accounts Payable		34,500
Common Stock ($10 par)		75,000
Retained Earnings..		25,800
Sales...		435,000
Sales Returns	10,500	
Purchases..	379,200	
Purchase Returns and Allowances.....................		12,000
Freight-In	7,500	
Depreciation Expense.....................................	8,400	
Other Operating Expenses.................................	30,000	
Total..	$607,500	$607,500

Other Information

Merchandise on hand July 1, 1988, had a retail price of	$ 31,800
Net purchases were marked to sell for	468,300
Net additional markups amounted to..........	13,650
Net markdowns amounted to..................	13,500

Required

1. Prepare a schedule calculating your estimate of the cost of ending inventory.
2. Prepare an income statement for the period July 1, 1988, through Apr. 30, 1989.
3. Prepare a balance sheet for Willie on Apr. 30, 1989.

(Check figure: Estimated ending inventory = $60,600)

Problem A9-8
Calculating the effects of
inventory errors on
incomes of 4 years

You have been hired as the inventory accounting clerk for Dlugatch, Inc. Your first task is to review the inventory records for the past 4 years and determine if there were any mistakes. You discover the following errors:

a. 1986 ending inventory was overstated because goods shipped to customers FOB shipping point were included. The overstatement amounted to $6,200.

b. 1986 sales were understated by $15,000 because sales of goods described in item (a) above were also omitted. These sales were erroneously recorded in 1987.

c. 1987 ending inventory was understated by $17,000 because goods out on consignment were omitted.

d. 1988 ending inventory was understated by $23,000. Employees neglected to count the inventory in a basement room.

e. 1989 purchases totaling $7,000 were not recorded. The bookkeeper had overlooked the invoice. The goods were included in ending inventory.

f. 1989 ending inventory was overstated by $4,000 because of an error in addition.

Required

Prepare a schedule showing the calculation of the correct net income for each of the 4 years. The reported net income for each year is shown below. Hint: Set up your solution paper as follows:

Description	1986	1987	1988	1989
Net income (loss) reported	$71,000	$43,500	$(7,200)	$36,000

Add or subtract the effects of each error in the appropriate columns; total each column to find corrected net income.

(Check figure: 1988 corrected net loss = $1,200)

**Problem A9-9
Calculating ending
inventory using periodic
and perpetual FIFO and
LIFO**

Pacific Co. has the following record of purchases and sales for its first month of operations, June, 1989:

Purchases			
Date	Units	Cost per Unit	Total Cost
June 2	200	$3.00	$ 600
10	80	3.25	260
17	240	3.50	840
23	80	3.75	300
30	40	4.00	160
Totals	640		$2,160

Sales	
Date	Units
June 13	100
20	160
27	40

Required

1. Calculate ending inventory and cost of goods sold using periodic FIFO and periodic LIFO.
2. Calculate ending inventory and cost of goods sold using perpetual FIFO and perpetual LIFO.

(Check figure: Cost of Goods Sold, perpetual LIFO = $1,030)

PROBLEMS: SET B

**Problem B9-1
Calculating the cost of
inventory using the gross
method**

Paynter's Personal Computers acquired the following computers during its first month of operations:

Aug. 2 Purchased 6 Desk Top Computers from Big Blu Computers, Inc. The list price of each computer was $3,000. Big Blu offered Paynter a 20% trade discount, and terms of 2/15, n/30. The computers were shipped FOB shipping point; the total freight bill was $750. Paynter paid for the inventory on Aug. 30.

5 Purchased 4 Einstein Portable Computers from Einstein Electronics. The computers listed for $2,500 each. The terms of the purchase were 3/10, n/60, 30-10 trade discount, and FOB destination. Freight charges totaled $470. Paynter had not paid Einstein on Aug. 31.

20 Purchased 15 Homegame Computers from Abacus Computers. The computers listed for $400 each and were shipped to Paynter FOB shipping point. Paynter received a 20% trade discount, a 5% quantity discount, and terms of 2/10, n/30. The computers were received on Aug. 25. Freight charges amounted to $475. Paynter paid for the purchase on Aug. 28.

Required

Assuming that Paynter uses the gross method of recording purchases, prepare clearly labeled schedules showing calculations of the cost of (1) the Desk Top Computers, (2) the Einstein Portable Computers, and (3) the Homegame Computers. Assume that the cash discount period begins on the purchase date, i.e., Aug. 2, Aug. 5, and Aug. 20. Note: Journal entries are not required.

(Check figure: Cost of the Homegame Computers = $4,943.80)

Problem B9-2
Preparing entries to record purchases under the gross and net methods

Keefer Communications made the following purchases and payments for inventory during December, 1989:

Dec. 4   Purchased 500 pushbutton telephones from Sound Transmission, Inc.; terms of the purchase were 2/10, n/30. The phones have a list price of $20 each.

    8   Purchased an assortment of desk- and wall-model rotary dial phones from Eastern Equipment Co. for $2,250. Terms of the purchase were 5/10, n/30.

  15   Paid Eastern Equipment the amount due.

  30   Paid Sound Transmission for the Dec. 4 purchase.

| Required |

Prepare journal entries to record Keefer's purchases and payments assuming that (1) the gross method is used to record purchases; (2) the net method is used to record purchases. Supporting calculations should be part of your journal entry explanations.

(Check figure: Purchase Discounts on the gross method will have a credit balance of $112.50)

Problem B9-3
Calculating ending inventory and cost of goods sold using FIFO, LIFO, and weighted average

Maryk Mart has the following inventory record for the month of January:

	Units	Cost per Unit	Total Cost
Inventory, Jan. 1	10	$10.00	$100.00
Purchase, Jan. 5	4	11.00	44.00
Purchase, Jan. 10	9	12.00	108.00
Purchase, Jan. 16	10	13.00	130.00
Purchase, Jan. 24	7	14.00	98.00

A count of the inventory on hand on Jan. 31 revealed that 18 units remained.

| Required |

Calculate ending inventory and cost of goods sold under the periodic FIFO, LIFO, and weighted average methods. Do not use the shortcut.

(Check figure: Ending Inventory under the FIFO method = $240)

Problem B9-4
Calculating ending inventory and cost of goods sold using FIFO, LIFO, and weighted average

Fuller Fire and Safety Equipment Co. experienced the following inventory-related transactions during the first quarter of 1989:

		Units	$ per Unit
Jan. 1	Inventory on hand	2,250	3.20
Jan. 1–15	Sales of inventory	750	8.00
Jan. 16	Purchase	500	3.30
Jan. 20	Defective inventory returned to vendor	100	3.30
Jan. 16–31	Sales of inventory	1,400	8.20
Feb. 4	Purchase	1,000	3.40
Feb. 13	Purchase	2,000	3.50
Feb. 1–15	Sales of inventory	700	8.50
Feb. 27	Purchase	500	3.48
Feb. 16–28	Sales of inventory	450	8.55
Mar. 17	Purchase	1,500	3.60
Mar. 25	Defective inventory returned to vendor	250	3.60
Mar. 1–31	Sales of inventory	1,300	8.60

| Required |

Prepare a schedule calculating the ending inventory and cost of goods sold for Fuller for the first quarter of 1989 using the periodic FIFO, LIFO, and weighted average methods. Use the shortcut method.   *(Check figure: Weighted average cost per unit = $3.40)*

Problem B9-5
Applying LCM on an item-by-item basis, and to inventory as a whole

Wouk's Cold Appliances is preparing financial statements for the year ended June 30, 1989. Wouk wants to use lower of cost or market to value ending inventory. The following inventory summary has been prepared:

Inventory Group	Inventory Item Number	Quantity	Cost (FIFO)	Market (Replacement Cost)
Freezers	1001	2	$ 140	$ 145
	1002	3	1,350	1,260
	1003	2	960	920
	1004	5	2,100	2,120
Refrigerators	2021	1	196	200
	2022	5	1,170	1,120
	2023	2	639	630
Ice makers	3041	1	150	142
	3042	4	896	920
	3043	2	368	360

Required

Calculate the amount of inventory that Wouk will show on the June 30, 1989, balance sheet, assuming that lower of cost or market is applied:
1. On an item-by-item basis
2. To the inventory as a whole

(Check figure: LCM applied to inventory as a whole = $7,817)

Problem B9-6
Using the gross profit method to estimate inventory lost in a flood

On Feb. 18, 1989, a flood destroyed much of the inventory of Harding Hardware Store. The total amount of merchandise that was salvaged amounts to $8,000. Harding asks you to help prepare an estimate of the loss in order to file a claim with the insurance company. You are handed the following schedule of data that has been gathered:

HARDING HARDWARE STORE
Income Statement
Year Ended November 30, 1988

Sales (net)...		$250,000
Cost of Goods Sold:		
Merchandise Inventory, Dec. 1, 1987......................	$ 34,000	
Purchases (net)......................................	152,000	
Goods Available for Sale	$186,000	
Merchandise Inventory, Nov. 30, 1988.....................	36,000	150,000
Gross Profit on Sales		$100,000
Operating Expenses		27,000
Net Income		$ 73,000
Sales (Dec. 1, 1988, through Feb. 18, 1989)...............		$ 44,000
Purchases (Dec. 1, 1988, through Feb. 18, 1989)		22,000

Required

Calculate the cost of the inventory lost in the flood.

(Check figure: Cost of inventory lost = $23,600)

Problem B9-7
Using the retail inventory method to estimate inventory; preparing an income statement and a balance sheet

Voles' Pool and Patio Store is applying for a loan at the Community National Bank. The bank has asked to see up-to-date financial statements. Vera Voles, owner of the store, explains to you that she isn't due to count her inventory for another 2 months — the end of the fiscal year. You volunteer to help prepare an income statement for her using the retail inventory method to estimate her ending inventory. Vera provides you with the following trial balance and additional information:

VOLES' POOL AND PATIO STORE Adjusted Trial Balance June 30, 1989	Debit	Credit
Cash...	$ 83,000	
Merchandise Inventory, Sept. 1, 1988	54,000	
Supplies on Hand	3,000	
Equipment	580,000	
Accumulated Depreciation: Equipment....................		$ 96,000
Accounts Payable		34,000
Common Stock ($1 par)		450,000
Retained Earnings.......................................		18,000
Sales...		420,000
Sales Returns...	20,000	
Purchases	120,000	
Purchase Discounts......................................		4,000
Freight-In	14,000	
Depreciation Expense	48,000	
Other Operating Expenses...............................	100,000	
Total	$1,022,000	$1,022,000

Other Information

Merchandise on hand on Sept. 1, 1988 had a retail price of	$108,000
Net purchases were marked to sell for	372,000
Net additional markups amounted to............	10,000
Net markdowns amounted to....................	30,000

Required

1. Prepare a schedule calculating your estimate of ending inventory.
2. Prepare an income statement for the period Sept. 1, 1988 – June 30, 1989.
3. Prepare a balance sheet for Vera as of June 30, 1989.

(Check figure: Estimated ending inventory = $24,000)

Problem B9-8
Calculating the effects of inventory errors of 4 years

You have been reviewing the inventory records of Jellybelly, Inc., for the last 4 years. Your investigation has revealed the following errors:

a. 1986 ending inventory was understated by $6,300 because goods purchased FOB shipping point were omitted.

b. 1987 sales were overstated by $5,000 because sales shipped to customers FOB destination were included. (These goods had not been included in cost of goods sold for 1987.) The sales should have been recorded in 1988. (The goods were included in cost of goods sold for 1988.)

c. 1987 ending inventory was overstated by $1,500. The cost of goods in on consignment was inadvertently included in ending inventory.

d. 1988 ending inventory was overstated by $2,250. Employees counted one bin of merchandise twice.

e. 1989 ending inventory was understated by $1,000. Goods out on consignment were not included.

Reported income (loss) in each of the last four years was: 1986 = $30,000; 1987 = $17,800; 1988 = $9,000; 1989 = ($1,000).

Required

Prepare a schedule showing the calculation of corrected net income for each of the 4 years. Hint: Set up your solution paper as illustrated below:

Description	1986	1987	1988	1989
Net income reported	$30,000	$17,800	$9,000	($1,000)

Add or subtract the effects of each error in the appropriate columns; total each column to find corrected net income.

(Check figure: 1988 corrected net income = $13,250)

**Problem B9-9
Calculating ending
inventory using periodic
and perpetual FIFO and
LIFO**

Strawberry Imports provides you with the following data about its purchases and sales for the month of April, 1989, its first month of operations:

Purchases			
Date	**Units**	**Cost per Unit**	**Total Cost**
Apr. 1	100	$2.50	$250
5	40	2.55	102
15	120	2.70	324
24	40	2.80	112
30	20	2.85	57
Totals	320		$845

Sales	
Date	**Units**
Apr. 8	50
17	80
29	20

Required

1. Calculate ending inventory and cost of goods sold using periodic FIFO and periodic LIFO.
2. Calculate ending inventory and cost of goods sold using perpetual FIFO and perpetual LIFO.

(Check figure: Cost of Goods Sold, perpetual LIFO = $399)

DECISION PROBLEM

For the past several years you have been employed by the First National Bank of Kansas City as a loan officer. As part of your responsibilities you are to assure that the bank's loan portfolio is invested such that it maximizes the bank's return on invested funds while minimizing its exposure. Generally this precludes you from loaning more than $1,000,000 to any one industry in the local area.

On Oct. 18, 1989, you had a most unusual day. Four companies in the same industry each approached you with a request for a $1,000,000 loan. Each supplied you with audited financial statements reflecting the results of operations of their first year of business, which ended on Sept. 30, 1989. These statements appear below:

	Chief	Arrowhead	Stram	Blue Jay
Sales	$15,300,000	$15,300,000	$15,300,000	$15,300,000
Cost of Goods Sold	12,037,500	11,650,000	12,750,000	12,550,000
Gross Profit	$ 3,262,500	$ 3,650,000	$ 2,550,000	$ 2,750,000
Operating Expenses	1,700,000	1,700,000	1,700,000	1,700,000
Net Income	$ 1,562,500	$ 1,950,000	$ 850,000	$ 1,050,000

The four companies buy and sell optical laser equipment to a variety of telephone companies in the United States and abroad. Sales for the four companies averaged $170 per unit for the year. The companies buy the equipment from a sole supplier located in Tulsa, Oklahoma. Prices charged by the supplier for 1988–1989 were:

TULSA LASER PRICE DATA
(per unit)
Established Price for the Month

October, 1988	$110	February, 1989	$125	June, 1989	$160
November, 1988	120	March, 1989	130	July, 1989	162
December, 1988	100	April, 1989	140	August, 1989	165
January, 1989	120	May, 1989	150	September, 1989	165

Purchases made by the four companies are analyzed below:

Chief		Arrowhead		Stram		Blue Jay	
Month	Units	Month	Units	Month	Units	Month	Units
Nov.	25,000	Nov.	10,000	Oct.	30,000	Oct.	20,000
Dec.	20,000	Feb.	50,000	Jan.	30,000	Nov.	35,000
Apr.	50,000	Apr.	40,000	Apr.	30,000	Mar.	25,000
July	25,000	May	20,000	Aug	30,000	June	40,000

Required

1. Determine the inventory method used by each of the four companies.

2. To which of the four companies will you loan the $1,000,000?

3. Assume that each of the four companies is subject to a 30% federal income tax. Would this change your answer in (2) above? How?

CHAPTER 10

Long-Lived Assets

Some of the things you should learn from studying this chapter are:

- How to recognize *long-lived assets* and distinguish between the two types, *tangible* and *intangible*
- Which assets are normally classified as *property, plant, and equipment* and why
- How to determine the cost of property, plant, and equipment assets
- To distinguish between a *capital expenditure* and a *revenue expenditure*
- How to calculate *depreciation* using the *straight-line, units-of-production, sum-of-the-years'-digits,* and *double declining-balance* methods
- To *record acquisition, depreciation,* and *disposal* of *property, plant, and equipment* assets
- To *calculate depletion* and prepare journal entries to *record depletion*
- The difference between *depreciation for financial accounting purposes* and *depreciation for income tax purposes*
- Which assets are normally classified as *intangibles* and why
- To calculate and prepare entries for *amortization* of intangible assets

We have already explained that all a firm's assets can be classified as either current assets or long-lived assets. Assets that will be used up in a firm's operations or are soon to be converted into cash (within 1 year or one operating cycle, whichever is longer) are current assets. All other assets, then, are long-lived assets. Long-lived assets provide benefits for more than 1 year or one operating cycle. Classifications of long-lived assets typically found on a balance sheet are investments; property, plant, and equipment; and intangibles. In this chapter we will cover two of these long-lived assets — property, plant, and equipment; and intangibles. Investments, that is, long-term investments representing long-lived assets, will be discussed in Chapter 14.

PROPERTY, PLANT, AND EQUIPMENT

Property, plant, and equipment assets are tangible long-lived assets owned by the business and used in its operations

Typical assets included in *property, plant, and equipment* are land, building, machinery, office equipment, delivery equipment, and natural resources—all tangible long-lived assets owned by a business and used in its operations.

Assets not considered as property, plant, and equipment include, for example, investments in stocks and bonds of other companies; patents (these are not tangible); land held for investment purposes (this asset is not used in the firm's operations); and buildings under construction (these are not yet used in the operations of the business).

Acquisition Cost

As you might well imagine, the cost of a long-lived asset that fits the category of property, plant, and equipment is more than the price tag on the asset itself. There will be many other costs that must be either necessarily or reasonably incurred to acquire the asset. There will also be some costs associated with the acquisition that may seem necessary or reasonable, but upon close examination, will be determined to be expenses that are chargeable elsewhere. Of course, it's the accountant's job to determine which costs are to become part of the total cost of the asset and which costs are not.

The general rule for determining the cost of inventory, cited in Chapter 9, applies equally to the cost of property, plant, and equipment assets:

General rule for determining acquisition cost

All reasonable and necessary costs to get an asset in position and condition ready for use may be included as part of the cost of the asset.

An example will illustrate how to determine which costs are part of the asset cost and which are not. Print-It Company incurred the following costs when it acquired a printing press:

1. Catalog list price $30,000
2. Trade discount 20%
3. Cash discount (terms 4/20, n/60) . . . .
4. Freight cost (terms FOB shipping point) . . . . $ 900
5. Insurance while in shipment   150
6. Repair cost. (Forklift operator dropped machine while clowning around during unloading. Repair was necessary before the machine could be placed in service. Because the damage occurred after receipt, the shipment insurance does not cover cost of repairs. Print-It must pay for repairs.)   2,500
7. Rewiring cost. (Accessible power was inadequate to supply the requirements of the new machine.)   250
8. Concrete slab cost. (It was necessary to pour a slab with bolts embedded in it. The machine was bolted to the slab to prevent excessive vibration.)   100
9. Consulting engineer's fee. (A consulting engineer was called in to thoroughly test the machine and demonstrate its operation.) . . .   500
10. Materials used in testing. (Cost of materials used by consulting engineer to test machine and demonstrate its operation.)   80

11. Maintenance cost. (Cost of materials needed during first month of operation.) 25

12. Operator's salary. (Salary during the first month of operation.) 800

The following analysis reflects the decisions made in applying the acquisition cost rule:

Description/Justification	Cost of Machinery: Charge to Machinery Account Amount	Not Cost of Machinery: Charge to Other Accounts Account Title	Amount
1 and 2. Catalog Price Less Trade Discount $30,000 less (.20)($30,000) = $30,000 less $6,000 =	$24,000		
3. Cash Discount ($24,000)(.04) = The cash price of the machine is $23,040 ($24,000 − $960). This amount is included in the cost of the machine. If Print-It chooses not to pay the cash price within the first 20 days— remember, the terms are 4/20, n/60—$24,000 will be due at the end of 60 days. Print-It will have borrowed the $23,040 from the seller for 40 days and paid $960 interest. *The cost of financing an asset is not part of the cost of the asset.* If Print-It elects to wait until the end of 60 days to pay, $23,040 will be charged to Machinery and $960 will be charged to Interest Expense. *The amount of the cash discount is always deducted, even if the buyer chooses not to take advantage of it.*	(960)		
4. Freight Cost Because the purchase was FOB shipping point, Print-It must pay the freight cost.	900		
5. Insurance While in Shipment Insurance paid to protect the asset while in shipment is a reasonable cost.	150		
6. Repair Cost The cost of these repairs are not covered by insurance. Although it is a necessary cost to get the machine into working order, *it is not a reasonable and necessary* cost in acquiring assets. Properly trained and supervised employees are expected to be careful in handling the company's assets.		Loss Due to Employee Negligence	$2,500
7. Rewiring Cost The cost of installing a special electric power line to supply the power needs of the machine is considered a reasonable and necessary cost. This cost is not considered part of the cost of the building, because the installation is designed to serve only this one machine. There is no assurance that it will be useful to others in the future.	250		
8. Concrete Slab The logic for adding this cost to the machine is the same as for the cost of the specially installed power line.	100		

(continued)

Description/Justification	Cost of Machinery: Charge to Machinery Account	Not Cost of Machinery: Charge to Other Accounts	
	Amount	Account Title	Amount
9. Consulting Engineer's Fee Setting the machine to perform to Print-It's special needs is a reasonable cost incurred in getting the machine into initial operation.	500		
10. Materials Used in Testing This is cost necessary to the consulting engineer's task. Materials used in normal production after the machine is operational become part of the expense of operations.	80		
11 and 12. Maintenance Cost and Operator's Salary These costs were incurred after the machine became operational; therefore they are operating costs, *not* acquisition costs.		Maintenance Expense Salary Expense	25 800
Total cost of machine	$25,020		

The following entry records all of Print-It's costs. It summarizes the total costs of acquiring the machine, and identifies each of the other costs associated with but not part of the total machine cost.

Dec. 1–31	Machinery	25,020	
	Loss Due to Employee Negligence	2,500	
	Maintenance Expense	25	
	Salary Expense	800	
	Cash		28,345

To record the cost of the printing press, costs incidental to its acquisition, and costs of operating it during December.

The Print-It Company example shows many of the common costs incurred in acquiring long-lived assets such as machinery and equipment. The following are some of the common acquisition costs for other property, plant, and equipment assets:

Common acquisition costs associated with various property, plant, and equipment assets

Land   Land is an asset that is considered to have an unlimited useful life. Costs of surveying to determine the boundaries of the land, costs incurred in removing old buildings, title insurance and legal fees, and other costs of a permanent nature such as draining swampy land or filling to level land, all are considered part of the cost of land.

Land improvement   The cost of driveways, sidewalks, shrubbery, sprinkler systems, and parking lots are all recorded in one account called Land Improvements. These items differ from land in that each has a limited useful life.

Buildings   The cost of a building includes construction costs, architectural fees, insurance (for fire, theft of materials, and natural disasters) while under construction, building permit fees, cost of surveying for the purpose of locating the building on the land, and the cost of grading associated with the construction of a basement or providing adequate drainage of surface water.

Natural resources Mineral deposits, oil wells, and timberland are material resources that exist in a natural state (natural resources). The cost of these natural resources includes the costs associated with acquiring land, including the natural resource borne by the land, as well as, for example, the cost of building access roads, sinking mine shafts, laying rail tracks into the mine, and other costs incurred in getting ready to extract the resource.

Leased assets Businesses often sign contracts to rent assets for a long period of time (5, 10, 25, or more years). These contracts are called leases. Certain lease contracts are considered to be equivalent to buying the asset—if a firm leased an automobile for 5 years, and if the expected useful life of the car is 5 years, the company can be said to have obtained all of the benefits of owning the asset. These kinds of leased assets are recorded just as if the company actually owned them.

Thus far, we have kept the discussion simple: Either we haven't indicated how property, plant, and equipment assets are paid for, or we tended to suggest that they were acquired with cash or on short-term credit. In the real world, long-lived assets are extremely costly and, of course, are also acquired in exchange for other assets, on long-term credit, or in exchange for an ownership interest in the business. Or they may be acquired through a combination of all these possibilities.

No matter what the arrangement for acquiring the asset, it should be recorded at its market value—the cash price specified—on the date it is formally acquired. The total cost of the asset includes all reasonable and necessary costs to get an asset in position and condition ready for use.

Lump-Sum Acquisitions

Cost is allocated to each asset acquired in a group purchase by the relative-value allocation method

Occasionally, a business may acquire several assets for one price. In such cases it is necessary to allocate the one lump-sum cost among the several assets. Normally, this is done by a *relative-value allocation,* such as the one illustrated as follows.

Delta, Inc., acquired land, a building, and machinery from Calamity Company for $1,000,000. A professional appraiser valued each of the assets at the following amounts: land, $800,000; building, $560,000; and machinery, $240,000. The $1,000,000 is allocated among the assets as follows:

Asset	Appraised Value	Percent of Total Appraised Value	×	Total Cost	=	Cost Allocated to Asset
Land	$ 800,000	$800,000/$1,600,000 = 50%	×	$1,000,000	=	$ 500,000
Building	560,000	$560,000/$1,600,000 = 35%	×	1,000,000	=	350,000
Machinery	240,000	$240,000/$1,600,000 = 15%	×	1,000,000	=	150,000
Totals	$1,600,000	100%				$1,00,000

The following entry would be made to record the acquisition:

Mar. 15	Land..	500,000	
	Building...	350,000	
	Machinery.......................................	150,000	
	Cash...		1,000,000
	To record acquisition of land, building, and machinery.		

Observe that the appraised value is $1,600,000 and the actual cost is $1,000,000. Although the assets were appraised at $600,000 over actual cost, they are recorded at cost. They are not recorded at the value someone says they are worth. Recording them at cost is objective and verifiable.

Capital vs. Revenue Expenditures

Capital expenditures benefit several periods; revenue expenditures benefit only one period

Cost incurred for, or associated with, assets that will provide economic benefits over several accounting periods are called *capital expenditures.* All capital expenditures associated with a particular asset are added to the cost of that asset.

Costs incurred that will provide economic benefits only during the current accounting period are called *revenue expenditures.* Revenue expenditures are recorded in expense accounts.

At the time an asset is acquired, all of the costs meeting the requirements of the general acquisition-cost rule are considered capital expenditures. For example, in the Print-It Company illustration, the invoice price less discounts, plus the costs of freight, insurance during shipment, rewiring, concrete slab, consulting engineer's fee, and materials used in testing are all proper acquisition costs and are therefore capital expenditures.

Some expenditures incurred after the asset is acquired and placed in service may also be considered capital expenditures, for example, the cost of replacing a truck engine with a more fuel-efficient one; the cost of adding a solar-powered heating unit to a building; the cost of overhauling a machine's motor; and the cost of resurfacing a parking lot.

Revenue expenditures consist primarily of the costs of regular maintenance, cleaning, and minor repairs. Examples of revenue expenditures include the costs of oil, grease and other lubricants, light bulbs, window panes, oil filters, tires, and the salaries of custodians and mechanics who perform regular maintenance functions.

It is important to distinguish between capital expenditures and revenue expenditures because they affect the measurement of income differently.

Capital expenditures are allocated to income over the several years during which they provide benefits (i.e., the single capital expenditure is spread out over a number of years). If a capital expenditure is erroneously treated as a revenue expenditure and entirely expensed during the current period, current expenses will be too high and therefore income will be too low. In subsequent years, when part of the capital expenditure should have been expensed, expenses will be too low and income will be too high. There will be a mismatching between expenses and revenues.

Revenue expenditures incorrectly charged to an asset account will also mismatch expenses and revenues, in this case causing the opposite effect: Expenses on the current income statement will be understated and thus current income will be overstated.

Depreciation

Depreciation is the allocation of a tangible asset's cost over its useful life

When someone says something like, "My new car is now one year old and it has depreciated $2,000," what they are talking about is a decrease in the market value of the asset. This is *not* what accountants mean by depreciation. In accounting, *depreciation* means the allocation of the cost of a tangible asset over its useful economic life.

When a company purchases a tangible long-lived asset, it is really buying a large bundle of service benefits that will be provided by that asset over time in the future. These future service benefits enable the asset's owner to earn revenue by providing a place (buildings) in which to manufacture, store, and sell the products, by furnishing a means (machines) of fashioning and packaging the product, or by providing a way (trucks) to deliver goods. As an asset is used over time, the bundle of future service benefits available from it becomes smaller and smaller. The part of the original cost of the asset that is assigned to the bundle of service benefits that have been used up is called depreciation.

An example of how depreciation expense is recorded is shown by the following entry:

Dec. 31 Depreciation Expense 10,000
             Accumulated Depreciation 10,000
             To record depreciation for the year.

What Causes Depreciation?

Physical wear-and-tear and obsolescence are the two causes of depreciation

The common causes of depreciation are physical wear-and-tear and obsolescence. In today's rapidly developing technological economy, obsolescence is a more important consideration than physical deterioration. For example, Pitch Company purchases a computer for $800,000. In evaluating how to depreciate that cost, Pitch Company first has to decide how many years the machine will last. Management observes that, with proper maintenance, it will continue processing information for a period of 20 years. But management also knows that the computer industry will probably develop a more efficient machine that will handle Pitch's increased information needs more efficiently within 5 years. For the current computer, the useful life to Pitch will be 5, *not* 20, years. At the end of the 5 years, Pitch will probably be able to sell its computer to a smaller company whose information needs it can serve adequately. The asset will not have deteriorated much at all, but it will be obsolete for Pitch's purposes. For other businesses it will not be obsolete.

Management's estimate of an asset's useful economic life is an essential ingredient in calculating depreciation.

How Much Depreciation Should Be Recorded?

There are several methods of determining how to depreciate the cost of an asset over its useful economic lifetime. That is, there are different ways of determining the cost to be allocated to each year of its life. We will demonstrate how to use each of these different methods using the same basic information:

Acquisition cost of asset $125,000

Estimated salvage value (what we can sell the asset for at the end of its useful life) . . . , ... $15,000

Estimated useful life in years . . . . 10 years

Estimated useful life in units of output (the total units we can expect the machine to produce during its useful life) . . . . 220,000 units

Straight-Line Depreciation

Straight-line depreciation assumes that we receive equal benefits from an asset each day of the asset's life. Straight-line depreciation, then, allocates an equal part of the total cost to each day of an asset's useful life. We usually record depreciation on a monthly or annual basis rather than daily. The basic idea is that straight-line recognizes the same amount of depreciation per unit of time — whatever that unit of time is. Here is the straight-line depreciation formula and the yearly depreciation for our $125,000 asset:

The straight-line method relates depreciation to the passage of time

$$\text{Straight-line depreciation per year} = \frac{\text{acquisition cost} - \text{estimated salvage value}}{\text{estimated useful life in years}}$$

$$= \frac{\$125,000 - \$15,000}{10 \text{ years}}$$

$$= \frac{\$110,000}{10 \text{ years}}$$

$$= \$11,000 \text{ per year}$$

Depreciation will be the same amount, $11,000, for each full year of the asset's life. The straight-line method assumes that an equal amount of the asset's total service benefits are used up each year.

Figure 10-1 on page 404 shows graphically how the straight-line method works.

Units-of-Output Depreciation

The units-of-output method is used for assets whose useful life is limited by physical wear-and-tear rather than obsolescence. This method is used for assets that are physically worn out before they become obsolete. According to the units-of-output method, as an asset produces a unit of output, it also uses up some of the service benefits available from the asset. Each unit produced uses up the same amount of the asset's service benefits. The more units the asset produces in a period, the greater the service benefits it uses up in that period. What all this simply means is that the part of the asset's total cost to be depreciated in a period depends directly on the number of units the asset produces in that period.

The units-of-output method relates depreciation to the using up of service benefits

The units-of-output method would be appropriate for a delivery truck. The truck will not become obsolete; it will deliver products year after year until it is worn out. The more it is used, the more quickly it will be worn out, and the greater will be the depreciation. The units of output for a delivery truck are tons of goods delivered per mile per period. The service benefits used would be measured in miles driven per period.

To use the units-of-output depreciation method, it is essential to have some way of measuring the asset's output during a particular period of time. For our delivery truck an odometer measures the miles driven. Automatic counters are used on production line machinery, and devices that record flying hours are used for company airplanes.

Returning to our basic example, assume that 10,000 units are produced in year 1 and 24,000 units in year 2. The depreciation for each of these years is calculated as follows:

$$\text{Units-of-output depreciation per unit} = \frac{\text{acquisition cost} - \text{estimated salvage value}}{\text{estimated total lifetime units of production}}$$

$$= \frac{\$125,000 - \$15,000}{220,000 \text{ units}}$$

$$= \frac{\$110,000}{220,000 \text{ units}}$$

$$= \$0.50 \text{ per unit}$$

Year 1 depreciation = 10,000 units $\times$ $0.50 per unit = $ 5,000

Year 2 depreciation = 24,000 units $\times$ $0.50 per unit = $12,000

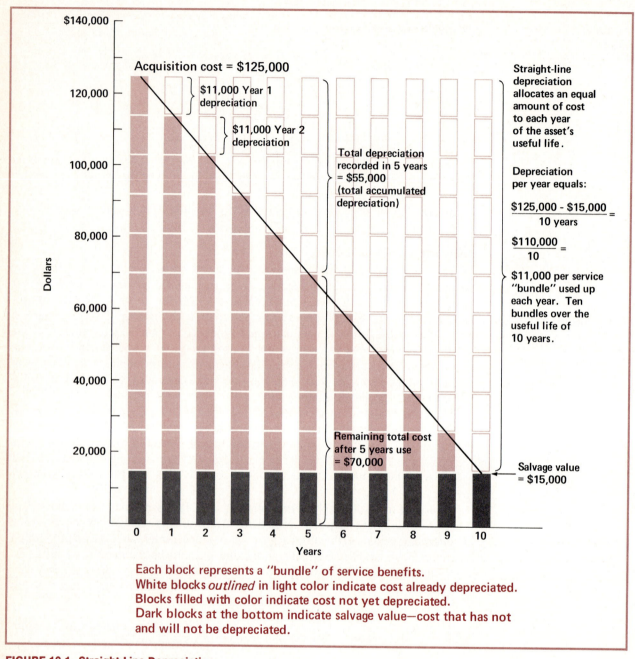

Acquisition cost = $125,000

{ $11,000 Year 1 depreciation

{ $11,000 Year 2 depreciation

Total depreciation recorded in 5 years = $55,000 (total accumulated depreciation)

Remaining total cost after 5 years use = $70,000

Salvage value = $15,000

Straight-line depreciation allocates an equal amount of cost to each year of the asset's useful life.

Depreciation per year equals:

$$\frac{\$125,000 - \$15,000}{10 \text{ years}} =$$

$$\frac{\$110,000}{10} =$$

$11,000 per service "bundle" used up each year. Ten bundles over the useful life of 10 years.

Each block represents a "bundle" of service benefits.
White blocks *outlined* in light color indicate cost already depreciated.
Blocks filled with color indicate cost not yet depreciated.
Dark blocks at the bottom indicate salvage value—cost that has not and will not be depreciated.

FIGURE 10-1 Straight-Line Depreciation

The sum-of-the-years'-digits method allocates more depreciation to early years of an asset's life and less to the later years

Sum-of-the-Years'-Digits Depreciation

The basic idea behind the sum-of-the-years'-digits method is that more service benefits are received in the early years of an asset's life when it is new, and fewer benefits are received each year as the asset grows older.

The sum-of-the-years'-digits (SYD) method assigns more depreciation expense to the early years of the asset's life and less to later ones. It is a method of "accelerated depreciation."

The procedure for calculating SYD depreciation for our basic example is outlined in the following steps:

STEP 1: Determine the sum of the digits of the years of the asset's useful life.

$$1 + 2 + 3 + 4 + 5 + 6 + 7 + 8 + 9 + 10 = 55$$

An easy way to determine the sum of the digits

Of course, you can see how cumbersome this process would be for an asset with say a 15-, 20-, or 25-year life. A shortcut formula that yields the same results as the more tedious addition process is:

$$\text{Sum of the digits} = n\left(\frac{n+1}{2}\right)$$

where n = number of years in the asset's life.

$$10\text{-year sum of the digits} = 10\left(\frac{10+1}{2}\right)$$

$$= 10(5.5)$$

$$= 55$$

STEP 2: Determine the asset's acquisition cost and salvage value, and the difference between these two amounts. In the example these are given as $125,000 and $15,000, respectively, and the difference is $110,000.

STEP 3: Multiply the difference between cost and salvage by a fraction composed of a numerator representing the number of years of life remaining at the beginning of the current year and a denominator representing the sum of the digits determined in step 1. The largest fraction represents the largest proportion of the cost to be depreciated in year 1. The lowest fraction represents the smallest proportion of the cost to be depreciated in year 10, the last year.

Year of Asset's Life	Years Remaining in Asset's Life	Fraction = $\dfrac{\text{Years Remaining}}{\text{Sum of the Years' Digits}}$	
1	10	Highest proportion depreciated	$\frac{10}{55}$
2	9		$\frac{9}{55}$
3	8		$\frac{8}{55}$
4	7		$\frac{7}{55}$
5	6		$\frac{6}{55}$
6	5		$\frac{5}{55}$
7	4		$\frac{4}{55}$
8	3		$\frac{3}{55}$
9	2	Lowest proportion depreciated	$\frac{2}{55}$
10	1		$\frac{1}{55}$
55 = Sum of the years' digits			$\frac{55}{55} = 100\%$

Depreciation expense under the sum-of-the-years'-digits method for each of the 10 years would be:

Year	Fraction	×	Cost − Salvage ($125,000 − $15,000)	=	Depreciation Expense
1	$\frac{10}{55}$		$110,000		$ 20,000
2	$\frac{9}{55}$		110,000		18,000
3	$\frac{8}{55}$		110,000		16,000
4	$\frac{7}{55}$		110,000		14,000
5	$\frac{6}{55}$		110,000		12,000
6	$\frac{5}{55}$		110,000		10,000
7	$\frac{4}{55}$		110,000		8,000
8	$\frac{3}{55}$		110,000		6,000
9	$\frac{2}{55}$		110,000		4,000
10	$\frac{1}{55}$		110,000		2,000
				Total depreciated	$110,000

SYD depreciation decreases by a constant amount each year

Note that after the depreciation for the first few years has been calculated, you can see that the depreciation expense decreases by a constant amount ($2,000) each year. Subsequent years' depreciation may be determined merely by deducting this constant amount. For example, year 3 depreciation = $16,000, year 4 depreciation = $16,000 less the constant $2,000 = $14,000.

Sum-of-the-years'-digits is an appropriate method for assets that provide more service benefits in the early years of their lives and less in later years. Many assets are efficient when first purchased but become less efficient as time passes. This decrease in utility may be caused by technological obsolescence or by increasing maintenance costs that become necessary because of the accumulated effects of physical wear-and-tear. Copying machines and computers are examples of assets that are depreciated by an accelerated depreciation method such as sum-of-the-years'-digits.

Figure 10-2 is a graphic illustration of how the sum-of-the-years'-digits method works.

Double Declining-Balance Depreciation

Another method for accelerating the depreciation, even more during the early years than the sum-of-the-years'-digits method, is declining-balance depreciation, or a simplified version commonly referred to as the ***double declining-balance method.*** This method is based on the same idea as the sum-of-the-years'-digits method and is used for assets that provide even more consumable service benefits in the early years, therefore requiring more depreciation in those years.

Double declining-balance depreciation allocates even more depreciation to the early years of an asset's life than SYD

Declining-balance depreciation, like the other depreciation methods, looks at (1) the acquisition cost, (2) an estimate of the life of the asset, and (3) its estimated salvage value. Plugging that information into a complex formula and solving it yields a percentage. Starting with the acquisition cost, this percentage is applied to that cost to determine the depreciation expense for the first year. The same percentage is applied to the remaining cost of the asset after the first year to determine the depreciation expense for the second year. And so on. Applying the same percentage to the remaining cost of the asset in each subsequent year—the declining balance—allocates the depreciation expense each year in such a way that the balance of the cost of the asset declines precisely to the salvage value at the end of the estimated lifetime. Hence, the name "declining-balance depreciation."

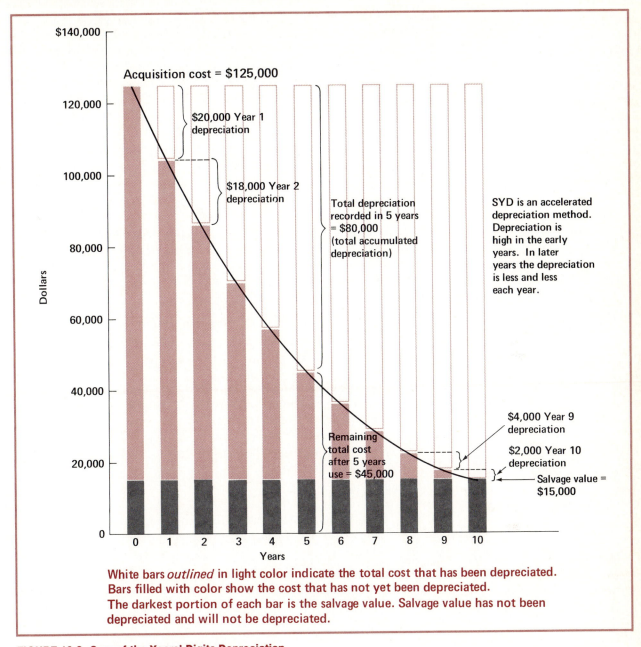

Acquisition cost = $125,000

$20,000 Year 1 depreciation

$18,000 Year 2 depreciation

Total depreciation recorded in 5 years = $80,000 (total accumulated depreciation)

SYD is an accelerated depreciation method. Depreciation is high in the early years. In later years the depreciation is less and less each year.

Remaining total cost after 5 years use = $45,000

$4,000 Year 9 depreciation

$2,000 Year 10 depreciation

Salvage value = $15,000

Dollars

Years

White bars *outlined* in light color indicate the total cost that has been depreciated.
Bars filled with color show the cost that has not yet been depreciated.
The darkest portion of each bar is the salvage value. Salvage value has not been depreciated and will not be depreciated.

FIGURE 10-2 Sum-of-the-Years'-Digits Depreciation

The double declining-balance method uses twice the straight-line depreciation rate

This precise declining-balance method can be replaced with a very simple and reasonably close approximation, which makes the complex formula unnecessary and which brings us to what we mean by "double declining-balance depreciation."

Instead of a complex formula, calculate the percentage that would result if you used the straight-line method—*but* double that percentage and apply it to the remaining balance (book value) each year.

Returning to our basic example to see how this works, consider the following steps:

Double declining-balance procedure

STEP 1: Determine, as for a straight-line method, the percentage used to calculate the depreciation expense in each year of its useful life. The percentage is the reciprocal of the number of years of useful life; that is,

$$\frac{1}{\text{number of years of useful life}}$$

For example, an asset with a 10-year life has a straight-line depreciation rate or percentage of $\frac{1}{10}$ or 10% in each year.

STEP 2: Double the percentage rate calculated in step 1.

$$2 \times \tfrac{1}{10} = \tfrac{2}{10} \text{ or } 20\%$$

Hint: Whenever the rate contains a repeating decimal, use the fraction rather than the decimal equivalent. For example, $\frac{1}{3} = .333$ (use $\frac{1}{3}$), $\frac{1}{12} = .0833$ (use $\frac{1}{12}$). Using the fraction will make your calculations easier and more accurate.

STEP 3: Apply this percentage rate to the acquisition cost of the asset (*do not* deduct salvage). This will yield year 1 depreciation expense.

$$\text{Year 1 depreciation expense} = 20\% \times \$125,000$$
$$= \$25,000$$

STEP 4: For each succeeding year multiply the percentage calculated in step 2 by the book value at the beginning of that year. (Remember, book value is cost minus all prior depreciation.)
(*a*) Year 2 depreciation expense = 20% ($125,000 − $25,000) = $20,000
(*b*) Year 3 depreciation expense = 20% ($125,000 − $25,000 − $20,000) = $16,000
(*c*) And so on

The schedule below shows the depreciation for each of the 10 years. Note that the double declining-balance method will not usually depreciate the cost down to exactly

Year	Book Value at Beginning of Year (cost − prior depreciation)	× Depreciation Rate =	Double Declining-Balance Depreciation Expense
1	$125,000	.20	$ 25,000
2	100,000	.20	20,000
3	80,000	.20	16,000
4	64,000	.20	12,800
5	51,200	.20	10,240
6	40,960	.20	8,192
7	32,768	.20	6,554
8	26,214	.20	5,243
9	20,971	.20	4,194
10	16,777	*	1,777

Total depreciated $110,000

* Note: Since salvage is $15,000, the final-year depreciation is limited to $1,777 ($16,777 − $15,000), *not* .20 × $16,777 = $3,355.

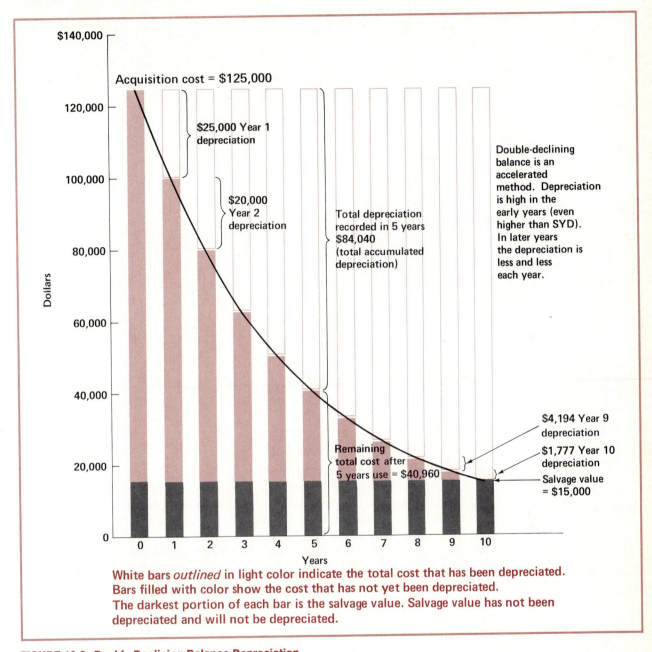

Acquisition cost = $125,000

$25,000 Year 1
depreciation

$20,000
Year 2
depreciation

Total depreciation
recorded in 5 years
$84,040
(total accumulated
depreciation)

Double-declining
balance is an
accelerated
method. Depreciation
is high in the
early years (even
higher than SYD).
In later years
the depreciation is
less and less
each year.

Remaining
total cost after
5 years use = $40,960

$4,194 Year 9
depreciation

$1,777 Year 10
depreciation

Salvage value
= $15,000

White bars *outlined* in light color indicate the total cost that has been depreciated.
Bars filled with color show the cost that has not yet been depreciated.
The darkest portion of each bar is the salvage value. Salvage value has not been
depreciated and will not be depreciated.

FIGURE 10-3   Double Declining-Balance Depreciation

*Be careful not to depreciate
an asset to an amount
below its salvage value*

salvage value over the useful life. (Remember, the double declining-balance rate is
just an approximation of the precise declining-balance rate.) It may be necessary,
then, to adjust the amount of depreciation in the final year so as not to depreciate
below the salvage value. Sometimes it may be necessary to record no depreciation in
the final year or years of the asset's useful life. *When using the double declining-balance method, depreciate down to salvage value and then stop depreciating.*

The double declining-balance method of depreciation is reviewed in Figure 10-3.

Depreciation Methods Compared

The straight-line, sum-of-the-years'-digits, and double declining-balance methods produce depreciation expense amounts that follow a pattern. We have shown you these patterns for each method numerically and graphically. As a review let's look at all three methods side by side, first in a table and then graphically as illustrated in Figure 10-4.

$$\text{Total amount to be depreciated} = \text{acquisition cost less salvage}$$
$$= \$125,000 - \$15,000$$
$$= \$110,000$$

Comparison of the yearly depreciation expense under three methods

Year	Straight Line	Sum of the Years' Digits	Double Declining Balance
1	$ 11,000	$ 20,000	$ 25,000
2	11,000	18,000	20,000
3	11,000	16,000	16,000
4	11,000	14,000	12,800
5	11,000	12,000	10,240
6	11,000	10,000	8,192
7	11,000	8,000	6,554
8	11,000	6,000	5,243
9	11,000	4,000	4,194
10	11,000	2,000	1,777
	$110,000	$110,000	$110,000

Depreciation — Balance Sheet Disclosure

Earlier, we indicated that depreciation expense is recorded by debiting a Depreciation Expense account and crediting an Accumulated Depreciation account. Because depreciation is a measure of how much of an asset's service benefits have been used, why not just credit the asset account? Why bother with an Accumulated Depreciation account? Perhaps the following illustration will help answer these questions.

Suppose that you come across the following disclosure of the property, plant, and equipment section on a balance sheet:

Property, Plant, and Equipment:	
Land	$1,000,000
Building	500,000
Total	$1,500,000

*(Note: This is **not** the correct disclosure of the Building asset.)*

Reporting the building in this way doesn't give the balance sheet reader enough information. Any one of a number of underlying factual situations might exist. Let's look at two extreme possibilities for this same disclosure:

Possibility 1		
Property, Plant, and Equipment:		
Land		$1,000,000
Building	$15,000,000	
Less: Accumulated Depreciation......................	14,500,000	500,000
Total		$1,500,000
Possibility 2		
Property, Plant, and Equipment:		
Land		$1,000,000
Building	$650,000	
Less: Accumulated Depreciation......................	150,000	500,000
Total		$1,500,000

In this case, the building is nearly fully depreciated (describes Possibility 1)

In this case, the building is only partially depreciated (describes Possibility 2)

The original disclosure, which we should see as an incorrect way to report a depreciable asset, does show a total of $1,500,000 of property, plant, and equipment assets, but it does not reveal whether the building is almost fully depreciated as is the case in possibility 1, or if it has a large proportion of its cost still to be depreciated as is

FIGURE 10-4
A Comparison of the Straight-Line, Sum-of-the-Years'-Digits, and Double Declining-Balance Methods of Determining Depreciation
Each depreciation line shows the decline in book value from acquisition cost to salvage value.

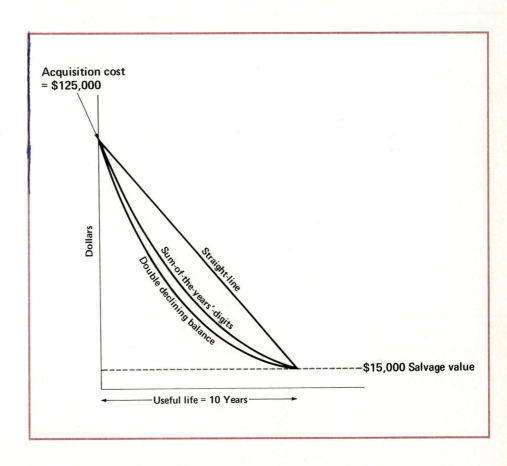

the case in possibility 2. Specific information about depreciation is very important to the statement reader.

If possibility 1 is the actual situation, it could mean that the company is going to need a new building in the near future. The company, therefore, is either going to have to raise a large sum of money to purchase one or perhaps lease a new building.

If possibility 2 is the actual situation, the company can continue to operate for some time before its present building will be worn out.

*Why we use an
Accumulated Depreciation
contra account*

The disclosure of the Accumulated Depreciation contra account gives the statement reader the information necessary to make a rough approximation of the portion of the asset used up and an idea of how long it will be before the company will have to make a large capital outlay to replace it.

Property, Plant and Equipment:		
Land		$ 5,000,000
Building	$12,000,000	
Less: Accumulated Depreciation......................	1,500,000	10,500,000
Machinery	$ 2,300,000	
Less: Accumulated Depreciation......................	1,800,000	500,000
Office Equipment	$ 250,000	
Less: Accumulated Depreciation......................	45,000	205,000
Total		$16,205,000

(Note: This is the correct way to disclose property, plant, and equipment assets.)

The depreciation method used for each type of asset and its estimated life are indicated in footnotes to the financial statements. Depreciation Expense appears on the income statement.

Depreciation and Cash

Depreciation spreads an asset's cost over its useful life. The accountant accomplishes this by debiting an expense account and crediting a contra-asset account at the end of each period.

The point we want to make here is that cash is never a part of a depreciation transaction. Any depreciation expense entry clearly shows that Cash is neither debited nor credited.

Furthermore, an Accumulated Depreciation account shows the total portion of an asset's cost that has been charged to expense through the end of a current period — that is, it represents that part of the asset's total available bundle of service that has been used up. Perhaps this is the best way to think of an Accumulated Depreciation account. It should help to make clear that accumulated depreciation does not represent accumulated cash. Sometimes students get the idea that Accumulated Depreciation is an account that sets aside cash for replacing the asset. Not so.

*Recording depreciation
does not provide cash for
replacing an asset*

The cost of replacing assets may be financed through borrowing, by leasing, or by using cash that has been set aside for this purpose. None of these transactions has anything to do with depreciation.

Depreciation and Income Taxes

The depreciation methods discussed thus far are those that have been used traditionally to measure depreciation expense for the purpose of preparing income statements and balance sheets. These methods attempt to allocate an asset's cost over its useful life in proportion to the benefits received in each year.

In preparing financial statements we are bound by the rules of good accounting theory. In preparing income tax returns we are required to use the rules specified in the tax laws. Sometimes tax rules and good accounting theory agree; many times they do not. Depreciation is one area in which we probably use different calculations for financial accounting purposes from those we use for tax purposes. You have learned the financial accounting methods; now let's take a simplified look at the tax rules.

Beginning with the 1987 tax law, depreciable assets were classified as having 3-year, 5-year, 7-year, 10-year, 15-year, 20-year, $27\frac{1}{2}$-year, and $31\frac{1}{2}$-year write-off periods. (We will call these tax lives.) Certain types of assets were placed into each of these eight classifications. Almost always the actual useful life of an asset is longer than the tax life. For example, the 5-year tax life includes cars and light-duty trucks; and the $31\frac{1}{2}$-year tax life includes nonresidential property.

In calculating tax depreciation for assets purchased after 1986, you may use the accelerated cost recovery system (ACRS) or a straight-line method. To calculate ACRS depreciation you simply take the cost of the asset (do *not* deduct salvage value) and multiply by a percentage in the table below. The percentage used depends on the tax life of the property and the year of the asset's life. The percentages to be used in each year of 3-year, 5-year, and 7-year tax life assets are shown below:

	3-Year Tax Life	5-Year Tax Life	7-Year Tax Life
Year 1	33.33%	20.00%	14.28%
Year 2	44.44	32.00	24.49
Year 3	14.82	19.20	17.49
Year 4	7.41	11.52	12.50
Year 5		11.52	8.92
Year 6		5.76	8.92
Year 7			8.92
Year 8			4.48
Total	100.00%	100.00%	100.00%

To find 1989 tax depreciation for an automobile purchased for $16,000 any time during 1989, you simply multiply 20% × $16,000 and derive $3,200 as your depreciation deduction. In 1990 and 1991 your deductions will be $5,120 (32% × $16,000) and $3,072 (19.20% × $16,000), respectively.

The tax law still allows you to use straight-line depreciation for tax purposes, but the calculations are a little different from the straight-line method you already know. The differences are:

1. You ignore the actual life and use the 3-, 5-, 7-, 10-, etc., year tax lives.

2. You ignore salvage value.

3. You must take $\frac{1}{2}$ year's depreciation in the first year no matter when during the year the asset was purchased. This also means that you will take $\frac{1}{2}$ year's depreciation in the last year.

DOUBLE STANDARD

by Jill Andresky

One of the old standbys for financial officers when times got tough has always been to try to pick up earnings by slowing depreciation charges.

Last year's Accelerated Cost Recovery System only made that easier by effectively permitting companies to depreciate plant and equipment at different rates for tax and accounting purposes. Says Ronald Murray, Coopers & Lybrand's director of accounting and SEC technical services: "Now you can have a slower book depreciation schedule, which helps financial statements, and yet still stay with fast depreciation for tax purposes, which helps cash flow."

Changing depreciation schedules can make quite a difference for a company. Inland Steel, which recently slowed down its depreciation, will reduce this year's losses by $43 million. (Inland made only $57 million last year.)

The easiest way to lower depreciation charges is to switch from accelerated depreciation to straight-line, where the same sum gets written off every year.

Those companies who want to lower their depreciation even further in hard times can switch to the units-of-output method, where charges are tied not to time but to production volume. In this way a plant running at 40% of capacity generates 60% lower depreciation charges. Ernst & Whinney's Denny Beresford, partner in charge of accounting standards, expects that more companies will follow the lead of Inland Steel by switching to units-of-output depreciation.

For the investor, several questions remain so far unresolved. What about the problem of technological obsolescence, for example? Any slow method of depreciation might well encourage management to keep a piece of machinery in operation long after

far superior replacements become available. The risk is great with units of output, especially in slow times.

Beresford raises a related issue: quality of earnings. "Some people would view a company that uses accelerated depreciation as being more conservative in its financial reporting and thus having a higher quality of earnings," he comments. IBM, for example, is still using the so-called sum-of-the-years'-digits method, which raises depreciation charges dramatically in the early years of an asset's life and then slows down as time goes on. As Beresford puts it: "A company changing away from accelerated to straight line might be viewed by some people as reporting at that time lower quality earnings."

Source: Forbes, Nov. 22, 1982, page 178.

Companies may change depreciation methods during an asset's life, if they have good theoretical justification for doing so. This article points out that some companies switch methods for apparently no reason other than to make their income statement income higher.

How does fast tax depreciation "help cash flow"? Use of ACRS depreciation means that taxable income will be lower than income statement income. Thus, the company will pay less income taxes—a cash savings.

The article implies that companies whose assets are not fully depreciated will continue to use them even though technologically superior assets exist. This short-sighted decision making may hurt the company in the long run. You will learn more about using accounting information to make *good* business decisions in the second volume of this two volume set, *Managerial Accounting*.

Tax straight-line depreciation for our 5-year-life asset automobile would be as follows:

Year 1	$16,000/5 years $\times \frac{1}{2}$ year	=	$ 1,600
Year 2	$16,000/5 years	=	3,200
Year 3	$16,000/5 years	=	3,200
Year 4	$16,000/5 years	=	3,200
Year 5	$16,000/3 years	=	3,200
Year 6	$16,000/5 years $\times \frac{1}{2}$ year	=	1,600
Total tax depreciation			$16,000

ACRS and tax straight-line depreciation usually offer a tax advantage. Since the tax life of an asset is generally shorter than the actual useful life, the depreciation deduction on the tax return is higher in the early years of an asset's life than the depreciation expense on the income statement—the higher the tax deduction, the lower the taxes due in those early years. Of course the time will come when the depreciation deduction on the tax return reaches zero while the depreciation deduction on the income statement continues. When this happens, the taxes due will be higher than the tax expense. What all this means is that, by using the tax depreciation methods, we have *postponed* the payment of taxes—a definite advantage when you remember that we have those dollars to invest until the taxes are due in a later year.

Our purpose in introducing you to tax depreciation is to emphasize that financial accounting and tax accounting are often very different and to show you that as a businessperson it may be important for you to know the major differences between accounting and tax rules. More information about income taxes is contained in the Appendix.

Depletion

For the purpose of explaining the basic idea behind depreciating an asset, we suggested that the asset might be considered as a total bundle of services that are used up during its lifetime. Depletion is like depreciation, although it is less conceptual and more tangible. You can see the service bundles being used up.

The same idea behind depreciation is applied to the depletion of a natural resource. A natural resource is what its name implies: It is a resource existing naturally —not constructed by humans. Examples of typical natural resources are deposits of coal, oil, iron ore, phosphate, and other minerals. These natural resources are typically used as raw materials in the production of other goods.

A quantity of a natural resource can be considered as consisting of a total bundle of materials—tons of coal, barrels of oil, etc.—available from it. As these materials are removed, a part of the natural resource is used up—depleted. The amount of the materials used up can be measured with a fair amount of accuracy. **Depletion** is the allocation of the cost of the part of a natural resource estimated to be used up in an accounting period. Depletion is calculated in exactly the same way as the units-of-output depreciation is calculated—and it is the only acceptable way to calculate depletion (there are no accelerated ways of calculating depletion).

Depletion is the allocation of the cost of a natural resource over its life as it is physically used up

The cost and salvage value of the natural resource are determined, along with an estimate of the total number of units (tons, barrels, etc.) that it is capable of producing. The cost less salvage is divided by the estimated total units. The result is depletion per unit produced. The following is an example.

Eureka Mining Co. paid $3,800,000 for a piece of land, including mining rights. Geologists estimated that 15,000,000 tons of uranium could be mined from this plot. Appraisers estimated that the land could be sold for $800,000 after mining is completed. Eureka mined 1,000,000 tons of uranium in year 1 and 3,000,000 tons in year 2.

The calculation of depletion per unit, and the journal entries to record the depletion in each year, are as follows:

$$\text{Depletion per ton} = \frac{\text{cost of property} - \text{salvage value of property}}{\text{total number of tons of uranium}}$$

$$= \frac{\$3,800,000 - \$800,000}{15,000,000 \text{ tons}}$$

$$= \frac{\$3,000,000}{15,000,000 \text{ tons}}$$

$$= \$0.20 \text{ per ton}$$

Year 1
Dec. 31   Depletion Expense.................................... 200,000
         Uranium Mining Property   200,000
         To record depletion for year 1. ($0.20 per ton × 1,000,000
         tons = $200,000)

Year 2
Dec. 31   Depletion Expense.................................... 600,000
         Uranium Mining Property   600,000
         To record depletion for year 2. ($0.20 per ton × 3,000,000
         tons = $600,000)

Observe that the asset was credited in this case rather than a contra-asset account. This is customary, probably because a mineral deposit is not replaceable in the same way that a machine or a building is. Exploration and discovery are necessary, if replacement is possible at all.

Footnotes to the financial statements will provide the reader with information about the number of tons mined in the current period and the total number of tons still in the ground.

Disposal of Property, Plant, and Equipment

As assets wear out, become obsolete, or are no longer needed, the business may decide to sell them or trade them in on new ones.

An asset "depreciates" up to the point in time when it is no longer in use or until it is fully depreciated — whichever comes first. By *fully depreciated* we mean that all of the cost except salvage value has been depreciated. Theoretically, when an asset is fully depreciated, all of those bundles of service benefits have been used up. If a mistake has been made in estimating an asset's useful life, the company may still be using it even though it may be fully depreciated. When this happens, we stop recording depreciation but leave the cost of the asset and its accumulated depreciation on the company's financial records. When the company stops getting benefits from the asset, it is sold, traded, or written off.

Example A: Asset Written Off at the End of the Period

Flax Co. owns a machine that had cost $20,000. Accumulated depreciation through Dec. 31, 1989, is $20,000.

The machine is fully depreciated; it doesn't even have a salvage value. (It would cost more to sell it than it would be worth.) Flax takes it to the city dump.

The machine is written off by the following entry:

*Writing off a fully
depreciated machine*

Dec. 31   Accumulated Depreciation: Machine 20,000
         Machine...   20,000
         To write off a fully depreciated machine removed from service
         and disposed of.

Example B: Asset Sold Immediately after the End of the Period

Ogle, Inc., owns a machine that had cost $100,000 and had accumulated depreciation through Dec. 31, 1989, of $45,000. The machine was sold on Jan. 1, 1990, for $70,000.

The gain or loss on the sale is calculated as follows:

Selling price of asset..		$70,000
Less: Book value of asset:		
Cost	$100,000	
Less: Accumulated depreciation...........................	45,000	55,000
Gain on sale of asset		$15,000

When we sell an asset for more than its book value, we record a gain

Jan. 1	Cash...	70,000	
	Accumulated Depreciation: Machine.......................	45,000	
	Machine		100,000
	Gain on Sale of Machine		15,000
	To record sale of machine on Jan. 1, 1990.		

Observe that the machine was removed from the general ledger by crediting the Machinery account for its *cost*.

Accumulated depreciation on this machine was eliminated by debiting Accumulated Depreciation: Machine for the total recorded through Dec. 31, 1989.

The Gain on Sale of Machine would be shown on the income statement under "Other Gains and Losses." Losses on sales (or exchanges) of assets also would be presented in this section of the income statement.

Example C: Asset Sold during an Accounting Period

Hawke Co. owns a building that originally cost $189,000, has an estimated useful life of 10 years, and has a $9,000 salvage value. The building was purchased on Jan. 1, 1984, and was used continuously until it was sold on Oct. 1, 1990, for $65,000.

The building was shown on the Dec. 31, 1989, balance sheet as follows:

Building...	$189,000	
Less: Accumulated Depreciation	108,000*	$81,000

* Calculation of accumulated depreciation, using straight-line depreciation:

$$\frac{\$189,000 - \$9,000}{10 \text{ years}} \times 6 \text{ years } (1984-1989) = \$18,000 \text{ per year} \times 6 \text{ years} = \$108,000$$

Partial year depreciation must be recorded when an asset is sold during a year

For the year in which the building is sold, the depreciation must be recorded for the part of the year that the asset was used. In this case, the building was used for 9 months, up through Sept. 30, the day before the sale. This adjustment will bring total lifetime accumulated depreciation right up to date prior to recording the sale.

1990			
Oct. 1	Depreciation Expense	13,500	
	Accumulated Depreciation: Building....................		13,500
	To record 9 months depreciation.		
	[($189,000 − $9,000)/10 years = $18,000 per year $\times \frac{9}{12}$ = $13,500]		

To calculate the gain or loss on the sale:

<table>
<tr><td>Selling price of building...</td><td></td><td>$65,000</td></tr>
<tr><td>Less: Book value of building:</td><td></td><td></td></tr>
<tr><td>   Cost...</td><td>$189,000</td><td></td></tr>
<tr><td>   Less: Total accumulated depreciation since acquisition</td><td></td><td></td></tr>
<tr><td>   ($108,000 + $13,500) ....</td><td>121,500</td><td>67,500</td></tr>
<tr><td>Loss on sale of building...</td><td></td><td>$ (2,500)</td></tr>
</table>

When we sell an asset for less than its book value, we record a loss

The entry to record the sale is:

```
1990
Oct. 1   Cash .................................................   65,000
         Accumulated Depreciation: Building.......................  121,500
         Loss on Sale of Building ................................   2,500
              Building ..........................................            189,000
         To record sale of building.
```

When recording sales of long-lived assets, remember:

Guidelines for recording the sale of a long-lived asset

1. Record its depreciation from the date acquired up to the day of sale.

2. Recognize the gain or loss on the sale.

A gain is indicated when we receive more for an asset than its book value (book value = original cost less accumulated depreciation).

A loss is indicated when we receive less for an asset than its book value.

When assets are traded for similar ones, a loss may be recorded, but not a gain

Similarly, when an asset is traded in on a new one, depreciation is recorded up to the date of the trade. Such a trade is commonly a transaction in which the old asset plus some cash is exchanged for a new asset much like the old one. If the old asset is traded for a new one of a *similar type,* the cost of the new asset equals the book value of the old asset (original cost minus its accumulated depreciation) plus the amount of cash given. In no case may the new asset be carried at more than its actual fair market value. This fair market value limitation may result in a *loss* being recorded on the trade. Good accounting theory prohibits the recognition of gains on trades of similar assets when cash is paid out. The following examples will clarify these rules governing trades of similar assets.

Example D: Asset Traded for a Similar One—No Gain or Loss Indicated

Fiske, Inc., traded a delivery van that originally cost $12,500 and has an accumulated depreciation of $8,500 for a new van having a fair market price of $19,000. (The van's list price is $21,500, but it has been selling for $19,000 regularly at dealers in the area.) Fiske agreed to give the old van and $15,000 in exchange for the new one. The cost of the new van is:

The cost of a new asset cannot be higher than its fair market value

<table>
<tr><td>Cost of old van ....</td><td>$12,500</td></tr>
<tr><td>Less: Accumulated depreciation on old van ....</td><td>8,500</td></tr>
<tr><td>= Book value of old van ....</td><td>$ 4,000</td></tr>
<tr><td>+ Cash paid..</td><td>15,000</td></tr>
<tr><td>= Cost of new van ....</td><td>$19,000</td></tr>
</table>

In this case the cost of the new van is equal to its fair market price. That is, the book value of the two assets given up (old van, $4,000 plus cash, $15,000) is the same as the fair market price ($19,000 for a new van).

Let's calculate the gain or loss as we did in the previous examples:

No gain or loss is recognized when the book value of the assets given equal the fair market value of the asset received

Exchange value of old van (selling price of old van is the value we receive — the market value of the new van)	$ 19,000
Less book value of all assets given:	
Book value of old van ($12,500 − $8,500)	(4,000)
Book value of cash given	(15,000)
Gain or (loss)	$ -0-

The entry to record the exchange is:

Jan. 2	Delivery Equipment (new van)	19,000	
	Accumulated Depreciation (on old van)	8,500	
	Delivery Equipment (old van)		12,500
	Cash		15,000
	To record trade of old van for a new one.		

Example E: Asset Traded for a Similar One — Gain Indicated but Not Recorded

Assume the same facts as in Example D except that Fiske acquires the new van in exchange for the old van and $10,000 cash. The cost of the new van is:

Book value of old van ($12,500 − $8,500)	$ 4,000
+ Cash paid	10,000
= Cost of new van	$14,000

When the fair market value of the asset acquired is higher than the book value of the assets given, the cost of the new asset equals the book value of the assets given

Our gain or loss calculation reveals that a gain is indicated:

Exchange value of old van (selling price of old van is the value we receive — the market value of the new van)	$ 19,000
Less book value of all assets given:	
Book value of old van ($12,500 − $8,500)	(4,000)
Book value of cash given	(10,000)
Gain or (loss)	$ 5,000

No gain is recorded when assets are exchanged

Good accounting theory says that we cannot recognize this gain because we didn't sell the old asset for cash or another current asset. This is said to be an "unrealized" gain because we didn't receive a liquid asset such as cash.

Since we can't recognize the gain, we can't record the new van at its fair market value—$19,000—we must record it at the book value of the assets we gave for it—$14,000 ($4,000 old van plus $10,000 cash).

The entry to record the exchange is:

Jan. 2	Delivery Equipment (new van)	14,000	
	Accumulated Depreciation (old van)	8,500	
	Delivery Equipment (old van)		12,500
	Cash		10,000
	To record trade of old van for a new one.		

Example F: Asset Traded for a Similar One—Loss Indicated and Recorded

Assume the same facts as in Example D except that Fiske acquires the new van in exchange for the old van and $18,000. The cost of the new van is $19,000. The prior method of calculation would yield a cost of $22,000:

Cost of old van	$12,500
Less: Accumulated depreciation on old van	8,500
= Book value of old van	$ 4,000
+ Cash paid	18,000
= Cost of new van (tentative)	$22,000

When the fair market value of the asset acquired is lower than the book value of the assets given, the cost of the new asset equals the fair market value of the asset acquired

Fiske can't record the new van at $22,000 because this is more than it is worth—it has a fair market value of $19,000. Generally accepted accounting principles will not allow Fiske to record the van at more than its fair market value.

The gain or loss calculation sheds some light on what really happened:

Exchange value of old van (selling price of old van is the value we receive—the market value of the new van)	$ 19,000
Less book value of all assets given:	
Book value of old van ($12,500 − $8,500)	(4,000)
Book value of cash given	(18,000)
Gain or (loss)	$ (3,000)

Fiske will be required to record a loss on this transaction because the book value of the two assets given up (the old van, $4,000 plus cash, $18,000) is $3,000 more than the value of the asset acquired ($19,000). The entry to record the exchange is:

Jan. 2	Delivery Equipment (new van)	19,000	
	Accumulated Depreciation (old van)	8,500	
	Loss on Trade of Equipment	3,000	
	Delivery Equipment (old van)		12,500
	Cash		18,000
	To record trade of old van for a new one.		

Losses may be recorded when assets are exchanged

The justification for requiring the recognition of a loss but not allowing the recognition of a gain is the principle of conservatism. The ***principle of conservatism*** requires that losses should be recognized when incurred, but gains should be deferred until cash or another liquid asset is received.

Remember to follow these rules when recording an exchange of one long-lived asset for a similar one:

Rules for recording exchanges of similar long-lived assets

1. Cost of the new asset is recognized and recorded as the *lesser* of:
   a. The book value of all assets given to acquire the new one, or
   b. The fair market value of the new one.

2. Gains are not recognized on exchanges of similar assets. (Gains are recognized on sales of assets.)

3. Losses are recognized on exchanges of similar assets.

4. Depreciation of old assets given up must be recorded up to the date of the trade.

INTANGIBLE ASSETS

Intangible assets lack physical substance and are not held for investment

.

Long-lived assets that (1) lack physical substance and (2) are not held for investment are classified as *intangible assets.*

Short-lived assets such as accounts receivable and prepaid expenses lack physical substance and are not investments but they are not classified as intangible assets — they are classified as current assets.

Similarly, long-term investments in stocks and bonds are not classified as intangibles — they are classified according to their purpose; they are investments.

Cost of Intangible Assets

The acquisition cost of intangible assets is determined by using the same general rule as for property, plant, and equipment:

The same cost rule is used for intangible and tangible assets

All reasonable and necessary costs to get an asset in position and condition ready for use may be included as part of the cost of the asset.

An intangible can be acquired, such as a patent bought from an inventor, or it can be created internally such as a copyright for an advertising jingle created by an employee of your advertising department. In either case, the cost of acquisition or the cost of development is included as part of an intangible's total cost. Legal fees, costs of filing documents with government agencies and costs of defending ownership, are other costs commonly associated with intangibles.

Because it is sometimes difficult to establish the existence of an asset that lacks physical substance, we must be very careful in the case of internally created intangibles. When we spend money we may be buying future benefits (an asset) or we may be deriving all benefits now (an expense). If we charge an amount to an asset account when an expense should have been used, we have understated expenses on the income statement and overstated net income.

Factors to consider in determining the cost of various intangible assets

The following are some common intangibles and the problems in measuring their cost and the using up of this cost.

Patents are exclusive rights granted by the U.S. government permitting one person or firm to manufacture, use, and sell a certain product. Polaroid film is a good example of a product manufactured under a patent. The owner of a patent may allow others to make and sell the product, usually charging a fee for this right. A patent is granted for a period of 17 years, although the product it protects may become obsolete in a much shorter time. When that happens the patent's useful life may be less than its 17-year legal life.

The costs of bringing successful suits against those who seek to copy a product — patent infringement suits — are considered a part of the cost of the patent. Unsuccessful patent infringement suits mean that the court ruled that the defendants didn't copy your product, or if they did, that they had a right to do so. The result of an unsuccessful suit may be that you no longer have a patent.

Patents can be purchased from their owners. Patents purchased from others are good only until the originally granted 17-year life expires. For example, a 16-year-old patent if purchased will provide rights to the purchaser for only one more year.

Copyrights are rights granted by the U.S. government for the exclusive use of a literary or artistic work for the creator's life plus 50 years. The copyright gives the creator, heirs, or persons to whom the right has been sold the exclusive right to publish or reproduce the work for this period of time.

The cost of obtaining a copyright is very small, only the cost of completing a form and the payment of a small fee to the U.S. Copyright Office. The cost of a copyright purchased from an author, however, may be very high. Can you imagine how much it might cost to purchase the copyright to the *Star Wars* movies?

Goodwill represents a number of intangible advantages such as superior operating efficiency, an unusually well-trained sales force, excellent client relations or public relations, an outstanding reputation or image in the marketplace, and an advantageous location. A firm that has all or many of these advantages has *goodwill* and will earn a higher return on its income-producing assets than will a firm having the same assets but not having goodwill.

Goodwill is recorded only when it is purchased

Goodwill is one of those internally created assets that is almost impossible to value, especially with any degree of objectivity. Nevertheless, goodwill can be acquired—but not by itself—it comes along with all the other tangible and intangible assets comprising the firm acquired. And, it is only at acquisition that goodwill can be objectively valued, and that's when it is recorded. The value of goodwill is the part of the total acquisition cost that cannot be assigned to the other assets acquired, as the following example illustrates.

Roof Company agreed to purchase all of the assets of Branch, Inc., for $530,000. The net assets (total assets minus total liabilities) on Branch's balance sheet were $385,000 and their fair market value, the amount for which they could be sold, at the time totaled $505,000. The negotiated price of Branch was higher than the total market value of the individual assets because Branch had consistently been able to earn a much higher rate of return on its assets than other firms in the industry. Roof Company therefore recorded goodwill of $25,000 (acquisition price of total asset package $530,000 less the total market value of the assets acquired $505,000 = $25,000).

Franchises are rights to sell a specific brand of products or services in a certain geographic area. Franchise agreements to operate a fast food restaurant such as McDonalds or Burger King probably come to mind immediately. Many municipalities grant franchises to private firms to provide such services as garbage removal, cable television, and electric power. The cost of the franchise includes payments made in advance of operating the franchised business, and legal fees for preparing contracts specifying the terms of the franchise agreement.

Trademarks are exclusive rights to use a certain name or symbol for an unlimited future period. For a new trademark, the initial cost of these assets may be quite small, consisting of the artist's fee to develop a symbol and a nominal filing fee to register the trademark with a government agency. The cost of acquiring an established and a well-known trademark may involve substantial sums—imagine what it would cost to purchase the name Coke or Pepsi, if this were even possible.

Organization costs are expenditures made in establishing a business. Organization costs include attorney's fees for drawing up a partnership agreement or articles of incorporation (the legal document creating a corporation), and fees paid to state and local governments to register as a business organization. The costs of organizing a business provide benefits for the life of the business. These costs are considered to be an intangible asset.

Amortization of Intangibles

Amortization is the process of allocating the cost of an intangible over its useful life

The process of allocating the cost of an intangible asset over all the periods it provides benefits is called *amortization.* Intangibles are normally amortized on a straight-line basis unless some other system can be shown to be clearly preferable. Straight-line amortization is identical to straight-line depreciation:

$$\text{Amortization per year} = \frac{\text{cost of intangible asset} - \text{salvage value}}{\text{number of years of useful life}}$$

Straight-line amortization is calculated just like straight-line depreciation

The *cost* of specific intangibles is determined by applying the general acquisition-cost rule.

Generally, an intangible asset has no *salvage value.* At the end of an intangible's life there is nothing of value left.

The *useful life* of an intangible may be much less than its legal life; a patent, for example, may provide benefits for 5 years instead of the legal maximum of 17. In any case, authoritative accounting rules establish an arbitrary maximum of 40 years for the amortization of any intangible. A copyright with a possible 90-year life usually loses substantially all of its economic usefulness over a period of 40 years or less. Goodwill has such an indeterminate life that some maximum was needed.

For example, Lee Company purchased a patent from Grant, Inc., for $17,500. The remaining legal life of the patent is 12 years, but Lee believes that it will be useful for only 7 years. The calculation of the amortization and the annual journal entry to record amortization is as follows:

$$\text{Amortization per year} = \frac{\$17,500 - 0}{7 \text{ years}} = \$2,500 \text{ per year}$$

Dec. 31 Patent Amortization Expense 2,500
          Patents 2,500
          To record patent amortization for the year.

Accumulated amortization accounts are not customarily used for intangibles, since these assets are difficult if not impossible to replace at the end of their useful lives. Appropriate footnotes disclose the estimated useful lives of intangibles.

CHAPTER SUMMARY

Property, plant, and equipment is a balance sheet classification that includes all *tangible long-lived assets* owned by a business and used in its operations to help produce revenues. The acquisition cost of a tangible long-lived asset includes all reasonable and necessary costs to get it in position and condition ready for use. Common property, plant, and equipment assets include land, buildings, machinery, equipment, and natural resources.

Expenditures made after the acquisition may be added to the cost of the asset— *capital expenditures*—or charged to expense—*revenue expenditures.* The asset account is increased whenever the expenditure benefits several future accounting periods. An expense account is debited when only the current accounting period is benefited.

Allocating the cost of a property, plant, and equipment asset (other than a natural resource) over its useful life is called *depreciation.* Depreciation results from physical wear-and-tear as well as from technical obsolescence.

Straight-line depreciation allocates an equal cost to each time period; *units-of-output depreciation* allocates an equal cost to each unit produced.

The *sum-of-the-years'-digits* and *double declining-balance* methods recognize higher depreciation amounts in the early years of an asset's life when it is more productive and requires less maintenance; as a result, lower depreciation is recognized in later years when the asset is less efficient.

Property, plant, and equipment assets are disclosed on the balance sheet at original cost. For assets other than land, an Accumulated Depreciation account is also shown as a subtraction from the cost amount. The difference between the balances in these two accounts—the asset and the accumulated depreciation—gives the statement reader a rough idea as to how long it will be before the asset must be replaced. This difference is the amount of the undepreciated cost.

Depreciation methods used for income tax calculations are different from those used in financial accounting. Tax laws assign an arbitrary life to assets instead of using their actual useful lives. *Accelerated cost recovery system (ACRS)* and a special form of straight-line depreciation are allowed for calculating tax depreciation.

Depletion is similar to depreciation; depletion is allocation of the cost of a natural resource that has been consumed. An equal cost is assigned to each unit produced.

When a property, plant, and equipment asset is sold, the depreciation must be accrued up until the date of sale. When the selling price exceeds its book value, a gain is recognized. If book value is larger than the selling price, a loss is recorded.

The balance sheet classification *Intangible Assets* includes a firm's long-lived assets that lack physical substance but are used in its operations. The acquisition cost of an intangible is amortized over its useful life, usually on a straight-line basis. A maximum life of 40 years is allowed. Common intangible assets are patents, copyrights, goodwill, and franchises.

IMPORTANT TERMS USED IN THIS CHAPTER

Accelerated cost recovery system (ACRS) A method of calculating depreciation for income tax purposes. The method may be used for assets placed in service after 1980. Depreciation each year is calculated by multiplying a prescribed percentage by the asset's cost. (page 413)

Accumulated depreciation The total part of the cost of a property, plant, and equipment asset that is considered to be "consumed" and that has been charged to depreciation expense. (page 410)

Amortization Allocation of the cost of an intangible asset over its useful life. (page 422)

Book value An asset's total cost less its accumulated depreciation. (page 418)

Capital expenditures Costs incurred for assets that provide benefits over several accounting periods. (page 401)

Copyright A right granted by the U.S. government for the exclusive use of a literary or artistic work for the creator's life plus 50 years. (page 421)

Depletion Allocation of a natural resource's cost estimated to be used up in a time period. An equal cost is assigned to each unit of natural resource extracted. (page 415)

Depreciation Allocation of the total cost of a tangible long-lived asset over its useful life. (page 401)

Double declining-balance depreciation A system of allocating an asset's cost over its useful life in decreasing amounts each year. Depreciation per year is calculated by multiplying a fixed percentage (twice the straight-line rate) by the asset's declining book value. (page 406)

Franchise The exclusive right to sell a specific brand of products or services in a certain geographic area. (page 422)

Goodwill If the acquisition price of a business is more than the fair market value of its net assets, the excess is the cost of that business's goodwill. (page 422)

Intangible assets Assets that lack physical substance but that are an important part of a business's operations. (A balance sheet classification.) (page 421)

Organization costs Costs incurred to establish a business. (page 422)

Patent A right granted by the U.S. government for the exclusive manufacture, use, and sale of a certain product for a 17-year period. (page 421)

Property, plant, and equipment Tangible long-lived assets owned by a business and used in its operations. (A balance sheet classification.) (page 397)

Relative-value allocation The allocation of the total cost of a group of assets among each asset based on the value of each asset relative to the value of the whole group. (page 400)

Revenue expenditures Costs incurred that benefit only the current accounting period. (page 401)

Straight-line depreciation A system of depreciating an asset's cost that allocates an equal amount of cost in each time period of the asset's useful life. Depreciation per period = (cost − salvage value) ÷ estimated useful life. (page 402)

Sum-of-the-years'-digits depreciation A system of depreciation that allocates a decreasing cost to each successive period in the asset's life. Depreciation for a period = [number of years left in the asset's life (as of the beginning of the year) ÷ the sum of the digits of the asset's useful life] × (cost − salvage value). (page 404)

Trademark Exclusive right to use a certain name or symbol for an unlimited future period. (page 422)

Units-of-output depreciation A system of depreciation that allocates an equal cost to each unit produced. Depreciation per period = (number of units produced this period) × [(cost − salvage value) ÷ useful life stated in units]. (page 403)

QUESTIONS

1. What is the general rule for determining the cost of a long-lived asset? Give examples of at least four costs that would be included in the cost of a building.

2. Explain why cash discounts are always deducted in determining the cost of a long-lived asset, even if the company doesn't take advantage of the cash discount.

3. Pilot, Inc., purchased a machine for $48,000 cash. When the machine arrived, it had to be stored in a local warehouse because the room to house the new machine was still under construction. Should the storage charges of $550 be added to the cost of the machine or should they be expensed? Explain.

4. The cost of freight on a machine acquired on Dec. 31, 1988, was debited to Miscellaneous Expense rather than Machinery. What effect will this error have on 1988 income? 1989 income?

5. What are the two most common causes of depreciation? Which cause is most crucial in determining the useful life of an asset in the contemporary U.S. economy? Explain.

6. Curlew Co. shows the following on its Dec. 31, 1989, balance sheet:

Building	$250,000	
Less: Accumulated Depreciation.	75,000	$175,000

Does this tell the statement reader that Curlew's building is worth $250,000? $175,000? Explain.

7. What is meant by the term *accelerated depreciation?* List two accelerated depreciation methods.

8. At times the amount of depreciation indicated by the double declining-balance formula will not be the depreciation recorded. Under what conditions must the amount indicated by the formula be adjusted? Explain.

9. Winger Co. shows a truck with a cost of $23,000 and an accumulated depreciation of $8,700. How much cash has been set aside for the replacement of the truck through the depreciation process? Explain.

10. When an asset's cost and its accumulated depreciation are equal in amount, the asset is said to be fully depreciated. Are the asset and the accumulated depreciation accounts removed from the financial records when this happens? Explain.

11. Baker Co. used straight-line depreciation for financial statements and an accelerated method for income tax returns. This amounts to keeping "two sets of books" and is illegal. Do you agree? Explain.

12. What is ACRS depreciation? For what purpose is ACRS depreciation used?

13. What is the difference between depreciation and depletion? Is accelerated depletion allowed?

14. Under what conditions will a company record a loss on an asset that is traded or sold?

15. Accounts Receivable, Investment in City of Charleston Bonds, and Copyrights are examples of assets that lack physical substance. Which of these will appear under the heading "Intangible Assets" on the balance sheet? Explain why those omitted would not be classified among intangible assets.

16. How does amortization differ from depreciation? What method of amortization is most widely used?

17. Over what time period is an intangible asset amortized?

18. Auden, Inc., has been manufacturing computer furniture for 10 years. Auden has consistently earned a much higher rate of return on its assets than its competitors. Auden is widely recognized as the most successful firm in the industry. Would you expect goodwill to exist in Auden's business? Explain. Where would you expect to find goodwill on Auden's financial statements? Explain.

EXERCISES

**Exercise 10-1
Calculating the cost of a
computer**

Melville Company purchased a new computer from Analog Computers. The following costs were incurred:

List price of the computer...	$100,000
Trade discount allowed to Melville....................................	10%
Cash discount allowed for payment within 30 days.....................	3%
Cost of air conditioning the room where the new computer is to be used. The computer requires a certain temperature and humidity to operate properly..	$ 1,250
Insurance on the computer. The policy covers damage from vandalism, fire, flood, and certain other natural disasters (3-year premium).............	360
Cost of 1-year maintenance contract. The computer will be serviced weekly by Analog technicians	2,080
Cost of rewiring needed to provide proper electric power................	420

Prepare a schedule that shows the calculation of the cost of the computer to Melville Company.

(Check figure: Cost of computer = $88,970)

Exercise 10-2
Using relative-value allocation

Herman, Inc., bought some assets from Gray Construction, which was disposing of its road construction division. The assets purchased and their appraised values appear below:

Asset	Appraised Value
Bulldozers	$ 50,000
Dump trucks	125,000
Scrapers	187,500
Excavators	262,500
Total	$625,000

Assuming that Herman paid $500,000 for all of the assets listed, prepare a schedule showing the calculation of the cost that would be assigned to each. Prepare the entry to record the acquisition.

(Check figure: Cost assigned to excavators = $210,000)

Exercise 10-3
Calculating units-of-output depreciation

Wilkes Co. purchased a company airplane on Jan. 1, 1989, for $204,000. Wilkes expects to use the plane for 5 years, at which time it will have a salvage value of $24,000. Wilkes believes that, with proper maintenance, the plane will fly approximately 7,500 hours during the 5 years. During 1989 and 1990, the plane flew 1,200 and 1,620 hours, respectively.

Prepare the entry to record depreciation for the years ended Dec. 31, 1989 and 1990, using the units-of-output method of depreciation. Present clearly labeled calculations to support your solution.

(Check figure: Units-of-output depreciation for 1990 = $28,800)

Exercise 10-4
Calculating sum-of-the-years'-digits depreciation

Morton, Inc., purchased equipment on Nov. 1, 1988, for $49,500. The equipment has an expected useful life of 5 years and an estimated salvage value of $4,500.

Calculate the depreciation expense for the years ended Oct. 31, 1989 and 1990, using the sum-of-the-years'-digits method. Prepare the journal entries to record the depreciation.

(Check figure: SYD depreciation for 1989 = $15,000)

Exercise 10-5
Calculating double declining-balance depreciation

On Jan. 1, 1989, Budd Company purchased a large power generator for $320,000. The generator is expected to last 5 years and to have a salvage value of $20,000.

Calculate the depreciation that would be recorded on Dec. 31, 1989 and 1990, using the double declining-balance method. Prepare journal entries to record the depreciation.

(Check figure: DDB depreciation for 1989 = $128,000)

Exercise 10-6
Calculating depletion

Red Pepper Mining Co. purchased and developed a mining site at a total cost of $3,000,000. Geologists estimate that 4,500,000 tons of iron ore are contained in the property. Red Pepper mined and sold 400,000 tons of iron ore during 1990. The sales price was $1.25 per ton. The salvage value of the property is estimated to be $75,000.

Calculate the depletion for 1990. Prepare entries to record depletion and to record the sale of the ore.

(Check figure: Depletion for 1990 = $260,000)

Exercise 10-7
Preparing entries to record sales of equipment

Seamore, Inc., sold a crane on Jan. 1, 1990. The crane had originally cost $600,000. Total depreciation recorded through Dec. 31, 1989, is $420,000.

Prepare the entry to record the sale of equipment at each of the following amounts: **(a)** $200,000, **(b)** $180,000, **(c)** $130,000.

[Check figure: Loss on sale of equipment (c) = $50,000]

Exercise 10-8
Preparing entries to record exchanges of assets

Vere, Inc., traded a pizza oven having a cost of $3,250 and an accumulated depreciation of $1,500 for a new pizza oven having a fair market value of $4,500.

Prepare the entry to record the acquisition of the new oven assuming that Vere was required to pay **(a)** $2,750 cash in addition to the old oven, **(b)** $2,000 cash in addition to the old oven, and **(c)** $3,100 cash in addition to the old oven. Show clearly labeled calculations to support your entries.

[Check figure: Cost of oven (b) = $3,750]

Exercise 10-9
Preparing entries to amortize intangibles

Spithead, Inc., purchased two intangible assets on Jan. 1, 1989. A patent was acquired for $27,200, and goodwill was purchased for $128,000 as part of the acquisition of Holmes Corp. The patent is a new one and has its full legal life remaining. The goodwill is expected to last for an indefinite time.

Prepare the amortization entries for Patents and Goodwill on Dec. 31, 1989, assuming that the patent is to be amortized over its legal life (no salvage value) and the goodwill is to be amortized over the maximum period allowed. Your entries should be supported by clearly labeled calculations.

(Check figure: Goodwill amortization expense = $3,200)

Exercise 10-10
Calculating ACRS, tax straight-line, financial accounting depreciation

On Jan. 1, 1989, Liverpool Corp. purchased some office furniture for $12,500. The furniture has a 10-year life for financial accounting purposes, but income tax laws arbitrarily assign it a 7-year life for income tax purposes. The furniture is expected to have a $2,500 salvage value.

Calculate 1989, 1990, and 1991 depreciation expense by each of the following methods: **(a)** ACRS, **(b)** tax straight-line, **(c)** financial accounting straight-line.

(Check figure: ACRS depreciation for 1989 = $1,785)

PROBLEMS: SET A

Problem A10-1
Calculating the cost of several assets

The management of Dansker Corp. has asked for your assistance in determining the cost of their property, plant, and equipment assets. Dansker began operations on Jan. 3, 1989. During the year the following transactions took place which management believes may relate to long-lived assets:

a. Paid $300,000 for land, building, and machinery. The land was appraised at $65,000, the building at $162,500, and the machinery at $97,500. Dansker was able to acquire the assets at less than their appraised value because the seller was badly in need of cash.

b. $250 was paid for title insurance on the land.

c. $1,000 was paid to drain a portion of the land and to haul in fill dirt so that the land could be used for a parking lot.

d. $500 was paid for a survey to determine the exact location of the driveways and parking lots to be constructed.

e. $11,000 was paid for grading and paving driveways and parking lots.

f. $2,400 was paid to a cleaning service to sweep the driveways and parking lots for the remainder of 1989.

g. $12,000 was paid to have a new roof put on the building. The roof is expected to last 20 years, which is also the remaining life of the building.

h. $7,250 was paid to have the motors in several of the machines overhauled.

i. $60 was paid to replace several window panes that were broken after Dansker moved into the building.

j. $250 was paid for a supply of oil, grease, and cleaning compounds that would be needed to assure efficient operation of the machines.

Required	Set up a solutions paper with the following column headings:

			Other Accounts	
Description	**Land**	**Buildings**	**Name**	**Amount**

For each of the 10 items listed in the problem, place the amount in the column indicating the correct account. If the amount should not be debited to either Land or Buildings, decide which account would be proper and place the account name and amount in the final column.

(Check figure: Buildings = $162,000)

**Problem A10-2
Calculating depreciation
under four different
methods**

On Jan. 1, 1987, Squeek Systems, Inc., purchased a large truck. Squeek estimates that the $315,000 truck will last for 6 years, at which time its salvage value will be $52,500. Squeek plans to use the truck for the following mileage each year: 1987, 150,000; 1988, 220,000; 1989, 220,000; 1990, 190,000; 1991, 150,000; 1992, 70,000.

Required	Calculate the amount of depreciation in each of the 6 years under

1. The straight-line method
2. The units-of-output method
3. The sum-of-the-years'-digits method
4. The double declining-balance method
Round to the nearest whole dollar.

(Check figure: Double declining-balance depreciation in 1989 = $46,667)

**Problem A10-3
Using different methods to
calculate depreciation on
various assets**

Innocent Manufacturing, Inc., purchased the following new assets on Jan. 1, 1989:

Asset	Cost	Salvage	Estimated Useful Life, Years
Paper shredder	$14,000	$1,500	5
Copying machine	18,500	2,500	4
Waste paper compactor	8,500	100	8

Required	For each of the assets listed above, determine:

1. The straight-line depreciation rate
2. The amount of depreciation expense for 1989 and 1990 using the straight-line method
3. The double declining-balance rate
4. The amount of depreciation expense for 1989 and 1990 using the double declining-balance method

*(Check figure: Double declining-balance depreciation
on the waste paper compactor for 1989 = $2,125)*

**Problem A10-4
Calculating depreciation
under three different
methods**

Indomitable Corp. has been in business for several years. On Dec. 31, 1989, the following major long-lived assets were on hand:

Buildings purchased June 30, 1979, for $2,800,000. Their estimated useful life and salvage values are 15 years and $130,000, respectively.

Delivery truck purchased Jan. 1, 1986, for $34,000. The truck had an estimated useful life of 5 years and a salvage value of $4,000.

Machinery purchased on Sept. 1, 1989, for $144,000. Engineers predict the useful life to be 12 years and the salvage value to be $6,000.

Indomitable uses the straight-line method for buildings, the sum-of-the-years'-digits method for delivery trucks, and the double declining-balance method for machinery.

Required

Calculate the depreciation expense that should be recorded for the year ended Dec. 31, 1989, for each of the assets.

(Check figure: 1989 depreciation on machinery = $8,000)

Problem A10-5
Recording sales and
exchanges of equipment

On Jan. 1, 1989, Kincaid Restaurant Corp.'s balance sheet lists the following equipment:

Baking Oven..	$ 9,000	
Less: Accumulated Depreciation	6,800	$ 2,200
Dishwasher...	$30,000	
Less: Accumulated Depreciation	6,000	24,000
Deep Fryer	$12,000	
Less: Accumulated Depreciation	9,000	3,000

The following transactions affecting equipment took place during 1989:

a. The baking oven was sold for $1,500.
b. The old dishwasher was traded in on a similar machine that operated more efficiently. The fair market value of the new washer was $38,000. In addition to giving the old dishwasher, Kincaid was required to pay $20,000 cash.
c. The old deep fryer was traded for a new one having a fair market price of $15,000. Kincaid was required to pay $10,000 in addition to the old fryer.

Required

Prepare journal entries to record each of the transactions described above. Each entry should be supported by clearly labeled calculations.

(Check figure: Loss on trading dishwasher = $6,000)

Problem A10-6
Recording depreciation
and disposals of
equipment

During 1989, Claggart's Garage disposed of several long-lived assets and acquired several others. Information relating to these transactions follows:

Jan. 1   Claggart traded an old wrecker having a cost of $45,000 and an accumulated depreciation of $15,000 for a new one having a fair market value of $68,000. Claggart was required to pay $40,000 in addition to the old wrecker.

May 1   Claggart sold an old engine diagnostic machine for $1,000. The machine cost $6,500 and had an accumulated depreciation on Jan. 1, 1989, of $4,200. Claggart uses the straight-line method of depreciation. The machine has an estimated useful life of 5 years and a $500 salvage value.

Oct. 1   Claggart sold an air compressor for $25 as scrap. The machine was purchased on Sept. 30, 1984, for $1,500; it was estimated to have a useful life of 5 years and a salvage value of $240. Depreciation had been correctly recorded through Dec. 31, 1988.

Nov. 1   Claggart traded a front-end alignment machine for a new one having a fair market value of $7,500. The old machine had been purchased on Jan. 1, 1982, for $4,500. The estimated useful life of the old machine was 12 years; the estimated salvage value was $180. Accumulated depreciation on Jan. 1, 1989, was $2,520. Claggart was required to pay $5,500 in addition to the old machine.

Required

Prepare the entry to record each of the transactions listed above. You may also need an entry to record depreciation for part of the year. Assume that Claggart has not recorded any depreciation since Dec. 31, 1988. Your entries should be supported by clearly labeled calculations.

(Check figure: Cost of new alignment machine = $7,180)

Problem A10-7
Recording acquisition and amortization of intangible assets

Ratcliffe Corp. began business in 1989. The controller has listed the following transactions and events that she is unsure about:

Jan. 1   Paid attorney $1,250 to draw up articles of incorporation and file them with the state government.

May 1   Purchased a franchise to sell Mainsail yachts. $12,000 cash was paid; the balance of $15,000 is due within 1 year.

July 1   Paid $2,000 to a songwriter to write the words and music for a theme song for the company's advertising. Ratcliffe acquired the copyright as a part of the fee.

Oct. 1   Paid $500 to an artist to design a logo for the company. This logo was registered at an additional cost of $50.

Dec. 31   Ratcliffe has had such a successful first year that management feels that some goodwill has been created. The firm's management team estimates the value of this goodwill to be at least $3,500.

Required

1. Analyze each of the transactions and events. Prepare all necessary journal entries. If no entry is required, write "no entry" and give the reason none is needed.
2. Prepare entries needed on Dec. 31 to amortize the intangible assets. Assume that all the intangibles are to be amortized over a 10-year period.

(Check figure: Franchise amortization expense = $1,800)

Problem A10-8
Answering questions about property, plant, and equipment as presented on a balance sheet

The Jenkins & Associates, Inc., balance sheet for 1989 shows one column for the current year and another for the previous year. The long-lived assets section is reproduced below:

	Dec. 31, 1989	Dec. 31, 1988
Property, Plant, and Equipment:		
Land	$ 960,000	$1,030,000
Building	$2,500,000	$2,800,000
Less: Accumulated Depreciation	(360,000)	(400,000)
Net Book Value of Building	$2,140,000	$2,400,000
Equipment	$ 420,000	$ 420,000
Less: Accumulated Depreciation	(150,000)	(120,000)
Net Book Value of Equipment	$ 270,000	$ 300,000
Total Property, Plant, and Equipment	$3,370,000	$3,730,000
Intangibles:		
Franchises	$ 36,000	$ 40,000

Required

Prepare answers to the following questions about Jenkins' long-lived assets. Your answers should be supported by calculations.

1. What is the most logical explanation for the change in the Land account?
2. One building costing $300,000 and having an accumulated depreciation of $100,000 was sold for $196,000 during 1989. What is the amount of depreciation expense on buildings for 1989?
3. Assuming that no equipment was bought or sold during 1989, what is the amount of depreciation expense on equipment during 1989?
4. Assuming that no franchise was bought or sold during 1989, what is the amount of franchise amortization expense for 1989?

(Check figure: Depreciation expense on buildings = $60,000)

PROBLEMS: SET B

Problem B10-1
Calculating the cost of several assets

Graveling, Inc., debits an account called Long-Lived Assets for the purchase of any asset that is expected to last longer than 1 year. During its first year of operations Graveling made the following debits to Long-Lived Assets:

a. $400,000 was paid for a parcel of land.
b. $13,100 was paid for title insurance and legal fees related to the purchase of the land.
c. $28,000 was paid to have the land cleared, filled, and leveled so that it would be suitable for use.
d. $6,400 was paid for a survey to determine the exact placement of a building on the land.
e. $1,000 was paid for a building permit.
f. $300,000 was paid to an architect to design the building and supervise construction.
g. $1,600,000 was paid to a contractor to erect the building.
h. $284,000 was paid for paving parking lots and driveways.
i. $207,000 was paid for landscaping.
j. $32,800 was paid to erect a fence around the property.

Required

Set up a solutions paper with the following headings:

Description	Land	Buildings	Land Improvements

For each of the 10 items listed in the problem, place the amount in the column indicating the correct property, plant, and equipment account.

(Check figure: Cost of buildings = $1,907,400)

Problem B10-2
Calculating depreciation under four different methods

Edward Fairfax Vere, Inc., purchased a machine for $32,000 on Jan. 1, 1987. Vere expects to use the machine for 4 years, at which time its estimated salvage value will be $2,000. Production from the machine over the 4 years is budgeted at the following levels: 1987, 10,000 units; 1988, 20,000 units; 1989, 40,000 units; 1990, 5,000 units.

Required

Calculate the amount of depreciation in each of the 4 years of the asset's life under:

1. The straight-line method
2. The units-of-output method
3. The sum-of-the-years'-digits method
4. The double declining-balance method

(Check figure: Double declining-balance depreciation for 1989 = $4,000)

Problem B10-3
Using different methods to calculate depreciation on various assets

The Handsome Sailor Company acquired the following new assets on Jan. 1, 1988:

Asset	Cost	Salvage	Estimated Useful Life, Years
Office furniture	$150,000	$ 15,000	5
Telephone system	210,000	30,000	6
Building	900,000	100,000	20

Required

For each of the assets listed above, determine:

1. The straight-line depreciation rate
2. The amount of depreciation expense for 1988 and 1989 using the straight-line method
3. The double declining-balance rate
4. The amount of depreciation expense for 1988 and 1989 using the double declining-balance method

(Check figure: 1989 double declining-balance depreciation for the building = $81,000)

Problem B10-4
Calculating depreciation
under three different
methods

Avenger, Inc., began operations on Jan. 1, 1989. During the first year of business the following asset purchases were made:

Jan. 1   Equipment was acquired at a cost of $380,000. Engineers predict the useful life of the equipment to be 15 years and salvage value to be $20,000.

Feb. 1   A building was purchased for $800,000. The building has an expected useful life of 20 years and a salvage value of $50,000.

Mar. 1   A fleet of delivery vans was acquired for $72,000. The vans should last 5 years and have a salvage value of $10,000.

Avenger uses the straight-line method for buildings, the sum-of-the-years'-digits method for equipment, and the double declining-balance method for trucks.

Required

Prepare a schedule showing the 1989 and 1990 depreciation for each of the assets listed above. Clearly labeled calculations should be shown to support your solution.

(Check figure: SYD depreciation on equipment for 1990 = $42,000)

Problem B10-5
Recording sales and
exchanges of various
assets

Billy Budd & Co.'s Dec. 31, 1988, balance sheet includes the following property, plant, and equipment assets:

Land...		$750,000
Building...................................	$1,800,000	
Less: Accumulated Depreciation	1,600,000	200,000
Refrigeration Equipment	$ 460,000	
Less: Accumulated Depreciation	220,000	240,000
Delivery Trucks	$ 125,000	
Less: Accumulated Depreciation	100,000	25,000

The following transactions affecting property, plant, and equipment assets took place on Jan. 1, 1989:

a. The land and building were sold for $1,175,000. Billy Budd has decided to lease space as soon as an acceptable facility can be located.
b. The old refrigeration equipment was traded on similar units with a larger capacity. The fair market price of the new assets was $650,000. Billy Budd was required to pay $450,000 in addition to giving the old equipment.

c. The old delivery trucks were traded for new ones. Billy Budd was required to pay $150,000 in addition to trading the old trucks. The new trucks have a fair market value of $182,000.

Required

Prepare journal entries to record each of the Jan. 1, 1989, transactions. Each entry should be supported by clearly labeled calculations.

(Check figure: Cost of new trucks = $175,000)

Problem B10-6
Recording depreciation and disposal of various assets

During 1989, Ustinov Airlines engages in the following transactions relating to property, plant, and equipment assets:

Jan. 1   Ustinov traded a computer that had cost $400,000 and had accumulated depreciation of $140,000 for a new computer having a fair market value of $640,000. Ustinov was required to pay $400,000 in addition to the old computer.

Apr. 1   Ustinov sold a building for $250,000. The building cost $300,000 and has accumulated depreciation of $100,000 on Jan. 1, 1989. Ustinov uses the straight-line method of depreciation. The building was estimated to have a useful life of 20 years and a salvage value of $20,000.

June 30   Ustinov sold old baggage carts for $125 as scrap. The carts were purchased on July 1, 1984, for $3,000; they were estimated to have a useful life of 5 years and a salvage value of $200. Accumulated depreciation on Jan. 1, 1989, was $2,520. The straight-line method is used.

Sept. 30   Ustinov traded an old airplane for a new one having a fair market price of $5,000,000. The old airplane had been purchased on Feb. 1, 1980, for $2,000,000, had no salvage value, and was fully depreciated as of Jan. 1, 1989. Ustinov was required to pay $4,950,000 in addition to giving the old airplane.

Required

Prepare the entry to record each of the transactions listed above. You may also need an entry to record depreciation for part of the year. Assume that Ustinov has not recorded any depreciation since Dec. 31, 1988. Your entries should be supported by clearly labeled calculations.

(Check figure: June 30 entry, loss on disposal of baggage carts = $75)

Problem B10-7
Recording acquisition and amortization of intangible assets

Rights-of-Man Enterprises is a diversified company involved in many different business ventures. Selected transactions for 1989 are described below:

Jan. 1   Acquired a patent for an artificial sweetener made from mango juice. The patent cost $96,000 and is expected to have an economic life of 16 years.

Apr. 1   Purchased a 5-year franchise to sell popcorn with exotic flavors from Tropicpop, Inc. The franchise price was $18,000; one-third of the price was paid in 1989; the remainder is due within 1 year.

June 30   Purchased an operating delicatessen. Goodwill purchased as part of the transaction totaled $50,000.

Nov. 1   Purchased a copyright for a play entitled *The Basket Case* for $18,000. The copyright is expected to have a useful life of 10 years.

Required

1. Prepare entries to record each of the transactions listed above.
2. Prepare the appropriate amortization entries on Dec. 31, 1989. Assume that the goodwill is to be amortized over the maximum number of years.

(Check figure: Copyright amortization expense = $300)

**Problem B10-8
Answering questions
about property, plant, and
equipment as presented
on a balance sheet**

Ryan, Inc.'s year-end balance sheet shows one column for the current year and another
column for the previous year. The long-lived assets appear on Ryan's 1989 balance sheet as
follows:

	Dec. 31, 1989	Dec. 31 1988
Property, Plant, and Equipment:		
Land	$ 400,000	$310,000
Building	$ 500,000	$500,000
Less: Accumulated Depreciation	(125,000)	(87,500)
Net Book Value of Building	$ 375,000	$412,500
Machinery	$ 75,000	$125,000
Less: Accumulated Depreciation	30,000	40,000
Net Book Value of Machinery	$ 45,000	$ 85,000
Total Property, Plant, and Equipment	$ 820,000	$807,500
Intangibles:		
Patents	$ 100,000	$130,000

Required

Prepare answers to the following questions about Ryan's long-lived assets. Your answers
should be supported by calculations.

1. What is the most logical explanation for the change in the Land account?
2. Assuming that no buildings were bought or sold during 1989, what is the amount of
depreciation expense on the buildings during 1989?
3. One piece of machinery costing $50,000 and having an accumulated depreciation of
$12,500 was sold for $37,500 during 1989. What is the amount of depreciation expense on
machinery during 1989?
4. Assuming that no patents were bought or sold during 1989, what is the amount of patent
amortization expense for 1989?

(Check figure: Depreciation expense on buildings = $37,500)

DECISION PROBLEM

Much of the heavy equipment of Central States Development Corporation is in need
of replacement. The equipment was acquired on Jan. 1, 1979, when several local
contractors formed the corporation. Four thousand shares of the corporation's stock
were issued in exchange for equipment valued on that date at $1,200,000. The
equipment was expected to have a 10-year life. To buy the same equipment today
would cost $1,850,000.

The president of the company suggests that the equipment be acquired from the
manufacturer by borrowing $1,600,000 from the bank at 10% interest. The loan
would be repaid over the 10-year expected life of the new equipment. The extra
$250,000 would come from the corporate Cash account.

The vice president of the company does not agree with this plan. He contends that
only $650,000 would have to be financed, since the company would have the other
$1,200,000 in cash as a result of the depreciation taken on the original heavy equip-

ment. These funds have been set aside for exactly this purpose, he argues. That is why the corporation charged depreciation expense each and every year of its 10-year life.

Over the 10-year period the corporation has recorded sales amounting to $8,000,000 and has had cost of goods sold totaling $4,000,000. At year-end on Dec. 31, 1989, accounts receivable of $50,000 are outstanding and accounts payable relating to cost of goods sold items amount to $30,000. In addition, operating expenses of $1,000,000 were incurred, with $20,000 unpaid on Dec. 31, 1989. Depreciation on the equipment is not included in these figures.

Required	1. Prepare summary journal entries reflecting the acquisition of the equipment, sales, cost of goods sold, operating expenses, depreciation (scrap value is 0), and payment of dividends. The corporation's policy is to pay dividends each year exactly equal to net income.

2. Determine the amount of cash on hand on Dec. 31, 1989.

3. Is the vice president right? Did depreciation provide funds for the equipment replacement? Explain.

G · A · A · P

Generally Accepted
Accounting Principles
Reviewed
and Expanded

Some of the things you will learn about when studying this section are:

- Why generally accepted accounting principles are necessary
- Who is responsible for developing generally accepted accounting principles and how they are developed
- How generally accepted accounting principles are enforced
- What the objectives of financial reporting are
- How financial reporting meets certain qualitative characteristics
- What the basic underlying assumptions of accounting are

Over the past 10 chapters we have introduced you to a number of generally accepted accounting principles—GAAP. We haven't provided you with an overall picture of generally accepted accounting principles until now because you weren't ready for it. Now you are—you have a good grasp of the financial accounting model and its purpose. You now have the background that you need to understand why we do what we do in accounting, that is, how the principles relate to the accounting process.

THE NEED FOR GAAP

Generally accepted accounting principles are the ground rules of accounting

In the Introduction to this text, we briefly introduced generally accepted accounting principles, suggesting that they are the ground rules of accounting. They assure us that similar economic events will be reported in the same manner by everyone. And when several acceptable alternatives exist for recording an economic event—say, inventory cost flows or depreciation—these ground rules require us to disclose which alternative was used in the financial statements. Since everyone must follow GAAP, the result is a consistent system of financial reporting that provides users of financial statements with information that is reliable, understandable, and comparable to prior years and among companies. Without these ground rules there would be chaos in financial reporting. General Motors might use the FIFO inventory method, Ford might use LIFO, and neither might tell us which it used. How could we meaningfully compare the two companies? We couldn't. And that's the point. That's why we need GAAP.

AUTHORITATIVE SUPPORT FOR GAAP

Who tells us what GAAP are? Even more important, who tells us that we must follow GAAP? What happens if we don't?

Back in the Introduction we said that the authority of GAAP rests on their acceptance by the accounting profession. And that's true, but it's not quite the whole story.

You know that the independent auditor—the CPA—provides statement users with an assurance that the statements represent fairly the results of operations and the financial condition of the company. The auditor gives this assurance, which is really an objective opinion, after examining the accounting records. And the auditor's opinion of the statements' fairness is an integral part of the statements themselves.

In that opinion the auditor must say whether or not the financial statements are presented fairly and prepared in accordance with GAAP. Why? Because the auditor must follow the pronouncements of the accounting profession to remain and practice in it. Failure to follow the pronouncements is cause for expulsion—the state board of accountancy could remove the CPA's license to practice public accounting.

One of the pronouncements is found in the American Institute of Certified Public Accountants (AICPA) *Statements on Auditing Standards*. It says that the auditor's report must state whether the financial statements are presented in accordance with GAAP. Another pronouncement, found in the AICPA Code of Professional Ethics, states that the CPA must not express an opinion that financial statements are in conformity with GAAP if the statements contain any departure from an accounting principle issued by the Financial Accounting Standards Board (FASB) or the old Accounting Principles Board (APB). The CPA may not issue an opinion stating that a set of financial statements is in conformity with GAAP when it is not. And without that opinion from the CPA, users cannot rely on the fairness of the financial statements.

The pronouncements of the public accounting profession and the regulations of the SEC provide authoritative support for GAAP

Many companies fall under the regulations of the Securities and Exchange Commission (SEC). And the SEC has direct legal power to force these companies to follow its accounting rules—failure to comply could mean a trip to jail. Most of the SEC's accounting rules are the same as those of the FASB and APB because the SEC has adopted them as their rules. The SEC normally looks to the FASB to establish accepted accounting principles.

GAAP, then, has authoritative support from two sources:

1. Indirectly, from the CPAs who must follow professional accounting pronouncements

2. From the SEC, which has legal authority to enforce compliance with these same pronouncements

THE MEANING AND DEVELOPMENT OF GAAP

Let's look more closely at the meaning of GAAP. Yes, they are the ground rules of accounting. But let's be more specific.

Generally accepted accounting principles is a technical accounting term. It includes conventions, concepts, standards, rules, principles, and procedures that are necessary to define accepted accounting practice at a particular time. That's how the profession itself explains GAAP in one of its pronouncements. Furthermore, generally accepted accounting principles are principles that have *substantial authoritative support*. The APB *Opinions* and FASB *Standards* constitute substantial authoritative support. But there is substantial authoritative support from outside the APB and FASB. Other authoritative support comes from the following:

- APB and FASB interpretations of *Opinions* and *Standards*
- Industry audit guides
- Industry accounting practices
- APB *Statements*
- AICPA statements of position
- Pronouncements of the SEC
- Accounting textbook and articles

There is no one single source for GAAP

Unfortunately, there isn't just one single source of generally accepted accounting principles. There have been a number of attempts, all unsuccessful thus far, to develop a single source. However, the FASB has completed a major project — called the ***conceptual framework study*** — that contains many of the principles. Several parts of the study are discussed in the following sections.

THE CONCEPTUAL FRAMEWORK STUDY

The Objectives of Financial Statements

The first part of the conceptual framework study is concerned with the objectives of financial reporting. Why are financial statements needed? Who needs them? What are the backgrounds of the people who need the financial statements? And what information do they need and how should it be presented so that they can understand it? This part of the study was completed in 1978.

Useful Information for Decisions

Financial reporting should provide useful information to investors and creditors

Financial reporting should provide information that is useful to present and potential investors and creditors. That's the first objective of a financial statement. The FASB listed only present and potential investors and creditors as users. Why? There are many more users — the IRS, the SEC, and management, to name a few. But is there any question in your mind about the ability of these groups to get whatever financial information they need concerning the company? Of course not. The IRS and the SEC have legal authority to get what they want — you either provide the requested information or go to jail. And management can get what they want: Employees provide the requested information or they are fired. Only investors and creditors do not have this direct access, so it is for these groups that financial statements are prepared.

The financial statements are the end product of the accounting activity. They represent the classification and summarization of many financial transactions, some of which are very complex. There simply isn't any way these activities can be presented in the financial statements so that everyone — we mean everyone from a skilled financial analyst to the unskilled small investor — can understand what they mean. The FASB assumes that readers of financial statements have a basic background in business and economics and will take the time and effort to study the statements and related notes. This, by the way, includes you.

Useful Information for Assessing Cash Flows

Financial reporting should provide useful information for assessing cash flows

The second objective of financial statements is that financial reporting should provide information that is useful in assessing cash flows. What we're concerned with is the amounts, timing, and uncertainty of the net cash inflow to the company. We're interested because people invest to increase their cash. The final test investors look at is whether or not they received more cash from an investment than they spent on it. And they want information that will help them choose between receiving cash now (selling their stock) or at some future date. They need information that will help them assess the risk that the amounts and timing of future cash receipts will not be as expected.

Useful Information about Balance Sheet Items and Changes in Them

Financial reports should help investors and creditors assess strengths and weaknesses of business entities

The third and last objective of financial statements is that financial reporting should provide information about the economic resources (assets); the claims to those resources (liabilities and owners' equity); and the effects of transactions, events, and circumstances that change resources and claims to those resources. That's the way the FASB puts it. Investors want this information to help them assess the company's strengths and weaknesses; to assess the company's liquidity (ability to convert assets to cash) and solvency (ability to pay its bills); and to evaluate information about the company's performance during the period.

Qualitative Characteristics

The second part of the conceptual framework study is concerned with examining the characteristics that make accounting information useful. This part of the study was completed in the spring of 1980.

1. Usefulness

Financial information must be useful to those who want it, but not too costly for those who prepare it

Usefulness, of course, is the most important characteristic of any reported information. People want accounting information that's useful — but what's useful to one user may not be as useful to another. Accounting standards must be set to require that just the right amount of information is reported in a financial statement. Well, now, exactly what does "just the right amount of information" mean? It doesn't mean *exactly* anything. What it does mean generally is that (1) the information must be useful to most of the people who want to use it, and (2) preparing that useful information won't be a burdensome (cost, time, complexity) task for those who have to prepare it.

2. Understandability

To be useful, financial information must be understandable

If you can't understand the accounting information given to you, it isn't useful even though it may be relevant to whatever decision you want to make. Let's expand on an example used by the FASB when they explain the term *understandability.* Suppose you're a vegetarian on a summer trip to Paris. Ordering a meal from a menu will present you with a problem. The waiter provides you with useful information relevant to your decision — the information is there on the menu in French. But if you can't understand it, it's useless.

Accounting information must be presented in a manner that investors and creditors understand. But, as we said before, it is assumed that investors and creditors have a basic knowledge of business and economics and that they will spend time and effort in studying the financial statements.

3. Relevance

To be useful, financial information must be relevant

For information to be relevant it must have a bearing on a decision to be made — it must make a difference in that decision. Return to the vegetarian example. Assume that you ask the waiter for a menu printed in English. He returns with an English menu of meat dishes. Now you have information that is understandable, but not useful or relevant. Finally, the waiter brings an English vegetable menu — this is both relevant and useful for your decision. You can now select whatever dish suits your vegetarian fancy.

4. Reliability

Accounting information should be reliable. That means it should be free from error. And it should be free from any bias of those who are providing it. For information to be reliable we must be able to prove — to *verify* — that it is free from error and bias. If different accountants working independently but using the same accounting methods arrive at the same results, the information is verified and proved to be reliable. Accounting information must always be able to stand the test of independent verification.

Be careful what conclusions you draw from the reliability characteristic. You can be sure that the tablets in a bottle of aspirin conform to the formula written on the side of the bottle. And you can be sure that the amounts reported on a set of financial statements are reliable. But the reason that you relied on the aspirin was the claim that two tablets would cure your headache — that was *relevant* information. The reliability of the formula was irrelevant. Accounting information does not claim to cure your financial headaches; it just claims that the information in the accounting bottle conforms to the accounting measurement formulas.

5. Timeliness

We must receive financial information in time to make decisions, otherwise the information is irrelevant and useless

Accounting information will be irrelevant and useless if we don't have it in time to make decisions. We must have accounting information before it loses its capacity to influence decisions. How fast information loses this capacity depends on the decision to be made. Accounting information needed for a corporate takeover bid (such as U.S. Steel buying Marathon Oil) may have value for only a few days or even hours. Information needed for the annual report would have value over a much longer period of time.

Sometimes we have to sacrifice precision for timeliness because approximate information now is more useful than precise information later. For example, isn't that what we do with the estimate of uncollectible accounts? We could know the exact amount of accounts that prove uncollectible if we just waited awhile. But by then the information would no longer be useful.

6. Verifiability

Financial information must be verifiable in order to be reliable

Accounting information must be susceptible of being reviewed by others. And when others can review independently the information contained in purchase invoices, sales invoices, property deeds, transfers of title, and other similar documents and arrive at the same values reported in the financial statements, the information is said to be verified. It's the ability to review the underlying documents that the verifiability characteristic is concerned with, not the results of the review. If the underlying documents are not available, the information reported on the financial statements can't be verified. And that means it can't be relied upon.

7. Neutrality

Financial information cannot favor one group over another group

Accounting information should not favor one group of users or preparers over another group. It should be free from bias. Both in making and in using accounting standards, the major concern should be the relevance and reliability of the information, not how that information affects one group or another.

Postponing the recording of purchases made in the last week of December until January would be reflected on the income statement by higher reported earnings for the current year. The higher reported earnings would reflect favorably on management this year. Neutrality would require that purchases be recorded when acquired, regardless of the effect on management's reported performance.

8. Comparability

Accounting information is useful if it is comparable

Usefulness is enhanced if accounting information can be compared with similar information for the same company through time, and similar information among companies at the same time. The principal reason for developing accounting standards is to reduce the use of different accounting methods. The use of many different accounting methods is what makes comparisons difficult.

Comparisons enable users to detect and explain similarities and differences among companies, and to evaluate the performance of each over time.

9. Completeness

In order to be reliable, financial information must be complete

For accounting information to be reliable, of course, it must be complete. Completeness implies that nothing material is left out that would be vital to investors or creditors in assessing the underlying events and conditions of the business. Of course, we have to consider what is material and what is the additional cost of getting additional information. Materiality and costs are limiting factors on completeness. Relevance determines what the limit is. A map for buried treasure may be complete in every detail but two—the name of the person making the map and the approximate value of the treasure. The irrelevance of the first omission and the cost of getting that information preclude obtaining it. But certainly the relevance of the second omission dictates that some effort should be made to obtain that missing information before investing substantial time and money to recover the treasure.

THE STRUCTURE OF GAAP

Remember what we said before about generally accepted accounting principles: They are conventions, concepts, standards, rules, principles, and procedures that are necessary to define accepted accounting practice at a particular time. About a dozen of these form a structure from which all the rest are derived. We can organize these into three areas: basic assumptions, basic principles, and basic modifiers.

Basic Assumptions

GAAP rests on four basic assumptions or concepts.

1. The business entity concept

2. The accounting period concept

3. The going concern concept

4. The stable-dollar concept

The Business Entity Concept

Accountants consider business entities as separate and distinct from their owners

A business entity is considered for accounting purposes as separate and distinct from its owners. Each business entity is treated for accounting purposes as generating its own revenue, incurring its own expenses, owning its own assets, and owing its own liabilities. Now that's not legally true if the entity is a proprietorship or a partnership. Accountants report on the economic substance of activities, and that may not always reflect the legal form.

Exhibit 1 depicts what we mean by the business entity concept. The exhibit shows the business activities of Joe Alex, who is very successful.

Year	1988				1989				1990				1991		
Quarter	1	2	3	4	1	2	3	4	1	2	3	4	1	2	3
Individual:															
Alex Himself															
Proprietorship:															
Alex Real Estate Agency															
Partnership:															
Alex and Zack, Consulting															
Corporations:															
Alex Motor Company															
Alex Body Company															
Alex Glass Company															
Alexmobile Company															

Accountants emphasize economic substance over legal form when preparing financial information for business entities

Joe operates a real estate agency. It's a proprietorship, which means that the agency doesn't have a legal existence. Its assets are Joe's assets as far as the law is concerned. The Alex Real Estate Agency assets are available to Joe's personal creditors if they can't be satisfied from his individual assets, and vice versa. If Joe can't pay his personal creditors, they can go to court to sue, if necessary, to be paid out of the Alex Real Estate Agency assets. The same goes for the real estate agency creditors. If they aren't paid, they can sue to be paid out of Joe's personal assets.

For accounting purposes, however, we ignore the legal form and, as Joe's accountants, prepare separate sets of financial statements for Joe the individual and the Alex Real Estate Agency.

Joe Alex and Barbara Zack are partners in a consulting firm. That's a business entity and we would prepare a set of financial statements for it also. Legally, of course, the assets of the partnership are available to *both* Joe's personal creditors and Barbara's personal creditors, just as Joe's assets are available for the proprietorship.

Several years ago Joe developed a fuel-efficient automobile that he calls the Alexmobile. Joe now owns a business that manufactures the Alexmobile. He organized it as a corporation. What he actually did was first to organize the Alex Motor Company, whose objective was providing financial and marketing activities for the Alexmobile. He became the principal stockholder but sold 40% of the stock to 1,000 interested investors. Then he set up three other corporations. The stock of these companies is all owned by the Alex Motor Company. The Alex Body Company provides auto frames, the Alex Glass Company provides windows, and the Alexmobile Company manufactures the car. Each of the four corporations is a legal entity. Each owns its own assets and owes its own debts. Each generates its own revenue and incurs its own expenses. Each prepares its own set of financial statements.

But Alex Motor Company owns 100% of the other three. Investors and creditors are interested in what the group as a whole has done. So when financial statements are prepared for the investors and creditors, the four sets of statements are combined — we call it *consolidated* — and only one set of statements is issued. The business entity is the whole group, even though there are four corporations. Economic substance is emphasized over legal form.

The Accounting Period Concept

We would know exactly how well all of Joe Alex's business ventures did from the time he started each if we waited until he sold his last real estate, consulted with his last client, and manufactured and sold the last Alexmobile. We could then precisely measure the revenue and expenses, the assets and liabilities. But of course we can't wait — Joe wants to know how he is doing *now* and at *frequent intervals* as long as he is in business. So do his creditors and the investors in Alex Motor Company.

Unfortunately for us accountants, Joe's business ventures don't stop operating when Joe wants financial statements. (Joe is very happy about that; he doesn't want anything to stop.) So we have to stop Joe's business artificially at frequent intervals to make the financial statements. And, as you know, we will stop the business *on paper* at the end of selected time intervals — years and quarters for Joe, his creditors, and investors; and monthly for Joe. These periods, although artificial, are timely and provide a consistent frame of reference to measure Joe's activities and to compare those measurements with previous periods and other companies.

The life of a business entity is broken up into frequent segments (years, quarters, and months) for accounting purposes

When we divide the life of a business entity into short segments, we are going to lose exactness. But it is the timeliness qualitative characteristic that makes accounting information useful, even if we have to approximate some of that information.

We prepare annually a complete set of financial statements with related footnotes for investors and creditors. However, only the major items of the income statement are reported to investors and creditors on interim statements — that means quarterly (or monthly, but we don't give investors and creditors monthly statements).

Refer back to Exhibit 1. This time look at the column headings 1988, 1989, and 1990. The years ended 1988, 1989, and 1990 represent the periods of time for which we will issue complete financial statements for each of Joe's business entities. Notice in the exhibit that each year is divided into four quarters, representing the periods of time for which we will issue interim statements for the businesses. We probably won't issue a fourth-quarter report because at the end of that quarter it's time to make the annual report.

The Going Concern Concept

Joe established his various business ventures assuming that they would have a long life. He fully expects each of them to continue in business as far in the future as he can see — through good times and bad, profits and losses — and that over their continued existence, there will be mostly good times and profits.

Accountants assume that business entities will remain in business long enough to allocate the cost of assets over the periods of time that entities expect to use these assets

Accountants similarly assume that a business entity will continue in existence for a long time. They call this assumption the ***going concern assumption,*** which is the rationale behind recording probable future economic benefits as assets rather than as expenses. For example, we record a building or a patent as an asset because we assume that we will be in business long enough to allocate the cost of the item to the periods of time we use it. If we did not make this assumption we would charge off the building and patent as expenses in the year we bought them. And that would really mess up the income statement. We would be matching this year's revenue with this year's expenditures — not expenses — with a resulting figure that would not provide us with much meaning.

The Stable-Dollar Concept

Money is a common unit of measure that we can use to record economic transactions and prepare financial statements. Everybody understands money — it's universally available, it's certainly relevant to financial transactions, and it's easy to use. Imagine trying to see how well Xerox did this year if the unit of measure were chickens or automobiles or wheat. These last three items have value, and as such can certainly be used to measure other goods. But they are not *common* economic denominators—only money is.

When preparing the basic financial reports, accountants ignore the changing value of the dollar

But money—the dollar—as a measure of economic activity does not have a constant value over time. Actually, the value of a dollar has decreased over time, especially in recent years. It is not time that causes the change in the value of money, but economic events. The dollar is not constant like units of physical measure. A mile or a quart always measure exactly the same; they are precise. These measures will not change when there is a shortage of oil, a surplus of corn, a Democratic majority in the House, or a military crisis in the Middle East. But the value of the dollar will.

Several ways have been proposed to deal with the change in the value of the dollar, so that financial reports today can be meaningfully related to financial reports in the past. The alternatives are to adjust the values on the financial statements for replacement values or price-level changes or both. But there are problems with these approaches. Adjusting for replacement values causes us concern because we would be leaving the comfortable area of objective verifiable evidence to support statement values. And adjusting for price-level changes causes us concern about the appropriateness of one index for measuring many different factors that cause changes in prices.

Basic Principles

The six principles that form the framework for the practice of accounting rest on the four basic assumptions. These principles are as follows:

1. The cost principle
2. The matching principle
3. The revenue-recognition principle
4. The expense-recognition principle
5. The full disclosure principle
6. The consistency principle

1. The Cost Principle

The cost principle is based on objective verifiable evidence

Exchange prices offer us objective, verifiable evidence of values for the goods and services we may exchange with others. On the day that exchanges are made we record the exchange prices in our accounting records. We call these prices **historical costs.** As time goes on, the values for the items we acquired may increase. But we will not record these increases in values, for several reasons.

One major reason is that we no longer have that objective verifiable evidence as to the item's new value. Yes, we know it's worth more and some expert can tell us what he or she thinks it's worth. So can another expert, whose valuations will not be the same as the first expert's. You see, their opinions are subjective, not objective. Therefore, the increase in value cannot be verified by independent parties. And that's very important, because the values on the financial statements must be capable of being verified so that investors and creditors can rely on the financial statements. Independent auditors will insist on verifying items in the accounting records before they issue their opinion. In verifying values, the auditors will look to various source documents for their objective evidence—purchase invoices, titles of ownership, property deeds, brokers' advices, and such items.

A second reason we use historical costs is that we have acquired goods and services for use in our operations, and once acquired the price we paid for them is relevant — not what they're worth today. We will assign the *costs* we paid to those periods of time that have received the benefit of the goods or services we acquired. There is substantial disagreement over this point. Some say that the values today are relevant and should be measured and disclosed (as mentioned previously, this topic of replacement costs and price-level-adjusted data will be discussed later in the text).

Very simply, what we mean by the cost principle is that we will record goods and services at the prices we paid for them and will not change those values at a later date when prices increase.

2. The Matching Principle

Revenue and expenses are matched to measure net income

How well did we do? That's a question often asked by management, investors, and creditors. (The answer is on the income statement.) It's asked more often than the question, What resources do we have? (The answer is on the balance sheet.) For this reason, the income statement is considered more important than the balance sheet — not that the balance sheet isn't important; it is. But the income statement is more important. It measures a company's earnings by comparing revenue with expenses. Expenses incurred in a particular time period are compared — matched — with the revenue earned during the same time period. Expenses are incurred because they directly or indirectly are responsible for generating revenue.

3. The Revenue-Recognition Principle

Earning revenue is a process that takes place over an extended period of time

Revenue is the inflow of assets that results from producing goods or rendering services. But exactly when do we record revenue? The earning of revenue does not take place all at one point in time — the *earning process* extends over a considerable length of time.

For example, let's look at Joe Alex Real Estate Agency. Joe has to do a number of things to earn revenue. He has to advertise, he has to take clients to see houses, he has to obtain clients who wish to sell houses, he has to help his clients finance the sale or purchase of the houses — he has a host of things to do. But specifically when should Joe recognize revenue?

Accountants answer this question by saying that revenue should be recognized when both of the following conditions are met:

a. The earning process is essentially complete, and

b. An exchange has taken place.

We can usually recognize revenue when title passes

For most companies these conditions are met at the time the goods are sold or services are rendered. This is called the ***point-of-sale method of recognizing revenue.*** For Joe Alex Real Estate Agency, revenue is recognized at the point in time when the title to the house passes from one client to the other.

But there are some exceptions to the general rule — and for good reasons.

Consider first the problem of the ***installment sales method of recognizing revenue.*** Many things are sold on an installment sales basis. We sell a $600 appliance to a customer today and receive a down payment of $100. The appliance is delivered and the $500 balance will be paid in installments over the next 36 months (plus interest, of course). Since the sale was made today, we should recognize $600 of revenue. We should also recognize the expenses of selling the appliance, and that would include an estimate of the bad debts expense (based on all the appliances we sold this year).

*Revenue is sometimes not
recognized until cash is
received*

But what if we can't estimate the amount of accounts that will not pay us? Then we *will not* recognize revenue when the sale is made. What we will do is to recognize revenue a little bit at a time as the cash payments are received. This is a very conservative approach, and the reason we use it is because we are not sure that the receivables we booked when the sale was made are ever going to be collected.

Another exception concerns contract projects—very common in the construction industry. Let's look at a new business Joe Alex just started. It's a construction company, and Joe has a contract to build a nuclear aircraft carrier for the U.S. government for $4 billion. It will take about 6 years to build the carrier. Now, if we follow the point-of-sale method, Joe's construction company will show no profits for the first 5 years. But in year 6, when the sale takes place, the company will show a profit. And what a profit!! Don't you think the economic facts are really distorted? Was the construction company doing poorly for the first 5 years? Certainly not, with the contract it has. Do you think Joe will have any problem selling the aircraft carrier? Of course not—the U.S. government must buy it for the agreed price when it's complete according to the specifications. It's all spelled out in the contract Joe and Uncle Sam signed before the work started.

*Sometimes revenue is
recognized as a long-term
project is being constructed*

What the construction company will do is to recognize revenue over the 6-year life of the project. How? Based on reasonable estimates of the project's progress. The amount of revenue to be recognized in any year is determined by comparing the costs incurred that year to the total estimated costs for the entire project. The resulting percentage is applied against the total revenue for the project, and that tells us how much revenue to recognize. This is called the ***percentage-of-completion method of recognizing revenue.***

*And sometimes revenue is
recognized when
production is complete*

One more exception to recognizing revenue at the point of sale is called the ***production method of recognizing revenue.*** Here revenue is recognized when production is complete even though a sale hasn't been made. We can use this method only when we are dealing with businesses where we are sure products will be sold—businesses that produce things like precious metals (gold, silver, uranium), or certain government-supported farm products (corn, wheat, soybeans).

4. The Expense-Recognition Principle

Here we are concerned with the point in time when a cost becomes an expense. Everything we acquire is a cost before it becomes an expense. We show costs on the balance sheet as assets—they are ***unexpired costs,*** meaning we have paid them but we haven't yet gotten any economic benefts from them. We show expenses on the income statement—they are ***expired costs,*** meaning we paid for them and have received the economic benefts represented by the cost. But when do we move costs from the balance sheet to show them as expenses on the income statement?

We recognize expenses in three ways:

*Expenses are recognized by
direct association, by
rational allocation, and by
immediate recognition*

a. Certain costs become expenses because we can ***associate*** them ***directly*** with revenue. When Joe Alex sells an Alexmobile, at that time the costs of the car—which are reflected as inventory on the company's balance sheet—become expenses, recorded under cost of goods sold on the income statement.

b. Certain costs become expenses by ***systematic and rational allocation.*** If we can't associate costs directly with revenue, the next best approach is to assign the costs to expenses over time periods in some reasonable manner. That's basically the idea behind the depreciation of buildings and equipment and the amortization of intangibles.

c. Some costs don't fit the first method and are too elusive to apply the second — these costs we recognize as expenses ***immediately,*** as soon as incurred. Joe Alex's salary is a good example. As the president of Alex Motor Company, Joe's salary should be allocated to those periods of time that receive the benefits of his efforts. Now, if Joe is really concerned about his ongoing concern, he spends some of his time on this year's activities, but probably more of his time planning future years' activities. It would be impossible to track Joe's current salary and activity to results to come in future years. For example, while singing in the shower, Joe thinks of a jingle to advertise the 1991 Alexmobiles. Time expired: 2 minutes. Two minutes of Joe's time this year is worth $15.75. To allocate that to 1991 is impossible. (Well, nothing is impossible. It's just not practical to try to determine this information.) The practical solution is to expense Joe's salary in total this year.

5. The Full Disclosure Principle

Information relevant to users must be disclosed in the statements or in the footnotes

Investors and creditors have every right to expect that the financial statements they are using contain all the significant economic and financial information that is relevant to their understanding of the entity's financial status. That's what we mean by full disclosure. This information can be communicated in the financial statements or in the notes that supplement them.

Full disclosure does not mean that everything must be disclosed. That would be too costly. A balance must be maintained between the cost of disclosing information and its relevance to users. Basically, if the information will make a difference in investor or creditor decisions, it should be disclosed.

6. The Consistency Principle

Consistency requires that the same generally accepted accounting principles are used period after period for the same accounting events

Accounting information is useful if it can be compared with similar information for the same company through time and with similar information between companies at the same time. But you have seen in the first 10 chapters that there are alternative generally accepted accounting principles for a number of areas — inventories, depreciation, and uncollectibles, for example. For accountants, the consistency principle means that the same accounting method will be applied to accounting events from period to period. If we choose LIFO inventory, we would expect to continue using LIFO year after year. We can't use FIFO in year 2 and average cost in year 3.

Does that mean that a company can never switch to another accounting method? No, companies can and in fact do change accounting methods — but only if they can demonstrate that the new method is preferable to the old one. Of course, if a change is made, the full disclosure principle would require that the nature and effect of the accounting change and the reason for the change must be disclosed in the financial statements when the change is made.

Basic Modifiers

We can't always follow the basic principles blindly. Sometimes practical considerations force us to modify our basic principles. The following are three basic modifiers:

1. Materiality

2. Conservatism

3. Industry practices

Materiality

The concept of materiality is relative—what is material to one company may be immaterial to another

Let's consider a few examples to develop the idea of materiality. In the first one, we'll go back to the Alexmobile Company. The engineering department has recommended—and the idea is accepted—to install an additional part on one of the engine assembly machines. This is not a repair; it's a new part. The cost is $14.11. Now, the cost principle requires us to record the part as an asset and allocate its cost over the 12-year remaining life of the machine. But do you think it's worth the effort to record as an asset the $14.11 and then depreciate it? Of course not. It would probably cost more in accounting effort to capitalize the part than the part is worth.

Also in the Alexmobile Company, at year-end the accounts receivable subsidiary ledger has a balance that is $150,000 greater than the control account. That's pretty big—or is it? We can't tell until we know the size of the accounts receivable. Let's say that the control account has a balance of $1,500,000. So the $150,000 difference is 10% and that's material. But now let's say the general ledger control account is $150,000,000. Now the $150,000 difference is only .1%, and when compared to the $150,000,000 it's small—it's not material.

Materiality is a relative thing. The way accountants apply the materiality principle is to determine whether or not they think the item in question will affect decisions of users of the financial statements. If it does, then it's material and must be reported in accordance with generally accepted accounting principles.

We may sometimes find that while an individual transaction is immaterial, a series of related immaterial transactions are material in the aggregate.

Conservatism

Conservatism to accountants means that when they cannot decide between two alternatives they will select the alternative that will understate net assets and net income

In recording business transactions, we look to GAAP for guidance. We often find several alternative ways we can record the transactions, and we select the alternative that we feel most fairly represents the economic substance of the transaction. That method is preferable, based on our considerable experience and judgment in selecting accounting alternatives.

But there are times when there is no clear-cut alternative. When this happens we will then select the most conservative alternative. By *conservative* we generally mean least likely to overstate net assets and net income. If we are uncertain, it's better to err by understating rather than overstating these items.

Industry Practices

Almost every major industry has some peculiarity about it that requires careful consideration when determining how to report the economic affairs of the companies in that industry in accordance with GAAP. Most often we can reconcile the peculiarity with generally accepted accounting principles. But in some cases we can't, and then we have to rely on what is generally accepted within the industry and work within that as the modifier to GAAP.

Perhaps the best example of an industry practice is found in the meatpacking industry, where market values are used to measure inventories of the various cuts of meat. It's just impossible to allocate the costs of a steer to the various by-products in any meaningful way.

QUESTIONS

1. Why do we need generally accepted accounting principles?

2. How are generally accepted accounting principles enforced?

3. Specifically what does the term *generally accepted accounting principles* mean?

4. What is the *conceptual framework study?*

5. What are the basic objectives of financial statements?

6. "General-purpose financial statements are prepared so that the general public should be able to understand them." Evaluate this statement.

7. The second project of the conceptual framework study is called "Qualitative Characteristics of Accounting Information." What was the purpose of the project? List the qualitative characteristics.

8. The most important characteristic of accounting information is usefulness. How do the other characteristics relate to usefulness?

9. About a dozen generally accepted accounting principles form a structure from which all the other generally accepted accounting principles are derived. Explain this structure.

10. The Buick automobile is a popular domestic automobile, and its manufacture is financed by numerous investors and creditors. But these investors and creditors never see Buick's balance sheet and income statement. Why not?

11. "Financial statements do not precisely measure revenue, expenses, assets, and liabilities." Explain this statement.

12. "Basic accounting principles rest on the basic assumptions of accounting. For example, the cost principle rests upon the going concern concept." Explain.

13. "The stable-dollar concept prohibits companies from providing investors and creditors with important relevant information." Evaluate this statement.

14. Revenue is recognized when the earning process is essentially complete and an exchange has taken place. Generally, this is at the point of sale, but there are three exceptions to this general rule. Why?

15. The matching principle requires that revenue earned in a particular time period be compared with those expenses incurred during the same time period that were directly or indirectly responsible for generating the revenue. Specifically how are expenses recognized?

16. What does the full disclosure principle mean to investors and creditors?

17. "Atlas Company adopted the FIFO method of inventory costing in 1954 when it first started business. The company wishes to switch to the LIFO method this year but can't because it would violate the consistency principle." Evaluate this statement.

18. "Sometimes practical considerations cause the basic principles to be modified." Explain.

Accounting for Partnerships and Corporations

Throughout out study in the first 10 chapters, we have not been overly concerned with the form of business ownership. From Chapter 1 to Chapter 10 we never really dealt with owners' equity because we had enough to do studying assets and liabilities. In Part Four of *Financial Accounting* it is time to learn about accounting for partnerships and corporations.

The assets, liabilities, revenues, and expenses are accounted for in the same way for proprietorships, partnerships, and corporations. What you've learned thus far about these items doesn't change. What does change is the way we account for owners' equity. The next two chapters will focus on accounting for the owners' equity of partnerships and corporations. The last two chapters of Part Four will show how to account for corporate long-term liabilities and investments, and how two corporations may be combined into one.

A partnership is a voluntary business association of two or more individuals. The partners must decide how they are going to share profits and losses, what procedures to follow when a new partner enters or an old partner withdraws, and what to do if the partnership is liquidated. You will learn the accounting procedures needed to record these events in the accounting records.

A corporation is an artificial being created by law. Corporations sell common stock and sometimes preferred stock to acquire assets to use in their operations. You will learn the various ways that corporations sell stock, how they borrow money, how they distribute earnings to stockholders as dividends, and how they report the various ownership claims in the stockholders' equity section of the balance sheet.

One corporation may buy the stock of another corporation. If it purchases enough stock, it owns the other company. You will learn how to account for these investments and how we may put the financial statements of two corporations together and report them as one business entity.

CHAPTER 11

Partnerships and Corporations

We wrote this chapter for you to learn the following things by studying it:

- The reasons individuals may wish to form partnerships and corporations and the characteristics of each
- Why assets are recorded at their fair value upon partnership formation
- The various methods of determining how partnership profits and losses are distributed
- The general steps that are followed in organizing a new corporation
- What common stock is, and the rights of a common stockholder
- How to record issuing common stock on a *subscription basis*
- What we mean by *treasury stock* and *donated capital*
- The difference between *par, stated, market,* and *book* value of stock

Up to this point we have concentrated on certain limited objectives. First, we introduced the principal financial statements, the income statement, statement of retained earnings, and balance sheet. Next, we discussed the manner in which business transactions are recorded and summarized to generate these financial statements. Following this we considered the basic elements of the financial statements. So far we have studied assets, liabilities, and their related revenues and expenses. Now it's time to complete the study of the basic elements by discussing the capital accounts.

Remember that in Chapter 1 we discussed the three main types of business entities: proprietorships, partnerships, and corporations. We have not found it necessary to distinguish among these three types of entities. Accounting for assets and liabilities is *not* dependent on the form of a business organization. Consequently, we used very simple corporations in the first 10 chapters. In this chapter we are concerned with partnerships and corporations.

Accounting for assets and liabilities does not depend on the form of business organization

PARTNERSHIPS

A partnership is a voluntary association of individuals to operate a business for profit

If three members of your class decide to form together as a group to wash cars for $5 per car, that's a partnership. It's a partnership because the Uniform Partnership Act—which most states have adopted—says it is. The act defines a ***partnership*** as "an association of two or more persons to carry on, as co-owners, a business for profit." This act governs the formation and operation of partnerships.

You have all come into contact with businesses formed as partnerships. Perhaps your first exposure to a partnership was your visit to your medical doctor and your dentist. If these professionals did not conduct their businesses alone, they conducted them as partnerships. The partnership form of business is common to the professions. So we see public accounting and law firms, as well as medical and dental practices, operated as partnerships. Many small manufacturing, assemblying, wholesale, retail, and service companies are also organized as partnerships.

Most professional associations are organized as partnerships

People join together to form partnerships for a number of reasons. Some of us have more organizational and managerial ability than others. Some of us have more knowledge and experience than others. Some of us have more money than others. A partnership utilizes the combined abilities, experiences, and capital of the partners to make the business stronger than if only one individual owned it. Perhaps the prime reason individuals seek partners is to obtain additional capital.

Partnerships are formed to utilize the combined abilities, experiences, and capital of the partners

For the professions, until recently, the corporate form of organization was denied in many states. Since a personal service was rendered, it was felt that the corporate form generated a feeling of impersonality and provided protection against lawsuits for poor-quality work. In a corporation only the money invested in the corporation by the stockholders is subject to attack in a lawsuit. That's not true for the partners in a partnership. Not only is the money they invested in the partnership subject to attack, but also their personal and other business assets. Many states have enacted legislation allowing professional organizations to incorporate. Even so, the largest of the partnerships, the international certified public accounting firms, have not elected to become corporations. Most of these firms have in excess of 1,500 partners, and several have more than 2,000 partners.

Partnerships will present us with a number of interesting accounting problems, but before we can get you started in partnership accounting, there are a number of things you need to know about partnerships.

PARTNERSHIP CHARACTERISTICS

A partnership is like a proprietorship in that it is not considered to be a separate legal entity. The partners are the individual legal entities. And the characteristics of partnerships all relate to this fact.

Ease of Formation

It's easy to form a partnership

As we said before, if two or more of us agree to start a business, any business, with the object of earning a profit, we have created a partnership. We don't need permission from the county commissioners, nor the IRS, nor the SEC, nor the state attorney general, nor anyone else to form a partnership. We just do it. In fact we don't even need a written contract between the partners. An oral agreement is all that is needed. It's very easy to form a partnership, just do it.

Voluntary Association

Partnerships are voluntary associations of individuals

No one can force us into a partnership. A partnership is a voluntary association. We are legally responsible for the business acts of our partners, and that legal responsibility extends beyond whatever funds we may have invested in the partnership. It extends to our personal and other business assets. So you can see it would be unfair and unreasonable to force us into partnerships with people we don't like or trust. We should *and do* have the right to select those people we wish to associate with in a partnership.

Articles of Partnership

A partner's written agreement is called the articles of partnership

All we need to form a partnership is an oral agreement. But we would be well advised to formalize the partner relationship by a written agreement. This is called the **articles of partnership.** Some of the things we would need to include in this document would be:

- The manner in which we share profits or losses
- The amount each of us is to invest
- The amount each of us may withdraw
- How new partners are to be admitted
- How old partners are allowed to withdraw

Mutual Agency

Each partner can act for the partnership; that's mutual agency

If you do business with a partnership you have a right to assume that the partner you are talking to has the authority to bind the partnership to whatever legal business transaction the two of you are talking about. Unless, of course, you are told or notified otherwise. The partners are all agents for the partnership. That means that each partner can act for the partnership. That's where the term **mutual agency** comes from. Here's how this concept works. The city of Bethlehem, Pennsylvania, may enter into an agreement with Mr. Garcia of Weinstein, Garcia, and Trovanivich for an audit of the city's general fund, knowing that Mr. Garcia has full authority to bind his CPA firm to a contract. But if the city were to enter into a contract with Mr. Garcia for the sale of sewerage pipes to the city, the city would not expect this to be binding on the CPA firm, since the transaction is not within the scope of an accounting firm's business. (Of course, Mr. Garcia would not enter into the second transaction, since he would not be considered independent in his relationship with the city when performing the audit to fulfill the first contract.)

So you can see that it is very important to select your partners carefully. Mutual agency coupled with unlimited liability could cause you a good deal of grief if you select an irresponsible or unethical partner.

Unlimited Liability

Unlimited liability makes each partner personally responsible for the partnership obligations

Suppose things don't go well for your partnership and you can't pay your bills. What then? Well, your creditors can look to the partnership assets for the settlement of their claims and if the assets aren't enough, what then? Your individual assets — that's what. Creditors can seek satisfaction from the personal assets of the individual partners. This is the **umlimited liability** characteristic of a partnership. If the personal assets of some of your partners are exhausted, the creditors can come to you and the remaining partners to settle whatever debts are still unpaid.

Limited Life

A partnership is dissolved whenever a new partner is admitted, a partner withdraws, dies, is incapacitated, or bankrupt. It has a limited life

The life of a partnership is limited. A partnership dissolves when one of the partners withdraws, dies, is forced into personal bankruptcy, or becomes incapacitated. A partnership is also dissolved when the specific objective for which the partnership was formed is achieved. If the articles of partnership specify the life of the partnership to be for a certain period of time, when that time has expired the partnership is dissolved. Of course the partnership may be dissolved by the decision of any one of the partners. The admission of a new partner also dissolves the old partnership.

You should realize that the dissolution of a partnership does not mean that the business operations are interrupted. Large partnerships, such as the regional and national CPA firms and certain law firms, provide in the partnership agreement for the manner in which the admission of new partners and the retirement of old partners is to be handled. You and I are generally unaware of the retirement, withdrawal, or admission of partners to the partnership of these firms.

Co-ownership of Property

Partnership assets are owned jointly by all the partners

When a partnership is formed, some of you may invest cash, some may invest office equipment or other assets, some may simply invest their talents. But whatever assets are invested become the property of all the partners. The partner contributing the asset no longer retains any personal right to that asset. The assets are owned jointly by all of you so when a partnership is terminated, the individual partners may not receive back the same assets they contributed. Of course, if it is agreeable to all the partners, the assets may be given back to those who contributed them. Often, however, the partners settle their claims against the partnership by the distribution of cash.

Income Participation

Profits and losses are distributed equally unless specified otherwise

It's important that you specify in the articles of partnership how the profits and losses are to be shared between the partners. How this is done is a matter of mutual consent among all the partners. But if you don't have an agreement, profits and losses will be distributed equally.

ADVANTAGES AND DISADVANTAGES OF PARTNERSHIPS

The partnership form of business organization offers a number of advantages

The partnership form of organization may offer you certain advantages over operating by yourself as a proprietorship or even operating with other individuals as owners organized as a corporation. These are some of the advantages:

1. *Capitalization*   The amount of money invested by the owners of the business is called its *capitalization.* The more owners, the more capital. This is one of the main reasons you may wish to have a partner—for his or her money, to help finance your business activities.

2. *Talent*   The more partners you have, the more talent you have. Of course, more people will share the profits. The advantage of having more talent is that you can utilize the unique skills and abilities of several people. Each of you can specialize in an area of the business that can best use your talents.

3. *Ease of formation*   It's so easy for you to form a partnership. You and the other partners just say you are a partnership and you are. That's not the case if you want to operate as a corporation. You must go through a formal legal process to be incorporated.

4. *Cost of organization*   The only cost you will have in becoming a partnership is the legal fee to have the articles of partnership drawn up. If you choose not to do this, you have no costs at all. Incorporating requires cash outlays for the application to the state in which you wish to be incorporated plus legal fees for filing the application and for preparation of the corporate charter and bylaws.

5. *Tax advantages*   Your partnership is not a legal entity. And that means it doesn't have to pay income taxes. You pay income taxes on your personal income including your share of the partnership income. However, certain corporations can elect to be taxed as if they were partnerships. That's called the Subchapter S option.

6. *Informality*   Corporations require formal legal procedures to do many of the things that you can do as a partnership without such rigidity. For example, in a corporation the distribution of income requires a board of directors' meeting to declare a dividend before payment can be made to the stockholders. In a partnership, you and the other partners may withdraw funds without such legal action.

7. *Less government supervision*   Generally partnerships have less government supervision than corporations.

Operating as a partnership has some disadvantages

Organizing as a partnership does have advantages, but it also has a number of disadvantages. They are:

1. *Loss of freedom*   You can't run a partnership as you would a proprietorship. As sole owner of a business you answer to no one. But with a partnership you must answer to your partners, and they to you. You have mutual agency and unlimited liability. This requires mutual agreement on the affairs of the partnership.

2. *Limited life*   If one of your partners dies or withdraws, the partnership is dissolved. That does not mean, however, that your business is over. You have most likely provided for this situation in the articles of partnership.

3. *Unlimited liability*   Corporations are legal entities and as a result are legally responsible for their actions, but only to the extent of their capitalization. Partnerships are not legal entities, so you and the other partners are legally responsible for your partnership's actions. As you now know, once the partnership assets are used to settle creditors' claims, your personal assets and those personal assets of your partners, may be required to settle any unsatisfied creditors' claims.

4. *Mutual agency*   Let's put it this way: A fool is one who has a fool as a partner. You're responsible for his acts, and with unlimited liability if he acts the fool, you pay for it.

5. *Capitalization*   If you need large sums of money to operate your business, the corporate form of organization is a much better vehicle for raising what you need. That's because you can sell shares of stock to a *large number of people* who are interested in a good investment for their money but don't want to become involved in the operations of the business.

6. *Tax disadvantages*   Depending on your income, you might pay more income taxes as a partnership than if you organized as a corporation. Since this is subject to whatever tax laws and tax rates are currently in effect, we can't give any hard-and-fast rule. Each partnership has to look at its own situation.

PARTNERSHIP ACCOUNTING

Accounting for business transactions with external parties for a partnership is the same as we learned for a proprietorship or for that matter for a corporation. Assets, liabilities, revenues, and expenses are all recorded according to the generally accepted accounting principles discussed in the first 10 chapters. It is in the owners' equity section that we see differences.

Partnership accounting requires that we establish a separate capital and a separate withdrawal account for each partner. The manner in which we distribute the net income or loss between the partners is unique for partnerships and differentiates a partnership from a corporation.

In the rest of this section we are going to introduce you to the following problems of partnership accounting: partnership formation, income distribution of a partnership, and partnership financial statements.

Partnership Formation

When a partnership is formed, a journal entry is made to record the assets contributed by each partner and the liabilities of each partner that are assumed by the partnership. If only cash is contributed and no liabilities are assumed, the problem of valuation is simple. The entry we would make to record the formation of a partnership in this situation would be simply to debit cash and credit the two partners' capital accounts like this:

A separate capital account is needed for each partner

Cash	25,000	
Jones, Capital		10,000
Smith, Capital		15,000
To record cash investments by Smith and Jones.		

But what if, in addition to cash, other assets are contributed? Then we have a valuation problem. At what value should we record the assets? The original cost? The book value of the assets on the individual partner's books? The fair value today? Some other value?

Assets are valued at their fair values on the day they are contributed to the partnership

Our generally accepted accounting principles tell us what to do. Specifically, the historical cost concept would require that assets contributed by individual partners be valued at their fair value on the date they are transferred to the partnership. What constitutes a fair value is, of course, subject to the mutual agreement of the partners.

Let's look at the firm of Ortiz and Mervine to see how we would account for the formation of a new partnership when cash and other assets are contributed. On July 1 of the current year, Mary Ortiz and Bill Mervine agree to combine their competing sporting goods stores and form a partnership. The partners are to contribute the assets of their previous stores. It is agreed that the liabilities of the proprietorships will be assumed by the partnership. A capital account is established for each partner with a credit balance equal to the total assets less the total liabilities contributed by that partner. These are the journal entries to open the accounts of the partnership:

Contribution of cash and other assets in forming a partnership

July 1	Cash...	3,500	
	Accounts Receivable	6,200	
	Merchandise Inventory	12,700	
	Store Supplies on Hand...................................	900	
	Accounts Payable		2,400
	Mary Ortiz, Capital		20,900
	To record investment of Mary Ortiz.		

1	Cash...	1,700	
	Accounts Receivable	7,300	
	Merchandise Inventory	9,100	
	Store Equipment..	6,500	
	Building	25,200	
	Land	10,000	
	Accounts Payable		4,500
	Mortgage Payable.......................................		26,200
	Bill Mervine, Capital		29,100

To record investment of Bill Mervine.

The values of the assets, other than cash, are the amounts both Mary and Bill agreed upon. The amounts represent the fair values as of July 1 of the store supplies, inventories, equipment, building, and land. The Accounts Receivable balance represents the face amount of only those receivables from the proprietorships that can reasonably be expected to be collected. Accounts that have only a small chance of collectibility are not transferred to the partnership.

The values of the assets other than cash will not agree with the amounts recorded in the books of the two proprietorships. That's because the values have increased (or perhaps decreased) since they were first acquired by Mary or Bill. That's what happened with the land Bill contributed. He paid $8,000 for it 5 years ago. And the building cost him $17,000 to build shortly after he purchased the land. Those were the values recorded on the books of Bill Mervine's Sporting Goods Store. The building has $4,200 of accumulated depreciation recorded also. But the fair value of the building today is $25,200, and that's what goes on the partnership books — not the original cost of $17,000, nor the book value of $12,800 ($17,000 − $4,200) — but the fair value today. Since the building has increased in value over the past 5 years, Bill is the one who should receive the credit for the increase. And he does this by recording the building at $25,200 and crediting his capital account for a similar amount.

Income Distribution of a Partnership

You and your partners can distribute your partnership income any way you want. What you will most likely consider is the services performed by each partner, the talent and capital contributed, and perhaps the length of time in the partnership.

You can adjust for differences in time devoted to the business and managerial or technical ability by providing *allowances* for salaries. Partnership salaries are merely a means to distribute partnership profits in an equitable manner; they are not salaries in the legal sense of the word. You and the other partners are owners of the business entity, not employees.

Salaries and interest allowances are a means of equitably distributing partnership profit

You can adjust for differences in capital contributions by *allowing* interest on the capital balances. Interest allowed in this manner is not interest expense on borrowed funds; it is again a *means to achieve an equitable distribution* of profits.

Most often you will find that partners share earnings (or losses) in one of these three general ways:

1. An established ratio

2. The capital investment relationship

3. Salary and interest allowances, the remainder in an established ratio

Established Ratio

Remember that if the articles of partnership are silent as to the manner of profit distribution, profits and losses are to be distributed equally. Any other ratio must be established by the partnership agreement. Whatever ratio you agree upon is an attempt to adjust for service and capital contributions.

For example, when Mary Ortiz and Bill Mervine formed their sporting goods partnership, they agreed to share profits in the ratio of 75% for Ortiz and 25% for Mervine ($\frac{3}{4}$ and $\frac{1}{4}$ or a 3:1 ratio). The income for their first one-half year of operation was $8,000. Here is how it was distributed:

Profit distribution by a fixed ratio

	Division of Profit
Mary Ortiz ($8,000 × .75)	$6,000
Bill Mervine ($8,000 × .25)	2,000
Net income	$8,000

The net income of $8,000 appeared as a credit balance in the Expense and Revenue Summary account after the normal closing entries were made. Then the Expense and Revenue Summary account was closed like this:

Recording partnership profit

Dec. 31	Expense and Revenue Summary..........................	8,000
	Mary Ortiz, Capital.....................................		6,000
	Bill Mervine, Capital...................................		2,000
	To close the expense and revenue summary account and distribute partnership profits.	

If Mary or Bill had made any withdrawals during the year, an entry debiting their respective withdrawal accounts would have been made. Then the withdrawal accounts would have been closed to their capital accounts, just like proprietorship accounting.

Capital Investment Relationship

Maybe the reason your partnership makes a profit is closely related to the amount of capital you and your partners have invested. If that's true, you should consider sharing those profits based on the partners' beginning or average capital balances.

The firm of Adams and Hancock share profits that way; let's see how it works. Adams and Hancock have beginning capital account balances of $20,000 and $40,000, respectively. During the year Adams invested an additional $10,000 on Apr. 1 and withdrew $5,000 on Oct. 1. Hancock withdrew $5,000 on July 1 and invested $25,000 additional capital on Oct. 1. Their capital accounts look like this:

Adams, Capital				Hancock, Capital			
		Bal.	20,000			Bal.	40,000
Oct. 1	5,000	Apr. 1	10,000	July 1	5,000	Oct. 1	25,000
		Bal.	25,000			Bal.	60,000

Beginning Ratio   The partnership earned $21,000 this year and if profits were to be divided according to the beginning capital account relationship, Adams would get one-third. That's because his beginning capital ($20,000) is one-third of the total beginning capital ($20,000 + $40,000). Hancock would then receive two-thirds

($40,000 ÷ $60,000). The journal entry the firm would have to make to record the profits would be:

Profit distribution based on beginning capital account ratios

Dec. 31   Expense and Revenue Summary 21,000
           Adams, Capital.......................................   7,000
           Hancock, Capital   14,000
           To close the expense and revenue summary account and to distribute profits.

Average Capital Balances Ratio   But Adams and Hancock elected not to distribute their profits based on the beginning capital account ratio. Instead they chose to use the *average* capital balance ratio. That's because they think it is more equitable since they make material investments and withdrawals during the year. The calculation of the average capital balance is a little more complex than one may think at first glance. Adding the beginning and ending balances and dividing by 2 will not properly state the average capital balance. We can show you this by a simple example.

Tom and Jane are partners. On Jan. 1, Tom has a zero balance in his capital account while Jane has $10. Eleven months go by with no change. Then, on Dec. 1, Tom invests $10 and Jane withdraws $10. So at year-end, Dec. 31, Tom has a $10 balance in his capital account and Jane has zero. When we add the beginning and ending balances for both Tom and Jane and divide each by 2, the result is a $5 average for each of them. But Jane had her $10 invested for 11 months of the year while Tom had $10 invested for only 1 month. The point is that we must consider the length of time that capital is invested in the partnership.

The way we consider time is by calculating something called *dollar-months.* Dollar-months is the result obtained by multiplying the dollar investment by the length of time those dollars are invested. That's the way Adams and Hancock did it. Adams had $20,000 invested from Jan. 1 to Apr. 1; then he invested an additional $10,000, bringing his capital balance to $30,000. On Oct. 1 he withdrew $5,000, reducing his account to $25,000. His total dollar-months were determined by this calculation:

Calculation of a partner's total dollar-months, which is divided by 12 to determine the average capital balance

Dollars	Months	Dollar-Months
$20,000	3	$ 60,000
30,000	6	180,000
25,000	3	75,000
Total		$315,000

Average capital balance = $315,000 ÷ 12 months = $26,250

The $20,000 invested from Jan. 1 to Apr. 1 (3 months) is equivalent to $60,000 dollar-months ($20,000 × 3). From Apr. 1 to Oct. 1 (6 months) he had $30,000 invested, equivalent to $180,000 dollar-months ($30,000 × 6). And during the last 3 months (Oct. 1 to Dec. 31) he had $25,000 invested or $75,000 dollar-months ($25,000 × 3).

Adams' average capital balance for the year was determined by dividing his total $315,000 dollar-months by the 12 months of the year—$26,250.

For Hancock the total dollar-months were:

Dollar-months calculation for the second partner

	Dollars	Months	Dollar-Months
	$40,000	6	$240,000
	35,000	3	105,000
	60,000	3	180,000
	Total		$525,000

Average capital balance = $525,000 ÷ 12 months = $43,750

His beginning balance of $40,000 remained in the partnership for 6 months (Jan. 1 to July 1), resulting in $240,000 dollar-months. Then on July 1 he withdrew $5,000, reducing his capital balance to $35,000 until Oct. 1. This was another $105,000 dollar-months ($35,000 × 3), and finally, on Oct. 1 he invested $25,000, bringing his capital balance up to $60,000 for the last 3 months of the year—that meant still another $180,000 dollar-months ($60,000 × 3). So his average capital balance was $43,750—the total $525,000 dollar-months divided by 12 months.

The firm's profits of $21,000 were distributed to Adams and Hancock based on the ratio of their average capital balances. Adams' portion of the $70,000 total average capital balance ($26,250 + $43,750) was 37.5% ($26,250 ÷ $70,000) and Hancock's was 62.5% ($43,750 ÷ $70,000). So Adams got $7,875 ($21,000 × .375) and Hancock $13,125 ($21,000 × .625), which was distributed to the partners by this entry:

Profit distribution based on average capital balances

Dec. 31   Expense and Revenue Summary 21,000
     Adams, Capital....................................... 7,875
     Hancock, Capital..................................... 13,125
  To close the expense and revenue summary account and distribute profits.

Allowance for Salaries and Interest

Perhaps your partnership has partners who contribute different things. Joe may provide the money you need to start up. You are going to spend all your waking hours on the partnership business, and Melissa is the smart one. We can set up an arrangement to compensate each of you fairly for your unique contribution. We can give credit for salaries to you and Melissa for your time and her talent. And we can give credit to Joe for interest on his money. Remember, you and Melissa are not being paid salaries, nor is Joe being paid interest. This is just a way of distributing profits (hopefully there are some) to each of you in an equitable manner. Any profits left over after allowing for salaries and interest are to be distributed to the three of you equally, because we have already adjusted for differences in your capital, time, and talents.

The differences in partner's capital, time, and talent can be compensated for by allowing for salaries and interest in the partnership distribution agreement

Let's look at the partnership of Reese, Stankey, and Hodgers to see how this arrangement works. The partnership earned $100,000 this year. Reese devotes full time to the partnership affairs and is allowed a salary of $22,000 for his managerial ability. Stankey spends only 30 hours per week in the business and is therefore given credit for only $15,000 of salary. Hodgers also spends 30 hours per week in the business, but it's his technical know-how that makes the partnership go. He is given credit for a salary of $25,000. Interest of 10% is allowed on the partners' beginning capital balances—$40,000, $50,000, and $20,000, respectively—and the remaining profits are split equally. Here is how the $100,000 partnership net income is distributed:

	REESE, STANKEY, AND HODGERS Income Distribution Schedule Year Ended December 31, 1989			
Allowance	**Reese**	**Stankey**	**Hodgers**	**Totals**
Interest	$ 4,000	$ 5,000	$ 2,000	$ 11,000
Salary	22,000	15,000	25,000	62,000
Totals	$26,000	$20,000	$27,000	$ 73,000
Remainder	9,000	9,000	9,000	27,000
Net income	$35,000	$29,000	$36,000	$100,000

Calculation of profit distribution allowing for interest and salaries

After the credit of $11,000 is allowed for interest and the $62,000 for salaries, a balance of $27,000 ($100,000 − $11,000 − $62,000) remains to be distributed equally to the three partners ($9,000 each).

The general journal entry to record the profit distribution would look like this:

Profit distribution based on allowances for interest and salaries

Dec. 31	Expense and Revenue Summary	100,000	
	Reese, Capital.....................................		35,000
	Stankey, Capital...................................		29,000
	Hodgers, Capital		36,000
	To close the expense and revenue summary acount and distribute partnership profits.		

Don't forget that interest and salaries *have not* been paid to the partners. The allowances for interest and salaries are only a means of determining how the net income for the period should be distributed.

What happens if the interest and salary allowances exceed net income? It doesn't matter; the income distribution is done the same way. Let's say that in 1990 Reese, Stankey, and Hodgers had a partnership income of $46,000 and it is distributed as follows:

Calculation of profit distribution when interest and salary allowances exceed net income

	REESE, STANKEY, AND HODGERS Income Distribution Schedule Year Ended December 31, 1990			
Allowance	**Reese**	**Stankey**	**Hodgers**	**Totals**
Interest	$ 4,000	$ 5,000	$ 2,000	$11,000
Salary	22,000	15,000	25,000	62,000
Totals	$26,000	$20,000	$27,000	$73,000
Remainder	(9,000)	(9,000)	(9,000)	(27,000)
Net income	$17,000	$11,000	$18,000	$46,000

Notice that the total allowances for interest and salaries exceeds net income by $27,000 ($73,000 − $46,000) and that this negative excess is distributed equally to the individual partners in the same manner as the positive excess was last year. The result is a reduction of $9,000 for each partner after allowing for interest and salary.

The profit distribution journal entry would be:

Profit distribution based on allowances for interest and salaries which exceed net income

Dec. 31	Expense and Revenue Summary	46,000
Reese, Capital.......................................		17,000
Stankey, Capital....................................		11,000
Hodgers, Capital		18,000
To close the expense and revenue summary account and distribute partnership profits.		

Partnership Financial Statements

The financial statements of a partnership and a proprietorship are similar. The income statements are identical in format except that on the partnership income statement the income distribution may be presented on the bottom portion of the statement. This is shown for the Reese, Stankey, and Hodgers partnership like this:

The income distribution may be shown on a partnership income statement

REESE, STANKEY, AND HODGERS		
Income Statement		
Year Ended December 31, 1989		
Sales		$787,000
Less: Sales Discounts......................................	$11,400	
Net Income		$100,000
Income Distribution:		
Reese	$35,000	
Stankey ...,...	29,000	
Hodgers...	36,000	$100,000

We are also going to need a statement of partners' capital accounts. This statement provides the partners with summarized information that shows the increases and decreases in their respective capital accounts during the year as well as the beginning and ending balances. It looks like this:

The statement of partners' capital accounts shows the investment, income distributions, and withdrawals of each partner

REESE, STANKEY, AND HODGERS				
Statement of Partners' Capital Accounts				
Year Ended December 31, 1989				
	Reese	**Stankey**	**Hodgers**	**Totals**
Capital, Jan. 1, 1989	$ 40,000	$50,000	$20,000	$110,000
Add: Investments	60,000			60,000
Net Income	35,000	29,000	36,000	100,000
	$135,000	$79,000	$56,000	$270,000
Less: Withdrawals	22,000	18,000	27,000	67,000
Capital, Dec. 31, 1989	$113,000	$61,000	$29,000	$203,000

The balance sheet of a partnership differs from that of a proprietorship only in the capital section. A partnership with few partners will have a capital account for each partner reflecting the partner's ending capital balance. But one with many partners will show only one account — Partners' Capital — which is the total of all the individual partners' accounts. Of course the partnership will maintain subsidiary accounts, one for each partner, to support the total in the control account — Partners' Capital.

SURVIVAL OF THE FITTEST

While there are many types of partnerships in the United States, CPA and law firms are the most numerous. They generally have the most employees and the most partners. Every year thousands of accounting and law graduates enter their profession's most prestigious firms. And 8 to 10 years later only a few remain and are admitted to partnership. Writing in the Jan. 3, 1983, *The Wall Street Journal,* Barbara Rosen points out that "making partner at a top New York law firm isn't easy. Not making it is tougher."

For those prestigious New York law firms partnership consideration comes up about seven years after graduation. For CPA firms it's a little longer. Data from Columbia University shows that of 246 lawyers entering 10 New York law firms in 1972 only 33 be-

came partners. What happened to the rest? Well most leave before seven years. Many entry level accountants and lawyers view the prestigious firms as a necessary training ground for their careers. They receive excellent training and exposure. This in turn provides them with many lucrative and challenging employment opportunities with their firm's clients. A number of individuals leave to set up their own CPA or law firms. And some stay, aspiring to partnership.

Still, of those remaining only a few will make partner. Technical ability is *not* the reason for rejection. These are all highly intelligent, highly motivated people, all top students in their graduating class. Further, if a staff member did not demonstrate technical ability they would have been dismissed

many years before. So what determines who is in and who is out?

Several factors could be the answer. Perhaps it's leadership ability, perhaps the ability to get along with colleagues, perhaps the ability to attract new clients. Or perhaps too many talented people are up for partnership at the same time. It could also be that bad economic times resulted in a poor financial year for the firm. Whatever the reason, for those rejected it is most likely the first time they have experienced failure and it is most certainly a situation for which coping is most difficult.

Source: The Wall Street Journal, Jan. 3, 1983, page 1.

Not everyone who enters a CPA or law firm will become a partner.

CORPORATIONS

A corporation is an artificial legal being

A **corporation** is an artificial legal being created by a government charter that endows it with certain powers. A corporation exists in the eyes of the law as though it were a person separate and distinct from the people who own it. It has many of the rights that a natural person possesses. It may own property, borrow money, sue and be sued, and in a sense it may even get "married" to another corporation through a merger. Corporations do not possess a natural citizen's rights to vote or to be elected to public office.

Corporations are the dominant form of business organization in the United States. While proprietorships and partnerships are probably more numerous, corporations own the largest amount of resources, produce and sell the most products, and employ the greatest number of individuals.

Some corporations are established by the federal government to operate in the public interest. An example is the Federal Deposit Insurance Corporation (FDIC), which insures the safety of many deposits in banks. The corporations you are most familiar with, those in business to make and sell products and services, are created under the laws of the various states. A corporation must meet the requirements set forth by the state in which it is incorporated. A company may incorporate in one state, having its main office in another state, and operate in many states. The Coca-Cola Company, for instance, is incorporated in Delaware, has its primary executive offices in Georgia, and operates in all 50 states (and in many foreign countries).

Articles of Incorporation

The articles of incorporation are written documents giving the state basic information about a proposed corporation

When you decide you want to do business as a corporation, you must apply to a state government for permission to be a corporation—to **incorporate.**

You begin the incorporation process by filing proposed articles of incorporation together with the required fee with the appropriate state office. A lawyer should be consulted in writing the proposed articles so that they will be in the proper form and will include all information required by state law. When these ***articles of incorpora-tion*** are approved, they become a part of the ***charter*** creating the corporation. The charter is the document issued by a state government giving a business the legal right to begin operating as a corporation.

Since each state has its own laws governing what should be included in the articles of incorporation, the contents of the articles will vary from state to state. Here are some of the things that are commonly included:

Corporations may have almost any name and any legal purpose

1. ***Name and purpose of the corporation*** Within certain limits you can choose almost any name for your corporation. You cannot, of course, call yourself the Ford Motor Corporation—another group has already picked that one.

   You may state your purpose narrowly—for example, you could say that you are establishing a corporation to sell peanuts at high school football games in Michigan. Or you may state your purpose broadly, so that you can diversify into many types of business without having to form a new corporation each time you want to begin a new type of business. For example, your purpose might be to enter into any lawful business activity permitted by the state of Michigan.

Capital stock is certificates of ownership in a corporation

2. ***Capital stock*** Ownership of a corporation is represented by shares of stock. Every corporation must have one type of stock, called ***common stock.*** In addition, other types, or classes, of stock may be sold.

   The charter must state the classes of stock that your corporation has permission to sell, the number of shares of each type that you are authorized to sell, what rights or special preferences are granted to each type of stock, and what restrictions are imposed upon each class.

   The amount of assets contributed by owners at the beginning of the new business must also be specified.

   We will discuss the various classes of stock and their rights and restrictions later in this chapter and the next.

The corporation must have an official address

3. ***Place of business*** You must specify the location of your principal office or place of business, so that an official address will be registered with the state. Your tax bills, lawsuits filed against you, and other legal correspondence will be sent to this legal address.

A corporation's life may be unending

4. ***Duration*** The life of your corporation must be defined. Although you may select a short life, such as 10 years, most corporations elect a perpetual—unending—life.

A corporation's governing body is its board of directors

5. ***Directors and officers*** You must list the names and addresses of the first governing body of your corporation, the board of directors, and its operating managers, the officers. After the corporation begins operations, the stockholders (owners) will meet and elect new members to the board of directors.

The people forming a new corporation are called incorporators

6. ***Incorporators*** The names and addresses of the individuals filing the articles of incorporation, the ***incorporators,*** must be listed. You must also disclose the number of shares of stock that each incorporator has agreed to buy and how the shares are to be paid for. Cash or some other asset—building, land, equipment—may be used to pay for shares.

If all the required information is properly presented, the state will issue a certificate of incorporation, or ***charter.*** Once you receive the charter, you may begin selling stock and operating your business.

Before we explain how to account for issuing stock, let's examine why the incorporators might have chosen the corporate form of business instead of a partnership, and how the management structure of a corporation appears.

Advantages of Corporations

Several characteristics of corporations may make this form of organization more desirable than either a partnership or a proprietorship:

1. *Greater amounts of capital can be raised*   Large numbers of individuals and institutions can more easily and efficiently acquire and dispose of ownership interests in a corporation than in a partnership. Many corporations have several million stockholders who have cumulatively invested more than $100 million.

2. *Owners' liability is limited*   Liability of the owners is limited to the amount invested in the corporation—the amount that each stockholder paid for his or her stock. Creditors having a claim against the corporation must be paid only from the assets of the corporation; personal assets of the stockholders are not available to creditors. In a partnership one or more partners must have unlimited liability, thus risking personal as well as business assets.

3. *Ownership shares are easily transferred*   After the initial sale of stock, shares may be transferred in private sale transactions, traded (sold) on established securities markets such as the New York Stock Exchange, or given away. The only involvement of the corporation in these transactions is in keeping an up-to-date list of the names and addresses of the stockholders.

   The billions of dollars changing hands daily through sales of stock on the New York Stock Exchange and the American Stock Exchange do not flow into the coffers of the corporations whose stock is being traded. Corporations acquire capital, cash, and other assets only upon a new issuance of stock or upon the sale of stock previously reacquired. Of course, corporations may also borrow money by issuing bonds or by getting a loan from a bank or other financial institution.

   Sale of a partnership interest is usually a much more complex affair. Remember, each new partner must be acceptable to all of the old partners.

4. *Continuity of existence*   Continuity of existence refers to the unlimited life of a corporation. The transfer of ownership shares does not affect the corporation's ability to operate routinely over decades. In contrast, a partnership's life ends each time a new partner enters or an old one retires. Continuity of existence makes long-term borrowing easier for a corporation than for partnerships and proprietorships.

Disadvantages of Corporations

If the corporate form were preferable in every way, there would be little reason for proprietorships and partnerships to exist. Anyone thinking of forming a corporation should also consider its negative characteristics:

1. *Double taxation exists*   The income of a corporation is taxed twice. Corporate income is taxed for the first time when it is earned by the entity. As an artificial person the corporation enjoys the natural citizen's obligation to pay income taxes. We will discuss some of the many special rules that apply to corporate tax returns in the Appendix.

   Corporate income is taxed a second time when it is distributed to shareholders. All dividends are taxed to individuals at a rate dependent on their level of income. Thus, the corporate income is taxed twice — once when the corporation earns it, and a second time when the stockholder receives it as dividends. Only after this double tax is paid is the corporate income available for the individual owner to spend.

Income is taxed only once in a partnership. Individual partners pay income taxes at personal income tax rates when the income is earned. The partnership entity is not required to pay income taxes. Some small corporations may avoid double taxation by electing to be taxed as partnerships. These **Subchapter S corporations** will be discussed in the Appendix.

Let's look at the example below and compare the amounts that an individual owner of a corporation and of a partnership will have to spend after taxes.

We have made some simplifying assumptions in this example. The point is still valid, however: Corporate income is taxed twice and ultimately provides less spendable cash for its owners than if the business were operated as a partnership.

2. **Government regulation is extensive** Corporations are subject to more government regulations than either proprietorships or partnerships. One federal agency that regulates all publicly owned corporations is the Securities and Exchange Commission. It has influence over the activities of only a very few partnerships.

The SEC regulates publicly held corporations

The Securities and Exchange Commission (SEC) has the responsibility for seeing that truthful information is presented to potential investors in corporate stocks. Subject to certain minimum size limitations, a corporation planning to sell stock to the public must file extensive information about its business activities, directors, operating performance (income), and financial position (balance sheet). After careful review by SEC staff members, this factual information can be made public by the corporation. The public can then study the data and decide whether to purchase stock from the corporation. The corporation must also file quarterly financial reports (called *10Q's*) and annual financial reports (called *10K's*) with the SEC. These reports are also available to stockholders and other interested parties.

Compliance with the regulations of the SEC and the various other federal, state, and local agencies is often an expensive and time-consuming activity.

The Facts Assumed for Our Example:

This example shows the effect of double taxation on corporate owners

	The Corporation	The Partnership
Number of owners	10 stockholders	10 partners
Net income (assume all of it is taxable)	$200,000	$200,000
Tax rate for the business	34%	0%
Tax rate for the owners	15%	15%

The Comparison:

Tax paid by each business:		
Net income	$200,000	$200,000
Tax rate	× .34	× 0
Tax paid	$ 68,000	$ 0

Amount distributed to each owner:		
Income before tax	$200,000	$200,000
Income tax	(68,000)	0
Income after tax	$132,000	$200,000
Divide by number of owners	÷ 10	÷ 10
Amount received by each owner	$ 13,200	$ 20,000
Tax paid by each owner:		
Amount received by the owner	$ 13,200	$ 20,000
Income tax rate	× .15	× .15
Tax paid	$ 1,980	$ 3,000
Amount available to spend:		
Amount received	$ 13,200	$ 20,000
Less: Income taxes paid	(1,980)	(3,000)
Amount the owner can spend	$ 11,220	$ 17,000

Corporate Organization Structure

The organization structure of most large corporations follows the same basic pattern. You will find that this pattern is modified somewhat to fit the needs of specific organizations. But, if you understand this basic structure, you will have a good grasp of the various parts of the corporate structure.

Figure 11-1 shows the basic corporate organization structure and an explanation of the function of each group in the structure.

Stockholders

The stockholders are the owners of the corporation. Most state corporation laws give the stockholders certain rights. These stockholder rights usually include the following:

A list of stockholder rights

1. The right to receive a certificate as evidence of ownership interest, and to transfer such shares as they choose through either sale or gift.

2. The right to vote at stockholders' meetings for the election of directors and on other such matters as may be brought before the stockholders for action.

3. The right to purchase a portion of any new shares issued such that they will own the same percentage of the total shares after the new issuance of stock as before. This **preemptive right** may be given up in some cases by a vote of the stockholders. One such case may exist when a special stock purchase plan (stock option plan) is initiated to reward top-level executives.

4. The right to receive dividends declared by the board of directors. This distribution of profits usually takes the form of cash, but other assets may be distributed as well.

5. The right to receive assets upon dissolution of the corporation if any remain after the creditors have been paid.

THIS CONCERN OFFERS STOCKHOLDERS A LITTLE TASTE OF THEIR INVESTMENTS

By Matt O'Connor

Tired of reading annual reports? George M. Chester thought he had a solution, but he ran into a problem.

Mr. Chester is president of Wisconsin Securities Co. of Delaware, a Milwaukee investment company with $40 million in assets and 231 stockholders.

In a recent letter to shareholders Mr. Chester wrote, "Each printed annual report costs the company $5. In our opinion no annual report is worth a fraction of this amount." Instead, he offered all 231 holders "a sample from one of our investments," urging them to "think of all the time and expense this will save you and us and the Securities and Exchange Commission."

Enclosed with the letter was a reply post card offering shareholders the choice of the company's annual report or a $5 10-ounce can of ginger cookies made by a company Wisconsin Securities invested $80,000 in last December.

"A DISASTER"

Mr. Chester, a wealthy 61-year-old lawyer who raises llamas as a hobby, likes to quip that he came up with the cookie scheme to "divert" stockholders from worrying about Wisconsin Securities' investment in Armco, Inc., the Ohio steel company, an investment he describes as "a disaster." Wisconsin Securities holds 400,000 shares in Armco. (Over several years, Armco's stock price dropped to $14 a share from $40 a share on the New York Stock Exchange, but it is up to about $19 currently.)

Early returns were running 2 to 1 in favor of the cookies, although Frederick Ott, a stockholder and friend of Mr. Chester, said he wanted a report because Mr. Chester usually includes Mr. Ott's name, along with a quote from Mr. Ott saying, "something stupid."

REMEMBER RULE 30d-1

But Mr. Chester had also sent a copy of his

shareholder letter to the SEC. And last week he had a call from its Chicago office informing him that under Rule 30d-1 of the Investment Company Act of 1940 he must send every shareholder an annual report.

Mr. Chester doesn't dispute the findings. "They said I could send the cookies too, and shareholders could eat the cookies while they read the report," he says. Undeterred, he's sending shareholders both the report and the cookies.

And he has big plans for 1988. Wisconsin Securities has a $7.4 million investment in an Ohio foundry with a plant in Scotland. The plant is next door to a whisky distillery. So Mr. Chester will be sending shareholders—along with the annual report, of course—a $25 bottle of Scotch single-malt whisky called Glenturret.

Source: The Wall Street Journal, Mar. 12, 1984, page 31.

In this chapter extensive government regulation is discussed as a disadvantage of the corporate form of business. As this humorous article shows, the regulations were created for the protection of the investing public. A single stockholder holding a small number of shares has very little power in a corporation. The Securities and Exchange Commission has the authority to enforce the various securities laws, which are designed, in part, to make sure that publicly owned corporations provide owners and prospective owners with factual information about corporate activities.

Compliance with the regulations of the SEC may be expensive and time-consuming, but it is the price corporations must pay to protect the investing public from unsavory or misguided corporate managers.

Common stockholders are the primary owners of a corporation

Stockholders normally acquire one of two basic types of stock as evidence of their ownership interest: common or preferred.

Common stock represents the primary ownership of the corporation. Common stockholders possess all of the rights listed above. More than any other security holders, they reap the rewards or suffer the consequences of a volatile stock market. If only one class of stock is issued, it is common stock.

When stock is sold and paid for in full, the owner is sent a stock certificate showing how many shares he or she owns. At this point the stock is said to be *issued.*

Figure 11-2 shows a common stock certificate.

Preferred stock is a less risky investment than common stock because preferred stockholders have special privileges

Preferred stock is issued by many corporations to appeal to investors who are unwilling to take all the risks involved in common stock ownership. The rights of the common stockholder are modified to provide the preferred stockholder with certain advantages not available to common stockholders; e.g., dividends are paid to preferred stockholders before any are paid to the common stockholders. At the same time, preferred stockholders give up some of the privileges accorded to common stockholders, e.g., the right to vote for members of the board of directors. We will take a closer look at preferred stock in Chapter 12.

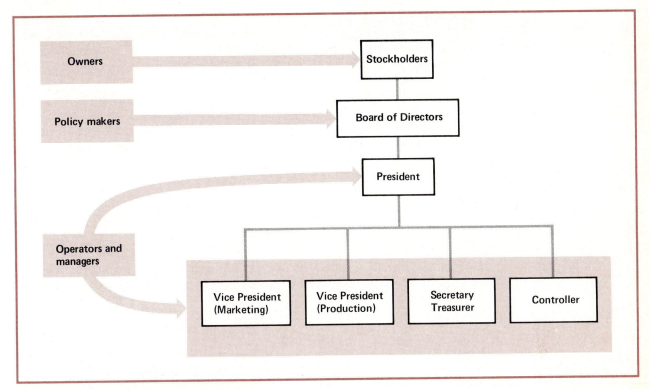

FIGURE 11-1 Corporate Organization Structure

**FIGURE 11-2
Common Stock Certificate**

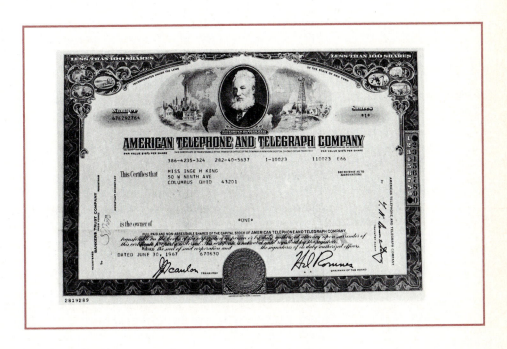

Board of Directors

The board of directors (1) makes policy, (2) evaluates managers, and (3) makes other decisions they are required by law to make

The board of directors, elected by the stockholders, is responsible for the management of the corporation. The board usually delegates the power to make operating decisions and to run the day-to-day activities of the business to a professional management team.

The board normally confines its attention to making policy, reviewing management performance, and acting on matters that can legally be decided only by the board. Decisions to expand the business by introducing a new product or by opening operations in a new geographic area are examples of major policy decisions. Declaring that dividends will be paid to stockholders is an action that can be taken legally only by the board.

President and Other Operating Officers

The president and other officers operate the corporation

The president, various vice presidents, the secretary-treasurer, and the controller are responsible for carrying out the policies set by the board.

They operate the corporation by supervising the purchase (or manufacture) of the product, and by selling and distributing the product. They hire employees, prepare budgets, arrange short-term borrowing, and attend to all the other details necessary to run a business.

ORGANIZING A CORPORATION AND SELLING STOCK

As we discuss accounting problems relating to organizing a corporation and selling stock, we follow the experiences of Bill and Betsy Prince and two of their friends in establishing a computer store.

PC CITY, INC.

Bill and Betsy Prince and two of their friends decide to go into the business of selling personal computers, software, and computer supplies. After discussing the merits of various types of business organizations, they elect to incorporate as PC CITY, Inc. A lawyer and a CPA are hired to prepare the articles of incorporation, to set up the accounting system, and to advise them regarding the various tax forms they will need to file. Within a short time the articles of incorporation are approved and the charter is received. The corporation is ready to sell stock.

The charter of incorporation authorizes PC CITY to issue 100,000 shares of $10-par stock.

Par versus No-Par Stock

A par or stated value may be set at the time stock is authorized

Many state laws require that stock have a par value. **Par value** is an amount determined arbitrarily and in no way is intended to reflect the actual market value of the stock. In some states par value defines an amount of **legal capital** that must be retained in the business. The amount represented as legal capital cannot be distributed to stockholders except when the corporation is liquidated. A corporation is liquidated when it goes out of business, pays all its debts, and gives any remaining assets to the stockholders.

Par and stated values are arbitrary—they do not reflect what the stock is worth

Due to the confusion among investors as to the actual meaning of par value, many states now permit the issuance of **no-par stock.** Some of these states allow the board of directors to arbitrarily select a **stated value.** If this is done, the stock is said to be **no-par with a stated value.** A stated value serves the same purpose as par value. But since stated value is not printed on the stock certificates, there is less risk of confusion.

In accounting for the issuance of stock, the par or stated value, if any, is recorded in the Common Stock account. This method preserves the legal capital in a separate account and makes balance sheet disclosure easier. Any amount received over and above par or stated value is credited to Paid-In Capital in Excess of Par (or Stated Value). Since par or stated value is usually set at a nominal amount, common stock is rarely sold for less than that value. No-par stock without a stated value is accounted for simply by crediting Common Stock for its sale price.

Selling Stock for Cash

Common Stock is credited for the par or stated value of the stock sold

Each of the four PC CITY incorporators agree to purchase 5,000 shares for $15 per share. The entry to record this sale on Jan. 5, 1989 — 20,000 shares (4 × 5,000) — of stock is as follows:

Jan. 5   Cash.. 300,000
                Common Stock   200,000
                Paid-In Capital in Excess of Par.....................   100,000
         To record the sale of 20,000 shares of $10-par stock for $15
         per share to the incorporators. (20,000 shares × $15 =
         $300,000)

If the PC CITY, Inc., stock had been no par with no stated value, the sale would have been recorded by debiting Cash and crediting Common Stock for $300,000.

Selling Stock by Subscription

Corporations wishing to sell stock to the public may choose to sell the shares on subscription. In a *subscription sale,* a subscriber agrees to purchase a specified number of shares at an agreed price. The subscriber makes a down payment when he or she signs the subscription contract; the balance is paid in installments. The subscriber receives no shares until he or she pays the contract price in full.

Stock sold on subscription is paid for in installments

On Jan. 30, 1989, PC CITY, Inc., sells subscriptions to 5,000 shares of stock at $18 per share. A 20% down payment is received at the time the subscription contract is signed. The remainder is due in two equal installments on Mar. 1 and Apr. 1, 1989.

Jan. 30   Stock Subscriptions Receivable 72,000
          Cash.. 18,000
                Common Stock Subscribed.........................   50,000
                Paid-In Capital in Excess of Par....................   40,000
          To record the sale of subscriptions to 5,000 shares of $10-par
          common stock and the receipt of a 20% down payment:
          (5,000 × $18) = $90,000 × 20% = $18,000.

A current asset, Stock Subscriptions Receivable, is debited for the unpaid balance of the subscription contract. A temporary stockholders' equity account, Common Stock Subscribed, is credited for the par or stated value of the shares subscribed. This account will remain only until the shares are paid in full and certificates are issued. Common Stock Subscribed is shown in the stockholders' equity section immediately below the Common Stock account. Paid-In Capital in Excess of Par is credited for the difference between the subscription price and the par value.

PC CITY, Inc., receives the two subscription installments.

Mar. 1	Cash	36,000	
	Stock Subscriptions Receivable		36,000
	To record receipt of first installment.		
Apr. 1	Cash	36,000	
	Stock Subscriptions Receivable		36,000
	To record receipt of second installment.		

When subscribers pay the installments due, the entry is similar to that which is made when customers pay on account: Cash is debited, and the receivable is credited.

When the subscription price is paid in full, the stock is issued

PC CITY, Inc., issues the shares for the fully paid subscriptions.

Apr. 1	Common Stock Subscribed	50,000	
	Common Stock		50,000
	To record the issuance of 5,000 shares of $10-par common stock.		

When subscriptions have been paid in full, we remove the temporary account, Common Stock Subscribed, and credit Common Stock. Remember that Common Stock Subscribed was originally credited for the *par value* of the subscribed shares. Par value, then, is the amount we transfer to the Common Stock account.

Selling Stock for Noncash Consideration

Occasionally stock is issued in exchange for services or assets. Transactions of this type are especially common in small corporations.

Stock sold for noncash assets is valued at either the market value of the stock or the market value of the asset

The selling price of the stock in this type of transaction is considered to be either the fair market value of the stock or the fair market value of the service or asset, whichever can be determined more objectively.

The fair market value of the stock being sold is usually more objective when the stock is actively traded on a stock exchange. To find the market value, you would simply call a stockbroker or check *The Wall Street Journal* for a stock price quotation. This quotation will provide an objective measure of the values exchanged in your noncash transaction.

Appraisal values of the services or assets received for the stock are more reliable when stocks are inactively traded. Stock in small, closely held corporations may change hands rarely, if at all. No current, bargained market value will be available for these shares.

The par or stated value of the stock should never be used as a measure of the selling price. Remember, these amounts are nominal and are arbitrarily determined when the corporation is formed. Par or stated value rarely reflects the current value of either the stock issued or the asset received.

Issuing Stock in Exchange for Services

A corporation may issue shares in exchange for legal, accounting, architectural, or other services.

PC CITY, Inc., issues 100 shares of stock to J. Barrister in exchange for legal services rendered in drawing up the articles of incorporation.

Apr. 2	Organization Cost.. 1,800	
	Common Stock	1,000
	Paid-In Capital in Excess of Par........................	800
	To record issuance of 100 shares of stock in exchange for legal services: $18 \times 100 = \$1,800$.	

The amount we used in the preceding entry could have been determined in two ways:

1. The current market price of the stock issued could be used as a measure of the value of the services received. Since PC CITY stock is not actively traded on a stock exchange, and since no sale of the stock has been negotiated since January, we will look for another measure of value.

2. The normal fee for performing this type of legal service could be used if this fee is well known. We will assume for this example that PC CITY's articles are not complex and that lawyers have a fairly standard fee of $1,800 for preparing simple articles of incorporation. We will also want to check to see if this value seems reasonable based on earlier selling prices of the stock. The stock sold in January for $18 per share and this stock also is being valued at $18 per share; this amount is certainly reasonable. If the value in this transaction were $50 per share, we would want to reconsider the method of choosing our stock value.

$1,800 is a well-known, standard fee for the type of service PC CITY received, and the amount is reasonable. We used $1,800 to record the value of the services received and the stock issued.

Organization Cost is debited for the costs of organizing a new corporation

Organization Cost is debited. This intangible asset is charged for legal fees, amounts paid to the chartering state, costs of printing the stock certificates, and other amounts expended in organizing a new corporation.

Organization Cost, like all intangible assets, must be amortized over its useful life, subject to a maximum of 40 years. Many corporations amortize organization costs over 5 years because this is the life they use on their income tax return. Since the amount of the amortization per year is relatively small (not material), no serious mismatching problems are created by using this short life.

Issuing Stock in Exchange for Assets

Often in smaller corporations a prospective stockholder will contribute assets that the corporation needs in its operations in exchange for stock.

PC CITY issues 500 shares of stock to Rods and Plots for 1 acre of land.

Sept. 1	Land... 12,000	
	Common Stock.....................................	5,000
	Paid-In Capital in Excess of Par	7,000
	To record issuance of 500 shares of stock in exchange for 1 acre of land. (Land appraised at $12,000.)	

Approximately 5 months have elapsed since PC CITY last issued stock, on Apr. 2, 1989. Since the stock is not actively traded, the old market value may not accurately reflect the current worth of the stock. In most cases no standard price is available for land because each piece is unique. In such instances we use one or more independent appraisals to establish an estimate of the asset's market value. We use this appraised value as the selling price of the stock and the acquisition price of the land.

CORPORATIONS: TREASURY STOCK

Treasury stock is the corporation's own stock that it has reacquired

A corporation may reacquire its own stock by purchasing it on a stock exchange (through a stockholder) or by a private transaction with an individual stockholder. This repurchased stock is called **treasury stock.**

Treasury stock may be purchased for later issuance to executives or employees under a stock option or stock purchase plan, for the purpose of buying out a disgruntled shareholder, or for a variety of other reasons.

While shares are held in the treasury, they do not possess the rights of outstanding shares—they cannot vote or receive dividends.

Purchase of Treasury Stock for Cash

PC CITY, Inc., repurchases 50 shares of stock at $25 per share.

Sept. 15	Treasury Stock	1,250	
	Cash		1,250
	To record acquisition of 50 shares of stock at $25 per share.		

Treasury Stock is a negative stockholders' equity account

Treasury Stock is debited for the cost of the reacquired shares. Since these shares are to be held for only a short time and not retired, the transaction reflects a temporary reduction in total stockholders' equity. We show this temporary reduction by reporting Treasury Stock on the balance sheet as a contra- (negative) stockholders' equity account. Remember, the par value and any amounts originally received in excess of par still appear in the Common Stock and Paid-In Capital in Excess of Par accounts.

At the end of this chapter we will show you exactly how treasury stock is shown in the stockholders' equity section.

Purchase of Treasury Stock for Noncash Assets

The cost of treasury stock is either the fair value of assets given or the fair value of the stock acquired

The corporation may give some asset other than cash for the stock it is buying back. The cost of the treasury stock in these transactions is the fair value of the assets given or the fair value of the stock being purchased, whichever is more objectively determinable. This rule should sound familiar. We used it for deciding the selling price of stock for noncash assets or services.

The corporation's assets are carried in the accounting records at cost. Or, sometimes they are carried at cost less accumulated depreciation, depletion, or amortization. They do not appear on the corporation's books at their market value.

When we use these assets to buy treasury stock, we must make two journal entries: one to revalue the asset — increase it or decrease it to its fair value — and a second to record the purchase of the treasury stock. The effect of these two entries will be the same as if we had sold the asset for cash and then used the cash to purchase treasury stock.

PC CITY exchanges one-half of the acre of land acquired on Sept. 1 for 300 shares of stock. The $\frac{1}{2}$ acre of land is appraised at $7,500.

Sept. 20	Land	1,500	
	Gain from Increasing Land to Fair Value..............		1,500
	To increase $\frac{1}{2}$ acre of land from $6,000 cost to $7,500 fair value.		
20	Treasury Stock	7,500	
	Land		7,500
	To record exchange of land for 300 shares of common stock.		
	Cost basis per share = $7,500 ÷ 300 shares = $25 per share.		

When we record the asset revaluation, we will recognize a gain or loss — just as we would if the asset had been sold for cash. This gain or loss account is shown on the income statement under Other Gains and Losses.

The gain or loss we record is a gain or loss on the disposal of an asset, not on the purchase of treasury stock.

Sale of Treasury Stock above Cost

PC CITY sells 20 shares of treasury stock for $30 per share. The treasury stock had been purchased for $25 per share.

Sept. 30	Cash	600	
	Treasury Stock		500
	Paid-In Capital from Treasury Stock		100
	To record sale of 20 shares of treasury stock that originally cost $25		
	for $30 each.		

Paid-In Capital from Treasury Stock is credited when we sell treasury stock for more than its cost

    A corporation may decide to sell treasury stock to an employee or to another person who wants to invest in the business. The treasury stock may be sold for more than the corporation originally paid. In this case we must do the following: (1) Debit Cash to record the asset we receive; (2) credit Treasury Stock to decrease this account — we no longer have the treasury stock; and (3) credit Paid-In Capital from Treasury Stock to record the amount we receive over and above what we originally paid for the treasury stock. Paid-In Capital from Treasury Stock specifically identifies the source of the new paid-in capital.

    When we sell an asset for more than its cost, we record a gain. Treasury stock is not an asset. *Corporations are not allowed to recognize gains or losses as a result of buying and selling their own stock.* Corporate income results from carrying on the business of the company, not from speculating in or attempting to manipulate the price of its own stock.

Sale of Treasury Stock below Cost

PC CITY sells 20 shares of treasury stock for $22 per share.

Oct. 31   Cash 440
          Paid-In Capital from Treasury Stock 60
              Treasury Stock 500
          To record sale of 20 shares of treasury stock that originally cost $25
          for $22 each.

When treasury shares are sold for less than their cost, we must record a decrease in stockholders' equity. This decrease is charged to:

Treasury stock sold for less than its cost reduces Paid-In Capital from Treasury Stock, then Retained Earnings

1. Paid-In Capital from Treasury Stock, until its balance reaches zero; then to
2. Retained Earnings (an account showing the accumulated income of the corporation).

In no case should such decreases be reported on the income statement as a loss.

In our illustration, PC CITY created Paid-In Capital from Treasury Stock when it sold treasury stock on Sept. 30. We then debit that account for the $60 excess of the cost of the treasury stock over the amount PC CITY sold it for on Oct. 31. If the Sept. 30 transaction had not occurred, PC CITY would not have had Paid-In Capital from Treasury Stock. In that case we would have debited the $60 to Retained Earnings.

Notice that in all cases we debit Treasury Stock for the cost of shares acquired and credit it for cost when the shares are resold. When all treasury shares have been disposed of, Treasury Stock will have a zero balance.

We have summarized accounting for treasury stock in Exhibit 11-1 on page 479.

CORPORATIONS: DONATED CAPITAL

Shares of stock or assets may be donated to a corporation

Profit-making corporations may receive donations of assets or of shares of their stock. Stockholders may donate shares in order for the corporation to have stock available to sell to raise additional capital or to use in stock option plans designed to keep or attract outstanding management talent. The cost of these treasury shares is zero; therefore we make no formal journal entry to record the acquisition. A memorandum entry is often made in the general journal to note officially the fact that shares were received. This stock is treasury stock with no cost.

PC CITY receives 50 shares of common stock as a donation.

Nov. 5   Memorandum: Received 50 shares of donated common stock.

If donated shares are later sold, Cash is debited and Donated Capital is credited for their sales price.

Cities and counties often donate land and occasionally other assets to attract new industry to operate in their locality. When new industry moves into a geographic area, the area benefits through increased employment and by receiving the taxes that the company pays. The company benefits by having the use of an asset at no cost.

EXHIBIT 11-1
Accounting for Treasury Stock
Rules for buying treasury stock

When Buying Treasury Stock:	
For Cash	Record treasury stock at the amount of cash given.
For Noncash Assets	Revalue the asset you give to its fair value. When you increase or decrease the asset, record a gain or loss.
	Record treasury stock at the fair market value of the asset given or the fair market value of the stock. Use the one of these values that is most objectively measured.

Rules for selling treasury stock

When Selling Treasury Stock:	
For More Than It Cost	Remove the cost of treasury stock from the accounts.
	Record the extra amount received as Paid-In Capital from Treasury Stock.
For Less Than It Cost	Remove the cost of treasury stock from the accounts.
	Decrease stockholders' equity for the excess of the cost over the selling price of the treasury stock by:
	1. Debiting Paid-In Capital from Treasury Stock.
	2. When the balance in Paid-In Capital from Treasury Stock is zero, debiting Retained Earnings.

PC CITY receives the donation of an old building from the City of Parrish. The building will be moved by the city from its present site to PC's land. PC CITY will use the building as a retail store and also refurbish the structure and maintain it as a historical landmark. The fair value of the building in its present condition is $15,000.

Dec. 15 Building 15,000
          Donated Capital 15,000
        To record donation of building by the city of Parrish.

Donated Capital is the paid-in capital account used to reflect the value of assets donated

Assets donated to the company are recorded at their fair value when they are received. Donated Capital, a stockholders' equity account, is credited to record the source of the asset entering the pool of resources that management has to use.

STOCKHOLDERS' EQUITY ON THE BALANCE SHEET

A review of the disclosure of the stockholders' equity accounts discussed in this chapter will help you visualize the effect that each stockholders' equity transaction has on the balance sheet. Our discussion is based on the PC CITY, Inc., stockholders' equity section as it appears after the entries illustrated in this chapter.

First, let's look at PC CITY's general ledger (page 481) to see how each stockholders' equity account will appear after we post all the transactions.

When we have posted all of the entries to the general ledger accounts and found the balance of each account, we are ready to prepare financial statements.

Stockholders' equity accounts are shown on the balance sheet. Here is what PC CITY's balance sheet stockholders' equity section looks like:

Stockholders' Equity		
Paid-In Capital:		
Common Stock, $10 par, 100,000 shares authorized, 25,600 shares issued, 25,240 shares outstanding (360 shares are in the treasury)......		$256,000
Additional Paid-In Capital:		
Paid-In Capital in Excess of Par	$147,800	
Paid-In Capital from Treasury Stock	40	
Donated Capital	15,000	
Total Additional Paid-In Capital		162,840
Total Paid-In Capital		$418,840
Earned Capital:		
Retained Earnings (amount assumed)............................		12,600
Total..		$431,440
Less: Treasury Stock (360 shares) at cost		(7,750)
Total Stockholders' Equity		$423,690

The major objective of the stockholders' equity section is to report the capital of the corporation by source—where the assets came from. For this reason we divide stockholders' equity into two basic subsections: paid-in capital and earned capital. ***Paid-in capital*** measures the resources contributed by owners and others. ***Earned capital,*** retained earnings, reflects the resources that have been earned by the corporation since it began, minus any earnings paid out as dividends. We will discuss earned capital in Chapter 12.

The paid-in capital subsection is divided into two categories, one showing the par or stated value of stock issued or subscribed and the other disclosing amounts contributed in excess of par, or contributed through other transactions. Observe that we report several important pieces of information for common stock:

1. The *par or stated value,* or the fact that it is no-par stock

2. The number of shares *authorized* by the articles of incorporation

3. The total number of shares that have been *issued* by the corporation at any time

4. The total number of shares *outstanding*—in the hands of stockholders

5. The number of shares held *in the treasury*

The par or stated value of any stock subscribed but not issued immediately follows common stock. All of PC's subscribed stock has been paid for and issued, so we didn't have Common Stock Subscribed on PC CITY's balance sheet.

The second paid-in capital category, additional paid-in capital, contains a listing of the accounts that arose either as a result of stockholders paying more than par or stated value for their shares, or from other contributed-capital transactions. Donated capital and increases in paid-in capital resulting from treasury stock transactions are examples of additional paid-in capital. Generally accepted accounting principles also allow donated capital to be shown in a separate stockholders' equity section. We're including it with additional paid-in capital for simplicity. This listing of accounts accomplishes our goal of reporting sources of all corporate capital.

The temporary contra-stockholders' equity account, Treasury Stock, is subtracted from the total of paid-in and earned capital.

PC CITY, INC.
General Ledger — Stockholders' Equity Accounts
December 31, 1989

Common Stock ($10 par)

		Jan. 5 (20,000 shs)	200,000
		Apr. 1 (5,000 shs)	50,000
		Apr. 2 (100 shs)	1,000
		Sept. 1 (500 shs)	5,000
		Dec. 31 Bal.	
		(25,600 shs)	256,000

Paid-In Capital in Excess of Par

		Jan. 5	100,000
		Jan. 30	40,000
		Apr. 2	800
		Sept. 1	7,000
		Dec. 31 Bal.	147,800

Common Stock Subscribed

Apr. 1 (5,000 shs)	50,000	Jan. 30 (5,000 shs)	50,000
		Dec. 31 Bal.	0

Donated Capital

		Dec. 15	15,000
		Dec. 31 Bal.	15,000

Treasury Stock

Sept. 15 (50 shs)	1,250	Sept. 30 (20 shs)	500
Sept. 20 (300 shs)	7,500	Oct. 31 (20 shs)	500
Nov. 5 (50 shs)	0		
Total (400 shs)	8,750	Total (40 shs)	1,000
Dec. 31 Bal. (360 shs)	7,750		

Paid-In Capital from Treasury Stock

Oct. 31	60	Sept. 30	100
		Dec. 31 Bal.	40

STOCK VALUE

The word "value" is used in several different ways when applied to common stock. The purpose of this final section of the chapter is to review the concepts of par value, stated value, and market value and to introduce you to two new terms—book value and liquidation value.

Par Value and Stated Value

Par value is an arbitrary amount per share set by the charter of incorporation. Par value is usually a nominal amount and does not reflect the actual value of a share of stock. Some states use par value to set the minimum amount of capital (legal capital) that must be retained in the business. Legal capital cannot be distributed to the stockholders except when the corporation is liquidated.

Stated value is also an arbitrary amount per share, but it is set by the board of directors instead of the charter of incorporation. Unlike par value, stated value is not printed on the stock certificate, so there is less risk of investors mistakenly believing that stated value is the stock's worth. Like par value, some states use stated value to establish the legal capital of the corporation.

Market Value

A stock's market value is the amount that a share of stock is selling for. Market value is determined by investor expectations about the future of the company and future general economic conditions. Such things as expected company earnings, expected dividend payments, the general financial condition of the company, expected future interest rates, and expected changes in tax rates may influence an investor's decision about the worth of a share of stock. In Chapter 16 we will discuss several tools that an investor can use in analyzing the financial condition of a company.

Book Value

The *book value per share* of stock is the claim against a company's assets represented by one share of stock. Book value per share is calculated by dividing total stockholders' equity (which is just total assets minus total liabilities) by the total number of shares of stock *outstanding* plus any shares subscribed but not yet issued. Treasury shares are not outstanding, so they are omitted. The book value per share of PC CITY's stock would be calculated as follows:

$$\frac{\text{Total stockholders' equity}}{\text{Total shares outstanding}} = \frac{\$423,690}{25,240 \text{ shs}} = \$16.79 \text{ per share}$$

PC CITY has no subscribed but unissued shares. If it did, the number of these shares would be added to the shares outstanding.

Liquidation Value

The *liquidation value* of a share of stock is the amount that a stockholder will receive if the corporation ceases operations, sells all of its assets, pays off all of its liabilities, and distributes the remaining cash to the stockholders. Since some of the assets will be sold at a gain and others at a loss, the liquidation value cannot be determined in advance of the sale of the assets.

Liquidation value can be higher or lower than book value before the liquidation process begins (remember, stockholders' equity goes up when the company has gains and down when it has losses). If PC CITY sold its assets for $380,000, a $43,690 loss would be incurred:

Selling price	$ 380,000
Less: Book value of net assets	(423,690)
Gain (loss) on sale of net assets	$ (43,690)

When the loss is deducted from retained earnings, total stockholders' equity would be reduced by $43,690. The liquidation value per share would be $15.06 [($423,690 − $43,690) ÷ 25,240 shs]. The book value before this process began was $16.79. The assets had a historical cost value of $16.79 per share, but when they were sold they proved to be worth only $15.06 per share.

CHAPTER SUMMARY

Our discussion of the principles of accounting has reached a point where it is essential that the three major types of business entities be distinguished. A study of the capital accounts cannot be undertaken without understanding the differences between proprietorships, partnerships, and corporations.

Partnerships are defined as "an association of two or more persons to carry on, as co-owners, a business for profit." They are a very common form of business organization for the professions, that is, law, medicine, and accounting. Small business entities in the wholesale and retail trades as well as in manufacturing also use the partnership form of organization.

A major reason for an individual businessperson to seek a partner is to obtain additional capital. Individuals also find it advantageous to combine their experience, knowledge, organizational, and managerial abilities.

When choosing the appropriate form of business organization, whether to incorporate or to be a partnership, individuals must consider the characteristics of each form and the advantages and disadvantages resulting from these characteristics. Advantages of the partnership are: the ability to generate more capital than proprietorships, the combination of talents, the ease of formation, the low cost of organizing, certain tax advantages, its informality, and relatively less government regulation than corporations.

The disadvantages of partnerships are: the loss of freedom of action, its limited life, its unlimited liability to the partners, the fact that each partner is a mutual agent for all other partners, the limited amount of capital that can be raised comparative to a corporation, and certain tax disadvantages.

When a partnership is formed, a separate capital account must be established for each partner. Assets contributed by the partners are to be valued at their fair value on the date the partnership is formed. This is the historical cost concept. All partners must agree on the valuations assigned to the various assets.

Profits and losses of a partnership are distributed to the individual partners in accordance with the provisions contained in the *articles of partnership.* If no such provision exists, profits and losses are distributed equally. Provisions generally consider differences in services performed and capital contributed. Provisions for profit and loss distribution may provide for distribution in certain *fixed ratios,* by *capital balance relationships,* or by considering *salary or interest equivalents.*

Corporations are the dominant business form in our economy. These legal beings are established by state charters after the incorporators file acceptable articles of incorporation and pay the proper fee. The *articles of incorporation* spell out the corporation's name and purpose for existence; the types of stock that it can issue, including number of shares and par value; the location of the principal corporate office; and the corporation's permitted legal life. In addition, the names and addresses of the first board of directors and the incorporators are listed.

Advantages that corporations have over proprietorships and partnerships are as follows: (1) They can raise greater amounts of capital; (2) their owners have limited liability; (3) their owners can easily transfer ownership shares; and (4) they have almost unlimited lives. Double taxation and extensive government regulation are the two primary disadvantages of corporations.

The corporate organizational structure has the stockholders on top, followed by the board of directors and then the president and other operating officers. Stockholders possess certain legal rights as owners of the corporation. Among the most important of these rights are:

1. The right to receive stock certificates.
2. The right to vote in corporate elections. (They elect the board of directors.)
3. The right to maintain their proportionate ownership (the preemptive right).
4. The right to receive dividends.
5. The right to receive residual assets upon dissolution.

The *board of directors* is responsible for managing the corporation. The board's attention is usually confined to broad matters of policy, reviewing management performance, and other matters that only they can legally perform.

The *management officers* operate the business in conformity with the board of directors' policies.

The gathering of capital needed to operate the corporation begins with the sale of common stock. Common stock may be sold for cash, on a subscription basis, or in exchange for services or noncash assets. The par or stated value, if any, of the issued stock is credited to the Common Stock account. Any amount received in excess of par or stated value is recorded in an additional paid-in capital account.

Stock repurchased by a corporation is called *treasury stock.* Since treasury stock may be acquired for a variety of purposes, it is held in a temporary contra-stockholders' equity account until it is needed. Reissuance of treasury stock above its cost creates additional paid-in capital. Reissuance below cost decreases paid-in capital and, in some cases, earned capital.

Donated capital may take the form of stock or other assets. Donations of stock are recorded by a memorandum entry; Donated Capital is credited when these shares are subsequently sold. Donations of assets are recorded at the fair value of the asset.

The stockholders' equity section of the balance sheet is divided into categories which are structured like this:

Paid-In Capital:
  Capital Stock
  Additional Paid-In Capital

Earned Capital
Less: Treasury Stock

IMPORTANT TERMS USED IN THIS CHAPTER

Articles of incorporation The written documents filed with a state government outlining basic information about the corporation, including its name, purpose, capital structure, and the names of individuals involved in its beginning. (page 465)

Articles of partnership A formal written contract between the partners in a partnership that establishes responsibilities, commitments, and the manner in which profits and losses are to be distributed. (page 455)

Authorized stock The total capital stock that may be issued by the corporation as stipulated in the aticles of incorporation. The classes of stock, par value, and total number of shares are specified. (page 466)

Board of directors The group of individuals elected by the stockholders and entrusted with the responsibility for managing a corporation. (page 472)

Book value per share The claim against a company's assets represented by each share of stock. Book value per share is calculated as follows: total stockholders' equity ÷ total shares outstanding. (page 482)

Capital stock Certificates of ownership issued by a corporation. Capital stock may refer to common stock or preferred stock or both. (page 466)

Charter The document issued by a state government that gives a business the legal right to begin operating as a corporation. (page 466)

Common stock A class of capital stock that represents the basic ownership of a corporation. Common stock carries the right to vote, share in earnings, maintain proportionate ownership share, and receive residual assets in liquidation. (page 470)

Corporation An artificial legal being created by government charter and possessing many of the rights of a natural person. (page 465)

Donated capital The value of assets or shares of capital stock given to a corporation. (page 478)

Earned capital The total income of the corporation since its incorporation, minus dividends paid to shareholders. (page 480)

Income distribution The manner in which partnership profits and losses are allocated to the individual partners. (page 459)

Issued stock Shares of capital stock that have been sold at some point in the corporation's history. See *authorized stock* and *outstanding stock.* (page 470)

Legal capital An amount of paid-in capital that must be retained in the corporation. Minimum legal capital, defined by state law, usually consists of the par value or stated value of the issued stock. (page 472)

Limited life The characteristic of a partnership that dissolves the partnership with the admission of a new partner, the withdrawal of a partner, or the death of a partner. (page 456)

Liquidation value per share The claim against a company's cash represented by each share of stock. Liquidation value per share can be determined only after all assets have been sold and all liabilities have been paid. (page 482)

Market value per share The amount that a share of stock is selling for on the open market. (page 482)

Mutual agency The authority of each partner in a partnership to legally bind all other partners to contracts. (page 455)

Organization cost An intangible asset consisting of the legal fees, state charter fees, and other costs incurred in creating a corporation. (page 475)

Outstanding stock Shares of capital stock in the hands of stockholders. (page 482)

Paid-in capital The amount of resources invested in the corporation by its stockholders, contributed through donation, and received as a result of certain treasury stock transactions. (page 480)

Par value An arbitrary per-share amount specified in the articles of incorporation (and printed on the face of each stock certificate). Usually defines the legal capital of the corporation. (page 472)

Partnership An association of two or more persons to carry on, as co-owners, a business for profit. (page 454)

Preferred stock A class of capital stock that carries certain rights that have priority over those of common stock. Priority rights to dividends and to distributions of assets in liquidation are typical. (page 470)

Stated value An arbitrary per-share amount specified by official action of the board of directors for no-par stock. May define the legal capital of the corporation. (page 472)

Stock subscription A method of selling capital stock in which a purchaser signs a contract agreeing to buy a specified number of shares at a negotiated price. The stock is normally paid for in installments. (page 473)

Stockholder Owner of shares of capital stock. (page 469)

Treasury stock Shares of capital stock reacquired and held by the issuing corporation. (page 476)

Unlimited liability The legal obligation making each partner in a partnership personally responsible for the partnership's obligations. (page 455)

QUESTIONS

1. Over the past several years Martha Jones and Rapheal Garcia have operated a profitable flower shop. They are currently thinking of admitting Peter Knowles into their partnership. Explain why this action is under consideration.

2. What does the term *articles of partnership* refer to? Why is it considered necessary?

3. Distinguish between the terms *limited life* and *unlimited liability*.

4. Define the term *mutual agency*.

5. What is a partnership?

6. When forming a partnership, why is it necessary to value assets contributed by the partners at their fair value on the date of formation?

7. Partners are not paid salaries but rather are *allowed* a salary. Explain.

8. How can a partnership agreement provide for an equitable distribution of profits and losses when the individual partners have different amounts of capital invested in the partnership?

9. Briefly explain how a corporation is created. Is it more difficult to create a partnership or a corporation? Explain.

10. How does the liability of a partner differ from the liability of a stockholder? Explain.

11. It is usually easier to transfer ownership interest in a corporation than to transfer ownership interest in a partnership. Explain why this is true.

12. Explain how the income of a corporation is taxed twice.

13. Explain the stockholders' *preemptive right.*

14. What activities are normally engaged in by a corporation's board of directors?

15. One Corp.'s stock has a par value of $1 per share; Two Corp.'s stock has a stated value of $1; Three Corp.'s stock has no par or stated value. Explain how the sale of one share of stock for $5 would be accounted for by each corporation.

16. Corporation A's stock has a par value of $1. Corporation B's stock has a par value of $10. Which stock is worth more? Explain.

17. How does a sale of stock on a subscription basis differ from a sale of stock for immediate cash?

18. How is each of the following shown on a corporation's balance sheet: Stock Subscriptions Receivable, Common Stock Subscribed?

19. What are organization costs? How are organization costs shown on the balance sheet?

20. Recently 100,000 shares of a large corporation's stock traded on the New York Stock Exchange for $50 per share. How much will the corporation receive as a result of this transaction? Explain.

21. Oz Corp. exchanged 100 shares of its $10-par common stock for some office furniture. Explain how Oz should determine the proper amount for this transaction.

22. What is treasury stock? How is treasury stock shown on a corporation balance sheet?

23. Kermit Corp. purchased treasury stock for $100 and later sold it for $125. How will this $25 "gain" be reported on the financial statements?

24. Squires Corp. received a pickup truck and 100 shares of its own stock as a donation from a stockholder. Explain the amount that would be assigned to Donated Capital in each of these cases.

25. Explain the difference between paid-in capital and earned capital.

26. What is meant by authorized stock, issued stock, and outstanding stock? Explain.

27. Is it possible to have more shares of stock issued than outstanding? Explain.

28. Herix stock has a book value of $38.20 per share. Does this mean that, if the corporation liquidates, each stockholder will receive $38.20 for each share of stock owned?

EXERCISES

**Exercise 11-1
Forming a partnership**

Effective Apr. 1, 1989, Ann and Betty agree to form a partnership from their two respective proprietorships. The balance sheets presented below reflect the financial position of each proprietorship as of Mar. 31, 1989.

	Ann	Betty
Assets		
Cash..	$ 400	$ 1,000
Accounts Receivable...........................	2,400	1,400
Merchandise Inventory	6,600	8,400
Prepaid Rent	—	800
Store Equipment..............................	8,000	6,000
Accumulated Depreciation	(3,000)	(3,600)
Building.......................................	25,000	—
Accumulated Depreciation	(5,000)	—
Land..	12,000	
Totals...	$46,400	$14,000
Liabilities and Owners' Equity		
Accounts Payable	$ 1,500	$ 600
Mortgage Payable	12,000	—
Ann, Capital..................................	32,900	—
Betty, Capital.................................	—	13,400
Totals...	$46,400	$14,000

As of Apr. 1,1989, the fair value of Ann's assets are: Merchandise Inventory, $5,400; Store Equipment, $3,000; Building, $50,000; and Land $20,000.

For Betty the fair value of the assets on the same date are Merchandise Inventory, $9,000; Store Equipment, $1,300; and Prepaid Rent, $0.

All other items on the two balance sheets are stated at fair values.

From this information, present general journal entries to record the opening of the partnership accounts.

(Check figure: Ann, Capital, $67,700)

**Exercise 11-2
Determining partnership profit**

The Back Bay Hardware Company is owned by Bill and Allen. This year the hardware company reported a $75,000 profit. Determine each partner's share of the profits under each of the following assumptions:

a. Nothing is mentioned in the partnership agreement concerning the sharing of profits.
b. Bill is to receive two-fifths of the profits, Allen three-fifths.

(Check figure: Allen, $45,000)

c. Profits are to be shared by Bill and Allen in a 3:1 ratio.

**Exercise 11-3
Calculating average capital balances**

From the information presented below concerning Thomas and Margie's capital accounts, determine the average capital balance of each partner:

Thomas, Capital		Margie, Capital	
Balance, Jan. 1	$20,000	Balance, Jan. 1	$70,000
Investment, Apr. 1	40,000	Withdrawal, Mar. 1	30,000
Withdrawal, Oct. 1	20,000	Withdrawal, July 1	10,000

Exercise 11-4
Distributing partnership profits

The partnership agreement among Bart, Gleason, and Stevens provides that the distribution of profits and losses shall be determined allowing a 20% rate of return on average capital balances; salary allowances of $34,000, $50,000, and $46,000, respectively; and the remainder equally. Average capital balances for the current year were: Bart, $60,000; Gleason, $100,000; and Stevens, $40,000.

a. Prepare an income distribution schedule assuming that the income for the year was $185,000.

(Check figure: Bart income: $51,000)

b. Prepare an income distribution schedule assuming that the income for the year was $155,000.

(Check figure: Gleason income: $65,000)

Exercise 11-5
Selling par-value stock

Prepare the proper journal entry to record each of the following 1989 transactions and events. If no entry is required, write, "No Entry."

July	1	Kent, Inc., received a charter of incorporation that authorizes the issuance of 500,000 of $5-par stock.
	12	Issued 40,000 shares for $6 per share.
	23	Issued 3,000 shares for $10 per share.

Exercise 11-6
Selling stated-value stock

Backwater Company was incorporated early in 1989. The following events occurred during January:

Jan.	2	Received a charter of incorporation from the state of Minnesota. The charter authorizes Backwater to issue 100,000 shares of no-par stock. The Backwater board of directors votes to set a stated value of $1 on each share.
	7	10,000 shares of stock were sold for $17,800.
	25	10,000 shares of stock were sold for $24,300.

Prepare journal entries to record the transactions and events above. If no entry is required, write, "No Entry."

Exercise 11-7
Selling no-par stock

Best Value Used Cars, Inc., began business in 1989. The following events and transactions occurred during the first month of operations:

Oct.	2	A charter of incorporation was received from the state of New Jersey. The charter authorized the sale of 1 million shares of no-par stock.
	10	Issued 5,000 shares of stock for $5 per share.
	29	Issued 3,500 shares of stock for $1 per share.

Prepare journal entries to record the transactions and events above. If no entry is required, write, "No Entry."

Exercise 11-8
Recording stock sold on subscription

Prepare the proper journal entries to record each of the following 1989 transactions:

Feb. 3	Beltways, Inc., sold subscriptions for 600 shares of $2-par common stock. The subscription price of $12 per share is to be paid in three installments: $4 down at the time of the subscription, and $4 at the beginning of March and April.
Mar. 1	Beltways collected the first installment.
Apr. 1	Beltways collected the second installment and issued the stock.

Exercise 11-9
Calculating total paid-in capital

May, Inc., is authorized by its charter to issue 100,000 shares of no-par stock. During its first year of operations 60,000 shares were sold for $15 per share.

June Corp. is authorized by its charter to issue 500,000 shares of $5-par stock. During its first year of operations June sold 10,000 shares for $20 per share and 40,000 shares for $17.50 per share.

July, Inc., is authorized by its charter to issue 1 million shares of no-par stock. July's board of directors adopted a stated value of $1 per share. During July's first year of operations 100,000 shares were sold for $500,000 and 80,000 shares were sold for $400,000.

Prepare schedules showing the calculation of common stock, additional paid-in capital, and total paid-in capital for May, June, and July, respectively. Your calculations should be clearly labeled.

(Check figure: Total paid-in capital for May = $900,000)

Exercise 11-10
Issuing stock for cash and noncash consideration

Homecare, Inc., was authorized by its charter of incorporation to issue 400,000 shares of $1-par common stock. Prepare entries to record each of the following 1989 transactions. Explain why you chose the amount that you did for the account debited.

Aug. 1   Homecare sold 40,000 shares of stock for $15 per share.

     2   Homecare issued 400 shares to Used Machinery in exchange for a tractor. The advertised price of the tractor was $6,995.

   16   Homecare issued 200 shares to G. Hernandez for services rendered in the process of applying for a charter of incorporation.

Dec. 31   20,000 shares were issued for a plot of land to be used as a plant nursery. The land was appraised by two independent appraisers at $240,000 and $260,000.

(Check figure: Land was debited for $250,000)

Exercise 11-11
Treasury stock transactions

Victory, Inc., has the following stock outstanding on Dec. 31, 1988:

Common Stock, $10 par, 1,000,000 shares authorized, 400,000 shares issued
and outstanding. $4,000,000
Paid-In Capital in Excess of Par Value. 5,000,000

Prepare journal entries to record the following transactions that took place in 1989:

Mar. 10   Victory repurchased 1,000 shares for $22.50 per share.
June 19   Victory sold 600 of the shares purchased on Mar. 10 for $26.00 per share.
Oct. 2   Victory sold the remaining 400 shares purchased on Mar. 10 for $20 per share.

(Check figure: Paid-In Capital from Treasury Stock, June 19 entry = $2,100)

Exercise 11-12
Recording acquisition of treasury stock for noncash assets

Downtown Corp. has offered to exchange some used assets for shares of Downtown common stock. During 1989 the following exchanges took place:

Nov. 2   Downtown traded a forklift with a market value of $9,000 for 200 shares of stock. The forklift had a cost of $15,000 and an accumulated depreciation on the day of the exchange of $8,500.

Dec. 1   Downtown exchanged a trailer having a cost of $37,500 and an accumulated depreciation on the date of the trade of $17,000 for 400 shares of stock. The trailer has a fair value of $19,200.

Prepare entries to revalue each of the assets and to record acquisition of the treasury stock.

(Check figure: Loss from Decreasing Trailer to Fair Value = $1,300)

Exercise 11-13
Calculating book value per share of common stock

The Dec. 31, 1989, McBee Corp. stockholders' equity section appears as follows:

Paid-In Capital:	
Common Stock, $10 par, 100,000 shares authorized, 60,000 shares issued and outstanding	$600,000
Paid-In Capital in Excess of Par	204,000
Total Paid-In Capital	$804,000
Earned Capital:	
Retained Earnings	18,000
Total Stockholders' Equity	$822,000

Calculate the book value per share of McBee's common stock.

(Check figure: Book value per share = $13.70)

PROBLEMS: SET A

Problem A11-1
Forming a partnership

Arkin and Zello are competitors selling heavy equipment. They believe that they can increase their business and reduce their costs by combining the two proprietorships into a partnership. An agreement is reached between the two to form a partnership commencing May 1 of the current year. Arkin will work full time, Zello only 20 hours per week. Consequently, the partners agree to share profits and losses in a 2 : 1 ratio and to contribute and maintain capital in a corresponding ratio.

The balance sheets of the two proprietorships as of Apr. 30 are presented below:

Balance Sheets April 30, 1989	Arkin	Zello
Assets		
Cash	$ 21,000	$ 15,000
Accounts Receivable	194,600	84,600
Less: Allowance for Doubtful Accounts	(11,200)	(7,200)
Merchandise Inventory	230,800	150,400
Prepaid Rent	—	3,000
Office Supplies	15,200	2,000
Land	20,000	—
Building	64,000	—
Less: Accumulated Depreciation	(16,000)	—
Office Equipment	12,000	31,000
Less: Accumulated Depreciation	(3,000)	(6,600)
Repair Equipment	86,000	—
Less: Accumulated Depreciation	(34,000)	
Total Assets	$579,400	$272,200
Liabilities and Owners' Equity		
Notes Payable	$ 60,000	$ —
Accounts Payable	85,000	55,800
Mortgage Payable	100,000	—
Arkin, Capital	334,400	—
Zello, Capital	—	216,400
Total Liabilities and Owners' Equity	$579,400	$272,200

The partners agree that the name of the partnership will be Arkin and Zello Equipment Company. They also agree to the following:

a. Concerning the transfer of Arkin's assets and liabilities:

1. The Accounts Receivable are to be valued at $151,200 and the Allowance for Doubtful Accounts stated at a zero balance to commence the new partnership.
2. Merchandise Inventory is to be reduced by $52,600.
3. Office Supplies are to remain as stated.
4. Land is to be established at its fair value of $54,000.
5. Fixed assets are to be recorded as follows: Office Equipment, $8,000; Building, $96,000; and Repair Equipment, $62,000.
6. One-half of the notes payable are to be considered personal notes due Arkin. All other liabilities are accepted by the partnership.

b. Concerning the transfer of Zello's assets and liabilities:

1. A write-off of $16,200 of Accounts Receivable is required. As with Arkin, Zello's Allowance for Doubtful Accounts is to be stated at a zero balance.
2. Merchandise Inventory is to be increased by $3,600.
3. The Prepaid Rent is for the building Zello occupies. The partnership plans to build a new structure in the near future and will continue to rent, occupying two locations, until the new building is complete.
4. Office Supplies are to be as stated.
5. Office Equipment is to be valued at $20,000.
6. Accounts Payable are accepted as stated.

| **Required** |

1. Prepare the general journal entries to record the formation of the new partnership.

   (Check figure: Zello withdraws $21,300, leaving a $185,300 capital balance)

2. For the 8 months ending Dec. 31, the partnership reports a profit of $300,000. During this time period Arkin has withdrawn $75,000 and Zello $37,500. Prepare a statement of the partners' capital accounts.

   (Check figure: Total capital, Dec. 31 = $743,400)

**Problem A11-2
Determining profit
distribution, different
partnership agreements**

During the year 1989 the accounting firm of Paton, Hatfield, and Montgomery earned a profit of $416,250. Paton had a capital balance on Jan. 1 of $75,000; he invested an additional $15,000 on Mar. 31; withdrew $30,000 on Sept. 30; and invested $22,500 on Oct. 31.

Hatfield's balance on Jan. 1 was $90,000. This was increased by $45,000 on Feb. 28 and reduced to $81,000 on July 31, remaining at $81,000 until year-end.

Montgomery had a capital investment amounting to $60,000 on Jan. 1. This was doubled on Apr. 30 and reduced by $30,000 on Aug. 31.

| **Required** |

Determine the profit distribution for each of the five different assumptions listed below:

1. Profits are distributed to the partners equally.
2. Profits are distributed in an 8:4:3 ratio.
3. Profits are distributed in the ratio of the Jan. 1, 1989, capital balances.
4. Profits are distributed in the ratio of the average capital balances.
5. Profits are distributed allowing 10% interest on the average capital balances; salaries of $39,000, $27,000, and $33,000, respectively; and the remainder shared equally.

[Check figure: Paton's share of profits: (1) $138,750; (2) $222,000; (3) $138,750; (4) $123,750; (5) $143,750]

Problem A11-3
Determining profit distribution, different profit levels

The partnership agreement among Reagan, Carter, and Ford provides the following:

a. An allowance of 15% on the average partners' capital shall be provided for interest equivalents. The average capital balances for 1989 are $240,000, $300,000, and $180,000, respectively.

b. Salary equivalents shall be $105,000 for Reagan, $90,000 for Carter, and $120,000 for Ford.

c. A bonus of 10% of any profits is to be allowed for Reagan.

d. The remainder is to be distributed equally.

Required

Prepare an income distribution schedule for each of the following levels: (1) $600,000 profit; (2) $450,000 profit; (3) $45,000 loss.

[Check figure: Reagan's share of profits: (1) $240,000; (2) $180,000; (3) $15,000 loss]

Problem A11-4
Preparing entries related to issuance of stock

Laton, Inc., was recently chartered by the state of New York. Transactions relating to the issuance of common stock during 1989 are described below:

Aug. 4   Laton, Inc., received a charter of incorporation from the state of New York. Laton was authorized to issue 2 million shares of no-par common stock. The board of directors voted to establish a stated value of $5 per share.

6   Issued 60,000 shares for $540,000 cash.

7   Issued 1,000 shares to Steinburg and O'Leary, Attorneys at Law, in payment for legal services rendered in preparing the articles of incorporation.

Sept. 1   Issued 2,000 shares to Ramona Chaffin in exchange for a plot of land. The land's value has been established by independent appraisers at $18,500.

24   10,000 shares of stock were sold for $11 per share cash.

27   1,500 shares of stock were issued to Vernon Pope in exchange for some office equipment. The equipment will be used in rented offices until a new building can be constructed.

Dec. 10   Polk City donated a building valued at $250,000 to Laton. Laton has agreed to move the building and preserve its basic architectural style. The moving is expected to be completed by Dec. 20, 1989.

Required

Prepare journal entries to record each of the transactions described above. If no entry is necessary, write "No Entry." Calculations should be included as part of your journal entry explanation where appropriate.

(Check figure: The Aug. 7 entry includes a debit to Organization Cost of $9,000)

Problem A11-5
Recording stock sold on subscription

Toth Company has been authorized to issue 500,000 shares of $2-par common stock. Toth's 1989 stock issuance transactions are described below:

Apr. 1   Toth sold subscriptions for 150,000 shares of stock. The shares have a subscription price of $10 each. Twenty percent of the subscription price was received as a down payment.

May 6   200,000 shares were sold for $1,200,000.

12   Subscribers paid an installment amounting to 40% of the subscription price.

June 6   1,000 shares were exchanged for a full-page advertisement in a national magazine. The ad appeared in the June 10 edition. The rate charged for such an advertisement is $65,000.

12   The final 40% of the subscription price was received and the stock was issued.

Required

Prepare journal entries to record the transactions described above. Calculations should be included as part of your journal entry where appropriate.

**Problem A11-6
Recording purchases and
sales of treasury stock**

The Dec. 31, 1989, stockholders' equity section of Jung Corp.'s balance sheet is as follows:

Stockholders' Equity	
Paid-In Capital:	
Common Stock, $5 par, 200,000 shares authorized, 150,000 shares issued and outstanding.	$ 750,000
Paid-In Capital in Excess of Par.	187,500
Total Paid-In Capital.	$ 937,500
Earned Capital:	
Retained Earnings.	545,500
Total Stockholders' Equity	$1,483,000

Required

Prepare Jung Corp.'s journal entries to record the following transactions that took place during January, 1989:

Jan.	4	Purchased 24,000 shares of Jung's stock for $168,000.
	15	Sold 4,000 shares of the treasury stock for $8 per share.
	25	Sold 14,000 shares of the treasury stock for $6.50 per share.
	31	Sold the remaining 6,000 shares of treasury stock for $7 per share.

**Problem A11-7
Preparing T-account
entries to record
stockholders' equity
transactions; preparing a
stockholders' equity
section**

Titan Tires, Inc., was incorporated in 1989. The following events and transactions relate to the company's stockholders' equity accounts during the first year of its existence:

Jan.	6	The charter of incorporation was received authorizing Titan to issue 500,000 shares of $10-par common stock.
	7	50,000 shares of stock were issued to the incorporators for $750,000 cash.
	21	Subscriptions to 50,000 shares were sold. The subscription price of $18 per share is to be received as follows: one-third on Jan. 21, one-third on Feb. 15, and one-third on Mar. 15. The one-third down payment was received.
Feb.	5	200 shares of stock were issued to Rubin and Perot, Attorneys at Law, in payment for legal services received in establishing the corporation. A value of $3,600 was deemed to be proper.
	15	The one-third installment due on the subscribed stock was received.
Mar.	1	Titan purchased 5,000 shares from one of the incorporators for $18 per share.
	15	The final installment was received on the subscribed shares. The shares were issued.
	31	Titan sold 2,000 shares of treasury stock for $21 per share.
Apr.	15	Titan received 2 acres of land adjoining the city dump as a used-tire recycling center. The land, having a fair market value of $20,000, was donated by Twin City.
	30	Titan traded a patent with a book value of $4,000 and a fair market value of $8,200 for 400 shares of Titan common stock.
May	27	Titan sold 1,000 shares of the treasury stock purchased on Mar. 1 for $17 per share.

The balance of the Retained Earnings account after all 1989 entries is $28,000. (Establish an account with this balance.)

Required

1. Prepare T-account entries for each of the events and transactions above. Do not make entries in general journal form. Set up T-accounts and post your entries directly to the T-accounts.
2. Prepare the stockholders' equity section of the Titan Tire balance sheet. You should include all appropriate disclosures discussed in this chapter.

(Check figure: Total stockholders' equity = $1,662,400)

Problem A11-8
Preparing the stockholders' equity section of a balance sheet

The following stockholders' equity accounts were included on the Dec. 31, 1989, trial balance of Lance, Inc. Each account has a normal balance.

Common Stock Subscribed	$ 10,000
Paid-In Capital from Treasury Stock	48,000
Retained Earnings	144,000
Paid-In Capital in Excess of Par	900,000
Treasury Stock (2,000 shares) at Cost	24,000
Common Stock	300,000
Donated Capital	44,000

Lance was authorized by its charter of incorporation to issue 400,000 shares of $5-par common stock.

Required

Prepare the stockholders' equity section of Lance, Inc.'s balance sheet in good form.

(Check figure: Total stockholders' equity = $1,422,000)

Problem A11-9
Calculating information missing from the stockholders' equity section

The following stockholders' equity section was prepared by Hart Corp.'s accounting department.

Stockholders' Equity	
Common Stock, no par, 20,000 shares issued	$ 50,000
Common Stock Subscribed	5,000
Paid-In Capital in Excess of Stated Value	47,000
Donated Capital	8,000
Retained Earnings	38,000
Total	$148,000
Less: Treasury Stock (300 shares)	(1,305)
Total Stockholders' Equity	$146,695

The stockholders' equity section omitted several important facts that may be calculated by using the information given.

Required

Answer each of the following questions using the data given in the stockholders' equity section above. Show calculations where appropriate.

1. What is the stated value per share of common stock?
2. What is total paid-in capital?
3. How many shares of common stock have been subscribed but not issued?
4. How many shares of common stock are outstanding?
5. How much was paid for each share of treasury stock?
6. What was the average amount paid for the common shares issued and subscribed? (Round your answer to the nearest cent.)
7. What is the book value per share of common stock?

(Check figure: Average amount paid for the shares issued and subscribed = $4.64)

PROBLEMS: SET B

Problem B11-1
Forming a partnership

The feed and supply store operated by John Abrems has been very successful. As a result he feels it is an appropriate time to expand operations. John contacts Ann Brown, who owns a warehouse and the land it stands on, and offers to form a partnership to be called Abrems and Brown Feed and Supply Store. Brown accepts and the partnership is formed on July 1, 1989.

Presented below is the trial balance of Abrems Feed and Supply Store as of June 30, 1989:

Cash..	$ 45,900	
Accounts Receivable	420,600	
Allowance for Doubtful Accounts..................		$ 23,400
Merchandise Inventory	202,500	
Prepaid Rent	5,850	
Store Equipment..	78,000	
Accumulated Depreciation		19,500
Notes Payable		66,000
Accounts Payable		101,100
Abrems, Capital..		542,850
Totals...	$752,850	$752,850

The partners agree to share profits and losses equally and decide that each will invest an equal amount in the partnership. Abrems and Brown agree that Brown's land is worth $90,000 and her building $300,000. Brown is to contribute cash in an amount to bring her capital account equal to Abrems.

Agreement is reached by the two partners on the following items concerning the transfer of Abrems Feed and Supply Store to the partnership.

a. Accounts Receivable in the amount of $61,200 are to be written off and the Allowance for Doubtful Accounts eliminated.

b. Merchandise Inventory is to be decreased by $26,400.

c. The Prepaid Rent is for the warehouse used by Abrems. All merchandise will be transferred to Brown's building. No refund will be received on the unused rent paid in advance.

d. The store equipment has a fair value of $60,000.

e. All other items, assets and liabilities, are to be transferred at their book values.

Required

1. Prepare the general journal entries to record the formation of the new partnership.

(Check figure: Brown's cash contribution = $83,400)

2. At the end of the year, Dec. 31, 1989, a profit of $178,000 is shown. Each partner has made withdrawals of $49,000. Prepare a statement of the partners' capital accounts.

(Check figure: Total capital, Dec. 31, 1989 = $1,028,600)

Problem B11-2
Determining profit distribution, different partnership agreements

During their first year of operations, the partnership of Ferris, Getty, and Holland earned $45,450. Summarized below is the activity of the individual partners' capital accounts:

	Ferris	Getty	Holland
Capital, Jan. 1	$10,000	$15,000	$20,000
Mar. 31, Investment	10,000		
May 31, Withdrawal		(2,500)	
June 30, Investment			2,500
July 31, Withdrawal		(2,500)	
Oct. 31, Investment		3,000	
Oct. 31, Withdrawal			(7,500)
Capital, Dec. 31	$20,000	$13,000	$15,000

| **Required** | Determine the partners' share of the partnership profits under the assumption that profits are shared: |

1. Equally
2. In a 5:2:2 ratio
3. In the ratio of the Jan. 1 capital balances
4. In the ratio of the average capital balances
5. Allowing for 10% interest on the average capital balances; salaries of $9,650, $7,600, and $8,150, respectively; and the remainder equally

[Check figure: Holland's share of profits = (1) $15,150; (2) $10,100; (3) $20,200; (4) $18,000, (5) $15,150]

Problem B11-3
Determining profit distribution, different profit levels)

The partnership agreement of Orthello, Hamlet, and MacBeth provides for the following: Profits and losses shall be distributed by allowing 10% interest on average capital balances and salaries of $37,500, $67,500, and $22,500, respectively; MacBeth is entitled to a bonus of 5% of reported profits (if any); any remainder is to be shared equally.

Average capital balances for 1989 are: Orthello, $300,000; Hamlet, $225,000; and MacBeth, $450,000.

| **Required** | Prepare income distribution schedules for each of the following levels of income: (1) $270,000; (2) $225,000; (3) $(22,500) loss. |

[Check figure: MacBeth's share of income: (1) 91,500; (2) $75,000; (3) ($15,000) loss]

Problem B11-4
Preparing entries related to issuance of stock

Lincoln Corp. was granted a charter by the state of Nebraska. 1989 transactions related to the issuance of common stock are described below:

Jan. 10   Lincoln Corp. received its charter of incorporation from the state of Nebraska. Lincoln was authorized to issue 200,000 shares of no-par common stock. The board of directors established a stated value of $50 per share.

     15   Sold 30,000 shares for $1,620,000.

     21   Issued 2,000 shares to Barnes, Lopez and Stein, Attorneys at Law, as payment for legal services rendered in preparing the articles of incorporation.

Feb. 15   Issued 1,000 shares to Robert Cawthon for a piece of land. The land had been appraised by several independent appraisers at an average of $55,000.

Mar. 15   8,000 shares were sold for $56 per share.

     18   Issued 1,000 shares to Olive Griffin in exchange for a portable modular building. The building will be used for office space until a more permanent structure can be built.

Apr. 1   Gothom City donated 50 acres of land appraised at $4,500 per acre to Lincoln Corp. The land is to be used as the site for Lincoln's primary manufacturing facility.

| **Required** | Prepare journal entries to record each of the transactions described above. If no entry is necessary, write "No Entry." Calculations should be included as part of your journal entry explanation where appropriate. |

(Check figure: The Jan. 21 entry included a debit to Organization Cost of $108,000)

Problem B11-5
Recording stock sold on subscription

Atlanta, Inc., has been authorized to issue 250,000 shares of $20-par stock. The following 1989 transactions relate to the initial issuance of Atlanta stock.

July 1   Atlanta sold subscriptions for 50,000 shares of stock. The shares have a subscription price of $30 per share. One-third of the subscription price was received as a down payment.

     15   20,000 shares were sold for $640,000.

Aug. 1 An installment amounting to one-third of the subscription price was received.
  24 100 shares of stock were exchanged for a new two-way radio system having a fair market value of $3,100.
Sept. 1 The final one-third of the subscription price was received and the stock issued.

Required

Prepare journal entries to record the transactions described above. Calculations should be included as part of your journal entry explanation where appropriate.

**Problem B11-6
Recording purchases and
sales of treasury stock**

Pennsy Promotions, Inc., has the following stockholders' equity on the Dec. 31, 1988, balance sheet:

Stockholders' Equity	
Paid-In Capital:	
Common Stock, $10 par, 50,000 shares authorized, 25,000 shares issued and outstanding.	$ 250,000
Paid-In Capital in Excess of Par.	600,000
Total Paid-In Capital.	$ 850,000
Earned Capital:	
Retained Earnings.	400,000
Total Stockholders' Equity.	$1,250,000

Required

Prepare Pennsy Promotions' journal entries to record the following transactions that took place during January, 1989:

Jan. 3 Purchased 5,000 shares of Pennsy Promotions stock for $40 per share.
  6 Sold 1,500 shares of the treasury stock for $44 per share.
  10 Sold 2,500 shares of the treasury stock for $36 per share.
  20 Sold 1,000 shares of the treasury stock for $40 per share.

**Problem B11-7
Preparing T-account
entries to record
stockholders' equity
transactions; preparing a
stockholders' equity
section**

The following events and transactions relate to the stockholders' equity accounts of the Mobile Company for 1989:

Jan. 3 The charter of incorporation was received authorizing Mobile to issue 200,000 shares of $2.50-par common stock.
  5 16,000 shares were sold to the incorporators of the business for a total of $200,000.
  15 Subscriptions to 24,000 shares were sold. The subscription price was $15 per share; one-third of the total was received as a down payment.
  31 2,000 shares were issued to the firm's attorneys in payment for legal services rendered in drawing up the articles of incorporation. A value of $15 per share was deemed appropriate.
Feb. 1 One-third of the subscription price of the subscribed shares was received.
  15 Mobile Company purchased 4,000 shares from one of the incorporators for $14 per share.
Mar. 1 The final balance due was received on the subscribed shares. The shares were issued.
  20 Mobile Company sold 1,000 shares of treasury stock for $17.50 per share.
  30 Mobile gave a patent with a book value of $2,000 and a fair market value of $11,200 in exchange for 800 shares of Mobile common stock.
Apr. 15 Mobile sold 1,000 shares of the treasury stock purchased on Feb. 15 for $13.50 per share.
Sept. 30 Mobile received 10 acres of land from the city of Hanover. The land has a market value of $25,000.

The balance of the Retained Earnings account after all 1989 entries is $16,400. (Establish an account with this balance.)

| **Required** | 1. Prepare T-account entries for each of the events and transactions above. Do not make entries in general journal form. Set up the T-accounts you need and post your entries directly to the T-accounts.
2. Prepare the stockholders' equity section of the Mobile Company balance sheet. You should include all appropriate disclosures discussed in this chapter. |

(Check figure: Total Paid-In Capital = $618,000)

Problem B11-8
Preparing the
stockholders' equity
section of a balance sheet

The following stockholders' equity accounts were included in the Dec. 31, 1989, trial balance of Palmer, Inc.:

	Debit	**Credit**
Paid-In Capital from Treasury Stock...		$ 25,000
Retained Earnings...		175,000
Common Stock Subscribed...		50,000
Paid-In Capital in Excess of Par...		200,000
Common Stock, $5 par...		250,000
Donated Capital...		80,000
Treasury Stock (450 shares) at Cost...	$11,250	

Palmer was authorized by its charter of incorporation to issue 100,000 shares of $5-par common stock.

| **Required** | Prepare the stockholders' equity section of Palmer, Inc.'s, balance sheet in good form. |

(Check figure: Total Stockholders' Equity = $768,750)

Problem B11-9
Calculating information
missing from the
stockholders' equity
section

The following stockholders' equity section was prepared by the bookkeeper for General Corp.:

Stockholders' Equity	
Common Stock, $20 par...	$ 100,000
Common Stock Subscribed...	10,000
Paid-In Capital in Excess of Par...	440,000
Donated Capital...	85,000
Retained Earnings...	365,000
Total...	$1,000,000
Less: Treasury Stock (150 shares)...	(15,300)
Total Stockholders' Equity...	$ 984,700

The stockholders' equity section omitted several important facts that may be calculated by using the information given.

| **Required** | Answer each of the following questions, using the data given in the stockholders' equity section above. Show calculations where appropriate. |

1. How many shares of common stock have been issued?
2. What is total paid-in capital?
3. How many shares of common stock have been subscribed but not yet issued?
4. How many shares of common stock are outstanding?
5. How much was paid for each share of treasury stock?
6. What was the average amount paid for the common shares issued and subscribed?
7. What is the book value per share of common stock?

(Check figure: Common stock issued = 5,000 shares)

DECISION PROBLEM

Charlie Engine is the president of an engineering firm having 20 equal stockholders, each shareholder holding one share of stock. This past year the corporation had profits of $2,900,000. Charlie is considering changing the corporation to a partnership because he has heard that he and the other 19 engineers partners will retain more money after taxes under the partnership form of organization.

Assume that the corporation distributes the entire earnings to each shareholder every year and that each engineer is taxed individually at 33%. Assume further that the corporation is taxed at a rate of 34%. Stockholders (partners) are taxed on their individual returns at a rate of 33%.

1. Prepare an analysis that will enable the partners to see how much money each would receive under the partnership and corporate forms of business ownership.

2. Discuss the advantages and disadvantages of the corporate form of organization for the engineering firm.

CHAPTER 12

Corporations: Retained Earnings, Preferred Stock, and Earnings per Share

After studying this chapter you should understand:

- What retained earnings are
- Why retained earnings are appropriated and the effect of appropriating them
- How to prepare a statement of retained earnings
- Cash, property, stock, and liquidating dividends — what they are, and how they are accounted for
- What special privileges are normally given to preferred stock and how it is accounted for
- How to prepare a complex stockholders' equity section of a balance sheet
- The concepts of primary and fully diluted earnings per share and how earnings per share is shown on the income statement

RETAINED EARNINGS

Retained Earnings shows the income accumulated since the corporation's beginning that is still held by the corporation

Retained Earnings is a stockholders' equity account that shows the income accumulated since the corporation's beginning and still retained in the business. It's the accumulated income that the corporation still has.

When you think of $58 million of retained earnings, visions of large piles of cash may flash through your mind. To understand what retained earnings is, you must forget that vision. Retained earnings is not cash; it is not any specific asset. Retained earnings merely shows where a certain dollar amount of assets originally came from.

The diagram of a corporation balance sheet shown at the top of the next page helps illustrate this concept.

You should see by studying this balance sheet that:

> **Assets** are resources
>
> **Liabilities and Stockholders' Equity are sources of resources**

Retained earnings is not an asset; it shows where assets came from

The amount shown as retained earnings doesn't mean that we have that amount of cash on hand. In fact, retained earnings is *not* any asset. It shows where an amount of assets originally came from — the income earned by the corporation.

DUNLAP CORP.
Balance Sheet
December 31, 1989

Assets		Liabilities and Stockholders' Equity	
		Liabilities	
Assets are the *resources* (cash, inventory, land, buildings, patents) that a corporation has to use in earning income.	$587,000	Liabilities show the *source* of some of the assets—those paid for by borrowing money.	$200,000
		Stockholders' Equity Paid-In Capital	
		Paid-In Capital shows a *source* of some assets— those invested by stockholders.	300,000
		Retained Earnings	
		Retained Earnings shows a *source* of assets—those paid for out of the income earned by the corporation.	87,000
Total Assets	$587,000	Total Liabilities and Stockholders' Equity	$587,000

The Creation of Retained Earnings

Retained Earnings is created as the final step of closing all corporate income accounts. Expenses and revenues are closed into the Expense and Revenue Summary account. The balance of Expense and Revenue Summary is the income (credit balance) or loss (debit balance) for the period. Expense and Revenue Summary is a temporary account showing a single period's operating results. This account is closed into Retained Earnings, a permanent account accumulating the operating results of all periods since the corporation began. The following closing entry establishes a positive Retained Earnings balance:

Retained Earnings is created when Expense and Revenue Summary is closed

Dec. 31	Expense and Revenue Summary	87,400	
	Retained Earnings		87,400
	To close Expense and Revenue Summary into Retained Earnings.		

Retained Earnings can have a negative (accumulated debit) balance. This debit balance in Retained Earnings is called a *deficit.* A deficit occurs when accumulated losses are greater than accumulated profits.

Retained Earnings—Appropriations

When a company earns large profits for several years, the Retained Earnings balance will grow rapidly. Stockholders may become restless and begin to wonder why the assets generated through earnings are not being distributed as dividends.

Some of the reasons why management may be accumulating assets are:

■ To expand productive capacity by constructing a new factory building

■ To purchase the assets of another corporation in order to expand into new markets

■ To meet the requirements of a state law requiring that assets be held because the corporation holds a large amount of its own repurchased stock—treasury stock

Reasons for accumulating earnings should be communicated to stockholders

Management needs to communicate the reason for not paying larger dividends to stockholders before they become too irate. This communication may be accomplished by a footnote to the financial statements or by appropriating retained earnings.

An appropriation is accomplished by simply transferring an amount from the unrestricted Retained Earnings account (called *Retained Earnings: Unappropriated*) into a restricted Retained Earnings account (called *Retained Earnings: Appropriated*). The Kimberly Company example illustrates this process.

Kimberly Company plans to build a new warehouse in 5 years. The board of directors decides to appropriate $70,000 of retained earnings on Dec. 31, 1986, and each succeeding Dec. 31 through 1990. Construction of the new building is to take place in 1991. The appropriation entry for each Dec. 31 is:

Retained earnings may be appropriated to communicate why they are being accumulated

1986–1990		
Dec. 31	Retained Earnings: Unappropriated	70,000
	Retained Earnings: Appropriated for Plant Expansion	70,000
	To record a restriction placed upon retained earnings.	

Appropriating retained earnings does not set aside assets

An appropriation of retained earnings has no effect on assets and no effect on total retained earnings. Note that the entry in the Kimberly illustration involves two Retained Earnings accounts—no asset account is debited or credited.

Since no specific fund of assets is set aside by appropriating retained earnings, Kimberly Company will have $350,000 ($70,000 × 5 years) of appropriated retained earnings on Dec. 31, 1990, but it may still lack sufficient cash to construct a new building. *Remember, appropriating retained earnings communicates a restriction on retained earnings; it does not set aside a fund of assets.*

Here's how we show an appropriation of retained earnings in the stockholders' equity section of the balance sheet:

KIMBERLY COMPANY
Stockholders' Equity
December 31, 1990

Paid-In Capital:		
Common Stock, $10 par, 100,000 shares authorized, issued, and outstanding.		$1,000,000
Earned Capital:		
Retained Earnings: Unappropriated.	$540,000	
Retained Earnings: Appropriated for Plant Expansion.	350,000	
Total Earned Capital		890,000
Total Stockholders' Equity		$1,890,000

When the restriction on retained earnings is no longer needed, we remove the appropriation by debiting the Retained Earnings: Appropriated account and crediting the Retained Earnings: Unappropriated account. When the plant expansion is completed, Kimberly Company removes the restriction by the following entry:

Dec. 31 Retained Earnings: Appropriated for Plant Expansion 350,000
        Retained Earnings: Unappropriated   350,000
    To remove restriction placed upon retained earnings.

Many corporations believe that the disclosure of appropriated retained earnings does more to confuse stockholders than to inform them. These firms disclose retained earnings restrictions by explaining them in a footnote.

Financial statement footnotes often contain important supplemental information not found in the financial statements. Investors should study these notes carefully.

The illustration below shows how Kimberly's stockholders' equity section and related footnote would look if this method of disclosure is chosen.

The reason for accumulating retained earnings may also be shown in a footnote

---

KIMBERLY COMPANY
Stockholders' Equity
December 31, 1990

Paid-In Capital:
  Common Stock, $10 par, 100,000 shares authorized, issued, and
    outstanding $1,000,000

Earned Capital:
  Retained Earnings (see Note 3) 890,000

Total Stockholders' Equity $1,890,000

A footnote showing a restriction of retained earnings

Note 3. Retained earnings restrictions.
The corporation has been limiting the payment of dividends because of a planned plant expansion. Retained earnings restricted for this purpose amount to $350,000.

Retained Earnings — Prior Period Adjustments

To understand prior period adjustments, we must first understand why an adjustment is needed. Adjustments are needed to correct errors we have made in the past. Let's examine how errors affect the accounts.

An error in an income statement account ends up in Retained Earnings

Assume that an error was made in an income statement account 3 years ago (Salary Expense was understated by $25,000).

The income statement account — Salary Expense — was closed into Expense and Revenue Summary at the end of the year. The error is transferred to Expense and Revenue Summary.

Expense and Revenue Summary was then closed into Retained Earnings. The effect of the error is now in Retained Earnings. Retained Earnings is a permanent balance sheet account that is carried forward from year to year — it is not closed.

The correction of Retained Earnings for an error made in a prior year is called a prior period adjustment

The effect of the error, then, must still be in Retained Earnings. More specifically, the current beginning balance of Retained Earnings is wrong if the prior year's error was not corrected. The process of correcting this beginning balance of Retained Earnings we call making a ***prior period adjustment.***

The Hopper Hale illustration shows you how to record a prior period adjustment.

In 1988, Hopper Hale Corporation's bookkeeper debited Advertising Expense and credited Cash when she should have debited Land and credited Cash. The effect of this $25,000 error was to overstate 1988 Advertising Expense and therefore understate 1988 income by $25,000. Land is also understated by $25,000.

The error was discovered in 1989 by an astute auditor. We make the following entry to correct the error:

```
1989
Dec. 31   Land .................................................  25,000
                  Retained Earnings: Unappropriated.................        25,000
          To correct an error made on the 1988 income statement.
```

Hopper Hale's entry involved a debit to Land and a credit to Retained Earnings because those are the two accounts that are still wrong in 1989. Remember that the 1988 Advertising Expense account was closed to Retained Earnings in 1988, so it is Retained Earnings that is wrong in 1989 — not Advertising Expense.

Prior period adjustments may increase or decrease Retained Earnings

Prior period adjustments may increase Retained Earnings, as it did in the Hopper Hale example, or decrease Retained Earnings. You must analyze the effects of each error and decide whether Retained Earnings is too high or too low. Once you make this determination, you will know whether the prior period adjustment requires a debit or a credit to Retained Earnings.

Retained Earnings: A Recap

There are only a few types of transactions that affect Retained Earnings: Unappropriated. We have explained all of them except one — dividends.

When assets are distributed to stockholders as dividends, Retained Earnings is debited and an asset is credited. After we finish looking at Retained Earnings, we will examine dividends in detail. The only thing you need to know now is that Retained Earnings is debited when dividends are declared.

Now you have seen all of the reasons for debiting and crediting Retained Earnings: Unappropriated. We have summarized these reasons for you in the following T-account:

All the reasons why Retained Earnings may increase or decrease

Retained Earnings: Unappropriated	
Decreases	**Increases**
Net loss for the period	Net income for the period
Negative prior period adjustments	Positive prior period adjustments
Dividends declared (cash, property, and stock)	Cancellation of appropriations of retained earnings
Negative effects of certain treasury stock sales (see Chapter 13)	
Additional appropriations of retained earnings	

Statement of Retained Earnings

The statement of retained earnings is one of the four financial statements published by corporations in annual reports to their stockholders.

We have already discussed two of these four statements — the balance sheet and income statement. You will study the third — the statement of cash flows — in Chapter 15. Now let's look at the fourth — the statement of retained earnings.

The statement of retained earnings shows what happened to the Retained Earnings account during a period

The statement of retained earnings shows what has happened to the Retained Earnings account during the time period covered by the statement. The 1989 statement of retained earnings for Hopper Hale Corporation shows the disclosure of a prior period adjustment as well as income and dividends for the period:

HOPPER HALE CORPORATION **Statement of Retained Earnings** **Year Ended December 31, 1989**	
Retained Earnings, Jan. 1, 1989	$417,000
Prior Period Adjustment:	
Correction of 1988 Error	25,000
Retained Earnings, Jan. 1, 1989 Corrected	$442,000
Add: Net Income for 1989	62,500
Total	$504,500
Deduct: Dividends Declared during 1989	(82,500)
Retained Earnings, Dec. 31, 1989	$422,000

The ending balance of Retained Earnings shown in the statement of retained earnings is the amount that appears in the stockholders' equity section of the balance sheet.

Corporations with retained earnings appropriations may present a statement of retained earnings which includes a section for unappropriated retained earnings and sections to disclose the changes in each appropriation. The Springdale Company statement below illustrates such a report:

A statement of retained earnings showing unappropriated and appropriated retained earnings

SPRINGDALE COMPANY **Statement of Retained Earnings** **Year Ended June 30, 1989**		
Retained Earnings: Unappropriated:		
Balance, July 1, 1988		$1,450,000
Add: Net Income for the Year	$295,000	
Removal of Contingencies Appropriation	125,000	420,000
Total		$1,870,000
Deduct: Dividends Declared	$148,000	
Appropriation for Plant Expansion	50,000	(198,000)
Balance, June 30, 1989		$1,672,000
Retained Earnings Appropriated for Plant Expansion:		
Balance, July 1, 1988		$ 200,000
Add: Appropriation during the Year		50,000
Deduct (none)		-0-
Balance, June 30, 1989		$ 250,000
Retained Earnings Appropriated for Contingencies:		
Balance, July 1, 1988		$ 125,000
Add: (none)		-0-
Deduct: Transfer Back to Unappropriated		(125,000)
Balance, June 30, 1989		-0-

Springdale Company has the following earned capital on the June 30, 1989, balance sheet:

Earned Capital:	
Retained Earnings: Unappropriated	$1,672,000
Retained Earnings: Appropriated for Plant Expansion	250,000
Total Earned Capital	$1,922,000

DIVIDENDS ON COMMON STOCK

Dividends are distributions of earned capital to stockholders

Dividends are distributions of the earned capital of a corporation to its stockholders. These dividends may take the form of cash, assets other than cash, or additional shares of the corporation's stock.

The declaration and payment of dividends is at the discretion of the board of directors. Some corporations have a policy of paying regular, consistent amounts as dividends. Generally, owners of these corporations purchase their stock because they know they can count on the regular receipt of dividends. They use these regular cash inflows from dividends to pay living expenses. Railroads and utilities are examples of industries that pay regular quarterly dividends.

At the other extreme, some corporations seldom, if ever, pay dividends to stockholders. These corporations use all of the assets generated by earnings to expand the business. Stockholders purchase shares in these growth industries primarily to benefit from the increasing market value of the corporation's stock. The electronics industry is an example of a rapidly growing field in which corporations pay few, if any, dividends.

Three points in time are important in the distribution of any dividend: (1) the declaration date, (2) the record date, and (3) the payment date.

The declaration date is the day the board of directors votes to distribute a dividend

The **declaration date** is the day that the board of directors meets and votes to distribute a dividend. The form of the dividend (cash, other assets, or stock), the amount of the dividend, and the record and payment dates are specified at this meeting. At this point the board has legally committed the corporation to pay the dividend. An accounting entry is required on this date to record the obligation.

On the record date a list of stockholders who will receive the dividend is compiled

The **record date** is the day that the list of the names and addresses of the stockholders is compiled. These are the specific owners who will receive the dividend when paid. This date is normally 2 or 3 weeks later than the declaration date. No accounting entry is necessary on the record date because no further financial transaction or commitment has taken place.

On the payment date the dividend is distributed

The **payment date** is the day on which the dividends are sent to the shareholders. An accounting entry is necessary on this date to record the payment of cash, or the distribution of noncash assets or stock.

Cash Dividends

A company must have retained earnings and cash to pay a cash dividend

The majority of dividends paid are cash dividends. These distributions may be made at any time but they typically occur at the end of a quarter or a year. Two items are needed before the board of directors should consider declaring a cash dividend — earned capital and cash.

Most state laws require that dividends be declared out of accumulated earnings, not out of the capital that was invested by owners. The stockholders' equity section in Chapter 11 illustrated that paid-in capital and earned capital are accounted for separately and clearly distinguished on the balance sheet. The board should have little trouble determining whether adequate earned capital exists.

The existence of earned capital does not guarantee that cash exists. The company may have reinvested the assets realized through earnings in inventory or property, plant, and equipment assets. It may have used some of these assets to repay debt.

If the board sees that extra cash will be available after meeting operating needs and that earned capital exists as represented by the balance in Retained Earnings, they may declare a cash dividend.

The following illustration shows what we do on the declaration, record, and payment date.

On May 1, 1989, the board of directors of Clark, Inc., met and declared a cash dividend. The $1.50 per share is to be paid on May 31 to stockholders of record on May 15. Clark has 100,000 shares of common stock outstanding.

May 1	Dividends..	150,000	
	Dividends Payable..............................		150,000
	To record declaration of cash dividend of $1.50 per share on 100,000 shares of outstanding stock.		

May 15 No entry is required on the record date.

31	Dividends Payable..................................	150,000	
	Cash		150,000
	To record payment of the dividend declared on May 1.		

On May 1 we debited a temporary account called Dividends. This account is closed into Retained Earnings at the end of the year by the following entry:

Dec. 31	Retained Earnings: Unappropriated....................	150,000	
	Dividends		150,000
	To close Dividends account for all dividends declared during the year.		

As you can see, the declaration of the dividend eventually resulted in a reduction of Retained Earnings. Some companies choose not to use a Dividends account; instead, they debit Retained Earnings when the dividend is declared. *In the remaining illustrations and problems for this chapter, we will follow this procedure of debiting Retained Earnings when a dividend is declared.*

The Dividends Payable account that we used is a current liability because we pay the dividend in a short period of time.

The declaration and payment of a cash dividend reduces the total assets and the total equities of the corporation. The decrease in Cash reduces total assets; the decrease in Retained Earnings (either directly, or by closing the Dividends account) reduces stockholders' equity.

Property Dividends

A distribution of assets other than cash is called a property dividend

Occasionally we distribute assets other than cash as dividends. Inventory, land, and equipment have all been used for this purpose. The basic requirements of cash dividends also apply to property dividends—we must have adequate earned capital, assets must exist that we can distribute, and the dividend must be declared by the board of directors.

The amount of a property dividend is the fair market value of the assets distributed

With property dividends we have to solve a problem that we didn't have with cash dividends—at what amount should we record the dividend? Generally accepted accounting principles tell us that the proper amount is the *fair market value* of the assets that will be distributed.

The fact that we carry our assets in the accounting records at cost, or cost less accumulated depreciation, means that we will need to revalue the assets. When we revalue, we will recognize a gain or loss to increase or decrease the asset to its fair value. How do we know what fair value is? We use price quotations, known selling prices, or appraisals.

The effect of revaluing the asset is the same as if we had sold the asset and then distributed the proceeds as a cash dividend.

The Aztec Company example shows you the correct accounting for a property dividend:

The board of directors of Aztec Company declared a property dividend consisting of 10 acres of vacant land costing $10,000 which the company is not using. Since the company has 10 shareholders each of whom owns an equal number of shares, the 10 acres will be divided evenly among them. The dividend was declared on Sept. 15, payable on Oct. 15 to stockholders of record on Oct. 1. Independent appraisals set the current fair value of the property at $16,000.

The entries associated with revaluing an asset and distributing it as a property dividend

Sept. 15	Land...	6,000	
	Gain to Increase Land to Fair Market Value..........		6,000
	To increase land from cost, $10,000, to market value of $16,000.		
15	Retained Earnings: Unappropriated	16,000	
	Property Dividend Payable		16,000
	To record *declaration* of a property dividend consisting of 10 acres of land with a current appraised value of $16,000.		
Oct. 1	*Record date*—no entry required.		
15	Property Dividend Payable	16,000	
	Land..		16,000
	To record *distribution* of the property dividend.		

Aztec did not realize a gain as a result of declaring the dividend but as a result of revaluing the asset. The Gain to Increase Land to Fair Market Value would be shown on the income statement among "other gains and losses."

Property dividends have the same effect on the balance sheet as cash dividends. Total assets decrease because some asset—Land, for example—is paid out. Total stockholders' equity is lower because Retained Earnings is decreased.

Stock Dividends

Remember we said that three things were necessary for a cash or property dividend—an asset to distribute, earned capital, and a declaration by the board of directors. What happens when we have plenty of earned capital and a board willing to declare a dividend but no assets to distribute? The board may declare a stock dividend.

A stock dividend involves issuing additional shares of the corporation's own stock

A **stock dividend** consists of issuing additional shares of the corporation's own stock to its stockholders on a pro rata basis.

For example, Irving Akard owns 10 shares of Tribune Company stock. When the Tribune Company declares and issues a 20% stock dividend. Irving receives 2 additional shares. Since each other shareholder receives a 20% dividend, the total number of shares increases by 20%. Each shareholder has the same proportionate ownership after the dividend was declared as before:

Each stockholder owns the same percentage of the corporation before and after a stock dividend

Total shares outstanding before dividend	100 shares
Total shares issued in 20% stock dividend	20 shares
Total shares outstanding after dividend	120 shares

Irving owned 10% of the Tribune Company before the dividend was declared (10% × 100 shares = 10 shares) and after the dividend was distributed (10% × 120 shares = 12 shares).

What did Irving gain as a result of the stock dividend? *Nothing!* He owned 10% of the company before and after the dividend. He now has more "pieces of paper" to represent the same ownership. If he desires to realize cash out of the stock dividend, he must sell shares and thus reduce his percentage of ownership in the corporation — something he could have done even before the dividend.

Why, then, do corporations issue stock dividends? The two most commonly given reasons are:

The reasons for issuing a stock dividend

1. **To reduce the market price of the stock.** When a large number of new shares are issued (over 25% more), the total number of shares of the corporation's stock available in the marketplace is increased to such an extent that the market price of each share drops. The lower market price per share makes the stock more affordable for individuals with small amounts to invest.

2. **To distribute something to the shareholders when all cash and noncash assets are needed in the business.** In a growing corporation the distribution of a stock dividend is a way of notifying stockholders that these retained earnings have been distributed in the form of additional shares of stock and that they will never be distributed in the form of cash or other assets.

In spite of the questionable value of stock dividends, many corporations issue them and thus we must understand the proper accounting procedures for them. The effect of a stock dividend on the balance sheet is to reduce earned capital and to increase paid-in capital. The amount we record depends on the size of the dividend.

We will use the Hastings Company information below to illustrate the correct recording of a small stock dividend and a large stock dividend.

HASTINGS COMPANY
Stockholders' Equity before Stock Dividend
June 30, 1989

Paid-In Capital:
  Common Stock, $10 par, 200,000 shares authorized, 120,000 shares
    issued and outstanding... $1,200,000
  Paid-In Capital in Excess of Par.................................... 300,000
      Total Paid-In Capital... $1,500,000

Earned Capital:
  Retained Earnings.. 940,000

Total Stockholders' Equity $2,440,000

Small Stock Dividends

Small stock dividends: issue fewer than 20–25% new shares

Small stock dividends involve the issuance of new shares amounting to less than 20 to 25% of the shares previously outstanding. In the case of a small stock dividend, we assume that too few new shares are issued to affect the market value of the stock. Each new share, then, has a value equal to the market value of each of the shares previously outstanding. This market value is considered the proper amount to use to account for a small stock dividend.

On July 1, 1989, the Hastings Company board of directors declared a 5% stock dividend to be distributed on Aug. 15 to stockholders of record on July 20. Hastings' stock was trading for $18 per share on July 1.

Small stock dividends are recorded at the market value per share on the declaration date

July 1	Retained Earnings (6,000 shares × $18)..................	108,000	
	Stock Dividend Distributable (6,000 shares × $10).....		60,000
	Paid-In Capital in Excess of Par (6,000 shares × $8)....		48,000
	To record *declaration* of a 5% stock dividend (5% × 120,000 shares = 6,000 new shares).		

Our declaration entry debits Retained Earnings just as we did for property dividends. The amount of the debit is the value of the shares we will issue—the number of new shares we will issue multiplied by the market value of each share.

Stock Dividend Distributable is credited for the par value (or stated value) of the new shares issued. Paid-In Capital in Excess of Par is credited for the amount by which market value of the stock exceeds par (or stated value). Stock Dividend Distributable is a temporary stockholders' equity account that we use until the stock is issued (see the Aug. 15 entry below).

We do not credit a liability account in this case because no true liability exists. A liability is an obligation that requires the disbursement of assets or the performance of a service for its satisfaction. We have no such obligation. The board of directors has committed the corporation to issue additional shares of common stock, not to pay out assets or perform services; this commitment, therefore, fails to meet the definition of a liability.

July 20   No journal entry is required on the *record* date.

Aug. 15   Stock Dividend Distributable 60,000
          Common Stock   60,000
          To record distribution of 6,000 shares of stock as a dividend.

When we issue the dividend, we remove the temporary stockholders' equity account Stock Dividend Distributable and increase Common Stock. We have now replaced the temporary stockholders' equity account with a permanent one.

The effect of this stock dividend was to move $108,000 out of earned capital into paid-in capital. Total assets and total stockholders' equity remain unchanged.

Let's look at Hastings' Stockholders' Equity section before and after the small stock dividend:

This illustration shows the effect of a small stock dividend on stockholders' equity

		Before Small Stock Dividend	After Small Stock Dividend
	Common stock	$1,200,000	$1,260,000
	Paid-in capital in excess of par	300,000	348,000
Total paid-in capital increased $108,000.	Total paid-in capital	$1,500,000	$1,608,000
Total retained earnings decreased $108,000.	Retained earnings	940,000	832,000
Total stockholders' equity is unchanged.	Total stockholders' equity	$2,440,000	$2,440,000

Hastings does have 6,000 more shares of common stock outstanding after the dividend.

Large Stock Dividends

Large stock dividends: issue more than 20–25% new shares

A large stock dividend is a pro rata distribution of new shares amounting to more than 20 to 25% of the stock previously outstanding. When we distribute a large stock dividend, we place so many additional shares into the marketplace that the market price of the stock will probably drop. Since we don't know how large this drop will be, we use the par value of the shares issued as the amount for recording the new shares.

Large stock dividends are recorded at the par value of the shares issued

Let's assume that, instead of issuing a 5% stock dividend, Hastings' board declared a 40% stock dividend.

On July 1, 1989, the Hastings Company board of directors declared a 40% stock dividend (*instead* of the 5% dividend in the illustration above). The shares will be distributed on Aug. 31 to stockholders of record on Aug. 1. Hastings' stock was trading for $18 per share on July 1.

July 1	Retained Earnings (48,000 shares × $10 par) 480,000	
	Stock Dividend Distributable	480,000
	To record the *declaration* of a 40% dividend (40% × 120,000 shares = 48,000 new shares).	
Aug. 1	No journal entry is required on the *record* date.	
31	Stock Dividend Distributable 480,000	
	Common Stock	480,000
	To record the *distribution* of a large stock dividend.	

Our entries to record a large stock dividend are exactly the same ones we use for a small stock dividend—with one exception. We won't need to credit Paid-In Capital in Excess of Par because there is no excess—the large stock dividend is recorded at par.

The effect of this large stock dividend is to move $480,000 out of earned capital into paid-in capital. Total assets and total stockholders' equity are unchanged.

Again, here is Hastings' stockholders' equity section before and after the dividend:

This illustration shows the effect of a large stock dividend on stockholders' equity

		Before Large Stock Dividend	After Large Stock Dividend
Common stock and total paid-in capital increased by $480,000	Common stock	$1,200,000	$1,680,000
	Paid-in capital in excess of par	300,000	300,000
	Total paid-in capital	$1,500,000	$1,980,000
Retained earnings decreased by $480,000	Retained earnings	940,000	460,000
Total stockholders' equity is unchanged	Total stockholders' equity	$2,440,000	$2,440,000

Hastings now has 48,000 more shares outstanding but the same total stockholders' equity.

Liquidating Dividends

Liquidating dividends are not dividends as we have been using the term. We have been using dividends to mean distributions out of earned capital—giving the owners some of the accumulated income of the corporation.

*Liquidating dividends
distribute paid-in capital
to the stockholders*

Liquidating dividends are pro rata distributions of paid-in capital (not earned capital) to the stockholders. We are giving the owners back some of the assets they invested in the company.

Liquidating dividends are paid only when a corporation is permanently reducing its size, or when it is going out of business.

The board of directors must exercise care to declare liquidating dividends only when they are allowed by state statutes. Many of these laws require approval by the stockholders or a court of law. In some states the directors are personally liable for any illegally declared liquidating dividends.

Dividends and Treasury Stock

No dividends are paid on treasury stock. This includes cash dividends, property dividends, stock dividends, and liquidating dividends. When a corporation owns treasury stock, it is holding shares of its own stock. To pay dividends on treasury stock would amount to the corporation paying itself a dividend—a useless exercise.

Stock Splits

*In a stock split old shares
are replaced with a larger
number of new ones*

A ***stock split*** occurs when the board of directors, acting with the permission of the state, reduces the par or stated value of all of its common stock. We accomplish this reduction by issuing additional new shares for each old share held by a stockholder.

Like large stock dividends, the purpose of a stock split is to put many new shares into the marketplace and thus reduce the market price per share.

When we distribute a stock split, the *only* amounts that change on the balance sheet are the number of shares authorized, issued, and outstanding and the par or stated value per share. The dollars assigned to Common Stock, Paid-In Capital in Excess of Par, Retained Earnings, and the other stockholders' equity accounts remain the same.

Because no monetary amounts are involved, we need only a memorandum entry to record a stock split.

The Firebrand Corporation example below and on page 515 demonstrates the effects of a stock split.

FIREBRAND CORPORATION
Stockholders' Equity
September 30, 1989
(before stock split)

Paid-In Capital:	
Common Stock, $1 par, 50,000 shares authorized, issued, and outstanding	$ 50,000
Paid-In Capital in Excess of Par	130,000
Total Paid-In Capital.	$180,000
Earned Capital:	
Retained Earnings	315,000
Total Stockholders' Equity.	$495,000

THE STOCK SPLIT

On Oct. 1, 1989, Firebrand received permission to issue a 4 for 1 stock split. Four new shares of $0.25-par-value stock are issued for each old share of $1-par-value stock. 200,000 (50,000 × 4) shares of $0.25 ($1 ÷ 4)-par-value stock are now authorized.

Oct. 1   Memorandum. $1-par-value common stock is split 4 for 1. New par value $0.25 per share for 200,000 authorized shares.

FIREBRAND CORPORATION
Stockholders' Equity
October 2, 1989
(after stock split)

The effect of a stock split on stockholders' equity

Paid-In Capital:	
Common Stock, $0.25 par, 200,000 shares authorized, issued, and outstanding	$ 50,000
Paid-In Capital in Excess of Par	130,000
Total Paid-In Capital	$180,000
Earned Capital:	
Retained Earnings	315,000
Total Stockholders' Equity	$495,000

A stockholder who previously owned 100 shares of Firebrand stock would now own 400 shares. Stock can be split 10 for 1, 2 for 1, or 1½ for 1 or in any other way the corporation desires.

The steps for calculating the new par or stated value and the new number of shares are:

1. Divide the par value per share by the number of new shares replacing one old share. In the Firebrand example we divided $1 by 4 new shares = $0.25 per share.

2. Multiply the number of shares authorized, issued, and outstanding by the number of new shares replacing one old share. In the Firebrand example we multiplied 50,000 old shares by 4 = 200,000 new shares.

If the corporation owns treasury stock at the time of the split, the treasury stock must be split as well. If Firebrand had owned 5,000 shares of treasury stock before the split, it would have 20,000 shares (4 × 5,000) after the split. The par value of this stock is also adjusted to $0.25 per share.

The purpose of a stock split is to reduce the market price per share of stock

The purpose of a stock split is to attract a larger number of investors by decreasing the market price of the stock. Stock on the national stock exchanges is normally bought and sold in 100-share lots. Smaller numbers of shares may be traded, but the broker's commission for handling such transactions is relatively high. You would need $9,000 to buy 100 shares of stock priced at $90 per share. A 2 for 1 split would reduce the needed cash to about $4,500 and a 4 for 1 split to $2,250.

SQUEEZE PLAY

by Robert McGough

Gilbert McDougald played shortstop for the New York Yankees during the 1950s, and in his best year he batted .311. This summer, in a different sort of game, he and a partner went 1 for 3,000, and they shouldn't have any difficulty scoring.

McDougald and Norman Rockwell, who are executive vice president and president of Metropolitan Maintenance Co., took their company private by forcing a 1-for-3,000 reverse stock split on their minority shareholders. For every 3,000 old shares, one new share was issued. But anyone who had fewer than 3,000 shares received only cash for his stock, and well below book value at that. Only McDougald and Rockwell owned more than 3,000 shares, so the two of them now own all the stock of the Nutley, N.J., company.

A nice squeeze play. Says Darrell Patrick of S. J. Wolfe & Co., a stockbroker for one of the former shareholders: "That's a ripoff of the shareholders. There's no other way to define it."

Metropolitan Maintenance has a $16 million (1983 sales) business providing maintenance, cleaning, and security services for commercial buildings. But having

sold stock in 1972, it found being public wasn't what it wanted, as a languishing price made its shares a poor tool for acquisitions. With only 175 shareholders left this year, it finally decided to get rid of the annoyance. Ousting the outsiders has a tax advantage: It will enable Metropolitan to become a Subchapter S corporation, meaning that McDougald and Rockwell will pay individual income taxes on the profits but no corporate taxes.

"There were very, very few complaints from the stockholders," claims the company's attorney. The company paid $37 per share for fractional shares, scarcely more than half the book value of $72 ($58 excluding goodwill). Earnings per share were up 89% in 1983 to $5.93, and were still climbing at mid-1984. A great time, it would appear, to buy the company.

M. J. Whitman & Co., a New York City financial consulting firm hired by the company for $7,500 to make an appraisal, affirmed that $37 per share was fair. Martin Whitman's defense: "I thought the company was a piece of crap." Noting that Metropolitan at one point appraised its own shares at $26, Whitman says, "My conscience is clear." The proxy did mention that "the opinion of the board of directors

must be considered in light of the fact that the board is controlled by Messrs. Rockwell and McDougald, who constitute two of the company's three directors." Nobody can complain about inadequate disclosure.

Warner National Corp., a savings and loan in Ohio, recently did a 1-for-16 reverse split, which will leave only three shareholders. Surgical Appliance Industries, a manufacturer in Cincinnati, is working on a 1-for-50,000 split that will leave only two shareholders. Crystal Tissue, a Middletown, Ohio, wrappings outfit, has proposed a 1-for-4,000 reverse split, but this has been delayed because some outsiders have expressed interest in taking over the entire company. Presumably the minority shareholders will share equally in that reward, although there is no guarantee that the new buyer won't simply pick up the control shares and leave outsiders in the cold.

Great values can frequently be found in thinly traded companies that have been ignored by Wall Street. But securities laws do not offer much protection from reverse splits and other freeze-outs.

Source: Forbes, Nov. 19, 1984, pages 54, 56.

In this chapter you learned that a stock split is a way of putting more shares into the marketplace and thus reducing the market price per share. You now know that a reverse stock split operates in just the opposite manner — it reduces the number of shares in the market and can force stockholders to be "eliminated" by having the corporation buy out old shares that can't be "traded in" for new shares issued in the reverse split. As a result, control of the corporation can be concentrated in the hands of only a few individuals. When only a few people own the corporation's stock, it will cease to be bought and sold on stock exchanges. When this happens, the corporation is said to be private, or closely held.

Sometimes a large stock dividend is distributed to accomplish the same purpose as a stock split. The advantage of using a stock split rather than a large stock dividend is that more shares may be distributed without affecting retained earnings. Thus we preserve the retained earnings balance for future dividend distributions.

PREFERRED STOCK

We have discussed common stock, the primary ownership shares of a corporation. Now it's time to turn our attention to preferred stock, a second type of equity security sold by many corporations to raise capital.

The authorization to issue preferred stock is included in the articles of incorporation. The authorization provides for:

1. Par value or the stipulation that the stock is to be no par

2. The total number of shares authorized

3. The annual dividend rate or amount

4. The characteristics that the stock is to possess (voting rights, dividend privileges, liquidation preferences, etc.)

Preferred stock offers its owners certain privileges that common stock owners do not have

Preferred stock appeals to a different group of investors than common stock. This is true because preferred stock offers its owners certain privileges (or preferences) not enjoyed by common stockholders.

The corporation offers stock with preferences to reduce the risks of investing. Preferred stock is less risky than common stock. You may be tempted to invest in preferred stock when you wouldn't invest in common. You will understand why preferred stock is less risky when we discuss its characteristics.

Characteristics of Preferred Stock

The characteristics of preferred stock are spelled out in the charter of incorporation. Remember, the charter is the legal document that creates the corporation and specifies the types of equity securities it can issue.

We will discuss characteristics relating to (1) dividends, (2) voting rights, (3) conversion privileges (the stockholders' right to trade preferred stock for another security), (4) callability (the corporation's right to buy back the preferred stock), and (5) liquidation preference.

Dividends

Preferred stockholders receive dividends before common stockholders receive any

Dividends on preferred stock are normally stated as a percentage of par value or a specified number of dollars per year if the stock has no par value. 6% preferred stock with a par value of $100 would pay a $6-per-year dividend—if declared by the board of directors. $3.50 preferred stock would refer to no-par stock paying a dividend of $3.50 annually.

You should understand that dividends on preferred must be declared by the board of directors before they can be paid and, like common dividends, they are not automatic. If the board pays any dividends during a year, however, preferred shareholders will receive their dividends before any are paid to common shareholders.

What if the board chooses not to declare a preferred dividend in a given year? If the preferred stock is *cumulative,* the dividends must be paid in a later year before any distributions can be made to common stockholders. Past dividends "owed" to preferred stockholders are called dividends in *arrears.* These obligations are not liabilities until the dividend is declared by the directors. We disclose the existence of this obligation in the footnotes to the financial statements.

Holders of *noncumulative* preferred stock would lose the right to receive dividends not declared in the current year.

This illustration shows that cumulative preferred dividends must be paid before common receives any

Arrow, Inc., has 10,000 shares of 8%, $100-par preferred stock and 100,000 shares of $1-par common stock outstanding. The preferred stock is cumulative but no dividends were declared in 1986, 1987, or 1988. The following calculation shows the amount that must be paid to preferred stockholders in 1989 before any dividends can be paid to common:

Dividends due each year: (8% × $100 par × 10,000 shares)	$ 80,000
Number of years in arrears: 1986, 1987, 1988	× 3
Total dividends in arrears	$240,000
Add: 1989 dividend	80,000
Total that must be paid before any distribution to common	$320,000

Assuming the same facts except that the preferred stock is noncumulative, Arrow would be required to pay only the $80,000 1989 dividend before distributions could be made to common.

Preferred stockholders are normally limited to receiving the amount of dividends specified—the 8% of $100 in the Arrow example. If this is the case, the stock is referred to as **nonparticipating.**

The corporation may also be authorized to issue participating preferred stock. **Participating preferred** gives the stockholder the right to receive the specified dividend and to receive more when dividends are paid to common stockholders. When all distributions are made, participating preferred will receive the same percentage of par value as the common stockholders for current dividends.

If there are dividends in arrears, cumulative, participating preferred will receive a higher percentage of par value than common stockholders.

To help you in allocating a cash dividend between preferred and common stockholders, we have provided the following step-by-step procedure:

You should use this procedure to allocate dividends between preferred and common stock

1. If preferred is cumulative, give preferred all dividends in arrears. (Noncumulative preferred does not receive dividends in arrears.)

2. Give preferred its current year's dividend percentage or amount.

3. Give common a matching current dividend. (By "matching" we mean the same percentage of its par value as preferred received.)

4. If preferred stock is participating, allocate all remaining dollars in this way:

Additional percentage of par allocated to common and preferred:

$$\frac{\textbf{Number of dollars remaining to be distributed}}{\textbf{Total par value of common and preferred stock}} = \begin{array}{c}\textbf{additional \% of par to give}\\\textbf{to each}\end{array}$$

$$\textbf{Additional \% of par} \times \textbf{total par value of preferred} = \begin{array}{c}\textbf{amount allocated}\\\textbf{to preferred}\end{array}$$

$$\textbf{Additional \% of par} \times \textbf{total par value of common} = \begin{array}{c}\textbf{amount allocated}\\\textbf{to common}\end{array}$$

Remember, if preferred is nonparticipating, all remaining dollars go to the common stockholders.

Follow this step-by-step approach as you study the examples we have provided. First an illustration where preferred is noncumulative and participating:

This illustration allocates dividends between common and preferred stockholders assuming that preferred is noncumulative and participating

Mason Company has the following stock outstanding on Dec. 31, 1989:

7% Noncumulative, participating preferred stock, $100 par, 2,000 shares authorized, issued, and outstanding..........................	$ 200,000
Common stock, $10 par, 100,000 shares authorized, issued, and outstanding...	1,000,000
Total preferred and common stock	$1,200,000

Mason declared a $108,000 dividend that would be allocated to preferred and common as follows:

	Preferred	Common	Total
Total outstanding stock (par)	$200,000	$1,000,000	$1,200,000
Total dividend declared			$ 108,000
First, regular preferred dividend [(7%)($200,000 par)]	$ 14,000		(14,000)
Amount remaining			$ 94,000
Second, matching common dividend [(7%)($1,000,000)]		$ 70,000	(70,000)
Amount remaining			$ 24,000
Third, remainder allocated to give each the same rate ($24,000 ÷ $1,200,000 = 2%):			
(2%)($200,000)	4,000		(4,000)
(2%)($1,000,000)......................		20,000	(20,000)
Amount remaining			$ -0-
Total distribution	$ 18,000 + $	90,000 = $	108,000

Each class of stock received a 9% dividend on par value. The $108,000 is a 9% dividend based on total par value of both preferred and common.

Now let's look at a more complex example. In this one the preferred stock is both cumulative (with dividends in arrears) and participating.

This illustration allocates dividends between common and preferred stockholders assuming preferred is cumulative and participating

Elfin Company has the following stock outstanding on Dec. 31, 1989:

8% Cumulative, participating preferred stock, $100 par, 500 shares authorized, issued, and outstanding	$ 50,000
Common stock, $1 par, 150,000 shares authorized, issued, and outstanding	150,000
Total preferred and common stock...............................	$200,000

Elfin did not declare or pay any dividends during 1988; therefore, there are $4,000 (8% × $50,000) preferred dividends in arrears.

Elfin declared a 1989 dividend of $30,000, which would be allocated to preferred and common as follows:

	Preferred	Common	Total
Total outstanding stock (par).................	$50,000	$150,000	$200,000
Total dividend declared......................			$ 30,000
First, preferred dividend in arrears............	$ 4,000		(4,000)
Amount remaining..........................			$ 26,000
Second, regular current preferred dividend [(8%)($50,000 par)].........................	4,000		(4,000)
Amount remaining..........................			$ 22,000
Third, matching common dividend [(8%)($150,000)]..........................		$ 12,000	(12,000)
Amount remaining..........................			$ 10,000
Fourth, remainder allocated to give each the same percentage ($10,000 ÷ $200,000 = 5%):			
(5%)($50,000).............................	2,500		(2,500)
(5%)($150,000)............................		7,500	(7,500)
Amount remaining..........................			$ -0-
Total distribution...........................	$10,500 +	$ 19,500 =	$ 30,000

Notice that the matching common dividend only matches the percentage received by preferred shareholders for the current year. Dividends in arrears are not matched.

In this illustration preferred shareholders received a 21% total distribution (8% for 1988 arrears and 13% for 1989). Common stockholders received a 13% total distribution. The current dividend of 13% is the same for both classes of stock.

Voting Rights

Voting rights are not ordinarily given to preferred stockholders. They are not allowed to vote in the election of members to the board of directors, or on other matters that require a vote of the stockholders.

Some state laws may permit us to issue voting preferred stock. Voting, then, is a special privilege that may be included in the characteristics of preferred stock.

Conversion Privilege

An owner of convertible preferred stock has the right to turn in his or her preferred shares to the corporation and receive common shares in their place. The number of common shares to be received is specified on the preferred stock certificate.

For example, K. Houston owns 100 shares of 8% noncumulative preferred stock convertible into common at the rate of one share of preferred for three shares of common. At any time Houston may submit her 100 preferred shares and receive 300 shares of common. The corporation can't make her convert; the decision is hers.

We assume that preferred stock is nonconvertible unless the corporation specifically adds this special feature.

Callability

Callable preferred stock may be retired by the corporation by paying the stockholder a predetermined amount — the **call price.**

The preferred stock certificate usually provides that the stock will become callable at some future date. The call price typically exceeds the original issue price.

For example, on Jan. 1, 1989, J. Nall purchases 100 shares of 6% cumulative preferred stock for $12 per share. The stock is callable at any time after Jan. 1, 1993, at $25 per share.

Now the corporation has the option. At any time after Jan. 1, 1993, it can retire Nall's stock by paying him $25 per share. Nall can neither force the corporation to retire his stock, nor can he refuse to let the corporation purchase it at the call price.

As you probably observed, the callability provision is not so much a privilege for the preferred stockholder as it is a right for the corporation. The corporation has an easy way of removing the obligations imposed upon it by having preferred stock outstanding. For example, if there is no preferred stock, there are no preferred dividends to pay.

Liquidation Preference

In case of liquidation, creditors receive assets first, then preferred stockholders, and finally common stockholders

All preferred stock includes a liquidation preference. This feature means that, if the corporation decides to cease operations and distribute its assets to creditors and owners, the preferred stockholders will receive assets in settlement of their claims before common stockholders are entitled to any assets.

The liquidation preference doesn't guarantee that preferred shareholders will receive all of the assets to which they are entitled. First the creditors must be paid, then any remaining assets can be used to settle preferred stockholder claims. If any assets are left, they can be distributed to common stockholders.

How much are preferred stockholders entitled to receive? This is a difficult question to answer since the amount depends on state law. In general, preferred shareholders will receive any dividends in arrears (if preferred is cumulative), and the par or stated value per share. Some states also require that the paid-in capital in excess of par (or stated value) be returned to the preferred shareholders on a pro rata basis.

In order to be successful in raising capital by issuing preferred stock, management must put together a "package" of preferences. Their objective will be to offer sufficient appeal to investors without placing an undesirable burden on the corporation or the common stockholders.

All preferred stock will have dividend and liquidation preferences. We must decide whether to add cumulative, participating, convertibility, and voting privileges — or possibly impose a callable restriction.

If we can raise the needed capital by selling nonvoting, noncumulative, nonparticipating preferred, there is no reason to offer voting, cumulative, participating, or convertibility rights.

Accounting for Preferred Stock

We account for preferred stock just like we did common stock

We account for preferred stock just like we did for common stock. The only difference is in the account titles we use. We substitute the accounts Preferred Stock, Paid-In Capital in Excess of Par: Preferred, Preferred Stock Subscribed, and Subscriptions Receivable: Preferred for the corresponding accounts applicable to common stock.

For example, the sale of 100 shares of $10 par preferred stock for $25 per share would be entered in the general joural like this:

Jan. 5   Cash 2,500
              Preferred Stock 1,000
              Paid-In Capital in Excess of Par: Preferred 1,500
          To record the sale of 100 shares of $10 par preferred stock.

We don't usually purchase preferred stock as treasury stock. If we do, we use the same procedures to account for it as we used for common treasury stock in Chapter 11.

THE STOCKHOLDERS' EQUITY SECTION ILLUSTRATED

We have completed our look at the various accounts that may appear in the stockholders' equity section of the balance sheet.

Now we will show you how each of the stockholders' equity accounts we discussed in this chapter and the last look on the balance sheet. In addition, we've added the descriptive information (shares authorized, issued, outstanding, par value, etc.) needed for fair disclosure. See the illustration at the top of page 523.

EARNINGS PER SHARE

If you own stock in a large corporation, you will be interested in how well that corporation is doing. One measure of corporate success is the amount of income it earns. You know, of course, that this information is available on the income statement.

Earnings per share is one measure of a corporation's success

Suppose you looked at the corporate income statement and found a net income of $127,000 reported there. Would that make you happy? You would certainly feel better than if you saw a net loss of $127,000. But in order to decide just how good you should feel, you would need to evaluate this amount in several ways.

We will look at one such evaluation, earnings per share, here. In Chapter 16 we will discuss a number of others.

Earnings per share (EPS), in its simplest form, is the net income earned by a corporation divided by the number of common shares outstanding. If Wise, Inc., earns $127,000 and has 10,000 shares outstanding during the year, the EPS is $12.70 ($127,000 ÷ 10,000). If there are 100,000 shares outstanding, the EPS is $1.27 ($127,000 ÷ 100,000).

You can see that just knowing total net income is not enough. You will also be interested in knowing how much that net income is when spread over all of the shares of stock. The more stock there is outstanding, the less beneficial the income is to each shareholder.

Authoritative financial accounting standards require disclosure of earnings per share on the face of the income statements of all corporations whose stock is publicly traded (sold on a stock exchange or over-the-counter). Closely held corporations, such as those whose stock is owned by the members of a family, are not required to disclose earnings per share amounts. Proprietorships and partnerships do not disclose earnings per share — remember, they do not issue stock so they have no shares.

This stockholders' equity section shows all of the accounts discussed in Chapters 11 and 12

MODEL CORPORATION
Stockholders' Equity
September 30, 1989

Paid-In Capital:

6% Preferred Stock, $100 par, noncumulative, nonvoting, participating, 10,000 shares authorized, 4,000 shares issued and outstanding	$ 400,000	
6% Preferred Stock Subscribed, $100 par, 500 shares	50,000	
Total Preferred Stock		$ 450,000
Common Stock, no par, stated value $25, 100,000 shares authorized, 60,000 shares issued, 58,500 shares outstanding (1,500 shares in the treasury)	$1,500,000	
Common Stock Subscribed, no par, stated value, $25, 1,000 shares	25,000	
Common Stock Dividend Distributable, 5,950 shares, no par, $25 stated value per share	148,750	
Total Common Stock		1,673,750

Additional Paid-In Capital:

Paid-In Capital in Excess of Par: Preferred	$ 45,000	
Paid-In Capital in Excess of Stated Value: Common	750,000	
Paid-In Capital from Treasury Stock	25,000	
Donated Capital	135,000	
Total Additional Paid-In Capital		955,000
Total Paid-In Capital		$3,078,750

Earned Capital:

Retained Earnings: Unappropriated		$ 875,000	
Retained Earnings: Appropriated:			
For Plant Expansion	$250,000		
For Contingencies	125,000		
Total Appropriated		375,000	
Total Earned Capital			1,250,000
Total Paid-In and Earned Capital			$4,328,750
Less: Treasury Stock: Common (1,500 shares at cost)			(67,500)
Total Stockholders' Equity			$4,261,250

Historical Earnings per Share

Corporations with simple capital structures report only historical earnings per share amounts. A ***simple capital structure*** means that the corporation has no convertible preferred stock, convertible bonds, or stock options outstanding that could cause the corporation to issue additional shares of stock. Before we go further, let's be sure you have an idea what convertible securities and stock options are.

Corporations with simple capital structures report only historical EPS

Convertible preferred stock and convertible bonds are securities that can be turned in to the corporation by their owners. In return the corporation must give the owners a predetermined number of shares of common stock. Thus, these securities can cause the corporation to issue more shares of common stock.

Stock options are arrangements that allow an individual, usually an executive of the company, to purchase stock at a price lower than she would have to pay if she bought it through a stockbroker. This stock option discount is a reward for the executive's efforts in making the company successful. Stock option plans may also cause the corporation to issue stock. When the executive elects to exercise her option and pay for the stock, the corporation must issue the shares.

Historical earnings per share calculations ignore the potential new shares that the corporation may be required to issue. By definition, in a simple capital structure, the corporation has no convertible securities or stock option plans.

Historical earnings per share is calculated by the following formula:

$$\textbf{Historical EPS} = \frac{\textbf{net income} - \textbf{preferred dividends}}{\textbf{weighted average common shares outstanding}}$$

Earnings per share is really per *common* share. Preferred dividends must be subtracted from reported net income to derive that portion of the income available to common stockholders. (Remember, preferred dividends must be paid before any distributions may be made to common stockholders.)

We use weighted average common shares outstanding during the year in the calculation in an attempt to equate the shares outstanding with the income produced by the resources received when those shares were sold. We would distort EPS if income on resources available for only 3 months were divided by shares assumed to be outstanding for a full year. The weighted average approach avoids this distortion by dividing income earned on resources used for 3 months by shares outstanding for 3 months.

The Branch, Inc., example shows you how to calculate weighted average shares outstanding. Study it and then we'll discuss the procedure we used.

This illustration shows how to calculate weighted average shares outstanding

Branch, Inc., had 100,000 common shares outstanding on Jan. 1, 1989. The following common stock transactions took place during the year: Mar. 1, sold 12,000 shares; June 30, sold 4,000 shares; November 1, repurchased 6,000 shares as treasury stock:

Date	Shares Outstanding	×	Months	=	Share-Months
1989					
Jan. 1	100,000		2		200,000
Mar. 1	112,000		4		448,000
June 30	116,000		4		464,000
Nov. 1	110,000		2		220,000
Total					1,332,000

Weighted average common shares outstanding
1,332,000 ÷ 12 months = 111,000

In calculating Branch's weighted average shares, we simply weighted the shares by the number of months that Branch had use of the assets provided from selling those shares:

The 100,000 shares outstanding from Jan. 1 to Mar. 1 (2 months) is equivalent to 200,000 share-months (100,000 × 2).

From Mar. 1 to June 30 (4 months) 112,000 shares were outstanding, equivalent to 448,000 share-months (112,000 × 4).

From June 30 to Nov. 1 (4 months) 116,000 shares were outstanding, equivalent to 464,000 share-months (116,000 × 4).

During the last 2 months, Nov. 1 to Dec. 31, 110,000 shares were outstanding or 220,000 share-months (110,000 × 2).

The weighted average common shares is determined by dividing the total 1,332,000 share-months by the 12 months of the year resulting in 111,000.

When we bought treasury stock — the 6,000 shares — we used resources. Branch didn't have as many resources at its disposal to earn income because some assets were used to buy treasury stock. We, then, subtracted these shares purchased on Nov. 1 after weighting them by the $\frac{1}{6}$ $(\frac{2}{12})$ of a year that Branch was without the assets used to purchase them.

If Branch's 1989 net income were $235,320 and no preferred stock was outstanding, the 1989 historical EPS would be:

$$1989 \text{ Historical EPS} = \frac{\$235,320 - 0}{111,000 \text{ shares}} = \$2.12 \text{ per share}$$

Primary and Fully Diluted Earnings per Share

Corporations with complex capital structures are required to report two prospective earnings per share amounts — primary earnings per share and fully diluted earnings per share. A corporation with a *complex capital structure* has securities outstanding that may cause the issuance of additional shares of common stock.

Corporations with complex capital structures must report primary and fully diluted EPS

Holders of convertible bonds or convertible preferred stock can submit their securities at any time and receive common shares. Holders of stock options may, at their descretion, pay an exercise price and receive common stock. Earnings per share calculated without considering these potential issuances may present a misleading picture to investors.

For example, suppose that you are evaluating Apex Corporation. Earnings per share is $4.15 without considering potential issuances. If new shares could be issued and the exercise of stock options is included, earnings per share would be $2.95. Would you make the same investment decision with the knowledge of the $2.95 amount as you would if only the $4.15 figure were available?

To provide investors with knowledge of the potential effects of convertible securities and options, authoritative financial accounting standards require that certain assumptions be made about these possible stock issuances. We must calculate earnings per share *as if* the potential issuance of common stock actually did occur.

Primary EPS includes the most likly issuances of stock

Primary earnings per share is calculated including the effects of securities that are *most likely* to cause issuances of new stock. *Fully diluted earnings per share* considers *all* potential new issuances. Fully diluted EPS thus yields the lowest possible earnings per share amount.

Fully diluted EPS includes all potential issuances of stock

The rules for determining whether potential shares should be included in primary or fully diluted EPS (or both) are complex. A consideration of these detailed requirements is left for the intermediate accounting course.

The following illustration will give you a general idea of the procedures followed in calculating primary and fully diluted EPS.

This illustration shows how primary and fully diluted EPS are calculated

The information below pertains to Valentine, Inc.:

Net income for 1989	$284,800
Weighted average common stock outstanding	80,000 shares
Preferred dividends paid in 1989	$ 8,800
New shares that may be issued if convertible preferred is converted	9,000 shares
New shares that may be issued if stock options are exercised	12,000 shares

Assume that effects of stock options are included in calculating both primary and fully diluted EPS and that the effect of convertible preferred is included in calculating fully diluted EPS only. The stock options are included in both primary and fully diluted because they are likely to cause issuance of common stock in the future.

The convertible preferred stock is not as likely to be converted; but since the possibility exists, the potential for new shares must be included in calculating fully diluted earnings per share.

$$\text{1989 Primary EPS} = \frac{\text{net income} - \text{preferred dividends}}{\text{wt. avg. common shares outstanding} + \text{likely new issuances}}$$

$$= \frac{\$284,800 - \$8,800}{80,000 \text{ shs} + 12,000 \text{ shs}}$$

$$= \frac{\$276,000}{92,000 \text{ shs}}$$

$$= \$3.00 \text{ per share}$$

$$\text{1989 Fully diluted EPS} = \frac{\text{net income (see note below)}}{\text{wt. avg. common shs outstanding} + \text{all possible new issuances}}$$

$$= \frac{\$284,800}{80,000 \text{ shs} + 12,000 \text{ shs} + 9,000 \text{ shs}}$$

$$= \frac{\$284,800}{101,000 \text{ shs}}$$

$$= \$2.82 \text{ per share}$$

Note: Preferred dividends are not deducted because this calculation is being made *as if* the preferred stock were converted. If conversion had taken place, no dividends would have been paid.

The bottom of the Valentine income statement would have the following information disclosed:

Net Income	$284,800
Primary Earnings per Common Share	$3.00
Fully Diluted Earnings per Common Share	$2.82

Our calculation of Valentine's primary EPS assumes that:

The convertible preferred stock is unlikely to be converted. We ignore the potential effects of conversion—issuing more shares and not paying preferred dividends.

The options are likely to be exercised. We include the potential effect of issuing 12,000 more shares to the individuals who could exercise these options at any time.

Our assumptions change a little when we calculate Valentine's fully diluted EPS. We now assume that:

The convertible preferred stock may be converted. We include the potential effects of this conversion. If the preferred stock were converted at the beginning of 1989, no preferred dividends would have been paid; so we don't deduct any. If the preferred stock were converted, more common shares (9,000) would be outstanding; so we add these potential new shares to the shares that were outstanding.

The options are still likely to be exercised. We still include the effect of issuing 12,000 more common shares.

CHAPTER SUMMARY

The *Retained Earnings* account is created when the Expense and Revenue Summary account is closed. Retained Earnings, then, accumulates the net income of the corporation from its inception. Reductions in this accumulation occur when dividends are declared and as the result of some treasury stock transactions. Corrections of prior years' errors may cause an increase or decrease in the Retained Earnings balance.

At times the board of directors may restrict a certain amount of retained earnings from distribution as dividends. These restrictions may be communicated by footnote explanation or by appropriating retained earnings.

All changes in retained earnings are shown in a financial statement called the statement of retained earnings. This statement together with the income statement and balance sheet constitute the three major statements we have discussed so far.

Corporations may distribute earned capital in the form of cash, noncash assets, or additional shares of stock. These *dividend distributions* must be declared by the board of directors; a list of eligible stockholders is prepared on the record date; and distribution takes place on the payment date. Adequate retained earnings and distributable assets must exist before a board of directors will consider declaring a dividend.

Liquidating dividends are distributions of paid-in capital of the corporation in the form of assets. These distributions must also be declared by the board of directors. Liquidating dividends are not dividends in the true sense of the word because they are not distributions of earnings.

Preferred stock is a second class of equity security that may be issued to raise capital. Since it carries many privileges not accorded to common stockholders, preferred stock is a lower-risk investment security than common. Among the privileges that may be included are preference in dividend distributions, preference in asset distributions upon liquidation, convertibility, accumulation of undeclared dividends, and participation with common stockholders in extra dividends. A group of privileges will be packaged by the corporation to appeal to a sufficiently large group of investors to raise the needed capital.

Earnings per share amounts must be published in the income statements of corporations whose stock is publicly traded. Corporations with simple capital structures report only historical earnings per share. Corporations that have convertible securities and stock options outstanding are required to issue additional shares of common stock upon demand of these security holders. For this reason these companies must report *primary earnings per share* reflecting the effects of the most likely new share distributions and *fully diluted earnings per share* taking into account all potential common stock issuances.

IMPORTANT TERMS USED IN THIS CHAPTER

Callable preferred stock Preferred stock that may be retired by the issuing corporation by paying the shareholder a predetermined amount—the call price. (page 521)

Complex capital structure A corporate structure that includes securities that may cause the company to issue common stock. Public corporations with complex capital structures must report primary and fully diluted earnings per share at the bottom of their income statements. (page 525)

Convertible securities Preferred stocks or bonds that carry the privilege, at the option of the holder, of being submitted to the corporation in exchange for a specified number of common shares. Preferred stocks and bonds without this privilege are nonconvertible. (page 525)

Cumulative preferred stock Preferred stock on which undeclared dividends of one year become corporate obligations of future years. All prior and current unpaid dividends must be paid before distributions can be made to common stockholders. Preferred stock without this privilege is noncumulative. (page 517)

Declaration date The date on which the board of directors votes to distribute a dividend. (page 507)

Deficit Retained Earnings with a debit (negative) balance. (page 502)

Dividends Pro rata distributions of corporate earned capital in the form of cash, noncash assets, or the corporation's own stock. (page 507)

Earnings per share Net income available to the common stockholder divided by the weighted average common shares outstanding. (page 522)

Fully diluted earnings per share Net income available to the common stockholder divided by actual common shares outstanding and all potential new issuances of common shares. Fully diluted earnings per share is the lowest possible earnings per share amount. (page 525)

Liquidating dividend Distributions of corporate paid-in capital. These distributions are not dividends in the true sense of the word because they do not distribute earnings. (page 514)

Liquidation preference The right of preferred stockholders to receive assets in the liquidation process before common stockholders may receive any assets. (page 521)

Participating preferred stock Preferred stock having the privilege of sharing in dividends with common stockholders after both groups have been paid a specified percentage of par. Preferred stock not having this privilege is nonparticipating. (page 518)

Payment date   The date on which previously declared dividends are distributed to stockholders. (page 507)

Primary earnings per share   Net income available to common stockholders divided by common shares outstanding plus the most likely issuances of new shares. (page 525)

Prior period adjustment   An adjustment of the beginning balance of Retained Earnings as a result of correcting an accounting error committed in an earlier period. (page 504)

Property dividend   The pro rata distribution of earned capital to stockholders in the form of assets other than cash. (page 508)

Record date   The date on which owners of stock are identified as those eligible to receive a previously declared dividend. (page 507)

Retained Earnings   A stockholders' equity account representing the accumulated income of a corporation since its beginning. Prior period adjustments, all dividends declared, and certain other adjustments must be deducted in calculating the current balance of this account. (page 501)

Retained Earnings: Appropriated   A stockholders' equity account that reflects a restriction imposed on retained earnings by the board of directors. Appropriated retained earnings are not available for dividend distributions. (page 503)

Simple capital structure   A corporate structure that contains no securities that may cause the company to issue common stock. Public corporations with simple capital structures must report historical earnings per share. (page 523)

Stock dividends   A pro rata distribution of earned capital in the form of additional shares of the company's own common stock. (page 509)

Stock split   A reduction of the par or stated value of the authorized stock and a simultaneous increase in the number of shares authorized, issued, and outstanding. (page 514)

QUESTIONS

1. Explain what takes place on the dividend *declaration date, record date,* and *payment date.* On which of these dates is an accounting entry necessary?

2. The board of directors must declare a dividend before one may be distributed. What two additional items must be present before a dividend is paid?

3. What is the effect on assets, liabilities, and stockholders' equity of declaring *and* issuing each of the following types of dividends:

   a. Cash dividend?
   b. Property dividend?
   c. Stock dividend?

4. What is the basic difference in accounting for small and large stock dividends?

5. Liquidating dividends do not result in a reduction of retained earnings. Why not?

6. Bolo Corp. stock is currently selling on the stock exchange for $232 per share. Explain two different actions that could be taken by the board of directors to reduce the price of the Bolo shares.

7. Brodgen Co. has a Retained Earnings account with a $35,400 debit balance. Explain how the negative balance could have come about. What is the proper term for negative retained earnings?

8. Mullins Corp. appropriates $25,000 of retained earnings each year to build a new warehouse. After 5 years, how much cash will Mullins have accumulated? Explain.

9. Lamb, Inc., has a total retained earnings of $594,600. $480,600 is appropriated for contingencies. What is the maximum dividend that the Lamb board of directors can declare? Explain.

10. The Zeta Corp. board of directors wishes to place restrictions on retained earnings to limit the amount that can be used for dividends. In what two ways may these restrictions be shown in the corporation's annual report?

11. What are *prior period adjustments?* How are they disclosed in the financial statements?

12. Why do corporations issue both common and preferred stock?

13. From the point of view of an investor, is cumulative or noncumulative preferred stock more desirable?

14. Both callable and convertible preferred stock have provisions that may result in the retirement of preferred stock. What is the primary difference between callable and convertible preferred?

15. The accountant for King, Inc., calculated historical, primary, and fully diluted earnings per share. Which of these would you expect to be the highest? Lowest?

16. Perry Corp. has a complex capital structure. Which earnings per share amounts must Perry report? On which financial statement are earnings per share amounts shown?

EXERCISES

Exercise 12-1
Recording a cash dividend

Byte Corp.'s board of directors declared a $50,000 cash dividend on Sept. 1, 1989, payable on Oct. 1, to stockholders of record on Sept. 15. Prepare all appropriate entries needed on the declaration, record, and payment dates.

Exercise 12-2
Recording a property dividend

Sunset Inc.'s board of directors voted to distribute some surplus office equipment to its 10 stockholders as a dividend. Each stockholder will receive a desk, chair, and electric typewriter. The office equipment to be distributed cost $25,000 and has accumulated depreciation at the time of declaration of $3,500. The current value of the equipment is $20,000. The property dividend was declared on Mar. 1, 1989, distributable on Apr. 1, to stockholders of record on Mar. 15. Prepare all appropriate entries needed on the declaration, record, and distribution dates.

(Check figure: On Mar. 1 Retained Earnings is debited for $20,000)

Exercise 12-3
Recording a small stock dividend

The McDowell Inc., board of directors voted on June 1, 1989, to declare a 10% stock dividend, distributable on July 1, to stockholders of record on June 15. On June 1, McDowell had 500,000 shares of $1 par common stock authorized; 50,000 shares were issued and outstanding. McDowell stock was selling for $3 per share on June 1. Prepare the appropriate journal entries needed on June 1, June 15, and July 1.

(Check figure: On July 1 Common Stock is credited for $5,000)

Exercise 12-4
Recording a large stock dividend

The Gossage Corp. board of directors voted on Nov. 1, 1989, to declare a 40% stock dividend, distributable on Dec. 31, to stockholders of record on Dec. 1. Gossage's charter authorizes the issuance of 200,000 shares of $5 par common stock. As of Nov. 1, 1989, 50,000 shares of common stock are issued and outstanding. The market price of Gossage stock on Nov. 1 is $6.50 per share. Prepare any entries needed on the declaration, record, and payment dates.

(Check figure: Debit to Retained Earnings on Nov. 1 = $100,000)

Exercise 12-5
Indicating the effect of various transactions on stockholders' equity categories

For each of the independent transactions listed below, indicate the dollar effect on Common Stock, Paid-In Capital in Excess of Par, and Retained Earnings. Indicate increases with a plus (+), decreases with a minus (−), and no effect with a zero (0).

Transaction	Common Stock	Paid-In Capital in Excess of Par	Retained Earnings
Example: $1 par common stock is sold for $5 per share.	+	+	0
a. A cash dividend is declared and paid.			
b. A small stock dividend is declared and paid.			
c. A property dividend is declared and distributed (book value of property = $2,000, fair market value = $1,800).			
d. Retained earnings of $50,000 is appropriated for plant expansion.			
e. A 2 for 1 stock split is implemented.			
f. Expense and Revenue Summary with a $46,000 debit balance is closed.			
g. A large stock dividend is declared and distributed.			

Exercise 12-6
Dividing a dividend between preferred and common stockholders

On Dec. 1, 1989, Home Delivery Corp. has 60,000 of 3%, $10 par cumulative, nonparticipating preferred stock and 75,000 shares of no-par common stock outstanding. The common stock has a stated value of $10 per share.

The Home Delivery board of directors declared a $125,000 cash dividend on Dec. 1, 1989, payable on Dec. 31, to stockholders of record on Dec. 1. Home Delivery did not pay dividends in 1985, 1986, 1987, or 1988.

Prepare a schedule showing how the $125,000 dividend will be split between the preferred and common stockholders.

(Check figure: Common stock gets a $35,000 dividend)

Exercise 12-7
Calculating earnings per share

Springer Inc., reported net income for 1989 of $330,000. 110,000 common shares were outstanding during the entire year. Since Springer is a large publicly held corporation, it is required to report earnings per share on its income statement each year. The following additional information is available:

a. Cash dividends of $22,000 were paid to holders of convertible preferred stock in 1989.
b. If convertible preferred stock is converted, 40,000 new common shares may be issued.
c. The convertible preferred stock is not likely to be converted so the new shares are not included in the calculation of primary earnings per share. Since a possibility for conversion exists, they must be included in the calculation of fully diluted earnings per share.

Prepare a schedule showing the calculation of primary and fully diluted earnings per share for 1989.

(Check figure: Primary earnings per share = $2.80)

Exercise 12-8
Calculating the weighted average of stock outstanding

Wilmet Corp. compiled the following information about its common stock for the year 1989:

Jan. 1	500,000 shares of common stock were outstanding.
Apr. 1	20,000 previously unissued shares of common stock were sold.
July 1	5,000 shares of common stock were purchased for the treasury.
Oct. 1	5,000 shares of treasury stock were issued for a parcel of land.
Dec. 1	12,000 previously unissued shares of common stock were sold.

Calculate the weighted average number of common shares outstanding during 1989.

(Check figure: Weighted average shares outstanding during 1989 = 514,750)

Exercise 12-9
Calculating earnings per share

Jason Fleece Wool Inc., reported 1989 income of $434,450. The accountant calculated a weighted average of 364,000 common shares outstanding during the year. The following additional facts are known about Jason:

a. $16,000 of dividends were paid on convertible preferred stock. If the stock is converted, 44,112 new common shares will be issued. It is not likely that this stock will be converted but it is possible.

b. $10,000 of dividends were paid on nonconvertible preferred stock.

c. Executives of the corporation have the right to acquire 25,000 shares of common stock by exercising stock options. It is considered likely that these options will be exercised.

Calculate Jason's primary and fully diluted earnings per share for 1989.

(Check figure: Fully diluted earnings per share = $0.98)

PROBLEMS: SET A

Problem A12-1
Recording dividends on common and preferred stock

King Corp. had the following stock outstanding on Dec. 31, 1988:

10% Preferred Stock, $40 par, 10,000 shares authorized, issued and outstanding	$ 400,000
Common Stock, $10 par, 500,000 shares authorized, 100,000 shares issued and outstanding	1,000,000

King has traditionally paid the preferred dividend in equal quarterly installments. Common dividends have followed an irregular pattern.

King's board of directors took the following dividend actions during 1989:

Mar. 1	The board declared the quarterly preferred dividend of $1 per share (10% × $40 × ¼).
15	Those owning preferred stock on this date will receive the preferred dividend.
31	The quarterly cash dividend is distributed to preferred stockholders.
Dec. 1	Since King has been having cash flow problems, the board declared no dividends in the second and third quarters. The board voted on Dec. 1 to declare the remaining preferred dividends for the second, third, and fourth quarters of the year. The market price per share of preferred stock was $60 on Dec. 1.
2	The board declared a 15% stock dividend on common stock. The market price per common share was $25 on Dec. 2.
15	Preferred and common stockholders of record on this day will receive dividends. On this day the market price of preferred stock is $62 and the market price of common stock is $27.
30	The common stock dividend was distributed. The market price of common stock was $26 per share on Dec. 30.
31	The cash was distributed to preferred stockholders.

Required

Prepare general journal entries to record the transactions and events listed above. If no entry is needed on a particular date, write "No Entry."

(Check figure: Dec. 1 dividend declared for preferred stockholders = $30,000)

**Problem A12-2
Recording retained
earnings appropriation,
property dividend, and
stock split**

Imperial Inc.'s balance sheet stockholders' equity section on Dec. 31, 1988, appears below:

Paid-In Capital:
Common Stock, $15 par, 200,000 shares authorized,
150,000 shares issued, 145,000 shares outstanding (5,000 shares
in treasury)... $2,250,000
Additional Paid-In Capital:
Paid-In Capital in Excess of Par $750,000
Paid-In Capital from Treasury Stock 50,000   800,000
Total Paid-In Capital $3,050,000

Earned Capital:
Retained Earnings Unappropriated.................................... 4,550,000
Total $7,600,000
Less: Treasury Stock (5,000 shares), at cost........................... (150,000)
Total Stockholders' Equity $7,450,000

The following events took place during 1989:
a. During March the Imperial board of directors voted to appropriate $100,000 for future
plant expansion.
b. During June a property dividend was declared and distributed. Maize Corp. stock which
Imperial had owned as an investment was distributed to the Imperial stockholders. The
per-share book value and market value of the Maize stock on the date of declaration were
$4.00 and $4.50, respectively. Four shares of Maize stock will be distributed for each share
of Imperial stock owned.
c. During August a 3 for 1 stock split was implemented.
d. Income for the year (*excluding* any effect of **a** through **c** above) was $267,900. (You must
adjust the $267,900 for any income statement items in **a** through **c**.)

Required

Prepare Imperial's stockholders' equity section on Dec. 31, 1989, after giving effect to the
information in **a** through **d** above. Your solution should be supported by schedules showing
how each amount was derived.

(Check figure: Retained Earnings Unappropriated = $2,397,900)

**Problem A12-3
Recording various
transactions and events
affecting Retained
Earnings**

On Jan. 1, 1989, Hood Guitar Inc., had a Retained Earnings: Unappropriated account with a
credit balance of $240,000, and Retained Earnings Appropriated for Contingencies with a
credit balance of $40,000. The following events occurred during 1989:

Apr. 15   Since the possibility of a strike has past, the board of directors voted to remove
$20,000 of Appropriated Retained Earnings and return this amount to the Unap-
propriated account.

July 12   The board of directors voted to pay a cash dividend totaling $62,500 on Sept. 1 to
stockholders of record on Aug. 1.

Aug. 9   A review of the Land account reveals that $36,000 which was debited to Land in
1986 should have been debited to Property Tax Expense. (Handle the correction
as a prior period adjustment.)

Sept. 1   The dividend declared on July 12 was paid.

Oct. 15   The board of directors voted to appropriate retained earnings for plant expansion
in the amount of $25,000.

Dec. 31   After closing all revenue and expense accounts for the year, Expense and Revenue Summary has a debit balance of $14,250.

Required

1. Prepare general journal entries to record each of the 1989 events and transactions outlined
above.
2. Prepare a statement of retained earnings for the year ended Dec. 31, 1989.

(Check figure: Retained Earnings: Unappropriated, Dec. 31, 1989 = $122,250)

Problem A12-4
Allocating dividends between preferred and common stockholders under various assumptions

Perez Equipment Corp. has the following capital stock outstanding on Dec. 31, 1989:

8% Preferred Stock, $5 par, 10,000 shares authorized, issued and outstanding..	$ 50,000
Common Stock, $1 par, 500,000 shares authorized, 450,000 shares issued and outstanding...	450,000

Perez did not declare or pay dividends during 1986, 1987, or 1988.

Required

Prepare schedules showing the amount of 1989 dividends to be received by preferred and by common stockholders under each of the following independent assumptions:

1. Preferred stock is cumulative and nonparticipating. A $40,000 dividend is declared and paid in 1989.

2. Preferred stock is noncumulative and participating. A $50,000 dividend is declared and paid in 1989.

(Check figure: Total amount received by preferred stockholders = $5,000)

3. Preferred stock is cumulative and participating. A $72,000 dividend is declared and paid in 1989.

Problem A12-5
Reproducing journal entries affecting Retained Earnings by looking at the statement of retained earnings

---

R. R. JENKINS INC.
Statement of Retained Earnings
For Year Ended December 31, 1989

Retained Earnings Unappropriated:		
Balance Jan. 1, 1989		$370,000
Prior Period Adjustment: To correct a 1987 error in recording insurance expense. Insurance Expense was debited when a cash payment was made; Notes Payable should have been debited		9,250
Balance Jan. 1 as adjusted		$379,250
Add: Net Income for the Year.............................	$60,000	
Reduction of Appropriation for Contingencies	50,000	110,000
Total		$489,250
Deduct: Dividend Declared and Paid (cash dividend on preferred stock)...................................	$30,000	
Dividend Declared and Distributed (small stock dividend on $5 par common stock, 5,000 shares distributed)...................................	47,500	(77,500)
Balance Dec. 31, 1989...		$411,750
Retained Earnings Appropriated for Contingencies:		
Balance Jan. 1, 1989		$125,000
Add: (none)		-0-
Deduct: Appropriation removed during 1989.........................		(50,000)
Balance Dec. 31, 1989...		$ 75,000

Required

Examine Jenkins' statement of retained earnings for 1989 and prepare in general journal form all of the entries that affected the Retained Earnings account during the year. Dates may be omitted from your entries. (Prepare declaration and distribution entries for any dividends.)

(Check figure: Your solution should contain seven entries)

Problem A12-6
Indicating the effect on balance sheet categories of various events and transactions

Required

For each of the *independent* (unrelated) transactions below, enter the dollar effect in each column of the solutions sheet. Show increases by placing a plus (+) in front of the amount, decreases by placing a minus (−) in front of the amount, and no effect by placing a zero (0) in the column. Headings for the columns and an example are shown below:

Description	Total Assets	Total Liabilities	Total Common Stock	Total Additional Paid-In Capital	Total Retained Earnings	Total Stockholders' Equity
Example: Corp. declared a cash dividend of $20,000	0	+$20,000	0	0	−$20,000	−$20,000

a. Corp. sold 2,000 shares of $5 par common stock for $12 per share.

b. Corp. sold 500 shares of $5 par common stock on subscription for $15 per share. A one-third down payment was received.

c. Corp. declared a 10% stock dividend. 100,000 shares of $5 par common stock were outstanding on the declaration date. The market price of the stock is $9 per share.

d. Corp. paid a $10,000 cash dividend which was declared last year.

e. Corp. collected $500 due on a common stock subscription and issued common stock with a par value of $2,500.

f. Corp. distributed 5,000 shares of $5 par common stock in payment of a stock dividend. (The 30% dividend had been declared in the previous year when the market value of the stock was $12.50 per share.)

g. Corp.'s board of directors implemented a 4 for 1 stock split. Before the split, 10,000 shares of $20 par common stock were outstanding.

h. Corp. purchased 5,000 shares of its own $5 par common stock for $8 per share.

i. Corp.'s board of directors voted to appropriate $50,000 of retained earnings for plant expansion.

j. Corp. corrected a $30,000 error which was made in a prior year. An entry to record sales had erroneously been credited to Donated Capital. (Cash was correctly debited.)

Problem A12-7
Recording transactions in stockholders' equity T-accounts, preparing a stockholders' equity section

Spinner Distributing Inc., has the following stockholders' equity on June 30, 1988:

Common Stock, $10 par, 100,000 shares authorized, 30,000 shares issued and
outstanding .... $ 300,000
Paid-In Capital in Excess of Par 245,000
Retained Earnings: Unappropriated..................................... 555,000
Total Stockholders' Equity.. $1,100,000

The following transactions occurred during the following fiscal year:

1988

July	8	Purchased 500 shares of common stock for the treasury, $11,500.
Sept.	21	Declared a cash dividend of $1 per share to stockholders of record on Oct. 15.
Nov.	1	Paid the cash dividend.
	26	Sold 10,000 shares of common stock on subscription. The subscription price was $25 per share. A 30% down payment was received.
Dec.	21	Sold the treasury stock for $28 per share. (The stock was originally issued for $17 per share.)

1989

Jan.	26	Collected half of the remaining balance on the stock subscriptions.
Feb.	14	Appropriated $150,000 of retained earnings for plant expansion.
Mar.	26	Collected the balance due on the stock subscriptions and issued the shares.
Apr.	3	Issued 10,000 shares of stock with a market value of $31 per share in exchange for a piece of land. No objective market price is available for the land.
May	4	Declared a 10% stock dividend distributable on July 1 to stockholders of record on June 15. The market price of the stock on May 4 was $32 per share.
June	19	Received a donation of a building which will be moved to the land acquired on Apr. 3. The building was valued at $42,000.
	30	Net income for the year was calculated to be $98,800.

Required

1. Set up the following stockholders' equity T-accounts:

    Common Stock
    Paid-In Capital in Excess of Par
    Common Stock Subscribed
    Common Stock Dividend Distributable
    Donated Capital
    Paid-In Capital from Treasury Stock
    Retained Earnings: Unappropriated
    Retained Earnings: Appropriated for Plant Expansion
    Treasury Stock

2. Enter the beginning balances in Common Stock, Paid-In Capital in Excess of Par, and Retained Earnings: Unappropriated.
3. Enter the transactions for the year in the appropriate T-accounts. (You may wish to set up the asset and liability accounts in addition to the stockholders' equity accounts listed above.) Identify each debit and credit by placing the date of the transaction next to the amount.
4. Prepare the stockholders' equity section of Spinners' balance sheet on June 30, 1989, in good form.

(Check figure: Total stockholders' equity = $1,773,800)

PROBLEMS: SET B

**Problem B12-1
Recording dividends on
common stock**

Barkley Incorporated's board of directors took the following actions during 1989 which affected stockholders' equity:

Jan.	1	The board of directors declared the annual cash dividend on the 100,000 shares of 6% noncumulative, nonparticipating $1 par preferred stock outstanding. The market price of the preferred stock was $5 on Jan. 1.
	1	The board declared a quarterly cash dividend of $1 per share to common stockholders. There were 250,000 shares of $10 par common stock outstanding. The market price per share of stock was $15 on Jan. 1.

Jan.	15	Common stockholders of record on this day will receive the cash dividend.
	31	Preferred stockholders of record on this day will receive the cash dividend.
Feb.	15	The cash dividend is distributed to common stockholders.
Mar.	1	The cash dividend is distributed to preferred stockholders.
Oct.	1	Since Barkley's cash position was unfavorable, no dividends on common stock were declared during the second and third quarters of the year. The board of directors voted to declare an 18% stock dividend in lieu of the fourth quarter cash dividend. The market price per share was $12 on Oct. 1.
Nov.	1	Common stockholders of record on this day will receive the stock dividend. The market price per share of stock was $12.50 on Nov. 1.
Dec.	15	The common stock dividend was distributed. The market price per share of common stock was $14 on December 15.

Required

Prepare the general journal entries to record the transactions and events listed above. If no entry is needed on a particular date, write "No entry."

(Check figure: Debit to Retained Earnings on Oct. 1 = $540,000)

**Problem B12-2
Recording retained earnings appropriation, property dividend, and stock split**

The Dec. 31, 1988, stockholders' equity section of Joyner Inc., appears below:

Paid-In Capital:
Common Stock, $5 par, 500,000 shares authorized,
100,000 shares issued, 95,000 shares outstanding
(5,000 shares in treasury). . . . . $ 500,000
Additional Paid-In Capital:
Paid-In Capital in Excess of Par $200,000
Donated Capital 20,000   220,000
Total Paid-In Capital . . . . $ 720,000

Earned Capital:
Retained Earnings: Unappropriated 1,750,000
Total $2,470,000
Less: Treasury Stock (5,000 shares) at cost . . . . (45,000)
Total Stockholders' Equity $2,425,000

The following events took place during 1989:
a. During January a property dividend was declared and distributed. Splash Pool Corp. stock which Joyner Inc., had owned as an investment was distributed to the Joyner stockholders. The per-share book value and fair market values of the Splash stock on the date of declaration were $1.10 and $1.15, respectively. Two shares of Splash stock will be distributed for each share of Joyner owned.
b. During April, a 2 for 1 stock split was implemented.
c. During December the Joyner board of directors voted to appropriate $40,000 of retained earnings for plant expansion.
d. Income for the year (*excluding* any effect of **a** through **c** above) was $326,000. (You must adjust the $326,000 for any income statement items contained in **a** through **c**.)

Required

Prepare Joyner's stockholders' equity section on Dec. 31, 1989, after giving effect to the information in **a** through **d** above. Your solution should be supported by schedules showing how each amount was derived.

(Check figure: Retained Earnings: Unappropriated = $1,827,000)

Problem B12-3
Recording various transactions and events affecting Retained Earnings

Devious Enterprises Inc., began 1989 with a Retained Earnings: Unappropriated account having a credit balance of $600,000, and Retained Earnings Appropriated for Plant Expansion of $240,000. The following occurred during 1989:

Feb. 15   A review of the Patent account reveals that a patent acquired in 1988 for $300,000 was not amortized. $30,000 Patent Amortization Expense should have been recorded in 1988. (Handle the correction as a prior period adjustment.)

Apr. 21   The board of directors voted to remove $100,000 of Appropriated Retained Earnings and return this amount to the Unappropriated account.

May 30   The board of directors voted to pay a cash dividend totaling $360,000 on June 30 to stockholders of record on June 15.

June 30   The dividend declared on May 30 was paid.

Sept. 18   Devious sold 2,000 shares of common stock which had been held in the treasury for $36,000. The treasury stock had cost $40,000. (Devious originally issued all common stock at par and no Paid-In Capital from Treasury Stock account exists.)

Dec. 31   After closing all revenue and expense accounts for the year, Expense and Revenue Summary has a debit balance of $136,000.

Required

1. Prepare general journal entries to record each of the 1989 events and transactions outlined above.
2. Prepare a statement of retained earnings in good form for the year ended Dec. 31, 1989.

(Check figure: Retained Earnings: Unappropriated, Dec. 31, 1989 = $170,000)

Problem B12-4
Allocating dividends between preferred and common stockholders under various assumptions

Creative Concepts Inc., has the following capital stock outstanding on Dec. 31, 1989:

6% Preferred Stock, $1 par, 100,000 shares authorized, issued, and outstanding...	$100,000
Common Stock, $5 par, 100,000 shares authorized, 80,000 shares issued and outstanding...	400,000

Creative Concepts did not declare or pay dividends in 1985, 1986, 1987, or 1988.

Required

Prepare schedules showing the amount of 1989 dividends to be received by preferred and by common stockholders under each of the independent assumptions below:
1. Preferred stock is cumulative and nonparticipating. A $42,000 dividend is declared and paid in 1989.
2. Preferred stock is noncumulative and participating. A $50,000 dividend is declared and paid in 1989.

(Check figure: Total amount received by common stockholders = $40,000)

3. Preferred stock is cumulative and participating. A $100,000 dividend is declared and paid in 1989.

Problem B12-5
Reproducing journal
entries affecting Retained
Earnings by looking at a
statement of retained
earnings

> **SHOPPER JOY INC.**
> **Statement of Retained Earnings**
> **For Year Ended December 31, 1989**
>
> Retained Earnings Unappropriated:
>
> | | | |
> |---|---:|---:|
> | Balance Jan. 1, 1989 | | $684,000 |
> | Prior Period Adjustment: To correct a 1988 error in recording sales revenue. Accounts Payable was credited on a cash sale rather than the Sales Revenue account. | | 5,000 |
> | Balance Jan. 1 as adjusted | | $689,000 |
> | Add: Net Income for the Year | | 134,000 |
> | Total | | $823,000 |
> | Deduct: Dividend Declared and Paid (cash dividend on preferred stock) | $ 56,000 | |
> | Dividend Declared and Distributed (small stock dividend on $10 par common stock, 20,000 shares distributed) | 480,000 | |
> | Appropriated for Self-Insurance | 30,000 | (566,000) |
> | Balance Dec. 31, 1989 | | $257,000 |
> | | | |
> | Retained Earnings Appropriated for Self-Insurance: | | |
> | Balance Jan. 1, 1989 | | $120,000 |
> | Add: Appropriation during 1989 | | 30,000 |
> | Deduct: (none) | | -0- |
> | Balance Dec. 31, 1989 | | $150,000 |

Required

Examine the Shopper Joy statement of retained earnings for 1989 and prepare in general journal form all of the entries that affected the Retained Earnings account for the year. Dates may be omitted from your entries. (Prepare declaration and distribution entries for any dividends.)

(Check figure: Your solution should contain seven entries)

Problem B12-6
Indicating the effect on
balance sheet categories
of various events and
transactions

Required

For each of the *independent* (unrelated) transactions that follow, enter the dollar effect in each column of the solutions paper. Show increases by placing a plus (+) in front of the amount, decreases by placing a minus (−) in front of the amount, and no effect by placing a zero (0) in the column. Headings for the columns and an example are shown below:

Description	Total Assets	Total Liabilities	Total Common Stock	Total Additional Paid-In Capital	Total Retained Earnings	Total Stockholders' Equity
Example: Inc. declared a cash dividend of $10,000	0	+$10,000	0	0	−$10,000	−$10,000

a. Inc. sold 1,000 shares of $10 par common stock for $18,400.

b. Inc.'s board of directors implemented a 3 for 1 stock split. Before the split, 50,000 shares of $10 par common stock were outstanding.

c. Inc. distributed 10,000 shares of $1 par common stock relating to a stock dividend. (The 40% dividend had been declared in the previous year when the market value of the stock was $2.25 per share.)

d. Inc. collected $2,500 due on a common stock subscription and issued common stock with a par value of $500.

e. Inc. sold 3,000 shares of common stock with a stated value of $2 per share for $12,500.

f. Inc. paid a $4,675 cash dividend which was declared last year.

g. Inc. purchased 5,000 shares of its $1 par common stock for $5 per share.

h. Inc. sold 100 shares of treasury stock for $2,000. The treasury stock had originally been purchased for $1,200.

i. Inc. declared a 40% stock dividend. 100,000 shares of $1 par common stock is outstanding on the declaration date. The market price of the stock is $2.50 per share.

j. Inc. sold 500 shares of $5 per common stock and subscription for $15 per share. A 10% down payment was received.

Problem B12-7
Recording transactions in stockholders' equity T-accounts, preparing a stockholders' equity section

Scofield Manufacturing Co. has the following stockholders' equity on Oct. 31, 1988:

Common Stock, $5 par, 200,000 shares authorized, 50,000 shares issued and outstanding	$250,000
Paid-In Capital in Excess of Par	150,000
Retained Earnings: Unappropriated	400,000
Total Stockholders' Equity	$800,000

The following transactions occurred during the following fiscal year:

1988
Nov. 5 Purchased 1,000 shares of common stock for the treasury, $10,000.

1989
Jan. 15 Declared a cash dividend of $0.50 per share payable Mar. 1 to stockholders of record Feb. 1.

Mar. 1 Paid the cash dividend.

25 Sold 5,000 shares of common stock on subscription. The subscription price was $8 per share. A 20% down payment was received.

Apr. 4 Sold the treasury stock for $12 per share. (The stock was originally issued for $8 per share.)

June 1 Collected half of the remaining balance on the stock subscriptions.

July 31 Appropriated $100,000 of retained earnings for a possible lawsuit loss.

Sept. 1 Collected the balance due on the stock subscription and issued the shares.

15 Issued 5,000 shares of stock in exchange for a forklift. The stock has a market value of $11 per share. No market price was available for the equipment.

30 Declared a 15% stock dividend distributable on Nov. 1 to the stockholders of record on Oct. 15. The market price of the stock on Sept. 30 was $12 per share.

Oct. 20 Received a donation of 10 acres of land valued at $25,000.

31 Calculated net income for the year at $166,000.

Required

1. Set up the following stockholders' equity T-accounts:

Common Stock
Paid-In Capital in Excess of Par
Common Stock Subscribed
Common Stock Dividend Distributable
Donated Capital
Paid-In Capital from Treasury Stock

Retained Earnings: Unappropriated
Retained Earnings: Appropriated for Lawsuit Loss
Treasury Stock

2. Enter the beginning balances in Common Stock, Paid-In Capital in Excess of Par, and Retained Earnings: Unappropriated.
3. Enter the transactions for the year in the appropriate T-accounts. (You may wish to set up the asset and liability accounts in addition to the stockholders' equity accounts listed above.) Identify each debit and credit by placing the date of the transaction next to the amount.
4. Prepare the stockholders' equity section of Scofield's balance sheet on Oct. 31, 1989 in good form.

(Check figure: Total stockholders' equity = $1,063,500)

DECISION PROBLEM

Golden Publishing was incorporated on Jan. 1, 1958, in South Bend, Indiana. The 150,000 shares of $10 par value stock sold for $27.50 and was acquired by corporate executives and many other interested investers. No one individual owns more than 10% of the stock.

Until Jan. 1, 1988, the publishing company earned on the average $3.50 per share and paid a consistent yearly cash dividend of $1.25 per share. On Jan. 1, 1988, the company paid a 10% stock dividend when the market price of the stock was $70 per share. Earnings for 1988 were $3.90 per share and a cash dividend of $1.25 was paid on Dec. 15, 1988.

On Jan. 1, 1989, the company discovered in its Munich, Germany warehouse the diary of Adolf Hitler. Prior to releasing this information to the financial press the company borrowed $5,000,000 from a major bank and together with corporate cash bought back 60% of the company's stock at $80 per share.

When the diary information was released to the financial press projections of future earnings were made by security analysts indicating that Golden Publishing would earn an estimated $1,023,000 and pay a record dividend of $3.10 per share.

Required

1. Prepare the stockholders' equity section for Golden Publishing as of Jan. 1, 1988, assuming that 450,000 shares of $10 par common stock was authorized and 150,000 shares were issued.
2. Prepare the stockholders' equity section for the company on Dec. 31, 1988, after the stock dividend, the 1988 earnings, and the dividends.
3. Assume on Dec. 31, 1987, the market price of the stock was $70 per share and on Jan. 2, 1988, it dropped to $63 per share. Determine the book value per share on each of these dates. Why is the market value per share different than the book value per share?
4. Assume that the company did in fact earn $1,023,000 for 1989 and did pay a $3.10 per share dividend. Prepare the stockholders' equity section as it would appear on Dec. 31, 1989. Compute the book value per share. Assume that the market value would be equal to 20 times earnings, compute the market value per share.
5. Why do you think that the publishing company bought back 60% of the stock? What do you think of the manner in which the company released the information about the diary?

CHAPTER 13

Corporations: Long-Term Liabilities

After studying this chapter you should understand the following:

- The comparative advantages and disadvantages of issuing bonds at different earnings levels
- The differences between the various types of bonds
- How to record the entries associated with a bond issue at par
- How the price of bonds can be determined using present value tables
- How to record the entries for a bond issue sold at a premium or discount
- How to amortize premiums or discounts by the *effective-interest* and *straight-line* methods
- How to record the entries associated with the *capitalization of a lease*

Financing the acquisition of plant assets is usually done on a long-term basis

In Chapter 8 we discussed the financing of the normal recurring operations of business entities. We saw that this was, for the most part, accomplished by the incurrence of current liabilities. Purchases of inventory are made on account; the use of labor is usually paid for weekly, biweekly, or semimonthly; temporary drains on cash are eased by the issuance of short-term notes. These everyday examples show the use of current liabilities in normal, recurring operations. However, situations arise that require substantial cash outlays, and these cannot be financed by the use of current liabilities. The acquisition of additional or replacement equipment or the construction of a new building are examples of such situations. Where do the funds come from to pay for these substantial cash outlays? Let's consider the case of the Lou Jergensen Mail-Order House.

Lou's company has done quite well over the past several years and he is thinking about expanding his business. He needs $250,000 to construct an addition on his building to handle the anticipated increase in the volume of mail orders. One thing Lou could do would be to use cash that he has retained in his business. Of course, in order to accumulate $250,000 Lou would have to severely limit the amount of dividends paid to the company's stockholders. An advantage of this plan is that Lou wouldn't need additional stockholders or creditors to help him. But like most small corporations, Lou's company just doesn't have the $250,000.

Large expenditures can be financed by the use of internal funds, funds obtained from additional investors, or borrowed funds

Something else Lou might try would be to issue additional stock to interested investors. They could invest the $250,000. But unless profits increase proportionately with the increase in the number of shares, the present stockholders' share of the corporation's earnings will be less than they were before the new stock was issued.

The third thing Lou's corporation could do would be to borrow the $250,000 from creditors on a long-term basis. There are several forms of long-term financing. Proprietorships, partnerships, and corporations may issue long-term notes, or may enter into long-term lease arrangements. In the case of corporations, bonds may be issued. The amount of funds that can be obtained from long-term notes or leases is typically less than that which can be obtained by the issuance of bonds. The reason for this is that long-term notes and leases are typically issued to a single investor or relatively few investors, such as a bank, a leasing company, or an insurance company. Bonds, on the other hand, are sold by underwriters who market them to many investors. But don't become misled into thinking that the amount of funds that can be obtained from notes or leases is insignificant. These instruments are often in the millions of dollars. It is not uncommon, however, for a large corporation to have a bond issue in the hundreds of millions of dollars.

If the $250,000 is obtained from creditors, there is a disadvantage. Interest and principal repayments must be made when due. An advantage of this method is that the present capital structure remains unchanged; that is, Lou and the rest of the present stockholders will not have to share ownership of the corporation with a new group of stockholders. Also, Lou's corporation can deduct the interest on the borrowed money on the corporate tax return.

Interest on borrowed funds is a tax-deductible item

We cannot establish a single rule that would determine which method of financing would be best for Lou or anyone else. We would have to consider many factors before selecting one means of long-term financing over the others. We can, however, prepare an analysis of the alternatives in a given situation that will help us choose the best alternative available. Such an analysis is presented in the following discussion.

Let us assume that $1 million of additional financing is required to build a new plant. At present there are 100,000 shares of common stock outstanding. The first alternative is to obtain the $1 million from retained earnings (assuming that there is $1 million in the corporate cash accounts). The second alternative is to find new investors and issue 50,000 additional shares of common stock worth $1 million. Alternative three is to obtain the money from a long-term note, lease, or bond issue

Financing Alternatives for Construction of New Plant

	From Retained Earnings (100,000 shares outstanding)		From Additional Stockholders (150,000 shares outstanding)		From Long-Term Creditors (100,000 shares outstanding)	
Earnings before interest and income taxes	$800,000	$500,000	$800,000	$500,000	$800,000	$500,000
Interest ($1,000,000 × 12%)					120,000	120,000
Earnings before income taxes	$800,000	$500,000	$800,000	$500,000	$680,000	$380,000
Income taxes at 34%	272,000	170,000	272,000	170,000	231,200	129,200
Net income	$528,000	$330,000	$528,000	$330,000	$448,800	$250,800
Earnings per share	$ 5.28	$ 3.30	$ 3.52	$ 2.20	$ 4.49	$ 2.51

requiring a 12% interest expense each year. We assume two earnings levels, $800,000 and $500,000, both before the interest expense and the income tax (assumed to be 34% of earnings before income taxes) have been deducted.

If you were a stockholder, *all other conditions being equal,* the first alternative would be the most attractive. Why? Because this alternative provides the highest earnings per share (EPS). At the $800,000 earnings level, EPS is $5.28, which exceeds both the $3.52 EPS projected if the $1 million is obtained from 50,000 new shares and the $4.49 EPS projected if the $1 million is obtained from long-term creditors. Also, the $3.30 EPS at the $500,000 earnings level under the first alternative exceeds the $2.20 and the $2.51 EPS under each of the other alternatives.

BONDS PAYABLE

Once the decision is made to obtain financing by means of issuing bonds, management of the corporation (proprietorships and partnerships do not issue bonds) must next decide what type of bonds to issue. Most corporations do not have the expertise to market their own securities. They usually work with an **investment banker** who provides a service of developing a marketable product—the bonds—and then selling it to the public. This process is called **underwriting** the new issue, which is why investment bankers are often called **underwriters.** The underwriter will help the corporation determine the type of bonds to issue, the interest rate the bonds should carry, the maturity date of the bonds, and other important matters. The bonds are usually sold to the underwriter, or to several underwriters, who in turn sell the bonds to interested investors at a somewhat higher price. Rather than buying the bonds, the underwriter may contract to sell the bonds on a commission basis. Or, the corporation may sell the bonds directly to a large institution such as an insurance company.

Underwriters help corporations issue bonds. They provide advice on the type of bonds to issue, the interest rate to pay, and when the bonds should mature

The corporation enters into a contract with an agent, called the **trustee,** representing the bondholders. It is the duty of the trustee to assure the bondholders that the corporation is fulfilling its responsibilities under the contract. The contract is referred to as a **trust indenture** or **bond indenture** and is called the **deed of trust.** The trustee is typically a large bank.

A bond indenture is a contract between the bond trustee and the corporation

In order to make the bond widely marketable so that large sums of money can be generated, bonds are commonly issued in units of $1,000 each. The amount of the bond, $1,000, is called its **face** or **par value.** The bond indenture will provide for the payment of periodic interest on the face value of the bond. Most bonds pay interest on a semiannual basis. Prices of bonds are expressed for trading purposes per $1,000 of face value. *Priced at 98* means that a $1,000 bond will sell for $980, 98% of $1,000. If a $1,000 bond is quoted at $102\frac{1}{4}$, it will sell for $1,022.50 ($102\frac{1}{4}$% of $1,000).

Interest on bonds is usually paid twice a year

A corporation may issue either **secured** or **unsecured bonds.** A secured bond provides the bondholder with a claim on a specified asset in the event the corporation does not fulfill its responsibilities under the terms of the bond indenture. The pledged or mortgaged assets are typically equipment or buildings. Unsecured bonds are issued on the general credit rating of the issuing corporation and are called **debenture bonds.** Only the financially strongest businesses can issue bonds on the basis of their name alone.

Bonds can be secured or debenture, term or serial, callable or convertible

Term or **serial bonds** may be issued. Term bonds are those in which the entire bond issue matures on a specified date in the future called the **maturity date.** Serial bonds mature at various dates over the bond contract. For example, a $50 million serial bond issue dated 1989 might provide for $10 million of bonds to mature commencing in 2000 and each year thereafter through 2004.

Bonds may have a *callable* or a *convertible feature.* Callable bonds provide the corporation with the right to redeem the bonds prior to their maturity date. When bonds are called, usually the bond indenture provides that a penalty be paid by the issuing entity. This is in the form of a call price, which is slightly higher than the face of the bonds. Convertible bonds provide the bondholder with the right to exchange his or her bonds for an ownership interest in the business entity.

Bonds Issued at Par

After a corporation has decided on the type of bonds to issue, the amount, the interest rate, the interest payment dates, and the maturity date, and the owners of the corporation approve, the trust indenture is prepared and the bonds are printed and issued. Let's use an example at this point to illustrate the accounting for bonds.

Assume that the Karlton Company issues $5 million of 20-year, 12% bonds on May 1, 1989, at par with interest payable semiannually on Nov. 1 and May 1. The entry to record the issuance of the bonds would be as follows:

Bonds sold at par

1989			
May 1	Cash...	5,000,000	
	Bonds Payable...................................		5,000,000
	To record the sale of $5,000,000 of 20-year 12% bonds at par.		

On Nov. 1, the first semiannual interest payment is due. This will amount to $300,000, computed as follows: $5,000,000 \times 12\% \times \frac{6}{12}$ year $= \$300,000$. The entry to record the interest payment is recorded as follows:

The first bond interest payment

1989			
Nov. 1	Bond Interest Expense................................	300,000	
	Cash...		300,000
	To record payment of semiannual interest on bonds payable.		

At the end of the accounting period, Dec. 31, the interest expense applicable to November through December, 1989, must be accrued and the liability for interest payable must be recorded. This entry would be recorded as follows:

Bond interest adjusting entry

1989			
Dec. 31	Bond Interest Expense	100,000	
	Bond Interest Payable.............................		100,000
	To record accrued interest on bonds payable. Interest is computed as follows: $5,000,000 \times 12\% \times \frac{2}{12}$ yr.		

Assuming that the business entity does not use reversing entries, the journal entry to record the May 1, 1990, interest payment would be as follows:

The second bond interest payment

1990			
May 1	Bond Interest Payable................................	100,000	
	Bond Interest Expense	200,000	
	Cash...		300,000
	To record payment of semiannual interest on bonds payable. Interest expense is computed as follows: $5,000,000 \times 12\% \times \frac{4}{12}$ yr.		

Throughout the life of the bonds, the entries made on Nov. 1, Dec. 31, and May 1 will be repeated year after year until May 1, 2009, when the bonds are finally retired by the following entry:

Retirement of bonds at maturity

2009
May 1	Bonds Payable	5,000,000	
	Cash		5,000,000
	To record payment of bonds payable at maturity.		

Bonds Sold between Interest Payment Dates

According to the trust indenture, bond interest payments are required to be paid on specified dates. These dates are printed on the bond certificates. Bonds may be sold, however, on any date. Thus, it is highly likely that bonds will be sold on a date other than a bond interest payment date. When this occurs, it is necessary to add to the price of the bond the interest accrued on the bond. To illustrate, assume that the Karlton Company bonds from the previous example were sold on July 1, 1989, rather than May 1. The investors must pay, in addition to the $5 million for the bonds, an additional $100,000 for the 2 months' accrued interest ($5,000,000 \times .12 \times \frac{2}{12}$)— which will be re-earned on the next interest payment date. The entry to record the sale of the bonds on July 1 would be as follows:

Bonds sold 2 months after issue date. Two months' interest must also be sold

1989
July 1	Cash	5,100,000	
	Bond Interest Payable		100,000
	Bonds Payable		5,000,000
	To record the sale of $5,000,000 of 20-year, 12% bonds at par plus 2 months' accrued interest.		

Karlton Company is obligated, by the terms of the trust indenture, to make a semiannual interest payment on Nov. 1 in the amount of $300,000. Karlton can pay no other amount but $300,000. When the interest payment is received by the bondholders, they will have been paid effectively for 4 months' interest. They have paid Karlton for 2 months' interest on July 1, but have received 6 months' interest on Nov. 1. The entry to record the interest payment on Nov. 1 is presented below:

The first bond interest payment

1989
Nov. 1	Bond Interest Payable	100,000	
	Bond Interest Expense	200,000	
	Cash		300,000
	To record payment of semiannual interest on bonds payable.		

Notice that the entry eliminates the Bond Interest Payable established from the July 1 entry and records interest expense for only 4 months.

The entry made on July 1 could have been recorded in a slightly different manner. Rather than crediting the Bond Interest Payable account for the accrued interest, the Bond Interest Expense account could have been credited in *anticipation* of the Nov. 1 debit from the semiannual interest payment. The July 1 entry would then appear as follows:

Bond interest payable could be recorded in Bond Interest Expense account	1989
	July 1 Cash 5,100,000
	           Bond Interest Expense 100,000
	           Bonds Payable 5,000,000
	        To record the sale of $5,000,000 of 20-year, 12% bonds at
	        par plus 2 months' accrued interest.

The Nov. 1 entry is then recorded simply as follows:

Recording the first bond interest payment	1989
	Nov. 1 Bond Interest Expense 300,000
	           Cash 300,000
	        To record payment of semiannual interest on bonds payable.

The result, of course, is that after the Nov. 1 entry is made, the balance in Bond Interest Expense is $200,000, reflecting 4 months' interest expense, as can be seen in the following account:

Bond Interest Expense			
1989 Nov. 1	$300,000	1989 July 1	$100,000
Bal.	$200,000		

Accounting for Bonds Issued at a Discount

More often than not, bonds are sold at a price ,hat differs from their par value. Bonds sold at a price greater than their par value are said to be sold at a ***premium.*** Bonds sold at a price lower than their value are said to be sold at a ***discount.***

Let's assume that the Karlton bonds that were issued on May 1, 1989, were issued at a price that was less than the $5 million face value. Specifically, let's assume that the bonds were sold for a price of $4,333,413 — $666,587 less than the face value. This $666,587 difference is the *discount.* Generally accepted accounting principles require that the liability account Bonds Payable must be recorded at the face value, $5,000,000. A contra-liability account, Discount on Bonds Payable, must then be established to adjust the face value of the bonds to the amount of cash received from selling the bonds. We would record the general journal entry on May 1, 1989, when the bonds are issued, as follows:

Bonds issued at a discount	May 1 Cash 4,333,413
	        Discount on Bonds Payable 666,587
	           Bonds Payable 5,000,000
	        To record the sale of $5,000,000 of 20-year, 12% bonds,
	        maturing May 1, 2009.

If a balance sheet were prepared on this date, the information pertaining to the bonds would be presented in the long-term liabilities section like this:

Long-Term Liabilities:
    12% Bonds Payable Due May 1, 2009 .... $5,000,000
    Less: Discount on Bonds Payable 666,587 $4,333,413

The carrying value of a bond is the difference between its face value and the discount

The $4,333,413 representing the difference between the $5,000,000 face value and the $666,587 discount, is called the **carrying value** of the bonds.

Now, let's move ahead to May 1, 2009, when the bonds are retired—the $5,000,000 face value of the bonds is paid to the creditors and the bonds are canceled. On that date Karlton Company will issue a check in the amount of $5,000,000 and record this entry:

2009

May 1   Bonds Payable   5,000,000

    Cash   5,000,000

    To record the retirement of $5,000,000 of 20-year, 12%

    bonds due this date.

What about the Discount on Bonds Payable account? If we no longer have the bonds, we should no longer have the discount! The Discount on Bonds Payable has a debit balance and the account must be credited to eliminate the debit balance. But when the credit is made, what do we debit? Three possibilities exist.

First, let's consider a second entry on May 1, 2009. Karlton has to pay $5,000,000 to retire the bonds, but received only $4,333,413 on May 1, 1989, when the money was borrowed. We could record a loss on the retirement of the bonds. Or perhaps we should not call it a loss but a fee paid for the use of money—interest expense. But was this fee incurred all on one date—May 1, 2009?

Well, what if we made a second entry on the date the bonds were issued—May 1, 1989? We could credit Discount on Bonds Payable and debit a loss on the sale of the bonds for the $666,587. Again, what we are doing is paying for the use of money, and that's interest expense. But was the $666,587 all incurred on May 1, 1989?

Bond discounts must be amortized over the life of the bonds

The $666,587 would seem to have been logically incurred over the period of time Karlton Company used the money—20 years, or 240 months. And that's the third alternative: Allocate the discount over the life of the bonds—in this case, $2,777 per month ($666,587 ÷ 240). This process is called **amortization.**

You may ask why bonds are sold at a price that is less—or more—than their face value. Well, when bonds are sold—say, the Karlton bonds—they have a stated interest rate in the bond indenture. And that rate is on the face of the bond certificates—12% for the Karlton bonds. Karlton Company *must* pay 12% interest on the bonds (6% on each of the two semiannual interest payment dates).

What if, when Karlton tries to sell its bonds, the interest rate that other companies are willing to pay on their bonds is 14%? Who would buy Karlton's bonds? Nobody. So Karlton must do something to sell its bonds. It can't change the 12% rate that it must pay as specified by the bond indenture, but it can change the *price* of the bonds—the amount the bonds sell for. Karlton will sell the bonds at a price investors are willing to pay. That price will be such that an investor will earn a 14% return on the investment. Selling the Karlton bonds at $4,333,413, and paying 12% interest a year—actually 6% every 6 months—on the $5,000,000 for 20 years, will give the investor a 14% return. (The section on present value later in this chapter will show you how this was calculated.) So you see the reason bonds are sold at a discount is to adjust the interest rate specified in the bond indenture—which is too low—to the rate of interest investors are willing to pay.

We don't have to amortize the bond discount every month; we can do it on bond interest payment dates and on the year-end closing dates. That's what Karlton will do. So, on the first bond interest payment date—Nov. 1, 1989—Karlton will record the interest expense as the sum of the cash paid, $300,000 ($5,000,000 × 12% × $\frac{6}{12}$

year), plus 6 months' amortization of the discount, $16,665 ($666,587 × $\frac{6}{240}$). That's a total interest expense for the 6 months of $316,665 ($300,000 + $16,665). Here's the general journal entry:

The first bond interest payment and amortization of the discount

1989			
Nov. 1	Bond Interest Expense	316,665	
	Discount on Bonds Payable		16,665
	Cash		300,000
	To record payment of semiannual interest on bonds ($5,000,000 × 12% × $\frac{6}{12}$ mo) and amortization of bond discount ($666,587 × $\frac{6}{240}$ mo).		

The Dec. 31 adjusting entry required to accrue the bond interest payable and to amortize the discount would be recorded like this:

The bond interest adjusting entry and amortization of the discount

1989			
Dec. 31	Bond Interest Expense	105,555	
	Discount on Bonds Payable		5,555
	Bond Interest Payable		100,000
	To record accrual of bond interest payable ($5,000,000 × 12% × $\frac{2}{12}$ mo) and amortization of bond discount ($666,587 × $\frac{2}{240}$ mo)		

The Dec. 31 balance sheet would show the carrying value of the bond as follows:

Long-Term Liabilities:		
12% Bonds Payable Due May 1, 2009	$5,000,000	
Less: Discount on Bonds Payable	644,367	$4,355,633

The balance in the discount account has been reduced to $644,367 ($666,587 − $16,665 − $5,555) by the amortization process.

On May 1, 1990, we will pay the semiannual interest payment of $300,000 and amortize 4 months' discount, Jan. 1 to Apr. 30. The following entry will be used to record this payment:

The second bond interest payment and amortization of the discount

1990			
May 1	Bond Interest Payable	100,000	
	Bond Interest Expense	211,110	
	Discount on Bonds Payable		11,110
	Cash		300,000
	To record payment of semiannual interest on bonds and amortize bond discount ($666,587 × $\frac{4}{240}$ mo).		

Notice that we have debited Bond Interest Payable for $100,000, thus eliminating the liability we accrued on Dec. 31, 1989.

Over the remaining life of the bonds we will make entries on May 1 and Nov. 1 identical to the ones made on May 1, 1990, and Nov. 1, 1989, just illustrated. And on Dec. 31 of each year we will make an accrual identical to the one made on Dec. 31, 1989.

Accounting for Bonds Issued at a Premium

Bonds may be sold at a premium, that is, at a price that exceeds par value. The reason for selling bonds at a premium is that the marketplace is reflecting a different

If the market rate of interest is less than the nominal rate, bonds will sell at a premium

market interest rate than that specified in the bond indenture. This is the same reason why bonds are sold at a discount. What determines whether bonds sell at a discount or at a premium is the relationship of the market rate of interest to the rate specified in the bond contract. If the market rate of interest is greater than the rate specified in the bond contract, the **nominal** rate, the bond will sell for a discount. On the other hand, if the market rate of interest is less than the nominal rate, bonds will sell at a **premium.**

Let's now assume the latter to be the case—that the Karlton bonds sell for $5,857,956 on May 1, 1989. A premium of $857,956 results because the market rate of interest must have been less than the nominal rate of 12%. We would record the following entry on May 1, 1989, the bond issue date:

Sale of bonds at a premium

1989			
May 1	Cash	5,857,956	
	Premium on Bonds Payable		857,956
	Bonds Payable		5,000,000
	To record the sale of $5,000,000 of 20-year, 12% bonds, maturing May 1, 2009.		

On this date the information relating to the bonds would be presented in the long-term liabilities section of the balance sheet as follows:

Long-Term Liabilities:		
12% Bonds Payable Due May 1, 2009	$5,000,000	
Plus: Premium on Bonds Payable	857,956	$5,857,956

The carrying value of the bond, $5,857,956, is the sum of the $5,000,000 face value and the $857,956 premium.

We will have to amortize the premium over the period of time the bond is outstanding, just as we did with the discount. And we will again do this on bond interest payment dates and at year-end. Consequently, the Nov. 1, 1989, bond interest payment and premium amortization would be recorded as follows:

The first bond interest payment and amortization of premium

1989			
Nov. 1	Bond Interest Expense	278,551	
	Premium on Bonds Payable	21,449	
	Cash		300,000
	To record payment of semiannual interest on bonds ($5,000,000 $\times$ 12% $\times \frac{6}{12}$ mo) and amortization of bond premium ($857,956 $\times \frac{6}{240}$ mo).		

This time the interest expense is the difference between the cash paid $300,000, and the $21,449 amortization of the premium ($857,956 $\times \frac{6}{240}$). When we had a discount, the interest expense was the sum of the cash and the amortization of the discount.

On Dec. 31, 1989, the bond interest payable must be accrued and the premium must be amortized. The entry to accomplish this would be recorded as follows:

Bond interest adjusting entry and amortization of premium

1989			
Dec. 31	Bond Interest Expense	92,850	
	Premium on Bonds Payable	7,150	
	Interest Payable		100,000
	To record accrual of bond interest payable and amortization of bond premium ($857,956 $\times \frac{2}{240}$ mo).		

The balance sheet on Dec. 31 would reflect the following carrying value of the bond:

Long-Term Liabilities:
12% Bonds Payable Due May 1, 2009 .... $5,000,000
Plus: Premium on Bonds Payable 829,357 $5,829,357

The premium account of $857,956 on May 1, 1989, has been reduced by the amortization of $21,449 on Nov. 1, 1989, and $7,150 on Dec. 31, 1989.

The interest payment on May 1, 1990, of $300,000 and the 4-month amortization of the premium we will record like this:

The second bond interest payment and amortization of premium

1990
May 1   Bond Interest Payable.................................... 100,000
        Bond Interest Expense 185,701
        Premium on Bonds Payable 14,299
            Cash 300,000
        To record the payment of semiannual interest on bonds and
        amortization of bond premium ($857,956 $\times \frac{4}{240}$ mo).

The bond interest payments on each Nov. 1 and May 1 over the remaining life of the bonds will be identical to the ones made on May 1, 1990, and Nov. 1, 1989. Each Dec. 31 accrual entry each year will be identical to the one made on Dec. 31, 1989.

PRESENT VALUE AND LONG-TERM LIABILITIES

The time value of money considers the relationship among time, money, and interest rates

In our discussion of bonds payable to this point we have ignored a very significant factor: the fact that money has a time value. The promise to pay $5 million 20 years hence is not the same thing as paying $5 million today. Nor is paying $300,000 every 6 months for forty 6-month periods over 20 years equivalent to paying $12 million ($300,000 $\times$ 40) today. *Money has a time value.* What is the time value of money? It is the value that equates the $5 million 20 years hence to its *present value* today. It considers the future cash item (the $5 million), the appropriate interest rate, and the length of time between today and the receipt or payment of the future cash item.

Everyone can see that a $5 million deposit made today is worth more than a $5 million deposit made 1 year from today. The deposit made today will earn interest for 1 year, and the interest plus the initial deposit of $5 million will, of course, exceed the $5 million deposited 1 year hence.

If the interest rate was 12%, the $5 million deposit made today would accumulate to $5,600,000 1 year hence—$5,000,000 + (12%)($5,000,000). The $5,600,000 is called the **amount.** The $5 million deposit made today is called the **present value.** If we know that $5,600,000 is available 1 year hence and money is worth 12%, then we know that the present value today of the $5,600,000 is $5,000,000.

The present value of any amount, for any period of time, at any interest rate, can be found by multiplying the amount by the factor $1/(1 + i)^n$. The value i represents the interest rate *per period.* The value n is the number of periods.

Present value tables have been prepared as an aid to calculating present values. Such a table is illustrated in Table 13-1. We can find the value of the factor $[1/(1 + i)^n]$ for 1 period at 12% by looking in Table 13-1 at the intersection of the $n = 1$ row and the $i = 12\%$ column. The factor is .892. To six decimal places the factor is .892857. The table (like Table 13-2) has been truncated to three decimal places to facilitate the computations in your homework problems. Multiplying the six-decimal factor .892857 times $5,600,000 results in the present value 5,000,000. If we had used the .892 truncated figure we would have computed the present value as

TABLE 13-1   Present Value of $1

$$p_{\overline{n}|i} = \frac{1}{(1+i)^n}$$ Lumpsum

n \ i	1%	2%	3%	4%	5%	6%	7%	8%	9%	10%	12%	15%	20%
1	0.990	0.980	0.970	0.961	0.952	0.943	0.934	0.925	0.917	0.909	0.892	0.869	0.833
2	0.980	0.961	0.942	0.924	0.907	0.889	0.873	0.857	0.841	0.826	0.797	0.756	0.694
3	0.970	0.942	0.915	0.888	0.863	0.839	0.816	0.793	0.772	0.751	0.711	0.657	0.578
4	0.960	0.923	0.888	0.854	0.822	0.792	0.762	0.735	0.708	0.683	0.635	0.571	0.482
5	0.951	0.905	0.862	0.821	0.783	0.747	0.712	0.680	0.649	0.620	0.567	0.497	0.401
6	0.942	0.887	0.837	0.790	0.746	0.704	0.666	0.630	0.596	0.564	0.506	0.432	0.334
7	0.932	0.870	0.813	0.759	0.710	0.665	0.622	0.583	0.547	0.513	0.452	0.375	0.279
8	0.923	0.853	0.789	0.730	0.676	0.627	0.582	0.540	0.501	0.466	0.403	0.326	0.232
9	0.914	0.836	0.766	0.702	0.644	0.591	0.543	0.500	0.460	0.424	0.360	0.284	0.193
10	0.905	0.820	0.744	0.675	0.613	0.558	0.508	0.463	0.422	0.385	0.321	0.247	0.161
11	0.896	0.804	0.722	0.649	0.584	0.526	0.475	0.428	0.387	0.350	0.287	0.214	0.134
12	0.887	0.788	0.701	0.624	0.556	0.496	0.444	0.397	0.355	0.318	0.256	0.186	0.112
13	0.878	0.773	0.680	0.600	0.530	0.468	0.414	0.367	0.326	0.289	0.229	0.162	0.093
14	0.869	0.757	0.661	0.577	0.505	0.442	0.387	0.340	0.299	0.263	0.204	0.141	0.077
15	0.861	0.743	0.641	0.555	0.481	0.417	0.362	0.315	0.274	0.239	0.182	0.122	0.064
16	0.852	0.728	0.623	0.533	0.458	0.393	0.338	0.291	0.251	0.217	0.163	0.106	0.054
17	0.844	0.714	0.605	0.513	0.436	0.371	0.316	0.270	0.231	0.197	0.145	0.092	0.045
18	0.836	0.700	0.587	0.493	0.415	0.350	0.295	0.250	0.211	0.179	0.130	0.080	0.037
19	0.827	0.686	0.570	0.474	0.395	0.330	0.276	0.231	0.194	0.163	0.116	0.070	0.031
20	0.819	0.672	0.553	0.456	0.376	0.311	0.258	0.214	0.178	0.148	0.103	0.061	0.026
21	0.811	0.659	0.537	0.438	0.358	0.294	0.241	0.198	0.163	0.135	0.092	0.053	0.021
22	0.803	0.646	0.521	0.421	0.341	0.277	0.225	0.183	0.150	0.122	0.082	0.046	0.018
23	0.795	0.634	0.506	0.405	0.325	0.261	0.210	0.170	0.137	0.111	0.073	0.040	0.015
24	0.787	0.621	0.491	0.390	0.310	0.246	0.197	0.157	0.126	0.101	0.065	0.034	0.012
25	0.779	0.609	0.477	0.375	0.295	0.232	0.184	0.146	0.115	0.092	0.058	0.030	0.010
26	0.772	0.597	0.463	0.360	0.281	0.219	0.172	0.135	0.106	0.083	0.052	0.026	0.008
27	0.764	0.585	0.450	0.346	0.267	0.207	0.160	0.125	0.097	0.076	0.046	0.022	0.007
28	0.756	0.574	0.437	0.333	0.255	0.195	0.150	0.115	0.089	0.069	0.041	0.019	0.006
29	0.749	0.563	0.424	0.320	0.242	0.184	0.140	0.107	0.082	0.063	0.037	0.017	0.005
30	0.741	0.552	0.411	0.308	0.231	0.174	0.131	0.099	0.075	0.057	0.033	0.015	0.004
31	0.734	0.541	0.399	0.296	0.220	0.164	0.122	0.092	0.069	0.052	0.029	0.013	0.003
32	0.727	0.530	0.388	0.285	0.209	0.154	0.114	0.085	0.063	0.047	0.026	0.011	0.002
33	0.720	0.520	0.377	0.274	0.199	0.146	0.107	0.078	0.058	0.043	0.023	0.009	0.002
34	0.712	0.510	0.366	0.263	0.190	0.137	0.100	0.073	0.053	0.039	0.021	0.008	0.002
35	0.705	0.500	0.355	0.253	0.181	0.130	0.093	0.067	0.048	0.035	0.018	0.007	0.001
36	0.698	0.490	0.345	0.243	0.172	0.122	0.087	0.062	0.044	0.032	0.016	0.006	0.001
37	0.692	0.480	0.334	0.234	0.164	0.115	0.081	0.057	0.041	0.029	0.015	0.005	0.001
38	0.685	0.471	0.325	0.225	0.156	0.109	0.076	0.053	0.037	0.026	0.013	0.004	0.001
39	0.678	0.461	0.315	0.216	0.149	0.103	0.071	0.049	0.034	0.024	0.012	0.004	0.001
40	0.671	0.452	0.306	0.208	0.142	0.097	0.066	0.046	0.031	0.022	0.010	0.003	0.000
41	0.665	0.444	0.297	0.200	0.135	0.091	0.062	0.042	0.029	0.020	0.009	0.003	0.000
42	0.658	0.435	0.288	0.192	0.128	0.086	0.058	0.039	0.026	0.018	0.008	0.002	0.000
43	0.651	0.426	0.280	0.185	0.122	0.081	0.054	0.036	0.024	0.016	0.007	0.002	0.000
44	0.645	0.418	0.272	0.178	0.116	0.077	0.050	0.033	0.022	0.015	0.006	0.002	0.000
45	0.639	0.410	0.264	0.171	0.111	0.072	0.047	0.031	0.020	0.013	0.006	0.001	0.000
46	0.632	0.402	0.256	0.164	0.105	0.068	0.044	0.029	0.018	0.012	0.005	0.001	0.000
47	0.626	0.394	0.249	0.158	0.100	0.064	0.041	0.026	0.017	0.011	0.004	0.001	0.000
48	0.620	0.386	0.241	0.152	0.096	0.060	0.038	0.024	0.015	0.010	0.004	0.001	0.000
49	0.614	0.378	0.234	0.146	0.091	0.057	0.036	0.023	0.014	0.009	0.003	0.001	0.000
50	0.608	0.371	0.228	0.140	0.087	0.054	0.033	0.021	0.013	0.008	0.003	0.000	0.000

TABLE 13-2 Present Value of an Ordinary Annuity of $1

$$P_{\overline{n}|i} = \frac{1 - \dfrac{1}{(1 + i)^n}}{i}$$

annuity

n	1%	2%	3%	4%	5%	6%	7%	8%	9%	10%	12%	15%	20%
1	0.990	0.980	0.970	0.961	0.952	0.943	0.934	0.925	0.917	0.909	0.892	0.869	0.833
2	1.970	1.941	1.913	1.886	1.850	1.833	1.808	1.783	1.759	1.735	1.690	1.625	1.527
3	2.940	2.883	2.828	2.775	2.723	2.673	2.624	2.577	2.531	2.486	2.401	2.283	2.106
4	3.901	3.807	3.717	3.629	3.545	3.465	3.387	3.312	3.239	3.169	3.037	2.854	2.588
5	4.853	4.713	4.579	4.451	4.329	4.212	4.100	3.992	3.889	3.790	3.604	3.352	2.990
6	5.795	5.601	5.417	5.242	5.075	4.917	4.766	4.622	4.485	4.355	4.111	3.784	3.325
7	6.728	6.471	6.230	6.002	5.786	5.582	5.389	5.206	5.032	4.868	4.563	4.160	3.604
8	7.651	7.325	7.019	6.732	6.463	6.209	5.971	5.746	5.534	5.334	4.967	4.487	3.837
9	8.566	8.162	7.786	7.435	7.107	6.801	6.515	6.246	5.995	5.759	5.328	4.771	4.031
10	9.471	8.982	8.530	8.110	7.721	7.360	7.023	6.710	6.417	6.144	5.650	5.018	4.192
11	10.367	9.786	9.252	8.760	8.306	7.886	7.498	7.138	6.805	6.495	5.937	5.233	4.327
12	11.255	10.575	9.954	9.385	8.863	8.383	7.942	7.536	7.160	6.813	6.194	5.420	4.439
13	12.133	11.348	10.634	9.985	9.393	8.852	8.357	7.903	7.486	7.103	6.423	5.583	4.532
14	13.003	12.106	11.296	10.563	9.898	9.294	8.745	8.244	7.786	7.366	6.628	5.724	4.610
15	13.865	12.849	11.937	11.118	10.379	9.712	9.107	8.559	8.060	7.606	6.810	5.847	4.675
16	14.717	13.577	12.561	11.652	10.837	10.105	9.446	8.851	8.312	7.823	6.973	5.954	4.729
17	15.562	14.291	13.166	12.165	11.274	10.477	9.763	9.121	8.543	8.021	7.119	6.047	4.774
18	16.398	14.992	13.753	12.659	11.689	10.827	10.059	9.371	8.755	8.201	7.249	6.127	4.812
19	17.226	15.678	14.323	13.133	12.058	11.158	10.335	9.603	8.950	8.364	7.365	6.198	4.843
20	18.045	16.351	14.877	13.590	12.462	11.469	10.594	9.818	9.128	8.513	7.469	6.259	4.869
21	18.856	17.011	15.415	14.029	12.821	11.764	10.835	10.016	9.292	8.648	7.562	6.312	4.891
22	19.660	17.658	15.936	14.451	13.163	12.041	11.061	10.200	9.442	8.771	7.644	6.358	4.909
23	20.455	18.292	16.443	14.856	13.488	12.303	11.272	10.371	9.580	8.883	7.718	6.398	4.924
24	21.243	18.913	16.935	15.246	13.798	12.550	11.469	10.528	9.706	8.984	7.784	6.433	4.937
25	22.023	19.523	17.413	15.622	14.093	12.783	11.653	10.674	9.822	9.077	7.843	6.464	4.947
26	22.795	20.121	17.876	15.982	14.375	13.003	11.825	10.809	9.928	9.160	7.895	6.490	4.956
27	23.559	20.706	18.327	16.329	14.643	13.210	11.986	10.935	10.026	9.237	7.942	6.513	4.963
28	24.316	21.281	18.764	16.663	14.898	13.406	12.137	11.051	10.116	9.306	7.984	6.533	4.969
29	25.065	21.844	19.188	16.983	15.141	13.590	12.277	11.158	10.198	9.369	8.021	6.550	4.974
30	25.807	22.396	19.600	17.292	15.372	13.764	12.409	11.257	10.273	9.426	8.055	6.565	4.978
31	26.542	22.937	20.000	17.589	15.592	13.929	12.531	11.349	10.342	9.479	8.084	6.579	4.982
32	27.269	23.468	20.388	17.873	15.802	14.084	12.646	11.434	10.406	9.526	8.111	6.590	4.985
33	27.989	23.988	20.765	18.147	16.002	14.230	12.753	11.513	10.464	9.569	8.135	6.600	4.987
34	28.702	24.498	21.131	18.411	16.192	14.368	12.854	11.586	10.517	9.608	8.156	6.609	4.989
35	29.408	24.998	21.487	18.664	16.374	14.498	12.947	11.654	10.566	9.644	8.175	6.616	4.991
36	30.107	25.488	21.832	18.908	16.546	14.620	13.035	11.717	10.611	9.676	8.192	6.623	4.992
37	30.799	25.969	22.167	19.142	16.711	14.736	13.117	11.775	10.652	9.705	8.207	6.628	4.994
38	31.484	26.440	22.492	19.367	16.867	14.846	13.193	11.828	10.690	9.732	8.220	6.633	4.995
39	32.163	26.902	22.808	19.584	17.071	14.949	13.264	11.878	10.725	9.756	8.233	6.638	4.995
40	32.834	27.355	23.114	19.792	17.159	15.046	13.331	11.924	10.757	9.779	8.243	6.641	4.996
41	33.499	27.799	23.412	19.993	17.294	15.138	13.394	11.967	10.786	9.799	8.253	6.645	4.997
42	34.158	28.234	23.701	20.185	17.423	15.224	13.452	12.006	10.813	9.817	8.261	6.647	4.997
43	34.810	28.661	23.981	20.370	17.545	15.306	13.506	12.043	10.837	9.833	8.269	6.650	4.998
44	35.455	29.079	24.254	20.548	17.662	15.383	13.557	12.077	10.860	9.849	8.276	6.652	4.998
45	36.094	29.490	24.518	20.720	17.774	15.455	13.605	12.108	10.881	9.862	8.282	6.654	4.998
46	36.727	29.892	24.775	20.884	17.880	15.524	13.650	12.137	10.900	9.875	8.287	6.655	4.998
47	37.353	30.286	25.024	21.042	17.981	15.589	13.691	12.164	10.917	9.886	8.292	6.657	4.999
48	37.973	30.673	25.266	21.195	18.077	15.650	13.730	12.189	10.933	9.896	8.297	6.658	4.999
49	38.588	31.052	25.601	21.341	18.168	15.707	13.766	12.212	10.948	9.906	8.301	6.659	4.999
50	39.196	31.423	25.729	21.482	18.255	15.761	13.800	12.233	10.961	9.914	8.304	6.660	4.999

$4,995,200. For this reason we will use the six-decimal factors in the illustrations, but you can learn the concepts as well by using the truncated three-decimal factors when solving your homework problems.

As an aid in notation for solving present value problems, we will use the lowercase *p* to mean the present value of a single sum of money. The present value factor is represented by the symbol

$$p_{\overline{n}|i}$$

which we read as

*the present value of a single sum of money for **n** periods at **i** percent*

To express the present value of $5,600,000 at 12% for 1 period we would write:

$$p = \$5,600,000\ p_{\overline{1}|12\%}$$

Unless we tell you otherwise, interest is expressed at an annual rate. This means that you must take care when using the present value tables to *adjust the interest and the periods* when interest is compounded more frequently than annually. For example, assume that we wish to know the present value of $5,000,000 payable 20 years hence if interest is 12% compounded semiannually. Since interest is compounded twice a year and there are 20 years, the number of periods involved is 40. And the interest rate per period is 6%, the annual rate of 12% divided by the number of periods in a year. The present value is expressed as:

The present value of $5,000,000 due 20 years from now. Interest compounded twice a year

$$p = \$5,000,000\ p_{\overline{40}|6\%}$$
$$= \$5,000,000\ (.097222)$$
$$= \$486,110$$

Note the line under the first three figures to the right of the decimal point. This is the factor you will find in the table.

Let's try another example. This time let's find the present value of $100,000 payable 5 years hence if interest is 16% compounded quarterly. The present value is determined like this:

The present value of the $100,000 due 5 years from now. Interest compounded four times a year

$$p = \$100,000\ p_{\overline{20}|4\%}$$
$$= \$100,000\ (.456387)$$
$$= \$45,639$$

The Karlton Company incurred two separate obligations when it issued the $5,000,000, 12%, 20-year bonds on May 1, 1989. First, it promised to pay the face amount of the bonds, $5,000,000, twenty years hence. And second, it promised to pay interest of $300,000 ($5,000,000 × 12% × ½ year) every 6 months—on Nov. 1 and May 1—for the life of the bonds, 20 years. These two promises can be expressed on a time line as shown at the top of page 555.

The second promise represents a series of payments (40 in number) to be made at the *end of each period*. This is called an **ordinary annuity.** A present value table of ordinary annuity factors is presented in Table 13-2; it works the same way as Table 13-1 did. We use the capital letter *P* to represent the present value of an ordinary annuity and express the fact as:

An ordinary annuity is a series of payments made at the end of each period

$$P_{\overline{n}|i}$$

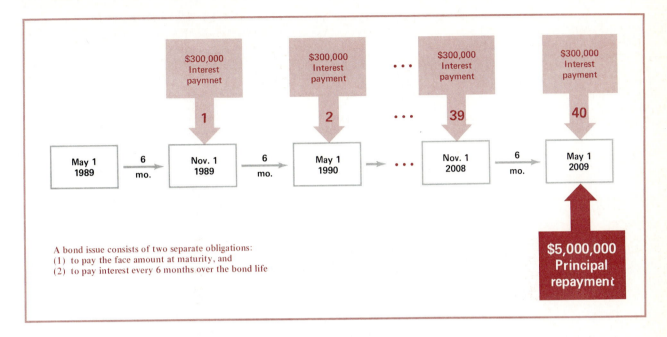

A bond issue consists of two separate obligations:
(1) to pay the face amount at maturity, and
(2) to pay interest every 6 months over the bond life

The present value of the $300,000 ordinary annuity of 40 payments at 12% per year (6% per period) would be calculated like this:

$$P = \$300,000 \ P_{\overline{40}|6\%}$$
$$= \$300,000 \ (15.046297)$$
$$= \$4,513,890$$

Now we can determine the present value of the $5,000,000, 12%, 20-year Karlton bonds. It is the sum of the present values of the two separate obligations — the present value of the promise to pay $5,000,000 twenty years hence and the promise to pay $300,000 twice a year for those 20 years. The present value of the bond is:

The present value of a $5,000,000, 20-year, 12% bond when the market rate of interest is 12%

$5,000,000 $p_{\overline{40}	6\%}$ = $5,000,000 (.097222)	= $ 486,110
$300,000 $P_{\overline{40}	6\%}$ = $300,000 (15.046297) =	4,513,890
Present value of the bonds		$5,000,000

You may be wondering, if the present value of the bonds is $5,000,000, which is also the face value, why bother with all these present value calculations? This is a good question. We have used the 12% interest rate to determine the present value of the bonds. Remember that 12% was the nominal rate — the rate specified in the bond indenture. Using the market rate to determine the present value of bonds when the market rate equals the nominal rate will always result in a present value that will equal the face value. It simply means that the bonds will sell at par.

If the market rate of interest equals the nominal rate, bonds will sell at their face value

But remember our discussion several pages back. Bonds will sell at a *discount* if the market rate of interest exceeds the nominal rate. And they will sell at a *premium* if the market rate of interest is less than the nominal rate.

If the Karlton bonds were issued at a time when the market rate of interest was 14%, the present value of the bonds would be:

The present value of a $5,000,000, 20-year, 12% bond when the market rate is 14%

$$\$5,000,000\ p_{\overline{40}|7\%} = \$5,000,000\ (.066780) \quad = \$\ \ 333,900$$
$$\$300,000\ P_{\overline{40}|7\%} = \quad \$300,000\ (13.331709) = \ \underline{\ \ 3,999,513}$$

Present value of the bonds $\$4,333,413$

This would be, all other economic factors being constant, the price the bonds would sell for. They would sell for a discount of $666,587 ($5,000,000 − $4,333,413).

And if the bonds were issued at a time when the market rate of interest was 10%, the selling price of the bonds would be as follows:

The present value of a $5,000,000, 20-year, 12% bond when the market rate is 10%

$$\$5,000,000\ p_{\overline{40}|5\%} = \$5,000,000\ (.142046) \quad = \$\ \ 710,230$$
$$\$300,000\ P_{\overline{40}|5\%} = \quad \$300,000\ (17.159086) = \ \underline{\ \ 5,147,726}$$

Present value of the bonds $\$5,857,956$

A premium of $857,956 results.

Do you see that in the discount and premium examples the market rate of interest was used to compute the present value? The market rate is called the ***effective*** rate of interest. The $5,000,000 face of the bond and the $300,000 semiannual interest payment cannot be changed since they are fixed by the terms of the trust indenture. The price the bonds sell for is changed by using the effective rate of interest.

The Effective-Interest Method of Amortizing Bond Discounts and Premiums

When we previously discussed accounting for bonds issued at discounts or premiums we amortized the discount or premium *equally* over the 40 periods. This is called the **straight-line method** of amortization. The amortization is the same for each 6-month period. While this method is easy, it does not reflect the effective interest rate. A method of amortization that does show the effective interest rate, the

The effective-interest method provides for a constant rate of interest each period

effective-interest method, is the preferred method and must be used unless the difference between the two methods is not material. The straight-line method provides an equal *amount of interest expense* each period. The effective-interest method provides for an equal *rate of interest* each period.

Interest expense is determined by multiplying the bond carrying value by the effective-interest rate

Here's how it works. The interest expense for each period is determined by multiplying the carrying value—the face value plus a premium or minus a discount—of the bond at the beginning of the period by the effective rate of interest. The amount of discount to be amortized is the difference between the interest expense and the interest payment for the period.

Let's refer back to the example where the Karlton bonds were sold at a discount to illustrate this process. We would calculate the interest expense for the first interest period ending on Nov. 1, 1989, like this:

Calculating interest expense

($5,000,000 face value − $666,587 discount) × 7% per period effective-interest rate
= $303,339 interest expense

Amortizing the discount is accomplished as follows:

Calculating discount amortization

$303,339 interest expense − $300,000 interest payment
= $3,339 discount amortization

TABLE 13-3   Karlton Company
Effective-interest method bond discount amortization schedule

Interest Period	A Interest Payment (face value × 6%)	B Interest Expense (Col. E × 7%)	C Discount Amortization (B − A)	D Unamortized Discount (D − C)	E Carrying Value of Bonds (face value − D)
May 1, 1989				$666,587	$4,333,413
Nov. 1, 1989	$300,000	$303,339	$ 3,339	663,248	4,336,752
May 1, 1990	300,000	303,573	3,573	659,675	4,340,325
Nov. 1, 1990	300,000	303,823	3,823	655,852	4,344,148
May 1, 1991	300,000	304,090	4,090	651,762	4,348,238
Nov. 1, 1991	300,000	304,377	4,377	647,385	4,352,615
May 1, 2008	300,000	340,815	40,815	90,400	4,909,600
Nov. 1, 2008	300,000	343,672	43,672	46,728	4,953,272
May 1, 2009	300,000	346,728	46,728	-0-	5,000,000

We now need to determine the amount of discount remaining after the amortization of the $3,339. This unamortized discount is $663,248 ($666,587 − $3,339) and is subtracted from the $5,000,000 face value of the bonds to arrive at the Nov. 1, 1989, carrying value of $4,336,752.

For the next interest period, May 1, 1990, the process is repeated. We take the bond carrying value, $4,336,752, times the 7% per period effective-interest rate to arrive at $303,573 interest expense. Subtracting the $300,000 interest payment from the interest expense determines the amount of discount amortization, $3,573, for the second interest period.

A bond discount amortization schedule, such as the one presented in Table 13-3 above for the Karlton Company bonds, is usually prepared for the life of the bonds when the bonds are issued.

Let's look at the amortization schedule a little differently. Perhaps that will make it easier to understand. On the date that the bonds were issued, two accounts would be created, namely, Bonds Payable for $5,000,000 and Discount on Bonds Payable for $666,587. Presenting these two accounts in T-accounts would look like this:

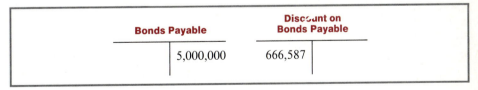

Bonds Payable	Discount on Bonds Payable
5,000,000	666,587

Now allow us the liberty of combining these two accounts into one *make-believe* account, which we will call Bond Carrying Value, which would look like this:

Bond Carrying Value
4,333,413

This is what is happening to the carryng value of the bonds over the first four interest periods:

	Bond Carrying Value		
			4,333,413
Cash Payment		Interest Expense	
(5,000,000)(.06)	300,000	(4,333,413)(.07)	303,339
			4,336,752
	300,000	(4,336,752)(.07)	303,573
			4,340,325
	300,000	(4,340,325)(.07)	303,823
			4,344,148
	300,000	(4,344,148)(.07)	304,090
			4,348,238

We can look at this concept of amortization using the effective-interest method still another way that may help you. This time let's use a diagram; see Figure 13-1.

What is happening is that the carrying value of the bond is increasing as it earns interest. And it earns interest *every day;* we just record the interest once every 6 months when a cash payment is made. Figure 13-1 shows that the initial carrying value of the bond increases to $4,636,752 ($4,333,413 + the interest of $303,339 for the first 6 months) and then is reduced by the cash payment of $300,000. The cash payment is made all at one time, so the reduction is shown as a straight drop to the new carrying value of $4,336,752. Each successive 6-month period first increases the carrying value by the interest, then reduces the carrying value by the cash payment. But each successive carrying value is a little larger than the previous one—until 20 years pass and the carrying value reaches $5,000,000, the maturity value of the bond.

FIGURE 13-1
Bond Discount
Amortization
Effective-interest method.

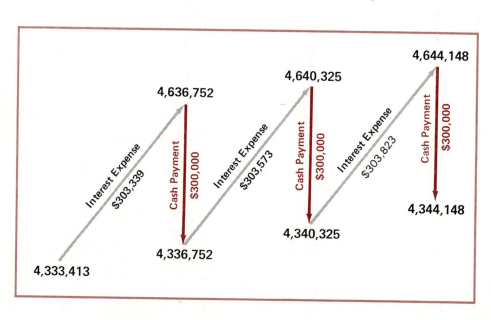

The first bond interest payment and discount amortization

Using the bond discount amortization schedule, let's compare the general journal entries required under the effective-interest and straight-line methods for the Nov. 1, 1989, interest payment, the Dec. 31, 1989, accrual, and the May 1, 1990, interest payment.

		Method Used	
		Effective-Interest	**Straight-Line**
1989			
Nov. 1	Bond Interest Expense	303,339	316,665
	Discount on Bonds Payable.............................	3,339	16,665
	Cash	300,000	300,000
	To record payment of semiannual interest on bonds and amortization of bond discount.		

The bond interest adjusting entry and discount amortization

Now compare the interest expense under both procedures. A significant difference, $13,326 ($316,665 − $303,339), exists. This is why the effective-interest method is required. It reflects the true interest cost and the straight-line method is only a convenience because it is easy. The Dec. 31 adjusting entry would be recorded like this:

		Method Used	
		Effective-Interest	**Straight-Line**
1989			
Dec. 31	Bond Interest Expense......................................	101,191	105,555
	Discount on Bonds Payable...............................	1,191	5,555
	Bond Interest Payable	100,000	100,000
	To record accrual of bond interest payable and amortization of bond discount.		

Can you determine how we arrived at the $1,191 discount amortization under the effective-interest method? Remember that the $5,555 straight-line amortization was calculated by taking $\frac{2}{240}$ of the initial $666,587 discount. This would be the same as taking $\frac{2}{6}$ of the $16,665 semiannual amortization. That's what we did for the effective-interest method, $\frac{2}{6}$ of the $3,573 second-period discount amortization (see Table 13-3). Amortization between interest payment dates under the effective-interest method is done on a straight-line basis.

The second bond interest payment and discount amortization

On May 1, 1990, the semiannual interest payment is recorded like this:

		Method Used	
		Effective-Interest	**Straight-Line**
1990			
May 1	Bond Interest Payable	100,000	100,000
	Bond Interest Expense.....................................	202,382	211,110
	Discount on Bonds Payable...............................	2,382	11,110
	Cash...	300,000	300,000
	To record payment of semiannual interest on bond and amortize bond discount.		

TABLE 13-4 Karlton Company
Effective-interest method bond premium amortization schedule

Interest Period	A Interest Payment (face value × 6%)	B Interest Expense (Col. E × 5%)	C Premium Amortization (A − B)	D Unamortized Premium (D − C)	E Carrying Value of Bonds (face value + D)
May 1, 1989				$857,956	$5,857,956
Nov. 1, 1989	$300,000	$292,898	$ 7,102	850,854	5,850,854
May 1, 1990	300,000	292,543	7,457	843,397	5,843,397
Nov. 1, 1990	300,000	292,170	7,830	835,567	5,835,567
May 1, 1991	300,000	291,778	8,222	827,345	5,827,345
Nov. 1, 1991	300,000	291,367	8,633	818,712	5,818,712
May 1, 2008	300,000	256,808	43,192	92,972	5,092,972
Nov. 1, 2008	300,000	254,649	45,351	47,621	5,047,621
May 1, 2009	300,000	252,381	47,621*	—	5,000,000

* Rounding ($2 error due to rounding)

If the Karlton Company bonds were issued on May 1, 1989, at a premium of $857,956, representing a 10% effective-interest rate, a bond premium amortization schedule such as the one illustrated in Table 13-4 would be prepared. This table is prepared in the identical manner as the bond discount amortization schedule. Using this schedule, we would record the comparative entries for Nov. 1, 1989, Dec. 31, 1989, and May 1, 1990, as follows:

Bond payment and adjusting entries for bonds issued at a premium

		Method Used	
		Effective-Interest	Straight-Line
1989			
Nov. 1	Bond Interest Expense...	292,898	278,551
	Premium on Bonds Payable..................................	7,102	21,449
	Cash...	300,000	300,000
	To record payment of semiannual interest on bonds and amortization of bond discount.		
1989			
Dec. 31	Bond Interest Expense...	97,514	92,850
	Premium on Bonds Payable..................................	2,486	7,150
	Interest Payable..	100,000	100,000
	To record accrual of bond interest payable and amortization of bond premium ($7,457 × ⅔ for effective-interest method).		
1990			
May 1	Bond Interest Payable...	100,000	100,000
	Bond Interest Expense..	195,029	185,701
	Premium on Bonds Payable..................................	4,971	14,299
	Cash...	300,000	300,000
	To record the payment of semiannual interest on bonds and amortization of bond premium.		

Financial Statement Disclosure of Bonds Payable

Bonds payable must be disclosed at their face values adjusted by separate accounts for unamortized discounts or premiums

Generally accepted accounting principles require that we classify bonds payable on the balance sheet as long-term liabilities. As we have previously illustrated, bonds payable are reported at their face value plus or minus their unamortized discount or premium. In addition, information as to their interest rate, maturity date, interest payment dates, collateral, etc., must be shown either parenthetically next to the account titles on the balance sheet or in a footnote to the financial statements.

If the business entity has several bonds outstanding they may be reflected on the balance sheet as one total, but a supporting schedule providing detailed information on each bond must accompany the financial statements.

Current maturities of bonds payable are transferred to the current liabilities section of the balance sheet *if* they are to be settled by the expenditure of a current asset or creation of a new current liability. However, if settlement is to be made by expending a noncurrent asset or by issuing a new long-term obligation, the current maturity should remain in the long-term liabilities section. A footnote would be required explaining the method of settlement.

LONG-TERM LEASES

There are times when business entities find it more advantageous to lease buildings and equipment on a long-term basis rather than to purchase them. Many of these lease arrangements are fairly simple, requiring the party receiving the right to use the asset, the **lessee,** to record rent expense when the periodic lease payment is made. Upon the completion of the lease term, the lessee has the option of either entering into a new lease, or vacating the building or returning the equipment to the **lessor.**

In recent years, however, leases have become much more flexible and consequently much more complex. Accounting for these new leases has given the accounting profession a very interesting challenge. While legal title to the leased property may remain with the lessor, the terms of the lease may indicate that the *economic substance* of the transaction is in essence a purchase. For instance, the lease may allow the lessee to purchase the asset for a bargain price at the end of the lease term. Under these circumstances the appropriate accounting treatment may not be simply to debit Rent Expense and credit Cash.

Accounting is concerned with the economic substance of a transaction rather than the legal form

Where the economic substance of the lease transaction indicates that the lessee has the rights and benefits of ownership, we must account for the transaction by recognizing the future economic benefits of the asset and by recognizing the obligation of the liability. This is called *capitalizing* the lease.

Let's see how this capitalization works. Pegasus Airline enters into a lease arrangement on Jan. 1, 1989, with the Athens Leasing Company to lease an airplane for 10 years. The terms of the lease requires Pegasus to make payments of $3,655.57 to Athens Leasing at the end of each quarter. Interest is considered to be 8%. The useful life of the aircraft is estimated to be 10 years. We will assume that the terms of this lease arrangement require capitalization of the lease.

We will record the following 1989 entries for Pegasus Airline:

Capitalizing a lease

Jan. 1 Leased Equipment 100,000
          Obligation under Capitalized Lease   100,000
      To record a capitalized lease for an airplane. Lease terms require
      quarterly payments of $3,655.57.

On this date Pegasus received an asset, which must be recorded on the books at its fair value. This value is determined by computing the present value of an annuity of 40 quarterly payments at 8% per annum, or 2% per quarter. Using Table 13-2 (page 553), we determine the value as follows:

The present value of a 10-year lease at $3,655.57 per quarter. Interest worth 8%

$$P = \$3,655.57 \; P_{\overline{40}|2\%}$$
$$= \$3,655.57 \; (\underline{27.355479})$$
$$= \$100,000$$

As of Jan. 1, 1989, the $100,000 also represents Pegasus' long-term liability to Athens Leasing.

The first lease payment is to be made on Mar. 31, at which date the following entry is made:

The first lease payment

1989
Mar. 31 Obligation under Capitalized Lease 1,655.57
       Interest Expense 2,000.00
          Cash..   3,655.57
       To record lease payment due this date. Interest is equal to
       $2,000.00: (.02) × ($100,000).

We record Interest Expense in the amount of $2,000, which we can consider interest for the use of the $100,000 "borrowed" funds for the 3-month period. We then reduce the long-term liability by $1,655.57 ($3,655.57 − $2,000.00), representing a repayment of the "principal."

In a similar manner we record the other three payments for the year. The general journal entries for these three payments are summarized below:

	Date					
	June 30		**Sept. 30**		**Dec. 30**	
	Dr	Cr	Dr	Cr	Dr	Cr
Obligation under Capitalized Lease	1,688.68		1,722.45		1,756.90	
Interest Expense	1,966.89		1,933.12		1,898.67	
Cash		3,655.57		3,655.57		3,655.57
To record payment due.						

Lease payment entries

Interest expense is computed as follows:

June 30	($100,000.00 − $1,655.57)(.02).............................	$1,966.89
Sept. 30	($100,000.00 − $1,655.57 − $1,688.68)(.02)..................	1,933.12
Dec. 31	($100,000.00 − $1,655.57 − $1,688.68 − $1,722.45)(.02)........	1,898.67

At the end of the year, Pegasus must record depreciation on its leased equipment just as it does for equipment that it owns. The depreciation adjusting entry assuming straight-line depreciation would be recorded as follows:

Recording depreciation on leased equipment

Depreciation Expense on Leased Equipment......................... 10,000
    Accumulated Depreciation on Leased Equipment   10,000
To record depreciation on leased equipment of $100,000: ($100,000 ÷ 10).

COMPUTERLAND'S VALUABLE NOTE PAYABLE

ComputerLand is owned by the William H. Millard family. The Oakland, California company operates nearly 800 outlets all over the world. Prior to building the ComputerLand empire, Mr. Millard founded and operated another company called Information Management Science Associates, Inc. (IMS). That company created a manufacturing subsidiary that went bankrupt in 1979. Included among the $1.9 million of liabilities of the subsidiary was a $250,000 promissory note payable due in May of 1981. The note was issued to the Marriner & Co. venture capital group in 1976 to help keep IMS going. The promissory note was originally convertible into shares of IMS but an agreement signed by Mr. Millard granted Marriner

the right to convert the note into any other company Millard might establish.

Mr. Millard paid all the scheduled interest payments on the note until May 1981 when he attempted to pay off the principal amount of the note to Marriner & Co. Meanwhile the note was sold to Micro/Vest (for $300,000 plus another $100,000 payable if the note were eventually converted into stock) and this company informed Mr. Millard in March of 1981 that it intended to exercise the conversion provision and convert the note into 20% of ComputerLand's stock. Mr. Millard contended that the agreement was only temporary and that the note could only be converted into shares of IMS. The dispute went to court.

Micro/Vest sold shares in the note to dozens of outsiders including William Agee and Mary Cunningham formerly of the Bendix Corporation. Mr. Millard contended that these individuals had no interest in the case other than to buy shares in the outcome of the lawsuit. Micro/Vest contended that selling the shares in the note was necessary to finance the $1.3 million legal fees.

In early 1985 a jury in Oakland awarded Micro/Vest a 20% interest in ComputerLand plus $115 million in punitive damages.

Source: Michael Brody, "ComputerLand's Suddenly Poorer Boss," *Fortune,* Apr. 15, 1985. Copyright © 1985 by Time, Inc. All rights reserved.

In addition to bonds and leases, notes payable are often issued on a long-term basis. One such note issued by ComputerLand caused a considerable amount of controversy.

On the Dec. 31, 1989, balance sheet, Pegasus would show the capitalized lease as follows:

Plant, Property, and Equipment:		
Leased Asset	$100,000	
Less: Accumulated Depreciation on Leased Asset	10,000	$90,000

and the obligation would be presented like this:

Long-Term Liabilities:	
Obligations under Capitalized Lease	$93,176.40

This value was computed as follows:

Obligation on Jan. 1, 1989		$100,000.00
Reduction of obligations:		
Mar. 31	$1,655.57	
June 30	1,688.68	
Sept. 30	1,722.45	
Dec. 31	1,756.90	6,823.60
Obligation on Dec. 31, 1989		$ 93,176.40

CHAPTER SUMMARY

In this chapter we were concerned with the measurement and disclosure of, and accounting for, long-term liabilities. The decision to obtain long-term financing rests on many complex interrelated factors, not the least of which is the effect on net income per owner. Since bond interest payments must be paid when due, projected earnings after a bond issue has been made must be sufficient to provide each owner with a greater return than was received prior to the bond issue. If this is not the case, it may be more advantageous to obtain long-term financing by accepting additional owners.

Various types of bonds can be issued by a business entity seeking outside financing. The bonds can be *secured* or *unsecured, term* or *serial, callable* or *convertible.* Market conditions, the relative strength of the business entity at the time the bonds are to be issued, and the purpose for which the requested financing is to be used all are determining factors in selecting the type of bonds to be issued.

When bonds are issued, a contract between the issuing entity and a *trustee,* called a *bond indenture,* is prepared. The trustee, usually a large bank, acts as an agent for the bondholders.

Bonds may be issued at *par,* at a *discount,* or at a *premium.* The price paid for bonds is dependent on the *market rate of interest* at the time the bonds are issued. If the market rate is equal to the nominal rate called for in the bond contract, the bonds are issued at par. If, however, the market rate exceeds the nominal rate, the bonds will sell for a discount. Conversely, if the market rate is less than the nominal rate, the bonds will sell for a premium.

Given the market rate of interest, the price bonds sell for can be determined by the use of *present value techniques.* The price will be the sum of the present value of the face of the bond and the present value of the stream of contractual interest payments, both discounted at the market rate of interest.

The amount of discount or premium involved in the issuance of a bond must be amortized to periodic interest expense over the life of the bonds. Two accounting alternatives accomplish this process: the *effective-interest method* and the *straight-line method.* The straight-line method can be used only when the difference in results obtained under this method and under the effective-interest method is considered to be immaterial.

Bonds are more often than not sold between interest payment dates. In this case the price of the bonds will include the amount of accrued interest from the last interest payment date. At the end of the accounting period, bond interest must be accrued to achieve a proper matching of periodic expense and a recognition of the liability to pay interest due.

An alternative to long-term financing by means of bonds is by leasing. While legal title remains with the lessor, certain types of leases provide in substance the same rights and benefits to the lessee as to the owner of property. In these cases the appropriate accounting treatment requires that the lease be *capitalized.*

IMPORTANT TERMS USED IN THIS CHAPTER

Amortization The allocation process of writing off bond premiums or discounts to Interest Expense over the life of the bond issue. (page 548)

Bond indenture A contract between the business entity issuing bonds and the bondholders. Also called **deed of trust.** (page 544)

Callable bonds Bonds that may be redeemed by the issuing corporation prior to maturity. (page 545)

Convertible bonds Bonds that may be exchanged at the bondholders' option for an ownership interest in the business entity. (page 545)

Debenture bonds Bonds that are unsecured; they are issued on the general credit rating of the business entity. (page 544)

Deed of trust See **bond indenture.**

Effective-interest method The method used to amortize bond discounts and premiums over the life of the bond issue, by use of the interest rate in effect at the time the bonds were issued. (page 556)

Effective interest rate The interest rate found in the marketplace at the time bonds are issued. It is this rate that is used to determine the present value of a bond and to amortize bond discount and premiums. (page 556)

Face value of bonds The amount that will be paid to bondholders at the maturity date of the bonds. (page 544)

Investment banker An individual or firm that helps market a bond issue. Often known as an **underwriter.** (page 544)

Lease capitalization The recording of the present value of future lease payments as an asset and liability on the balance sheet. (page 561)

Nominal interest rate The rate of interest specified in the bond contract. (page 550)

Ordinary annuity A series of payments commencing 1 period hence and terminating at the end of the last period. (page 554)

Present value techniques The procedures for finding the value of money today under assumed rates of interest. (page 551)

Secured bonds Bonds that provide the bondholder with a claim on a specified asset in the event the business entity does not fulfill its responsibilities under the terms of the bond indenture. (page 544)

Serial bonds Bonds that mature at various successive dates over the life of the bond contract. (page 544)

Straight-line method A method used to amortize bond discounts or premiums evenly over the life of the bond issue. (page 556)

Term bonds Bonds that mature in total at the maturity dates specified in the bond contract. (page 544)

Trustee Typically, a bank acting as an agent for the bondholders that has entered into a contract with a business entity issuing bonds. (page 544)

Underwriter See **investment banker.**

Unsecured bonds See **debenture bonds.**

QUESTIONS

1. What are the advantages and disadvantages to the present owners of a business entity of obtaining additional financing by issuing bonds?

2. Distinguish between term and serial bonds; and convertible and callable bonds.

3. When a business entity issues bonds it incurs two separate liabilities. Explain.

4. How are bond prices determined?

5. What is the difference between accounting for bond premiums and discounts using the effective-interest method and the straight-line method?

6. Why must bond discounts or premiums be amortized?

7. How are bond discounts or premiums reflected on the balance sheet?

8. More often than not bonds are issued between interest payment dates. What accounting problems does this cause?

9. On June 1 the Dickens Company issues a $1,500,000, 10%, 20-year bond in a 12% market. The bonds are dated Apr. 1 and interest is payable semiannually.

   a. What is the face amount of the bonds?
   b. Did the bond sell for a premium or a discount?
   c. How much is the accrued interest on June 1, the date of issue?
   d. How much interest was paid on the first interest payment date?
   e. What is the nominal interest rate?
   f. What is the effective interest rate?
   g. What is the maturity value of the bond?
   h. Without prejudice to any previous answer, assume that the bond sold for a discount of $70,000. What would be the carrying value on the date of issue?

10. It really does not matter how a company amortizes bond premiums or discounts. The company can select either the effective-interest method or the straight-line method. Comment.

11. What is an ordinary annuity?

12. Several years ago the Irving Company issued a $100,000 bond. Interest is payable semiannually. The carrying value of the bond on Jan. 1 of the current year was $98,612. The amount of interest expense recorded for this year was $3,945, while the cash payment of interest was $3,500.

   a. Did the bonds initially sell for a premium or a discount?
   b. What is the carrying value of the bonds at the end of the current year?

13. What does the term capitalization mean when discussing a lease contract?

14. Assume that a lease contract requires capitalization of the asset at $100,000 and that an 8% interest factor was used to determine the present value of the lease payment. If the lease requires annual payments of $12,000 and the asset has a 10-year life, determine the amounts that will appear on the financial statements at the end of the first year of the lease.

EXERCISES

Exercise 13-1
Determining earnings per share under different capital structures

Courageous Company and Southern Cross, Ltd., each have Bonds Payable and Stockholders' Equity that totals $8,000,000. Courageous has $3,000,000 of Bonds Payable and Southern Cross $3,000,000 of Stockholders' Equity. Courageous has 250,000 shares outstanding and Southern Cross has 200,000. Assuming that the bonds were issued at par and have a 12% interest rate, and that income taxes are 40% of taxable income, determine the amount of earnings per share if income before bond interest expense is first $700,000, then $1,800,000.

(Check figure: At the $700,000 level, earnings per share, Southern Cross, Ltd. = $0.30)

Exercise 13-2
Determining bond selling prices

The Intrepid Company issues $4,500,000 of 14%, 20-year bonds on Oct. 1, 1989. Interest is paid on Oct. 1 and Apr. 1. Compute the price the bonds will sell for if the market rate is first 12%, then 16%.

(Check figure: At 16% = $3,963,060)

Exercise 13-3
Journal entries for bonds
issued at par

On May 1, 1989, the Constellation Company issued at par a $300,000, 20-year, 12% bond payable. Semiannual interest is paid on May 1 and Nov. 1 of each year. Prepare the general journal entries (without explanations) relating to the bond for the years 1989 and 1990.

Exercise 13-4
Journal entries for bonds
issued at a premium

On Apr. 1, 1989, the Columbia Corporation issued $900,000 of 10%, 20-year bonds receiving $924,000 cash. Interest is paid on Apr. 1 and Oct. 1 of each year. Prepare the general journal entries (without explanations) relating to the bond for the year 1989 using the straight-line method to amortize the premium.

Exercise 13-5
Bond discount
amortization schedule and
journal entries

The Weatherly Company issued $4,000,000 of $2\frac{1}{2}$-year, 11% bonds on Jan. 1, 1989, at a time when the market interest rate was 12%. The bonds sold for $3,915,753. Interest is payable semiannually. Prepare a bond premium amortization schedule (round to the nearest whole dollar) for the $2\frac{1}{2}$ years and the general journal entry (without explanation) to record the July 1, 1989, interest payment and discount amortization using the effective-interest method.

Exercise 13-6
Journal entries for bonds
issued between interest
payment dates

On Dec. 1, 1989, the Ranger Company issued $600,000 of 20-year, 12% bonds at par. The bonds were dated Oct. 1 and pay interest semiannually. Prepare the entry to record the issuance of the bonds, the Dec. 31, 1989, adjusting entry, and the Apr. 1, 1990, interest payment relating to the Ranger bonds.

Exercise 13-7
Journal entries for a
capitalized lease

Rainbow Corporation leases certain nautical equipment from Endeavour, Ltd. The lease must be capitalized due to the terms of the lease contract. The lease payments of $550 are to be paid to Endeavour at the end of every month for the next 3 years commencing 30 days from today's date, Oct. 1, 1989. Money is considered to be worth 12% and the equipment has an estimated life of 4 years. Prepare the entry to record the lease, to record the first payment (Oct. 31, 1989), and to record the depreciation of the leased asset on Dec. 31, 1989 (round to the nearest whole dollar).

(Check figure: Leased equipment = $16,559)

PROBLEMS: SET A

Problem A13-1
Earnings per share for
different capital structures

The stockholders of Martin Motors are considering expanding their business. They have decided that they will issue both additional stock and bonds such that their capital structure (the sum of the stockholders' equity and bonds payable) will total $30,000,000. The bonds will be issued at par value. Mr. Martin, the company president, feels that the best arrangement would be to issue $15,000,000 of 10% bonds, $5,000,000 of 12% bonds, and the remainder in stock. Mr. McCormack, the financial vice president, thinks that it would be better to issue only $8,000,000 of the 10% bonds, $7,000,000 of the 12% bonds, and have $15,000,000 in common stock. Under Mr. Martin's plan there would be 200,000 shares of stock outstanding while Mr. McCormack thinks that there should be 300,000 shares of stock. A 40% tax rate would apply to Martin Motors under either plan.

Required

1. Determine the amount of earnings per share under each plan for earnings before interest and taxes of $2,500,000 and $8,000,000.

(Check figure: At the $8,000,000 level, earnings per share under Mr. McCormack's plan = $12.72)

2. At what income level would the earnings per share be equal under both plans?

(Check figure: $3,020,000)

Problem A13-2
Journal entries for a bond issued between interest payment dates

O'Neil Products received permission from the Securities and Exchange Commission to issue at par $30,000,000 of 16%, 20-year bonds dated Nov. 1, 1989. The bonds were not issued until Dec. 1, 1989. Interest payment dates are Nov. 1 and May 1.

| *Required* |

Prepare without explanations all the general journal entries relating to the bond issue for the years 1989 and 1990. Include the year-end adjusting entries and closing entries for the interest expense.

Problem A13-3
Journal entries for a bond issued at a premium

On June 1, 1989, the Colfax Company issued $4,000,000 of 20-year, 12% bonds. Interest is paid semiannually on June 1 and Dec. 1 of each year. The bonds sold for $4,181,200. The Colfax Company follows the policy of amortizing bond premiums and discounts on the straight-line basis and on bond interest payment dates.

| *Required* |

Prepare without explanations the general journal entries for the year 1989 relating to the bond transactions.

(Check figure: Premium amortization per month = $755)

Problem A13-4
Journal entries for a bond issued at a discount

The Pennington Corporation, on May 1, 1989, issued $400,000, 12%, 10-year bonds receiving $389,200 cash proceeds on that date. Interest is payable semiannually on May 1 and Nov. 1. The bonds are due May 1, 1999.

| *Required* |

1. Prepare without explanations the general journal entries for the years 1989 and 1990 relating to the bond transactions assuming that the straight-line method of amortizing bond discounts is used and that the discount is amortized on bond interest dates.
2. How will the bonds be presented on the Dec. 31, 1990, balance sheet?

(Check figure: Unamortized discount = $9,000)

Problem A13-5
Effective-interest method: journal entries for a bond issued at a discount

The Trumbull Company received $2,200,097 on Apr. 1, 1989, for the issuance of $3,000,000, 20-year, 10% bonds dated Apr. 1, 1989. The bonds were sold in a 14% market and pay interest every 6 months. Trumbull uses the effective-interest method of amortizing bond discounts.

| *Required* |

Prepare without explanations the general journal entries for the years 1989 and 1990 relating to the bond issue.

(Check figure: Bond Interest Expense on Dec. 31, 1990 = $77,454)

Problem A13-6
Effective-interest method: journal entries for a bond issued at a premium

Winthrop Wingtip Shoes issued $1,500,000, 13%, 10-year bonds to yield 12% on Mar. 1, 1989, receiving $1,586,024 cash on that date. The bonds pay interest semiannually (Mar. 1 and Sept. 1). Winthrop uses the effective-interest method to amortize bond premiums.

| *Required* |

1. Prepare without explanations the general journal entries for 1989 and 1990 relating to the bond transactions.
2. How will the bonds be presented on the Dec. 31, 1989, balance sheet?

(Check figure: Unamortized bond premium = $76,720)

Problem A13-7
Determine bond selling prices

| *Required* |

Compute the bond selling prices for each of the following:
1. $4,000,000, 20-year, 11.5% bonds priced to yield 10% interest paid semiannually.
2. $2,500,000, 5-year, 17% bonds priced to yield 16% interest paid quarterly.
3. $4,500,000, 30-year 13.5% bonds priced to yield 12% interest paid annually.

(Check figures: 1. $4,514,570; 2. $2,583,938; 3. $5,041,913)

Problem A13-8
Journal entries for a
capitalized lease

On Sept. 1, 1989, Bankhead Data Service leased from Longworth Computers a model 720 computer under a lease that requires capitalization. Payments of $2,500 must be made at the end of every month for 3 years. The asset has an estimated economic life of 4 years and will be depreciated over that period of time. Interest of 12% is to be used for the capitalization.

Required

1. Prepare the general journal entries without explanations for the year 1989 pertaining to the lease for Bankhead Data Service. Round your answers to the nearest whole dollar.
2. What accounts pertaining to the lease will appear on the Dec. 31, 1989, financial statements?

(Check figure: Interest Expense = $2,965)

PROBLEMS: SET B

Problem B13-1
Earnings per share for
different capital structures

Due to a large increase in the demand of their product line, Little Rock Business Machines, Inc., is considering expanding their plant capacity by raising additional funds. The funds will come from several sources, a 20-year, 14% bond issue, a 10-year 16% bond issue, and a common stock issue. The amount of each issue is the subject of the Nov. 15, 1989, board of directors meeting. Ms. Patterson, the chairperson of the board, feels that $40,000,000 of financing is needed and is of the opinion that $15,000,000 should come from the 14% bonds, $10,000,000 from the 16% bonds, and the remainder from the stock which would result in a total of 350,000 shares of stock.

Mr. Williamson, the president of the company, feels that the total capitalization is fine but the mix is wrong. He would like to see the 14% bonds increased to $20,000,000, the 16% bonds increased to $15,000,000, and only $5,000,000 come from common stock. His plan would result in a total of 200,000 shares of stock.

Required

1. Compute the amount of earnings per share of common stock under each of the two plans assuming that earnings before interest and taxes (40%) are first $6,000,000; then assume the level increases to $20,000,000.

(Check figure: At the $6,000,000 level, under Ms. Patterson's plan, the earnings per share are $3.94)

2. At what income level would the earnings per share be equal under both plans?

(Check figure: $7,200,000)

Problem B13-2
Journal entries for a bond
issued between interest
payment dates

On Mar. 1, 1989, the Sacramento Company was authorized to issue at par $20,000,000 of 18%, 30-year bonds dated Mar. 1, 1989. However the bonds were not issued until May 1, 1989. Interest on the bonds is paid semiannually on Mar. 1 and Sept. 1.

Required

Record (without explanations) the general journal entries relating to the bond issue for the years 1989 and 1990 including the year-end adjusting and closing entries.

Problem B13-3
Journal entries for a bond
issued at a discount

The Denver Corporation issued $9,000,000 of 30-year 14% bonds on Apr. 1, 1989. Interest is payable semiannually on Apr. 1 and Oct. 1 of each year. The bonds sold for $8,940,000. Bond premiums and discounts are amortized on the straight-line basis and on bond interest payment dates by the Denver Corporation.

Required

Prepare without explanations the general journal entries for the year 1989 relating to the bond transactions.

(Check figure: Discount amortization, Dec. 31 = $500)

Problem B13-4
Journal entries for bonds
issued at a premium

The Hartford Corporation issued $3,000,000 of 16%, 20-year bonds on Feb. 1, 1989, receiving $3,180,000 on that date. Interest is payable on Feb. 1 and Aug. 1 of each year.

| Required |

1. Prepare without explanations the general journal entries for the years 1989 and 1990 relating to the bond issue assuming the straight-line method of amortizing bond premiums is used and that the bond premiums are amortized on interest payment dates.
2. How will the bonds be presented on the Dec. 31, 1990, balance sheet?

(Check figure: Unamortized premium = $162,750)

Problem B13-5
Effective-interest method:
journal entries for a bond
issued at a discount

Dover Dog Food, Inc., received $627,192 on May 1, 1989, for the issuance of $800,000, 20-year, 14% bonds dated May 1, 1989. The bonds were sold in an 18% market and pay interest semiannually. The company uses the effective-interest method of amortizing bond discounts.

| Required |

Prepare without explanations the general journal entries for the years 1989 and 1990 relating to the bond issue. Round your answers to the nearest whole dollar.

(Check figure: Bond Interest Expense on Dec. 31, 1990 = $18,860)

Problem B13-6
Effective-interest method:
journal entries for a bond
issued at a premium

On Apr. 1, 1989, the Tallahassee Times issued $1,000,000 of 10-year 15% bonds receiving $1,052,550. The bonds, which were dated Apr. 1, 1989 and pay interest semiannually, have an effective interest of 14%.

| Required |

1. Prepare the general journal entries without explanations for the years 1989 and 1990 relating to the bonds. Assume that the effective-interest method of amortizing bond premiums is used. Round your answers to the nearest whole dollar.
2. How will the bonds be presented on the Dec. 31, 1990, balance sheet?

(Check figure: Unamortized Bond Premium = $47,493)

| Required |

Problem B13-7
Determining bond selling
prices

For each of the following three independent cases you are to compute the bond selling prices:
1. $250,000, 5-year, 13% bond priced to yield 16%, interest is paid quarterly.
2. $450,000, 20-year, 15½% bond priced to yield 12%, interest is paid semiannually.
3. $800,000, 30-year, 15% bond priced to yield 15%, interest is paid annually.

(Check figures: 1. $224,419; 2. $568,379; 3. $800,000)

Problem B13-8
Journal entries for a
capitalized lease

Atlanta Airways entered into a lease contract with Honolulu Leasing Company on Oct. 1, 1989, for the lease of several aircraft. According to the terms of the lease the lease must be capitalized. On the last day of every month Atlanta Airways is required to pay Honolulu Leasing $1,200,000 for the next 4 years. The aircraft have an estimated economic life of 10 years. Interest of 12% is to be used for the capitalization.

| Required |

1. Without explanations prepare the general journal entries for the year 1989 pertaining to the lease for Atlanta Airways.
2. What accounts pertaining to the lease will appear on the Dec. 31, 1989, financial statements?

(Check figure: Interest Expense = $1,344,624)

DECISION PROBLEM

The Red River Petrochemical Company is considering acquiring an existing plant from the DinoSor Oil Company. The facility could be acquired for $12,000,000 by issuing that amount of common stock, corporate bonds, or by leasing the facility from the present owners.

| **Required** | What must the board of directors of Red River Petrochemical consider before deciding which alternative to select? |

CHAPTER 14

Corporations: Investments and Consolidations

Some of the things you should understand after you study this chapter are:

- The reasons that one corporation invests in stocks and bonds of other corporations
- How to account for investments in bonds at the time of acquisition, while the corporation owns them, and at the time of sale
- The cost, lower-of-cost-or-market, and equity methods of accounting for investments in stock
- The reasons for issuing consolidated financial statements
- The purchase method of accounting for the acquisition of a subsidiary
- How to prepare consolidated balance sheets under the purchase method on the date of acquisition
- What minority interest is and how it is reported on consolidated balance sheets and income statements

Anyone can buy stocks and bonds traded on the securities exchanges — corporations are no exception. Corporations have the right to own property. The word property is just another name for assets. An investment in bonds or stock is an asset just like merchandise inventory, land, or patents.

Corporations buying stocks and bonds through brokers are really buying the stocks and bonds from other investors. These previous owners have held the stocks or bonds for a time, earned dividends or interest on them, and are now selling them because they need cash for some purpose. Corporations may also buy stocks and bonds directly from another corporation that is issuing the securities. It is of no consequence to the investor corporation whether the stocks or bonds are purchased from previous owners or from the issuing corporation; the entries to account for the investment are exactly the same.

In Chapter 7 you learned about short-term investments in stocks and bonds. Excess cash that is expected to be only temporarily available is used to purchase these short-term investments.

In this chapter we will discuss long-term investments in bonds and stocks — the reasons for making these investments and how to account for them.

INVESTMENTS IN BONDS

Reasons for Investing in Bonds

Corporations often accumulate large amounts of cash for future expansion of manufacturing, warehousing, or sales facilities, or for a variety of other reasons. The cash, while it is being accumulated for its intended use, should be put to work earning a return for the corporation. A corporation may decide to invest in bonds for the following reasons:

1. Bonds pay a higher rate of interest over a longer period than do savings accounts or government securities.

2. Bonds are a safer investment than stocks. Interest must be paid to owners of bonds each year. Dividends on stock are paid to stockholders at the discretion of the board of directors of the company issuing the stock. Also, in case of liquidation, an owner of bonds (a creditor of the issuing corporation) will receive a higher priority in the distribution of assets than an owner of stock.

Accounting for Investments in Bonds

Bonds Purchased at Par

Bonds purchased at par value earn the printed rate of interest

When bonds are purchased at their par value, the interest we earn will be at the rate printed on the face of the bond. The interest we earn will also equal the amount of cash interest we receive. The way we record the purchase of bonds and the interest earned is shown in the following example.

KNAVE CUTLERY CO.

Knave Cutlery Co. purchased ten, $1,000, 18% bonds of Fizz Cola, Inc., on Jan. 1, 1989. The bonds pay interest on Dec. 31 and June 30 each year. Knave paid $10,000 for the bonds. Knave purchased the bonds through a securities exchange broker who acquired them from another individual. Knave did not buy the bonds from Fizz Cola.

Jan. 1	Investments in Bonds...................................	10,000	
	Cash...		10,000
	To record purchase of Fizz Cola bonds as a long-term investment.		
June 30	Cash..	900	
	Interest Income		900
	To record semiannual interest received on Fizz bonds ($10,000 × 18% × ½ year = $900).		

On Dec. 31, Knave will make an identical entry to the June 30 one. In fact, Knave will make this entry each June 30 and Dec. 31 as long as it owns the bonds.

Did you notice that Knave bought the bonds on the day after the interest had been paid to the previous owner of the bonds? This assumption made our illustration simple. Let's make it a little more complex by assuming that Knave buys these same bonds on Mar. 1, 1989.

If we buy bonds between interest dates, we must pay the previous owner the interest he has earned since the last interest payment date.

As the new owner of the bonds on the next interest payment date, we will receive cash for a full 6 months' interest. We must be careful to recognize as income only the amount we earn—the interest income for the time that we have owned the bonds.

Here are Knave's entries for bonds purchased between interest dates:

Entries for bonds bought between interest dates

Mar. 1	Investment in Bonds	10,000	
	Interest Receivable	300	
	Cash		10,300

To record purchase of Fizz Cola bonds as a long-term investment ($10,000 \times 18\% \times \frac{2}{12} = \$300$).

June 30	Cash	900	
	Interest Receivable		300
	Interest Income		600

To record semiannual interest received on Fizz bonds ($10,000 \times 18\% \times \frac{6}{12} = \$900$).

On Mar. 1 Knave bought two things: (1) $10,000 of Fizz Cola bonds, and (2) the right to receive $300 earned by the old owner. Knave didn't earn the $300, so Knave must be careful not to record it as income. Knave debited Interest Receivable for the $300 because Knave will receive this amount along with another $600 on June 30.

On June 30 when Knave receives the $900 from Fizz, $300 of it pays back Knave for the amount given to the old owner. $600 is earned by Knave for holding the bonds for 4 months ($10,000 \times 18\% \times \frac{4}{12} = \$600$).

On Dec. 31, 1989, Knave will debit Cash and credit Interest Income for $900. This entry will be made each 6 months for as long as Knave owns the bonds.

The diagram below will help you visualize the transactions we have illustrated and discussed.

	Dec. 31, 1988	March 1, 1989	June 30, 1989	Dec. 31, 1989
Cash interest	$900 interest received by old owner from Fizz	$300 interest paid to old owner by Knave	$900 interest received by Knave from Fizz	$900 interest received by Knave from Fizz
Interest earned	$900 interest (6 months) earned by old owner	$300 interest (2 months) earned by old owner	$600 interest (4 months) earned by Knave	$900 interest (6 months) earned by Knave

Bonds Purchased at a Discount or Premium

You learned in Chapter 13 that bonds are often issued at amounts below or above their par value. Let's review the reasons for the existence of discounts and premiums.

Bonds sell for less than par (a ***discount***) when the interest rate in the market—the rate paid by competing bonds—is higher than the rate printed on the bonds.

Bonds sell at a discount when the market rate of interest is higher than the printed rate

Knave would be foolish to pay the same price for Fizz Cola bonds paying 18% as for Hybrid, Inc.'s bonds paying 20%. To compensate, the Fizz Cola bonds will sell for less than par. The buyer of those bonds will still receive the par value when they mature. The difference between par and the selling price is the extra interest income earned by the investor.

Bonds sell at a premium when the market rate of interest is lower than the printed rate

Bonds sell for more than par (a *premium*) when the market rate of interest is lower than the rate printed on the bonds.

Assuming that Knave had bought the bonds when issued by Fizz, you can see that Fizz doesn't want to pay any higher rate than it has to. If the competing interest rate in the market is 16%, that's what Fizz is willing to pay. Since Fizz's printed rate is 18%, Fizz will simply charge the investor more for the bonds. Remember, the investor still receives only the par value at maturity. The extra amount paid by the investor serves to decrease the interest expense for Fizz and decrease the interest income earned by the investor.

Another thing you should remember from Chapter 13 is that we increase or decrease the interest each period by amortizing the discount or premium, respectively. You may also remember that there were two methods of amortization—straight-line and effective-interest.

Now let's use the Knave Cutlery Co. to illustrate accounting for discounts and premiums on investments in bonds.

Straight-Line Amortization of Discounts and Premiums

Assume that Knave Cutlery Co. purchased $300,000 (par value) of Comfort Corp. bonds maturing in 5 years. The bonds have a printed annual interest rate of 18%, which is paid semiannually on June 30 and Dec. 31.

The entries in parallel columns at the bottom of pages 576 and 577 show how Knave accounts for the bonds using straight-line amortization if they are purchased for $281,388 (a discount) or $320,070 (a premium).

There are some very important things you should learn from studying these entries:

Jan. 1   Knave records the investment in bonds at the amount paid. No separate discount or premium account is established. In Chapter 13 you did use a separate account. There is no theoretical reason for not using separate accounts—it's just customary not to use them for investments.

June 30 and Dec. 31   Knave receives $27,000 in cash because this amount is specified by the bond contract. The fact that the bonds were purchased at an amount other than par makes no difference.

The straight-line method amortizes the same amount of discount or premium each interest period

Knave determines the discount or premium to be amortized each period by dividing the total discount or premium by the number of 6-month periods remaining in the bond's life. The straight-line method amortizes the same amount each period.

Knave records amortization of the discount by debiting the Investment in Bonds account for $1,861.20 each period. Knave keeps doing this until the bonds mature or are sold. If Knave keeps the bonds until maturity, the Investment in Bonds account will be increased to par value—$300,000. Notice that the interest income recorded each period is more than the $27,000 cash received. This is logical—remember that when bonds are purchased at a discount, we earn a higher rate of interest (20%) than the printed rate (18%).

Knave records amortization of the premium by crediting the Investment in Bonds account. The effect of doing this over the 10 remaining periods will be to reduce the Investment account to $300,000. Interest income is less than the $27,000 cash received. This also makes sense—when we buy bonds at a premium we earn less interest (16%) than the printed rate (18%).

Effective-Interest Amortization of Discounts and Premiums The straight-line method amortizes an equal number of dollars each period and recognizes an equal amount of interest income each period. The effective-interest method recognizes interest income at the same rate each period but yields a different number of dollars each period.

You are already familiar with the effective-interest method from Chapter 13. The interest expense you recorded each period was calculated by multiplying the book value of the bonds at the beginning of the period by the effective interest rate. In this chapter you'll do essentially the same thing. To find the interest earned, multiply the balance in the Investment account at the beginning of the period by the effective interest rate.

Let's look at Knave's investment in those same Comfort Corp. bonds to see the effective-interest calculations and entries. (See top of pages 580 and 581.)

Again, let's highlight some important things you should learn from studying these entries:

Jan. 1 Knave records the purchase of bonds exactly the same way as when the straight-line method was used.

June 30 and Dec. 31 The $27,000 cash is still received at the end of each 6-month period.

Knave records the discount amortization by debiting the Investment account just as in the straight-line method. The amount is determined by:

The effective-interest method amortizes a different amount of discount or premium each interest period

1. Calculating interest income

$$\underset{\text{at beginning of period}}{\text{Balance of investment}} \times \text{effective interest rate} = \text{interest income}$$

Transaction	$300,000 Bonds Purchased at a *Discount* ($281,388) (effective interest rate = 20%)		
Jan. 1, 1990 Knave purchased Comfort bonds ($300,000 par) for cash	Investment in Bonds...................... Cash................................ To record purchase of Comfort bonds, par value = $300,000.	281,388.00	281,388.00
June 30, 1990 Knave received $27,000 semiannual interest ($300,000 × 18% × 6/12), and amortized the discount or premium	Cash..................................... Investment in Bonds...................... Interest Income .... To record receipt of semiannual interest and amortization of discount: Discount = $300,000 − $281,388 = Divide by number of periods (5 years × 2 periods per year) Amortization per period	27,000.00 1,861.20 $18,612.00 ÷ 10 $ 1,861.20	28,861.20
Dec. 31, 1990 Knave received $27,000 semiannual interest and amortized the discount or premium	Cash..................................... Investment in Bonds...................... Interest Income .... To record receipt of semiannual interest and amortization of discount.	27,000.00 1,861.20	28,861.20

2. Subtracting the cash received

Interest income − cash received = discount amortized

This procedure is repeated on Dec. 31. Remember, though, you must calculate a new Investment account balance before you determine the new interest income and amortization amounts.

Knave records the premium amortization by crediting the Investment account — this was also the same as we did for the straight-line method. The amounts of interest income and premium amortized are determined in the same way that we calculate them for discount amortization.

Knave's amortization of the discount or premium will bring the balance in the Investment account to $300,000 at the end of 5 years. So, the straight-line and effective-interest methods end up at the same place (a $300,000 balance); they just get there differently.

If Knave holds the bonds until they mature in 5 years, $300,000 will be received from Comfort. The following entry records this transaction:

Dec. 31	Cash	300,000
	Investment in Bonds..............................		300,000
	To record receipt of maturity value of Comfort Corp. bonds.	
	(We are assuming that Knave already recorded the 12/31/92	
	interest income and premium amortization.)	

Sale of Bond Investment

The sale of a bond investment before it matures is recorded by debiting the asset received (usually Cash), crediting Investment in Bonds for their carrying value, and debiting a loss (or crediting a gain).

$300,000 Bonds Purchased at a Premium ($320,070)
(effective interest rate = 16%)

Investment in Bonds	320,070	
Cash..		320,070
To record purchase of Comfort bonds, par value = $300,000.		

Cash..	27,000	
Investment in Bonds		2,007
Interest Income...		24,993
To record receipt of semiannual interest and amortization of premium:		

Premium = $320,070 − $300,000 =	$20,070
Divide by number of periods (5 years × 2 periods per year)	÷ 10
Amortization per period	$ 2,007

Cash..	27,000	
Investment in Bonds		2,007
Interest Income...		24,993
To record receipt of semiannual interest and amortization of		
premium.		

Let's use Knave again to illustrate. Assume that Knave bought the bonds for $320,070 on Jan. 1, 1990, and sold them for $312,500 on Jan. 1, 1991. The entry to record the sale is:

Bonds sold for more or less than their book value result in a gain or loss

1991			
Jan. 1	Cash...	312,500.00	
	Loss on Sale of Bonds	4,669.65	
	Investment in Bonds		317,169.65
	To record sale of Comfort bonds.		

Balance of Investment in Bonds on 1/1/91:

Cost 1/1/90	$ 320,070.00
Deduct premium amortized 6/30/90	(1,394.40)
Deduct premium amortized 12/31/90	(1,505.95)
Balance 1/1/91	$ 317,169.65

Loss on sale:

Sales price of investment................	$ 312,500.00
Deduct balance of investment 1/1/90.....	(317,169.65)
Loss on sale of investment	$ (4,669.65)

Losses and gains on sales of bonds are shown on the income statement as "Other Gains and Losses." Remember from Chapter 10 that losses and gains on the sale of long-lived assets (buildings, machinery, land) also are disclosed in this section of the income statement.

INVESTMENTS IN STOCK

Corporations may decide to purchase stock of other corporations for one or both of the following reasons:

Reasons for Investing in Stock

1. Investment

The corporation may wish to invest the cash it's accumulating for plant expansion or other reasons. Further, it may want to earn a higher rate of return than savings accounts, government securities, or even corporate bonds can offer. The corporation is willing to take a little more risk in exchange for higher earnings on its investment.

Common stocks are sometimes selected because their dividend payout rates are high or because their market values are expected to increase. The dividends received plus the increase in market value may be projected to be greater than the interest that could be earned by investing in interest-bearing securities such as bonds.

2. Acquisition

The corporation wants to acquire another corporation by purchasing its stock. Any one individual or entity that acquires enough voting stock of a corporation may elect a sufficient number of directors to significantly influence or even control the actions of the company. The ability to influence another corporation's actions may be especially important if that corporation supplies us with critical materials and supplies, or if it provides a crucial distribution system for our products. If the ownership percentage is high enough, the financial statements of the two corporations may be combined and treated as one entity for reporting purposes.

The next part of this chapter deals with accounting for investments in common stock. The remainder of the chapter is devoted to demonstrating the preparation of consolidated financial statements.

Accounting for Investments in Stock — The Cost Method

When less than 20% of another corporation is owned, the cost method is used

When the investor corporation is unable to exert significant influence over the actions of the investee corporation, the ***cost method*** of accounting, the mechanics of which are explained later, should be used. We presume that no significant influence exists when the investor owns less than 20% of the outstanding voting stock of the investee. The cost method is appropriate in those instances where a company is merely investing accumulated cash without attempting to acquire or control the investee.

The purchase of common stock, the receipt of dividends, and the disposal of the stock are three events typically encountered. The acquisition of stock should be recorded at cost, including brokerage fees and any other costs associated with the purchase. Cash and property dividends are recorded as income when declared by the board of directors of the investee corporation. The difference between the acquisition cost and the sale price of the investment is recognized as a gain or loss on the disposal of the investment. In the following example we will demonstrate the proper entries for each of these events.

Purchase of Stock Investment — Cost Method

The cost method records investments at cost

Robco, Inc., is setting aside $50,000 per year in a special fund for the modernization of its production facilities. The construction is expected to take place at the end of 5 years. In the meantime, the financial managers of Robco decide to invest the funds in common stocks. On June 15, 1990, Robco purchases 5,000 shares of Mammoth Motors Corporation stock, which is selling for $9.25 per share plus a broker's commission of $250. The 5,000 shares constitute 1% of Mammoth's 500,000 shares of outstanding stock. The entry to record the acquisition is:

June 15	Investment in Mammoth Motors Stock	46,500
	Cash		46,500
	To record acquisition of 5,000 shares at $9.25 per share plus a broker's commission of $250.	

Robco is purchasing stock on the open market (e.g., the New York or American Stock Exchange). The stock is not being acquired from Mammoth Motors but from another investor. Robco records the investment at cost without regard to the stock's par value, original issue price, or any other value.

Income on Stock Investment — Cost Method

The cost method recognizes income when dividends are received

On Oct. 1, the Mammoth board of directors declares a $0.25 per share quarterly dividend to stockholders of record on Oct. 15, payable Oct. 31. Robco's entries to record the dividend declaration and the receipt of the cash appear below:

Oct. 1	Dividends Receivable	1,250
	Dividend Income		1,250
	To record Mammoth's declaration of a $0.25 per share dividend [($0.25)(5,000 shares) = $1,250].	
31	Cash	1,250
	Dividends Receivable		1,250
	To record receipt of Mammoth Company dividend.	

	$300,000 Bonds Purchased at a *Discount* ($281,388) **(effective interest rate = 20%)**		

Jan. 1, 1990 Knave purchased Comfort bonds ($300,000 par) for cash	Investment in Bonds ....
	    Cash ....
	 To record purchase of Comfort bonds, par value = $300,000.
			281,388.00
			        281,388.00

June 30, 1990 Knave received semiannual interest ($300,000 × 18% × $\frac{6}{12}$), and amortized the discount or premium	Cash ....
	 Investment in Bonds ....
	    Interest Income........................
	 To record receipt of semiannual interest and amortization of discount:
	   Balance of investment
	     1/1/90....................
	   Effective interest rate
	     (20% × $\frac{6}{12}$).................
	   Interest income ....
	
	   Interest income ....
	   Less cash received..........
	   Discount amortized ....
		
		 $281,388.00
		
		 × 10%
		 $ 28,138.80
		
		 $ 28,138.80
		 (27,000.00)
		 $ 1,138.80
			27,000.00
			 1,138.80
			        28,138.80

Balance in the Investment account 7/1/90	Balance 1/1/90 .... Discount amortized .... Balance 7/1/90	$281,388.00 + 1,138.80 $282,526.80	

Dec. 31, 1990 Knave received $27,000 semiannual interest and amortized the discount or premium	Cash ....
	 Investment in Bonds ....
	    Interest Income........................
	 To record receipt of semiannual interest and amortization of discount:
	   Balance of investment
	     7/1/90....................
	     Effective interest rate ....
	   Interest income ....
	
	   Interest income ....
	   Less cash received..........
	   Discount amortized ....
		
		 $282,526.80
		 × 10%
		 $ 28,252.68
		
		 $ 28,252.68
		 (27,000.00)
		 $ 1,252.68
			27,000.00
			 1,252.68
			        28,252.68

The dividend income is recorded when the dividend is declared. It is on this date that the Mammoth board incurred a liability to pay the dividend and thus Robco is assured of receiving it.

On Nov. 5, Mammoth declares and issues a 20% stock dividend. Robco prepares a memorandum entry noting that additional shares are received. No income is recognized because no assets are distributed. Robco has more "pieces of paper" to represent the same 1% ownership interest. Robco now owns 6,000 of the 600,000 outstanding shares of Mammoth stock—still 1%. Robco prepares the following memorandum entry:

Nov. 5   Received 1,000 shares of Mammoth Motors common stock as the company's share of a 20% stock dividend.

$300,000 Bonds Purchased at a *Premium* ($320,070)
(effective interest rate = 16%)

Investment in Bonds	320,070.00	
Cash		320,070.00
To record puchase of Comfort bonds, par value = $300,000.		

Cash	27,000.00	
Investment in Bonds		1,394.40
Interest Income................................		25,605.60

To record receipt of semiannual interest and amortization
of premium:

Bond investment 1/1/90	$320,070.00
Effective interest rate (16% × $\frac{6}{12}$)	× 8%
Interest income	$ 25,605.60

Interest income	$ 25,605.60
Less cash received....................	(27,000.00)
Premium amortized..................	$ (1,394.40)

Balance 1/1/90	$320,070.00
Premium amortized....................	− 1,394.40
Balance 7/1/90	$318,675.60

Cash	27,000.00	
Investment in Bonds		1,505.95
Interest Income................................		25,494.05

To record receipt of semiannual interest and amortization
of premium:

Balance of investment 7/1/90	$318,675.60
Effective interest rate	× 8%
Interest income	$ 25,494.05

Interest income	$ 25,494.05
Less cash received....................	(27,000.00)
Premium amortized..................	$ (1,505.95)

Robco's total cost of $46,500 or $9.30 per share ($46,500 ÷ 5,000 shares) should now be distributed over 6,000 shares. The average cost of the Mammoth Motors stock is now $7.75 per share ($46,500 ÷ 6,000).

On Dec. 31, 1990, Mammoth Motors reports a net income of $780,000 ($1.30 per share). This information is of interest to Robco since it reflects how well Mammoth is performing. No journal entries are made by Robco to record this information since no income has been received. *The cost method recognizes income only upon the declaration of dividends by the investee.*

Sale of Stock Investment—Cost Method

On Mar. 1, 1991, Robco sells 1,200 shares of Mammoth stock at $8 per share less brokerage fees of $115. This disposal is recorded by the following entry:

Shares of stock may be sold for more or less than their cost resulting in a gain or loss

Mar. 1	Cash [($8 × 1,200 shares) − $115]............................	9,485
	Investment in Mammoth Motors Stock	
	($7.75 × 1,200 shares).....................................	9,300
	Gain on Sale of Mammoth Motors Stock....................	185
	To record the sale of 1,200 shares of Mammoth stock having a book value of $7.75 per share for $8.00 per share.	

Remember that following the stock dividend each share of Mammoth now has a cost basis of $7.75; therefore, the sale of 1,200 shares requires a credit to the Investment account of $9,300 (1,200 × $7.75). The difference between the cost and the net proceeds received is recorded as a gain or loss.

Lower-of-Cost-or-Market on Stock Investment—Cost Method

Lower-of-cost-or-market must be applied when the cost method is used

Robco's fiscal year ends on Apr. 30 each year. At this time the **lower-of-cost-or-market procedure** is applied to long-term investments in stocks as well as to the temporary investments in stocks we discussed in Chapter 7. Robco finds the total cost and the total market value of the group of stocks that it owns. If market value is below cost, the investment is reported on the balance sheet at this lower amount. No income statement loss is recognized, however, unless the decline in market value appears to be permanent. Assuming that the 4,800 shares (6,000 bought less 1,200 sold) of Mammoth Motors stock is Robco's only investment, the following entry is appropriate:

Cost of Mammoth shares on hand: 4,800 shares × $7.75 cost basis per share..	$37,200
Deduct: Market value of Mammoth shares on hand: 4,800 shares × $7.50 quoted market price (net of selling commissions) on Apr. 30, 1991	36,000
Unrealized loss	$ 1,200

Apr. 30	Unrealized Loss on Long-Term Investment in Stock	1,200
	Allowance to Reduce Long-Term Investment in	
	Stock to Market Value	1,200
	To record the fact that the market value of long-term investments in stock is $1,200 less than cost.	

Long-term investments would appear on Robco's balance sheet as follows:

Long-Term Investment:	
Investment in Stock (cost)...	$37,200
Less: Allowance to Reduce Investment in Stock to Market Value	(1,200)
Investment in Stock at Lower-of-Cost-or-Market.......................	$36,000

The unrealized loss is reported as a *negative* stockholders' equity account. This account may be shown among the additional paid-in capital accounts (Paid-In Capital in Excess of Par, Donated Capital, etc.) as a deduction.

Accounting for Investments in Stock — The Equity Method

The equity method is used when more than 20% of the stock of another corporation is owned

When an investor corporation exerts significant influence over the investee corporation, the *equity method* of accounting is used. We presume that the investor exerts significant influence when he acquires 20% or more of the investee's stock. If he has sufficient votes to elect members to the investee's board of directors, if he exchanges management personnel with the investee, or if he enters into substantial transactions with the investee, we say that these are further indications of significant influence.

The equity method accounts for the acquisition of stock at cost; recognizes income (or loss) as it is earned by the investee; reduces the Investment account when dividends are received; and records a gain or loss upon disposal of the stock. The following example will illustrate the equity method.

Purchase of Stock Investment — Equity Method

The equity method records investments at cost

On Jan. 1, 1989, Gracewill Corporation purchases 40,000 of the 100,000 outstanding shares of Sibyll, Inc., for $816,000, including all brokerage fees and taxes. The entry to record the acquisition is:

Jan. 1	Investment in Sibyll, Inc., Stock	816,000	
	Cash		816,000
	To record purchase of 40,000 shares (40%) of Sibyll, Inc., stock.		

We record the investment at cost just as we would if we were using the cost method.

Income on Stock Investment — Equity Method

The equity method recognizes income as it is earned by the investee

On Dec. 31, 1989, Sibyll reports a net income of $240,000. Under the equity method Gracewill recognizes 40% of these earnings at the time reported by Sibyll — not at the time Sibyll distributes them as dividends. Since the investor may exert significant influence over the investee, the investor may be able to control when dividends are paid and how much is distributed. If income were recognized by the investor at the time dividends were declared, the investor could possibly manipulate his net income by regulating the dividend declarations of the investee. *The equity method eliminates the possibility for manipulation by requiring the investor to recognize income (or loss) when it is earned by the investee.* Gracewill records its share of Sibyll's 1989 income as follows:

Dec. 31	Investment in Sibyll, Inc., Stock	96,000	
	Income from Investment in Sibyll, Inc.		96,000
	To record 40% equity in the $240,000 net income of Sibyll, Inc.		

Since Sibyll earned a $240,000 net income during 1989, its net assets (total assets minus total liabilities) increased by $240,000 and stockholders' equity (retained earnings) increased by $240,000. If Gracewill's Investment account is to continue to reflect a 40% equity in Sibyll's net assets, Gracewill's Investment account must be increased by $96,000 (40% of $240,000).

If a net loss is reported by the investee, the decrease in net assets is recorded by the investor by debiting a loss account and crediting (reducing) the Investment account.

Dividends from Investee — Equity Method

On Jan. 2, 1990, Sibyll, Inc., declares a $0.50 per share dividend. The dividend will be paid on Jan. 15 to stockholders of record on Jan. 7. Declaration and distribution of a cash or property dividend reduces the net assets of the investee. The investor, then, reduces the Investment account to record this fact. Also, since Gracewill records income when it is earned by Sibyll, any further income recognition when dividends are distributed would constitute double counting. Gracewill prepares the following entries to record the declaration and receipt of the dividend:

<table>
<tr><td rowspan="4" style="width:25%">When dividends are declared by an investee, the equity method requires that the Investment account be reduced</td><td>Jan. 2</td><td>Dividends Receivable ....</td><td>20,000</td><td></td></tr>
<tr><td></td><td style="padding-left:2em">Investment in Sibyll, Inc., Stock.........................</td><td></td><td>20,000</td></tr>
<tr><td></td><td>To record declaration of a $0.50 per share dividend by investee ($0.50 × 40,000 shares = $20,000).</td><td></td><td></td></tr>
<tr><td></td><td></td><td></td><td></td></tr>
</table>

Jan. 2   Dividends Receivable   20,000
         Investment in Sibyll, Inc., Stock.........................   20,000
    To record declaration of a $0.50 per share dividend by investee
    ($0.50 × 40,000 shares = $20,000).

Jan. 15   Cash   20,000
         Dividends Receivable   20,000
    To record receipt of cash dividend from Sibyll, Inc.

We handle stock dividends under the equity method exactly as we did under the cost method. A memorandum entry is sufficient to note the fact that additional shares of stock have been received. The ownership percentage and the equity in the net assets of the investee remain unchanged.

Sale of Stock Investment — Equity Method

An investor may sell some shares of the investee but still have a high enough ownership percentage to exercise significant influence. In such cases we determine the carrying value per share of the investment and record the difference between this carrying value and the selling price of the stock as a gain or loss.

When stock is sold for more or less than its carrying value, a gain or loss is recorded

On Jan. 17, 1990, Gracewill disposes of 10,000 shares of Sibyll at $23 per share. This transaction is recorded as follows:

Jan. 17   Cash ($23 × 10,000 shares)   230,000
         Investment in Sibyll, Inc., Stock......................   223,000
         Gain on Sale of Investment   7,000
    To record the sale of 10,000 shares of Sibyll, Inc.

The carrying value per share of investment is calculated as follows:

Acquisition cost..	$816,000
Portion of 1989 income......................................	96,000
Less dividends received	(20,000)
Balance of Investment account	$892,000
Divide by number of shares owned...........................	÷ 40,000 shs
Carrying value per share owned.............................	$ 22.30
Number of shares sold	× 10,000 shs
Carrying value of shares sold	$223,000

McLOUTH SETTLES EQUITY ACCOUNTING SUIT FILED BY SEC

(Believed the first of its kind)

The Securities and Exchange Commission accused McLouth Steel Corp. of incorrectly using the equity method of accounting in its financial statements. It is believed to be the first suit of its kind.

The SEC also accused the Detroit company of other accounting irregularities that the commission said resulted in overstated earnings and understated losses. The maker of flat-rolled steel products settled the charges by agreeing to a court order barring future violations of antifraud and periodic reporting sections of federal securities law. In settling the charges, the company didn't admit or deny wrongdoing.

The SEC suit, combined with a statement last month by the Financial Accounting Standards Board, will make it tougher for companies to use the equity method. Under that accounting procedure, if a company buys more than 20% of another concern and exercises "significant influence" over that concern, the investment company can include a prorated portion of the other company's earnings in its financial statements.

The SEC charged that although McLouth held 19.87% of Jewell Coal & Coke Co. the company didn't exercise significant influence over Jewell and shouldn't have included any of Jewell's profit in its financial statements between 1974 and 1978.

The commission cited a variety of factors to support its contention. The commission said that McLouth had tried and failed to get representation on Jewell's board and that Jewell had ignored McLouth's wishes on several significant corporate matters.

The FASB, elaborating last month on its 10-year-old equity accounting opinion, said those factors and others should be considered in deciding whether a company could use the equity method.

Companies often file stock-ownership reports with the SEC indicating that they plan to buy 20% of another company and to use the equity accounting method. But the SEC and the FASB are making it clear that the stock ownership alone isn't enough.

Sheldon Goldfarb, a SEC lawyer, said he believed the McLouth case was the first to raise this issue. He added that it was "significant" because companies filing stockownership reports will "have to look a little more closely" at whether they can use the equity methods.

The SEC said, for example, that McLouth hadn't been able to persuade Jewell to drop plans to spin off its coal operation from its coke manufacturing business.

And it took a suit, which eventually was settled, to get Jewell to increase its dividends, as McLouth wanted, the commission said.

The commission also said that McLouth failed to disclose that after the price of coke rose sharply in 1970, McLouth had to sue to force Jewell to continue to supply coke under a 10-year contract. The suit also was settled.

If McLouth hadn't used the equity accounting method, it could have included in its financial statements only the dividends that Jewell distributed. In 1975, the difference between the two procedures was $3.5 million or 55% of McLouth's pretax earnings, the SEC said.

McLouth sold its Jewell shares in 1978, the SEC said.

As part of the settlement McLouth agreed to have independent directors on its audit committee to review the company's internal accounting controls and accounting methods.

Source: The Wall Street Journal, June 18, 1981, page 7.

In our discussion of the cost and equity methods we mentioned that the equity method should be used only when the investor company exerts significant influence over the investee company. In this article you can see that the McLouth company management apparently used the equity method to recognize profits for its investment in Jewell Co. even though there was a great deal of tangible evidence that significant influence did not exist. The effect of this misapplication of the equity method was to overstate income.

The SEC felt that McLouth should have been using the more conservative cost method of accounting for its investment in Jewell Co. The cost method would have required McLouth to wait until dividends were declared by Jewell before recognizing profit.

Misapplication of generally accepted accounting principles may result in financial information that can be misleading to the investing public. One of the tasks of the SEC is to enforce the fair presentation of financial information.

If the ownership drops below 20%, or if significant influence ceases to exist for some other reason, the investor converts to the cost method of accounting for future periods.

The authoritative financial accounting standard covering marketable equity securities states that lower-of-cost-or-market is not appropriate when the investment is accounted for by the equity method. This makes sense—we are not carrying the investment at cost.

The Cost and Equity Methods Contrasted

The table below highlights the similarities and differences in accounting for long-term investments in stock by the cost and equity methods.

The Cost and Equity Methods Compared

Event	Cost Method	Equity Method
1. Common stock in another corporation is purchased.	Record at cost including brokerage and other fees.	Record at cost including brokerage and other fees.
2. Income (or loss) is reported by the investee.	No entry.	Record a portion of the investee's income or loss. The portion recorded is determined by the percentage of the investee we own.
3. End-of-year market price quotations are available for the investee's stock.	Apply the lower-of-cost-or-market method for the long-term investment.	No action is necessary. Lower-of-cost-or-market is not used.
4. Investee declares a cash or property dividend.	Record dividend income.	Record reduction in Investment account.
5. Investee declares a stock dividend.	Prepare memorandum entry noting the number of shares received.	Prepare memorandum entry noting the number of shares received.
6. Investor sells shares of investee.	Record difference between proceeds and cost per share as a gain or loss.	Record difference between proceeds and carrying value per share as a gain or loss.

CONSOLIDATED FINANCIAL STATEMENTS

The Parent and Subsidiary Relationship

When one corporation owns more than 50% of the stock of another, a parent–subsidiary relationship exists

If Corporation P owns a large enough percentage of the stock of Corporation S, it may not only exert significant influence over Corporation S—it may effectively control the activities of Corporation S. When this situation exists, the controlling corporation is referred to as the **parent** and the corporation being controlled is called the **subsidiary.** A parent and subsidiary relationship is generally assumed when one corporation owns more than 50% of the outstanding common stock of another.

How does P control S? Remember that each share of common stock we own gives us a vote in the election of the members of the board of directors. If P owns more than 50% of S, P can elect all of the people it wants to S's board. The S board members elected by P (and loyal to P) can then set operating policies and hire the managers to run S. P controls S.

The parent and subsidiary companies are separate legal entities. They may be in different industries, and from all outward appearances they may seem to have no relationship at all to each other. An investor purchasing shares in the parent company is really acquiring indirect ownership interest in one or more subsidiary companies as well. The investor must rely on the financial statements published by the parent to disclose the financial position and operating results of all corporations under the parent's control.

Since the parent owns more than 20% of the stock in each subsidiary corporation, the equity method of accounting is used to account for the investment in the parent company records. The equity method will yield a single amount on P's balance sheet, Investment in Subsidiary Corporation, and a single amount on P's income statement, Income from Investment in Subsidiary Corporation. These two individual amounts do not provide information about the subsidiary's various assets, liabilities, revenues, and expenses.

Investors' decisions may be influenced by the composition of the subsidiary's assets and liabilities. Some of the questions we might ask as investors include: Are the assets composed primarily of cash, receivables, and inventories, or do plant and equipment assets predominate? Are liabilities primarily current or long-term? What assets are pledged as collateral for liabilities?

We may also be curious about the subsidiary's revenues and expenses. Are revenues primarily from merchandise sales, or do disposals of nonoperating assets and miscellaneous income items play a major role? How significant is cost of goods sold expense in relation to administration and selling costs?

Consolidated financial statements show the parent and subsidiary companies as a single economic entity

Consolidated financial statements provide the investor with more information about the composition of subsidiary and parent financial reports. *Consolidated financial statements* are an attempt to portray the parent and subsidiary companies as a *single economic entity.* A single consolidated balance sheet shows all of the assets and liabilities of the parent and all subsidiary companies. A single consolidated income statement likewise discloses the revenues and expenses of the parent and all subsidiary companies.

The consolidation process may be accomplished by using the purchase or the pooling-of-interests method. The *purchase method* is used when a parent acquires the subsidiary's stock by using cash, other assets, or debt securities. The purchase method is also used if the subsidiary is acquired by exchanging the parent's stock for the subsidiary's stock *and* less than 90% of the subsidiary's stock is acquired. The *pooling method* is used when 90% or more of a subsidiary is acquired by an exchange of parent company stock for subsidiary stock *and* a number of other conditions are satisfied. In the business world, far more consolidations are accomplished using the purchase method.

We will demonstrate the basics of the purchase method in the remainder of this chapter. The pooling method and complex applications of the purchase method will be left for a more advanced accounting course.

Consolidation on the Date of Acquisition—100% Ownership

There are two important things you must understand about combining financial statements when one company *purchases* another:

The subsidiary's assets appear on the consolidated balance sheet at their fair market value

1. The subsidiary's assets are placed on the consolidated balance sheet at their cost to the parent corporation. When the parent company buys the assets of the subsidiary, it must pay the fair market value for these assets. This fair market value is the parent's cost.

   The parent's cost will probably be different from the carrying value on the books of the subsidiary company. Remember that the subsidiary's asset carrying value is its original cost (or its original cost minus accumulated depreciation). The market value of these assets may have changed substantially since the subsidiary acquired them.

   If the parent pays more for the subsidiary's assets than the total of their individual fair market values, the parent has purchased goodwill. This goodwill must also appear on the consolidated balance sheet.

The subsidiary's income earned after acquisition is consolidated

2. The subsidiary's income is combined with the parent's on the consolidated income statement (but only subsidiary income after acquisition). Revenues and expenses incurred by the subsidiary *before* the acquisition date are *not* included in determining the combined net income.

These two points are very logical if you remember that the purchase method assumes that one company is *buying* another at a point in time. The accounting, then, is similar to what we do when we buy any asset—record it at acquisition cost, and recognize profit that it earns only after we buy it.

The following illustration will show you how to prepare a consolidated balance sheet on the day the subsidiary is acquired. We don't have to be concerned with a consolidated income statement on the day of acquisition. A consolidated income statement on the day of acquisition is just a parent company statement, because the subsidiary's earnings up to the day of acquisition are not included.

Parent Company (Company P) acquired all of the outstanding stock of Subsidiary Company (Company S) on Jan. 1, 1990, for $100,000. The individual condensed balance sheets of Company P and Company S immediately after the acquisition are shown in Exhibit 14-1.

What did Company P buy for $100,000? An examination of Company S's balance sheet reveals that the *net assets* (assets minus liabilities) purchased have a carrying value of $85,000 ($125,000 − $40,000). Company P paid $15,000 in excess of the carrying value. We may attribute this $15,000 to the fact that S's carrying value of certain assets may be less than their market value. Or P may have purchased goodwill, an asset possessed by Company S but not listed on its balance sheet. In most cases both undervalued assets and goodwill exist.

EXHIBIT 14-1

<table>
<tr><td colspan="4" align="center">**COMPANY P AND COMPANY S**
Condensed Balance Sheets
January 1, 1990</td></tr>
<tr><td colspan="2" align="center">**Company P**</td><td colspan="2" align="center">**Company S**</td></tr>
<tr><td>Assets:</td><td></td><td>Assets:</td><td></td></tr>
<tr><td> Current Assets (total).....</td><td>$ 500,000</td><td> Current Assets (total).....</td><td>$ 50,000</td></tr>
<tr><td> Investment in S ....</td><td>100,000</td><td> Property, Plant, and</td><td></td></tr>
<tr><td> Property, Plant, and</td><td></td><td>   Equipment Assets (net)..</td><td>75,000</td></tr>
<tr><td>   Equipment Assets (net)..</td><td>1,000,000</td><td></td><td></td></tr>
<tr><td></td><td></td><td> Total Assets..............</td><td>$125,000</td></tr>
<tr><td> Total Assets..............</td><td>$1,600,000</td><td></td><td></td></tr>
<tr><td>Equities:</td><td></td><td>Equities:</td><td></td></tr>
<tr><td> Current Liabilities ....</td><td>$ 180,000</td><td> Current Liabilities ....</td><td>$ 5,000</td></tr>
<tr><td> Long-Term Liabilities....</td><td>520,000</td><td> Long-Term Liabilities....</td><td>35,000</td></tr>
<tr><td> Common Stock ....</td><td>700,000</td><td> Common Stock ....</td><td>60,000</td></tr>
<tr><td> Retained Earnings ....</td><td>200,000</td><td> Retained Earnings ....</td><td>25,000</td></tr>
<tr><td> Total Equities ....</td><td>$1,600,000</td><td> Total Equities ....</td><td>$125,000</td></tr>
</table>

Assume that an appraisal of Company S's assets shows land with a market value that is $5,000 higher than its carrying value. All other assets' market and carrying values are the same. We assume that the remaining $10,000 excess payment ($15,000 − $5,000) is for goodwill—we can't identify any other asset that we purchased.

Now that we have determined the market value of the various assets and the amount of goodwill, we can combine the balance sheets. We accomplish this combination by:

Steps in combining balance sheets on the date of acquisition using the purchase method

STEP 1: Eliminating the Investment account found on the parent company's balance sheet and the stockholders' equity accounts on the subsidiary's balance sheet. Any difference between these two amounts will be taken care of by steps 2 and 3 below.

STEP 2: Adding (or deducting) appropriate amounts to adjust all subsidiary assets and liabilities to their fair values.

STEP 3: Entering goodwill to account for any difference not explained by market value adjustments in step 2.

EXHIBIT 14-2

COMPANIES P AND S
Consolidated Balance Sheet—Purchase Method Worksheet
Time of Acquisition—100% Ownership
January 1, 1990

Accounts	Company P	Company S	Adjustments and Eliminations	Consolidated Balance Sheet
Assets:				
Current Assets	$ 500,000	$ 50,000		$ 550,000
Investment in S	100,000		(a) $(100,000)	
Goodwill			(b) + 10,000	10,000
Property, Plant, & Equip.	1,000,000	75,000	(c) + 5,000	1,080,000
Total Assets	$1,600,000	$125,000	(e) $ (85,000)	$1,640,000
Equities:				
Current Liabilities	$ 180,000	$ 5,000		$ 185,000
Long-Term Liabilities	520,000	35,000		555,000
Common Stock	700,000	60,000	(d) $ (60,000)	700,000
Retained Earnings	200,000	25,000	(d) (25,000)	200,000
Total Equities	$1,600,000	$125,000	(e) $ (85,000)	$1,640,000

Columns above are headed "Individual Company Balance Sheets" spanning Company P and Company S.

(a) The Investment account is eliminated. It is being replaced by S's various assets and liabilities.
(b) Goodwill is added because Company P paid $10,000 more for Company S's assets than their fair market value.
(c) $5,000 must be added because S's land was undervalued. Company P paid fair market value for the land.
(d) Company S's Common Stock and Retained Earnings are eliminated. The stockholders' equity accounts of Company P reflect the ownership of the consolidated entity.
(e) Note that asset adjustment total equals equity adjustment total.

The worksheet in Exhibit 14-2 illustrates this procedure.

Intercompany accounts are eliminated

Intercompany accounts may exist between a parent and a subsidiary. We must eliminate (offset) these against each other in the consolidation process. For example, if Company P had loaned Company S $10,000 during 1989, Company P would have a $10,000 receivable on its balance sheet and Company S would have a $10,000 payable on its balance sheet. This transaction gives the consolidated entity no right to receive cash from an outside party, nor does it create an obligation to pay an outside party. The consolidated entity owes itself $10,000. We take care of this illogical situation by removing both the receivable and payable in preparing the consolidated balance sheet.

Consolidation on the Date of Acquisition—Less than 100% Ownership

When the parent owns less than 100% of a subsidiary, a minority interest exists

When one company buys less than 100% of the stock of another, a ***minority interest*** exists. In most cases ownership of more than 50% of the subsidiary's stock will give the parent control and necessitate the preparation of consolidated financial statements. The individuals and corporations, other than the parent, who own stock in the subsidiary still have a claim against the subsidiary's assets—a minority interest. We show this minority interest in the stockholders' equity or liabilities section of the consolidated balance sheet. We must also identify part of all future consolidated income as belonging to minority shareholders.

Let's repeat the Company P and Company S illustration assuming that Company P purchased only 90% of Company S stock for $100,000. All other facts of the example are the same. The new worksheet is shown in Exhibit 14-3 below.

EXHIBIT 14-3

COMPANIES P AND S Consolidated Balance Sheet — Purchase Method Worksheet Time of Acquisition — 90% Ownership January 1, 1990				
Individual Company Balance Sheets				
Accounts	**Company P**	**Company S**	**Adjustments and Eliminations**	**Consolidated Balance Sheet**
Assets:				
Current Assets	$ 500,000	$ 50,000		$ 550,000
Investment in S	100,000		$(100,000)	
Goodwill			(a) + 19,000	19,000
Property, Plant, & Equip.	1,000,000	75,000	+ 4,500	1,079,500
Total Assets	$1,600,000	$125,000	$ (76,500)	$1,648,500
Equities:				
Current Liabilities	$ 180,000	$ 5,000		$ 185,000
Long-Term Liabilities	520,000	35,000		555,000
Common Stock	700,000	60,000	(b) $ (60,000)	700,000
Retained Earnings	200,000	25,000	(b) (25,000)	200,000
Minority Interest:				
Common Stock			(b) + 6,000	6,000
Retained Earnings			(b) + 2,500	2,500
Total Equities	$1,600,000	$125,000	$ (76,500)	$1,648,500

(a) Goodwill is greater than in Exhibit 14-2 because Company P is paying the same amount for a smaller portion of Company S's net assets.

(b) 10% of Company S's Common Stock and Retained Earnings is transferred to minority interest. Minority Interest appears on the published statement as one amount, $8,500.

We now assume that Company P is paying $100,000 for 90% of the $85,000 net assets of Company S. Since the same price is paid for less equity in Company S, Company P must be purchasing more goodwill. The revised calculation of goodwill follows.

Calculation of goodwill

Purchase price of 90% of Company S	$100,000
Deduct carrying value of 90% of the net assets of Company S (90% × $85,000)	(76,500)
Difference	$ 23,500
Deduct portion of difference attributable to undervalued Company S land purchased by Company P (90% × $5,000)	(4,500)
Portion of difference attributable to goodwill	$ 19,000

The minority interest on the consolidated balance sheet amounts to 10% of the stockholders' equity of Company S. In the consolidation process we eliminate 90% of Company S's Common Stock and Retained Earnings, leaving the 10% still owned by outside parties. We show minority interest on the consolidated balance sheet as a single amount rather than a separate total for each stockholders' equity account.

CHAPTER SUMMARY

Corporations purchase bonds issued by other corporations to earn interest on cash being accumulated for some future purpose. These bond investments may be purchased on the day they pay interest or at a time between interest payment dates.

Bond investments purchased at par earn interest at the printed rate. Bonds purchased at a discount earn interest at higher than the printed rate; those purchased at a premium earn interest at less than the printed rate. Bond discounts and premiums are not recorded in separate accounts.

Bond premiums and discounts must be amortized over the remaining life of the bonds. We use either the *straight-line* or the *effective-interest method* of amortization.

Bond investments may be held until maturity or sold at any time. If we sell a bond investment, we will recognize a gain or loss if the selling price is above or below the carrying value of the investment.

Corporations purchase stock in other corporations to earn a return on idle funds or to gain influence, and perhaps control, over the actions of other corporations.

The investor corporation uses the *cost method* to account for the common stock investment if no significant influence can be exercised over the investee. The *equity method* is used when significant influence can be exerted. Significant influence is presumed to exist in cases where more than 20% of the investee's stock is owned.

When an investor corporation controls an investee corporation, usually through ownership of more than 50% of the investee's common stock, we prepare *consolidated financial statements.* Consolidated financial statements report the financial position and operating results of the parent corporation and all subsidiaries as if they were one economic entity.

The *purchase method* is used when we acquire controlling interest in a subsidiary by using assets, or stock (if we acquire less than 90% of the subsidiary's stock in exchange for the parent's stock).

Consolidation under the purchase method involves:

1. Recording the subsidiary's assets on the combined balance sheet at their fair market value
2. Recognizing any goodwill purchased
3. Combining revenues and expenses of the parent and subsidiary beginning with the date of acquisition

The *pooling method* is required when we acquire controlling interest in a subsidiary by exchanging parent company stock for 90% or more of the subsidiary's stock.

When less than 100% of a subsidiary is acquired, we must disclose the *minority interest* claims against the assets and income of the subsidiary on the balance sheet and income statement respectively.

IMPORTANT TERMS USED IN THIS CHAPTER

Consolidated financial statements Financial statements that portray a parent and one or more subsidiary companies as a single economic entity. Consolidated statements are prepared when the parent owns more than 50% of the subsidiary's stock. (page 587)

Cost method A system of accounting used by investors to account for investments in investees over which the investor exerts no significant influence. (page 579)

Effective-interest method The method used to amortize discounts and premiums on bond investments over the remaining life of the bond by using the interest rate in effect at the time the bonds were purchased. (page 576)

Equity method A system of accounting used by investors to account for investment in investees over which the investor exerts significant influence. (page 583)

Goodwill The excess of the purchase price of a business over the total fair market value of the net assets of that business. (page 587)

Intercompany accounts Accounts arising from transactions between a parent and subsidiary corporation. Intercompany accounts are eliminated in the process of preparing consolidated financial statements. (page 589)

Minority interest The claim of the minority shareholders against the assets and income of a consolidated entity. (page 590)

Parent corporation An investor corporation that owns more than 50% of the common stock of an investee corporation. (page 586)

Pooling-of-interests method A system of preparing consolidated financial statements. This method must be used when the parent corporation exchanges its stock for 90% or more of the subsidiary's common stock and when other defined criteria are satisfied. (page 587)

Purchase method A system of preparing consolidated financial statements. This method must be used when the parent corporation acquires stock in a subsidiary by giving cash, other assets, or exchanging stock (if less than 90% of the subsidiary's stock is acquired in exchange for the parent's stock). (page 587)

Straight-line method A method used to amortize discounts or premiums on bond investments. This method amortizes an equal amount of discount or premium each year for the remainder of the bond's life. (page 575)

Subsidiary corporation A corporation that has more than 50% of its common stock owned by another corporation. (page 586)

QUESTIONS

Note: Questions with a * relate to consolidations.

1. Commercial Corp. paid $102,000 for a bond with a par value of $100,000. Why would Commercial be willing to pay more than par value for this bond investment?

2. Allday Inc., purchased a $10,000 par value bond for $9,750. Allday did not create a discount account when the investment was recorded. Must Allday still amortize a discount? Explain.

3. On Jan. 1, 1989, Kelly Corp. purchased bonds with a par value of $400,000 and maturing on Jan. 1, 1998. Assuming Kelly paid $347,000 for the bonds, what will be the balance of the Investment in Bonds account on Jan. 1, 1989, immediately after the purchase and on Dec. 31, 1998, immediately before they are redeemed by the issuer? Explain each of your answers.

4. Under what circumstances must the purchaser of a bond investment pay interest to the previous owner of the bond?

5. Why do corporations invest in stock of other corporations?

6. What percentage ownership of common stock must investors hold before they are presumed to have significant influence over an investee? Why is the determination of significant influence important?

7. Parrott Corp. acquired 40,000 shares of Sikes Inc., common stock for $5.75 per share plus an $11,500 brokerage fee. Assuming Parrott bought 10% of the outstanding Sikes stock, for how much would Parrott debit Investment in Stock? Would your answer be the same if Parrott had bought 40% of the Sikes stock? Explain.

8. Valley received notice of a dividend declaration by Aaron Inc., an investee. Valley made the following entry:

Dividend Receivable..	5,400	
Investment in Aaron Stock		5,400

To record declaration of dividend by Aaron Inc.

Which method is Valley using to account for the investment in Aaron? Explain.

9. Under what circumstances is the lower-of-cost-or-market method used in accounting for long-term investments in stock? Under what circumstances is this method not appropriate?

*10. Explain how a parent–subsidiary relationship comes into existence.

*11. Why are consolidated financial statements more useful to investors than parent-only financial statements?

*12. Kimco acquired 95% of the common stock of Conrad Co. by giving $2,000,000 cash. Should the purchase or pooling method be used in preparing consolidated financial statements? Explain.

*13. Parent, Inc., purchased all of the common stock of Sub Corp. for cash. The *net* assets of Sub have a book value of $325,000 and a fair market value of $460,000. Assuming the purchase method of consolidation, how much would Parent have to pay in order for $25,000 of goodwill to be reported on the consolidated balance sheet? Explain.

*14. What are intercompany accounts? Why are they eliminated in the consolidation process?

*15. Hugh Corp. owns 95% of the common stock of Smalley Inc. How is the claim of the owners of the other 5% of Smalley's stock reported on the consolidated financial statements? What is this claim called?

EXERCISES

Note: Exercises with * relate to consolidations.

Exercise 14-1
Recording the purchase of bonds with accrued interest

On Aug. 1, 1989, Thomas Co. purchased Oster Corp. bonds having a $200,000 par value and paying 12% annual interest. Interest is paid semiannually on June 30 and Dec. 31 each year. Thomas purchased the bonds for their par value plus accrued interest.

Prepare the entries Thomas would make on Aug. 1 and Dec. 31, 1989.

(Check figure: Credit to Cash on Aug. 1 = $202,000)

Exercise 14-2
Recording entries for bonds purchased at a discount using straight-line amortization

On Mar. 2, 1989, Hardy Corp. purchased Laurel Inc., bonds having a par value of $2,000,000. The bonds pay 18% annual interest on Mar. 1 and Sept. 1 and mature in 20 years. Hardy paid $1,928,720 for the bonds.

Prepare entries for Hardy on Mar. 2 and Sept. 1, 1989, assuming straight-line amortization is used.

(Check figure: Investment in Bonds is debited for $1,782 on Sept. 1, 1989)

Exercise 14-3
Recording entries for bonds purchased at a premium, using effective-interest amortization

On Mar. 2, 1989, Young Inc., purchased Green Co. 7% bonds having a par value of $500,000. The bonds pay interest on Mar. 1 and Sept. 1 each year. Young purchased the bonds for $521,324. At this price the bonds yield an effective interest rate of 6%.

Prepare Young's entries for the purchase on Mar. 2, 1989, and the first interest receipt on Sept. 1, 1989. Use the effective-interest method of amortization.

(Check figure: On Sept. 1, 1989, Investment in Bonds is credited for $1,860.28)

Exercise 14-4
Recording investment in stock events using cost and equity methods

On Feb. 1, 1989, Kiwi Inc., purchased 20,000 shares of White Corp. common stock for $13.50 per share plus a brokerage commission of $4,000. On June 1, 1989, White declared a $0.50 per share dividend to be paid on July 1, to stockholders of record on June 15.

Prepare any journal entries needed on Feb. 1, June 1, June 15, and July 1 to record these events assuming **(a)** the cost method, and **(b)** the equity method is used. If no entry is required on a given date write "No Entry."

(Check figure: Dividend income recognized using the cost method = $10,000)

Exercise 14-5
Calculating investment income using cost and equity methods

Castle Corp. owns 10,000 common shares (20%) of Bishop Corp. During 1989 Bishop reported income of $500,000 and declared dividends as follows:

Jan. 1 $0.55 per share payable on Feb. 1.
Apr. 1 $0.65 per share payable on May 1.
July 1   A 5,000-share (total) stock dividend distributable on Aug. 1.
Sept. 1 $0.75 per share dividend payable on October 1.

How much income from the investment will Castle report under **(a)** the cost method and **(b)** the equity method?

(Check figure: Income reported using the equity method = $100,000)

Exercise 14-6
Recording entries for investment in stock using the equity method

Owl Oil Co. owns 20,000 shares of Flo-tru Pumps Inc. The stock, representing 40% ownership of Flo-tru, was purchased for $178,200 on Oct. 1, 1989. Prepare journal entries for each of the following dates assuming Owl exerts significant influence over Flo-tru:

1989
Nov. 1   Flo-tru declares a $0.15 per share cash dividend.
Dec. 1   Flo-tru pays the dividend previously declared.
     31   Flo-tru reports a $9,000 net income for the year. Flo-tru stock is selling for $8.25 per share on the stock exchange.

1990

Jan. 15   Owl sells 5,000 shares of Flo-tru for $8.25 per share less a broker's commission of $250. Owl still exerts significant influence.

Dec. 31   Flo-tru reports a $14,000 net income for the year. Flo-tru stock is selling for $8.00 per share on the stock exchange.

(Check figure: Loss on sale of stock = $3,700)

Exercise 14-7
Making T-account entries
for investment using the
cost and equity methods

Keys Inc., purchases 1,000 shares (5%) of common stock of Black Corp. and 8,000 shares (25%) of Dome Inc., as long-term investments. The total cost, including brokerage fees, of the two investments are $233,500 and $793,600, respectively. Keys uses the cost method to account for Black and the equity method to account for Dome. The following transactions and events took place in the year immediately following the purchase of the stocks:

Jan. 15   Dome declared and paid a $2.40 per share cash dividend.
Apr.   1   Black declared and distributed a 10% stock dividend.
June 12   Keys sold 50 shares of Dome for $5,600 after deducting brokerage commissions.
July 31   Dome announced a 2 for 1 stock split.
Sept. 1   Dome declared and paid a $1 per share dividend.
Oct.   1   Keys purchased an additional 1,000 shares of Black for $101,300 plus $2,700 brokerage fee.
Dec. 31   Black and Dome report income of $86,000 and $320,000, respectively, for the year. (On Dec. 31 Keys owns 10% of Black and 24.8% of Dome.)

Determine a Dec. 31 balance for Investment in Black and for Investment in Dome. (*Hint:* Set up a T-account for each investment and enter appropriate increases and decreases. You need not make formal journal entries.)

(Check figure: Balance of Investment in Dome = $833,020)

Exercise 14-8*
Calculating goodwill
included in the purchase
of subsidiaries

Determine the amount of goodwill, if any, in each of the following acquisitions treated as purchases:

a. Chris Co. purchased 100% of the stock of Harp Inc., for $300,000. Harp's net assets had a book value of $180,000. Harp's copyrights were undervalued by $8,000 and land was undervalued by $110,000.

b. Star Inc., purchased 100% of the stock of Angelo Corp. for $750,000. Angelo's net assets have a carrying value of $815,000. Angelo's accounts receivable were overvalued by $32,000, merchandise inventory was overvalued by $38,000, and buildings were undervalued by $2,000.

(Check figure: Goodwill = $3,000)

c. Stanco purchased 100% of the stock of Stella Corp. for $1,680,000. Stella's assets have a carrying value of $2,200,000; Stella's liabilities totaled $800,000. The following Stella assets were undervalued: land by $90,000, buildings by $126,000, and equipment by $64,000.

Exercise 14-9*
Calculating goodwill and
minority interest in the
purchase of subsidiaries

a. Castro Corp. acquired 70% of Riggs Inc., for $320,000. At the time of the acquisition Riggs' net assets had a carrying value of $400,000 and a market value of $440,000. Compute the goodwill and the minority interest on the date of acquisition.

b. Chemicals Inc., acquired 75% of the assets of Plastics Corp. for $240,000. Plastics' net assets had a carrying value of $150,000. Plastics' patents were undervalued by $80,000; land was undervalued by $100,000. Merchandise inventory was overvalued by $18,000. Compute the goodwill and minority interest on the date of acquisition.

(Check figure: Minority interest = $37,500)

PROBLEMS: SET A

**Problem A14-1
Recording investments in
bonds at par and
calculating interest
income for the year**

Quincy Corp. follows a policy of investing the cash it is accumulating to build a new warehouse. The following bond investment transactions took place in 1989:

Jan. 1   Quincy purchased $40,000 of 16% Burr Corp. bonds. The bonds pay interest each
year on June 30 and Dec. 31. The bonds were purchased at par.

June 1   Quincy purchased $100,000 of 18% Hamilton Inc., bonds. The bonds pay interest
each year on Feb. 1 and Aug. 1. The bonds were purchased for $100,000 plus
accrued interest.

    30   Quincy received the semiannual interest on the Burr bonds.

Aug. 1   Quincy received the semiannual interest on the Hamilton bonds.

Dec. 31   Quincy received the semiannual interest on the Burr bonds.

    31   Quincy accrued 5 months' interest on the Hamilton bonds.

Required

1. Prepare general journal entries to record each of the transactions and events.
2. How much interest income did Quincy earn during 1989? Support your answer with clearly
labeled calculations.

(Check figure: Interest income for 1989 = $16,900)

**Problem A14-2
Recording investment in
bonds at premium using
the straight-line and the
effective-interest methods
of amortization**

On July 1, 1989, Carthage Corp. purchased Hannibal Inc., bonds having a par value of
$200,000 and paying 14% annual interest. The bonds mature in 10 years and pay interest on
June 30 and Dec. 31 each year. Carthage paid $222,766 for the bonds. This purchase price
means that Carthage will earn 12% annual effective interest.

Required

1. Assuming straight-line amortization is used, prepare Carthage's entries on July 1, 1989,
Dec. 31, 1989, and June 30, 1990.
2. Assuming effective-interest amortization, prepare Carthage's entries on July 1, 1989, Dec.
31, 1989, and June 30, 1990.

*(Check figure: Interest income on June 30, 1990,
under the effective-interest method = $13,327.92)*

**Problem A14-3
Recording investment in
bonds at discount using
straight-line and effective-
interest methods of
amortization**

On Jan. 1, 1989, Fairdale Co. purchased Langston Corp. bonds as a long-term investment. The
following data relate to these bonds:

Par value.. $200,000
Stated interest rate... 14% annual rate
Interest payment dates...................................... June 30 and Dec. 31
Remaining life of bonds..................................... 10 years
Purchase price $180,252
Effective interest rate earned................................ 16% annual rate

Required

1. Prepare Fairdale's entries on Jan. 1, June 30, and Dec. 31, 1989, assuming straight-line
amortization is used.
2. Prepare Fairdale's entries on Jan. 1, June 30, and Dec. 31, 1989, assuming effective-interest
amortization is used.

*(Check figure: Discount amortized on Dec. 31, 1989,
using the effective-interest method = $453.77)*

Problem A14-4
Preparing journal entries and balance sheet disclosures for investment in stock using cost and equity methods

Holley Inc., invests in common stock of other corporations. During 1989 and 1990 the following transactions took place:

1989

Jan. 1   Holley purchased 30,000 shares of Palmetto Co. for $2.50 per share plus $1,500 brokerage commission.

Dec. 1   Palmetto declared a $0.10 per share cash dividend payable on Jan. 15, 1990, to stockholders of record on Jan. 1, 1990.

     31   Palmetto reported a net income of $96,000 for the year. Palmetto's stock was trading for $2.75 at the close of the year.

1990

Jan. 15   Holley received the cash dividend from Palmetto.

Apr. 20   Holley sold 6,000 shares of Palmetto for $4.00 per share less a brokerage commission of $1,200.

Sept. 1   Palmetto declared a 20% stock dividend distributable on Oct. 1 to stockholders of record on Sept. 15.

Oct. 1   Holley received the new shares from Palmetto.

Dec. 31   Palmetto reported a net loss of $20,000 for the year. Palmetto stock was trading for $2.00 per share at the close of the year.

Required

1. Prepare general journal entries for Holley assuming the cost method is used to account for the investment.
2. Assuming the cost method, show what will appear under Investments on the balance sheet related to Investment in Palmetto on Dec. 31, 1989 and 1990. How much dividend income and other gains or losses will Holley report for 1989 and 1990?
3. Prepare general journal entries for Holley assuming the equity method is used to account for the investment. (*Note:* On Dec. 31, 1989, Holley owned 25% of Palmetto; on Dec. 31, 1990, Holley owned 20% of Palmetto.)
4. Assuming the equity method, show what will appear under Investments on the balance sheet related to the Investment in Palmetto on Dec. 31, 1989 and 1990. How much investment income and other gains and losses will Holley report for 1989 and 1990?

(Check figure: Balance of Investment in Holley on Dec. 31, 1990, under the equity method = $74,000)

Problem A14-5
Calculating the beginning balance of stock investment using the equity method when ending balance and transactions are known

On Dec. 31, 1989, Network International has the following long-term investment on the balance sheet:

Investment in Optics Inc. $700,250

The following additional information is available:

a. Network exerted significant influence over Optics during the entire year.
b. On Dec. 31, 1989, Network owned 35% (175,000 shares) of Optics' common stock.
c. Optics reported a net income of $620,000 for the year.
d. During August Optics declared and paid a $0.05 per share dividend.
e. During July Network purchased 25,000 shares of Optics for $81,250 plus a $1,250 brokerage fee. This transaction increased Network's ownership interest from 30% to 35% of Optics.
f. During February Optics declared and paid a $0.05 dividend.
g. During January Network sold 10,000 shares of Optics receiving a net of $31,500 after brokerage fees. Network recognized a gain of $3,700 on the sale. This transaction reduced Network's ownership from 32% to 30% of Optics.

Required

Prepare a schedule calculating the balance of Investment in Optics Inc., on Jan. 1, 1989. (*Note:* In this problem you must work backward to calculate the beginning-of-the-year amount.)

(Check figure: Balance of Investment on Jan. 1, 1989 = $444,800)

Problem A14-6*
Preparing a consolidation worksheet on the day of acquisition

Winston Co. purchased 100% of the stock of Bradey Corp. on Jan. 1, 1989. Immediately following the cash purchase separate balance sheets of the two companies appeared as follows:

WINSTON AND BRADEY
Balance Sheets
January 1, 1989
(000's omitted)

	Winston	Bradey
Assets		
Current Assets.......................................	$ 430	$ 25
Investment in Bradey	180	
Other Assets..	1,250	85
Total Assets..	$1,860	$110
Equities		
Liabilities..	$ 290	$ 35
Common Stock......................................	500	50
Retained Earnings	1,070	25
Total Equities	$1,860	$110

Required

Prepare a consolidated balance sheet worksheet on the date of the acquisition. Assume the fair market value of Bradey's current assets was $25,000 and of other assets was $145,000.

(Check figure: Total consolidated assets = $1,895)

Problem A14-7*
Preparing a consolidation worksheet on the day of acquisition when minority interest is included

Buckeye Inc., acquired 75% of Keystone Corp. for $600,000 cash. On Jan. 1, 1989, the date of acquisition, Keystone's inventory was undervalued by $100,000; all other asset carrying values and market values were approximately the same. Individual company balance sheets on the acquisition date are shown below:

BUCKEYE INC. AND KEYSTONE CORP.
Balance Sheets
January 1, 1989

	Buckeye	Keystone
Assets		
Current Assets.....................................	$2,160,000	$212,500
Investment in Keystone	600,000	
Other Assets	5,080,000	642,500
Total Assets......................................	$7,840,000	$855,000
Equities		
Current Liabilities	$ 990,000	$ 40,000
Long-Term Liabilities............................	1,250,000	125,000
Common Stock	4,000,000	375,000
Retained Earnings	1,600,000	315,000
Total Equities	$7,840,000	$855,000

Required

Prepare a worksheet to develop a consolidated balance sheet for Buckeye and Keystone on Jan. 1, 1989.

(Check figure: Minority interest = $172,500)

PROBLEMS: SET B

Problem B14-1
Recording investments in bonds at par and calculating interest income for the year

The board of directors of Electro Corp. decided to invest in corporate bonds. The following transactions took place in 1989:

Jan.   1   Electro purchased $10,000 of 14% Bull Implements Co. bonds. The bonds pay interest each year on June 30 and Dec. 31. The bonds were purchased at par.

Apr.   1   Electro purchased $100,000 of 12% Team Machine Inc., bonds. The bonds pay interest each year on Jan. 31 and July 31. The bonds were purchased for $100,000 plus accrued interest.

June 30   Electro received the semiannual interest on the Bull bonds.

July 31   Electro received the semiannual interest on the Team bonds.

Dec. 31   Electro received the semiannual interest on the Bull bonds.

31   Electro accrued 5 months' interest on the Team Inc., bonds.

Required

1. Prepare general journal entries to record each of the transactions and events.
2. How much interest income did Electro earn during 1989? Support your answer with clearly labeled calculations.

(Check figure: Interest income for 1989 = $10,400)

Problem B14-2
Recording investment in bonds at premium using the straight-line and effective-interest methods of amortization

On July 1, 1989, Bennett Enterprises purchased Olson Co. bonds having a par value of $300,000 and paying 12% annual interest. The bonds mature in 5 years and pay interest on June 30 and Dec. 31 each year. Bennett paid $322,878 for the bonds. This purchase price means that Bennett will earn 10% annual effective interest.

Required

1. Assuming straight-line amortization is used, prepare Bennett's entries on July 1, 1989, Dec. 31, 1989, and June 30, 1990.
2. Assuming effective-interest amortization is used, prepare Bennett's entries on July 1, 1989, Dec. 31, 1989, and June 30, 1990.

(Check figure: Interest income on June 30, 1990,
under the effective-interest method = $16,051.10)

Problem B14-3
Recording investments in bonds at discount using the straight-line and effective-interest methods of amortization

On Jan. 1, 1989, Reese Construction purchased Coast Concrete bonds as a long-term investment. The following data relate to these bonds:

Par value. $300,000
Stated interest rate. . . . . 12% annual rate
Interest payment dates. . . . . June 30 and Dec. 31
Remaining life of bonds. . . . . 5 years
Purchase price $278,814
Effective interest rate earned. . . . . 14% annual rate

Required

1. Prepare Reese's entries on Jan. 1, June 30, and Dec. 31, 1989, assuming straight-line amortization is used.
2. Prepare Reese's entries on Jan. 1, June 30, and Dec. 31, 1989, assuming effective-interest amortization is used.

(Check figure: Discount amortized on Dec. 31, 1989,
assuming the effective-interest method = $1,623.17)

Problem B14-4
Preparing journal entries and balance sheet disclosures for investment in stock using cost and equity methods

Terrace Industries invests in common stock of other corporations. The following transactions took place during 1989 and 1990:

1989

Jan. 15	Terrace purchased 6,000 shares of Circle E Corp. for $21.50 per share plus a $4,500 brokerage fee.
Dec. 31	Circle E declared a $1.30 per share cash dividend payable on Feb. 1, 1990, to stockholders of record on Jan. 15, 1990.
31	Circle E reported a net income of $164,000 for the year. Circle E's stock was trading for $22.50 per share at the close of the year.

1990

Feb. 1	Terrace received the cash dividend from Circle E.
May 15	Terrace sold 1,000 shares of Circle E for $28 per share less a brokerage commission of $1,500.
June 30	Circle E declared a 10% stock dividend distributable on Aug. 1 to stockholders of record on July 15.
Aug. 1	Terrace received the new shares from Circle E.
Dec. 31	Circle E reported a net income of $150,000 for the year. Circle E stock was trading for $19 per share at the close of the year.

Required

1. Prepare general journal entries for Terrace assuming the cost method is used to account for the investment. (Round any per share calculations to the nearest cent.)
2. Assuming the cost method, show what will appear under Investments on the balance sheet related to the Investment in Circle E on Dec. 31, 1989 and 1990. How much dividend income and other gains and losses will Terrace report for 1989 and 1990? (Round any per share calculations to the nearest cent.)
3. Prepare general journal entries for Terrace assuming the equity method is used to account for the investment. (*Note:* On Dec. 31, 1989, Terrace owned 30% of Circle E; on Dec. 31, 1990, Terrace owned 25% of Circle E.)
4. Assuming the equity method, show what will appear under Investments on the balance sheet related to the Investment in Circle E on Dec. 31, 1989 and 1990. How much investment income and other gains or losses will Terrace report for 1989 and 1990?

(Check figure: Balance of Investment in Circle E on Dec. 31, 1990, under the equity method = $183,250)

Problem B14-5
Calculating the beginning balance of stock investment using the equity method when ending balance and transactions for the year are known

On Dec. 31, 1989, Tiffany Equipment Co. has the following long-term investment on its balance sheet:

Investment in Crystal $1,013,500

The following additional information is available:

a. Tiffany exerted significant influence over Crystal during the entire year.
b. On Dec. 31, 1989, Tiffany owned 45% (225,000 shares) of the Crystal stock.
c. Crystal reported a net income of $850,000 for the year.
d. During November Crystal declared and paid a $0.15 per share cash dividend.
e. During October Tiffany sold 15,000 shares of Crystal receiving a net of $51,000 after brokerage fees. Tiffany recognized a $6,750 gain on the sale. This transaction reduced Tiffany's ownership interest from 48% to 45% of Crystal.
f. During May Crystal declared and paid a $0.15 per share cash dividend.
g. During February Tiffany purchased 5,000 shares of Crystal for a total of $16,500. This purchase increased Tiffany's ownership percentage from 47% to 48% of Crystal.

Required

Prepare a schedule calculating the balance of Investment in Crystal on Jan. 1, 1989. (*Note:* In this problem you must work backward to compute the beginning-of-the-year amount.)

(Check figure: Balance of Investment on Jan. 1, 1989 = $728,500)

Problem B14-6*
Preparing a consolidation worksheet on the day of acquisition

Britt Co. purchased 100% of the stock of Kory Corp. on Jan. 1, 1989. Immediately after the cash purchase separate balance sheets of the two companies appeared as follows:

BRITT AND KORY COMPANIES
Balance Sheets
January 1, 1989
(000's omitted)

	Britt	Kory
Assets		
Current Assets	$ 700	$ 80
Investment in Kory.	400	
Other Assets	1,640	300
Total Assets	$2,740	$380
Equities		
Liabilities.	$ 600	$120
Common Stock	1,600	200
Retained Earnings.	540	60
Total Equities.	$2,740	$380

Required

Assuming the fair market value of Kory's current assets was $80,000 and fair value of other assets was $360,000 on Jan. 1, 1989, prepare a consolidated balance sheet worksheet on the day of acquisition.

(Check figure: Total consolidated assets = $2,860)

Problem B14-7*
Preparing a consolidation worksheet on the day of acquisition when minority interest is included

Ellis Manufacturing acquired 80% of Pebble Stone Corp. for $475,000 cash. On Jan. 1, 1989, the date of the acquisition, Pebble's inventory was undervalued by $50,000; all other asset book and market values were approximately the same. Individual company balance sheets on the acquisition date are shown below:

ELLIS AND PEBBLE CORPS.
Balance Sheets
January 1, 1989
(000's omitted)

	Ellis	Pebble
Assets		
Current Assets.	$ 350	$200
Investment in Pebble.	475	
Other Assets	1,225	500
Total Assets.	$2,050	$700
Equities		
Current Liabilities	$ 175	$ 50
Long-Term Liabilities	500	150
Common Stock.	1,000	425
Retained Earnings	375	75
Total Equities	$2,050	$700

Required

Prepare a worksheet to develop a consolidated balance sheet for Ellis and Pebble on Jan. 1, 1989.

(Check figure: Minority interest = $100,000)

DECISION PROBLEM

After several months of negotiation Oklahoma Manufacturing acquired 80% of the outstanding stock of Citizens Company, thus effecting a majority control of Citizens Company. The arrangements were finalized on Apr. 1, 1989, when Oklahoma Manufacturing exchanged stock in its company to stockholders of Citizens Company, leaving 20% of Citizens stock outstanding. Both companies maintained their separate identities and serviced their respective customers as if they were separate companies, but from Apr. 1, 1989, to Dec. 31, 1989, the chairman of the board of directors of Oklahoma Manufacturing was in fact the chief operating officer of Citizens Company. One of Citizens' major customers is Oklahoma Manufacturing, accounting for about 30% of Citizens sales.

Sometime in late January, 1990, the financial statements of both Oklahoma Manufacturing and Citizens Company for the year ended Dec. 31, 1989, were completed. The comptroller of Oklahoma Manufacturing then prepared combined financial statements for the board of directors' meeting to be held on Feb. 1, 1990. These statements are presented below:

Balance Sheets December 31, 1989		
	Oklahoma	**Citizens**
Cash.	$ 60,000	$ 25,000
Accounts Receivable	170,000	82,000
Inventory	530,000	125,000
Investments	1,000,000	-0-
Property, Plant, and Equipment	5,000,000	1,000,000
Total Assets	$6,760,000	$1,232,000
Accounts Payable	$ 25,000	$ 10,000
Bonds Payable	3,225,000	250,000
Common Stock	750,000	100,000
Retained Earnings	2,760,000	872,000
Total Equities	$6,760,000	$1,232,000

(continued)

Income Statements
Year Ended
December 31, 1989

	Oklahoma	Citizens
Sales...	$1,500,000	$ 750,000
Cost of Service.................................	$ 800,000	$ 450,000
Operating Expenses	300,000	100,000
Total Costs and Expenses..................	$1,100,000	$ 550,000
Net Income	$ 400,000	$ 200,000

COMBINED COMPANIES
Balance Sheet
December 31, 1989

Cash...	$ 85,000
Accounts Receivable	252,000
Inventory	655,000
Investments	1,000,000
Property, Plant, and Equipment	6,000,000
Total Assets	$7,992,000
Accounts Payable	$ 35,000
Bonds Payable.................................	3,475,000
Common Stock.................................	850,000
Retained Earnings	3,632,000
Total Equities	$7,992,000

Income Statement
For the Year Ended 12/31/89

Sales...	$2,250,000
Cost of Service.................................	$1,250,000
Operating Expenses	400,000
Total Costs and Expenses..................	$1,650,000
Net Income	$ 600,000

Required   Comment on the financial statements prepared by the comptroller of Oklahoma Manufacturing.

Using Financial Statements

You have now learned about the three basic financial statements—the balance sheet, the income statement, and the statement of retained earnings. In Part Five of *Financial Accounting* you will learn to prepare the last major financial statement—the statement of cash flows—and to analyze the financial statements that are needed to evaluate a company's financial condition.

Where did the business get the cash it needed to operate? How did the business use its cash? These are important questions which can't be answered by studying the balance sheet and income statement. In Chapter 15 you will learn how to prepare a statement of cash flows. This new statement is designed to show the inflows and outflows of cash during a particular year.

Readers of a company's financial statements may want to know, "Will the company be able to pay its debts when they come due?" or "Does the company have more merchandise inventory than it can sell in a reasonable period of time?" or "Are selling expenses too high?" In Chapter 16, you will learn to analyze the financial statements and calculate various ratios that will help answer these and many other questions. You will also learn about financial statement footnotes, which provide supplemental information. The reader must have these supplemental facts to understand the company's financial condition.

The Statement of Cash Flows

By studying this chapter, you should learn the following:

- The purpose of the statement of cash flows
- The three information elements that are included in the statement of cash flows
- How to calculate cash provided by operations
- How to construct T-account working papers needed to prepare a formal statement of cash flows
- How to construct a worksheet to prepare a formal statement of cash flows
- How to prepare a formal statement of cash flows
- How to convert an accrual-basis income statement into a cash-basis income statement

In the previous 14 chapters you have learned about the balance sheet, the income statement, and the statement of retained earnings. You have studied how to measure and record assets, liabilities, stockholders' equity, revenue, expenses, gains, and losses.

Chapter 15 introduces you to a new financial statement—the statement of cash flows. In preparing this statement you will use all of the accounts that you've already learned about. You will learn to analyze these accounts and compile information that is not found in the other statements.

Generally accepted accounting principles specify that a complete set of annual financial statements must include:

A complete set of financial statements must include a statement of cash flows

A balance sheet

An income statement

A statement of retained earnings

A statement of cash flows

[607]

This requirement applies to all businesses—no matter how large or small.

Before we proceed with our discussion of the statement of cash flows, let's briefly review the purposes of the other financial statements.

The purpose of the *balance sheet* is to show the resources that a company has—its assets—and where those resources come from: borrowing—liabilities; investments by owners—paid-in capital; and accumulation of earnings—retained earnings. These resources and sources of resources are presented at one instant in time, the end of the accounting period.

The purpose of the *income statement* is to show the expenses incurred matched with the revenues earned. Gains and losses experienced during the period are also included.

The *statement of retained earnings* simply shows the beginning balance of retained earnings, the net income or loss for the period, dividends declared, and the ending balance of retained earnings.

We may find it difficult, if not impossible, to learn certain things from studying the three major statements. For example, to discover how a company's growth and expansion was financed, or what amount of cash was generated by operations, we would need to make a detailed analysis of the statements. We would also have to make a number of assumptions before we could even attempt to find out this information. The *statement of cash flows* is designed to fill this information gap left by other statements.

The Financial Accounting Standards Board (FASB) has stated that the objective of the statement of cash flows is to provide information about cash receipts and cash payments and to provide information about the **operating, investing,** and **financing activities** of a business.

The information provided by the statement of cash flows, together with the information contained in the three other financial statements, will help the user of the financial statements to

- Assess an entity's ability to generate positive future cash flows

- Assess an entity's ability to meet its obligations, its need for external financing, and its ability to pay dividends

- Assess the reasons for differences between income and associated cash receipts and payments

- Assess both the cash and noncash aspects of an entity's investing and financing transactions

The statement of cash flows provides information not shown in the other financial statements

The statement of cash flows provides information about cash receipts and payments as well as operating, investing, and financing activities

The statement of cash flows has three sections: operating activities; investing activities; and financing activities

The statement of cash flows is divided into three sections: *net cash flow from operating activities, cash flows from investing activities,* and *cash flows from financing activities.* In order to explain how the statement is prepared and in order to grasp the meaning of the statement we shall work first with a simple example to explain the three sections of the statement.

THE SIMPLE COMPANY

The Operating Section

Operating activities consist of delivering or producing goods for sale and providing services

The operating section of the cash flow statement, as explained by the FASB, consists of the activities of delivering or producing goods for sale and providing services. The cash flows from **operating activities** are generally the cash effects of transactions that enter into the determination of income. In order to see how the operating section is developed let's assume that a small company, we will call it The Simple Company, had the following balance sheet on Dec. 31, 1988:

THE SIMPLE COMPANY
Balance Sheet
December 31, 1988

Cash	$ 9,000
Accounts Receivable	20,000
Total Assets	$29,000
Common Stock	$15,000
Retained Earnings	14,000
Total Liabilities and Stockholders' Equity	$29,000

The company had just three transactions for the year 1989, these transactions were, in general journal entry form:

Accounts Receivable	40,000	
Sales		40,000
To record sales on account.		
Cash	45,000	
Accounts Receivable		45,000
To record the collection of accounts receivable.		
Expenses	25,000	
Cash		25,000
To record expenses.		

After these transactions have been recorded The Simple Company would prepare an income statement and a balance sheet such as presented below:

THE SIMPLE COMPANY
Income Statement
For the Year Ended December 31, 1989

Sales	$40,000
Expenses	25,000
Net Income	$15,000

THE SIMPLE COMPANY
Comparative Balance Sheets
December 31, 1989

	1989	1988
Cash	$29,000	$ 9,000
Accounts Receivable	15,000	20,000
Total Assets	$44,000	$29,000
Common Stock	$15,000	$15,000
Retained Earnings	29,000	14,000
Total Liabilities and Stockholders' Equity	$44,000	$29,000

In addition a statement of cash flows would be prepared and it would look like this:

THE SIMPLE COMPANY
Statement of Cash Flows
For the Year Ended December 31, 1989

Cash Flow from Operating Activities:	
Net Income	$15,000
Noncash Expenses and Revenues Included in Income:	
Decrease in Accounts Receivable	5,000
Net Cash Flow from Operating Activities	$20,000

A decrease in accounts receivable is added to net income in determining cash flows from operations

Notice that the statement of cash flows starts with the net income figure. This provides a reconciliation between the two statements. The decrease in Accounts Receivable of $5,000 is added to the net income to determine the amount of cash flows from operating activities for the year of $20,000.

Look on the comparative balance sheets and you can see that cash has indeed increased by $20,000. That's because $45,000 was collected from accounts receivable and $25,000 was paid for expenses. Those were the only transactions involving cash. But when the revenues (sales) were measured on the income statement $40,000 was used in the determination of the $15,000 net income, not the $45,000 collected. Accounts receivable decreased because the company collected $5,000 more cash from its customers in 1989 than it recorded as revenue.

What happened in 1989 was that The Simple Company collected $20,000 cash from 1988 sales, the Dec. 31, 1988, Accounts Receivable balance, and they collected $25,000 cash from the $40,000 1989 sales, leaving $15,000 uncollected as the ending Accounts Receivable balance. So, for the analysis of cash flows when accounts receivable decreases it means that the net income figure must be increased to arrive at the cash flows figure.

Now let's expand the illustration to include accounts payable and inventories. A revised Dec. 31, 1988, balance sheet is presented below with these two accounts, Inventory and Accounts Payable, added:

THE SIMPLE COMPANY
Balance Sheet
December 31, 1988

Cash	$ 9,000	
Accounts Receivable	20,000	
Inventory	10,000	
Total Assets		$39,000
Accounts Payable	$ 6,000	
Common Stock	15,000	
Retained Earnings	18,000	
Total Liabilities and Stockholders' Equity		$39,000

During the year 1989, let's assume the following transactions have occurred:

Accounts Receivable...	40,000	
Sales..		40,000

To record sales on account.

Cash..	45,000	
Accounts Receivable...		45,000

To record collection of accounts receivable.

Inventory..	35,000	
Accounts Payable...		35,000

To record acquisition of inventory.

Expenses (Cost of Goods Sold)......................................	25,000	
Inventory...		25,000

To record the cost of inventory sold.

Accounts Payable...	32,000	
Cash..		32,000

To record payment of accounts payable.

After these 1989 activities The Simple Company would record an income statement and a balance sheet as follows:

THE SIMPLE COMPANY
Income Statement
For the Year Ended December 31, 1989

Sales	$40,000
Expenses..	25,000
Net Income	$15,000

THE SIMPLE COMPANY
Comparative Balance Sheets

	Dec. 31	
	1989	**1988**
Cash	$22,000	$ 9,000
Accounts Receivable...	15,000	20,000
Inventory..	20,000	10,000
Total Assets..	$57,000	$39,000
Accounts Payable...	$ 9,000	$ 6,000
Common Stock	15,000	15,000
Retained Earnings	33,000	18,000
Total Liabilities and Stockholders' Equity	$57,000	$39,000

The statement of cash flows would now appear as follows:

THE SIMPLE COMPANY
Statement of Cash Flows
For the Year Ended December 31, 1989

Cash Flow from Operating Activities:	
Net Income...	$ 15,000
Noncash Expenses and Revenues Included in Income:	
Decrease in Accounts Receivable................................	5,000
Increase in Inventory	(10,000)
Increase in Accounts Payable	3,000
Net Cash Flows from Operating Activities.............................	$ 13,000

The net income figure is again adjusted by $5,000 for the decrease in Accounts Receivable. In addition the increase in Inventory of $10,000 must be subtracted and the increase in Accounts Payable of $3,000 must be added to net income to determine the $13,000 net cash flow from operating activities. The $13,000 is the difference between the Dec. 31, 1989, cash balance of $22,000 and the Dec. 31, 1988, cash balance of $9,000.

The expenses for 1989 amounted to $25,000, the cost of the inventory sold. But the amount of cash *expended* for these *expenditures* was $32,000, a difference of $7,000. And that is precisely the sum of the differences between the Inventory decrease ($10,000) and the Accounts Payable increase ($3,000). We will expand on this later in the chapter when we discuss the conversion of the accrual-basis income statement to the cash-basis income statement.

By adding or subtracting the differences in the Accounts Receivable, Inventory, and Accounts Payable accounts to the net income for the period a reconciliation can be made between the net income figure and the amount of cash flows from operations for the period.

The Investing Section

The FASB has defined investing activities as those that include lending money and collecting loans; acquiring and disposing of securities; and acquiring and selling productive assets.

In order to illustrate cash flows from *investing activities* we will need to add two more accounts to The Simple Company's balance sheet; Net Property, Plant, and Equipment and Investments. We are using the Net Property, Plant, and Equipment account rather than the individual accounts (Land, Buildings, Equipment, and their related accumulated depreciation accounts) so as to keep the illustration as brief as possible. The substance of the investing activity can be illustrated by using the Net Property, Plant, and Equipment item. Adding these two accounts to the Dec. 31, 1988, balance would result in the balance sheet shown at the top of the facing page. Notice that the addition of the Net Property, Plant, and Equipment account ($30,000) and Investments account ($5,000) was accomplished by increasing the Common Stock from $15,000 to $50,000 to make the balance sheet balance. Now, assuming that the cash flows from operating activities remain the same as before, three additional transactions will illustrate the cash flows from investing activities.

THE SIMPLE COMPANY
Balance Sheet
December 31, 1988

Cash	$ 9,000
Accounts Receivable	20,000
Inventory	10,000
Net Property, Plant, and Equipment	30,000
Investments	5,000
Total Assets	$74,000
Accounts Payable	$ 6,000
Common Stock	50,000
Retained Earnings	18,000
Total Liabilities and Stockholders' Equity	$74,000

They are as follows:

Cash	8,000	
Net Property, Plant, and Equipment		8,000
To record the sale of certain equipment at its book value.		

Net Property, Plant, and Equipment	4,000	
Cash		4,000
To record the acquisition of equipment.		

Investments	2,000	
Cash		2,000
To record the acquisition of bonds to be held as a long-term investment.		

The sale of the equipment was made at book value. This is to avoid temporarily the problem of dealing with a gain or loss. We will address that issue in a more complex example a little later in the chapter. None of these transactions affect the income statement so net income remains the same. But the 1989 balance sheet will change as will the cash flow statement. These two statements are presented below:

THE SIMPLE COMPANY
Comparative Balance Sheets

	Dec. 31,	
	1989	**1988**
Cash	$24,000	$ 9,000
Accounts Receivable	15,000	20,000
Inventory	20,000	10,000
Net Property, Plant, and Equipment	26,000	30,000
Investments	7,000	5,000
Total Assets	$92,000	$74,000
Accounts Payable	$ 9,000	$ 6,000
Common Stock	50,000	50,000
Retained Earnings	33,000	18,000
Total Liabilities and Stockholders' Equity	$92,000	$74,000

The net effect of these investing activities was to add $2,000 ($8,000 − $4,000 − $2,000) to the cash balance, $2,000 to the Investment account, and to deduct $4,000 from the Property, Plant, and Equipment account. This would result in the following cash flows statement:

THE SIMPLE COMPANY
Statement of Cash Flows
For the Year Ended December 31, 1989

Cash Flow from Operating Activities:		
Net Income...		$ 15,000
Noncash Expenses and Revenues Included in Income:		
Decrease in Accounts Receivable.................................		5,000
Increase in Inventory		(10,000)
Increase in Accounts Payable		3,000
Net Cash Flows from Operating Activities........................		$ 13,000
Cash Flow from Investing Activities:		
Proceeds from Disposal of Equipment......................	$ 8,000	
Purchase of Equipment....................................	(4,000)	
Purchase of Investment Bonds.............................	(2,000)	
Net Cash Provided by Investing Activities........................		2,000
Net Increase in Cash...		$ 15,000

The disposal of equipment, the purchase of equipment, and the purchase of investment bonds are investing activities

Now you can start to see the statement's usefulness. The statement is telling us that cash has increased by $15,000 this year. Check the comparative balance sheets and it has indeed increased by $15,000 (from $9,000 to $24,000). Specifically, cash has increased by $13,000 resulting from those activities associated with the normal operations of the company. And in addition, cash has increased by $2,000 due to certain investing activities, the purchase of plant and equipment, and the disposal of other equipment.

The Financing Section

The financing activity includes obtaining resources from owners and creditors, providing owners a return on and of their investment, and repaying creditors

The *financing activity,* according to the FASB, would include obtaining resources from owners and creditors; providing owners a return on, and a return of, their investment; and repaying creditors.

We need add only two more transactions to illustrate the last section of the cash flow statement. And we can use the same 1988 balance sheet as in the previous example. The two transactions are

Cash	10,000	
Common Stock		10,000

To record the issuance of common stock.

Retained Earnings	3,000	
Cash		3,000

To record the payment of dividends.

These transactions, together with those from the previous examples, will result in the following balance sheet and cash flow statements:

THE SIMPLE COMPANY
Comparative Balance Sheets

	Dec. 31,	
	1989	**1988**
Cash	$31,000	$ 9,000
Accounts Receivable	15,000	20,000
Inventory	20,000	10,000
Net Property, Plant, and Equipment	26,000	30,000
Investments	7,000	5,000
Total Assets	$99,000	$74,000
Accounts Payable	$ 9,000	$ 6,000
Common Stock	60,000	50,000
Retained Earnings	30,000	18,000
Total Liabilities and Stockholders' Equity	$99,000	$74,000

THE SIMPLE COMPANY
Statement of Cash Flows
For the Year Ended December 31, 1989

Cash Flow from Operating Activities:		
Net Income		$ 15,000
Noncash Expenses and Revenues Included in Income:		
Decrease in Accounts Receivable		5,000
Increase in Inventory		(10,000)
Increase in Accounts Payable		3,000
Net Cash Flows from Operating Activities		$ 13,000
Cash Flow from Investing Activities:		
Proceeds from Disposal of Equipment	$ 8,000	
Purchase of Equipment	(4,000)	
Purchase of Investment Bonds	(2,000)	
Net Cash Provided by Investing Activities		2,000
Cash Flow from Financing Activities:		
Proceeds from Issuing Common Stock	$10,000	
Dividends paid	(3,000)	
Net Cash Provided by Financing Activities		7,000
Net Increase in Cash		$ 22,000

Issuing common stock and paying dividends are financing activities

The cash flow statement is now complete. It tells us that during the year 1989 The Simple Company has had an increase in its Cash account of $22,000; $13,000 came from operations, $2,000 from investing, and $7,000 from financing activities.

The Simple Company example developed each of the three sections by first showing the transactions that affected that activity. You were then able to follow the transactions into the 1989 income statement and balance sheet and see how the cash flow statement was developed. Such is not the case in real life. The cash flow statement is made after the accounting period has ended and after the income statement and balance sheets have been prepared. This makes it more difficult to prepare the cash flow statement and that's the topic we need to discuss in the remainder of this chapter.

CONVERTING FROM THE ACCRUAL TO THE CASH BASIS

Before we consider a more complex example it is necessary to digress for a moment to consider how the *accrual-basis income* statement can be converted to a *cash-basis income* statement. The concepts used for this conversion will help you understand how the operating activities section of the statement of cash flows is developed.

The revenue realization and matching principles so important to accrual-basis income measurement are ignored in preparing a cash-basis income statement. Since generally accepted accounting principles require income statements for external use to be prepared on the accrual basis, cash from operations is normally derived by adjusting accrual-basis net income as follows:

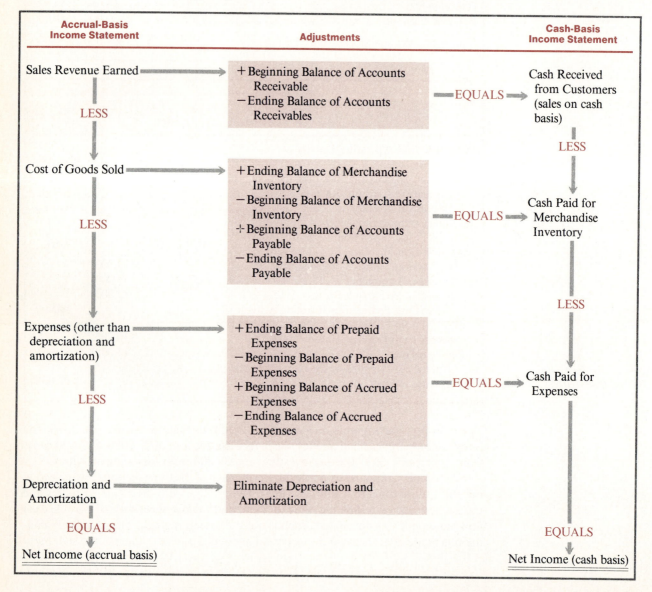

Remember as you look at the logic underlying each of these adjustments that we are interested in calculating cash inflows and cash outflows from income-oriented activities.

Cash Received from Customers

To accrual-basis Sales we add the beginning balance of Accounts Receivable. This will include cash collected on accounts receivable during the current year from sales that were reported on the accrual basis in prior years. From accrual-basis Sales we subtract the ending balance of Accounts Receivable. This will exclude credit sales on the current income statement that have not yet been collected.

Cash Paid for Merchandise Inventory

First we calculate net purchases by adding the ending balance of Merchandise Inventory to Cost of Goods Sold and deducting the beginning balance from Cost of Goods Sold.

Now that we know how much merchandise was purchased this year, we must calculate how much was actually paid for. This is accomplished by adding the beginning balance of Accounts Payable—we're assuming that purchases made last year were paid for this year. The process is completed by deducting the ending balance of Accounts Payable—we're removing an amount that is included in purchases this year that won't be paid for until next year.

Cash Paid for Expenses

We must analyze two types of balance sheet accounts in calculating this amount: prepaid expenses (Prepaid Rent, Prepaid Insurance, etc.) and accrued expenses (Salaries Payable, Utilities Payable, etc.).

To accrual income statement expenses we add the ending balance of prepaid expenses—the cash has been paid out this year but the expense won't be reported on the accrual basis until next year. From accrual income statement expenses we deduct the beginning balance of prepaid expenses—we're removing expenses that were included this year but paid for last year.

The beginning balance of accrued expenses is added because we're assuming we paid for these expenses this year even though they were reported on the accrual-basis income statement last year. We deduct the ending balance of accrued expenses—these expenses are on this year's income statement, but they won't be paid until next year.

Depreciation and Amortization

These expenses don't use any cash or any other current asset. We eliminate them in calculating cash from operations.

Cash from Operating Activities — A Shortcut

This method of computing cash flows from operating activities is called the direct method. We can derive cash from operations a little more quickly by using the following shortcut calculation which is commonly used and is called the indirect method:

Cash from operating activities may be derived also by adjusting accrual net income

Accrual-Basis Net Income

Deduct Increase in Accounts Receivable (or *Add* Decrease in Accounts Receivable)

Deduct Increase in Merchandise Inventory (or *Add* Decrease in Merchandise Inventory)

Deduct Increase in Prepaid Expenses (or *Add* Decrease in Prepaid Expenses)

Add Increase in Accounts Payable (or *Deduct* Decrease in Accounts Payable)

Add Increase in Accrued Expenses (or *Deduct* Decrease in Accrued Expenses)

Add Depreciation and Amortization Expenses for the Year

Cash-Basis Net Income

This calculation accomplishes the same thing that we did with the direct method. Now we're beginning with net income and adjusting it instead of adjusting each revenue and expense account on the income statement. The cash flow from operating activities on the statement of cash flows is determined using this shortcut procedure, the indirect method.

THE COMPLEX COMPANY: T-ACCOUNT APPROACH

The T-account and the worksheet approaches are two ways to develop a statement of cash flows

A more realistic example of preparing the statement of cash flows is now needed and The Complex Company example will fill that need. We will demonstrate two approaches to preparing the statement of cash flows: first, the T-account approach, which is easier to understand but less formal, and second, the formal worksheet approach. For both examples we will use the same data which consists of an income statement for the year ended Dec. 31, 1989, a statement of retained earnings for the year ended Dec. 31, 1989, and comparative balance sheets for 1988 and 1989. The statements are presented below and on the next page.

THE COMPLEX COMPANY
Condensed Income Statement
Year Ended December 31, 1989

Sales		$ 290,000
Cost of Goods Sold		(174,000)
Gross Profit on Sales		$ 116,000
Operating Expenses:		
Administrative Expenses	$ 45,000	
Selling Expenses	20,900	
Depreciation Expenses	12,000	
Patent Amortization Expense	1,000	(78,900)
Other Income and Expenses:		
Interest Expense	$(15,400)	
Gain on Sale of Land	2,500	(12,900)
Income before Income Taxes		$ 24,200
Income Tax Expense		(9,700)
Net Income		$ 14,500

THE COMPLEX COMPANY
Statement of Retained Earnings
Year Ended December 31, 1989

Balance, Jan. 1, 1989	$ 88,000
Add: Net Income for the Year	14,500
Deduct: Dividends Declared and Paid during 1989	(10,000)
Balance, Dec. 31, 1989	$ 92,500

THE COMPLEX COMPANY Balance Sheet			
	December 31,		Increase (Decrease)
	1989	**1988**	
Assets			
Current Assets:			
Cash.....................................	$ 50,000	$ 55,000	$ (5,000)
Accounts Receivable (net)...................	109,000	90,000	19,000
Merchandise Inventory	175,000	153,000	22,000
Prepaid Expenses	15,500	17,000	(1,500)
Total Current Assets	$ 349,500	$ 315,000	
Investments:			
Land Held for Investment...................	-0-	$ 27,500	(27,500)
Property, Plant, and Equipment:			
Land Used in Operations	$ 148,400	$ 100,000	48,400
Buildings.................................	465,000	415,000	50,000
Less: Accum. Deprec.: Building...........	(217,000)	(205,000)	(12,000)
Total Property, Plant, and Equipment....	$ 396,400	$ 310,000	
Intangibles:			
Patents	$ 5,000	$ 6,000	(1,000)
Total Assets	$ 750,900	$ 658,500	
Liabilities and Stockholders' Equity			
Current Liabilities:			
Accounts Payable	$ 69,000	$ 75,000	$ (6,000)
Accrued Liabilities	24,500	20,000	4,500
Total Current Liabilities	$ 93,500	$ 95,000	
Long-Term Liabilities:			
Bonds Payable.............................	$ 200,000	$ 200,000	-0-
Premium on Bonds Payable.................	29,400	30,000	(600)
Total Long-Term Liabilities.............	$ 229,400	$ 230,000	
Total Liabilities..............................	$ 322,900	$ 325,000	
Stockholders' Equity			
Common Stock, no par.....................	$ 335,500	$ 245,500	$ 90,000
Retained Earnings...........................	92,500	88,000	4,500
Total Stockholders' Equity.............	$ 428,000	$ 333,500	
Total Liabilities and Stockholders' Equity.......	$ 750,900	$ 658,500	

For the T-account approach a T-account is needed for each balance sheet account including a very large T-account for cash

The starting point for the T-account approach is to set up T-accounts for each *balance sheet* account and enter the beginning balance (BB) and ending balance (EB) as illustrated in Exhibit 15-1. Notice the very large T-account for cash, and how the account is divided into the three sections for the cash flow statement. As you may have guessed, the Cash T-account will contain all the information necessary to prepare the cash flow statement when we are done analyzing the T-accounts.

EXHIBIT 15-1

THE COMPLEX COMPANY
Statement of Cash Flows
T-Account Approach
(Before Analysis)

Cash			Accounts Receivable		
BB	55,000		BB	90,000	
	OPERATING ACTIVITIES		EB	109,000	

Beginning balance

			Merchandise Inventory		
			BB	153,000	
			EB	175,000	

Entries to explain the changes in cash will be entered here

			Prepaid Expenses		
	INVESTING ACTIVITIES		BB	17,000	
			EB	15,500	

Entries to explain the changes in accounts other than Cash will be entered in these accounts

			Accounts Payable		
	FINANCING ACTIVITIES		BB	75,000	
				EB	69,000

Ending balance

NONCASH INVESTING AND
FINANCING

			Accrued Liabilities		
				BB	20,000
EB	50,000			EB	24,500

Land Held for Investment			Land Used in Operations		
BB	27,500		BB	100,000	
EB	-0-		EB	148,400	

Buildings			Accum. Deprec.: Buildings		
BB	415,000			BB	205,000
EB	465,000			EB	217,000

Patents			Bonds Payable		
BB	6,000			BB	200,000
EB	5,000			EB	200,000

(continued)

	Premium on Bonds Payable	
	BB	30,000
	EB	29,400

Common Stock			**Retained Earnings**	
BB	245,500		BB	88,000
EB	335,500		EB	92,500

What we are going to do is to analyze the transactions made by The Complex Company in terms of their effects on cash flows. We will enter these transactions in the T-accounts as we analyze them. Beside each transaction we have provided a short version of the T-accounts affected in the margin of the text. The complete T-accounts with all the explanations are shown in Exhibit 15-2; you should be careful to examine this exhibit to see where the explanations are placed and to see how the completed analysis looks.

Entry Code Letter

A

Transaction

Cash Flows from Operations 14,500
      Retained Earnings 14,500

Description and Analysis

Reported income for the year was $14,500 as seen in the statement of retained earnings. The initial assumption is that all revenue involved is an inflow of cash and all expenses involved an outflow of cash. Adjustments will be made to determine the actual cash flows. Since a positive net income figure is reported, an inflow is the initial assumption. The entry then is to debit Cash (actually Cash in the operating activities section to reflect the assumed increase in cash) and to credit Retained Earnings.

Cash		
BB	55,000	
	Operating	Activities
A	14,500	

Retained Earnings		
	BB	88,000
	A	14,500

These entries are coded A as a reference. Look at Exhibit 15-2 (page 627).

We recommend that you start your analysis with the income for the year and then adjust this amount by the changes in the current assets and current liabilities. Notice in Exhibit 15-1 that the current accounts were all located near the Cash account.

Please understand that what we are doing is explaining how the accounts changed from the beginning to the ending balances. We are not actually recording the transactions in the accounts of The Complex Company. That has already been done during the course of the year. We are just using T-accounts as accountants do, for analytical purposes!

Entry Code Letter

B

Transaction

Accounts Receivable........................ 19,000
    Cash Flows from Operations..............   19,000

Description and Analysis

We are, in effect, converting from the accrual basis of accounting to the cash basis. Net income on the accrual basis is determined in accordance with generally accepted accounting principles. But cash flows from operations is determined simply by the difference between cash receipts from revenues and cash payments for expenses. Look at entry B in Exhibit 15-2.

When the Accounts Receivable account increases during the year that means that more accrual revenue has been earned than the amount of cash received. Thus, the accrual net income figure would be higher than the cash income figure. For this reason we must deduct the increase in receivables from the net income figure.

Notice the check mark in the Accounts Receivable account. That indicates that we have finished analyzing the account. The beginning balance of $90,000 plus the B adjustment of $19,000 determines the ending balance of $109,000.

Cash			
BB	55,000		
	Operating	Activities	
A	14,500	B	19,000

Accounts Receivable		
BB	90,000	
B	19,000	
EB	109,000 ✓	

Entry Code Letter

C

Transaction

Merchandise Inventory....................... 22,000
    Cash Flows from Operations..............   22,000

Description and Analysis

The increase in the Merchandise Inventory account indicates that during the year The Complex Company bought $22,000 more inventory than it sold. The net income figure must be reduced. Look at entry C in Exhibit 15-2.

Cash			
BB	55,000		
	Operating	Activities	
A	14,500	B	19,000
		C	22,000

Merchandise Inventory		
BB	153,000	
C	22,000	
EB	175,000 ✓	

Entry Code Letter

D

Transaction

Accounts Payable............................. 6,000
    Cash Flows from Operations..............   6,000

Description and Analysis

A decrease in Accounts Payable indicates that cash was paid out this period for purchases made in a prior period. Income must be reduced by this additional cash payout that does not appear on the income statement. Look at entry D in Exhibit 15-2.

Cash			
BB	55,000		
	Operating	Activities	
A	14,500	B	19,000
		C	22,000
		D	6,000

Accounts Payable			
D	6,000	BB	75,000
		✓EB	69,000

Entry Code Letter
E

Transaction

Cash Flows from Operations................... 1,500

    Prepaid Expenses.........................   1,500

Description and Analysis

A decrease in Prepaid Expenses means that some expenses on this period's income statement were paid for last period. They are noncash outflows for the current period. The decrease, then, must be added to current net income just as any other noncash expense would be. Look at entry E in Exhibit 15-2.

Cash

BB	55,000			
	Operating	Activities		
A	14,500	B	19,000	
E	1,500	C	22,000	
		D	6,000	

Prepaid Expenses

BB	17,000	E	1,500
EB	15,500 ✓		

Entry Code Letter
F

Transaction

Cash Flows from Operations................... 4,500

    Accrued Liabilities.......................   4,500

Description and Analysis

An increase in Accrued Liabilities means that some accrued expenses on this period's income statement will be paid for in future periods. Those expenses that did not require a current use of cash must be added to accrual-basis income. Look at entry F in Exhibit 15-2.

Cash

BB	55,000			
	Operating	Activities		
A	14,500	B	19,000	
E	1,500	C	22,000	
F	4,500	D	6,000	

Accrued Liabilities

		BB	20,000
		F	4,500
		✓EB	24,500

Entry Code Letter
G

Transaction

Cash Flows from Operations................... 12,000

    Accum. Deprec.: Building   12,000

Description and Analysis

Depreciation expense for the period was recorded by debiting Depreciation Expense, a noncash entry, and crediting Accumulated Depreciation. The analysis debits Cash Flows from Operations to accomplish the objective of adding back this noncash item to net income. Accumulated Depreciation is credited because this was the original noncash account credited. Look at entry G in Exhibit 15-2.

    Please, PLEASE understand that depreciation is not, IS NOT, a source of cash. We have simply adjusted the net income figure from the income statement by an item that DID NOT involve cash to determine the income from operating activities on a cash basis.

    Look at it this way. Assume a company has cash sales of $6,000 and the only expense it had was $1,000 of depreciation. That would be a net income of $5,000. In order to determine the amount of cash flows from operations (which we know is $6,000 from the cash sales) we would have to add back the $1,000 depreciation to the accrual-basis net income figure of $5,000 to arrive at the $6,000 cash flow from operations.

Cash

BB	55,000			
	Operating	Activities		
A	14,500	B	19,000	
E	1,500	C	22,000	
F	4,500	D	6,000	
G	12,000			

Accum. Deprec.: Buildings

		BB	205,000
		G	12,000
		✓EB	217,000

Entry Code Letter

H

Transaction

Cash Flows from Operations................... 1,000
    Patents..................................... 1,000

Description and Analysis

Patent amortization expense for the period was recorded by debiting the expense account and crediting Patents. Since this too is an expense not using cash, it must be added back to net income by debiting Cash Flows from Operations in the analysis entry. The credit in the analysis entry is to Patents since this was the original noncash credit. Look at entry H in Exhibit 15-2.

Cash

BB	55,000		
	Operating	Activities	
A	14,500	B	19,000
E	1,500	C	22,000
F	4,500	D	6,000
G	12,000		
H	1,000		

Patents

BB	6,000	H	1,000
EB	5,000 ✓		

Entry Code Letter

I

Transaction

Premium on Bonds Payable 600
    Cash Flows from Operations.............. 600

Description and Analysis

The original entry made by The Complex Company when interest was paid was as follows:

Interest Expense........................... 15,400
Premium on Bonds Payable 600
    Cash 16,000

The actual cash outflow was $16,000, but only $15,400 was reflected on the income statement as an expense due to the $600 premium amortization. The analysis entry is to debit Premium on Bonds Payable to reproduce the noncash part of the entry and credit Cash Flows from Operations to deduct $600 from income to reflect the correct amount of cash outflows associated with interest. Look at entry I in Exhibit 15-2.

Cash

BB	55,000		
	Operating	Activities	
A	14,500	B	19,000
E	1,500	C	22,000
F	4,500	D	6,000
G	12,000	I	600
H	1,000		

Premium on Bonds Payable

I	600	BB	30,000
		✓EB	29,400

Entry Code Letter

J

Transaction

Cash Flows from Investing.................... 30,000
    Cash Flows from Operations.............. 2,500
    Land Held for Investment................ 27,500

Description and Analysis

The original entry to record the sale of land was as follows:

Cash 30,000
    Gain on Sale of Land 2,500
    Land Held for Investment................ 27,500

The total cash inflow of $30,000 must be shown as an investing activity. Presently, $2,500 of this amount is included on the income statement as a gain. The credit to Cash Flows from Operations in the analysis entry deducts $2,500 from net income. The debit to Cash Flows from Investing for $30,000 shows that this amount will be reported in that section of the cash flow statement. The credit to the Land Held for Investment account of $27,500 reproduces the noncash part of the original entry. Look at entry J in Exhibit 15-2.

Cash

BB	55,000		
	Operating	Activities	
A	14,500	B	19,000
E	1,500	C	22,000
F	4,500	D	6,000
G	12,000	I	600
H	1,000	J	2,500
	Investing	Activities	
J	30,000		

Land Held for Investment

BB	27,500	J	27,500
EB	-0- ✓		

Entry Code Letter	Transaction		
K	Land Used in Operations......................	48,400	
	Cash Flows from Investing		48,400

Description and Analysis

A purchase of land for a parking area was recorded during this year. Land Used in Operations is debited to reproduce the noncash part of the entry. Cash Flows from Investing is credited to reflect the outflow of cash. Cash Flows from Operations is not affected since the purchase of land is not reflected on the income statement. Look at entry K on Exhibit 15-2.

Cash

BB	55,000		
	Operating	Activities	
A	14,500	B	19,000
E	1,500	C	22,000
F	4,500	D	6,000
G	12,000	I	600
H	1,000	J	2,500
	Investing	Activities	
J	30,000	K	48,400

Land Used in Operations

BB	100,000		
K	48,400		
EB	148,400 ✓		

Entry Code Letter	Transaction		
L-1	Noncash Investing and Financing	50,000	
	Common Stock		50,000
L-2	Buildings	50,000	
	Noncash Investing and Financing		50,000

Description and Analysis

A new building was acquired in exchange for common stock having a market value of $50,000. Cash is unaffected by this transaction, but since it is a significant activity it must be shown on the statement of cash flows. This is accomplished by showing the transaction as a noncash investing and financing activity. (Notice the new section included in the Cash account.) An entry to reproduce this transaction in the T-accounts would involve merely debiting Building and crediting Common Stock. This method would bury the entry among the noncash accounts and fail to highlight the data needed for preparation of the statement of cash flows.

The dilemma is solved by arbitrarily splitting the transaction into two parts: (1) issuing the stock and (2) acquiring the building. The two analysis entries above make use of noncash investing and financing activities to show the inflow of noncash resources from issuing common stock (entry L-1) and the outflow of noncash resources in acquiring the building (entry L-2). This procedure keeps all information needed to prepare the statement of cash flows in the analysis account. Look at entries L-1 and L-2 in Exhibit 15-2.

Cash

BB	55,000		
	Operating	Activities	
A	14,500	B	19,000
E	1,500	C	22,000
F	4,500	D	6,000
G	12,000	I	600
H	1,000	J	2,500
	Investing	Activities	
J	30,000	K	48,400
	Financing	Activities	

Noncash Investing and Financing

L-1	50,000	L-2	50,000

Buildings

BB	415,000		
L-2	50,000		
EB	465,000 ✓		

Common Stock

		BB	245,500
		L-1	50,000
		EB	335,500

Entry Code Letter

Transaction

M   Cash Flows from Financing.   40,000
     Common Stock   40,000

Description and Analysis

Notice that after transaction L-1 the Common Stock account does not balance to $335,500. That's because there is another transaction involving common stock. Specifically, The Complex Company sold stock for $40,000. This inflow of cash is reflected as Cash from Financing Activities. The analysis entry shows the inflow as a debit and the credit to Common Stock now explains how that account went from a beginning balance of $245,500 to the ending balance of $335,500. Look at entry M in Exhibit 15-2.

Cash

BB	55,000		
Operating		Activities	
A	14,500	B	19,000
E	1,500	C	22,000
F	4,500	D	6,000
G	12,000	I	600
H	1,000	J	2,500
Investing		Activities	
J	30,000	K	48,400
Financing		Activities	
M	40,000		
Noncash Investing and Financing			
L-1	50,000	L-2	50,000

Common Stock

		BB	245,500
		L-1	50,000
		M	40,000
		✓EB	335,500

Entry Code Letter

Transaction

N   Retained Earnings   10,000
     Cash Flows from Financing.   10,000

Description and Analysis

On the statement of retained earnings it is indicated that a $10,000 dividend was paid in 1989. This represents an outflow of cash, specifically Cash Flows from Financing Activities. Retained Earnings is debited to reproduce the noncash part of the entry and this will explain, together with the net income entry A, how Retained Earnings went from the beginning balance of $88,000 to the ending balance of $92,500. The credit to the Cash account in the cash flows from financing activities now completes all the transactions for the period. Look at entry N in Exhibit 15-2.

Cash

BB	55,000		
Operating		Activities	
A	14,500	B	19,000
E	1,500	C	22,000
F	4,500	D	6,000
G	12,000	I	600
H	1,000	J	2,500
Investing		Activities	
J	30,000	K	48,400
Financing		Activities	
M	40,000	N	10,000
Noncash Investing and Financing			
L-1	50,000	L-2	50,000
EB	50,000 ✓		

Retained Earnings

		BB	88,000
N	10,000	A	14,500
		✓EB	92,500

With this last transaction we should be able to add the debits in the Cash account, subtract the credits and have a balance, the ending balance, of $50,000. And that's precisely what we have.

Using the information contained in the Cash account from the analysis prepared in Exhibit 15-2 we can now prepare a statement of cash flows. This statement is illustrated in Exhibit 15-3.

EXHIBIT 15-2

THE COMPLEX COMPANY
Statement of Cash Flows
T-Account Approach
(After Analysis)

Cash

BB		55,000			
		Operating	**Activities**		
A	Net Income	14,500	B	Increase in Receivables	19,000
E	Decrease in Prepaid Expenses	1,500	C	Increase in Inventory	22,000
F	Increase in Accrued Liabilities	4,500	D	Decrease in Payables	6,000
G	Depreciation Expense	12,000	I	Amortization of Premium on Bonds Payable	600
H	Amortization of Patent	1,000	J	Gain on Sale of Land	2,500
		Investing	**Activities**		
J	Cash from Sale of Land	30,000	K	Cash for Purchase of Land	48,400
		Financing	**Activities**		
M	Cash from Sale of Common Stock	40,000	N	Cash Used to Pay Dividend	10,000

Noncash Investing and Financing

L-1	Noncash Resources from Issuance of Common Stock	50,000	L-2 Noncash Resources Used to Acquire Building	50,000
EB		50,000 ✓		

Accounts Receivable

BB	90,000	
B	19,000	
EB	109,000 ✓	

Merchandise Inventory

BB	153,000	
C	22,000	
EB	175,000 ✓	

Prepaid Expenses

BB	17,000	E	1,500
EB	15,500 ✓		

Accounts Payable

D	6,000	BB	75,000
		✓EB	69,000

Accrued Liabilities

		BB	20,000
		F	4,500
		✓EB	24,500

(continued)

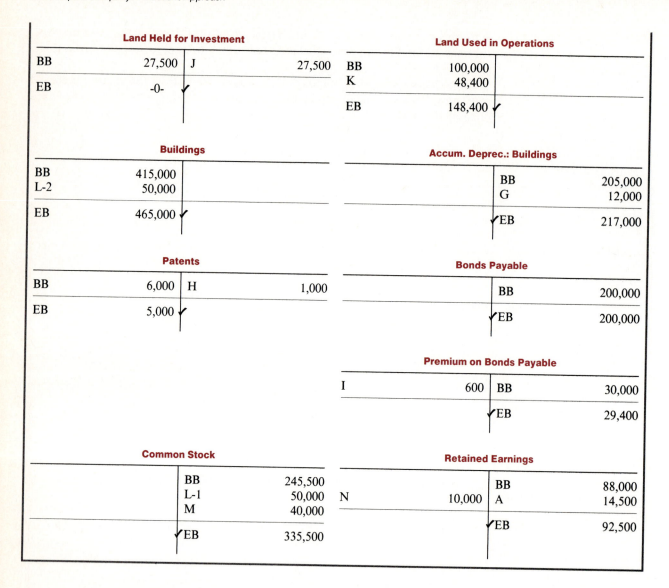

Land Held for Investment		
BB	27,500	J	27,500
EB	-0-		

Land Used in Operations	
BB	100,000
K	48,400
EB	148,400

Buildings	
BB	415,000
L-2	50,000
EB	465,000

Accum. Deprec.: Buildings	
BB	205,000
G	12,000
EB	217,000

Patents		
BB	6,000	H	1,000
EB	5,000		

Bonds Payable	
BB	200,000
EB	200,000

Premium on Bonds Payable		
I	600	BB	30,000
		EB	29,400

Common Stock	
BB	245,500
L-1	50,000
M	40,000
EB	335,500

Retained Earnings		
N	10,000	BB	88,000
		A	14,500
		EB	92,500

Notice in Exhibit 15-3, the statement of cash flows, how each section is prepared from the data in the Cash account of Exhibit 15-2. The cash flows from operating activities is a negative $16,600. The credits to the Cash account are listed in the cash flow statement as decreases. Cash flows from investing activities is a negative $18,400, and cash flows from financing activities is a positive $30,000.

Also notice how the noncash investing and financing activities are handled, on the bottom of the statement after the net cash decrease of $5,000 is presented.

The T-account approach is the fastest way to prepare the statement of cash flows

Preparing the statement of cash flows using the T-account approach, once you get used to it, is the fastest way to prepare the statement. The disadvantage of the T-account method is that it does not provide formal documentation of your work which is necessary to have in the files of preparing firms and/or certified public accountants. That's why the worksheet method is used.

EXHIBIT 15-3

THE COMPLEX COMPANY
Statement of Cash Flows
For the Year Ended December 31, 1989

Net Cash Flow from Operating Activities:		
Net Income...		$ 14,500
Noncash Expenses, Revenues, Losses, and Gains Included in Income:		
Increases:		
Decrease in Prepaid Expenses	$ 1,500	
Increase in Accrued Liabilities........................	4,500	
Depreciation Expense	12,000	
Patent Amortization	1,000	19,000
Decreases:		
Increase in Accounts Receivable......................	$ 19,000	
Increase in Merchandise Inventory....................	22,000	
Decrease in Accounts Payable.........................	6,000	
Amortization of Bond Premium.......................	600	
Gain on Sale of Land	2,500	(50,100)
Net Cash Flow from Operating Activities........................		$(16,600)
Cash Flows from Investing Activities:		
Increases: Cash from the Sale of Land......................	$ 30,000	
Decreases: Cash Used to Purchase Land....................	(48,400)	(18,400)
Cash Flows from Financing Activities:		
Increases: Cash from Sale of Common Stock................	$ 40,000	
Decreases: Cash Used to Pay Dividends	(10,000)	30,000
Net Decrease in Cash		$ (5,000)
Noncash Investing and Financing Activities:		
Acquisition of Building by Issuing Stock		$ 50,000

THE COMPLEX COMPANY: WORKSHEET APPROACH

A four-column worksheet is used for the worksheet approach to preparing the statement of cash flows

The worksheet approach formalizes the T-account approach. The starting point is to prepare a four-column worksheet with a listing of all the beginning balance sheet debit accounts and all the beginning balance sheet credit accounts entered in the first column. The second and third columns are left for the debit and credit entry analysis. In the fourth column are entered all the ending balance sheet debit and credits. See Exhibit 15-4 for an illustration of the starting worksheet. Be careful at this stage. The worksheet requires entering the beginning balances in the first column and the ending balances in the last column. This is exactly the opposite from the way these amounts will appear on the balance sheet; the most recent year will appear first (ending balances) on the balance sheet followed by last year's figures (beginning balances). Also, notice that on the worksheet we list all accounts with debit balances first, then those with credit balances. We won't be listing the accounts in exactly the same order that they appear on the balance sheet.

Check the mathematical accuracy of your amounts by adding accounts with debit balances and verifying that this total is the same as the total of the accounts with credit balances. For The Complex Company beginning debits and beginning credits equal $863,500, ending debits and credits equal $967,900. Study Exhibit 15-4 to see how The Complex Company worksheet looks at this point.

After entering the beginning and ending balances on the worksheet you need to write the major headings of the statement of cash flows on the bottom of the

EXHIBIT 15-4

THE COMPLEX COMPANY
Worksheet for the Statement of Cash Flows
For the Year Ended December 31, 1989

	Jan. 1, 1989 Balance	Summary of 1989 Entries Debit	Credit	Dec. 31, 1989 Balance
Debits				
Cash...	$ 55,000	*This column is for the*		$ 50,000
Accounts Receivable......................................	90,000	*beginning balances of the*		109,000
Merchandise Inventory.....................................	153,000	*balance sheet accounts*		175,000
Prepaid Expenses...	17,000			15,500
Land Held for Investment.................................	27,500			-0-
Land Used in Operations...................................	100,000			148,400
Buildings..	415,000			465,000
Patents..	6,000			5,000
Total Debits...	$863,500	*These middle columns are*		$967,900
Credits		*for analysis transactions*		
		that explain how the		
Accumulated Depreciation	$205,000	*accounts changed during*		$217,000
Accounts Payable	75,000	*the period*		69,000
Accrued Liabilities......................................	20,000			24,500
Bonds Payable	200,000			200,000
Premium on Bonds Payable	30,000			29,400
Common Stock	245,500			335,500
Retained Earnings......................................	88,000			92,500
Total Credits...	$863,500			$967,900

The bottom section of the worksheet is for adding items that will be used in the statement of cash flows

This column is for the ending balances of the balance sheet accounts

worksheet—leave space after each heading to enter the content of the statement as you do your analysis. Look at Exhibit 15-5 to see these headings on the completed worksheet. The headings would be

> Cash Flows from Operations
>> Net Income
>>> Add:
>>> Deduct:
> Cash Flows from Investing
>> Add:
>> Deduct:
> Cash Flows from Financing
>> Add:
>> Deduct:
> Noncash Investing and Financing

EXHIBIT 15-5

THE COMPLEX COMPANY
Worksheet for the Statement of Cash Flows
For the Year Ended December 31, 1989

	Jan. 1, 1989 Balance	Summary of 1989 Entries Debit	Summary of 1989 Entries Credit	Dec. 31, 1989 Balance
Debits				
Cash	$ 55,000		Z$ 5,000	$ 50,000
Accounts Receivable....................	90,000	B$ 19,000		109,000
Merchandise Inventory..................	153,000	C 22,000		175,000
Prepaid Expenses.......................	17,000		E 1,500	15,500
Land Held for Investment	27,500		J 27,500	-0-
Land Used in Operations................	100,000	K 48,400		148,400
Buildings	415,000	L-2 50,000		465,000
Patents................................	6,000		H 1,000	5,000
Total Debits	$863,500			$967,900
Credits				
Accumulated Depreciation	$205,000		G 12,000	$217,000
Accounts Payable......................	75,000	D 6,000		69,000
Accrued Liabilities....................	20,000		F 4,500	24,500
Bonds Payable	200,000			200,000
Premium on Bonds Payable	30,000	I 600		29,400
Common Stock	245,500		L-1 50,000	335,500
			M 40,000	
Retained Earnings	88,000	N 10,000	A 14,500	92,500
Total Credits.........................	$863,500			$967,900
Summary Entry Totals		$156,000	$156,000	
Cash Flows from Operations				
Net Income		A$ 14,500		
Add: Decrease in Prepaids		E 1,500		
Increase in Accrued Liab.......		F 4,500		
Depreciation Expense		G 12,000		
Patent Amortization		H 1,000		
Deduct: Increase in Receivables			B$ 19,000	
Increase in Inventory			C 22,000	
Decrease in Payables			D 6,000	
Amortization of Bond Premium			I 600	
Gain on Sale of Land........			J 2,500	
Cash Flows from Investing				
Add: Cash from Sale of Land........		J 30,000		
Deduct: Cash used to Purchase Land.....			K 48,400	
Cash Flows from Financing				
Add: Cash from Sale of Common Stock		M 40,000		
Deduct: Cash Used to Pay Dividends.....			N 10,000	
Noncash Investing and Financing				
Acquisition of Building for Common Stock		L-1 50,000	L-2 50,000	
Summary Entries Subtotals		$153,500	$158,500	
Net Decrease in Cash..................		Z 5,000		
Summary Entries Totals		$158,500	$158,500	

The analysis transactions are entered in the summary debit and credit columns in the following manner: Transaction A, the analysis of net income for the year, is entered in the credit column in the row containing the Retained Earnings account. The corresponding $14,500 debit is entered in the debit column in the net income row on the bottom of the worksheet under cash flows from operations.

We'll do two more: Transaction B analyzed the $19,000 change in Accounts Receivable. The debit is entered in the accounts receivable row while the credit is entered on the bottom of the worksheet under cash flows from operations in the increase in receivables row. The last transaction from the T-account approach was the payment of $10,000 dividends, transaction N. This is entered on the worksheet in the debit column in the row containing Retained Earnings. And it is entered on the bottom of the worksheet under cash flows from financing as a credit.

All of the other transactions are entered in a similar manner: Study Exhibit 15-5 and trace the transaction analysis entries to their respective debits and credits. With the worksheet approach we need one more debit and credit. After transaction N, the last transaction, we need to add the debit column and the credit column for the bottom portion of the worksheet. The debits total $153,500, while the credits total $158,500, a difference of $5,000. That's the decrease in the Cash account which has yet to be handled on the worksheet. That's why we need one more transaction on the worksheet. We've labeled it transaction Z and it's a debit on the very bottom of the worksheet in the net decrease in cash row and a credit at the very top in the cash row. Now we add the debits and credits for the balance sheet summary entries and get $156,000 proving the equality of the debits and credits.

Once the worksheet is complete it is a simple matter to then prepare the statement of cash flows from the bottom portion of the worksheet.

CHAPTER SUMMARY

The *statement of cash flows* is the fourth major financial statement that must be published for external users. The objective of this statement is to provide information about cash receipts and cash payments and to provide information about the *investing* and *financing activities* of a business. The information provided by the statement of cash flows together with the information contained in the three other financial statements help financial statement users assess: (1) an entity's ability to generate positive future cash flows; (2) an entity's ability to meet its obligations, its need for external financing, and its ability to pay dividends; (3) the reasons for differences between income and associated cash receipts and payments; and (4) both the cash and noncash aspects of an entity's investing and financing transactions.

The statement is divided into three major sections: *cash flows from operating activities, cash flows from investing activities,* and *cash flows from financing activities.* Cash flows from operating activities are generally the cash effects of transactions that enter into the determination of income. Cash flows from investing activities are those that include lending money, collecting loans, and acquiring or selling securities and productive assets. Cash flows from financing activities include obtaining resources from owners and creditors, providing owners a return on and a return of their investment, and repaying creditors.

The statement of cash flows can be prepared in one of two ways, the *T-account approach* or the *worksheet approach.* The T-account approach is easier and faster but it is not as formal as the worksheet approach, nor does the T-account approach provide documentation of the cash flow analysis.

When using the T-account approach you must establish a T-account for each balance sheet item, placing the beginning and ending balances in the T-accounts. A very large T-account must be prepared for cash since this account will eventually contain all the information necessary to prepare the statement. Entries are recorded in the T-accounts to reproduce, in summary form, the transactions that took place during the period. Whenever cash is involved it is placed in the Cash T-account in the appropriate operating, investing, or financing section of that T-account. The corresponding debit or credit is entered into the appropriate balance sheet account. The T-account approach is an orderly, efficient way of handling a large number of transactions in a complex situation.

The worksheet approach requires the preparation of a formal worksheet containing four columns. The first and the last columns contain the beginning and ending balance sheet account balances. The middle two columns are for the summary debit and credit analysis entries. The analysis entries that are entered in the middle two columns explain how the balance sheet account went from the beginning balance to the ending balance and on the bottom of the worksheet where they generate the statement of cash flows.

IMPORTANT TERMS USED IN THIS CHAPTER

Accrual-basis income   A measure of income that recognizes revenue as it is earned and matches expenses incurred in earning the revenue reported. (page 616)

Cash-basis income   A measure of income that recognizes revenue when cash is received and reports expenses when cash is paid out. (page 616)

Financing activity   Transactions entered into by a business entity that would include obtaining resources from owners and creditors, providing owners a return on and a return of their investment, and repaying creditors. (page 614)

Investing activity   Transactions entered into by a business entity that would include lending money and collecting loans, acquiring and selling securities, and acquiring and selling productive assets. (page 612)

Operating activity   Transactions entered into by a business entity that would include the delivering or producing of goods for sale and providing services. (page 608)

QUESTIONS

1. Why is the statement of cash flows needed when a company already issues a balance sheet, income statement, and statement of retained earnings?

2. How does the statement of cash flows help the user of financial statements?

3. The statement of cash flows contains three major sections. What are these sections and what information is contained in each?

4. When preparing a statement of cash flows net income must be adjusted to derive cash flows from operations. Why is this adjustment necessary?

5. Why is it logical to analyze balance sheet accounts when preparing to construct a statement of cash flows?

6. Towards the end of the chapter another section was added to the statement of cash flows. The section was called noncash investing and financing activities. What is the purpose of this section?

7. A statement in the financial press recently stated that a company had a source of cash flows of $150,000 from depreciation. Comment on this statement.

8. How does the calculation of cash-basis income differ from the calculation of accrual-basis income?

9. Explain the difference between determining cash flows from operations by the *direct* method and the *indirect* method.

10. In calculating cash flows from operations depreciation expense is added back to net income and amortization of premium on bonds payable is deducted from net income. Where are each of these pieces of information found in the T-accounts? (Which T-account, and on which side?)

11. Why is it necessary in the T-account analysis to split a financing and investing activity not affecting cash flows into two parts and analyze it as if it were two transactions?

12. What are the advantages and disadvantages of the T-account and the worksheet approaches to preparing the statement of cash flows?

13. A gain on the disposal of equipment would be reported as a deduction from net income on the statement of cash flows. Explain why?

14. A company recently acquired a desk-top computer, giving a 60-day note for the full price. How is this transaction reflected on the statement of cash flows?

EXERCISES

Exercise 15-1
Determining the cash-flow effect of changes in account balances on net income

Explain what effect each of the following changes in account balances would have on net income when determining cash flows from operations. Each item is to be considered independently.

Example: Accounts Receivable decreases by $11,500.
Effect: Net income is adjusted by adding $11,500.

a. Supplies Inventory decreases by $5,690.
b. Accounts Payable decreases by $3,200.
c. Accounts Receivable increases by $24,400.
d. Prepaid Insurance decreases by $1,800.
e. Merchandise Inventory increases by $15,500.
f. Income Taxes Payable increases by $6,100.
g. Allowance for Uncollectibles decreases by $2,800.

Exercise 15-2
Determining cash flows from operations

The Dodge Company reported net income for the year to be $27,000. Determine the cash flows from operations assuming the following information:

a. Accounts Receivable increased $3,000.
b. Accounts Payable increased $12,000.
c. Merchandise Inventory decreased $2,500.
d. Depreciation amounted to $5,000.

(Check figure: Cash flows from operations = $43,500)

Exercise 15-3
Re-creating entries and determining effect on cash flows from operations

The following transactions are among those entered into by Champion Inc., during 1989. Re-create the entry that Champion should have made and determine the effect of the entry on cash flows.

Example: Champion borrowed $10,000 from the bank on a long-term note.

Entry: Cash.. 10,000
            Notes Payable 10,000

Effect: Cash flows from investing activities increased by $10,000.

a. One hundred shares of Texas-T Oil Inc., was purchased for $21,000 as a long-term investment.

b. An account receivable in the amount of $1,080 was collected.

c. A building was purchased for $170,000. $10,000 cash was paid and a 90-day note was given for the balance.

d. A parcel of land having an original cost of $10,000 was sold for $17,000.

e. A customer's account with a $400 balance was written off as uncollectible (the allowance method is used).

f. Champion issued 1,000 shares of $2 par common stock for $2,460.

Exercise 15-4
Calculating cash flows
from operations

The 1989 income statement of Gull Paper Co. appears below:

GULL PAPER CO. Income Statement Year Ended December 31, 1989		
Sales		$240,000
Cost of Goods Sold		90,000
Gross Profit on Sales		$150,000
Operating Expenses:		
Advertising Expense	$14,000	
Depreciation Expense	36,000	
Patent Amortization Expense	5,000	
Salary Expense	56,000	111,000
Net Income		$ 39,000

Calculate the cash flows from operations for 1989. (Begin with net income and add back expenses not using cash.)

(Check figure: Cash flows from operations = $80,000)

Exercise 15-5
Stating where effect of
transactions would appear
on statement of cash flows

Each of the following transactions will result in cash flows from investing activities, cash flows from financing activities, or noncash investing and financing activities. Analyze each transaction and state which one of these three categories on the statement of cash flows will be affected.

a. $400,000 was borrowed by issuing bonds that mature in 20 years.

b. A dump truck with a book value of $3,500 was traded for stationery and other office supplies.

c. A $39,400 cash dividend was declared and paid.

d. A machine was acquired by issuing a 60-day note for the $8,000 purchase price.

e. Land was acquired by exchanging 10,000 shares of common stock for the property. The stock had a market price of $98,000.

f. A patent was sold for $12,500. A 30-day note was accepted for the total amount. (The book value of the patent was also $12,500.)

g. Equipment was purchased for $105,000.

h. Used machinery having a book value of $12,800 was traded for 100 shares of stock in another corporation. The stock acquired is to be held for an extended period.

i. An individual to whom the corporation owed $5,000 on a long-term note accepted a used copying machine in full payment of the debt.

j. Five hundred shares of common stock were sold on subscription. The subscription payments were due on the first day of each of the 3 months following the subscription sale. The subscription price totaled $75,000.

**Exercise 15-6
Preparing cash flows from operations section of the T-account for cash**

Turbo Products Inc., uses the T-account approach to prepare the working papers for the statement of cash flows. The following T-account was used to gather information about the cash flows from operations.

Cash			
(3) Depreciation Expense	50,000	(1) Net Loss for the Year	24,600
(4) Patent Amortization Expense	6,000	(2) Gain on Sale of Land	8,400
(6) Loss on Sale of Equipment	14,600	(5) Amortization of Premium on Bond Payable	19,000

Prepare the cash flows from operations section of the statement of cash flows.

(Check figure: Cash flows from operations = $18,600)

**Exercise 15-7
Converting items from accrual basis to cash basis**

Hobbs Inc., is attempting to convert its accrual-basis income into cash-basis income. For each of the following situations, perform the required conversion:

a. Sales on the accrual-basis income statement amounted to $172,500. Accounts Receivable at the beginning and end of the year totaled $97,500 and $115,000, respectively. Determine cash collected from customers on the cash-basis income statement.

(Check figure: Cash collected from customers = $155,000)

b. Advertising Expense on the accrual-basis income statement was $20,750. Prepaid Advertising increased from $7,000 at the beginning of the year to $8,000 at the end of the year. Determine the cash paid for advertising on the cash-basis income statement.

c. Salary Expense on the accrual-basis income statement was $27,900. Accrued Salaries Payable at the beginning and end of the year amounted to $780 and $1,180, respectively. Determine the cash paid for salaries on the cash-basis income statement.

d. Depreciation Expense on the accrual-basis income statement was $12,500. Accumulated Depreciation increased from $62,500 at the beginning of the year to $75,000 at the end. Calculate the Depreciation Expense on the cash-basis income statement.

PROBLEMS: SET A

**Problem A15-1
Preparing the cash flows from operating activity section**

In each of the three columns below are income statement data for the year ended Dec. 31, 1989:

	Company X	Company Y	Company Z
Sales Revenue..........................	$200,000	$125,000	$60,000
Cost of Goods Sold Expense	80,000	75,000	20,000
Patent Amortization Expense	3,000	6,000	—
Depreciation Expense: Machinery	9,000	10,000	1,750
Organization Cost Amortization Expense.......	750	—	250
Depreciation Expense: Building	16,500	9,500	4,200
Income Tax Expense......................	26,250	—	12,000
Salary Expense	25,000	15,500	7,500
Utilities Expense	13,500	7,300	3,800
Gain on Sale of Machine	—	—	2,000
Loss on Sale of Land.....................	—	2,700	—

Required

Prepare the cash flows from operating activities section of the statement of cash flows for Company X, Y, and Z, respectively. (Hint: First calculate net income for each of the three.)

(Check figure: Cash flows from operating activities, Company X = $55,250)

The 1989 financial statements of Asian Products Inc., are shown below:

ASIAN PRODUCTS INC.
Income Statement
Year Ended December 31, 1989
(000's omitted)

Sales..	$2,000
Cost of Goods Sold.......................................	(960)
Gross Profit on Sales.....................................	$1,040
Operating Expenses:	
Depreciation...	(120)
Other...	(440)
Net Income...	$ 480

ASIAN PRODUCTS, INC.
Comparative Balance Sheets
(000's omitted)

	December 31, 1989	1988
Assets		
Cash..	$ 60	$ 80
Accounts Receivable (net)...........................	750	500
Merchandise Inventory...............................	650	700
Land..	440	416
Building..	1,680	1,600
Accumulated Depreciation: Building...............	(340)	(220)
Total Assets...	$3,240	$3,076
Equities		
Accounts Payable.......................................	$ 384	$ 400
Noncurrent Liabilities..................................	40	420
Common Stock...	1,680	1,600
Retained Earnings......................................	1,136	656
Total Equities..	$3,240	$3,076

Additional information taken from the financial records of Asian Products:

a. Land costing $24,000 was acquired for cash.
b. $380,000 of noncurrent liabilities were paid off with cash.
c. Common stock was issued in exchange for a building with a fair market value of $80,000.

Required

Prepare a statement of cash flows in good form for the year ended Dec. 31, 1989. You need not prepare T-account working papers. All the information needed to prepare the statement is given in the income statement, balance sheets, and additional information above.

(Check figure: Cash flow from operating activities = $384,000)

**Problem A15-3
Preparing a statement of
cash flows**

Mainsea's 1989 financial statements appear below:

MAINSEA ENTERPRISES
Income Statement
Year Ended December 31, 1989
(000's omitted)

Sales..		$400
Cost of Goods Sold..		225
Gross Profit on Sales......................................		$175
Operating Expenses:		
Depreciation..	$33	
Other (including taxes).............................	92	125
Net Income..		$ 50

MAINSEA ENTERPRISES
Balance Sheet
(000's omitted)

	Dec. 31, 1989	Dec. 31, 1988	Increase (Decrease) in Account Balance
Assets			
Cash...	$ 89	$ 19	$ 70
Accounts Receivable.........................	108	58	50
Merchandise Inventory......................	123	88	35
Prepaid Expenses...........................	4	5	(1)
Land..	100	70	30
Building.....................................	500	400	100
Accumulated Depreciation	(103)	(70)	33
Total Assets................................	$ 821	$570	
Equities			
Accounts Payable...........................	$ 43	$ 49	(6)
Accrued Payables...........................	16	—	16
Bonds Payable (due 1995)	100	—	100
Common Stock	550	450	100
Retained Earnings..........................	112	71	41
Total Equities..............................	$ 821	$570	

Other relevant data:

a. Land was purchased for $30,000.
b. Bonds Payable in the amount of $100,000 were issued for a new building.
c. A $9,000 cash dividend was declared and paid.
d. Common stock was sold for $100,000 cash.

Required

Prepare a statement of cash flows using either the T-account approach or the worksheet approach as directed by your instructor.

(Check figure: Cash flows from operating activities = $9,000)

**Problem A15-4
Preparing a statement of
cash flows**

Potter Company condensed balance sheets for Dec. 31, 1988 and 1989, and the condensed
income statement for the year ended Dec. 31, 1989, are presented below:

**POTTER COMPANY
Income Statement (Condensed)
Year Ended December 31, 1989**

Sales..		$171,000
Cost of Goods Sold Expense...		70,650
Gross Profit on Sales		$100,350
Operating Expenses:		
Depreciation Expense: Building..........................	$12,500	
Depreciation Expense: Machinery........................	3,750	
Patent Amortization Expense.............................	600	
Other Selling and Administrative Expenses.................	24,000	40,850
Income before Tax		$ 59,500
Income Tax Expense		26,000
Net Income		$ 33,500

**POTTER COMPANY
Comparative Balance Sheets (Condensed)**

	Dec. 31	
	1989	**1988**
Assets:		
Current Assets:		
Cash..	$ 16,100	$ 2,650
Accounts Receivable	24,000	28,700
Allowance for Uncollectibles	(1,500)	(1,100)
Merchandise Inventory	40,750	27,250
Current Assets (total).................................	$ 79,350	$ 57,500
Property, Plant, and Equipment:		
Land	$103,500	$ 73,500
Building	210,000	150,000
Less: Accumulated Depreciation..........................	(45,000)	(32,500)
Machinery	112,500	112,500
Less: Accumulated Depreciation..........................	(21,250)	(17,500)
Total Property, Plant, and Equipment.................	$359,750	$286,000
Intangible Assets:		
Patent	$ 8,400	$ 9,000
Total Assets	$447,500	$352,500
Liabilities and Stockholders' Equity		
Current Liabilities:		
Accounts Payable	$ 12,500	$ 18,750
Salaries Payable...	6,500	3,750
Current Liabilities (total)............................	$ 19,000	$ 22,500
Noncurrent Liabilities:		
Bonds Payable (issued at par).............................	50,000	75,000
Total Liabilities..	$ 69,000	$ 97,500
Common Stock (no par)	$290,000	$200,000
Retained Earnings..	88,500	55,000
Total Stockholders' Equity	$378,500	$255,000
Total Liabilities and Stockholders' Equity....................	$447,500	$352,500

In addition the following information was compiled from the company's financial records:

a. A plot of land was purchased for $30,000 cash.
b. A new building was purchased for cash, $60,000.
c. Additional common stock was issued for $90,000 cash.
d. Bonds with a maturity value of $25,000 were retired when they matured.

Required

Prepare a statement of cash flows using either the T-account approach or the worksheet approach as directed by your instructor.

(Check figure: Cash flows from operating activities = $38,450)

Problem A15-5
Preparing a statement of cash flows

Siesta Fashions Inc., condensed balance sheets for 1988 and 1989 and the income statement for 1989 are shown below:

SIESTA FASHIONS INC. Comparative Balance Sheets (Condensed) (000's omitted)		
	Dec. 31,	
	1989	**1988**
Assets		
Current Assets:		
Cash	$ 115	$ 20
Accounts Receivable......................	240	200
Allowance for Uncollectibles......................	(25)	(15)
Merchandise Inventory......................	450	585
Prepaid Expenses......................	90	50
Current Assets (total)	$ 870	$ 840
Property, Plant, and Equipment:		
Land......................	$ 256	$ 156
Building......................	242	266
Less: Accumulated Depreciation	(84)	(104)
Machinery......................	300	140
Less: Accumulated Depreciation	(60)	(50)
Total Property, Plant, and Equipment	$ 654	$ 408
Total Assets......................	$1,524	$1,248
Liabilities and Stockholders' Equity		
Current Liabilities:		
Accounts Payable	$ 260	$ 210
Accrued Liabilities......................	86	70
Current Liabilities (total)......................	$ 346	$ 280
Noncurrent Liabilities:		
Bonds Payable (issued at par)	200	200
Total Liabilities	$ 546	$ 480
Preferred Stock......................	$ 160	$ -0-
Common Stock (no par)......................	600	600
Retained Earnings......................	218	168
Total Stockholders' Equity	$ 978	$ 768
Total Liabilities and Stockholders' Equity	$1,524	$1,248

SIESTA FASHIONS INC.
Income Statement (Condensed)
Year Ended December 31, 1989
(000's omitted)

Sales		$840
Cost of Goods Sold Expense		548
Gross Profit on Sales		$292
Operating Expenses:		
Selling Expenses	$152	
Administrative Expenses	64	
Depreciation Expense: Building	16	
Depreciation Expense: Machinery	10	242
Net Income		$ 50

In addition the following was compiled from the company's records:

a. A building was purchased for $40,000 cash.
b. Machinery for a new assembly line was purchased by giving the manufacturer preferred stock. The machinery acquired has a fair market value of $160,000.
c. A building was sold for $28,000. The building had originally cost $64,000 and had accumulated depreciation of $36,000.
d. Land was purchased for $100,000.

Required	Prepare a statement of cash flows using either the T-account approach or the worksheet approach as directed by your instructor.

(Check figure: Net increase in cash = $207,000)

Problem A15-6
Preparing a statement of cash flows

Lott Salt Co. financial statements for 1989 appear below:

LOTT SALT CO.
Income Statement
Year Ended September 30, 1989
(000's omitted)

Sales		$11,892
Cost of Goods Sold		(8,466)
Gross Profit on Sales		$ 3,426
Operating Expenses:		
Depreciation Expense: Building	$ 130	
Depreciation Expense: Equipment	46	
Other Operating Expenses	2,480	(2,656)
Income from Primary Operations		$ 770
Other Income and Expense:		
Interest Expense	$ (58)	
Gain on Sale of Building	32	(26)
Income before Tax		$ 744
Income Taxes		(230)
Net Income		$ 514

(continued)

LOTT SALT CO.
Statement of Retained Earnings
For Year Ended September 30, 1989
(000's omitted)

Retained Earnings Balance (10/1/88)	$1,024
Add: Net Income for the Year	514
Total	$1,538
Deduct: Dividends Declared and Paid	(194)
Retained Earnings (9/30/89).	$1,344

LOTT SALT CO.
Comparative Balance Sheets
(000's omitted)

	Sept. 30, 1989	Sept. 30, 1988	Increase (Decrease) in Account Balance
Assets			
Current Assets:			
Cash	$ 676	$ 608	$ 68
Accounts Receivable (net)	1,280	854	426
Merchandise Inventory.	888	1,034	(146)
Total Current Assets.	$ 2,844	$ 2,496	
Property, Plant and Equipment:			
Land.	$ 1,110	$ 860	250
Buildings	2,102	2,050	52
Less: Accumulated Depreciation	(1,010)	(1,032)	(22)
Equipment	1,460	1,460	-0-
Less: Accumulated Depreciation	(636)	(590)	46
Total Property, Plant, and Equipment	$ 3,026	$ 2,748	
Total Assets.	$ 5,870	$ 5,244	
Liabilities and Stockholders' Equity			
Current Liabilities:			
Accounts Payable.	$ 736	$ 900	(164)
Notes Payable.	200	280	(80)
Accrued Payables.	132	120	12
Total Current Liabilities.	$ 1,068	$ 1,300	
Noncurrent Liabilities:			
Notes Payable (due 6/30/95).	$ 280	-0-	280
Bonds Payable (due 12/31/99)	600	$ 600	-0-
Discount on Bonds Payable.	(72)	(80)	(8)
Total Noncurrent Liabilities	$ 808	$ 520	
Total Liabilities	$ 1,876	$ 1,820	
Stockholders' Equity:			
Common Stock (no par)	$ 2,650	$ 2,400	250
Retained Earnings.	1,344	1,024	320
Total Stockholders' Equity	$ 3,994	$ 3,424	
Total Liabilities and Stockholders' Equity	$ 5,870	$ 5,244	

An analysis of Lott's financial records revealed the following information:

a. A building costing $248,000 and having an accumulated depreciation of $152,000 was sold for $128,000. The $32,000 gain appears on the income statement.

b. Common stock was issued in exchange for 10 acres of land. The common stock and the land were fairly valued at $250,000.

c. The entry to record interest expense on the bonds was as follows:

Interest Expense...	58,000	
Cash..		50,000
Discount on Bonds Payable		8,000

(Less cash was used than is reflected in the Interest Expense account.)

d. $280,000 was borrowed from the bank; a note due in 1995 was signed.

e. An addition to the building costing $300,000 was constructed for cash.

f. Dividends of $194,000 were declared and paid.

| **Required** | Prepare a statement of cash flows using either the T-account approach or the worksheet approach as directed by your instructor. |

(Check figure: Net cash flows from operations = $154,000)

Problem A15-7
Calculating cash-basis net income

Hamilton Concrete Inc.'s 1989 income statement and comparative balance sheets for 1988 and 1989 appear below:

HAMILTON CONCRETE INC.
Income Statement
Year Ended June 30, 1989

Sales		$360,000
Cost of Goods Sold		150,000
Gross Profit on Sales		$210,000
Operating Expenses:		
Depreciation Expense.....................................	$70,000	
Other Operating Expenses................................	40,000	110,000
Net Income		$100,000

HAMILTON CONCRETE INC.
Comparative Balance Sheets

	June 30	
	1989	**1988**
Assets		
Cash	$ 60,000	$ 40,000
Accounts Receivable (net)...................................	120,000	160,000
Merchandise Inventory......................................	160,000	70,000
Noncurrent Assets (net)	300,000	110,000
Total Assets..	$640,000	$380,000

(continued)

Equities		
Accounts Payable	$ 80,000	$ 50,000
Accrued Salaries Payable	20,000	80,000
Noncurrent Liabilities	210,000	20,000
Total Liabilities	$310,000	$150,000
Paid-In Capital	$200,000	$200,000
Retained Earnings	130,000	30,000
Total Stockholders' Equity	$330,000	$230,000
Total Equities	$640,000	$380,000

Required

Calculate Hamilton Concrete's cash-basis net income for the year ended June 30, 1989.

(Check figure: Cash-basis net income = $90,000)

PROBLEMS: SET B

**Problem B15-1
Preparing the cash flows
from operations section**

In each of the three columns below are income statement data for the year ended Dec. 31, 1989:

	Company A	Company B	Company C
Sales Revenue	$160,000	$300,000	$400,000
Cost of Goods Sold Expense	60,000	180,000	200,000
Advertising Expense	12,000	16,000	40,000
Sales Commission Expense	6,000	30,000	60,000
Goodwill Amortization Expense	2,000	—	—
Depreciation Expense: Building	3,000	8,000	72,000
Depreciation Expense: Equipment	1,000	32,000	24,000
Patent Amortization Expense	3,600	40,000	—
Income Tax Expense	18,000	—	1,800
Loss on Sale of Machinery	1,600	—	—
Gain on Sale of Land	—	—	20,000

Required

Prepare the cash flows from operations section of the statement of cash flows for Company A, B, and C, respectively. (Hint: First calculate net income for each of the three.)

(Check figure: Cash flows from operations, Company B = $74,000)

**Problem B15-2
Preparing the statement
of cash flows**

The 1989 financial statements of Kord Enterprises Inc., are shown below:

KORD ENTERPRISES INC.
Income Statement
Year Ended December 31, 1989
(000's omitted)

Sales	$1,600
Cost of Goods Sold	820)
Gross Profit on Sales	$ 780
Operating Expenses:	
Depreciation	(40)
Other	(220)
Net Income	$ 520

(continued)

KORD ENTERPRISES INC.
Comparative Balance Sheets
(000's omitted)

	Dec. 31,	
	1989	**1988**
Assets		
Current Assets:		
Cash	$ 120	$ 150
Accounts Receivable (net)	320	80
Merchandise Inventory......................................	560	610
Current Assets (total)	$1,000	$ 840
Property, Plant, and Equipment:		
Land...	$ 280	$ 180
Building..	1,640	1,500
Accumulated Depreciation: Building	(120)	(80)
Total Property, Plant, and Equipment	$1,800	$1,600
Total Assets......................................	$2,800	$2,440
Equities		
Current Liabilities:		
Accounts Payable	$ 160	$ 80
Salaries Payable	200	220
Total Current Liabilities..............................	$ 360	$ 300
Noncurrent Liabilities......................................	80	400
Common Stock	1,540	1,440
Retained Earnings	820	300
Total Equities................................	$2,800	$2,440

Additional information taken from the financial records of Kord Enterprises:
a. A building costing $140,000 was aquired for cash.
b. Cash was used to pay off noncurrent liabilities amounting to $320,000.
c. Common stock was issued in exchange for land with a fair market value of $100,000.

Required

Prepare a statement of cash flows in good form for the year ended Dec. 31, 1989. You need not prepare T-accounts. All the information needed to prepare the statement is given in the income statement, balance sheets, and additional information above.

(Check figure: Cash flows from operations = $430,000)

Problem B15-3
Preparing a statement of cash flows.

Maxxco's 1989 financial statements are shown below:

MAXXCO INC.
Income Statement
Year Ended December 31, 1989
(000's omitted)

Sales		$800
Cost of Goods Sold		450
Gross Profit on Sales		$350
Operating Expenses:		
Depreciation	$ 65	
Other (including taxes)...................................	185	250
Net Income		$100

(continued)

MAXXCO INC.
Balance Sheet
(000's omitted)

	Dec. 31,		Increase (Decrease) in Account Balance
	1989	1988	
Assets			
Cash	$ 177	$ 38	$139
Accounts Receivable	217	116	101
Merchandise Inventory	245	176	69
Prepaid Expenses	9	11	(2)
Land	200	140	60
Building	1,000	800	200
Accumulated Depreciation...................	(205)	(140)	65
Total Assets	$1,643	$1,141	
Equities			
Accounts Payable.............................	$ 86	$ 97	(11)
Accrued Payables	33	-0-	33
Bonds Payable (due 1995)	200	-0-	200
Common Stock................................	1,100	900	200
Retained Earnings	224	144	80
Total Equities	$1,643	$1,141	

Other relevant data:
a. Land was purchased for $60,000 cash.
b. Bonds payable in the amount of $200,000 were issued for a new building.
c. A $20,000 cash dividend was declared and paid.
d. Common stock was issued for $200,000 cash.

Required

Prepare a statement of cash flows using the T-account approach or the worksheet approach as directed by your instructor.   *(Check figure: Cash flows from operations = $19,000)*

Problem B15-4
Preparing a statement of cash flows

Raines Inc., condensed balance sheets for Dec. 31, 1988 and 1989, and the condensed income statement for the year ended Dec. 31, 1989, are presented below:

RAINES INC.
Income Statement (Condensed)
Year Ended December 31, 1989

Sales..		$970,000
Cost of Goods Sold Expense		630,500
Gross Profit on Sales...		$339,500
Operating Expenses:		
Depreciation Expense: Building	$30,000	
Depreciation Expense: Equipment.....................	28,000	
Copyright Amortization Expense	7,000	
Other Selling and Administrative Expenses	22,500	87,500
Income before Tax		$252,000
Income Tax Expense.......................................		138,500
Net Income..		$113,500

(continued)

RAINES INC.
Comparative Balance Sheets (Condensed)

	Dec. 31	
	1989	**1988**
Assets		
Current Assets:		
Cash	$ 6,100	$ 3,650
Accounts Receivable	58,500	71,300
Allowance for Uncollectibles	(2,100)	(2,450)
Merchandise Inventory	140,000	127,500
Current Assets (total)	$ 202,500	$ 200,000
Property, Plant, and Equipment:		
Land	$ 196,000	$ 152,000
Building	672,500	610,000
Less: Accumulated Depreciation	(383,000)	(353,000)
Equipment	450,000	450,000
Less: Accumulated Depreciation	(73,000)	(45,000)
Total Property, Plant, and Equipment	$ 862,500	$ 814,000
Intangible Assets:		
Copyright	$ 49,000	$ 56,000
Total Assets	$1,114,000	$1,070,000
Liabilities and Stockholders' Equity		
Current Liabilities:		
Accounts Payable	$ 68,000	$ 89,000
Salaries Payable	12,500	11,000
Current Liabilities (total)	$ 80,500	$ 100,000
Noncurrent Liabilities:		
Bonds Payable (issued at par)	200,000	300,000
Total Liabilities	$ 280,500	$ 400,000
Common Stock (no par)	$ 550,000	$ 500,000
Retained Earnings	283,500	170,000
Total Stockholders' Equity	$ 833,500	$ 670,000
Total Liabilities and Stockholders' Equity	$1,114,000	$1,070,000

In addition, the following information was compiled from the company's financial records:

a. Additional land costing $44,000 was purchased for cash.
b. A new building was purchased for cash, $62,500.
c. Additional common stock was issued for $50,000.
d. $100,000 of outstanding bonds were retired at maturity.

| *Required* | Prepare a statement of cash flows using either the T-account approach or the worksheet approach as directed by your instructor. |

(Check figure: Cash flows from operations = $158,950)

Problem B15-5
Preparing a statement of cash flows

Advanced Filters Inc., condensed balance sheets for 1988 and 1989, and the income statement for 1989, are shown below:

ADVANCED FILTERS INC.
Comparative Balance Sheets (Condensed)
(000's omitted)

	Dec. 31,	
Assets	**1989**	**1988**
Current Assets:		
Cash	$ 12	$ 7
Accounts Receivable......................	63	59
Allowance for Uncollectibles.....................	(6)	(8)
Merchandise Inventory......................	135	101
Prepaid Expenses......................	8	11
Current Assets (total)	$ 212	$ 170
Property, Plant, and Equipment:		
Land......................	$ 604	$ 428
Building......................	1,560	1,400
Less: Accumulated Depreciation	(168)	(88)
Equipment	620	660
Less: Accumulated Depreciation	(216)	(200)
Total Property, Plant, and Equipment	$2,400	$2,200
Total Assets......................	$2,612	$2,370
Liabilities and Stockholders' Equity		
Current Liabilities:		
Accounts Payable	$ 110	$ 60
Accrued Liabilities......................	26	20
Current Liabilities (total)......................	$ 136	$ 80
Noncurrent Liabilities:		
Bonds Payable (issued at par)	180	20
Total Liabilities	$ 316	$ 100
Common Stock (no par)......................	$2,000	$2,000
Retained Earnings......................	296	270
Total Stockholders' Equity	$2,296	$2,270
Total Liabilities and Stockholders' Equity	$2,612	$2,370

ADVANCED FILTERS INC.
Income Statement (Condensed)
Year Ended December 31, 1989
(000's omitted)

Sales		$700
Cost of Goods Sold Expense		454
Gross Profit on Sales......................		$246
Operating Expenses:		
Selling Expenses	$70	
Administrative Expenses	40	
Depreciation Expense: Building......................	80	
Depreciation Expense: Equipment	30	220
Net Income		$ 26

In addition the following information was compiled from the company's records:

a. Equipment having a cost of $60,000 and accumulated depreciation of $14,000 was sold for $46,000.
b. A major addition to the building was constructed. The addition was "paid for" by giving the construction company a bond for $160,000 due in 3 years.
c. Land was purchased for $176,000.
d. Equipment was purchased for $20,000.

| **Required** | Prepare a statement of cash flows using either the T-account approach or the worksheet approach as directed by your instructor. |

(Check figure: Cash flows from operations = $155,000)

Problem B15-6
Preparing a statement of cash flows

Unlimited Products Inc., financial statements for 1989 appear below:

UNLIMITED PRODUCTS INC.
Income Statement
Year Ended June 30, 1989
(000's omitted)

Sales..		$12,780
Cost of Goods Sold...		(7,668)
Gross Profit on Sales..		$ 5,112
Operating Expenses:		
Depreciation Expense: Building.............................	$ 150	
Depreciation Expense: Equipment	75	
Other Operating Expenses..................................	3,474	(3,699)
Income from Primary Operations.........................		$ 1,413
Other Income and Expense:		
Interest Expense	$ 120	
Loss on Sale of Equipment.................................	45	(165)
Income before Tax.....................................		$ 1,248
Income Taxes...		(609)
Net Income...		$ 639

UNLIMITED PRODUCTS INC.
Statement of Retained Earnings
For Year Ended June 30, 1989
(000's omitted)

Retained Earnings Balance (7/1/88)	$	660
Add: Net Income for the Year		639
Total	$	1,299
Deduct: Dividends Declared and Paid		(204)
Retained Earnings (6/30/89)...................................	$	1,095

UNLIMITED PRODUCTS INC. Comparative Balance Sheets (000's omitted)			
	June 30,		**Increase (Decrease) in Account Balance**
	1989	**1988**	
Assets			
Current Assets:			
Cash	$ 1,230	$ 1,155	$ 75
Accounts Receivable (net)	2,520	2,580	(60)
Merchandise Inventory...........................	975	564	411
Total Current Assets	$ 4,725	$ 4,299	
Property, Plant, and Equipment:			
Land...	$ 1,455	$ 1,155	300
Buildings	3,210	3,210	-0-
Less: Accumulated Depreciation	(570)	(420)	150
Equipment....................................	2,700	2,565	135
Less: Accumulated Depreciation	(180)	(240)	(60)
Total Property, Plant, and Equipment	$ 6,615	$ 6,270	
Total Assets...................................	$11,340	$10,569	
Liabilities and Stockholders' Equity			
Current Liabilities:			
Accounts Payable.............................	$ 615	$ 720	(105)
Bank Loan Payable	-0-	450	(450)
Accrued Payables..............................	90	129	(39)
Total Current Liabilities....................	$ 705	$ 1,299	
Noncurrent Liabilities:			
Notes Payable (due 9/30/95)....................	$ 690	$ -0-	690
Bonds Payable (due 12/31/99)	3,000	3,000	-0-
Premium on Bonds Payable	600	660	(60)
Total Noncurrent Liabilities	$ 4,290	$ 3,660	
Total Liabilities	$ 4,995	$ 4,959	
Stockholders' Equity:			
Preferred Stock................................	$ 300	$ -0-	300
Common Stock (no par)........................	4,950	4,950	-0-
Retained Earnings	1,095	660	435
Total Stockholders' Equity	$ 6,345	$ 5,610	
Total Liabilities and Stockholders' Equity	$11,340	$10,569	

An analysis of Unlimited's financial records revealed the following information:

a. Equipment costing $405,000 and having an accumulated depreciation of $135,000 was sold for $225,000. The $45,000 loss appears on the income statement.

b. Preferred stock with a par value of $300,000 was issued for 40 acres of land.

c. The entry to record interest expense on the bonds was as follows:

Interest Expense	75,000	
Premium on Bonds Payable	60,000	
Cash...		135,000

(More cash resources were used than is reflected in the Interest Expense account.)

d. Borrowed $690,000 from the bank; a note due in 1995 was signed.
e. Equipment costing $540,000 was purchased for cash.
f. Dividends of $204,000 were declared and paid.

Required

Prepare a statement of cash flows using either the T-account approach or the worksheet approach as directed by your instructor.

(Check figure: Cash flows used in operations = $96,000)

Problem B15-7
Calculating cash-basis net income

Libbey Company's 1989 income statement and comparative balance sheets for 1988 and 1989, are shown below:

LIBBEY COMPANY Income Statement Year Ended September 30, 1989		
Sales		$180,000
Cost of Goods Sold		75,000
Gross Profit on Sales		$105,000
Operating Expenses:		
Depreciation Expense............................	$35,000	
Other Operating Expenses......................	20,000	55,000
Net Income		$ 50,000

LIBBEY COMPANY Comparative Balance Sheets		
	Sept. 30,	
	1989	**1988**
Assets		
Cash	$ 30,000	$ 20,000
Accounts Receivable (net)	60,000	80,000
Merchandise Inventory...............................	80,000	35,000
Noncurrent Assets (net)	150,000	55,000
Total Assets..	$320,000	$190,000
Equities		
Accounts Payable	$ 40,000	$ 25,000
Accrued Salaries Payable	10,000	40,000
Noncurrent Liabilities	105,000	10,000
Total Liabilities	$155,000	$ 75,000
Paid-In Capital...	$100,000	$100,000
Retained Earnings.....................................	65,000	15,000
Total Stockholders' Equity	$165,000	$115,000
Total Equities..	$320,000	$190,000

Required

Calculate Libbey Company's cash-basis net income for the year ended Sept. 30, 1989.

(Check figure: Cash-basis net income = $45,000)

CHAPTER 16

Financial Statement Analysis and Interpretation

By studying this chapter, you will learn:

- What *horizontal* and *vertical financial statement analyses* are
- How to prepare *comparative* and *common-size financial statements*
- How to calculate ratios indicating strength of earnings performance: *rate of return on total assets, rate of return on stockholders' equity, earnings per share,* and *price-earnings ratio*
- How to calculate ratios indicating long-term debt-paying ability: *times interest earned* and *debt-to-equity ratio*
- How to calculate ratios indicating the strength of a company's liquid position: *working capital, current ratio, quick ratio, accounts receivable turnover, number of days sales uncollected,* and *inventory turnover*
- The types of information commonly found in financial statement footnotes that assist in evaluating a company's performance and financial strength

You have studied the structure of financial statements throughout the first 15 chapters. Each component of the four major statements was traced from the original entry recording the data to the point where the item was ultimately disclosed in the appropriate financial statement category. In this chapter we will examine the finished financial statements to discover some of the types of information that can be obtained about the company's earnings performance, its financial structure, and its long- and short-term debt-paying ability.

A company's financial reporting goes beyond just the four financial statements. The auditor's report and the notes to the financial statements also provide valuable sources of information about the company's financial position and results of operations. The *auditor's report* contains the auditor's opinion about whether the presentations on the financial statements are fair within the boundaries of generally accepted accounting principles. Any significant departures from generally accepted accounting principles are noted in the audit report and their effect on the financial statements is quantified wherever possible. The auditor, an independent outside

The auditor's report contains an opinion about whether the financial statement presentations are fair

party, gives an opinion on the financial statements only after carefully reviewing and analyzing the statements and the supporting documents. A careful reading of the audit report provides important background information for the analysis of financial statements.

The notes to the financial statements should not be viewed as an extra bit of data tacked on to the end of the annual report. These notes are an integral part of the statements. They provide significant information found nowhere else in the statements. We will examine the content of some typical notes after we show you how to analyze the financial statements themselves.

COMPARATIVE FINANCIAL STATEMENTS AND TREND ANALYSIS

Horizontal analysis compares financial data of a company for several years

One approach to financial statement analysis is to compare the financial data of a single company for 2 or more years. This *horizontal analysis* makes it possible to focus attention on items that have changed significantly during the period you are reviewing. Comparison of an item over several periods with a base year may show a trend developing. A *base year* is a year chosen as a beginning point.

Comparative Financial Statements

Comparative financial statements compare financial data for 2 or more years

Comparative financial statements usually show financial statement data for 2 or more years, the increase or decrease in each item on the statement, and the percentage change as compared with the earliest year reported. Exhibit 16-1 and 16-2 show such comparative balance sheets and income statements for Most, Inc.

On comparative statements the most current year's information is normally presented in the first column. Successive columns show amounts for progressively earlier and earlier years. The Most, Inc., 2-year comparative statements show the amount of change in each statement item. These increases and decreases are calculated simply by subtracting 1988 amounts from 1989 amounts, e.g., Cash: $5,368 − $6,574 = −$1,206. The percentage increase or decrease in each statement amount is also disclosed in the final column. These percentages are calculated by dividing the amount of change by the earliest year amount, e.g., Cash: −$1,206 ÷ $6,574 = −18.3%. The analyst will give most attention to material comparative statement items that show a significant percentage change during the year. Merchandise inventory is an illustration of a material item showing a significant percentage change (24.1%). Marketable securities also had a large percentage increase (96.8%), but this item would be viewed as much less important because of its relatively small dollar amount.

Material items showing significant changes should be given careful attention

Generally speaking there were no dramatic shifts in the asset, liability, or stockholders' equity structure of Most. The following observations are among those that may be made:

1. The decrease in cash is accompanied by an increase in marketable securities, indicating that Most may be managing its idle cash better in 1989 by investing a larger part of it.

2. While merchandise inventory has increased significantly (24.1%), there appears to be no cause for alarm because sales have also experienced a large boost (28.1%). It is necessary to have more inventory on hand to meet the growing customer demand.

EXHIBIT 16-1

MOST, INC.
Comparative Balance Sheets
(000s omitted)

	December 31, 1989	December 31, 1988	Amount Increase (Decrease)	Percent Increase (Decrease)
Assets				
Current Assets:				
Cash.....	$ 5,368	$ 6,574	$(1,206)	(18.3)%
Marketable Securities.....	3,090	1,570	1,520	96.8
Accounts Receivable (less Allowance for Uncollectibles of $710 in 1989 and $814 in 1988).....	35,382	32,936	2,446	7.4
Merchandise Inventory	62,582	50,434	12,148	24.1
Prepaid Expenses.....	2,870	2,590	280	10.8
Total Current Assets.....	$109,292	$ 94,104	$15,188	16.1
Investments:				
Investment in Common Stock	$ 6,000	$ 6,000	—	—
Property, Plant, and Equipment:				
Land.....	$ 4,520	$ 4,300	$ 220	5.1
Building.....	72,540	72,540	—	—
Less: Accumulated Depreciation	(30,696)	(29,196)	1,500*	5.1
Equipment	18,907	16,717	2,190	13.1
Less: Accumulated Depreciation	(7,980)	(7,840)	140*	1.8
Total Property, Plant, and Equipment	$ 57,291	$ 56,521	$ 770	1.4
Total Assets.....	$172,583	$156,625	$15,958	10.2 %
Liabilities and Stockholders' Equity				
Current Liabilities:				
Accounts Payable	$ 24,235	$ 30,353	$(6,118)	(20.2)%
Accrued Payables.....	9,758	6,137	3,621	59.0
Income Tax Payable.....	2,040	1,425	615	43.2
Current Portion of Long-Term Debt.....	3,000	3,000	—	—
Total Current Liabilities	$ 39,033	$ 40,915	$(1,882)	(4.6)
Long-Term Liabilities:				
8% Mortgage Bonds Payable.....	$ 25,000	$ 28,000	$(3,000)	(10.7)
10% Unsecured Note Payable.....	5,000	—	5,000	†
Total Long-Term Liabilities	$ 30,000	$ 28,000	$ 2,000	7.1
Total Liabilities	$ 69,033	$ 68,915	$ 118	.2
Stockholders' Equity:				
5% Preferred Stock ($10 par)	$ 500	$ 500	—	—
Common Stock ($1 par).....	10,000	9,500	$ 500	5.3
Paid-In Capital in Excess of Par—Common Stock	35,843	30,053	5,790	19.3
Retained Earnings.....	57,207	47,657	9,550	20.0
Total Stockholders' Equity	$103,550	$ 87,710	$15,840	18.1
Total Liabilities and Stockholders' Equity	$172,583	$156,625	$15,958	10.2 %

* The amounts of the Accumulated Depreciation amounts increased. The effect of these increases is to decrease assets. Remember, Accumulated Depreciation is a contra asset.

† When an amount increases or decreases from zero to another number, the percentage change is infinitely large and therefore meaningless ($\frac{5,000}{0} = \infty$).

EXHIBIT 16-2

MOST, INC.				
Comparative Income Statements				
(000s omitted)				
	For the Year Ended December 31,		**Amount Increase (Decrease)**	**Percent Increase (Decrease)**
	1989	**1988**		
Net Sales.....	$ 862,915	$ 673,488	$189,427	28.1%
Cost of Goods Sold.....	(564,346)	(454,335)	110,011	24.2
Gross Profit on Sales	$ 298,569	$ 219,153	$ 79,416	36.2
Operating Expenses:				
Selling Expenses	$(212,062)	$(162,571)	$ 49,491	30.4
General and Administrative Expenses	(58,771)	(35,928)	22,843	63.6
Total Operating Expenses.....	$(270,833)	$(198,499)	$ 72,334	36.4
Other Income and Expenses				
Dividend Income	$ 516	$ 430	$ 86	20.0
Interest Expense	(3,120)	(3,016)	104	3.5
Net Other Income (Expense).....	$ (2,604)	$ (2,586)	$ 18	.7
Income before Income Taxes.....	$ 25,132	$ 18,068	$ 7,064	39.1
Income Tax Expense	(7,557)	(5,693)	1,864	32.7
Net Income	$ 17,575	$ 12,375	$ 5,200	42.0%
Earnings per Common Share.....	$1.80	$1.30		

3. There seems to be a slight shift from using debt to using equity to finance the company. Total liabilities increased only .2% while total stockholders' equity increased 18.1%. These changes occurred while total liabilities and stockholders' equity increased by 10.2%.

Comparative statements provide a means for alerting the analyst to significant shifts that require further attention. He or she will then employ the various techniques we will discuss later in this chapter to analyze those shifts.

Trend Analysis

Trend analysis is another type of horizontal examination that compares proportionate changes in selected financial statement information over time. The time period selected for comparisons is usually at least 5 years and may be as many as 10 or 20.

Trend percentages state selected financial data as a percentage of the same data in a base year

Trend percentages are calculated by selecting a year as a base year and calculating amounts of selected items in following years as percentages of the amount of the same item in the base year. (All amounts in the base year are set equal to 100%). To illustrate, selected income statement amounts for Most, Inc., for the years 1985 through 1989 are given below:

MOST, INC. Selected Income Statement Amounts for the Years Ended December 31, (000s omitted)					
	1989	**1988**	**1987**	**1986**	**1985**
Net Sales	$862,915	$673,488	$562,104	$401,982	$388,500
Gross Profit.	298,569	219,153	218,181	213,986	209,790
Net Income.	17,575	12,375	11,088	10,666	10,560

These amounts are converted into trend percentages by dividing the amount in a given year by the 1985 base year amount, e.g., Sales—1986: $401,982 ÷ $388,500 = 103%; 1987: $562,104 ÷ $388,500 = 145%, etc. The Most, Inc., trend percentages are tabulated below:

MOST, INC. Selected Income Statement Data Shown as Percentages of 1985 Base Year Years Ended December 31,					
	1989	**1988**	**1987**	**1986**	**1985**
Net Sales	222%	173%	145%	103%	100%
Gross Profit.	142	105	104	102	100
Net Income.	166	117	105	101	100

Comparisons of dollar amounts over the years indicate that sales, gross profit, and net income are increasing. Comparisons of the trend percentages reveal that gross profit has not increased nearly as rapidly as sales, indicating possibly that the cost of inventory has been increasing more quickly than the sales price. The percentage increase in net income is not nearly as great as the percentage increase in sales, but it generally exceeds the percentage increase in gross profit. One possible explanation for these trend relationships is that management is doing a good job of controlling either selling or general and administrative expenses, or both.

Trend percentages and comparative statements are used to get an overview of a company's performance

Trend percentages, like comparative financial statements, are used to get an overview of an entity's performance. This overview will highlight particular areas where further, more detailed analysis is needed. The analyst of Most, Inc.'s trend percentages, for example, would probably want to look into other ratios and comparisons relating to cost of goods sold and operating expenses.

COMMON-SIZE FINANCIAL STATEMENTS

Vertical analysis compares financial data within a single year

Relating financial statement items to each other within a single time period is referred to as *vertical analysis.* Common-size financial statements and financial ratios are two tools employed in vertical analysis. Common-size statements will be discussed in this section and financial ratios in the next.

EXHIBIT 16-3

		MOST, INC. **Common-Size Income Statements** **Years Ended December 31,**		
			1989	**1988**
Net Sales			100.00%*	100.00%
Cost of Goods Sold			(65.40)	(67.46)
Gross Profit on Sales			34.60	32.54
Operating Expenses:				
Selling Expenses			(24.58)	(24.14)
General and Administrative Expenses			(6.81)	(5.33)
Total Operating Expenses			(31.39)	(29.47)
Other Income and Expense:				
Dividend Income			.06	.06
Interest Expense			(.36)	(.45)
Net Other Income (Expense)			(.30)	(.39)
Income before Income Taxes			2.91	2.68
Income Tax Expense			(.88)	(.85)
Net Income			2.03%	1.83%

* Percentages have been rounded.

Common-size financial statements show each item on a statement as a percentage of a key item on that statement

Common-size financial statements show each item on a statement as a percentage of one key item on that statement. No dollar amounts appear. Each item on an income statement is usually stated as a percentage of net sales. Common-size balance sheets often state all amounts as a percentage of total assets or total equities.

Most, Inc., common-size income statements are shown in Exhibit 16-3. The computational technique is to take each item and divide by Sales of that year, e.g., Cost of Goods Sold 1989: $564,346 ÷ $862,915 = 65.40%; 1988: $454,335 ÷ $673,488 = 67.46%.

Common-size statements are useful for seeing how significant the components of a statement are. Dividend income and interest expense have a very minor effect on Most's net income (they are only .06% and .36% of 1989 sales), while cost of goods sold and selling expenses are of great significance (they are 65.4% and 24.58% of 1989 sales).

The vertical analysis of a single year's statements—common-size statements—may be combined with horizontal analysis—comparative statements—to detect significant changes in financial statement components from year to year. Exhibit 16-3 shows such comparative common-size statements. Perhaps the most notable change occurred in cost of goods sold (which went down from 67.46% to 65.40% of sales) and in operating expenses (which increased from 29.47% to 31.39% of sales). While these changes are not substantial, they bear watching in future periods to see if these trends continue.

Common-size statements can be used to compare companies of differing size

Common-size statements are especially helpful in comparing two companies that differ in size. Imagine comparing Most, Inc.'s income statement with that of the Blaque Company shown on page 658.

BLAQUE COMPANY
Income Statement
Year Ended December 31, 1989
(000s omitted)

Net Sales	$ 4,535,600
Cost of Goods Sold	(2,585,292)
Gross Profit on Sales	$ 1,950,308
Operating Expenses:	
Selling.	$ (689,411)
General and Administrative.	(317,492)
Total Operating Expenses.	$(1,006,903)
Income before Income Tax	$ 943,405
Income Tax Expense.	(452,834)
Net Income	$ 490,571

Blaque is so much larger that a comparison of any number on the two income statements seems meaningless. When Blaque's statement is converted to a common size, comparisons are possible:

BLAQUE COMPANY
Common-Size Income Statement
Year Ended December 31, 1989

Sales.	100.0%
Cost of Goods Sold	(57.0)
Gross Profit on Sales.	43.0
Operating Expenses:	
Selling	(15.2)
General and Administrative	(7.0)
Total Operating Expenses	(22.2)
Income before Income Tax	20.8
Income Tax Expense.	(10.0)
Net Income.	10.8%

Most, Inc.'s cost of goods sold (see Exhibit 16-3) is a much higher percentage of sales (65.4%) than is Blaque's (57.0%). If the companies are in the same industry, we may question whether the difference is due to volume buying, better inventory management, or possibly just a difference in the inventory costing method (Most may be using LIFO and Blaque FIFO). Blaque's selling expenses are a much lower percentage (15.2%) than Most's (24.58%). The analyst may question what possible efficiencies Blaque has discovered that have eluded Most. Differences in advertising policies, policies on commissions paid to sales representatives, or economies of scale could account for the differences.

Many industry trade associations gather statistics from member firms and produce common-size financial statements based on averages for businesses falling within a predetermined size category. For example, sporting goods stores with annual retail sales under $3 million might submit their income statements in a standardized format to a trade association, which would then compute average cost of goods sold and the other percentages for stores in this size range. These common-size statistics would provide one standard basis for comparisons that could be used to evaluate the relative performance of a company, in much the same way that Most was evaluated in comparison with Blaque.

FINANCIAL RATIO ANALYSIS

A *ratio* is the relationship between two amounts that results from dividing one by the other. The ratio of 1,000 to 500 would be $1{,}000 \div 500 = 2$, sometimes expressed as 2:1. This means that the first number is twice as large as the second. The ratio of 25 to 50 would be expressed as .5 ($25 \div 50$) or .5:1, signifying that the first number is half as large as the second. Ratio analysis can provide additional insights into the operating performance and financial position of Most, Inc.

Analysis of Earnings Performance

Stockholders and potential stockholders employ several ratios to help them evaluate management performance in using the resources of the entity to earn profits. Rate of return on total assets and rate of return on stockholders' equity are two such ratios.

Rate of return on total assets indicates management's efficiency in using all of the firm's resources

Rate of return (ROR) on total assets is a measure of management's efficiency in using all resources at its disposal. The formula for computing this ratio is as follows:

$$\text{Rate of return (ROR) on total assets} = \frac{\text{income before interest expense}}{\text{average total assets}}$$

Income before interest expense is used so that earnings will not be influenced by the manner in which the assets are financed. Interest is a cost of financing the business, not a cost of operating it. Average total assets reflect resources employed throughout the year, not those on hand at the beginning or at the end. This average could be computed by weighting the dollars of assets used by the number of days they are employed and dividing by 365. An approximation of this average may be obtained by adding the beginning and ending asset amounts and dividing by 2. This simplified technique will be used throughout the chapter wherever an average is required.

Most, Inc.'s return on total assets for 1989 is calculated as follows:

$$\text{ROR on total assets} = \frac{\text{net income} + \text{interest expense}}{(\text{total assets, beg. of year} + \text{total assets, end of year}) \div 2}$$

$$\text{ROR on total assets} = \frac{\$17{,}575{,}000 + \$3{,}120{,}000}{(\$156{,}625{,}000 + \$172{,}583{,}000) \div 2}$$

$$= \frac{\$20{,}695{,}000}{\$164{,}604{,}000} = .1257 \text{ or } 12.57\%$$

Most's management earned an average of 12.57% on each dollar of assets invested in the company.

Rate of return on common stockholders' equity indicates management's efficiency in using resources invested by common stockholders

Rate of return (ROR) on common stockholders' equity is a measure of management's effectiveness in using the resources invested by the common stockholders. This rate may be higher or lower than the return on total assets, depending on how judiciously management has combined debt and preferred stock with common stock in financing company's resources. The formula for computing this ratio is as follows:

$$\text{Rate of return (ROR) on} \atop \text{common stockholders' equity} = \frac{\text{net income} - \text{preferred dividends}}{\text{average common stockholders' equity}}$$

The earnings amount in the numerator excludes both payments to holders of debt (interest expense) and holders of preferred stock (preferred dividends). Thus the net income less preferred dividends is the net amount earned on the equity of the common stockholders. Average common stockholders' equity is an approximation of the amount invested by this group of owners throughout the year.

The following preliminary computations are made for Most, Inc.:

Preferred dividends:
Par value of preferred stock (at the time dividends are declared)......... $500,000
Dividend rate paid... 5%
Amount of preferred dividends...................................... $ 25,000

Average common stockholders' equity:			
Total stockholders' equity	− preferred stockholders' equity	= common stockholders' equity	
Jan. 1, 1989	$ 87,710,000 − $500,000	= $ 87,210,000	
+Dec. 31, 1989	103,550,000 − 500,000	= 103,050,000	
Total		= $190,260,000	
		÷2	
Average common stockholders' equity for 1989		= $ 95,130,000	

The rate of return on Most's common stockholders' equity for 1989 is as follows:

$$\text{ROR on common stockholders' equity} = \frac{\$17,575,000 - \$25,000}{\$95,130,000} = .1845$$

$$= 18.45\%$$

Favorable leverage exists when the company uses assets provided by creditors to earn a higher return for common stockholders

Since the 18.45% return on common stockholders' equity exceeds the 12.57% return on total assets, management has made effective use of ***leverage,*** or ***trading on the equity.*** Leverage or trading on the equity involves using the assets invested by common stockholders as collateral for debt financing (borrowing on notes or bonds) and limited-return equity financing (selling preferred stock) in an attempt to earn a higher return for the common stockholder. A simple example will help clarify this concept.

JOHN AND MABEL'S FRUIT STAND

John and Mabel Jones run a fruit and vegetable stand. They have $100 of their own money invested and earn a $5 profit (or 5% return). An additional $100 is borrowed from a friend at 6% interest. In order for John and Mabel to come out ahead on this loan, they must use the borrowed money to earn more than the $6 interest they will have to pay. Assuming that the net income on the $200 of assets is $7, the Jones' have used someone else's money to increase their return from 5% ($5 ÷ $100) to 7% ($7 ÷ $100). Remember, the $7 net income is *after* the interest expense deduction.

Rate of return on John and Mabel's total assets:

$$\frac{\text{Net income} + \text{interest expense}}{\text{Average total assets}} = \frac{\$7 + \$6}{(\$200 + \$200) \div 2} = \frac{\$13}{\$200}$$

$$= .065 \text{ or } 6.5\%$$

Rate of return on John and Mabel's stockholders' equity:

$$\frac{\text{Net income} - \text{preferred dividends}}{\text{Average common stockholders' equity}} = \frac{\$7 - \$0}{(\$100 + \$100) \div 2}$$

$$= \frac{\$7}{\$100} = .07 \text{ or } 7\%$$

Leverage, then, is simply an *attempt* to use funds supplied by nonowners to increase the return to owners. Any time the rate of return on common stockholders' equity exceeds the rate of return on total assets, leverage has been used to the stockholders' advantage.

Leverage may also work to the detriment of common stockholders. If the return on the borrowed and preferred stock capital is not sufficient to pay the interest and preferred dividends on that capital, some of the earnings that would normally be available to common stockholders are absorbed in making up the difference. Any time the rate of return on total assets is more than the rate of return on common stockholders' equity, leverage has been used to the detriment of the stockholders.

Earnings per share of common stock (EPS) is a measure of the income earned on each share of common stock. Calculation of this ratio was discussed in Chapter 12. The formula for a simple capital structure and the calculation of 1989 EPS for Most, Inc., are presented below.

Earnings per share of common stock shows the average dollars of income for each share of common stock

$$\textbf{EPS (simple capital structure)} = \frac{\text{net income} - \text{preferred dividends}}{\text{average number of common shares outstanding}}$$

$$\text{EPS} = \frac{\$17,575,000 - \$25,000}{(9,500,000 \text{ shs} + 10,000,000 \text{ shs}) \div 2}$$

$$= \frac{\$17,550,000}{9,750,000 \text{ shs}} = \$1.80$$

Earnings per share amounts must appear on the face of the income statements of public companies. Nonpublic (closely held, or nonpublicly traded) companies are not required to disclose earnings per share amounts. If you review Most, Inc.'s income statement in Exhibit 16-2, you will see that EPS is properly shown for 1989 and 1988.

Price-earnings ratio statistics are one more indicator of the earnings performance of common stock. The formula for calculating the price-earnings ratio is:

$$\text{Price-earnings ratio} = \frac{\textbf{market price per share of common stock}}{\textbf{earnings per share of common stock}}$$

Assuming a current market price of $27 for Most, Inc.'s stock, the price-earnings ratio would be as follows:

$$\text{Price-earnings ratio} = \frac{\$27}{\$1.80} = 15 \text{ or } 15:1$$

This simply means that Most's stock is currently selling for 15 times the amount that each share earned. Price-earnings ratios of 15 are not at all uncommon. A few range as high as 20 or more. The price-earnings ratio is the reflection of the stock market's assessment about the future earnings of the company. Investors have been willing to buy a share of stock for as many as 15 to 20 times the current per-share earnings because they feel that the future income growth of the firm will be sufficient to provide an adequate return on this investment. This return is normally received through a combination of dividends and an increased market value of the stock.

The price-earnings ratio reflects the stock market's assessment about the future earnings of the company

The dividend yield rate indicates the cash payout rate on the common stockholders' investment

Dividend yield rate shows the current year's dividends as a percentage of the current market price of the stock. This indication of the cash payout rate on an investment allows stockholders and potential stockholders to compare interest rates on certificates of deposit, corporate bonds, and other securities with this measure of return on common stock. The investor should be aware that dividend yield rates ignore the potential increase in the market value of common stock. For this reason the dividend yield rate should be combined with other statistics in making investment decisions.

The formula for calculating dividend yield rates and the 1989 dividend yield rate for Most, Inc., assuming that $8,000,000 dividends were paid to common stockholders, follows:

$$\text{Dividend yield rate} = \frac{\textbf{dividends per share of common stock}}{\textbf{current market price per share of common stock}}$$

$$\frac{\text{1989 Dividend yield}}{\text{rate for Most, Inc.}} = \frac{\$8,000,000 \div 10,000,000 \text{ shs}}{\$27} = \frac{\$0.80}{\$27} = .0296 \text{ or } 2.96\%$$

This relatively low dividend yield rate of 3% on Most, Inc., common stock would not be attractive to investors who count on cash flow from dividends to pay their living expenses. A potential Most, Inc., stockholder would probably be an individual who is more interested in speculating on the growth in the market value of the stock. This type of investor would rely more heavily on growth in earnings per share and recent trends in the market price of the stock than the dividend yield rate.

Analysis of Debt-Paying Ability

Creditors and potential creditors are interested in continuously monitoring a company's ability to pay interest as it comes due and to repay the principal of the debt at maturity. Times interest earned, debt to total assets ratio, and equity to total assets ratio are three statistics that provide information about this debt-paying ability. Later we will discuss several liquid position measures that indicate the ability to meet short-term debt responsibilities.

*Times interest earned tells
how many times a company
could pay its interest
expense with assets derived
from income*

Times interest earned is a ratio that indicates the margin of safety provided by current earnings in meeting the company's interest responsibilities. The formula for calculating this ratio is as follows:

$$\text{Times interest earned} = \frac{\text{income before interest expense and income taxes}}{\text{annual interest expense}}$$

Income before interest expense and income taxes is used because this is the amount that could be used to pay interest—provided it were available in the form of cash. Income taxes are excluded because interest is deductible in calculating income tax.

1989 times interest earned for Most, Inc., is as follows:

$$\text{Times interest earned} = \frac{\$17,575,000 + \$3,120,000 + \$7,557,000}{\$3,120,000}$$

$$= \frac{\$28,252,000}{\$3,120,000} = 9.1 \text{ times}$$

Most's income available to meet its interest responsibilities was about 9 times the amount of its interest expense. Usually if interest is covered several times, long-term creditors consider this an acceptable margin of safety. Most's times interest earned ratio should be quite satisfactory to its creditors.

*The debt to total assets
ratio indicates the
percentage of a company's
assets provided by creditors*

The ***debt to total assets ratio*** shows the percentage of the firm's assets financed by debt. The higher this percentage, the greater the risk that the company will be unable to meet its obligations when due. The debt to total assets ratio formula and the 1989 calculation for Most, Inc., follow:

$$\text{Debt to total assets ratio} = \frac{\text{total liabilities}}{\text{total assets}}$$

$$\text{Most, Inc., 1989 debt to total assets ratio} = \frac{\$69,033,000}{\$172,583,000} = .399 \text{ or } .40, \text{ or } 40\%$$

Forty percent of Most's total assets were financed by debt.

*The stockholders' equity to
total assets ratio shows the
percentage of a company's
assets provided by
stockholders*

The ***stockholders' equity to total assets ratio,*** sometimes called the ***equity ratio,*** shows the percentage of the firm's assets financed by stockholders. The higher this ratio, the smaller the risk that the company will be unable to meet its obligations when due. After a moment's reflection you should see that the debt to total assets ratio and the stockholders' equity to total assets ratio are complementary, that is, the two percentages should always add to 100%. This is true because all assets are financed by either debt or equity funds. The stockholders' equity to total assets ratio may be found by subtracting the debt to total assets ratio from 100%:

$$\text{Stockholders' equity to total assets ratio} = 100\% - \text{debt to total assets ratio}$$

$$\begin{array}{l}\text{1989 Most, Inc., stockholders'}\\ \text{equity to total assets ratio}\end{array} = 100\% - 40\% = 60\%$$

This ratio may also be calculated by the following formula:

$$\text{Stockholders' equity to total assets ratio} = \frac{\text{total stockholders' equity}}{\text{total assets}}$$

$$\begin{array}{l}\text{1989 Most, Inc., stockholders'}\\ \text{equity to total assets ratio}\end{array} = \frac{\$103,550,000}{\$172,583,000} = .60 \text{ or } 60\%$$

Sixty percent of Most's assets come from stockholders (including reinvested earnings) and 40% from creditors. This fact, coupled with the favorable leverage and times interest earned statistics, should be satisfactory to long-term creditors. Of course, each analyst will have standards in mind when financial analysis is begun. These standards may vary from analyst to analyst. Statistics satisfactory to one analyst may cause concern to another.

Analysis of Liquid Position

An analysis of a firm's liquid position provides indicators of its short-term debt-paying ability and of management's current operating efficiency. For this reason, *both* investors and creditors are particularly interested in these statistics.

Working capital is a measure of the liquid resources management has to use

Working capital is total current assets minus total current liabilities. A strong working capital position can be an advantage to a company attempting to obtain short-term credit at favorable interest rates. Investors and long-term creditors view a strong working capital position as indicating an ability to make expected dividend and interest payments in a timely manner. Most, Inc.'s working capital for 1989 is shown below:

Current assets	$109,292,000
−Current liabilities	39,033,000
=Working capital..	$ 70,259,000

The current ratio is one measure of a company's ability to pay its short-term debts

The **current ratio** is current assets divided by current liabilities. This statistic is often assigned great importance by creditors in making credit-granting decisions. The general formula and 1989 current ratio for Most, Inc., appear below:

$$\text{Current ratio} = \frac{\text{current assets}}{\text{current liabilities}}$$

$$\text{1989 Most, Inc., current ratio} = \frac{\$109,292,000}{\$39,033,000} = 2.80 \text{ or } 2.8:1$$

This means that for every dollar of current liabilities, Most has $2.80 of current assets. Many creditors feel that a current ratio of 2.0 is satisfactory. Relying too heavily on the current ratio may not be desirable, as the following illustration demonstrates:

The current ratios for Company A and B are calculated as follows:

	Company A	Company B
Current assets:		
Cash	$ 40,000	$175,000
Accounts receivable.........	60,000	125,000
Merchandise inventory......	180,000	95,000
Prepaid expenses	20,000	5,000
Total current assets	$300,000	$400,000
Current liabilities	$100,000	$200,000
Current ratio................	$300,000 ÷ $100,000 = 3	$400,000 ÷ $200,000 = 2

Company A's current ratio of $3:1$ is much better than Company B's $2:1$. If we inspect the composition of the current assets, we see that A's cash and accounts receivable are only one-third of total current assets, whereas three-fourths of B's current assets are composed of these two particularly liquid resources. In reality, B may be in a position to meet its current obligations as well, if not better, than A.

Company A could further improve its current ratio by merely paying off $40,000 of current liabilities with the $40,000 cash on hand. If this were done, the new current ratio would be:

$$\text{Company A current ratio (revised)} = \frac{\$300,000 - \$40,000}{\$100,000 - \$40,000} = \frac{\$260,000}{\$60,000} = \underline{\underline{4.33}}$$

This act of manipulating current assets close to the end of the time period can produce a ratio that may satisfy creditors while actually weakening the immediate liquid position of the company.

Limiting your analysis to too few statistics, relying on arbitrary rules of thumb, and not understanding the limitations behind the calculation of a ratio are pitfalls that you must carefully avoid.

The quick ratio is a measure of a company's immediate liquid position

The **quick ratio,** also known as the **acid-test ratio,** shows the relationship between highly liquid (quick) assets and current liabilities. Quick assets are those that may be converted directly into cash within a short period of time. These include cash, marketable securities, and receivables. Merchandise inventory is omitted because merchandise is normally sold on credit (converted into a receivable) and then the receivable must be collected before cash is realized. Thus inventory is two steps away from cash rather than just one. Prepaid expenses are also omitted because they are usually relatively small in amount and because they are used up in operations rather than converted into cash.

$$\textbf{Quick ratio} = \frac{\textbf{quick assets}}{\textbf{current liabilities}}$$

Most, Inc.'s quick assets ratio on Dec. 31, 1989, is as follows:

Cash...	$ 5,368,000
Marketable securities...	3,090,000
Accounts receivable (net)	35,382,000
Total quick assets	$43,840,000

$$\text{1989 Most, Inc., quick ratio} = \frac{\$43,840,000}{\$39,033,000} = 1.12 \text{ or } 1.12:1$$

Creditors generally use the rule of thumb that a quick ratio of $1:1$ is satisfactory. Most's quick ratio appears to be acceptable.

The quick ratio, when viewed with the current ratio, gives an idea of the influence of merchandise inventory and prepaid expenses. Looking at the Company A–Company B illustration again one can see that the quick ratio is a tipoff that Company A's current ratio may be misleading as a sole indicator of debt-paying ability.

	Company A	Company B
Quick assets:		
Cash.....................	$ 40,000	$175,000
Accounts receivable	60,000	125,000
Total quick assets	$100,000	$300,000
Quick ratio................	$100,000 ÷ $100,000 = 1	$300,000 ÷ $200,000 = 1.5

Company B has the stronger quick ratio and the weaker current ratio, indicating that merchandise inventory and prepaid expenses play a less important role in its current position than these assets do in Company A's.

Inventory turnover indicates how quickly a company sells its average investment in inventory

Inventory turnover shows how many times the average dollars invested in merchandise inventory were sold (turned over) during the year. This statistic when compared with the year-end merchandise inventory provides the analyst with a basis for judging whether the company has an excessive investment in merchandise at the end of the year. A too-large ending inventory may indicate that sales volume was not as high as expected near year-end, or possibly that management was inefficient in allowing too much unsold goods to accumulate. On the other hand, a large inventory may be present because of an unusually high sales volume expected near the beginning of the next period. In any case, the analyst will be wise to attempt to discover the reasons for low turnover and excessive ending inventory.

Inventory turnover is calculated by dividing cost of goods sold by average merchandise inventory. Cost of goods sold is used instead of sales because sales includes gross profit, while cost of goods sold, like merchandise inventory, does not. The general formula and the 1989 Most, Inc., inventory turnover follow:

$$\textbf{Inventory turnover} = \frac{\textbf{cost of goods sold}}{\textbf{average merchandise inventory}}$$

$$\text{1989 Most, Inc., inventory turnover} = \frac{\$564,346,000}{(\$50,434,000 + \$62,582,000) \div 2}$$

$$= \frac{\$564,346,000}{\$56,508,000} = 9.99 \text{ times}$$

Since Most's inventory turns over about 10 times per year, the year-end inventory should be about 10% of cost of goods sold. Most's inventory of $62,582,000 is a little above this amount (10%)($564,364,000) = $56,435,000. This excess is probably explained by Most's increasing sales volume.

Accounts receivable turnover indicates how quickly a company collects its average Accounts Receivable balance

Accounts receivable turnover indicates the number of times per year that the average balance of Accounts Receivable is collected. This ratio of sales on credit to average accounts receivable is calculated as follows:

$$\textbf{Accounts receivable turnover} = \frac{\textbf{credit sales}}{\textbf{average accounts receivable}}$$

Assuming that substantially all of Most, Inc.'s sales are on credit, the firm's 1987 receivables turnover is as follows:

$$\text{1989 Most, Inc., accounts receivable turnover} = \frac{\$862,915,000}{(\$32,936,000 + \$35,382,000) \div 2}$$

$$= \frac{\$862,915,000}{\$34,159,000} = 25.3 \text{ times}$$

Average age of receivables is another measure of how quickly a company collects its Accounts Receivable

This ratio takes on more meaning when used in the calculation of the statistic discussed next.

Average age of receivables provides a rough approximation of the average time that it takes to collect receivables. Average age of receivables is determined as follows:

$$\text{Average age of receivables} = \frac{365 \text{ days}}{\text{accounts receivable turnover}}$$

$$1989 \text{ average age of Most receivables} = \frac{365 \text{ days}}{25.3 \text{ times}} = 14.4 \text{ days}$$

Most, Inc., takes an average of 14 days to collect its receivables. If Most's credit terms are net 10 days, its collection efforts could be improved. If the credit terms are 15 or 30 days, Most's collection efforts appear to be excellent.

Creditors are interested in receivables turnover and the average age of receivables as indicators of how quickly the company's receivables are converted into the cash required for operations and debt repayment. Investors and creditors use receivables turnover as one more index of management efficiency.

INTERPRETATION OF FINANCIAL RATIOS

Ratios must be compared with some standard to be meaningful

A quick ratio of 1.12, an inventory turnover of 9.99, or a price-earnings ratio of 15 mean very little when considered in a vacuum. Financial ratios become relevant for decision making only when compared with some standards. Each analyst must decide on a set of standards for each ratio that he or she relies on to gauge the performance of the company being analyzed. Some common bases for establishing standards are considered below.

Company History

The company's ratios for past years may be used as a standard

Horizontal analysis has been defined as comparing financial data of a single company for 2 or more years. Comparative financial statements and trend analysis were presented as applications of horizontal analysis. Each of the financial ratios may be computed for a number of years and then compared to form an opinion about whether the company's performance is getting better or worse. If Most's inventory turnover has been 10, 12, and 16 during 1989, 1988, and 1987, respectively, the analyst should be concerned enough to attempt to discover the reason for the deterioration in this ratio. If management inefficiency seems to be the only plausible explanation, the analyst may expect continued problems that could lead to a decision to reject a credit application or not to invest in stock of the corporation.

A major limitation of comparing amounts and ratios for a single company is that there is no basis for a decision about the significance of these statistics. Some external standard is needed against which to measure the company's ratios. For example, if the average inventory turnover in Most's industry is 4, the turnover of 10 may appear excellent. If the industry average is 12, a turnover of 10 may be a cause for concern.

External Standards

Average ratios of other firms in the industry may be used as a standard

Ratio information about other companies is often used as a yardstick against which to compare the statistics of the firm being analyzed. These external data may be obtained by analyzing the financial statements of the other firms; by obtaining copies of industry averages from the publications of trade associations; by examining data on industry norms, average ratios, and credit ratings from credit agencies such as

Dun & Bradstreet; or by consulting statistics available in investment service publications such as *Annual Statement Studies* published by Robert Morris Associates.

Care must be taken in deciding which ratios are to be used as standards of comparison. Many companies are so diversified that it is difficult to identify one particular industry in which they operate. A current ratio or inventory turnover ratio for such a conglomerate would be meaningless for comparing with those statistics of another firm operating in only one industry.

In most industries comparability will be affected by size. Larger firms will be able to avail themselves of economies of scale and certain sophisticated quantitative management techniques that may not be practical for smaller ones. Smaller companies may be able to maintain closer client relations and better customer relations than the larger ones. These differences in operating techniques may influence different ratios in different ways. The larger firm, for example, may be expected to have a higher gross profit percentage and inventory turnover, while the smaller one may have a quicker receivables turnover and a lower percentage spent on advertising. Comparisons of similar size entities in the same industry is desirable whenever possible.

The differences in accounting methods employed in generating financial information may also influence the comparability of ratios and other statistics. Among the different principles that firms may employ are different inventory techniques, depreciation methods, estimates of useful lives, methods of accounting for income taxes, and revenue recognition procedures. It is a fairly easy matter to discover which methods a particular company is using. Adjusting the financial information to compensate for differences in accounting methods may prove to be a difficult, if not impossible, task.

NOTES TO FINANCIAL STATEMENTS

Footnotes provide valuable information about financial statements

Notes to the financial statements, commonly called *footnotes,* provide additional information that may greatly influence your overall judgment about the future potential of the company. Some of the more important footnotes are discussed in this section.

Accounting Policies

When a company selects from several acceptable methods, the accounting policy note tells which method was chosen

Authoritative generally accepted accounting principles require that all financial statements contain a note outlining the various accounting methods that the company has elected to use. The accounting policies note explains which accounting method was selected from among several acceptable ones, for example, FIFO or LIFO inventory methods, straight-line or double declining-balance depreciation. The *accounting policies note,* usually the first note to the financial statements, is helpful in deciding how comparable the financial statistics for two different companies are. The following illustration shows a typical accounting policies note:

SUMMARY OF ACCOUNTING POLICIES

Inventories   Inventories are stated generally at cost, which is not in excess of market. The cost of substantially all inventories is determined by the last-in, first-out (LIFO) method.

Depreciation and Depletion The cost of most manufacturing plant and equipment is depreciated using an accelerated method based primarily on a sum-of-the-years'-digits formula. The cost of mining properties is depreciated or depleted mainly by the units-of-production method.

Consolidation The financial statements include the consolidation of all wholly and majority-owned subsidiaries except the finance subsidiary. The finance company is so different from the other companies that, even though wholly owned, it is accounted for by the equity method. It appears as an investment on the balance sheet and in "other income" on the income statement.

Methods of accounting for research and development costs, recognition of warranty expenses, and translating foreign subsidiary statements into U.S. currency are not appropriate accounting policy disclosures because only one acceptable method can be used for each of these.

Contingencies

Financial statements are analyzed in order to form an opinion about how well a company has performed in the past and to make an estimate about how well it is expected to do in the future. A large potential lawsuit loss could significantly change your forecast about the future of the company. This vital information can be obtained by reading the contingencies note.

The contingencies note provides information about future events that may occur

A *contingency* is a future event that may occur but whose occurrence is not certain. The *contingencies note* must include a description of all future losses that are probable, reasonably possible, and in some cases even remote. Where an estimate or a range of estimates of the amount of loss can be made, these must also be disclosed.

The following contingencies note is a sample of the typical disclosures that may be made:

NOTE 7 CONTINGENCIES

Early in fiscal 1988, the Federal Trade Commission filed a formal complaint against the company and two other manufacturers of gudgeon twisters charging them with sharing an unlawful monopoly in violation of the Federal Trade Commission Act. The Commission seeks, among other things, divestiture of certain assets and royalty-free licensing of certain trademarks. The company denies that it has violated the Act and is vigorously defending its position. Trial is continuing before an Administration Law Judge of the Federal Trade Commission, and it is expected that the litigation will continue for some time at considerable expense.

A lawsuit has been filed against the company claiming damages from alleged environmental contamination by our Beaver Falls plant. The suit filed on Mar. 30, 1989, in the federal court in Pennsylvania alleges damages of $1,000,000. The State of Pennsylvania has moved to intervene as plaintiff in this case seeking $25,000,000 in compensatory and $1,000,000 in punitive damages. The company will vigorously defend against this lawsuit.

As you learned in Chapter 8, contingencies that are probable in nature and subject to reasonable estimation must be recognized as current period losses. The loss (or expense) must be shown on the income statement and the corresponding liability (or allowance account) must appear on the balance sheet. Bad debts and warranty expenses are illustrations of contingencies considered probable and subject to estimation.

Other Descriptive Notes

Other notes provide descriptive information about balance sheet and income statement items

Some information vital to the understanding of the financial statements is simply too long and detailed to be shown on the statements themselves. This information is usually shown in a descriptive note referenced to a particular item on the income statement or balance sheet. Typical are those providing supplementary information about the following:

Subject of Note	Information Included
Property, plant, and equipment	The types of assets included in this category, their estimated useful lives, and whether they are pledged as collateral for loans
Long-term liabilities	The effective interest rate, maturity dates, repayment terms, collateral for the debt, any restriction imposed by the creditor (such as a limitation on the amount of dividends the company can pay)

Other common descriptive notes relate to pension plans, income taxes, earnings per share calculations, and stock option plans.

OTHER SOURCES OF INFORMATION

Various publications provide general background information

The serious student of financial statement analysis will supplement all of the techniques described thus far with several other sources of financial and nonfinancial information. Magazines such as *Business Week* and *Forbes* and financial newspapers such as *The Wall Street Journal, Barrons,* and the *Commercial and Financial Chronicle* provide data on prospects for the economy as a whole and for various industries. In addition, articles on management personnel, company strategy, and significant legislation affecting the business community expand the analyst's background knowledge. Up-to-date quarterly operating results and current stock prices also appear in many of these publications.

Several research firms publish financial services that are available on a subscription basis. These are available in most university and large public libraries. We have already mentioned industry trade associations and credit-reporting bureaus as possible sources of information.

Many large corporations provide interview sessions for professional analysts who work for large stock brokerage firms, trust departments of banks, and other institutions that invest vast sums of money. While these sessions do provide an opportunity for the analysts to ask questions that may interest them and to hear management's hopes for the future of the company, they may not act as a means of communicating secret inside information to a chosen few money managers. Such activities would be illegal.

BANK GIVES LOAN TO CONCERN SELLING Xs

This is a true story. Only the bank and the borrower's names have been deleted to protect the innocent and avoid embarrassment.

A Beverly Hills, Calif., accounting firm recently gave a specimen financial statement to a woman business owner who subsequently became a client of the firm.

Months later she called Andrew Hillas, a partner at the CPA firm, Singer, Lewak, Greenbaum & Goldstein, to complain that her financial statement made no sense. Her Company's name was missing, replaced by a string of Xs, and the numbers were wrong.

"We hadn't done a financial statement for her," Mr. Hillas says. She had looked at the specimen he had given her earlier. And she had given it to her bank — a big one — in applying for a $50,000 loan. Even though the specimen was less than clear about the company's business (it says the "company is a California corporation engaged in the promotion and sale of xxxxx") and the results didn't jibe with the company's earlier years' results, she got the loan.

Source: The Wall Street Journal Nov. 14, 1983, page 33.

In the situation explained in this article the bank apparently did not examine a loan applicant's financial statements very carefully in making a large loan. If a closer examination had been made, the banker would have noticed that the statements were merely samples and not intended to represent the financial position of any real company. More rational investing and credit-granting decisions would be made if the techniques you learned in this chapter were used.

CHAPTER SUMMARY

The auditor's report, the financial statements, and the notes to the financial statements may be analyzed to provide the reader with insight into a company's earnings performance, the strength of its financial structure, its debt-paying ability, and the effect of inflation on its operations.

The *audit report* contains the auditor's independent opinion about whether the financial statements are presented fairly in conformity with generally accepted accounting principles. A careful study of this report may alert the reader to weaknesses in financial measurement of disclosure.

Financial statements may be analyzed *horizontally* and *vertically.* One horizontal approach compares balance sheets of several years expressed in dollars and percentages. A similar comparison is made of income statements of several years. Another horizontal approach, called *trend analysis,* compares proportionate changes in selected financial information over time. These proportionate changes are expressed as percentages of a designated base year. A third horizontal approach involves comparing financial ratios for several years in order to detect significant changes in them over time.

Vertical financial statement analysis involves comparing items on financial statements of a single period. *Common-size financial statements* state each component of the statements in terms of one other component. A common-size income statement usually states each component as a percentage of sales. A common-size balance sheet presents each item as a percentage of total assets.

Ratio analysis, another form of the vertical approach, may be used to examine earnings performance, debt-paying ability, and liquid position. The following ratios are commonly employed in these evaluations:

Earnings Performance

$$\text{Rate of return on total assets} = \frac{\text{income before interest expense}}{\text{average total assets}}$$

$$\begin{array}{c}\text{Rate of return on common}\\\text{stockholders' equity}\end{array} = \frac{\text{net income} - \text{preferred dividends}}{\text{average common stockholders' equity}}$$

$$\text{Earnings per share} = \frac{\text{net income} - \text{preferred dividends}}{\text{average number of common shares outstanding}}$$

$$\text{Price-earnings ratio} = \frac{\text{market price per share of common stock}}{\text{earnings per share of common stock}}$$

$$\text{Dividend yield rate} = \frac{\text{dividends per share of common stock}}{\text{current market price per share of common stock}}$$

Debt-Paying Ability

$$\text{Times interest earned} = \frac{\text{income before interest expense and income taxes}}{\text{annual interest expense}}$$

$$\text{Debt to total assets} = \frac{\text{total liabilities}}{\text{total assets}}$$

$$\text{Stockholders' equity to total assets} = \frac{\text{total stockholders' equity}}{\text{total assets}}$$

Liquid Position

$$\text{Current ratio} = \frac{\text{current assets}}{\text{current liabilities}}$$

$$\text{Quick ratio} = \frac{\text{quick assets}}{\text{current liabilities}}$$

$$\text{Inventory turnover} = \frac{\text{cost of goods sold}}{\text{average merchandise inventory}}$$

$$\text{Accounts receivable turnover} = \frac{\text{credit sales}}{\text{average accounts receivable}}$$

$$\text{Average age of receivables} = \frac{\text{365 days}}{\text{accounts receivable turnover}}$$

Ratios take on much more meaning when they can be compared to measures of what they "should be." Standards of comparison are usually obtained by analyzing financial statements of companies in the same industry and averaging the ratios thus determined. Industry averages may also be acquired from trade associations and financial research firms.

Ratio comparisons are most useful when the companies studied are in fact in the same industry, are of approximately the same size, and use similar accounting methods.

Notes to the financial statements are an integral part of the statements. Financial analysis is not complete until the notes have been carefully examined. Each company must disclose choices made from among different accounting methods in an *accounting policies note.* The accounting policies note is followed by notes providing detailed information about certain financial statement items such as property, plant, and equipment, and long-term debt. Events that may have a significant effect on future financial statements are disclosed in a *contingencies note.* Common contingencies include pending lawsuits and administrative complaints filed by regulatory agencies.

Background information about the firm, its industry, and the economy as a whole may be obtained from business magazines and newspapers, publications of financial research firms, industry trade associations, credit-rating bureaus, and interviews with management.

IMPORTANT TERMS USED IN THIS CHAPTER

Accounting policies note   A description of the various accounting methods that the company has selected to use in preparing its financial statements. Disclosure is made of only those methods selected from among several acceptable ones. (page 668)

Auditor's report   An independent auditor's opinion regarding the fairness of presentation of the financial statements. (page 652)

Common-size financial statement   A financial statement in which each component is stated as a percentage of one other component. A common-size income statement usually states each component as a percentage of sales. A common-size balance sheet presents each item as a percentage of total assets. (page 657)

Comparative financial statements   Presentation of financial statements of more than one period in columnar form. Changes between periods expressed in dollars or percentages may also be included. (page 653)

Contingency   A future event that may occur but whose occurrence is not certain. (page 669)

Horizontal analysis   Comparing the financial data of a single company for 2 or more years. (page 653)

Leverage   The use of debt or preferred stock financing in an attempt to earn a higher rate of return on common stockholders' equity than would have been possible without this financing. (page 660)

Ratio   The relationship of one number to another that is determined by dividing the first number by the second. (page 659)

Trading on the equity   See *Leverage.*

Trend analysis   The comparison of proportionate changes in selected financial information over time. These proportionate changes are expressed as a percentage of a designated base year. (page 655)

Vertical analysis   The comparison of items on financial statements of a single period. (page 656)

QUESTIONS

1. Does the auditor's report state that the financial statements present a true and correct picture of the company's financial position? Explain.

2. Can a horizontal analysis be made of a single year's financial statements? Explain.

3. What is the analyst attempting to learn by studying comparative financial statements?

4. Jon Investor is calculating trend percentages for sales and net income of Toco, Inc. If he selects 1988 as his base year, what will the trend percentages be for 1988? How will he calculate the trend percentages for 1989?

5. Explain how vertical analysis differs from horizontal analysis.

6. Which financial statement analysis tool would be most useful in comparing two companies of vastly differing size? Explain how this tool makes the comparison possible.

7. Willco's rate of return on total assets is 11%; explain what this rate tells the analyst.

8. What is favorable leverage? Is it present in a company that has a rate of return on total assets of 12% and a rate of return on common stockholders' equity of 10%? Explain.

9. Jarax, Inc., common stock has a dividend yield ratio of 8%; Jarax, Inc., bonds maturing in 20 years offer an effective interest rate of 12%. Explain what the dividend yield rate is. Explain why an investor might prefer the Jarax common stock over the Jarax bonds even though the yield rate on the stock is lower.

10. What does a times interest earned statistic of .95 mean? How would this statistic be evaluated by a long-term creditor? Explain.

11. Why is the quick ratio often a better measure of the very short-term liquid position of a company than the current ratio?

12. Explain how inventory turnover is used to evaluate the amount of inventory on hand at the end of a time period.

13. Clyde Co.'s average age of receivables is 35 days. Explain what additional information is necessary before this average can be evaluated as relatively good or bad.

14. List some external standards against which the performance of a company may be compared.

15. Briefly describe the type of information that you will find in an accounting policies note.

EXERCISES

Exercise 16-1
Preparing a common-size
income statement

Convert this income statement into a common-size statement that uses Sales as 100%:

MAYER CORP.		
Income Statement		
Year Ended September 30, 1989		
Sales		$180,000
Cost of Goods Sold		99,000
Gross Profit on Sales		$ 81,000
Operating Expenses:		
Selling Expenses.	$43,200	
General and Administrative Expenses.	16,200	59,400
Income before Income Taxes.		$ 21,600
Income Tax Expense.		9,720
Net Income		$ 11,880

(Check figure: Selling expenses = 24%)

Exercise 16-2
Calculating trend percentages

Pro Foods, Inc., is concerned about the level of its advertising and office salaries expense. Selected income statement data for the past 3 years appear below:

	1989	1988	1987
Sales..	$140,000	$60,000	$37,500
Gross profit..................................	89,600	37,200	22,500
Advertising expense	7,000	3,300	2,250
Office salaries expense	22,400	9,000	4,500
Net income...................................	30,800	13,800	9,000

Calculate trend percentages for Sales, Advertising Expense, and Office Salaries Expense. Use 1987 as a base year. Round to the nearest percent.

(Check figure: 1989 Advertising Expense = 311%)

Exercise 16-3
Calculating ROR on total assets and on stockholders' equity

The following data have been assembled from the financial statements of Rule, Inc.:

	Dec. 31, 1989	Jan. 1, 1989
Total assets.......................................	$180,000	$140,000
Total stockholders' equity........................	144,000	112,000
Total preferred stockholders' equity	30,000	30,000
Preferred dividends declared......................	2,400	—
Net income.......................................	20,000	—
Interest expense..................................	5,750	—

Calculate the following ratios:

a. Rate of return on total assets.
b. Rate of return on common stockholders' equity.

(Check figure: Rate of return on common stockholders' equity = 17.96%)

Exercise 16-4
Calculating EPS, P/E ratio, and dividend yield rate

N. Vester is in the process of analyzing the earnings performance of the Boulder Transport Corp. She has gathered the following data from Boulder's financial statements and from a report of the closing market prices of stock:

Net income for 1989...	$ 743,000
Preferred dividends declared during 1989...........................	60,000
Common dividends declared Dec. 31, 1989.........................	620,000
Number of shares of Boulder common stock outstanding:	
Jan. 1, 1989..	1,100,000 shs
Dec. 31, 1989..	1,300,000 shs
Market price per share of common stock on Dec. 31, 1989..............	$15

Calculate the following ratios relating to the Boulder stock:

a. Earnings per share of common stock

(Check figure: Earnings per share of common stock = $0.569)

b. The price-earnings ratio
c. The dividend yield rate of common stock

Exercise 16-5
Calculating times interest earned, debt to total assets ratio, and stockholders' equity to total assets ratio

The president of Tom's Toys, Inc., has asked you to gather some statistics about his company's debt-paying ability. You have compiled the following data:

Net income	$900,000
Income tax rate	40%
Interest expense	$100,000
Total liabilities	2,048,000
Total stockholders' equity	4,352,000

Using the data above, calculate:

a. Times interest earned

(Check figure: Times interest earned = 16 times)

b. Debt to total assets ratio
c. Stockholders' equity to total assets ratio

Exercise 16-6
Calculating working capital, current ratio, and quick ratio

The following information was taken from the balance sheet of Ready Corp.:

Cash	$13,250
Accounts receivable (net)	33,000
Merchandise inventory	40,000
Prepaid expenses	9,950
Accounts payable	25,200
Accrued payables	1,800
Notes payable (due in 6 months)	10,000

Calculate **(a)** working capital, **(b)** current ratio, and **(c)** quick ratio.

(Check figure: Current ratio = 2.6:1)

Exercise 16-7
Calculating inventory turnover, accounts receivable turnover, and average age of receivables

You have been assigned the task of evaluating Dorian, Inc.'s management of merchandise and receivables. You decide that inventory turnover, accounts receivable turnover, and average age of receivables statistics will prove valuable in your opinions. The following data are available from Dorian's annual report:

Merchandise inventory:	
Jan. 1	$ 245,000
Dec. 31	375,000
Accounts receivable:	
Jan. 1	250,000
Dec. 31	297,000
Cost of goods sold	2,480,000
Cash sales	1,000,000
Total sales	5,100,000
Dorian's credit terms	Net 30 days

a. Calculate inventory turnover, accounts receivable turnover, and average age of receivables.

(Check figure: Accounts receivable turnover = 15 times)

b. In your opinion, is Dorian doing a good job or a poor job of managing inventory and receivables? Explain.

Exercise 16-8
Finding missing balance sheet amounts using ratios

You are given the following ratios and amounts for the Turtle Corp. for 1989:

Current ratio	2.7
Quick ratio	1.17
Inventory turnover	3.4
Accounts receivable turnover	6.5

Cost of goods sold for 1989	$197,200
Credit sales for 1989	260,000
Accounts receivable, 1/1/89	38,200
Merchandise inventory, 1/1/89..	62,000

TURTLE CORP.
Schedule of Current Assets
and Current Liabilities
December 31, 1989

Current Assets:		
Cash		$ 5,000
Accounts Receivable...	(2)	
Merchandise Inventory	(3)	
Prepaid Insurance		7,200
Total Current Assets..	(1)	$
Current Liabilities:		
Accounts Payable	(4)	$
Accrued Payables..		5,000
Total Current Liabilities		$40,000

Supply the missing amounts in this schedule. Hint: Solve in numerical order (total current assets first, etc.).

(Check figure: Total current assets = $108,000)

PROBLEMS: SET A

Problem A16-1
Calculating liquid position, debt-paying ability, and earnings performance ratios

Poston, Inc.'s income statement and balance sheet for 1989 are presented below:

POSTON, INC.
Income Statement
Year Ended August 31, 1989

Sales		$150,000
Cost of Goods Sold:		
Merchandise Inventory, Sept. 1, 1988......................	$ 24,000	
Purchases (net)...	99,000	
Goods Available for Sale	$123,000	
Merchandise Inventory, Aug. 31, 1989.....................	18,000	
Cost of Goods Sold		105,000
Gross Profit		$ 45,000
Operating Expenses		24,000
Income from Operations		$ 21,000
Other Income and Expense:		
Interest Expense		7,000
Income before Tax..		$ 14,000
Income Tax Expense..		6,400
Net Income		$ 7,600

```
                        POSTON, INC.
                        Balance Sheet
                       August 31, 1989
```

Cash	$ 6,000
Marketable Securities	3,000
Accounts Receivable (net)	17,000
Merchandise Inventory...................................	18,000
Property, Plant, and Equipment (net)	160,000
Goodwill	6,000
Total Assets...	$210,000
Accounts Payable..	$ 16,000
Accrued Salaries Payable	2,000
Income Taxes Payable....................................	1,500
Other Accrued Payables	500
10% Note Payable (due in 2000)........................	70,000
Common Stock ($1 par).................................	80,000
Retained Earnings	40,000
Total Liabilities and Stockholders' Equity	$210,000

All sales were on credit. On Sept. 1, 1988, Poston had total assets of $240,000 (including accounts receivable of $13,000 and merchandise inventory of $24,000), total liabilities of $127,600, and total stockholders' equity of $112,400.

Required

1. Calculate the following liquid position ratios: current ratio, quick ratio, inventory turnover, and accounts receivable turnover.
2. Calculate the following ratios indicating debt-paying ability: times interest earned, debt to total assets ratio, and stockholders' equity to total assets ratio.

   (Check figure: Debt to total assets ratio = 42.9%)

3. Calculate the following earnings performance statistics: rate of return on total assets, and rate of return on common stockholders' equity.

Problem A16-2
Calculating percentage increase and decrease in comparative balance sheets

The following financial statements are included in the 1989 annual report of Federal Company:

```
                    FEDERAL COMPANY
               Comparative Balance Sheets
                    (000s omitted)
```

	June 30,	
	1989	**1988**
Assets		
Current Assets:		
Cash...	$ 31,600	$ 6,000
Accounts Receivable (net of Allowances for Uncollectibles of $560 in 1989 and $192 in 1988)	19,200	9,600
Merchandise Inventory	22,100	20,000
Total Current Assets	$ 72,900	$ 35,600

(continued)

Property, Plant, and Equipment:		
Land	$ 80,000	$ 90,000
Buildings	20,000	20,000
Less: Accumulated Depreciation	(2,700)	(2,500)
Equipment	15,000	14,000
Less: Accumulated Depreciation	(2,000)	(1,500)
Total Property, Plant, and Equipment	$110,300	$120,000
Intangibles:		
Patents	$ 1,500	$ 1,600
Total Assets	$184,700	$157,200

Liabilities and Stockholders' Equity		
Current Liabilities:		
Accounts Payable	$ 20,000	$ 16,600
Accrued Payables	3,500	3,000
Total Current Liabilities	$ 23,500	$ 19,600
Long-Term Liabilities:		
8% Note Payable (due 1992)	$ 12,000	—
10% Bonds Payable (due 1997)	81,000	81,000
Total Long-Term Liabilities	$ 93,000	$ 81,000
Total Liabilities	$116,500	$100,600
Stockholders' Equity:		
Common Stock, $1 par	$ 10,000	$ 10,000
Paid-In Capital in Excess of Par	26,400	26,400
Retained Earnings	31,800	20,200
Total Stockholders' Equity	$ 68,200	$ 56,600
Total Liabilities and Stockholders' Equity	$184,700	$157,200

FEDERAL COMPANY
Comparative Income Statements
Years Ended June 30,
(000s omitted)

	1989	1988
Net Sales	$160,000	$104,000
Cost of Goods Sold	59,200	37,500
Gross Profit on Sales	$100,800	$ 66,500
Operating Expenses:		
Sales Salary Expense	$ 25,800	$ 21,600
Utilities Expense	14,000	11,800
Advertising Expense	27,200	16,800
Other Expenses	5,000	4,200
Total Operating Expenses	$ 72,000	$ 54,400

(continued)

Other Income and Expense:		
Interest Expense..	$ 10,000	$ 8,600
Income before Income Taxes	$ 18,800	$ 3,500
Income Tax Expense......................................	7,200	1,200
Net Income..	$ 11,600	$ 2,300

Required

1. Comparative income statements and balance sheets for 1989 and 1988 are presented above. On your solutions paper, prepare columns showing the amount and percentage increase or decrease for each item on the statements.
2. Based on your solution for requirement (1), answer the following questions:
   a. What are the three balance sheet accounts that experienced the greatest percentage change? *cash*
   b. What three revenue or expense accounts on the income statement had the highest percentage change?
   c. Does the large increase in current assets appear to have been generated by profits for the year? Explain. *yes*
   d. Sales increased as compared with the prior year. Did expenses seem to increase proportionately also? Comment on any exceptions.

(Check figure: Income statement items with the highest percentage change = Income Tax Expense, Cost of Goods Sold Advertising Expense)

Problem A16-3
Completing the balance sheet and income statement

The following financial information is available for Dallas Machinery Corp.:

a. All sales were on credit.
b. The debt to total assets ratio is 52%.
c. Working capital is $828.
d. Net income is 14% of sales; gross profit is 65% of sales.
e. The only interest paid was on long-term debt.
f. Inventory turnover = 5. (Beginning inventory = $150.)
g. Accounts receivable turnover = 10. (Beginning accounts receivable = $240.)
h. 46% of the total cost of the building has been depreciated.

NI = .14sales
.14 392

Required

Complete the Dallas Machinery Corp. financial statements shown below. Round all calculations to the nearest dollar. (Hint: Determine the amounts in the order indicated by the numbers in parentheses on the statements.)

DALLAS MACHINERY CORP.
Income Statement
Year Ended December 31, 1989

Sales..	(1)	$ 2800
Cost of Goods Sold..	(3)	980
Gross Profit on Sales	(2)	1820
Operating Expenses	(15)	
Interest Expense	(14)	
Income before Income Taxes.................................	(4)	600
Income Tax Expense (34.67% of income before income taxes)............	(5)	208
Net Income		$392

392
NI = POT - TX
= POT - (T · PISS)
PBT(1 - T)
392 = X (1 - .3467)
392 = X(.6533)

DALLAS MACHINERY CORP.
Balance Sheet
December 31, 1989

Assets:

Cash		$ 418
Accounts Receivable (net)	(6)	
Merchandise Inventory..	(7)	
Building	(10)	
Accumulated Depreciation	(11)	( )
Total Assets..	(9)	$
Liabilities and Stockholders' Equity:		
Accounts Payable..	(8)	$
10% Bonds Payable (due 1997)...............................	(12)	
Common Stock		500
Retained Earnings	(13)	
Total Equities		$2,600

Problem A16-4
Selecting data needed
and calculating five ratios

The following financial data have been assembled for World Coatings, Inc., on Dec. 31, 1989:

Average total assets for 1989...	$400,000
Total stockholders' equity (average for 1989)	300,000
Common stock, $2 par...	175,000
8% preferred stock, $50 par...	75,000
Net income	31,000
Interest expense	3,000
Income tax expense (40% of income before income taxes)	
Market price of common stock, 12/31/89	$2.75
Market price of preferred stock, 12/31/89	$60

Common dividends were paid at the rate of $0.10 per share per quarter.
Preferred dividends were declared and paid.
No preferred stock or common stock was issued or reacquired during 1989.

Required

Using whatever data you need from the above list, calculate:
1. Rate of return on total assets
2. Rate of return on common stockholders' equity
3. Earnings per common share

(Check figure: Earnings per common share = $0.286)

4. Price-earnings ratio
5. Dividend yield rate

2. Calculate the following ratios indicating debt-paying ability: times interest earned, debt to total assets ratio, and stockholders' equity to total assets ratio.
3. Calculate the following earnings performance statistics: rate of return on total assets, and rate of return on common stockholders' equity.

Problem B16-2
Calculating percentage increase and decrease in comparative balance sheets

The following financial statements are included in the 1989 annual report of Aspin Company:

ASPIN COMPANY
Comparative Balance Sheets
(000s omitted)

	Sept. 30,	
	1989	**1988**
Assets		
Current Assets:		
Cash......	$ 7,200	$ 3,600
Accounts Receivable (net of Allowances for Uncollectibles of $120 in 1989 and $40 in 1988)	5,600	3,800
Merchandise Inventory	15,400	11,000
Total Current Assets	$ 28,200	$ 18,400
Property, Plant, and Equipment:		
Land	$ 50,000	$ 44,000
Buildings......	36,000	36,000
Less: Accumulated Depreciation......	(600)	(500)
Equipment......	7,000	6,000
Less: Accumulated Depreciation......	(200)	(100)
Total Property, Plant, and Equipment......	$ 92,200	$ 85,400
Intangibles:		
Copyrights	$ 2,900	$ 2,800
Total Assets	$123,300	$106,600
Liabilities and Stockholders' Equity		
Current Liabilities:		
Accounts Payable	$ 2,000	$ 8,000
Accrued Payables	1,300	1,000
Total Current Liabilities	$ 3,300	$ 9,000
Long-Term Liabilities:		
6% Note Payable (due 1991)......	$ 20,000	$ 20,000
12% Bonds Payable (due 1996)	20,000	—
Total Long-Term Liabilities......	$ 40,000	$ 20,000
Total Liabilities......	$ 43,300	$ 29,000
Stockholders' Equity:		
Common Stock, $10 par......	$ 20,000	$ 20,000
Paid-In Capital in Excess of Par......	8,000	8,000
Retained Earnings	52,000	49,600
Total Stockholders' Equity	$ 80,000	$ 77,600
Total Liabilities and Stockholders' Equity......	$123,300	$106,600

ASPIN COMPANY
Comparative Income Statements
Years Ended September 30,
(000s omitted)

	1989	1988
Net Sales	$68,400	$76,000
Cost of Goods Sold	24,472	26,600
Gross Profit on Sales	$43,928	$49,400
Operating Expenses:		
Sales Salary Expense	$10,944	$12,160
Utilities Expense	12,312	9,120
Other Selling Expenses	6,156	6,840
Other General Expenses	2,052	2,280
Total Operating Expenses	$31,464	$30,400
Other Income and Expense:		
Interest Expense	$ 3,600	$ 1,200
Income before Income Taxes	$ 8,864	$17,800
Income Tax Expense	3,988	8,010
Net Income	$ 4,876	$ 9,790

Required

1. Comparative income statements and balance sheets for 1989 and 1988 are presented above. On your solutions paper, prepare columns showing the amount and percentage increase or decrease for each item on the statements.
2. Based on your solution for requirement (1), answer the following questions:
   a. What are the four balance sheet accounts that experienced the greatest percentage change?
   b. What three revenue or expense accounts on the income statement had the highest percentage change?
   c. Does the large increase in current assets appear to have been generated by profits for the year? Explain.
   d. Sales decreased as compared with the prior year. Did expenses seem to decrease proportionately also? Comment on any exceptions.

(Check figure: Income statement items with the highest percentage change = Utilities Expense, Interest Expense, and Income Tax Expense)

Problem B16-3
Completing the balance
sheet and income
statement

The following financial information is available for Waco Sales, Inc.:

a. All sales were on credit.
b. The debt to total assets ratio is 55%.
c. Working capital is $1,310.
d. Net income is 9.0% of sales; gross profit is 30% of sales.
e. The only interest paid was on long-term debt.
f. Inventory turnover = 6 (beginning inventory = $500).
g. Accounts receivable turnover = 12 (beginning accounts receivable = $300).
h. 45% of the total cost of the building has been depreciated.

Required

Complete the Waco Sales, Inc., financial statements shown below. Round all calculations to the nearest dollar. (Hint: Determine the amounts in the order indicated by the numbers in parentheses on the statements.)

WACO SALES, INC.
Income Statement
Year Ended December 31, 1989

Sales.	(1)	$
Cost of Goods Sold.	(3)	
Gross Profit on Sales	(2)	
Operating Expenses	(15)	
Interest Expense	(14)	
Income before Income Taxes.	(4)	
Income Tax Expense (60% of income before income taxes)	(5)	
Net Income		$540

WACO SALES, INC.
Balance Sheet
December 31, 1989

Assets:		
Cash		$ 310
Accounts Receivable (net)	(6)	
Merchandise Inventory.	(7)	
Building	(10)	
Accumulated Depreciation	(11)	( )
Total Assets.	(9)	$
Liabilities and Stockholders' Equity:		
Accounts Payable.	(8)	$
6% Bonds Payable (due 1997)	(12)	
Common Stock		800
Retained Earnings	(13)	
Total Equities		$4,000

Problem B16-4
Selecting data needed
and calculating five ratios

The following financial data have been assembled for Retton Merchandising, Inc., on Dec. 31, 1989.

Average total assets for 1989	$250,000
Total stockholders' equity (average for 1989).	200,000
Common stock, $25 par	100,000
8% preferred stock, $5 par	50,000
Net income	15,000
Interest expense	1,000
Income tax expense (40% of income before income taxes)	
Market price of common stock, 12/31/89.	$1.10
Market price of preferred stock, 12/31/89.	$7.50
Common dividends were paid at the rate of $0.05 per share per quarter.	
Preferred dividends were declared and paid.	
No preferred stock or common stock was issued or reacquired during 1989.	

| **Required** | Using whatever data you need from the above list, calculate: |

1. Rate of return on total assets
2. Rate of return on common stockholders' equity

(Check figure: Rate of return on common stockholders' equity = 7.33%)

3. Earnings per common share
4. Price-earnings ratio
5. Dividend yield rate

Problem B16-5
Calculating liquidity ratios
for two firms and deciding
which should receive a
short-term loan

Front, Inc., and Center Company both sell machinery for washing large trucks. Both companies have applied for a short-term loan. Data from the Dec. 31, 1989, balance sheets appear below:

	Front, Inc.	Center Co.
Cash.	$ 55,000	$ 150,000
Marketable Securities.	3,600	120,000
Accounts Receivable (net).	61,400	90,000
Merchandise Inventory	360,000	240,000
Property, Plant, and Equipment (net).	700,000	750,000
Intangibles	3,000	—
Total Assets	$1,183,000	$1,350,000
Current Liabilities.	$ 120,000	$ 200,000
Long-Term Liabilities	200,000	200,000
Common Stock, $10 par	800,000	800,000
Retained Earnings.	63,000	150,000
Total Equities	$1,183,000	$1,350,000

Other Information:

	Front, Inc.	Center Co.
Accounts Receivable, Jan. 1, 1989	$ 78,600	$ 70,000
Merchandise Inventory, Jan. 1, 1989	320,000	260,000
1989 sales:		
Cash	516,000	240,000
Credit	684,000	960,000
1989 Cost of Goods Sold	1,054,000	700,000

| **Required** | 1. Calculate for each company the current ratio, quick ratio, inventory turnover, accounts receivable turnover, and average age of receivables. |

2. Which company would you recommend to receive the short-term loan? Explain.
3. What additional ratios would you consider if the companies were requesting a long-term loan? Explain.

(Check figure: Inventory turnover for Center Co. = 2.8)

DECISION PROBLEM

As a financial analyst for Webb Payner, a New York City investment banking firm, you have become interested in the activity of a company called Pace Electronics. The company is not listed on the New York Stock Exchange but is planning to do so shortly with the help of an investment banker, hopefully your firm. The company is somewhat guarded about their financial statements and you have been able to obtain only bits and pieces of information about the company. You will need a balance sheet and income statement in order to study the company further to determine if your firm should compete with other investment bankers for the right to represent Pace Electronics.

The following information is available:

Earnings per share	8.16
Accounts receivable turnover	25
Debt to asset ratio	.4
Quick ratio	.6 : 1
Common shares outstanding	20,000
Bond interest rate	12%
Return on marketable securities	10%
Corporate tax rate	40%
Inventory turnover	5
Current ratio	2 : 1
Working capital	$150,000
Par value per share	$5
Paid-in capital per share	$15

The year-end balances of Accounts Receivable and Inventories has remained relatively constant over the past several years.

In addition to the above information the following relationships are known:

The company maintains a 1 : 2 : 6 relationship between its Cash, Marketable Securities, and Accounts Receivable.

Prepaid Expenses amount to $\frac{1}{2}$ of Accounts Receivable.

Accounts Payable are four times Accrued Expenses.

The book value of the Buildings is twice that of the Equipment and both are 20% depreciated.

The book value of the Equipment is twice the cost of the Land.

Operating Expenses are $\frac{1}{3}$ of the Cost of Goods Sold.

All Sales are credit sales.

<table>
<tr><td>**Required**</td><td>Using the information provided prepare a balance sheet and income statement for the year ended Dec. 31, 1989, for Pace Electronics.</td></tr>
</table>

APPENDIX
Corporate Income Taxation

Did you know that about one-third of the income that large corporations earn is paid to the federal government in the form of income taxes? Not only does the federal government tax income, but so do most states. These taxes provide a substantial source of revenue for the various governments. For the federal government, half of its revenues come from income taxes. It may surprise you to know that individuals contribute about 38% of the total federal revenues while corporations contribute only 11%. But there are many, many more individuals paying taxes than there are corporations. When you consider that a corporation earning $1,000,000 will pay $340,000 in federal income taxes you can see that the corporate executives must understand fully the tax consequences of their management decisions if they are to maximize the return to the stockholders.

The foremost objective of corporate executives is to provide stockholders with the highest possible long-term return on the funds the stockholders entrusted to the corporation. This return must be done within the existing framework of various local, state, federal, and international laws. And it must be done ethically. Corporations must determine their tax liability in compliance with the federal tax laws and file corporate income tax returns. This is referred to as *tax compliance.* A knowledge of accounting is essential when complying with the provisions of the tax law. A knowledge of the tax laws is essential in keeping the tax liability as low as possible and, thus, stockholder returns high. Before entering into any business transaction the corporate executives must understand the tax consequence of that transaction. It may be that there is a provision in the tax law that will allow the transaction to be structured in a different manner, thus avoiding taxes. Congress wrote the tax law not only to raise revenues to operate the federal government, but also to encourage (or discourage) certain kinds of business activities. If there are provisions that will allow a corporation to avoid taxes it is the corporate executives' responsibility to be aware of these provisions and to utilize them. This is called *tax avoidance* (also known as legitimate tax planning) and is both legal and ethical. It is *tax evasion* that is a criminal act. Corporate executives found guilty of tax evasion on behalf of their corporations are subject to criminal prosecution.

In the area of income taxes, maximizing stockholder returns implies that income taxes be minimized and that calls for careful *tax planning.* In order to provide for tax planning, corporations must employ or engage individuals who are extremely knowledgeable about the tax laws. The individuals must advise the corporation on planning business transactions to minimize the tax effect of the transaction. And the corporation must maintain an adequate record of all business transactions to provide proof that the transactions have been reported properly.

Our discussion of corporate income taxes in this text must be very brief. Our purpose is simply to expose you to the major provisions of the tax laws that affect corporations. As the discussion proceeds bear in mind that the relationship between accounting and income taxes is very close. A large portion of the income tax provisions rests on accounting principles that we have already learned. But you must understand that the objectives of income taxation and financial reporting are not identical.

We all know the major objective of income taxes. It is to generate revenues to pay for the government services we use. The tax laws are also used to stimulate or slow down the national economy, and as a vehicle to attain certain social goals. By now we all know that financial accounting's objective is to report fairly a business entity's financial position and results of operations. Straight-line depreciation may be used on the income statement to properly measure net income, but an accelerated depreciation method would be used on the tax return to minimize the tax liability. So, you can see that there will be times that we will do one thing on the income statement and another on the tax return. We are not keeping two sets of books, we are simply reporting fairly to stockholders the results of operations of the company. And these operations reflect various tax planning decisions that will be disclosed in the footnotes to the financial statements.

THE CORPORATE TAX STRUCTURE

Corporate income taxes are determined by applying the appropriate corporate tax rate to the *corporate taxable income.* Corporate taxable income is determined by subtracting from *corporate gross income, ordinary deductions* and *special deductions.* Exhibit 1 reflects the composition of gross income, ordinary deductions, and special deductions.

EXHIBIT 1 Computation of Corporate Taxable Income

Gross Income:		Ordinary Deductions:		Special Deductions:	
• Gross profit		• Cost of goods sold		• Net operating losses	
• Dividends		• Salaries and wages			
• Interest	LESS	• Depreciation	LESS	• Dividends received deductions	EQUALS TAXABLE INCOME
• Royalties		• Bad debts		• Other special deductions	
• Net gain/loss on sales and exchanges		• Rents			
• Other income		• Taxes			
		• Interest			
		• Entertainment			
		• Amortization			
		• Insurance premiums			
		• Contributions			
		• Other expenses			

The corporate tax rate currently in effect is as follows:

Taxable Income	Tax Rate
0–$50,000	15%
$50,000–$75,000	25%
Over $75,000	34%

For taxable income between $100,000 and $335,000 there is a 5% *surtax* imposed to compensate for the lower levels of income where the tax rate was less than 34%. The effect of this surtax is that all corporations earning over $335,000 will, in effect, pay a flat tax rate of 34%. But for corporations earning more than $100,000 and less than $335,000 the *marginal tax rate* in this range will be 39%. To illustrate how this is accomplished consider a corporation with taxable income of exactly $335,000. The amount of corporate taxes would be computed as follows:

Taxable Income	Tax Rate	Corporate Income Taxes
$335,000	34%	$113,900
OR		
$50,000	15%	$ 7,500
$25,000	25%	6,250
$260,000	34%	88,400
($335,000 − $100,000)	5%	11,750
		$113,900

RECONCILIATION OF BOOK AND TAXABLE INCOME

As we mentioned above, the net income on the corporate financial statement and taxable income will differ. This difference is because certain accounting income items are excluded from the computation of taxable income, and certain accounting expenses are not deductible on the tax return. Two sets of books are not kept but the Internal Revenue Service does want to know why there is a difference between book income and taxable income.

In order to ensure that corporations with economic income pay some federal income tax, many corporations are subject to the alternative minimum tax (AMT) provision of the tax law. This topic is beyond the scope of our brief appendix.

Corporations are required to file their tax returns on a form called *Form 1120.* Schedule M-1 of the 1120 requires a reconciliation between book income and taxable income (before net operating losses and the dividends received deduction). Exhibit 2 is an example of the Schedule M-1 worksheet used for the reconciliation. We will use this worksheet to explain some of the major differences between accounting income and taxable income.

Gross Income

Sales

The Sales figure under column 1 "Profit and Loss Account" is the amount of sales reflected on the corporation's income statement, $4,560,000. Included in this figure is a sale to a customer amounting to $100,000 that provides for a cash payment of $30,000 this year and the $70,000 balance to be paid monthly over the next three years. It is not the corporation's usual policy to sell merchandise on the installment payment basis, but since this was such a large order the arrangement was made.

There is a tax advantage to this type of sale. The revenue does not have to be reported on the tax return until the cash is received. Since $30,000 cash was received this year, $70,000 does not have to be reported as taxable income on the corporate tax return. That is why adjustment (*a*) amounting to $70,000 in column 3 "Right-Hand Column" is on the Schedule M-1 worksheet. This adjustment is subtracted from the corporations' income statement income to arrive at the tax return's sales figure of $4,490,000.

EXHIBIT 2
Schedule M-1 Worksheet

	(1) Profit and Loss Account	(2) Left-Hand Column	(3) Right-Hand Column		(4) Taxable Income
Sales	$4,560,000		(*a*)	70,000	$4,490,000
Dividends	50,000				50,000
Interest: State Bonds	100,000		(*b*)	100,000	
Life Insurance Proceeds	1,000,000		(*c*)	1,000,000	
Total	$5,710,000				$4,540,000
Cost of Goods Sold	$1,950,000				$1,950,000
Salaries and Wages	870,000				870,000
Depreciation	550,000		(*d*)	400,000	950,000
Bad Debts	25,000	(*e*) $ 5,000			20,000
Interest	77,000				77,000
Entertainment	10,000	(*f*) 2,000			8,000
Amortization	125,000				125,000
Insurance Premiums	12,000	(*g*) 12,000			
Contributions	62,000	(*h*) 8,000			54,000
Federal Income Tax	6,900	(*i*) 6,900			
Total	$3,687,900				$4,054,000
Net Income	$2,022,100				
Taxable Income before Special Deductions					$ 486,000

Interest

The corporation has invested substantial excess funds in various state bond issues in order to earn interest on these otherwise idle funds. This year the interest amounted to $100,000. The federal tax law allows taxpayers (corporations are legal taxpayers) to exclude interest on obligations of a state, territory, or political subdivision from the computation of taxable income. Thus, adjustment (*b*) eliminates the $100,000 book income.

Life Insurance Proceeds

The corporation carries life insurance on its executives with the corporation named as the beneficiary. Unfortunately, early this year one of the executives had a heart attack and passed away. The proceeds of the policy amounted to $1,000,000.

Life insurance proceeds are not taxable income, but are considered to be accounting income and that is why adjustment (*c*) is made.

Ordinary Deductions

Cost of Goods Sold

The tax law allows businesses to use any of the generally accepted accounting methods of inventory valuation. However, if a business selects the LIFO method for the tax return it *must* also use LIFO on the income statement. In a period of rising inventory costs the LIFO method will result in the highest cost of goods sold and thus the lowest net income or taxable income. Our illustrative corporation has selected the LIFO method and consequently there is no difference between the book cost of goods sold and that reported on the tax return.

Depreciation

The corporation uses the straight-line method of depreciating its buildings and equipment. But, as you saw in Chapter 10, on the tax return they will use the accelerated cost recovery system (ACRS). This results in a difference of $400,000 for the current year and necessitates adjustment (*d*) on the Schedule M-1 worksheet.

Bad Debts

The tax law now does not allow taxpayers to use the "reserve" method of accounting for bad debts. The reserve method is the generally accepted accounting method of providing for an estimate of bad debts expense by providing for an allowance for uncollectibles. When the accounts are written off the allowance account is debited and Accounts Receivable is credited. The tax law requires taxpayers to take the deduction for bad debts expense when the Account Receivable is written off, not when the allowance is established. This amounts to a $5,000 difference for our corporation and is adjusted on the Schedule M-1 worksheet by adjustment (*e*).

Travel and Entertainment

This year the corporation incurred $10,000 of meal and entertainment expenses. The tax law allows a deduction for only 80% of this amount or $8,000, thus adjustment (*f*) is needed for the Schedule M-1 worksheet.

Insurance Premiums

The $1,000,000 proceeds from the life insurance policy were not taxable under federal tax laws. It follows then that since life insurance proceeds are not taxable, the premiums are not tax deductible. Adjustment (*g*) for $12,000 eliminates the insurance premium expense on the income statement.

Contributions

The amount of contributions that is allowed for a corporation as a tax deduction is limited to 10% of taxable income without considering the contributions. Total taxable revenues amount to $4,540,000. Total taxable deductions are $4,054,000 less the contributions allowed of $54,000 would be $4,000,000. Thus, taxable income not considering the contributions would be $540,000 and 10% of that figure is $54,000 the limit on contributions. The actual contributions were $62,000 requiring an $8,000 adjustment as seen in adjustment (*h*) on the Schedule M-1 worksheet.

Taxable Income before Special Deductions

The amount of taxable income before special deductions for the corporation would be the difference between the taxable revenues of $4,540,000 and the tax-deductible expenses of $4,054,000 or $486,000.

Special Deductions

Net Operating Losses

The net operating loss provision of the tax code provides a relief to those companies that suffer a tax operating loss. To illustrate this important provision assume that our company had operating taxable profits of $500,000 for its first 3 years of existence and sustained a loss of $3,400,000 last year, its fourth year of existence.

For the first 3 years the corporation would have paid taxes of $170,000 per year ($500,000 × 34%). No taxes would have been paid last year because of the loss. But let's look at the 4-year life of the company. The net effect over the 4 years is that the corporation has lost $1,900,000 [($3,400,000 − 3($500,000)]. Yet they have paid $510,000 in taxes!

The tax law allows corporations to carry back the loss for 3 years if they so elect. Any loss remaining after the election to carry back 3 years, or the entire loss if the carryback election is not made, can be carried forward for 15 years.

What this would mean for the $1,900,000 loss is that if the corporation elected to carry back 3 years $1,500,000 of the loss would be used to offset the first 3 years' income and the corporation would be entitled to a refund of $510,000 ($1,500,000 × 34%). In addition the corporation could offset next years' taxable income to the extent of $400,000.

Dividends Received

Corporations are allowed to reduce the amount of the dividends received and reported on the tax return by 80%. Our corporation reported $50,000 dividends received. In the determination of taxable income a $40,000 exclusion is allowed and only $10,000 will be reported.

Taxable Income

The amount of taxable income for the corporation would be computed as follows:

Federal Income Tax before Special Deductions	$486,000
Less: Special Deductions:	
Net Operating Loss Carryforward	(400,000)
Dividends Received Deduction	(40,000)
Taxable Income	$ 46,000

Federal Income Tax

For the current year the corporation's income tax would be $6,900 ($46,000 × 15%). This is reflected on the Schedule M-1 worksheet as adjustment (*i*)

SCHEDULE M-1 RECONCILIATION

Presented below is the Schedule M-1 reconciliation for the corporation:

Left-hand column:
1. Net income per books $2,022,100
2. Federal income tax 6,900
3. Excess of capital losses over capital gains.......................... -0-
4. Taxable income not recorded on books .... -0-
5. Expenses recorded on books, not deducted on return:

Bad debts	$ 5,000	
Entertainment	2,000	
Insurance premiums.............................	12,000	
Contributions....................................	8,000	27,000

6. Total of lines 1–5 .... $2,056,000

Right-hand column
7. Income recorded on books, not included in return:

Installment sales	$ 70,000	
Interest on state bonds............................	100,000	
Life insurance proceeds	1,000,000	$1,170,000

8. Deductions on return, not made on books:

Depreciation...	400,000

9. Total of lines 7 and 8 .... $1,570,000
10. Taxable income before special deductions (line 6 minus line 9) .... $ 486,000

SUBCHAPTER S CORPORATIONS

If you are a shareholder of a corporation, you face a double taxation problem. First, the income earned by the corporation is taxed. Then, as the income is distributed to you in the form of dividends, it is taxed as part of your personal income.

Certain corporations, having no more than 35 shareholders and meeting other requirements, may elect not to be subject to income tax. They are taxed similar to partnerships. These are referred to as Subchapter S corporations. Shareholders must report on their individual tax returns the dividends received from the corporations plus their pro rata shares of the corporation's undistributed taxable income. Salaries received from the corporation would, of course, also be included as gross income on the individual's return.

Taxpayers would generally elect the Subchapter S option if the amount of total tax on the individual return under Subchapter S is less than the tax on the individual return plus the corporate return. For example, assume that a corporation owned equally by four shareholders has taxable income for the current year of $640,000. Further assume that each of the shareholders is married and files a joint return and has personal income of $52,000 before consideration of the income (or dividends) of the corporation. The tax rates for individuals filing a joint return are:

Taxable Income	Rate
0–$29,750	15%
Over $29,750	28%

An additional tax of 5% is imposed on taxable income between $71,900 and $149,250.

If the Subchapter S option is not elected, the corporation's aftertax income would be determined as follows:

Corporate income before taxes	$640,000
Less: Income taxes ($640,000 × 34%)	217,600
Corporate Income after Taxes	$422,400

The corporation distributes the $422,400 income as dividends equally to the four shareholders, $105,600 to each. The amount of aftertax income for each of the four shareholders would be:

Taxable Income before Receiving Dividends	$ 52,000
Plus: Dividends	105,600
Taxable Income	$157,600
Less: Income Taxes ($157,600 × 28%)	44,128
Income after Taxes	$113,472

Under Subchapter S the amount of income after tax for each shareholder would be:

Taxable Income before Including Subchapter S Income	$ 52,000
Subchapter S Income ($640,000 ÷ 4)	160,000
Taxable Income	$212,000
Less: Income Taxes ($212,000 × 28%)	59,360
Income after Taxes	$152,640

Each shareholder is better off by $39,168 ($152,640 − $113,472) by electing the Subchapter S option.

INDEX

$$\text{Rate of return (ROR) on common stockholders' equity} = \frac{\text{net income} - \text{preferred dividends}}{\text{average common stockholders' equity}}$$

$$\text{Rate of return (ROR) on total assets} = \frac{\text{income before interest expense}}{\text{average total assets}}$$

$$\text{Times interest earned} = \frac{\text{income before interest and income taxes}}{\text{annual interest expense}}$$

$$\text{PS (simple capital structure)} = \frac{\text{net income} - \text{preferred dividends}}{\text{average number of common shares outstanding}}$$

$$\text{Dividend yield rate} = \frac{\text{dividends per share of common stock}}{\text{current market price per share of common stock}}$$

$$\text{Price-earnings ratio} = \frac{\text{market price per share of common stock}}{\text{earnings per share of common stock}}$$

$$\text{Debt to total assets ratio} = \frac{\text{total liabilities}}{\text{total assets}}$$

$$\text{Stockholder's equity to total assets ratio} = \frac{\text{total stockholders' equity}}{\text{total assets}}$$

$$\text{Accounts receivable turnover} = \frac{\text{credit sales}}{\text{average accounts receivable}}$$

$$\text{Average age of receivables} = \frac{\text{365 days}}{\text{accounts receivable turnover}}$$

$$\text{Inventory turnover} = \frac{\text{cost of goods sold}}{\text{average merchandise inventory}}$$

$$\text{Current ratio} = \frac{\text{current assets}}{\text{current liabilities}}$$

$$\text{Quick ratio} = \frac{\text{quick assets}}{\text{current liabilities}}$$